NEW YORK CITY

Where to Stay and Eat
for All Budgets

Must-See Sights
and Local Secrets

Ratings You Can Trust

Fodor's Travel Publications   New York, Toronto, London, Sydney, Auckland
www.fodors.com

FODOR'S NEW YORK CITY
Editor: William Travis

Editorial Production: Tom Holton
Editorial Contributors: Lynne Arany, Naomi Black, Stella Fiore, Melisse Gelula, Sarah Gold, Shannon Kelly, Melissa Klurman, Adam Kowit, Matthew Lombardi, Sara Marcus, Jacinta O'Halloran, Jennifer Paull, John Rambow, Robin A. Rothman, Nina Rubin, Tom Steele, Mark Sullivan
Maps: David Lindroth, *cartographer;* Rebecca Baer and Robert P. Blake, *map editors*
Design: Fabrizio La Rocca, *creative director;* Guido Caroti, *art director;* Moon Sun Kim, *cover designer;* Melanie Marin, *senior photo editor*
Production/Manufacturing: Colleen Ziemba
Cover Photo (pedicab, Times Square): Jeff Greenberg

SPECIAL SALES
This book is available for special discounts for bulk purchases for sales promotions or premiums. Special editions, including personalized covers, excerpts of existing books, and corporate imprints, can be created in large quantities for special needs. For more information, write to Special Markets/Premium Sales, 1745 Broadway, MD 6-2, New York, New York 10019, or e-mail specialmarkets@randomhouse.com.

AN IMPORTANT TIP & AN INVITATION
Although all prices, opening times, and other details in this book are based on information supplied to us at press time, changes occur all the time in the travel world, and Fodor's cannot accept responsibility for facts that become outdated or for inadvertent errors or omissions. So **always confirm information when it matters,** especially if you're making a detour to visit a specific place. Your experiences—positive and negative—matter to us. If we have missed or misstated something, **please write to us.** We follow up on all suggestions. Contact the New York City editor at editors@fodors.com or c/o Fodor's at 1745 Broadway, New York, NY 10019.

Be a Fodor's Correspondent

Your opinion matters. It matters to us. It matters to your fellow Fodor's travelers, too. And we'd like to hear it. In fact, we *need* to hear it.

When you share your experiences and opinions, you become an active member of the Fodor's community. That means we'll not only use your feedback to make our books better, but we'll publish your names and comments whenever possible. Throughout our guides, look for "Word of Mouth," excerpts of your unvarnished feedback.

Here's how you can help improve Fodor's for all of us.

Tell us when we're right. We rely on local writers to give you an insider's perspective. But our writers and staff editors—who are the best in the business—depend on you. Your positive feedback is a vote to renew our recommendations for the next edition.

Tell us when we're wrong. We're proud that we update most of our guides every year. But we're not perfect. Things change. Hotels cut services. Museums change hours. Charming cafés lose charm. If our writer didn't quite capture the essence of a place, tell us how you'd do it differently. If any of our descriptions are inaccurate or inadequate, we'll incorporate your changes in the next edition and will correct factual errors at fodors.com *immediately*.

Tell us what to include. You probably have had fantastic travel experiences that aren't yet in Fodor's. Why not share them with a community of like-minded travelers? Maybe you chanced upon a beach or bistro or B&B that you don't want to keep to yourself. Tell us why we should include it. And share your discoveries and experiences with everyone directly at fodors.com. Your input may lead us to add a new listing or highlight a place we cover with a "Highly Recommended" star or with our highest rating, "Fodor's Choice."

Give us your opinion instantly at our feedback center at www.fodors.com/feedback. You may also e-mail editors@fodors.com with the subject line "New York City Editor." Or send your nominations, comments, and complaints by mail to New York City Editor, Fodor's, 1745 Broadway, New York, NY 10019.

You and travelers like you are the heart of the Fodor's community. Make our community richer by sharing your experiences. Be a Fodor's correspondent.

Happy traveling!

Tim Jarrell, Publisher

CONTENTS

F 6 < **Contents**

Maps

CloseUps

ABOUT OUR WRITERS

New York native Lynne Arany is well-practiced in the art of uncovering the lesser-known gems in New York's cultural scene. Author of the *Little Museums* guidebook, contributor to the *New York Times,* and freelance travel writer and editor, she's covered areas from Scotland to the southwestern United States. But she most enjoys the serendipity of the search here at home.

Naomi Black arrived in New York two decades ago and hasn't stopped exploring. Her books include *Seashore Entertaining, 10 Terrific Parties, Dude Ranches of the American West,* and *The Ghost Town Storyteller,* among others. She's written about the New York area for *Travel & Leisure* to *Appalachia Bulletin.* When she can, she caves, dives, and learns about traveling from her two children.

Stella Fiore is an M.F.A. candidate in Writing at Sarah Lawrence College. She has covered New York's nightlife scene for *Shecky's New York Bar, Club & Lounge Guide 2005* and as an editor at IgoUgo.com, where she co-wrote and edited the company's first New York City guidebook, *IgoUgo's Real New York.*

Melisse Gelula has contributed to several New York City guides, including Fodor's *CityGuide New York* and Fodor's *New York City.* For this edition, she investigated the city's most wayward streets, and its most mercurial ones: Greenwich Village, the Lower East Side, and Brooklyn. Melisse has edited and written for dozens of travel guides and currently tracks down spas around the world for *Spa Finder Magazine.*

A full-time editor at Fodor's, Sarah Gold is also a writer; her work has appeared in such publications as *The New York Times, New York Magazine,* and *The Boston Globe.* When she's not staring at words on her computer screen or chasing deadlines, she all-too-regularly enjoys maxing out her credit cards in New York's fabulous shops.

Fodor's editor Jennifer Paull regularly scours the city for plum finds for the Shopping chapter, turning up everything from ostrich eggs to cult-favorite vinyl.

Former Upper West Sider Shannon Kelly jumped at the chance to revise the Uptown chapter for this edition, as it allowed her to wander the streets above 57th again, perpetuating the charade that she still lives there. Shannon has contributed to numerous Fodor's guides and to Fodors.com and is currently compiling a list of the best cupcakes in New York.

Melissa Klurman was happily able to indulge her passion for Frette sheets, plush robes, and deep soaking tubs while checking out the hotel scene for the Where to Stay chapter. A former Fodor's editor, Melissa is a freelance writer who has contributed to Fodor's *CityGuide New York* and *UpClose New York* in addition to her other job as mom to two-year-old Aidan.

Nightlife updater, proud Brooklynite, and sometime rock musician Sara Marcus writes about music and culture for *Time Out New York* and the *Advocate,* all while working towards a master's degree in creative writing at Columbia University. After nearly four years of obsessive concert-going in the Big Apple, she's grateful that her travel-writing debut gives her the opportunity to tell the world what she really thinks about every music venue in the city.

A New York City resident for 10 years, Fodor's editor Jacinta O'Halloran can elbow to the best view on the Empire State Building, haggle a good deal on New York City T-shirts, find a great pint of Guinness and a grand cup of tea, and anticipate seat-openings on the subway. She still looks up. Jacinta updated the Union Square to Murray Hill chapter.

East Villager John D. Rambow updated Smart Travel Tips, On the Calendar, Books & Movies, and portions of Nightlife and Exploring. A Fodor's editor by day, he loves New York history almost as much as its bars, restaurants, thrift stores, and museums. "The Bronx is up and the Battery's down" remains the best navigational advice he ever got.

At 5 feet, desperation not entitlement inspires entertainment editor/writer Robin A. Rothman to seek the best spots in NYC's bars and clubs. To secure them, she's known to gratuitously drop publication names like RollingStone.com, *Village Voice* and MTV to counteract the fact that the tallest man in any room will inevitably stand right in front of her. She continues to mourn Wetlands Preserve, Tramps, and Coney Island High.

For more than five years, Tom Steele has covered the New York entertainment and restaurant scenes for *Fodor's New York City, Time Out New York,* and *Out* magazine. He lives in Manhattan.

His work involves munching on spring rolls in Chinatown, creamy cannolis in the Bronx, and hot buttered biscuits in Harlem, so you won't hear any complaints from freelance writer Mark Sullivan. A former editor for Fodor's, he's written about his experiences in the Big Apple and elsewhere for the *New York Post, Budget Travel,* and *In Style.*

ABOUT THIS BOOK

Our Ratings

Sometimes you find terrific travel experiences and sometimes they just find you. But usually the burden is on you to select the right combination of experiences. That's where our ratings come in.

As travelers we've all discovered a place so wonderful that its worthiness is obvious. And sometimes that place is so experiential that superlatives don't do it justice: you just have to be there to know. These sights, properties, and experiences get our highest rating, **Fodor's Choice,** indicated by orange stars throughout this book.

Black stars highlight sights and properties we deem **Highly Recommended,** places that our writers, editors, and readers praise again and again for consistency and excellence.

By default, there's another category: any place we include in this book is by definition worth your time, unless we say otherwise. And we will.

Disagree with any of our choices? Care to nominate a place or suggest that we rate one more highly? Visit our feedback center at www.fodors.com/feedback.

Budget Well

Hotel and restaurant price categories from ¢ to $$$$ are defined in the opening pages of each chapter. For attractions, we always give standard adult admission fees; reductions are usually available for children, students, and senior citizens. Want to pay with plastic? **AE, D, DC, MC, V** following restaurant and hotel listings indicate if American Express, Discover, Diner's Club, MasterCard, and Visa are accepted.

Restaurants

Unless we state otherwise, restaurants are open for lunch and dinner daily. We mention dress only when there's a specific requirement and reservations only when they're essential or not accepted—it's always best to book ahead.

Hotels

Hotels have private bath, phone, TV, and air-conditioning and operate on the European Plan (a.k.a. EP, meaning without meals), unless we specify that they use the Continental Plan (CP, with a Continental breakfast), Breakfast Plan (BP, with a full breakfast), or Modified American Plan (MAP, with breakfast and dinner) or are all-inclusive (including all meals and most activities). We always list facilities but not whether you'll be charged an extra fee to use them, so when pricing accommodations, find out what's included.

Many Listings

★	Fodor's Choice
★	Highly recommended
⊠	Physical address
✛	Directions
⌖	Mailing address
☎	Telephone
🖷	Fax
⊕	On the Web
✉	E-mail
🎫	Admission fee
⊙	Open/closed times
⌐	Start of walk/itinerary
Ⓜ	Metro stations
▭	Credit cards

Hotels & Restaurants

🏨	Hotel
🛏	Number of rooms
⌂	Facilities
ⅼ◯ⅼ	Meal plans
✕	Restaurant
⌂	Reservations
🏛	Dress code
↘	Smoking
🍷	BYOB
✕🏨	Hotel with restaurant that warrants a visit

Outdoors

🏌	Golf
⛺	Camping

Other

♻	Family-friendly
🛈	Contact information
⇨	See also
⊠	Branch address
☞	Take note

Manhattan is, above all, a walker's city. Along its busy streets, an endless variety of sights unfolds everywhere you go. Attractions, many of them world-famous, crowd close together on this narrow island, and because the city can only grow up, not out, the new simply piles on top of the old. Manhattan's character changes every few blocks, so quaint town houses stand shoulder to shoulder with sleek glass towers, gleaming gourmet supermarkets sit around the corner from dusty thrift shops, and chic bistros inhabit the storefronts of soot-smudged warehouses. Many visitors, beguiled into walking a little farther, then a little farther still, often have stumbled upon their trip's most memorable moments.

Our walking tours cover a great deal of ground, yet they only scratch the surface of the city. If you plod dutifully from point to point, nose buried in this book, you'll miss half the fun. Look up at the tops of skyscrapers, and you'll see a riot of mosaics, carvings, and ornaments. Step into the lobby of an architectural landmark and study its features; take a look around to see the real people who work, live, or worship there today. Peep down side streets, even in crowded midtown, and you may find fountains, greenery, and sudden bursts of flowers. Find a bench or ledge on which to perch and take time just to watch the crowd passing by. New York has so many faces that every visitor can discover a different one.

New York is full of neighborhoods, some defined by a landmark or ethnic heritage, some barely in the same form in which they began, others invented for commercial gain and successfully spreading their boundaries. A few in-between blocks toss their hat in with whichever nearby area is hottest at the moment. This guide checks into all the boroughs of the Big Apple, but naturally focuses on the core, Manhattan. Its long, thin stretch is covered here from south to north, from Wall Street and the East Village to Morningside Heights and Harlem.

Getting Around

When it comes to getting around New York, you'll have your pick of transportation in almost every neighborhood. The subway and bus networks are thorough, although getting across town can take some extra maneuvering. If you're not pressed for time, take a public bus; they generally are slower than subways, but you can also see the city as you travel. Yellow cabs are abundant, except at the rush hour of 4:30–5 PM, when many are off duty (shift change time). Like a taxi ride, the subway is a true New York City experience and often the quickest way to get around. But New York is really a walking town, and depending on the time of day and your destination, hoofing it could be the easiest and most enjoyable option.

The map of Manhattan has a Jekyll-and-Hyde aspect. The rational Dr. Jekyll part prevails above 14th Street, where the streets form a regular grid pattern, imposed in 1811. Numbered streets run east and west (crosstown), and broad avenues, most of them also numbered, run north (uptown) and south (downtown). The chief exceptions are Broadway and the thoroughfares that hug the shores of the Hudson and East

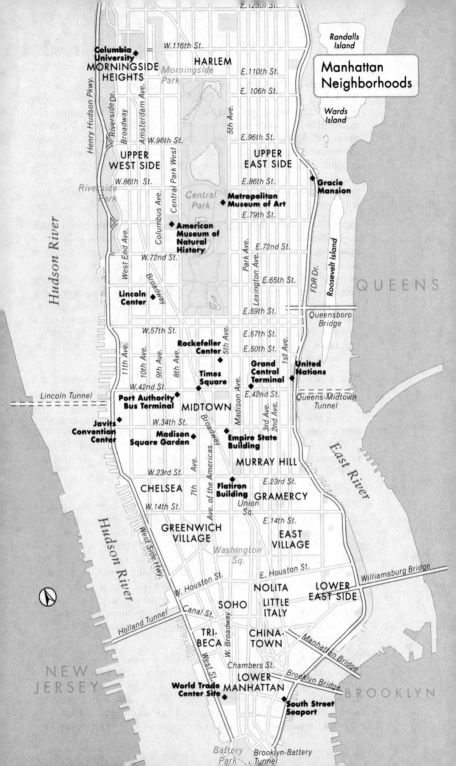

Manhattan Neighborhoods

Randalls Island

Wards Island

Roosevelt Island

QUEENS

Hudson River

East River

NEW JERSEY

BROOKLYN

MORNINGSIDE HEIGHTS
Columbia University
HARLEM
Morningside Park

UPPER WEST SIDE
UPPER EAST SIDE
Gracie Mansion

Central Park
Metropolitan Museum of Art
American Museum of Natural History

Riverside Park

Lincoln Center

Rockefeller Center
Times Square
Grand Central Terminal
United Nations

Port Authority Bus Terminal
MIDTOWN

Javits Convention Center
Madison Square Garden
Empire State Building
MURRAY HILL

CHELSEA
Flatiron Building
GRAMERCY
Union Sq.

GREENWICH VILLAGE
Washington Sq.
EAST VILLAGE

NOLITA
LOWER EAST SIDE

SOHO
LITTLE ITALY

TRI-BECA
CHINA-TOWN

World Trade Center Site
LOWER MANHATTAN
South Street Seaport

Battery Park

W. 116th St.
E. 128th St.
E. 110th St.
E. 106th St.
W. 96th St.
E. 96th St.
W. 86th St.
E. 86th St.
E. 79th St.
W. 72nd St.
E. 72nd St.
E. 65th St.
E. 59th St.
W. 57th St.
E. 57th St.
E. 50th St.
W. 42nd St.
E. 42nd St.
W. 34th St.
W. 23rd St.
E. 23rd St.
W. 14th St.
E. 14th St.
E. Houston St.
W. Houston St.
Canal St.
Chambers St.

Henry Hudson Pkwy.
Riverside Dr.
Broadway
Amsterdam Ave.
Columbus Ave.
Central Park West
Upper West Side
West End Ave.
5th Ave.
Park Ave.
Lexington Ave.
FDR Dr.
Queensboro Bridge
11th Ave.
10th Ave.
9th Ave.
8th Ave.
5th Ave.
Madison Ave.
3rd Ave.
2nd Ave.
1st Ave.
Queens-Midtown Tunnel
Lincoln Tunnel
Ave. of the Americas
7th Ave.
West Side Hwy.
Broadway
W. Broadway
Holland Tunnel
Williamsburg Bridge
Manhattan Bridge
Brooklyn Bridge
Brooklyn-Battery Tunnel

rivers. Broadway runs the entire length of Manhattan. At its southern-most end it follows the city's north–south grid; at East 10th Street it turns and runs on a diagonal to West 86th Street, then at a lesser angle until West 107th Street, where it merges with West End Avenue.

Below 14th Street—the area settled before the 1811 grid was decreed—Manhattan streets reflect the disordered personality of Mr. Hyde. They may be aligned with the shoreline, or they may twist along the route of an ancient cow path. Below 14th Street you'll find West 4th Street intersecting West 11th Street, Greenwich Street running roughly parallel to Greenwich Avenue, and Leroy Street turning into St. Luke's Place for one block and then becoming Leroy again. There's an East Broadway and a West Broadway, both of which run north–south and neither of which is an extension of plain old Broadway. Logic won't help you below 14th Street; only a good street map and good directions will.

You may also be confused by the way New Yorkers use *uptown, downtown,* and *midtown.* These terms refer both to locations and to directions. Uptown means north of wherever you are at the moment; downtown means to the south. But uptown, downtown, and midtown are also specific parts of the city. Unfortunately, no consensus exists about where these areas are: downtown may mean anyplace from the tip of lower Manhattan through Chelsea. Midtown is generally known to be between 34th and 59th streets.

A similar situation exists with *East Side* and *West Side.* Someone may refer to a location as "on the East Side," meaning somewhere east of 5th Avenue. A hotel described as being "on the West Side" may be on West 42nd Street. But when New Yorkers speak of the east side or the west side, they usually mean the respective areas above 59th Street on either side of Central Park. Be prepared for misunderstandings.

Wall Street & the Battery

Nearly at the southern tip of Manhattan and clustered around the New York and American stock exchanges, Wall Street is both the name of the downtown financial nexus and a thoroughfare. The grand and hulking architecture wedged into these blocks truly does merit comparison to canyons. The Dutch began the colony of Nieuw Amsterdam on these narrow streets, and a century and a half later, George Washington was sworn in on Wall Street as the United States first president. Luckily, the destruction that leveled the nearby World Trade Center did not physically damage the area. The absolute tip of the island is leafy Battery Park, full of war monuments and benches on which to rest and catch a harbor breeze.

The Seaport & the Courts

New York's days as a great 19th-century haven for clipper ships are preserved in lower Manhattan at South Street Seaport, centered on Fulton Street at the East River and crowned by the Brooklyn Bridge. On the cobblestone pedestrian streets and wooden docks, street performers compete with tall masted ships and retail stores for audiences' attention. Just blocks west of the seaport, you can take in the majestic court buildings of the City Hall area.

Little Italy & Chinatown

No longer the large community it once was, Little Italy is now basically confined to Mulberry Street between Canal and Broome streets. A few remaining Italian-American families and touristy eateries keep traditions alive, such as September's San Gennaro festival and summer sidewalk dining. Chinatown has grown north of its original boundary of Canal Street, spilling into much of what was once Little Italy, and also farther east into the Lower East Side, a formerly Jewish neighborhood. As you head east from Broadway along Canal Street, Chinese discount stalls and jewelry stores increase in number, and to the south, a carnival-like atmosphere reigns on the small streets, which are packed with purveyors of untold varieties of pungent fish, unusual vegetables, and pastries.

SoHo & TriBeCa

A neighborhood of cast-iron buildings and a few Belgian brick streets, SoHo (*So*uth of *Ho*uston Street) is bounded on its other three sides by Lafayette Street, Canal Street, and 6th Avenue. Artists transformed SoHo's late 19th-century factories into loft studios in the 1960s, and many of the galleries that followed have since been replaced by cushy restaurants and high-fashion boutiques. To the south and west, TriBeCa (the *Tri*angle *Be*low *Ca*nal Street) extends roughly as far as Murray Street and east to West Broadway. The broader streets of TriBeCa have a neighborhood feel, with a sprinkling of pricey restaurants and precious specialty shops, and many converted factory buildings.

Greenwich Village

The pattern of narrow, tree-lined streets known to New Yorkers simply as "the Village" remains true to its 19th-century heritage as a haven for bohemians, students, artists, actors, carousers, and tourists. Extending from 14th Street south to Houston Street and from the piers of the Hudson River east to 5th Avenue, it's one of the best parts of the city to wander for hours. Jazz clubs and piano bars line Grove Street, where literary legends have left their mark at old speakeasies and taverns. The Village is still stomping grounds of one of the largest gay communities in the country (specifically on Sheridan Square and Christopher Street).

The East Village & the Lower East Side

Once an edgy neighborhood of immigrants, artists, and punks, the East Village was hit with a wave of gentrification in the 1990s that is now lapping Avenue C, the penultimate avenue of sub-neighborhood Alphabet City. NYU students and young executives have joined the harmonious mélange that frequents the Polish and Ukrainian coffee shops, blackbox theaters, trendy pasta bars, and St. Mark's Place—a raggedy stretch of vintage stores, fetish shops, and sidewalk vendors. The area is bounded by 14th Street on the north, 4th Avenue or the Bowery on the west, Houston Street on the south, and the park-lined East River.

Saunter south of Houston Street and you'll enter the Lower East Side, once the cramped stepping-stone of many of New York's immigrant groups, and where the legacy of Jewish immigrants remains strongest in discount clothing, fabric, and design stores, and even a century-old knish bakery on Houston Street. Young clothing designers and hip bars and restaurants are now filling the storefronts of residential buildings on streets such as Eldridge and Ludlow.

Murray Hill, Flatiron District & Gramercy
In the nascent years of the skyscraper, two of New York's most distinctive structures wowed New Yorkers within the Flatiron District: the 21-story Fuller Building (now known as the Flatiron Building), wedged into the tight triangle created by 5th Avenue, Broadway, and 23rd Street; and the Metropolitan Life Insurance Company's 693-foot tower soaring above Madison Square Park. Within walking distance of this commercial area are the brownstone mansions and town houses of Gramercy, in the East 20s, and of Murray Hill, in the East 30s. Moneyed families such as the Roosevelts and Morgans made their homes here in the mid-19th century. The southern gateway to these neighborhoods is Union Square.

Chelsea
Like its London district namesake, New York's Chelsea maintains a villagelike personality, with quiet streets graced by renovated town houses. The neighborhood stretches from 6th Avenue west to the Hudson River, and from 14th Street to the upper 20s. Chelsea has always been congenial to writers and artists, and it has also embraced a multicultural population for decades; the neighborhood has largely supplanted the Village as the center of gay (mostly male) life in the city. The contemporary art scene thrives in spacious warehouse galleries west of 10th Avenue from West 20th to West 29th streets.

42nd Street
From west to east, this famous street is like a symphony of movements. It starts off slightly slow and seedy before a rapid crescendo to the tacky razzle-dazzle at Times Square, glaringly bright every day of the year. Thirty or so major Broadway theaters are nearby, in an area bounded roughly by West 41st and 53rd streets between 6th and 9th avenues. Before and after the show, critics, actors, directors, playwrights, and spectators come to dine on Restaurant Row (46th Street between 8th and 9th avenues) and along 9th Avenue in Hell's Kitchen. Midway across the island, the street's pulse gradually calms to the tree-lined stretch of Bryant Park and the New York Public Library. The pace picks up east of 5th Avenue, with high-rise offices, Grand Central Terminal, and the Chrysler Building. Finally, the strident energy subsides near the genteel residences of Tudor City, the stately United Nations headquarters, and the balcony over the East River.

Rockefeller Center & Midtown Skyscrapers
The 19-building complex known as Rockefeller Center inhabits 22 acres of prime real estate between 5th and 7th avenues and 47th and

52nd streets. The center is full of keepsake photo shots such as the ice-skating rink and towering Christmas tree fronting the GE building, the fan-staging area outside NBC's *Today Show,* and the pink-and-blue neon marquis of Radio City Music Hall. St. Patrick's Cathedral, Saks Fifth Avenue, and the rest of midtown's gleaming skyscrapers are just walk signs away.

5th Avenue & 57th Street
One of the world's great shopping districts, 5th Avenue north of Rockefeller Center, and 57th Street between Lexington Avenue and 7th Avenue are where some of the crème de la crème of designer boutiques and the biggest names in New York retailing. Follow Holly Golightly's lead in *Breakfast at Tiffany's* and come to look even if you know you won't buy. Music aficionados of different bandwidths make their way to West 57th Street for either Carnegie Hall or the Hard Rock Cafe.

The Upper East Side
Between Park and 5th avenues is where Old Money resides, and the tony restaurants and social clubs serve as extensions of luxurious town houses. Historic district designation has ensured that much of the Upper East Side between East 59th and 78th streets hasn't strayed from its turn-of-the-20th-century good taste, but whatever pushes the envelope of acceptability is sure to be on view at the Whitney Museum of American Art. Steel yourself for the clash of desire and resources when viewing the wares of Madison Avenue's haute couture boutiques.

Museum Mile
Once called Millionaire's Row, the stretch of 5th Avenue along Central Park between East 79th and 104th streets is still home to more millionaires—and billionaires—than any other street in the city. It earned its nickname Museum Mile for the world-class collections of art and artifacts scattered along its length. The only building built by Frank Lloyd Wright in New York is the Solomon R. Guggenheim Museum. Don't leave without visiting at least a few galleries in the largest art museum in the western hemisphere, the Metropolitan Museum of Art.

Central Park
This 843-acre patch of rolling countryside is where Manhattanites escape from the urban jungle and reconnect with nature. Nowhere does a rippled pond, peeping duckling, or crimson leaf seem more precious and remarkable than against a backdrop of high-rises. Central Park serves the city's most soothing vistas and opportunities for just about any outdoor activity. White clothing is required for the croquet course, and at the open-air disco just off the northeast corner of the Sheep Meadow, rollerbladers move with figure-skaters' liquid grace. Buskers, massage practitioners, and remote-controlled miniature sailboats are some of the other pleasant distractions. The rectangular park is bordered by 59th and 110th streets, and 5th Avenue and Central Park West.

The Upper West Side

Ornate prewar buildings line the residential boulevards of Riverside Drive, West End Avenue, and Central Park West and the commercial thoroughfare of Broadway, providing a stately backdrop for the lines of patrons awaiting a table during weekend brunch hours. Weaving between baby strollers, aspiring actors, and Juilliard students hustling off to their auditions and rehearsals, walk up busy Columbus Avenue at least as far as the American Museum of Natural History. At night, Lincoln Center for the Performing Arts is what draws many to the area.

Morningside Heights

Rising up between the Upper West Side and Harlem, Morningside Heights is home to the ivied buildings of Columbia University, one of the nation's oldest, and to the magnificent French Gothic Cathedral of St. John the Divine, which in addition to religious services sponsors music performances of all genres. Two of the most visited buildings alongside Riverside Park are here: Grant's Tomb and Riverside Church.

Harlem

An important influence on American culture, Harlem has been a hotbed of African-American and Hispanic-American culture and life for nearly a century. Music is a part of the cultural draw, be it gospel services at Baptist churches or amateur nights at the Apollo Theatre. The collection of the Schomburg Center for Research in Black Culture includes early jazz and blues recordings. Harlem extends north from 110th Street to about 145th Street (the border of Manhattanville); the most interesting sights on the West Side roughly between 116th and 135th streets.

GREAT ITINERARIES

New York City in 5 Days

Enjoying everything New York City has to offer during a short trip is more than a challenge, it's an impossibility. Whether your bent is sightseeing or shopping, museums or music, New York does indeed have it all. In five days you can see only the best of the best.

DAY 1

Begin a day dedicated to New York icons with a bird's-eye view atop the Empire State Building. Stroll up 5th Avenue past the leonine guardians of the New York Public Library and step inside to behold the gleaming Main Reading Room. Forty-second Street takes you east to the beaux arts Grand Central Terminal, a hub of frenetic activity and architectural wonder. Move on to the Chrysler Building, an art deco stunner, and continue east to the United Nations. Make your way west across 49th Street to the triumvirate of Saks Fifth Avenue, Rockefeller Center, and St. Patrick's Cathedral. Shopping, ice-skating at the Rockefeller rink, or visiting a nearby museum could fill your day until dusk, a good time to walk south on 7th Avenue toward the bright lights of Times Square.

⊘ Rush hour is a contact sport in Grand Central Terminal and Wednesday's foot traffic through Times Square can grind nearly to a standstill as audiences pour in and out of Broadway matinees.

DAY 2

Set off in search of history via ferry to the Statue of Liberty and Ellis Island. An early start helps you beat the crowds, and after a thorough visit, complete with guided tours, you can expect to return six hours later. Back in Manhattan, walk through the Wall Street area, home of the colonial-era Fraunces Tavern and mid-

19th-century Trinity Church. St. Paul's Chapel is Manhattan's oldest surviving church building and site of September 11 remembrances. Just north is the neo-Gothic Woolworth Building (don't miss the splendid gilded lobby) and City Hall. The perfect place to take in the sunset is the esplanade along Battery Park City, easily accessed via Chambers Street. For dinner, choose among TriBeCa's many restaurants.

⊘ There may be fewer crowds waiting for the ferry on weekdays.

DAY 3

Fine art and the finer things in life beckon, starting at the magnificent Metropolitan Museum of Art. You could easily spend a whole day here, but you'll exhaust yourself if you do. Luckily, just behind the museum lies beautiful Central Park, where you can collapse onto a bench, rowboat, or meadow and watch the world go by. For a romantic carriage ride through the park, hail a hansom cab at the park's south end, across from the Plaza hotel and the F.A.O. Schwarz toy store, both extravagances worth a peek. World-class shopping awaits on 5th Avenue and 57th Street.

⊘ The Metropolitan Museum of Art is closed Monday.

DAY 4

First thing this morning, head west to the American Museum of Natural History. Take a gander at the dinosaurs and stop by John Lennon's last home, the Dakota apartment building on Central Park West at 72nd Street. Walk into lush, green Central Park itself to see its Shakespeare Garden, Belvedere Castle, Bethesda Fountain, and Wildlife Center (more familiarly known as the Central Park Zoo). After your dose of fresh air, shop 'til you drop along 5th Avenue and 57th Street. Then treat

yourself to dinner followed by a performance at Carnegie Hall or Lincoln Center for the Performing Arts.

⊘ Do this any day.

DAY 5

Do what many New Yorkers like to do on their days off—wander. Make your way to Chinatown for a dim sum breakfast or tapioca-filled soft drink. From here head north to SoHo and NoLita for galleries and chic boutiques and restaurants. Farther east, the Lower East Side is a former immigrant enclave where you'll find the Lower East Side Tenement Museum and bargain shopping on Orchard Street. If you haven't eaten by now, hit a café a few blocks north in the happening East Village, home to yet more shops and vintage stores. From Union Square, walk up Broadway to the fashionable Flatiron District with its inimitable Flatiron Building. Have dinner in one of the neighborhood's noted restaurants.

⊘ This is fine any day, though many Orchard Street shops are closed Saturday.

If You Have More Time

Brooklyn has as much personality as Manhattan and provides a great view of the New York skyline from the Brooklyn Bridge and the Promenade in historic Brooklyn Heights. If you're here for the sunset, check out the evening's world-class entertainment at the Brooklyn Academy of Music. Other daytime attractions in the borough are the Brooklyn Museum of Art and the Brooklyn Botanic Garden, both right next to a subway line. Art galleries are sprouting in hip Williamsburg, a short train ride from Manhattan's 14th Street, and the world's most famous modern art is now being exhibited at the Museum of Modern Art's temporary home in Queens.

Back in Manhattan, another day sees another side of the city uptown. In Morningside Heights you'll find Riverside Park overlooking the Hudson and the Gothic work-in-progress Cathedral of St. John the Divine, as well as the ivory towers of Columbia University. Come back down to earth in Harlem, whose rich history is documented at the Schomburg Center near the famous Abyssinian Baptist Church. Other landmarks include the legendary Apollo Theatre, Striver's Row, the Studio Museum in Harlem, and soul-food restaurants such as Sylvia's.

If You Have 3 Days

For a small bite of the Big Apple, begin your first day at the Empire State Building, Metropolitan Museum of Art, and Central Park. Exit the park's south end at 5th Avenue and work your way through the stores until Rockefeller Center. Drop your loot at the hotel and then take a jaunt through neon-lit Times Square. On the second day take an early ferry trip to the Statue of Liberty and Ellis Island, and then walk the Wall Street area up until City Hall. Board an N or R train to 8th Street, where you can begin a tour of Washington Square Park and Greenwich Village. Follow the itinerary for Day 5 on your last day in town, which hits some great spots for clothing, art, and souvenirs.

A Kid's-Eye View of New York

New York bursts with fantastic activities and sights for tots and teenagers alike. Best of all, these stops appeal to adults as well. Two double-decker bus companies with hop-on, hop-off service and a water taxi service make getting around the city convenient and fun. Both have money-saving family packages that include Metro-Cards for public transportation, so consider your options when buying tickets.

DAY 1

Start off with a trip to that perennial favorite, the American Museum of Natural History, to see the genuinely awesome dinosaurs. Afterward take a subway ride down to 34th Street, in the front car for a cool view of the tracks. Teens might want to browse the affordable fashions at H & M, or you can head straight to the observatory deck of the nearby Empire State Building. Board a double-decker bus or take a subway down to SoHo, location of the New York City Fire Museum and the Children's Museum of the Arts. Adventurous eaters love dinner in Chinatown, where roast ducks hang in the windows and tapioca balls fill colorful shakes.
☺ The Children's Museum of the Arts is closed Monday and Tuesday.

DAY 2

Begin the day on the first ferry out to the Statue of Liberty and Ellis Island. In warm weather, head next to South Street Seaport, which serves up fast food, tall ships, chain stores, and street performers. In winter, take the double-decker bus up to Rockefeller Center where ice-skating and the Christmas tree are special treats. There's more fun to be had at the nearby Museum of Television and

Radio and at the high-tech Sony-Wonder Technology Lab in the Sony Building. And no kid's trip to New York City is complete without a pilgrimage to F.A.O. Schwarz. For a more affordable option on Broadway, see what family-friendly programming is on stage at the New Victory Theater. The high wattage of cleaned-up Times Square and 42nd Street, between 7th and 8th avenues, is free entertainment.
☺ Both the Museum of Television and Radio and SonyWonder Technology Lab are closed Monday, and the stage is dark at the New Victory Theater from Monday through Wednesday.

DAY 3

Cruise around Manhattan island this morning on the Circle Line, and when your tour's completed stop by the *Intrepid* Sea-Air-Space Museum. Pick up the subway at 8th Avenue for a trip to Central Park. There, check out the Wildlife Center and Children's Zoo, take a ride on the famous carousel, and catch a performance at the marionette theater in the Swedish Cottage. At the east side of the park, miniature boats skim the Conservatory Water. Afterward stop in at the Metropolitan Museum of Art to see the Temple of Dendur, the arms and armor, and oversize statues in the Greek galleries. As night falls, try one of the special kids' music programs at Lincoln Center for the Performing Arts or take in a movie on the huge screen at the nearby Sony IMAX Theater.
☺ The Metropolitan Museum of Art is closed Monday.

The Art Experience

For art lovers of every taste, there's no place like New York. There's so much to choose from, whether you favor the old masters,

abstract expressionism, or quirky conceptual installations. Monday can seem like a "Day Without Art," but there are some galleries and museums that take advantage of others' closed doors.

DAY 1

The first stop on every aesthete's schedule should be the Metropolitan Museum of Art. Limit yourself to a morning, then head for the many galleries along Madison Avenue between East 80th and 70th streets—be sure to stop in at both Gagosian and Knoedler & Co. Don't miss the masterpiece-heavy Frick Collection before strolling east to view the collections at the Asia Society and Museum. In the evening attend a performance at Lincoln Center for the Performing Arts, City Center, or Carnegie Hall. Then catch a cabaret act at Café Carlyle or the Oak Room.
☺ All these museums are closed on Monday, and galleries are often closed Sunday and Monday.

DAY 2

Spend a thoroughly modern morning at the Neue Galerie New York and Solomon R. Guggenheim Museum on 5th Avenue and then head east to the Whitney Museum of American Art. Spend the rest of the afternoon at the galleries along 57th Street, whose standouts include the Marlborough and Pace Wildenstein. Depending on your inclination, enjoy an evening of dinner and theater along the Great White Way, or taxi downtown for funkier performance art, a play, music, or a reading at a cutting-edge venue such as the Kitchen, P.S. 122, or La Mama Etc.
☺ Friday through Tuesday are the best days to do this tour in order to avoid any museum closures; galleries are often closed Sunday and Monday.

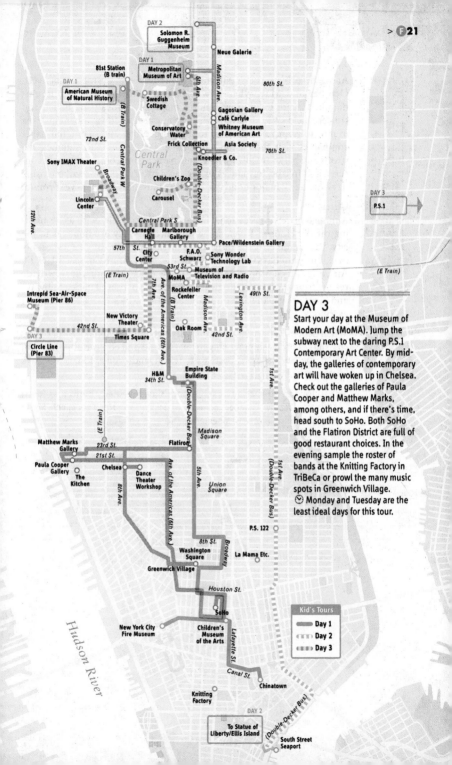

DAY 2

Solomon R. Guggenheim Museum

Neue Galerie

DAY 1

Metropolitan Museum of Art

80th St.

81st Station (B train)

DAY 1

American Museum of Natural History

Swedish Cottage

Gagosian Gallery
Café Carlyle
Whitney Museum of American Art

72nd St.

Conservatory Water

Frick Collection

Asia Society

70th St.

Central Park

Knoedler & Co.

Sony IMAX Theater

(Double-Decker Bus)

DAY 3

P.S.1

Children's Zoo

Lincoln Center

Carousel

12th Ave.

Central Park S

Carnegie Hall

Marlborough Gallery

57th St.

City Center

Pace/Wildenstein Gallery

F.A.O. Schwarz
Sony Wonder Technology Lab

(E Train)

53rd St.

MoMA

Museum of Television and Radio

(E Train)

Intrepid Sea-Air-Space Museum (Pier 86)

Rockefeller Center

49th St.

New Victory Theater

42nd St.

Oak Room

42nd St.

DAY 3

Circle Line (Pier 83)

Times Square

Empire State Building

DAY 3

Start your day at the Museum of Modern Art (MoMA). Jump the subway next to the daring P.S.1 Contemporary Art Center. By midday, the galleries of contemporary art will have woken up in Chelsea. Check out the galleries of Paula Cooper and Matthew Marks, among others, and if there's time, head south to SoHo. Both SoHo and the Flatiron District are full of good restaurant choices. In the evening sample the roster of bands at the Knitting Factory in TriBeCa or prowl the many music spots in Greenwich Village.
🕙 Monday and Tuesday are the least ideal days for this tour.

H&M
34th St.

Madison Square

Matthew Marks Gallery

23rd St.

Flatiron

21st St.

Paula Cooper Gallery

Chelsea

The Kitchen

Dance Theater Workshop

Union Square

P.S. 122

8th St.

Washington Square

La Mama Etc.

Greenwich Village

Houston St.

SoHo

New York City Fire Museum

Children's Museum of the Arts

Kid's Tours

— Day 1
⋯⋯ Day 2
⋯⋯ Day 3

Canal St.

Chinatown

Knitting Factory

DAY 2

To Statue of Liberty/Ellis Island

South Street Seaport

Hudson River

WHEN TO GO

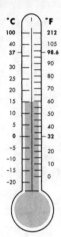

At one time, New York's cultural life was limited to the months between October and May, when new Broadway shows opened, museums mounted major exhibitions, and formal seasons for opera, ballet, and concerts held sway. Today, however, there are Broadway openings even in mid-July, and a number of touring orchestras and opera and ballet companies visit the city in summer. In late spring and summer, the streets and parks are filled with ethnic parades, impromptu sidewalk concerts, and free performances under the stars. Except for regular closing days and a few major holidays, the city's museums are open year-round.

Climate

Although there's an occasional bone-chilling winter day, with winds blasting off the Hudson River, snow only occasionally accumulates in the city. Late summer is the only really unpleasant time of year, especially the humid, hot days of August (when the temperature can reach 100°F). Air-conditioned stores, restaurants, theaters, and museums provide respite from the heat; so do the many green expanses of parks. Subways and buses are usually air-conditioned, but subway stations can be as hot as saunas.

When September arrives—with its dry "champagnelike" weather—the city shakes off its summer sluggishness. Mild and comfortable, autumn shows the city off at its best, with yellow-and-bronze foliage displays in the parks.

The following table shows each month's average daily highs and lows:
🔢 Forecasts **Weather Channel Connection** ☎ 900/932–8437 95¢ per minute from a Touch-Tone phone ⊕ www.weather.com.

Jan.	38F	3C	May	72F	22C	Sept.	76F	24C
	25	−4		54	12		60	16
Feb.	40F	4C	June	80F	27C	Oct.	65F	18C
	27	−3		63	17		50	10
Mar.	50F	10C	July	85F	29C	Nov.	54F	12C
	35	2		68	20		41	5
Apr.	61F	16C	Aug.	84F	29C	Dec.	43F	6C
	44	7		67	19		31	−1

NYC & Company–Convention and Visitors Bureau (✉ 810 7th Ave., between W. 52nd and W. 53rd Sts., 3rd fl., Midtown West ☎ 212/484–1222 ⊕ www.nycvisit.com) has exact dates and times for many of the events listed below, and the bureau's Web site has more information on all sorts of activities.

WINTER

Late December–early January	The nine-day New York National Boat Show, at the Jacob Javits Convention Center, shows off the latest in pleasure craft (power- and sailboats), yachts, and nautical equipment.
Early January	Hulking bikes of all varieties are on display at the New York International Motorcycle Show at the Jacob Javits Center.
Late January	Leading dealers in the field of visionary art—also sometimes called naïve art or art of the self-taught—exhibit their wares at the Outsider Art Fair at the Puck Building in SoHo.
Late January–early February	The Lunar New Year, celebrated over two weeks, includes extravagant banquets, a flower market, and a colorful paper-dragon dance that snakes through Chinatown.
Early February	In the Annual Fleet Empire State Building Run-Up invitational organized by the New York Road Runners Club, runners scramble up the 1,576 stairs from the lobby of the Empire State Building to the 86th-floor observation deck.
	Nearly 3,000 well-bred canines and their human overseers take over Madison Square Garden for the Westminster Kennel Club Dog Show, the nation's second-longest-running sporting event (after the Kentucky Derby).
February 14	On St. Valentine's Day, couples are married on the 80th floor of the Empire State Building.
March 17	New York's first St. Patrick's Day Parade took place in 1766, making this boisterous tradition one of the city's oldest annual events. The parade heads up 5th Avenue, from 44th Street to 86th Street.

SPRING

Late March	At the International Asian Art Fair, 50 dealers from around the world exhibit furniture, sculptures, bronzes, ceramics, carpets, jewelry, and more from the Middle East, Southeast Asia, and the Far East. Prices begin at $1,000.
	The Triple Pier Expo lures more than 600 antiques dealers to Piers 88, 90, and 92, which are filled with everything from art glass to furniture. There's a reprise of the event in November.

Late March– early April	The week before Easter, the Macy's Flower Show creates lush displays in its flagship emporium and sets its Broadway windows abloom. Exquisite flower arrangements are also on display in Rockefeller Center.
	The Jacob Javits Center is host to the annual New York International Auto Show, where hundreds of the latest and hottest cars, along with auto oddities, get drivers' motors running.
Easter Sunday	As in the classic Fred Astaire movie *Easter Parade,* you (or even your pet) can don an extravagant hat and strut up 5th Avenue in the Easter Promenade. The parade centers around St. Patrick's Cathedral, at 51st Street.
Early April	Every spring, the three-ring Ringling Bros. and Barnum & Bailey Circus comes to town. Just before opening night, the Animal Walk takes the show's four-legged stars from the train yard in Queens through the Queens Midtown tunnel and west along 34th Street to Madison Square Garden; it happens around midnight but is well worth waiting up for.
Mid-April	Since 1962 book-lovers have been hitting their jackpot at the Antiquarian Book Fair, held at the Park Avenue Armory on the Upper East Side. Nearly 200 book exhibitors display first editions, rare volumes, manuscripts, autographs, letters, atlases, drawings, and maps, with prices from $25 to more than $25,000.
Late April	The Cherry Blossom Festival at the Brooklyn Botanic Garden takes place during the trees' peak flowering and includes Taiko drumming groups, traditional Japanese dance and arts, and bento box lunches for picnicking.
Early May	About 30,000 cyclists turn out for the annual Bike New York: The Great Five Boro Bike Tour. The low-key, 42-mi tour begins in Battery Park and ends with a ride across the Verrazano-Narrows Bridge into Staten Island.
	The International Fine Art Fair brings dealers from all over the country to the Seventh Regiment Armory, where they show off exceptional paintings, drawings, and sculptures from the Renaissance to the 20th century.
Mid-May	On the second or third Saturday in May, booths of the Ninth Avenue Food Festival line 20 blocks of 9th Avenue (from 37th to 57th Street) and cook up every conceivable type of food. Most of 9th Avenue's many food stores and restaurants participate, selling samples of their wares as well as specially prepared delicacies.
Late May	Ships from the armed forces of the United States and from other countries join up with Coast Guard ships during Fleet Week for a parade up the Hudson River. After the ships dock, they are open to the public. The center of things for this event, held the week before Memorial Day, is the *Intrepid* Sea-Air-Space Museum.

	Since 1931, Memorial Day has marked the start of the Washington Square Outdoor Art Exhibit, an open-air arts-and-crafts fair with some 600 exhibitors who set up along the park and on surrounding streets. The action continues for two weekends, from noon to sundown.
Late May–July	The Downtown River to River Festival brings 500 music, dramatic, and arts performances to lower Manhattan. Many of the events are free.
Early June	The Belmont Stakes, New York's thoroughbred of horse races, and the final race of the Triple Crown, comes to Long Island's Belmont Park Racetrack.
Early June	During the National Puerto Rican Day Parade, dozens of energetic bands send their rhythms reverberating down 5th Avenue, as huge, sometimes raucous crowds cheer them on.
Mid-June	Nine of the major museums lining 5th Avenue from 82nd up to 104th Street waive their admission and have special late hours for the Museum Mile Festival, held the second Tuesday in June. Fifth Avenue is closed to traffic, and entertainers perform in the streets.
SUMMER	
Late June	JVC Jazz Festival New York brings giants of jazz and new faces alike to Carnegie Hall, Lincoln Center, Birdland, Bryant Park, and other venues around town.
	Lesbian & Gay Pride Week includes a film festival, concerts aplenty, and many other events. It culminates with the world's biggest annual gay pride parade, which heads down 5th Avenue and then to Greenwich Village on the last Sunday of the month.
Late June– August	On Monday nights filmgoers head to Bryant Park, the New York Public Library's "backyard," for the Bryant Park Summer Film Festival. The lawn turns into a picnic ground as fans of classic films claim space hours before the show begins, at dusk.
	Central Park SummerStage presents free weekday evening and weekend afternoon rock, blues, Latin, pop, African, and country music; dance; opera; and readings. Arrive early for a spot.
	Shakespeare in the Park, sponsored by the Joseph Papp Public Theater and staged in Central Park's Delacorte Theater, tackles the Bard and other classics, often with star performers.
	The New York Philharmonic plays free concerts in various city parks.
	Celebrate Brooklyn Performing Arts Festival brings pop, jazz, rock, classical, klezmer, African, Latin, and Caribbean multicultural music, as well as spoken-word and theatrical performances, to Prospect Park's Bandshell.

July	The streets around Brooklyn's Our Lady of Mt. Carmel Church are full of Italian festivities for two weeks, beginning the first Thursday in July. A highlight of the Festa del Giglio (Feast of the Lily) is Giglio Sunday, when men of the community parade down the street a 65-foot spire holding a band.
	Lincoln Center Festival is an international summer performance event lasting several weeks; it includes classical music concerts, contemporary music and dance presentations, stage works, and non-Western arts.
	From late June through July, Midsummer Night Swing transforms Lincoln Center's Fountain Plaza into an open-air dance hall. Top big bands provide jazz, Dixieland, R&B, calypso, and Latin rhythms for dancers of all ages; dance lessons are given each night.
	The Washington Square Music Festival is a series of Tuesday evening free outdoor classical, jazz, and big-band concerts.
July 4	Lower Manhattan celebrates Independence Day with the Great 4th of July Festival, which includes arts, crafts, ethnic food, and live entertainment. South Street Seaport also puts on a celebration.
	Macy's 4th of July Fireworks fill the night sky over the East River. The best viewing points are FDR Drive from East 14th to 41st streets (access via 23rd, 34th, and 48th streets) and the Brooklyn Heights Promenade. The FDR Drive is closed to traffic, but arrive early, as police sometimes restrict even pedestrian traffic.
August	Lincoln Center Out of Doors is a series of music, dance, and family-oriented events lasting almost the entire month.
	Harlem Week, the world's largest black and Hispanic festival, runs throughout the month. Come for the food, concerts, gospel events, a film festival, children's festival, an auto show, and a bike tour.
	The music of Mozart and his peers wafts through Lincoln Center during the Mostly Mozart festival. Afternoon and evening concerts are presented at reasonable prices.
Late August	The 10-day Howl! Festival, named in honor of the famous poem by beat poet (and East Village resident) Allen Ginsburg, includes more than 250 music, art, and theatrical performances. One highlight is Wigstock, a show of drag queen performances held in Tompkins Square Park.
Late August–early September	The U.S. Open Tennis Tournament, in Flushing Meadows–Corona Park, Queens, is one of the city's premier annual sport events.
Labor Day Weekend	A Caribbean revel modeled after the harvest carnival of Trinidad and Tobago, the West Indian American Day Carnival, in Brooklyn, is the centerpiece of a week's worth of festivities. Celebrations include salsa, reggae, and calypso music performances, as well as Monday's

	gigantic parade of floats, elaborately costumed dancers, stilt walkers, and West Indian food and music.
Early September	Broadway on Broadway, the official start of the theater season, brings some of the best new musical numbers to the streets for a free two-hour concert in Times Square.
September	Garlands and lights bedeck Little Italy's Mulberry Street and environs for the Feast of San Gennaro, the city's oldest, grandest, largest, and most crowded *festa*, held in honor of the patron saint of Naples.

FALL

Late September	Some 200 publishers set up displays along 5th Avenue from 42nd to 57th streets for New York Is Book Country, where you can buy new fall releases and unusual old books, meet authors, admire beautiful book jackets, and enjoy live entertainment and bookbinding demonstrations. Bring the kids.
Late September–mid-October	Begun in 1963, the New York Film Festival is the city's most prestigious annual film event. Cinephiles pack various Lincoln Center venues—advance tickets to afternoon and evening screenings are essential to guarantee a seat.
October–December	The Brooklyn Academy of Music (BAM) Next Wave Festival attracts artsy crowds with its program of local and international cutting-edge dance, opera, theater, and music. You can see such "regulars" as Phillip Glass, John Cale, Lou Reed, and the German dance-theater troupe of Pina Bausch.
October	The Columbus Day Parade, organized by the Italian-American Columbus Citizens Foundation, is held each year around October 12. It usually runs on 5th Avenue between 44th and 79th streets.
	Openhousenewyork, begun in 2003, allows curious locals and visitors alike to take free tours of nearly 100 government buildings, artists' studios, private apartments and institutions, and other interesting places. Many locations are otherwise closed to the public.
	Considered one of the world's top art fairs, the International Fine Art and Antique Dealers Show brings dealers from the United States and Europe, who show treasures dating from antiquity to the 20th century.
	The Feast day of St. Francis of Assisi (October 4) is commemorated at the Cathedral Church of St. John the Divine with the blessing of animals, both pets and the more exotic sort.
October 31	Thousands of revelers, many in bizarre but brilliant costumes or manipulating huge puppets, march up 6th Avenue (from Spring to West 23rd streets) in the rowdy Greenwich Village Halloween Parade.
Late October–early November	The Metropolitan National Horse Show, held on Pier 94 on the West Side, features the best in equestrian competition.

Early November	The New York City Marathon, the world's largest, begins on the Staten Island side of the Verrazano-Narrows Bridge and snakes through all five boroughs before finishing in front of Tavern on the Green in Central Park. New Yorkers turn out in droves to cheer on the runners.
November 11	On Veterans Day a parade marches down 5th Avenue to Madison Square Park. Following the parade, there's a service held at the Eternal Light Memorial in the park.
Thanksgiving Day	The Macy's Thanksgiving Day Parade is a New York tradition. The huge balloons float down Central Park West from West 77th Street to Broadway and Herald Square. The parade begins at 9 AM; when it comes to getting a good spot, the earlier the better.
Late November	Several days after Thanksgiving, an enormous Christmas tree is mounted in Rockefeller Center, just above the golden statue of Prometheus. Thousands of people gather to watch the ceremonial tree lighting.
Late November– early January	Every year the city's major department stores give their windows over to elaborate Christmas displays. Those on view at Barneys and Saks Fifth Avenue lean toward the inventive and the slightly satiric. The windows at Lord & Taylor and Macy's are more traditional—and generally more festive.
Late December	A Giant Hanukkah Menorah is lighted at Grand Army Plaza, near the southeast corner of Central Park.
New Year's Eve	The famous ball drop in Times Square is televised all over the world. Arrive early, and dress warm!
	In Central Park, a rowdy Midnight Run sponsored by the New York Road Runners Club begins at Tavern on the Green. One set of prizes is for the best costume.

PLEASURES & PASTIMES

Architecture Nothing evokes New York City more dramatically than its ever-evolving peaks of steel, glass, and concrete. Save yourself a cramped neck by beholding your favorite skyscraper from a distance, whether from the deck of a cruise boat or the Staten Island Ferry, or the boardwalk of another masterpiece of 19th-century architecture, the Brooklyn Bridge. Few buildings built prior to the mid-19th century have survived the perpetual swing of wrecking balls, but the Financial District has a few—St. Paul's Chapel, Trinity Church, and Federal Hall. Fans of art deco can wander in and out of the Empire State Building, the Chrysler Building, and Rockefeller Center. Modern buildings that play with curves include Philip Johnson's rose-color "Lipstick Building" at 3rd Avenue and East 53rd Street, Frank Lloyd Wright's Guggenheim Museum at 5th Avenue and East 89th Street, and the ski jump–like Grace Building by Skidmore, Owings & Merrill, at West 42nd Street, between 5th and 6th avenues.

Dining From early in the morning to the moment dinner is served, star chefs fuss over seasonings, sauces, and broths with which to seduce your tongue. For the fairest of prices, stand-up counters and narrow holes-in-the-wall deliver the authentic taste of faraway lands. New York, like Paris, is a movable feast. To enjoy it within a fine establishment such as those of chef Daniel Boulud or restaurateur Danny Meyer, make reservations well in advance, or on shorter notice, you may be able to slip in for a cost-saving, but just as delectable, lunch. Overspending your budget is not a prerequisite to eating well in this town. Sample kimchi at a Korean restaurant, snack on the crispest-ever french fries at a Belgian bistro, gobble up a pastrami sandwich or a bagel and schmear at a Jewish deli, or finally have a go at escargot or tripe at a 24-hour brasserie.

Museums The settings of New York's museums can be as impressive as their collections—from the *Intrepid* Sea-Air-Space Museum aboard an aircraft carrier on the Hudson River to the chunks of European monasteries that make up the Cloisters, a collection of medieval art and objéts. To better imagine the laundry lines, pushcarts, barrels, and clamor of Little Italy and the Lower East Side during the late 1800s, take a boat trip to the immigrant processing center–turned–museum, Ellis Island, or squeeze through the narrow rooms of the Lower East Side Tenement Museum. On the opposite end of the spectrum, the rich collections of industrial barons and financiers such as Henry Clay Frick and J. P. Morgan are on view in their former mansions and private libraries. But if the city held no other museum than the colossal Metropolitan Museum of Art, you could still occupy yourself for days roaming its labyrinthine corridors. A plethora of art museums cover every borough of the city, so familiarize yourself with their permanent and upcoming exhibitions to best prioritize your viewing.

Performing Arts New York has always been an epicenter of the arts. The city's nickname, "The Big Apple," is said to have been coined by jazz musicians, and you can hear them pour their soul into the great American music genre from the West Village's basements to Harlem's lounges. As the Times Square renaissance continues with no end in sight, Broadway's theaters are booked solid with shows that seem more rewarding every season. Just as vital and important as the blockbuster musicals is off-Broadway drama, where more than a few Tony Award–winning megahits originated. Tickets to productions that include actors as accomplished as Willem DaFoe, William H. Macy, and Frances McDormand are usually about half of those on the well-traveled Great White Way. Brooklyn hosts the world's most accomplished and avant-garde acting troupes, dance companies, and directors at the Brooklyn Academy of Music (BAM). Classical music is still centered on Manhattan's West Side, between Carnegie Hall and the New York Philharmonic at Lincoln Center.

Shopping Whether you're planning to run your credit cards up to the max or just window-shop, New York is a veritable shopping orgy. Everywhere, the ambience is part of the experience, and stores are stage sets—the elaborate Ralph Lauren mansion, the minimalist Calvin Klein boutique, super-charged NikeTown, endlessly eclectic ABC Carpet & Home. Bookstores are legion, including secondhand specialists like the Strand, with 8 mi of books. Even though you can get a lot of shopping done under one roof at Bloomingdales, Macy's, Saks Fifth Avenue, Henri Bendel, or Bergdorf Goodman, your feet will cover miles between their floors. SoHo and NoLita are where to go for pricy gifts and funky shoes and clothes, and the Meatpacking District now has hangers holding cuts of designer threads. Mayor Bloomberg may be cutting back on the city's recycling, but vintage and secondhand stores still freshen up castoffs from au-courant fashionistas of the *Sex and the City* vein.

FODOR'S CHOICE

The sights, restaurants, hotels, and other travel experiences on these pages are our editors' top picks—our Fodor's Choices. They're the best of their type in the area covered by the book—not to be missed and always worth your time. In the destination chapters that follow, you will find all the details.

LODGING

$$$$ Four Seasons. Towering over 57th Street, this I. M. Pei spire houses palatial, soundproof guest rooms with 10-foot ceilings, English sycamore walk-in closets, and blond-marble baths whose immense tubs fill in 60 seconds.

$$$ The Lowell. Many of the suites have working fireplaces in this small gem on a tree-lined Upper East Side street. The Pembroke Room serves a stunning tea, and the Post House is renowned for steaks.

$$$ Mercer Hotel. Imagine yourself in a minimalist SoHo loft apartment at this downtown hotel with dark African woods and high-tech light fixtures. The decadent two-person tubs, surrounded by mirrors, steal the show.

$$–$$$$ Inn at Irving Place. The tea salon of this grand pair of 1830s town houses near Gramercy Park evokes a gentler New York, as do the ornamental fireplaces, four-poster beds, and embroidered linens.

$$–$$$ W Times Square. This super-sleek 57-floor monolith with in-room DVD players puts a premium on futuristic style and ultrahip bustle in its restaurant and bar.

$$ Roger Williams Hotel. Its cavernous Rafael Viñoly–designed lobby—dubbed "a shrine to modernism" by *New York* magazine—highlights this stylish Murray Hill hotel.

¢–$$ The Gershwin. Young, foreign travelers flock to this budget hotel–cum–hostel, housed in a converted 13-story Greek revival building. Pop art on each floor augments the brightly colored rooms.

$ Howard Johnson's Express Inn. At the nexus of East Village and Lower East Side nightlife, the economical Express is perfect if you want to check out the downtown scene.

¢–$ Larchmont Hotel. Inside this beaux arts town house, rooms have a tasteful safari theme and share bathrooms. For the price and the old New York feel of West 11th Street, this Greenwich Village gem is all anyone needs.

RESTAURANTS

$$$$ Daniel. Daniel Boulud's grand dining room presents French classics as well as the chef's own brilliant inventions, such as scallops in black tie (dressed with truffles).

$$$$	**Gramercy Tavern.** Tom Colicchio's seasonal menu offers a respite from the fusion food that's trendy around town. There's an emphasis on game and fish roasted on the bone. Save room for dessert.
$$$$	**Jean Georges.** Dramatic picture windows give you a view of Central Park from this sleek, modernist dining room as Jean-Georges Vongerichten casts his culinary spell over some of the most astonishing dishes you'll ever taste.
$$$$	**Le Bernardin.** This trend-setting French seafood restaurant serves deceptively simple dishes, such as Spanish mackerel tartare with osetra caviar, in a plush, teak-paneled dining room.
$$$–$$$$	**Gotham Bar & Grill.** Chef Alfred Portale practically invented "New York architectural cuisine," and he remains the genre's best practitioner—not a drop of flavor is ever lost in the process of arranging the strikingly beautiful presentations.
$$–$$$$	**Craft.** Crafting your ideal meal here is like picking and choosing from a gourmand's well-stocked kitchen. The simple yet intriguing menu is exceptionally prepared.
$$–$$$	**Babbo.** This is Italian food as it was meant to be, updated, and after your first bite of the ethereal homemade pasta or tender suckling pig you'll know why critics rave.
¢–$$$	**Nobu.** Nobu Matsuhisa's dramatic food makes this New York's most famous Japanese restaurant. Both the classic Japanese sushi and the more contemporary dishes are worth waiting for (you'll have to reserve a month in advance).

AFTER HOURS

Bowery Ballroom. P. J. Harvey, Shelby Lynne, and Superchunk are among the performers who have appeared at this premier midsize concert venue.
Campbell Apartment. Enjoy a cocktail and executive high style from an overstuffed chair at this restored 1930 former elegant private office.
The Carlyle. At this discreetly sophisticated spot on the Upper East Side, Eartha Kitt and a host of others perform; Monday night belongs to Woody Allen and his clarinet.
Club Shelter. This warehouselike space is the home to some of the best dancing in the city.
Royalton. A hidden entrance and ultramodern decor make this a stylishly hip spot for sipping vodka and champagne.
Village Vanguard. The quintessential jazz venue, where you can still feel the vibes of Monk, Coltrane, and Davis.

ARCHITECTURE

Chrysler Building. An art deco, William Van Alen–designed master-piece built between 1928 and 1930, the Chrysler Building is one of New York's most iconic and beloved skyscrapers. It's at its best at dusk, when the stainless-steel spires glow, and at night, when its illuminated geometric design looks like the backdrop to a Holly-wood musical.

Empire State Building. Atop the 86th-floor observatory (1,050 feet high) you can see up to 80 mi on a clear day. But at night the city's lights are dazzling. The French architect Le Corbusier said, "It is a Milky Way come down to earth." The definitive New York icon is equally stunning from afar.

Grand Central Terminal. The world's largest railway station and the nation's busiest is, as critic Tony Hiss has said, "as a crossroads, a noble building . . . and an ingenious piece of engineering." Inside its majestic space, a celestial map of the zodiac constellations covers the robin's egg–blue ceiling (the major stars actually glow with fiber-optic lights).

CHURCHES

Cathedral Church of St. John the Divine. The largest Gothic cathedral in the world carries the Portal of Paradise, which depicts St. John witnessing the Transfiguration of Jesus, and 32 biblical characters, all intricately carved in stone. The cathedral has changing museum and art-gallery displays and presents a full calendar of secular (classical, folk, solstice) concerts.

FOR KIDS

Ice-skating, Rockefeller Center. The outdoor skating rink at Rockefeller Center is utterly romantic, especially when the enormous Christmas tree towers above.

MONUMENTS

Ellis Island Museum. If JFK airport seems daunting and chaotic, imagine disembarking into the international arrival hall at Ellis Island in the late 1800s. Interactive displays cover 400 years of immigration, the slave trade, and may provide links to your own ancestors. Enjoy a fabulous view and a stop at the Statue of Liberty while ferrying to the island.

abd**Statue of Liberty.** Presented to the United States in 1886 as a gift from France, she has become a near-universal symbol of freedom and democracy, standing a proud 152 feet high, on top of an 89-foot pedestal (executed by Richard Morris Hunt), on Liberty Island.

MUSEUMS

Metropolitan Museum of Art. Works of art from all over the world and every era of human creativity are part of this elegant and expansive treasure chest. When canvas and marble overwhelm you, turn to the temples, courtyard gardens, and silky dresses that also make up the collections.

Solomon R. Guggenheim Museum. Frank Lloyd Wright's landmark museum building displays an inspiring collection of impressionist works including Matisse and van Gogh. Changing exhibitions focus on artists ranging from Norman Rockwell to Jeff Koons.

QUINTESSENTIAL NEW YORK

Bethesda Fountain. Few New York views are more romantic than the one from the top of the magnificent stone staircase that leads down to the ornate, three-tier fountain in Central Park.

Cabaret. See a celebrity on stage or sitting next to you at one of the intimate cabaret rooms such as the Carlyle, Oak Room, or Joe's Pub.

SoHo. The elegant cast-iron buildings, occasional cobblestone street, art galleries, and clothing stores make this a wonderful area in which to shop, drink, and dream of a more glamorous life.

Walking over the Brooklyn Bridge. Begin admiring the Manhattan skyline from the Brooklyn Heights Promenade before setting out for a leisurely hour's stroll on the Brooklyn Bridge's boardwalk. Traffic is beneath you, and the views along the East River and harbor are wide open.

Washington Square Park. In a city without backyards, residents live their lives publicly, and if people-watching isn't entertainment enough in this Greenwich Village park, there are jugglers, magicians, and guitarists to circle round on the weekend.

A Yankees Game. Cheer on the winning Bronx Bombers alongside their devoted fans (or dare to root for the other team).

SHOPPING

Madison and 57th. Here's where the glossy flagships of international and American designers close ranks.

NoLita. One of the few neighborhoods that has withstood the chains, this is the place for unique boutiques.

ABC Carpet & Home. Each floor swarms with distinctive style, from the ornate accessories jumbled downstairs to the '60s mod squadrons above.

Barneys New York. Skate through for a cram session on the new darlings and the evergreen favorites of the design world.

B&H Photo Video and Pro Audio. Join the pros in perusing the equipment here.

Century 21. You can strike fashion gold among these packed racks of discounted goods.

Kate's Paperie. Wood pulp never looked so good as it does in these cards, wrapping papers, and albums.

Kiehl's Since 1851. The original source breeds cult-favorite lotions, conditioners, and cleansers.

Tiffany & Co. Talk about true blue—Tiffany's remains the consummate place for glittering gems and silver baubles.

THEME PARKS

Coney Island. Sideshows, old roller coasters, a boardwalk, a beach, and the original Nathan's Famous—what more could you ask for on a sunny afternoon in Brooklyn?

WHERE ART COMES FIRST

Brooklyn Academy of Music. America's oldest performing arts center is a premier performing arts mecca.

Carnegie Hall. A concert at this Italian Renaissance–style, 2,804-seat auditorium is a sublime experience.

Clementine. Works from up-and-coming artists are shown in this intimate Chelsea spot.

Film Forum. Come to watch anything from new releases to restored classics at this popular art-house-repertory theater.

Metropolitan Opera. From October to mid-April, this titan opera company performs with an intensity and quality that rival the world's finest symphonic orchestras.

WILDLIFE

The Bronx Zoo. One urban jungle deserves another. Only at the world's largest urban zoo is there room for gorillas to lumber around a 6½-acre simulated rain forest, or tigers and elephants to roam nearly 40 acres of open meadows.

SMART TRAVEL TIPS

Finding out about your destination before you leave home means you won't squander time organizing everyday minutiae once you've arrived. You'll be more street-wise when you hit the ground as well, better prepared to explore the aspects of New York City that drew you here in the first place. The organizations in this section can provide information to supplement this guide; contact them for up-to-the-minute details. Happy landings!

ADDRESSES

In Manhattan, the grid layout makes getting around easy. Avenues run north and south, with 5th Avenue dividing the east and west sides above 8th Street—the lower the address number on a street, the closer it is to 5th Avenue. The streets below 14th Street on the west and 1st Street on the east were settled before the grid system and follow no particular pattern.

To locate the cross street that corresponds to a numerical avenue address, or to find the avenue closest to a numerical street address, check the Web site below. (Cross streets for businesses are also listed in phone books.)

🔲 **Manhattan Address Locator** ⊕ www. manhattanaddress.com

AIR TRAVEL TO & FROM NEW YORK

Schedules and fares for air service to New York vary from carrier to carrier and, sometimes, from airport to airport. For the best prices and for nonstop flights, consult several airlines. Generally, more international flights go in and out of Kennedy Airport, more domestic flights go in and out of LaGuardia Airport, and Newark Airport serves both domestic and international travelers.

BOOKING

When you book, look for nonstop flights and remember that "direct" flights stop at least once. Try to avoid connecting flights, which require a change of plane. Two airlines may operate a connecting flight jointly, so ask whether your airline operates every segment of the trip; you may find that the carrier you prefer flies you only part of the way. To find more booking tips and to check prices and make online flight reservations, log on to www.fodors.com.

CARRIERS

There's an abundance of large and small airlines with flights to and from New York City.

Major Airlines Domestic carriers: **America West** ☎ 800/235-9292 ⊕ www.americawest.com. **American** ☎ 800/433-7300 ⊕ www.americanairlines.com. **Continental** ☎ 800/525-0280 ⊕ www.continental.com. **Delta** ☎ 800/221-1212 ⊕ www.delta.com. **Northwest/KLM** ☎ 800/225-2525 ⊕ www.nwa.com. **United** ☎ 800/241-6522 ⊕ www.united.com. **US Airways** ☎ 800/428-4322 ⊕ www.usairways.com.

International Carriers Air Canada ☎ 888/247-2262 ⊕ www.aircanada.ca. **Alitalia Airlines** ☎ 800/223-5730 ⊕ www.alitalia.com. **Austrian Airlines** ☎ 800/843-0002 ⊕ www.aua.com. **British Airways** ☎ 800/247-9297, 0870/85-098-50 in U.K. ⊕ www.ba.com. **Lufthansa** ☎ 800/399-5838 ⊕ www.lufthansa.com. **Qantas** ☎ 800/227-4500, 13-1313 in Australia ⊕ www.qantas.com. **Virgin Atlantic Airways** ☎ 800/862-8621, 01293/450-150 in U.K. ⊕ www.virgin-atlantic.com.

Smaller Airlines JetBlue ☎ 800/538-2583 ⊕ www.jetblue.com. **Midwest** ☎ 800/452-2022 ⊕ www.midwestairlines.com.

CHECK-IN & BOARDING

Always **find out your carrier's check-in policy.** Plan to arrive at the airport about two hours before your scheduled departure time for domestic flights and 2½ to 3 hours before international flights. You may need to arrive earlier if you're flying from one of the busier airports or during peak air-traffic times. To avoid delays at airport-security checkpoints, try not to wear any metal. Jewelry, belt and other buckles, steel-toe shoes, barrettes, and underwire bras are among the items that can set off detectors.

Assuming that not everyone with a ticket will show up, airlines routinely overbook planes. When everyone does, airlines ask for volunteers to give up their seats. In return, these volunteers usually get a several-hundred-dollar flight voucher, which can be used toward the purchase of another

ticket, and are rebooked on the next flight out. If there are not enough volunteers, the airline must choose who will be denied boarding. The first to get bumped are passengers who checked in late and those flying on discounted tickets, so get to the gate and check in as early as possible, especially during peak periods.

Always **bring a government-issued photo ID** to the airport; even when it's not required, a passport is best.

CUTTING COSTS

The least expensive airfares to New York City are priced for round-trip travel and must usually be purchased in advance. Airlines generally allow you to change your return date for a fee; most low-fare tickets, however, are nonrefundable. It's smart to call a number of airlines and check the Internet; when you are quoted a good price, book it on the spot—the same fare may not be available the next day, or even the next hour. Always check different routings and look into using alternate airports. Also, price off-peak flights, which may be significantly less expensive than others. Travel agents, especially low-fare specialists (⇨ Discounts & Deals), are helpful.

Consolidators are another good source. They buy tickets for scheduled flights at reduced rates from the airlines, then sell them at prices that beat the best fare available directly from the airlines. (Many also offer reduced car-rental and hotel rates.) Sometimes you can even get your money back if you need to return the ticket. Carefully read the fine print detailing penalties for changes and cancellations, purchase the ticket with a credit card, and confirm your consolidator reservation with the airline.

When you fly as a courier, you trade your checked-luggage space for a ticket deeply subsidized by a courier service. There are restrictions on when you can book and how long you can stay. Some courier companies list with membership organizations, such as the Air Courier Association and the International Association of Air Travel Couriers; these require you to become a member before you can book a flight.

Consolidators AirlineConsolidator.com ☎ 888/468-5385 ⊕ www.airlineconsolidator.com, for international tickets. **Best Fares** ☎ 800/880-1234 or 800/576-8255 ⊕ www.bestfares.com; $59.90 annual membership. **Cheap Tickets** ☎ 800/377-1000 or 800/652-4327 ⊕ www.cheaptickets.com. **Expedia** ☎ 800/397-3342 or 404/728-8787 ⊕ www.expedia.com. **Hotwire** ☎ 866/468-9473 or 920/330-9418 ⊕ www.hotwire.com. **Now Voyager Travel** ✉ 45 W. 21st St., Suite 5A, New York, NY 10010 ☎ 212/459-1616 🖷 212/243-2711 ⊕ www.nowvoyagertravel.com. **Onetravel.com** ⊕ www.onetravel.com. **Orbitz** ☎ 888/656-4546 ⊕ www.orbitz.com. **Priceline.com** ⊕ www.priceline.com. **Travelocity** ☎ 888/709-5983, 877/282-2925 in Canada, 0870/876-3876 in U.K. ⊕ www.travelocity.com.

🛈 **Courier Resources Air Courier Association/Cheaptrips.com** ☎ 800/280-5973 or 800/282-1202 ⊕ www.aircourier.org or www.cheaptrips.com; $34 annual membership. **International Association of Air Travel Couriers** ☎ 308/632-3273 ⊕ www.courier.org; $45 annual membership. **Now Voyager Travel** ✉ 45 W. 21st St., Suite 5A, New York, NY 10010 ☎ 212/459-1616 🖷 212/243-2711 ⊕ www.nowvoyagertravel.com.

ENJOYING THE FLIGHT

State your seat preference when purchasing your ticket, and then repeat it when you confirm and when you check in. For more legroom, you can request one of the few emergency-aisle seats at check-in, if you're capable of moving obstacles comparable in weight to an airplane exit door (usually between 35 pounds and 60 pounds)—a Federal Aviation Administration requirement of passengers in these seats. Seats behind a bulkhead also offer more legroom, but they don't have underseat storage. Don't sit in the row in front of the emergency aisle or in front of a bulkhead, where seats may not recline.

Ask the airline whether a snack or meal is served on the flight. If you have dietary concerns, request special meals when booking. These can be vegetarian, low-cholesterol, or kosher, for example. It's a good idea to pack some healthful snacks and a small (plastic) bottle of water in your carry-on bag. On long flights, try to maintain a normal routine, to help fight jet lag. At night, get some sleep. By day, eat light meals, drink water (not alcohol), and **move around the cabin** to stretch your legs. For additional jet-lag tips consult

Fodor's FYI: Travel Fit & Healthy (available at bookstores everywhere).

Smoking policies vary from carrier to carrier. Many airlines prohibit smoking on all of their flights; others allow smoking only on certain routes or certain departures. Ask your carrier about its policy.

FLYING TIMES

Some sample flying times are: from Chicago (2½ hours), London (7 hours), Los Angeles (6 hours), Sydney via Los Angeles (21 hours).

HOW TO COMPLAIN

If your baggage goes astray or your flight goes awry, complain right away. Most carriers require that you **file a claim immediately.** The Aviation Consumer Protection Division of the Department of Transportation publishes *Fly-Rights*, which discusses airlines and consumer issues and is available online. You can also find articles and information on mytravelrights.com, the Web site of the nonprofit Consumer Travel Rights Center.

🛈 **Airline Complaints Aviation Consumer Protection Division** ✉ U.S. Department of Transportation, Office of Aviation Enforcement and Proceedings, C-75, Room 4107, 400 7th St. SW, Washington, DC 20590 ☎ 202/366-2220 ⊕ airconsumer.ost.dot.gov. **Federal Aviation Administration Consumer Hotline** ✉ For inquiries: FAA, 800 Independence Ave. SW, Washington, DC 20591 ☎ 800/322-7873 ⊕ www.faa.gov.

RECONFIRMING

Check the status of your flight before you leave for the airport. You can do this on your carrier's Web site, by linking to a flight-status checker (many Web booking services offer these), or by calling your carrier or travel agent.

SECURITY

Due to increased security measures at area airports, many airlines request that passengers arrive a minimum of two hours before an international flight, and one hour before a domestic flight. Be sure to bring a government-issued photo identification, such as a passport or driver's license. There are tight restrictions on what is allowed in carry-on luggage (⇨ Packing).

Avoid wearing clothes with metal accessories and be prepared to remove your shoes for inspection.

AIRPORTS & TRANSFERS

The major air gateways to New York City are LaGuardia Airport (LGA) and JFK International Airport (JFK) in the borough of Queens, and Newark Liberty International Airport (EWR) in New Jersey. Cab fares are generally higher to and from Newark, and LaGuardia is closer to Manhattan and easier to navigate than JFK. The AirTrain link between Newark Airport and Penn Station in Manhattan makes the journey in less than 30 minutes.

🛈 Airport Information **JFK International Airport** ☎ 718/244-4444 ⊕ www.panynj.gov. **LaGuardia Airport** ☎ 718/533-3400 ⊕ www.laguardiaairport. com. **Newark Liberty International Airport** ☎ 973/961-6000 or 888/397-4636 ⊕ www. newarkairport.com.

AIRPORT TRANSFERS

Air-Ride provides detailed, up-to-the-minute recorded information on how to reach your destination from any of New York's airports. Note that if you arrive after midnight at any airport, you may wait a long time for a taxi. Consider calling a car service as there is no shuttle service at that time.

🛈 Transfer Information **Air-Ride** ☎ 800/247-7433 (800/AIR-RIDE) ⊕ www.panynj.gov/aviation.html.

TRANSFERS—CAR SERVICES

Car services can be a great deal because the driver will often meet you on the concourse or in the baggage-claim area and help you with your luggage. The flat rates and tolls are often comparable to taxi fares, but some car services will charge for parking and waiting time at the airport. To eliminate these expenses, other car services require that you telephone their dispatcher when you land so they can send the next available car to pick you up. New York City Taxi and Limousine Commission rules require that all car services be licensed and pick up riders only by prior arrangement; if possible, **call 24 hours in advance for reservations,** or at least a half day before your flight's departure. Drivers of nonlicensed vehicles ("gypsy cabs")

often solicit fares outside the terminal at in baggage claim areas. Don't take them: even if you do have a safe ride you'll pay more than the going rate.

For phone numbers, see (⇨ Taxis & Car Services) below.

TRANSFERS—TAXIS & SHUTTLES

Outside the baggage-claim area at each of New York's major airports are taxi stands where a uniformed dispatcher helps passengers find taxis (⇨ Taxis and Car Services). Cabs are not permitted to pick up fares anywhere else in the arrivals area, so if you want a taxi, take your place in line. Shuttle services generally pick up passengers from a designated spot along the curb.

New York Airport Service runs buses between JFK and LaGuardia airports, and buses from those airports to Grand Central Terminal, Port Authority Bus Terminal, Penn Station, Bryant Park, and hotels between 31st and 60th streets in Manhattan. Fares cost between $12 and $15. Buses operate from 6:15 AM to 11:10 PM from the airport; between 5 AM and 10 PM going to the airport.

SuperShuttle vans travel to and from Manhattan to JFK, LaGuardia, and Newark. These blue vans will stop at your home, office, or hotel. Courtesy phones are at the airports. For travel to the airport, the company requests 24-hour advance notice. Fares range from $15 to $19 per person.

🛈 Shuttle Service **New York Airport Service** ☎ 718/875-8200 ⊕ www.nyairportservice.com. **SuperShuttle** ☎ 212/258-3826 ⊕ www. supershuttle.com.

TRANSFERS FROM JFK INTERNATIONAL AIRPORT

Taxis charge a flat fee of $45 plus tolls (which may be as much as $6) to Manhattan only, and take 35–60 minutes. Prices are roughly $16–$55 for trips to most other locations in New York City. You should also tip the driver.

AirTrain JFK links to the A subway line's Howard Beach station, and to Long Island Railroad's (LIRR) Jamaica Station, which is adjacent to the Sutphin Boulevard/Archer Avenue E/J/Z subway station, with connections to Manhattan. The light rail system runs 24 hours, leaving from the Howard Beach and the LIRR stations station every 4–8 minutes during peak times and every 12 minutes during low traffic times. From midtown Manhattan, the longest trip to JFK is via the A train, a trip of under an hour that costs $2 in subway fare in addition to $5 for the AirTrain. The quickest trip is with the Long Island Railroad (about 30 minutes), for a total cost of about $12. When traveling to the Howard Beach station, be sure to take the A train marked FAR ROCKAWAY or ROCK-AWAY PARK, **not** LEFFERTS BOULEVARD.

🚊 **JFK Transfer Information AirTrain JFK** ⊕ www.airtrainjfk.com. **Long Island Railroad** Jamaica Station ⊠ 146 Archer Ave., at Sutphin Ave. ☎ 718/217-5477.

TRANSFERS FROM LAGUARDIA AIRPORT

Taxis cost $20–$30 plus tip and tolls (which may be as high as $6) to most destinations in New York City, and take at least 20–40 minutes.

For $2 you can ride the M-60 public bus (there are no luggage facilities on this bus) to 116th Street and Broadway, across from Columbia University on Manhattan's Upper West Side. From there, you can transfer to the No. 1 subway to midtown. Alternatively, you can take Bus Q-48 to the Main Street subway station in Flushing, where you can transfer to the No. 7 train. Allow at least 90 minutes for the entire trip to midtown.

TRANSFERS FROM NEWARK AIRPORT

Taxis to Manhattan cost $40–$65 plus tolls ($5) and take 20 to 45 minutes. "Share and Save" group rates are available for up to four passengers between 8 AM and midnight—make arrangements with the airport's taxi dispatcher. If you're heading to the airport from Manhattan, a $15 surcharge applies to the normal taxi rates and the $5 toll.

AirTrain Newark is an elevated light rail system that connects to New Jersey Transit and Amtrak trains at the Newark Liberty International Airport Station. Total travel time to Penn Station in Manhattan is approximately 20 minutes and costs $11.55

if you connect to a New Jersey train (it costs significantly more to connect to an Amtrak train). AirTrain runs from 5 AM to 2 AM daily.

Before heading to Manhattan, the AirTrain makes a stop at Newark's Penn Station. The five-minute ride here costs $6.80. From Newark Penn Station you can catch PATH trains, which run to Manhattan 24 hours a day. PATH trains run every 10 minutes on weekdays, every 15 to 30 minutes on weeknights, and every 20 to 30 minutes on weekends. After stopping at Christopher Street, one line travels along 6th Avenue, making stops at West 9th Street, West 14th Street, West 23rd Street, and West 33rd Street. Other PATH trains connect Newark Penn Station with the World Trade Center site. PATH train fare is $1.50.

Olympia Trails buses leave for Grand Central Terminal and Penn Station in Manhattan about every 20 minutes until midnight. The trip takes roughly 45 minutes, and the fare is $12. Between the Port Authority or Grand Central Terminal and Newark, buses run every 20 to 30 minutes. The fare is $12.

🚊 **Newark Airport Information AirTrain Newark** ☎ 888/397-4636 ⊕ www.airtrainnewark.com. **Olympia Trails** ☎ 212/964-6233 or 877/894-9155 ⊕ www.olympiabus.com. **PATH Trains** ☎ 800/234-7284 ⊕ www.pathrail.com.

BOAT & FERRY TRAVEL

The Staten Island Ferry runs across New York Harbor between Whitehall Street next to Battery Park in lower Manhattan and St. George terminal in Staten Island. The free 25-minute ride gives you a view of the Financial District skyscrapers, the Statue of Liberty, and Ellis Island.

New York Water Taxi, in addition to serving commuters, shuttles tourists to the city's many waterfront attractions between the west and east sides and lower Manhattan, the South Street Seaport, and Brooklyn's waterfront parks. The hop-on, hop-off ticket (good for two days) is $20 for adults.

FARES & SCHEDULES

🚊 **Boat & Ferry Information New York Water Taxi** (NYWT) ☎ 212/742-1969 ⊕ www.newyorkwatertaxi.com. **Staten Island Ferry** ☎ 718/815-2628 ⊕ www.siferry.com.

BUS TRAVEL TO & FROM NEW YORK CITY

Most long-haul and commuter bus lines feed into the Port Authority Bus Terminal, on 8th Avenue between West 40th and 42nd streets. You must purchase your ticket at a ticket counter, not from the bus driver, so give yourself enough time to wait in a line. Six bus lines, serving northern New Jersey and Rockland County, New York, make daily stops at the George Washington Bridge Bus Station from 5 AM to 1 AM. The station is connected to the 175th Street Station on the A line of the subway, which travels down the West Side of Manhattan.

🛈 Bus Information **Adirondack, Pine Hill, and New York Trailways** ☎ 800/225-6815 ⊕ www. trailways.com. **Bonanza Bus Lines** ☎ 888/751-8800 ⊕ www.bonanzabus.com. **Greyhound Lines Inc.** ☎ 800/231-2222 ⊕ www.greyhound.com. **New Jersey Transit** ☎ 800/772-2222 ⊕ www.njtransit. com. **Peter Pan Trailways** ☎ 413/781-2900 or 800/237-8747 ⊕ www.peterpanbus.com. **Shortline** ☎ 800/631-8405 ⊕ www.shortlinebus.com. **Vermont Transit** ☎ 800/552-8737 ⊕ www. vermonttransit.com.

🛈 Bus Stations **George Washington Bridge Bus Station** ✉ 4211 Broadway, between 178th and 179th Sts., Washington Heights ☎ 800/221-9903 ⊕ www. panynj.gov. **Port Authority Bus Terminal** ✉ 625 8th Ave., at 42nd St., Midtown West ☎ 212/564-8484 ⊕ www.panynj.gov.

BUS TRAVEL WITHIN NEW YORK CITY

Most city buses follow easy-to-understand routes along the Manhattan street grid. Routes go up or down the north–south avenues, or east and west on the major two-way crosstown streets: 96th, 86th, 79th, 72nd, 57th, 42nd, 34th, 23rd, and 14th. Most bus routes operate 24 hours, but service is infrequent late at night. Traffic jams can make rides maddeningly slow, especially along 5th Avenue in midtown and the Upper East Side. Certain bus routes provide "Limited-Stop Service" during weekday rush hours, which saves travel time by stopping only at major cross streets and transfer points. A sign posted at the front of the bus indicates it has limited service; ask the driver whether the bus stops near where you want to go before boarding.

To find a bus stop, **look for a light-blue sign (green for a limited bus)** on a green pole; bus numbers and routes are listed, with the stop's name underneath.

FARES & SCHEDULES

Bus fare is the same as subway fare: $2. MetroCards (⇨ Public Transportation) allow you one free transfer between buses or from bus to subway; when using a token or cash, you can **ask the driver for a free transfer coupon,** good for one change to an intersecting route. Legal transfer points are listed on the back of the slip. Transfers generally have time limits of two hours. You cannot use the transfer to enter the subway system.

Route maps and schedules are posted at many bus stops in Manhattan and at major stops throughout the other boroughs. Each of the five boroughs of New York has a separate bus map; they're available from some station booths, but rarely on buses. The best places to obtain them are the MTA booth in the Times Square Information Center, or the information kiosks in Grand Central Terminal and Penn Station.

🛈 Bus Information **Metropolitan Transit Authority (MTA) Travel Information Line** ☎ 718/330-1234, 718/330-4847 for non-English speakers ⊕ www. mta.nyc.ny.us. **MTA Status information hotline** ☎ 718/243-7777, updated hourly.

PAYING

Pay your bus fare when you board, with exact change in coins (no pennies, and no change is given) or with a MetroCard.

BUSINESS HOURS

New York is very much a 24-hour city. Its subways and buses run around the clock, and plenty of services are available at all hours and on all days of the week.

BANKS

Most banks are open weekdays 9 AM–3 PM or 9 AM–3:30 PM; some have late hours one day a week or are open on Saturday or even Sunday. *See* Mail & Shipping for post office hours.

MUSEUMS & SIGHTS

Museum hours vary greatly, but most of the major ones are open Tuesday–Sunday and keep later hours on Tuesday, Thursday, or Friday evenings.

PHARMACIES

Pharmacies are generally open early in the morning and remain open until at least 6 PM or 7 PM. Most chain drugstores, including Duane Reade, CVS, and Rite-Aid, have a number of locations that keep late hours or are open 24 hours.

SHOPS

Stores are generally open Monday–Saturday from 10 AM to 6 PM or 7 PM, but neighborhood peculiarities do exist and many retailers remain open until 8 PM or even later. Sunday hours are common in most areas of the city. Many stores on the Lower East Side and on West 47th Street (the Diamond District) close on Friday afternoon and all day Saturday for the Sabbath, but some are open Sunday.

CAMERAS & PHOTOGRAPHY

Photography opportunities abound in New York, and you may have to shoot fast or several times if you want to avoid passersby filling the frame. Some people may be sensitive about having their picture taken without their consent, so ask their permission first. The *Kodak Guide to Shooting Great Travel Pictures* (available at bookstores everywhere) is loaded with tips.

🖪 Photo Help **Kodak Information Center** ☎ 800/242-2424 ⊕ www.kodak.com.

EQUIPMENT PRECAUTIONS

Don't pack film or equipment in checked luggage, where it is much more susceptible to damage. X-ray machines used to view checked luggage are extremely powerful and therefore are likely to ruin your film. Try to ask for hand inspection of film, which becomes clouded after repeated exposure to airport X-ray machines, and keep videotapes and computer disks away from metal detectors. Always keep film, tape, and computer disks out of the sun. Carry an extra supply of batteries, and be prepared to turn on your camera, camcorder, or laptop to prove to airport security personnel that the device is real.

CAR RENTAL

Rates in New York City begin at around $40 a day and $200 a week for an economy car with air-conditioning, automatic transmission, and unlimited mileage. This includes the state tax on car rentals, which is 13.62%. Rental costs are lower just outside New York City, specifically in places like Hoboken, New Jersey, and Yonkers, New York. The Yellow Pages are also filled with a profusion of local car-rental agencies, some renting secondhand vehicles. If you're traveling during a holiday period, make sure that a confirmed reservation guarantees you a car.

🖪 Major Agencies **Alamo** ☎ 800/327-9633 ⊕ www.alamo.com. **Avis** ☎ 800/331-1212, 800/879-2847 or 800/272-5871 in Canada, 0870/606-0100 in U.K., 02/9353-9000 in Australia, 09/526-2847 in New Zealand ⊕ www.avis.com. **Budget** ☎ 800/527-0700, 0870/156-5656 in U.K. ⊕ www.budget.com. **Dollar** ☎ 800/800-4000, 0800/085-4578 in U.K. ⊕ www.dollar.com. **Hertz** ☎ 800/654-3131, 800/263-0600 in Canada, 0870/844-8844 in U.K., 02/9669-2444 in Australia, 09/256-8690 in New Zealand ⊕ www.hertz.com. **National Car Rental** ☎ 800/227-7368, 0870/600-6666 in U.K. ⊕ www.nationalcar.com.

CUTTING COSTS

For a good deal, book through a travel agent who will shop around. Also, price local car-rental companies—whose prices may be lower still, although their service and maintenance may not be as good as those of major rental agencies—and research rates on the Internet. Consolidators that specialize in air travel can offer good rates on cars as well (⇨ Air Travel). Remember to ask about required deposits, cancellation penalties, and drop-off charges if you're planning to pick up the car in one city and leave it in another. If you're traveling during a holiday period, also make sure that a confirmed reservation guarantees you a car.

🖪 Local Agencies **New York Rent-A-Car** ☎ 212/799-1100 ⊕ www.nyrac.com.

INSURANCE

When driving a rented car you are generally responsible for any damage to or loss of the vehicle. You also may be liable for any property damage or personal injury that you may cause while driving. Before you rent, see what coverage you already have under the terms of your personal auto-insurance policy and credit cards.

For about $9 to $25 a day, rental companies sell protection, known as a collision- or loss-damage waiver (CDW or LDW), that eliminates your liability for damage to the car; it's always optional and should never be automatically added to your bill. In New York State, if you're renting a vehicle for more than 48 hours, you may choose to cancel the LDW coverage within 24 hours of signing the rental agreement. (To do so you must bring the car, which is subject to inspection, to one of the rental company's branches.)

REQUIREMENTS & RESTRICTIONS
In New York you must be 18 to rent a car. Although rental agencies based in New York are technically required to rent to qualified drivers under 25, hefty surcharges of as much as $115 a day may effectively remove this option. Surcharges in New Jersey tend to be lower.

When picking up a car, non-U.S. residents will need a reservation voucher for any prepaid reservations that were made in the traveler's home country, a passport, a driver's license, and a travel policy that covers each driver.

SURCHARGES
Before you pick up a car in one city and leave it in another, ask about drop-off charges or one-way service fees, which can be substantial. Also inquire about early-return policies; some rental agencies charge extra if you return the car before the time specified in your contract while others give you a refund for the days not used. To avoid a hefty refueling fee, fill the tank just before you turn in the car, but be aware that gas stations near the rental outlet may overcharge. It's almost never a deal to buy the tank of gas that's in the car when you rent it; the understanding is that you'll return it empty, but some fuel usually remains. Surcharges may apply if you're under 25 or if you take the car outside the area approved by the rental agency. You'll

pay extra for child seats (about $8 a day), which are compulsory for children under five, and usually for additional drivers (up to $25 a day, depending on location).

CAR TRAVEL
If you plan to drive into Manhattan, try to avoid the morning and evening rush hours (a problem at the crossings into Manhattan) and lunch hour. The deterioration of the bridges to Manhattan, especially those spanning the East River, mean repairs will be ongoing for the next few years. Listen to traffic reports on the radio (⇨ Media) before you set off, and don't be surprised if a bridge is partially or entirely closed.

Driving within Manhattan can be a nightmare of gridlocked streets, obnoxious drivers and bicyclists, and seemingly suicidal jaywalkers. Narrow and one-way streets are common, particularly downtown, and can make driving even more difficult. The most congested streets of the city lie between 14th and 59th streets and 3rd and 8th avenues.

GASOLINE
Fill up your tank when you have a chance—gas stations are few and far between in Manhattan. If you can, **fill up at stations outside of the city,** where prices are anywhere from 10¢ to 50¢ cheaper per gallon. The average price of a gallon of regular unleaded gas is $2.50, at this writing. In Manhattan, you can refuel at stations along the West Side Highway and 11th Avenue south of West 57th Street and along East Houston Street. Some gas stations in New York require you to pump your own gas; others provide attendants. In New Jersey, the law requires that an attendant pump your gas.

PARKING
Free parking is difficult to find in midtown, and violators may be towed away literally within minutes. All over town, parking lots charge exorbitant rates—as much as $23 for two hours (this includes an impressive sales tax of 18.625%). If you do drive, **use your car sparingly in Manhattan.** Instead, park it in a guarded parking garage for at least several hours; hourly rates decrease somewhat if a car is left for a significant

amount of time. If you find a spot on the street, be sure to **check parking signs carefully.** Rules differ from block to block, and they're nearly all confusing.

ROAD CONDITIONS

New York City streets are in generally good condition, although there are enough potholes and bad patch jobs to make driving a little rough in some areas, as on Canal Street. Road and bridge repair seems to go on constantly, so you may encounter the occasional detour or a bottleneck where a three-lane street narrows to one lane. Heavy rains can cause street flooding in some areas, most notoriously on the Franklin Delano Roosevelt Drive (known as the FDR and sometimes as East River Drive), where the heavy traffic can grind to a halt when lakes suddenly appear on the road. Traffic can be very heavy anywhere in the city at any time, made worse by the bad habits—double-parking, sudden lane changes, etc.—of some drivers. Many drivers don't slow down for yellow lights here—they speed up to make it through the intersection.

RULES OF THE ROAD

On city streets the speed limit is 30 mi per hour, unless otherwise posted. No right turns on red are allowed within city limits, unless otherwise posted. Be alert for one-way streets and "no left turn" intersections.

The law requires that front-seat passengers wear seat belts at all times. Children under 16 must wear seat belts in both the front and back seats. Always **strap children under age four into approved child-safety seats.** It is illegal to use a handheld cell phone while driving in New York State. Police will immediately seize the car of anyone arrested for DWI (driving while intoxicated) in New York City.

CHILDREN IN NEW YORK

Even though much of New York is focused on the adult pursuits of making money and then spending it, kids can run riot in this city, too. Cultural institutions include programs for introducing children to the arts, large stores put on fun promotional events, and many attractions, from skyscrapers to museums, engage the whole family. For listings of children's events, consult *New York* magazine, and *Time Out New York.* The Friday *New York Times* "Weekend" section also includes children's activities. Other good sources on happenings for youngsters are the monthly magazines *New York Family* and *Big Apple Parent,* both available free at toy stores, children's museums, and other places around town where parents and children are found. The Web site goCityKids includes listings of what's going on. If you have access to cable television, check the local all-news channel New York 1, where you'll find a spot aired several times daily that covers current and noteworthy children's events. *Fodor's Around New York City with Kids* (available in bookstores everywhere) can help you plan your days together.

If you are renting a car, don't forget to arrange for a car seat when you reserve. For general advice about traveling with children, consult *Fodor's FYI: Travel with Your Baby* (available in bookstores everywhere).

🄵 Publications & Web Sites **Big Apple Parent** ⊕ www.parentsknow.com. **goCityKids** ⊕ www. gocitykids.com. **New York Family** ⊕ www. parenthood.com.

BABYSITTING

The Baby Sitters' Guild will schedule sightseeing tours for a flat fee of $100. Regular babysitting rates are $17 an hour for one child, $20 for two children, and $25 for three children, plus a $4.50 transportation charge ($7 after midnight). More than 16 languages are spoken by staff members. Minimum booking is for four hours, and infants cost extra. Cash and travelers' checks are accepted.

🄵 Agency **Baby Sitters' Guild** ☎ 212/682-0227 ⊕ www.babysittersguild.com ⊙ Daily 9-9.

FLYING

Experts agree that it's a good idea to use safety seats aloft for children weighing less than 40 pounds. Airlines set their own policies: if you use a safety seat, U.S. carriers usually require that the child be ticketed, even if he or she is young enough to ride free, because the seats must be strapped into regular seats. And even if you pay the full adult fare for the seat, it may be worth it, especially on longer trips. Do **check your airline's policy about using safety seats during takeoff and landing.** Safety seats are not allowed everywhere in the plane, so get your seat assignments as early as possible.

When reserving, request children's meals or a freestanding bassinet (not available at all airlines) if you need them. But note that bulkhead seats, where you must sit to use the bassinet, may lack an overhead bin or storage space on the floor.

LODGING

Before you consider using a cot or fold-out couch for your child, ask just how large your hotel room is—New York City rooms tend to be small. Most hotels in New York allow children under a certain age to stay in their parents' room at no extra charge, but others charge for them as extra adults; be sure to find out the cutoff age for children's discounts.

PUBLIC TRANSPORTATION

Children shorter than 44 inches ride for free on MTA buses and subways. If you're pushing a stroller, don't struggle through a subway turnstile; **ask the station agent to buzz you through the gate** (the attendant will ask you to swipe your MetroCard through the turnstile nearest the gate). Keep a sharp eye on your young ones while on the subway. At some stations there is a gap between the train doors and the platform. During rush hour crowds often try to push into spaces that look empty—but are actually occupied by a stroller. Unfortunately New York riders are not known to give up their seats for children, for someone carrying a child, or for much of anyone else.

SIGHTS & ATTRACTIONS

Places that are especially appealing to children are indicated by a rubber-duckie icon (🐤) in the margin.

COMPUTERS ON THE ROAD

The Web site JiWire allows you to find Wi-Fi hotspots in hotels, libraries, parks, and other locations throughout the city.
📶 JiWire ⊕ www.jiwire.com.

CONCIERGES

Concierges, found in many hotels, can help you with theater tickets and dinner reservations: a good one with connections may be able to get you seats for a hot show or prime-time dinner reservations at the restaurant of the moment. You can also turn to your hotel's concierge for help with travel arrangements, sightseeing plans, services ranging from aromatherapy to zipper repair, and emergencies. **Always tip** a concierge who has been of assistance (⇨ Tipping).

CONSUMER PROTECTION

Whether you're shopping for gifts or purchasing travel services, **pay with a major credit card** whenever possible, so you can cancel payment or get reimbursed if there's a problem (and you can provide documentation). If you're doing business with a particular company for the first time, contact your local Better Business Bureau and the attorney general's office in your state and (for U.S. businesses) the company's home state as well. Have any complaints been filed? Finally, if you're buying a package or tour, always consider travel insurance that includes default coverage (⇨ Insurance).
📶 BBBs **Council of Better Business Bureaus** ✉ 4200 Wilson Blvd., Suite 800, Arlington, VA 22203 ☎ 703/276-0100 🖷 703/525-8277 ⊕ www. bbb.org.

CUSTOMS & DUTIES

IN AUSTRALIA

Australian residents who are 18 or older may bring home A$400 worth of souvenirs and gifts (including jewelry), 250 cigarettes or 250 grams of cigars or other tobacco products, and 1,125 ml of alcohol (including wine, beer, and spirits). Residents under 18 may bring back A$200 worth of goods. Members of the same family traveling together may pool their allowances. Prohibited items include meat products. Seeds, plants, and fruits need to be declared upon arrival.
📶 **Australian Customs Service** 🏛 Regional Director, Box 8, Sydney, NSW 2001 ☎ 02/9213-2000, 1300/363263, 02/9364-7222, 1800/020-504 quarantine-inquiry line 🖷 02/9213-4043 ⊕ www.customs. gov.au.

IN CANADA

Canadian residents who have been out of Canada for at least seven days may bring in C$750 worth of goods duty-free. If you've been away fewer than seven days but more than 48 hours, the duty-free allowance drops to C$200. If your trip lasts 24 to 48 hours, the allowance is C$50. You may not pool allowances with family members. Goods claimed under the C$750 exemption may follow you by mail; those claimed under the lesser exemptions must accompany you. Alcohol and tobacco products may be included in the seven-day and 48-hour exemptions but not in the 24-hour exemption. If you meet the age requirements of the province or territory through which you reenter Canada, you may bring in, duty-free, 1.5 liters of wine or 1.14 liters (40 imperial ounces) of liquor or 24 12-ounce cans or bottles of beer or ale. Also, if you meet the local age requirement for tobacco products, you may bring in, duty-free, 200 cigarettes and 50 cigars. Check ahead of time with the Canada Customs and Revenue Agency or the Department of Agriculture for policies regarding meat products, seeds, plants, and fruits.

You may send an unlimited number of gifts (only one gift per recipient, however) worth up to C$60 each duty-free to Canada. Label the package UNSOLICITED GIFT—VALUE UNDER $60. Alcohol and tobacco are excluded.

🔲 **Canada Customs and Revenue Agency** ⊠ 2265 St. Laurent Blvd., Ottawa, Ontario K1G 4K3 ☎ 800/461-9999 in Canada, 204/983-3500, 506/636-5064 ⊕ www.ccra.gc.ca.

IN NEW ZEALAND

All homeward-bound residents may bring back NZ$700 worth of souvenirs and gifts; passengers may not pool their allowances, and children can claim only the concession on goods intended for their own use. For those 17 or older, the duty-free allowance also includes 4.5 liters of wine or beer; one 1,125-ml bottle of spirits; and either 200 cigarettes, 250 grams of tobacco, 50 cigars, or a combination of the three up to 250 grams. Meat products, seeds, plants, and fruits must be declared upon arrival to the Agricultural Services Department.

🔲 **New Zealand Customs** ⊠ Head office: The Customhouse, 17-21 Whitmore St., Box 2218, Wellington ☎ 09/300-5399 or 0800/428-786 ⊕ www.customs.govt.nz.

IN THE U.K.

From countries outside the European Union, including the United States, you may bring home, duty-free, 200 cigarettes, 100 cigarillos, 50 cigars, 100 cigarillos, or 250 grams of tobacco; 1 liter of spirits or 2 liters of fortified or sparkling wine or liqueurs; 2 liters of still table wine; 60 ml of perfume; 250 ml of toilet water; plus £145 worth of other goods, including gifts and souvenirs. Prohibited items include meat products, seeds, plants, fruits, and dairy products.

🔲 **HM Customs and Excise** ⊠ Portcullis House, 21 Cowbridge Rd. E, Cardiff CF11 9SS ☎ 0845/010-9000, 0208/929-0152 advice service, 0208/929-6731, 0208/910-3602 complaints ⊕ www.hmce.gov.uk.

DISABILITIES & ACCESSIBILITY

New York has come a long way in making life easier for people with disabilities. At most street corners, curb cuts allow wheelchairs to roll along unimpeded. Many restaurants, shops, and movie theaters with step-up entrances have wheelchair ramps. And though some New Yorkers may rush past those in need of assistance, you'll find plenty of people who are more than happy to help you get around.

Hospital Audiences maintains a Web site with information on the accessibility of many landmarks and attractions. A similar list, "Tourist and Cultural Information for the Disabled," is available from New York City's Web site. Big Apple Greeters has tours of New York City tailored to visitors' personal preferences. The Andrew Heiskell Braille and Talking Book Library houses an impressive collection of braille, large-print, and recorded books in a layout designed for people with vision impairments.

🔲 **Local Resources Andrew Heiskell Library** ⊠ 40 W. 20th St., between 5th and 6th Aves., Flatiron District Ⓜ F or V to 23rd St. ☎ 212/206-5400, 212/206-5458 TDD ⊕ www.nypl.org/branch/lb. **Big Apple Greeters** ⊠ 1 Centre St., Suite 2035, Lower

Manhattan, New York, NY 10007 ☎ 212/669-2896 ⊕ www.bigapplegreeter.org. **Hospital Audiences** ☎ 212/575-7676 ⊕ www.hospaud.org. **New York City** ☎ 311 in New York City, 212/639-9675 (212/NEW-YORK) outside of New York ⊕ www.nyc.gov.

HOTEL RESERVATIONS

When discussing accessibility with an operator or reservations agent, ask hard questions. Are there any stairs, inside *or* out? Are there grab bars next to the toilet *and* in the shower/tub? How wide is the doorway to the room? To the bathroom? For the most extensive facilities meeting the latest legal specifications, opt for newer accommodations. If you reserve through a toll-free number, consider also calling the hotel's local number to confirm the information from the central reservations office. Get confirmation in writing when you can.

LODGING

Despite the Americans with Disabilities Act, the definition of accessibility seems to differ from hotel to hotel. Some properties may be accessible by ADA standards for people with mobility problems but not for people with hearing or vision impairments, for example.

If you have mobility problems, ask for the lowest floor on which accessible services are offered. If you have a hearing impairment, check whether the hotel has devices to alert you visually to the ring of the telephone, a knock at the door, and a fire/emergency alarm. Some hotels provide these devices without charge. Discuss your needs with hotel personnel if this equipment isn't available, so that a staff member can personally alert you in the event of an emergency.

If you're bringing a guide dog, get authorization ahead of time and write down the name of the person with whom you spoke.

SIGHTS & ATTRACTIONS

Most public facilities in New York City, whether museums, parks, or theaters, are wheelchair-accessible. Some attractions have tours or programs for people with mobility, sight, or hearing impairments.

TRANSPORTATION

Other than at major subway exchanges, most stations are still all but impossible to navigate; people in wheelchairs should stick to public buses, most of which have wheelchair lifts and "kneelers" at the front to facilitate getting on and off. Bus drivers will provide assistance.

Reduced fares are available to all disabled passengers displaying a Medicare card. Visitors to the city are also eligible for the same Access-a-Ride program benefits as New York City residents. Drivers with disabilities may use windshield cards from their own state or Canadian province to park in designated handicapped spaces.

🚩 Complaints **Aviation Consumer Protection Division** (⇨ Air Travel) for airline-related problems. **Departmental Office of Civil Rights** ✉ For general inquiries, U.S. Department of Transportation, S-30, 400 7th St. SW, Room 10215, Washington, DC 20590 ☎ 202/366-4648 🖷 202/366-9371 ⊕ www.dot.gov/ost/docr/index.htm. **Disability Rights Section** ✉ NYAV, U.S. Department of Justice, Civil Rights Division, 950 Pennsylvania Ave. NW, Washington, DC 20530 ☎ ADA information line 202/514-0301, 800/514-0301, 202/514-0383 TTY, 800/514-0383 TTY ⊕ www.ada.gov. **U.S. Department of Transportation Hotline** ☎ For disability-related air-travel problems, 800/778-4838 or 800/455-9880 TTY.

TRAVEL AGENCIES

In the United States, the Americans with Disabilities Act requires that travel firms serve the needs of all travelers. Some agencies specialize in working with people with disabilities.

🚩 Travelers with Mobility Problems **Access Adventures/B. Roberts Travel** ✉ 206 Chestnut Ridge Rd., Scottsville, NY 14624 ☎ 585/889-9096 ⊕ www.brobertstravel.com ✍ dltravel@prodigy.net, run by a former physical-rehabilitation counselor. **Accessible Vans of America** ✉ 9 Spielman Rd., Fairfield, NJ 07004 ☎ 877/282-8267, 888/282-8267, 973/808-9709 reservations 🖷 973/808-9713 ⊕ www.accessiblevans.com. **CareVacations** ✉ No. 5, 5110-50 Ave., Leduc, Alberta, Canada, T9E 6V4 ☎ 780/986-6404 or 877/478-7827 🖷 780/986-8332 ⊕ www.carevacations.com, for group tours and cruise vacations. **Flying Wheels Travel** ✉ 143 W. Bridge St., Box 382, Owatonna, MN 55060 ☎ 507/451-5005 🖷 507/451-1685 ⊕ www.flyingwheelstravel.com.

🚩 Travelers with Developmental Disabilities **New Directions** ✉ 5276 Hollister Ave., Suite 207, Santa Barbara, CA 93111 ☎ 805/967-2841 or 888/967-2841

🖨 805/964-7344 ⊕ www.newdirectionstravel.com.
Sprout ✉ 893 Amsterdam Ave., New York, NY 10025
☎ 212/222-9575 or 888/222-9575 🖨 212/222-9768
⊕ www.gosprout.org.

DISCOUNTS & DEALS

Numerous tourist-oriented publications available at hotels, stores, and attractions have coupons good for discounts of all kinds, from restaurants and shopping to sightseeing and sporting activities. Cut-rate theater tickets are sold at TKTS (⇨ The Performing Arts *in* Chapter 8) booths in Times Square and South Street Seaport. Some major museums have evenings with free or pay-what-you-wish admission one day a week.

Be a smart shopper and compare all your options before making decisions. A plane ticket bought with a promotional coupon from travel clubs, coupon books, and direct-mail offers or purchased on the Internet may not be cheaper than the least expensive fare from a discount ticket agency. And always keep in mind that what you get is just as important as what you save.

DISCOUNT RESERVATIONS

To save money, look into discount reservations services with Web sites and toll-free numbers, which use their buying power to get a better price on hotels, airline tickets (⇨ Air Travel), even car rentals. When booking a room, always **call the hotel's local toll-free number** (if one is available) rather than the central reservations number—you'll often get a better price. Always ask about special packages or corporate rates.

🛈 Airline Tickets **Air 4 Less** ☎ 800/AIR4LESS, low-fare specialist.

🛈 Hotel Rooms **Accommodations Express** ☎ 800/444-7666 or 800/277-1064 ⊕ www.acex.net. **Central Reservation Service (CRS)** ☎ 800/555-7555 or 800/548-3311 ⊕ www.crshotels.com. **Hotels.com** ☎ 800/246-8357 ⊕ www.hotels.com. **Quikbook** ☎ 800/789-9887 ⊕ www.quikbook.com. **Steigenberger Reservation Service** ☎ 800/223-5652 ⊕ www.srs-worldhotels.com. **Turbotrip.com** ☎ 800/473-7829 ⊕ www.turbotrip.com.

PACKAGE DEALS

Don't confuse packages and guided tours. When you buy a package, you travel on your own, just as though you had planned the trip yourself. Fly-drive packages, which combine airfare and car rental, are often a good deal. In cities, ask the local visitor's bureau about hotel and local transportation packages that include tickets to major museum exhibits or other special events.

SIGHTSEEING

Consider purchasing a CityPass, a group of tickets to six top-notch attractions in New York—the Empire State Building, the Guggenheim Museum, the American Museum of Natural History, the Museum of Modern Art, Circle Line Cruises, and the *Intrepid* Sea-Air-Space Museum. The $53 pass, which saves you half the cost of each individual ticket, is good for nine days from first use. It also allows you to beat long ticket lines at some attractions. You can buy a CityPass online or at any of the participants' ticket offices.

🛈 **CityPass** ☎ 707/256-0490 recorded information ⊕ www.citypass.com.

EMERGENCIES

Dial 911 for police, fire, or ambulance services in an emergency (TTY is available for persons with hearing impairments).

🛈 Hospitals **Bellevue** ✉ 1st Ave., at E. 27th St., Gramercy ☎ 212/562-4141. **Beth Israel Medical Center** ✉ 1st Ave. at E. 16th St., Gramercy ☎ 212/420-2000. **Lenox Hill Hospital** ✉ 100 E. 77th St., between Lexington and Park Aves., Upper East Side ☎ 212/434-3030. **New York Presbyterian Hospital** ✉ 525 E. 68th St., at York Ave., Upper East Side ☎ 212/746-5454. **NYU Hospital Downtown** ✉ 170 William St., between Beekman and Spruce Sts., Lower Manhattan ☎ 212/312-5000. **NYU Medical Center** ✉ 550 1st Ave., at E. 32nd St., Murray Hill ☎ 212/263-7300. **St. Luke's-Roosevelt Hospital** ✉ 10th Ave. at 59th St., Midtown West ☎ 212/523-4000. **St. Vincent's Hospital** ✉ 7th Ave. and W. 12th St., Greenwich Village ☎ 212/604-7000.

🛈 24-Hour Pharmacies **CVS** ✉ 342 E. 23rd St., between 1st and 2nd Aves., Gramercy ☎ 212/505-1555 ✉ 630 Lexington Ave., at E. 53rd St., Midtown East ☎ 917/369-8688 ⊕ www.cvs.com. **Rite-Aid** ✉ 301 W. 50th St., at 8th Ave., Midtown West ☎ 212/247-8384 ⊕ www.riteaid.com.

GAY & LESBIAN TRAVEL

Attitudes toward same-sex couples are very tolerant in Manhattan and many parts of Brooklyn, perhaps less so in other parts of the city. Chelsea, Greenwich Village, and Hell's Kitchen are the most prominently gay neighborhoods, but gay men and lesbians feel right at home almost everywhere. The world's biggest gay pride parade takes place on 5th Avenue the last Sunday in June.

PUBLICATIONS

For listings of gay events and places, check out *HX, Next,* and the *Gay City News,* all distributed free on the street and in many bars and shops throughout Manhattan. Magazines *Paper* and *Time Out New York* have a gay-friendly take on what's happening in the city. For details about the gay and lesbian scene, consult *Fodor's Gay Guide to the USA* (available in bookstores everywhere).

🔢 Local Information **Gay & Lesbian Switchboard of NY** ☎ 212/989-0999 or 888/843-4564 ⊕ www. glnh.org. **Lesbian, Gay, Bisexual & Transgender Community Center** ⊠ 208 W. 13th St., between 7th and 8th Aves., Greenwich Village ☎ 212/620-7310 ⊕ www.gaycenter.org.

🔢 Gay Publications **Gay City News** ⊕ www. gaycitynews.com. **HX** ⊕ www.hx.com. **Next** ⊕ www.nextmagazine.net.

🔢 Gay- & Lesbian-Friendly Travel Agencies **Different Roads Travel** ⊠ 8383 Wilshire Blvd., Suite 520, Beverly Hills, CA 90211 ☎ 323/651-5557 or 800/429-8747 (Ext. 14 for both) 🖷 323/651-5454. **Kennedy Travel** ⊠ 130 W. 42nd St., Suite 401, New York, NY 10036 ☎ 212/840-8659 or 800/237-7433 🖷 212/730-2269 ⊕ www.kennedytravel.com. **Now, Voyager** ⊠ 4406 18th St., San Francisco, CA 94114 ☎ 415/626-1169 or 800/255-6951 🖷 415/626-8626 ⊕ www.nowvoyager.com. **Skylink Travel and Tour/Flying Dutchmen Travel** ⊠ 1455 N. Dutton Ave., Suite A, Santa Rosa, CA 95401 ☎ 707/546-9888 or 800/225-5759 🖷 707/636-0951, serving lesbian travelers.

GUIDEBOOKS

Plan well and you won't be sorry. Guidebooks are excellent tools—and you can take them with you. You may want to check out color-photo-illustrated *Fodor's Exploring New York City* and *Compass American Guides: Manhattan,* thorough on culture and history, and pocket-size *Citypack New York City,* with a large city map. *Flashmaps New York City* is loaded with detailed theme maps. All are available at online retailers and bookstores everywhere.

HOLIDAYS

Major national holidays are New Year's Day (Jan. 1); Martin Luther King Day (3rd Mon. in Jan.); Presidents' Day (3rd Mon. in Feb.); Memorial Day (last Mon. in May); Independence Day (July 4); Labor Day (1st Mon. in Sept.); Columbus Day (2nd Mon. in Oct.); Thanksgiving Day (4th Thurs. in Nov.); Christmas Eve and Christmas Day (Dec. 24 and 25); and New Year's Eve (Dec. 31).

INSURANCE

The most useful travel-insurance plan is a comprehensive policy that includes coverage for trip cancellation and interruption, default, trip delay, and medical expenses (with a waiver for preexisting conditions).

Without insurance you'll lose all or most of your money if you cancel your trip, regardless of the reason. Default insurance covers you if your tour operator, airline, or cruise line goes out of business—the chances of which have been increasing. Trip-delay covers expenses that arise because of bad weather or mechanical delays. Study the fine print when comparing policies.

U.K. residents can buy a travel-insurance policy valid for most vacations taken during the year in which it's purchased (but check preexisting-condition coverage).

Always **buy travel policies directly from the insurance company;** if you buy them from a cruise line, airline, or tour operator that goes out of business you probably won't be covered for the agency or operator's default, a major risk. Before making any purchase, review your existing health and home-owner's policies to find what they cover away from home.

🔢 Travel Insurers In the U.S.: **Access America** ⊠ 2805 N. Parham Rd., Richmond, VA 23294 ☎ 800/284-8300 🖷 804/673-1491 or 800/346-9265 ⊕ www.accessamerica.com. **Travel Guard International** ⊠ 1145 Clark St., Stevens Point, WI 54481 ☎ 715/345-0505 or 800/826-1300 🖷 800/955-8785 ⊕ www.travelguard.com.

FOR INTERNATIONAL TRAVELERS

For information on customs restrictions, *see* Customs & Duties.

CAR RENTAL

When picking up a rental car, non-U.S. residents need a reservation voucher for any prepaid reservations that were made in the traveler's home country, a passport, a driver's license, and a travel policy that covers each driver.

CONSULATES

⚡ Australia **Australian Consulate General** ✉ 150 E. 42nd St., 34th fl., between Lexington and 3rd Aves., Midtown East, New York, NY 10017-5612 ☎ 212/351-6500 🖷 212/351-6501 ⊕ www. australianyc.org.

⚡ Canada **Consulate General of Canada** ✉ 1251 Ave. of the Americas, between W. 49th and W. 50th Sts., Midtown West, New York, NY 10020-1175 ☎ 212/596-1628 🖷 212/596-1790 ⊕ www.canada-ny.org.

⚡ New Zealand **New Zealand Consulate-General** ✉ 222 E. 41st St., between 2nd and 3rd Aves., 19th fl., Midtown East, New York, NY 10017-6702 ☎ 212/832-4038 🖷 212/832-7602.

⚡ United Kingdom **British Consulate-General** ✉ 845 3rd Ave., between E. 51st and E. 52nd Sts., Midtown East, New York, NY 10022 ☎ 212/745-0200 🖷 212/754-3062 ⊕ www.britainusa.com/ny.

CURRENCY

The dollar is the basic unit of U.S. currency. It has 100 cents. Coins are the copper penny (1¢); the silvery nickel (5¢), dime (10¢), quarter (25¢), and half-dollar (50¢); and the golden $1 coin, replacing a now-rare silver dollar. Bills are denominated $1, $5, $10, $20, $50, and $100, all mostly green and identical in size; designs and background tints vary. In addition, you may come across a $2 bill, but the chances are slim.

CURRENCY EXCHANGES

Although most visitors from foreign countries are likely to use ATMs to get American money, currency-exchange booths are also available throughout Manhattan. They are especially common in touristy areas such as Grand Central Terminal (main concourse) and Times Square. Banks will also exchange money, but they have shorter hours (many banks close at 3 PM on weekdays and shut down entirely on weekends).

⚡ Exchange Offices **Chase Foreign Money Exchange** ☎ 888/242-7384 ⊕ www.chase.com. **Travelex** ☎ 800/287-7362 ⊕ www.travelex.com.

ELECTRICITY

The U.S. standard is AC, 110 volts/60 cycles. Plugs have two flat pins set parallel to each other.

EMERGENCIES

For police, fire, or ambulance, **dial 911** (0 in rural areas).

INSURANCE

Britons and Australians need extra medical coverage when traveling overseas.

⚡ Insurance Information In the U.K.: **Association of British Insurers** ✉ 51 Gresham St., London EC2V 7HQ ☎ 020/7600-3333 🖷 020/7696-8999 ⊕ www.abi.org.uk. In Australia: **Insurance Council of Australia** ✉ Insurance Enquiries and Complaints, Level 12, Box 561, Collins St. W, Melbourne, VIC 8007 ☎ 1300/780808 or 03/9629-4109 🖷 03/9621-2060 ⊕ www.iecltd.com.au. In Canada: **RBC Insurance** ✉ 6880 Financial Dr., Mississauga, Ontario L5N 7Y5 ☎ 800/668-4342 or 905/816-2400 🖷 905/813-4704 ⊕ www.rbcinsurance.com. In New Zealand: **Insurance Council of New Zealand** ✉ Level 7, 111-115 Customhouse Quay, Box 474, Wellington ☎ 04/472-5230 🖷 04/473-3011 ⊕ www.icnz.org.nz.

MAIL & SHIPPING

You can buy stamps and aerograms and send letters and parcels in post offices. Stamp-dispensing machines can occasionally be found in airports, bus and train stations, office buildings, drugstores, and the like. You can also deposit mail in the stout, dark blue, steel bins at strategic locations everywhere and in the mail chutes of large buildings; pickup schedules are posted. You can deposit packages at public collection boxes as long as the parcels are affixed with proper postage and weigh less than one pound. Packages weighing one or more pounds must be taken to a post office or handed to a postal carrier.

For mail sent within the United States, you need a 37¢ stamp for first-class letters weighing up to 1 ounce (23¢ for each additional ounce) and 23¢ for postcards.

You pay 80¢ for 1-ounce airmail letters and 70¢ for airmail postcards to most other countries; to Canada and Mexico, you need a 60¢ stamp for a 1-ounce letter and 50¢ for a postcard. An aerogram—a single sheet of lightweight blue paper that folds into its own envelope, stamped for overseas airmail—costs 70¢.

To receive mail on the road, have it sent c/o General Delivery at your destination's main post office (use the correct five-digit ZIP code). You must pick up mail in person within 30 days and show a driver's license or passport.

PASSPORTS & VISAS

When traveling internationally, carry your passport even if you don't need one (it's always the best form of ID) and **make two photocopies of the data page** (one for someone at home and another for you, carried separately from your passport). If you lose your passport, promptly call the nearest embassy or consulate and the local police.

Visitor visas aren't necessary for Canadian or European Union citizens, or for citizens of Australia who are staying fewer than 90 days.

🔊 Australian Citizens **Passports Australia** ☎ 131-232 ⊕ www.passports.gov.au. **United States Consulate General** ✉ MLC Centre, Level 59, 19–29 Martin Pl., Sydney, NSW 2000 ☎ 02/9373-9200, 1902/941-641 fee-based visa-inquiry line ⊕ usembassy-australia.state.gov/sydney.

🔊 Canadian Citizens **Passport Office** ✉ To mail in applications: 200 Promenade du Portage, Hull, Québec J8X 4B7 ☎ 819/994-3500 or 800/567-6868, 866/255-7655 TTY ⊕ www.ppt.gc.ca.

🔊 New Zealand Citizens **New Zealand Passports Office** ✉ For applications and information, Level 3, Boulcott House, 47 Boulcott St., Wellington ☎ 0800/22-5050 or 04/474-8100 ⊕ www.passports.govt.nz. **Embassy of the United States** ✉ 29 Fitzherbert Terr., Thorndon, Wellington ☎ 04/462-6000 ⊕ usembassy.org.nz. **U.S. Consulate General** ✉ Citibank Bldg., 3rd fl., 23 Customs St. E, Auckland ☎ 09/303-2724 ⊕ usembassy.org.nz.

🔊 U.K. Citizens **U.K. Passport Service** ☎ 0870/521-0410 ⊕ www.passport.gov.uk. **American Consulate General** ✉ Danesfort House, 223 Stranmillis Rd., Belfast, Northern Ireland BT9 5GR ☎ 028/9032-8239 🖷 028/9024-8482 ⊕ usembassy.org.

uk. **American Embassy** ✉ For visa and immigration information or to submit a visa application via mail (enclose an SASE), Consular Information Unit, 24 Grosvenor Sq., London W1 1AE ☎ 09055/444-546 for visa information (per-minute charges), 0207/499-9000 main switchboard ⊕ usaembassy.org.uk.

TELEPHONES

All U.S. telephone numbers consist of a three-digit area code and a seven-digit local number. Within many local calling areas, you dial only the seven-digit number. Within some area codes, you must dial "1" first for calls outside the local area. To call between area-code regions, dial "1" then all 10 digits; the same goes for calls to numbers prefixed by "800," "888," "866," and "877"—all toll-free. For calls to numbers preceded by "900" you must pay—usually dearly.

For international calls, dial "011" followed by the country code and the local number. For help, dial "0" and ask for an overseas operator. The country code is 61 for Australia, 64 for New Zealand, 44 for the United Kingdom. Calling Canada is the same as calling within the United States. Most local phone books list country codes and U.S. area codes. The country code for the United States is 1.

For operator assistance, dial "0." To obtain someone's phone number, call directory assistance at 555–1212 or occasionally 411 (free at many public phones). To have the person you're calling foot the bill, phone collect; dial "0" instead of "1" before the 10-digit number.

At pay phones, instructions often are posted. Usually you insert coins in a slot (usually 25¢–50¢ for local calls) and wait for a steady tone before dialing. When you call long-distance, the operator tells you how much to insert; prepaid phone cards, widely available in various denominations, are easier. Call the number on the back, punch in the card's personal identification number when prompted, then dial your number.

INTERNET SERVICES

You can check your e-mail or surf the Internet at cafés, copy centers, and libraries. By far the most well equipped and probably most convenient is easyInternetCafé in Times Square, which has a staggering 650 computer terminals; it's open from 7 AM to 1 AM, seven days a week. The nearby Times Square Information Center (*see* Visitor Information) has free terminals for checking e-mail. In addition, many public entities and businesses, including public libraries and some McDonald's and Starbucks, now provide wireless Internet access. The organization NYCwireless keeps track of free Wi-Fi hotspots in the New York area.

⚡ Internet Cafés **Cyber Cafe** ⊠ 250 W. 49th St., between 8th Ave. and Broadway, Midtown West ☎ 212/333-4109 ⊕ www.cyber-cafe.com. **easyInternetCafé** ⊠ 234 W. 42nd St., between 7th and 8th Aves., Midtown West ☎ 212/398-0724 ⊕ www.easyinternetcafe.com. **www.web2zone** ⊠ 54 Cooper Sq., East Village ☎ 212/614-7300 ⊕ www.web2zone.com.

⚡ Other Internet Locations **New York Public Library-Mid-Manhattan Library** ⊠ 455 5th Ave., at E. 40th St., Midtown East ☎ 212/340-0833 ⊕ www.nypl.org. **NYCwireless** ⊕ www.nycwireless.net. **Times Square Information Center** ⊠ 7th Ave. between 46th and 47th Sts., Midtown West ☎ 212/768-1560 ⊕ www.timessquarenyc.org ⊙ Daily 8-8.

LIMOUSINES

You can rent a chauffeur-driven car from one of many limousine services. Companies usually charge by the hour or a flat fee for sightseeing excursions.

⚡ Limousine Services **Carey Limousines** ☎ 212/599-1122 or 800/336-0646 ⊕ www.ecarey.com. **Concord Limousines, Inc.** ☎ 718/965-6100 ⊕ www.concordlimo.com. **London Towncars** ☎ 212/988-9700 or 800/221-4009 ⊕ www.londontowncars.com.

MAIL & SHIPPING

Most post offices are open weekdays 8 AM–5 PM or 8 AM–6 PM and Saturday from 9–4. There are dozens of branches in New York. The main post office on 8th Avenue is open daily 24 hours.

⚡ Post Offices **Grand Central Terminal** ⊠ 450 Lexington Ave., between 44th and 45th Sts., Midtown East 10017 ☎ 800/275-8777 ⊕ www.usps.gov. **J.A. Farley General Post Office** ⊠ 8th Ave. at W. 33rd St., Midtown West 10001 ☎ 800/275-8777 ⊕ www.usps.gov.

MEDIA

NEWSPAPERS & MAGAZINES

The major daily newspapers in New York are the *New York Times* and the *Wall Street Journal,* both broadsheets, and the *Daily News* and the *New York Post,* which are tabloids. The *Village Voice* and the *New York Press* are both free weeklies. Local magazines include the *New Yorker, New York,* and *Time Out New York.* All of these are widely available at newsstands and shops around town.

RADIO & TELEVISION

Some of the major radio stations include *WBGO-FM* (88.3; jazz), *WBLS-FM* (107.5; R&B), *WFMU-FM* (91.1; freeform music), *WKTU-FM* (103.5; urban), *WPLJ* (95.5; pop and rock), *WQXR-FM* (96.3; classical), and *WXRK-FM* (92.3; rock).

Talk stations include *WNEW-FM* (102.7), *WNYC-AM* (820; National Public Radio), *WNYC-FM* (93.9; NPR and classical), *WNYE-FM* (91.5), and *WOR-AM* (710). News stations include *WABC-AM* (770), *WCBS-AM* (880), and *WINS-AM* (1010).

The city has its own 24-hour cable TV news station, New York 1 (Channel 1), available through Time Warner Cable, with local and international news announcements around the clock. Weather forecasts are broadcast "on the ones" (1:01, 1:11, 1:21, etc.).

From 8 to 11 each evening, the public station WNYC (channel 25) broadcasts a block of shows about local fashion, music, history, and events around town.

MONEY MATTERS

In New York, it's easy to get swept up in a debt-inducing cyclone of $60 per person dinners, $100 theater tickets, $20 nightclub covers, and $300 hotel rooms. But one of the good things about the city is that there's such a wide variety of options, you can spend in some areas and save in others. Within Manhattan, a cup of coffee can cost from 75¢ to $4, a pint of beer from $5 to $8, and a sandwich from $6 to $10. Generally, prices in the outer boroughs are lower than those in Manhattan.

The most generously bequeathed treasure of the city is the arts. The stated admission fee at the Metropolitan Museum of Art is a suggestion; those who can't afford it can donate a lesser amount and not be snubbed. Many other museums in town have special times during which admission is free. The Museum of Modern Art, for instance, is free on Friday 4–8. In summer a handful of free music, theater, and dance performances, as well as films (usually screened outdoors) fill the calendar each day.

Prices throughout this guide are given for adults. Substantially reduced fees are almost always available for children, students, and senior citizens. For information on taxes, *see* Taxes.

ATMS

Cash machines are abundant throughout all the boroughs and are found not only in banks but in many grocery stores, laundries, delis, and hotels. Many bank ATMs charge users a fee around $1.50, and the commercial ATMs in retail establishments may charge more. Be careful to remain at the ATM until you complete your transaction, which may require an extra step after receiving your money.

CREDIT CARDS

Throughout this guide, the following abbreviations are used: **AE**, American Express; **D**, Discover; **DC**, Diners Club; **MC**, MasterCard; and **V**, Visa.

🎫 Reporting Lost Cards **American Express** ☎ 800/992-3404. **Diners Club** ☎ 800/234-6377. **Discover** ☎ 800/347-2683. **MasterCard** ☎ 800/ 622-7747. **Visa** ☎ 800/ 847-2911.

PACKING

In New York, a few restaurants still require men to wear jackets and ties. In general, New Yorkers tend to dress a bit more formally than their Midwest or West Coast counterparts for special events. Jeans and sneakers are acceptable for casual dining and sightseeing just about anywhere in the city. Always **bring sneakers or other flat-heeled walking shoes** for pounding the New York pavement.

In spring and fall, pack at least one warm jacket and sweater, since moderate daytime temperatures can drop after nightfall. Bring shorts for summer, which can be quite humid. You need a warm coat, hat,

scarf, and gloves in winter; boots for often slushy streets are also a good idea.

Pack light—porters and luggage trolleys can be hard to find at New York airports. And bring a fistful of quarters to rent a trolley.

In your carry-on luggage, pack an extra pair of eyeglasses or contact lenses and enough of any medication you take to last a few days longer than the entire trip. You may also ask your doctor to write a spare prescription using the drug's generic name, as brand names may vary from country to country. In luggage to be checked, **never pack prescription drugs, valuables, or undeveloped film.** And don't forget to carry with you the addresses of offices that handle refunds of lost traveler's checks. Check *Fodor's How to Pack* (available at online retailers and bookstores everywhere) for more tips.

To avoid customs and security delays, carry medications in their original packaging. Don't pack any sharp objects in your carry-on luggage, including knives of any size or material, scissors, nail clippers, and corkscrews, or anything else that might arouse suspicion.

To avoid having your checked luggage chosen for hand inspection, don't cram bags full. The U.S. Transportation Security Administration suggests packing shoes on top and placing personal items you don't want touched in clear plastic bags.

CHECKING LUGGAGE

You're allowed to carry aboard one bag and one personal article, such as a purse or a laptop computer. Make sure what you carry on fits under your seat or in the overhead bin. Get to the gate early, so you can board as soon as possible, before the overhead bins fill up.

Baggage allowances vary by carrier, destination, and ticket class. On international flights, you're usually allowed to check two bags weighing up to 70 pounds (32 kilograms) each, although a few airlines allow checked bags of up to 88 pounds (40 kilograms) in first class. Some international carriers don't allow more than 66 pounds (30 kilograms) per bag in business class and 44 pounds (20 kilograms) in economy. On domestic flights, the limit is usually 50 to 70 pounds (23 to 32 kilograms) per bag. In general, carry-on bags shouldn't exceed 40 pounds (18 kilograms). Most airlines won't accept bags that weigh more than 100 pounds (45 kilograms) on domestic or international flights. Expect to pay a fee for baggage that exceeds weight limits. Check baggage restrictions with your carrier before you pack.

Airline liability for baggage is limited to $2,500 per person on flights within the United States. On international flights it amounts to $9.07 per pound or $20 per kilogram for checked baggage (roughly $640 per 70-pound bag), with a maximum of $634.90 per piece, and $400 per passenger for unchecked baggage. You can buy additional coverage at check-in for about $10 per $1,000 of coverage, but it often excludes a rather extensive list of items, shown on your airline ticket.

Before departure, itemize your bags' contents and their worth, and label the bags with your name, address, and phone number. (If you use your home address, cover it so potential thieves can't see it readily.) Include a label inside each bag and **pack a copy of your itinerary.** At check-in, make sure each bag is correctly tagged with the destination airport's three-letter code. Because some checked bags will be opened for hand inspection, the U.S. Transportation Security Administration recommends that you leave luggage unlocked or use the plastic locks offered at check-in. TSA screeners place an inspection notice inside searched bags, which are resealed with a special lock.

If your bag has been searched and contents are missing or damaged, file a claim with the TSA Consumer Response Center as soon as possible. If your bags arrive damaged or fail to arrive at all, file a written report with the airline before leaving the airport.

🚩 Complaints **U.S. Transportation Security Administration Contact Center** ☎ 866/289–9673 ⊕ www.tsa.gov.

PUBLIC TRANSPORTATION

When it comes to getting around New York, you have your pick of transportation in almost every neighborhood. The subway and bus networks are extensive, especially in Manhattan, although getting across town can take some extra maneuvering. If you're not pressed for time, take a public bus (⇨ Bus Travel Within New York City); they generally are slower than subways, but you can also see the city as you travel. Yellow cabs (⇨ Taxis & Car Services) are abundant, except during the evening rush hour, when many drivers' shifts change. Like a taxi ride, the subway (⇨ Subway Travel) is a true New York City experience; it's also often the quickest way to get around. But New York is really a walking town, and depending on the time of day and your destination, hoofing it could be the easiest and most enjoyable option.

During weekday rush hours (from 7:30 AM to 9:30 AM and 5 PM to 7 PM) **avoid the jammed midtown area,** both in the subways and on the streets—travel time on buses and taxis can easily double.

Subway and bus fares are $2, although reduced fares are available for senior citizens and people with disabilities during non-rush hours.

You pay for mass transit with a Metro-Card, a plastic card with a magnetic strip. After you swipe the card through a subway turnstile or insert it in a bus's card reader, the cost of the fare is automatically deducted. With the MetroCard, you can **transfer free** from bus to subway, subway to bus, or bus to bus. You must start with the MetroCard and use it again within two hours to complete your trip.

MetroCards are sold at all subway stations and at some stores—look for an "Authorized Sales Agent" sign. The MTA sells two kinds of MetroCards: unlimited-ride and pay-per-ride. Seven-day unlimited-ride MetroCards ($24) allow bus and subway travel for a week. If you will ride more than 13 times, this is the card to get.

The one-day unlimited-ride Fun Pass ($7) is good from the day of purchase through 3 AM the following day. It's only sold by neighborhood MetroCard merchants and MetroCard vending machines at stations (not through the station agent). When you purchase a pay-per-ride card worth $10 or more, you get a 20% bonus—six rides for the price of five. Unlike unlimited-ride cards, pay-per-ride MetroCards can be shared between riders; unlimited-ride MetroCards can only be used once at the same station or bus route in an 18-minute period.

You can buy or add money to an existing MetroCard at a MetroCard vending machine, available at most subway station entrances (usually near the station booth). The machines accept major credit cards and ATM or debit cards. Many also accept cash, but note that the maximum amount of change they will return is $6.

F Schedule & Route Information Metropolitan Transit Authority (MTA) Travel Information Line ☎ 718/330-1234, 718/596-8585 travelers with disabilities ⊕ www.mta.nyc.ny.us.

RESTROOMS

Public restrooms in New York are few and far between; some are very clean, and some are filthy. Facilities in Penn Station and Grand Central Terminal are not only safe but fairly well maintained. Because of concerns about vandalism and other crime, restrooms in most subway stations have been largely sealed off. Two clean pay toilets (25¢) are at the adjacent Herald and Greeley squares on West 34th and West 32nd streets.

Head for midtown department stores, museums, or the lobbies of large hotels to find the cleanest bathrooms. Public atriums, such as those at the Citicorp Center and Trump Tower, also provide good public facilities, as do Bryant Park and the many Barnes & Noble bookstores and Starbucks coffee shops in the city. If you're in the area, the Times Square Information Center, on Broadway between 46th and 47th Street, can be a godsend.

Restaurants usually allow only their patrons to use their restrooms, but if you're dressed well and look as if you belong, you can often just sail right in. Be aware that cinemas, Broadway theaters, and concert halls have limited amenities, and there are often long lines before performances and during intermissions.

SAFETY

New York City is one of the safest large cities in the country. However, do not let yourself be lulled into a false sense of security. As in any large city, travelers in New York remain particularly easy marks for pickpockets and hustlers.

After 9/11, security was heightened throughout the city. Never leave any bags unattended, and expect to have you and your possessions inspected thoroughly in such places as airports, sports stadiums, museums, and city buildings.

Ignore the panhandlers on the streets and subways, people who offer to hail you a cab (they often appear at Penn Station, the Port Authority, and Grand Central), and limousine and gypsy cab drivers who (illegally) offer you a ride.

Keep jewelry out of sight on the street; better yet, **leave valuables at home.** Don't wear gold chains or gaudy jewelry, even if it's fake. Men should **carry their wallets in their front pants pocket** rather than in their back pockets. When in bars or restaurants, never hang your purse or bag on the back of a chair or put it underneath the table.

Avoid deserted blocks in unfamiliar neighborhoods. A brisk, purposeful pace helps deter trouble wherever you go.

The subway runs round-the-clock and is generally well trafficked until midnight (and until at least 2 AM on Friday and Saturday nights), and overall it is very safe. If you do take the subway at night, ride in the center car, with the conductor, and wait on the center of the platform or right in front of the station agent. Watch out for unsavory characters lurking around the inside or outside of stations, particularly at night.

When waiting for a train, **stand far away from the edge of the subway platform,** especially when trains are entering or leaving the station. Once the train pulls into the station, **avoid empty cars.** While on the train don't engage in verbal exchanges with aggressive riders, who may accuse others of anything from pushing to taking up too much space. If a fellow passenger makes you nervous while on the train, trust your instincts and **change cars.** When disembarking, stick with the crowd until you reach the street.

Travelers Aid International helps crime victims, stranded travelers, and wayward children, and works closely with the police.
⚂ Travelers Aid ⊠ JFK International Airport, Terminal 6 ☎ 718/656-4870 ⊠ Newark International Airport, Terminal B ☎ 973/623-5052 ⊕ www. travelersaid.org.

LOCAL SCAMS

Someone who appears to have had an accident at the exit door of a bus may flee with your wallet or purse if you attempt to give aid. The individual who approaches you with a complicated story is probably playing a confidence game and hopes to get something from you. **Beware of people jostling you in crowds,** or someone tapping your shoulder from behind. Never play or place a bet on a sidewalk card game, shell game, or other guessing game—they are all rigged to get your cash, and they're illegal.

SENIOR-CITIZEN TRAVEL

The Metropolitan Transit Authority (MTA) offers lower fares for passengers 65 and over. Show your Medicare card to the bus driver or station agent, and for the standard fare ($2) you will be issued a MetroCard and a return-trip ticket.

To qualify for age-related discounts, mention your senior-citizen status up front when booking hotel reservations (not when checking out) and before you're seated in restaurants (not when paying the bill). Be sure to have identification on hand. When renting a car, ask about promotional car-rental discounts, which can be cheaper than senior-citizen rates.
⚂ Educational Programs Elderhostel ⊠ 11 Ave. de Lafayette, Boston, MA 02111-1746 ☎ 877/426-8056, 978/323-4141 international callers, 877/426-2167 TTY ☐ 877/426-2166 ⊕ www.elderhostel.org.
⚂ MTA Reduced Fare hotline ☎ 718/243-4999 ⊕ www.mta.nyc.ny.us.

SIGHTSEEING TOURS

A guided tour can be a good way to get a handle on this sometimes overwhelming city, to explore out-of-the-way areas to which you might not want to venture on your own, or get in-depth exposure to a particular facet of the city's history, inhabitants, or architecture.

BOAT TOURS

In good weather, a Circle Line Cruise is one of the best ways to get oriented. Once you've finished the three-hour, 35-mi circumnavigation of Manhattan, you'll have a good idea of where things are and what you want to see next. Narrations are as interesting and individual as the guides who deliver them. The Circle Line operates daily, and the price is $28. Semi-Circle cruises, more limited tours of two hours, also run daily; they cost $23.

NY Waterway runs two-hour harbor cruises for $26. Dates and times vary, but the cruises run year-round. The 90-minute Twilight Cruise ($21) operates from early May through early November the Harbor Cruise, which covers the same territory during the day, operates year-round.

Several cruises leave from South Street Seaport's Pier 16. The cargo schooner *Pioneer,* owned by the South Street Seaport Museum, makes two-hour voyages Tuesday through Sunday, from after Memorial Day through mid-September. Reservations, which can be made no more than two weeks in advance, are a good idea. The fare is $25.

Circle Line Downtown runs hour-long sightseeing tours of New York Harbor and lower Manhattan; they cost $20.
⚂ Circle Line Cruise ⊠ Pier 83 at W. 42nd St., Midtown West ☎ 212/563-3200 ⊕ www. circleline42.com. **NY Waterway** ⊠ Pier 17 at South St. Seaport, Lower Manhattan ⊠ Pier 78 at W. 38th St. and 12th Ave., Midtown West ☎ 800/533-3779 ⊕ www.nywaterway.com. *Pioneer* ⊠ Pier 16 at South St. Seaport, Lower Manhattan ☎ 212/748-8786 ⊕ www.southstseaport.org. **Circle Line Downtown** ⊠ Pier 16 at South St. Seaport, Lower Manhattan ☎ 212/269-5755 ⊕ www. circlelinedowntown.com.

BUS TOURS

Gray Line New York runs a number of "hop-on, hop-off" double-decker bus tours in various languages, including a downtown Manhattan loop, upper Manhattan loop, Harlem gospel tour, and evening tours of the city. Packages include entrance fees to attractions and one-day MetroCards. The company also books sightseeing cruises, as well as day trips to

Atlantic City, Hyde Park, the Woodbury Common outlet mall, and other locations in the New York area.

🚊 **Gray Line New York** ⊠ Port Authority Bus Terminal, 625 8th Ave., at 42nd St., Midtown West 📞 800/669-0051 ⊕ www.graylinenewyork.com. **Gray Line Visitor Center** ⊠ 777 8th Ave., at 47th St., Midtown West.

HELICOPTER TOURS

Liberty Helicopter Tours has six pilot-narrated tours from $63 per person as well as $120–$849 for a tour of up to four people. Some tours depart from Pier 6 in Lower Manhattan.

🚊 **Liberty Helicopter Tours** ⊠ Heliport, W. 30th St. at 12th Ave., Midtown West 📞 212/967-6464 ⊕ www.libertyhelicopters.com.

PRIVATE GUIDES

Arthur Marks creates customized tours on which he sings show tunes about the city. Private group tours start at $350; you may wish to enquire about group tours, which Marks gives from May through November.

Walk of the Town tailor tours to the participants' to your interests; special themes include "Cops, Crooks, and the Courts," "When Harlem was Jewish," and "The Lullaby of Broadway." Tours are available by appointment only; most start at $300.

🚊 **Arthur Marks** 📞 212/673-0477. **Walk of the Town** 📞 212/222-5343.

SPECIAL-INTEREST TOURS

Central Park Walking Tours cover the park daily. Some of its 90-minute tours are thematic, investigating such features as prominent trees and the park's unique bridges and arches. Bite of the Big Apple Central Park Bicycle Tour organizes two-hour bicycle trips through Central Park with stops along the way, including Strawberry Fields and the Belvedere Castle. One tour is devoted to areas of the park used in movies.

Harlem Spirituals leads combination bus and walking tours and Sunday gospel trips to Harlem. The Lower East Side Tenement Museum runs a tour of the Lower East Side, retracing its history as an immigrant community; it's available weekends, April through December.

Opera buffs can tour scenery and costume shops and the stage area on Metropolitan Opera House Backstage Tours.

The South Street Seaport Museum has tours of historic ships and the waterfront, as well as predawn forays through the fish market.

The Times Square Alliance runs a free tour of the Times Square area that takes you to theaters and other sights in the area. Tours leave Friday at noon from the Times Square Information Center.

🚊 **Bite of the Big Apple** 📞 212/541-8759 ⊕ www.centralparkbiketour.com. **Central Park Walking Tours** 📞 212/721-0874 ⊕ www.centralparkwalkingtours.com. **Harlem Spirituals** 📞 212/391-0900 or 800/660-2166 ⊕ www.harlemspirituals.com. **Lower East Side Tenement Museum** 📞 212/431-0233 ⊕ www.tenement.org. **Metropolitan Opera House Backstage** 📞 212/769-7020 ⊕ www.metguild.org/education. **South Street Seaport Museum** 📞 212/748-8590 ⊕ www.southstseaport.org. **Times Square Information Center** ⊠ 7th Ave. between 46th and 47th Sts., Midtown West 📞 212/768-1560 ⊕ www.timessquarenyc.org.

WALKING TOURS: GUIDED

The wisecracking PhD candidates of Big Onion Walking Tours lead themed tours such as "Revolutionary New York" and its famous "multiethnic eating tours" in addition to neighborhood walks. The Downtown Alliance conducts free, history-rich tours of the Wall Street area on Thursday and Saturday at noon. Meet on the steps of the U.S. Custom House at Bowling Green.

The Municipal Art Society conducts a series of walking tours on weekdays and both bus and walking tours on weekends. Tours emphasize the architecture and history of particular neighborhoods. New York City Cultural Walking Tours have covered such sundry topics as buildings' gargoyles and the old Yiddish theaters of the East Village. Tours are run every Sunday from March to December; private tours can be scheduled throughout the week. Urban Explorations runs tours with an emphasis on architecture and landscape design. Chinatown is a specialty.

The Urban Park Rangers conducts free weekend walks and workshops in city parks. The knowledgeable Joyce Gold has been conducting tours since 1976. Regular historical walks include Harlem, Gramercy Park, and the Lower East Side. The contributions of immigrants and artists to various neighborhoods are often highlighted in other tours.

Big Onion Walking Tours ☎ 212/439-1090 ⊕ www.bigonion.com. **Downtown Alliance** ☎ 212/606-4064 ⊕ www.downtownny.com. **Joyce Gold** ☎ 212/242-5762 ⊕ www.nyctours.com. **Municipal Art Society** ☎ 212/935-3960, 212/439-1049 recorded information ⊕ www.mas.org. **New York City Cultural Walking Tours** ☎ 212/979-2388 ⊕ www.nycwalk.com. **Urban Explorations** ☎ 718/721-5254. **Urban Park Rangers** ☎ City of New York: 311 in New York City, 212/639-9675 (212/NEW-YORK) outside of New York ⊕ www.nycparks.org.

WALKING TOURS: SELF-GUIDED

Talking Street's two audio tours of New York City are delivered to you via a number you call on your cell phone. Comedian Jerry Stiller's coverage of the Lower East Side emphasizes the turbulent period around 1900; a walking tour of Lower Manhattan and the World Trade Center site is narrated by actress Sigourney Weaver. Both tours cost $5.95 and take less than two hours to complete; you can buy them, using a credit card, over the phone or on the company's Web site.

The SoundWalk line of audio tours covers unusual sights in a nonstuffy way. They get you off the main drags and on to the nonobvious parts of such areas as the Bronx, Times Square, and Dumbo. The tours sell for around $20 and are available as downloadable audio files as well as CDs.

For a narrated tour of Central Park, pick up a three-hour audio guide from the bike rental shop Pedal Pusher. It costs $10 for the day.

Pedal Pusher ✉ 1306 2nd Ave., between E. 68th and E. 69th Sts., Upper East Side ☎ 212/288-5592. **SoundWalk** ☎ www.soundwalk.com. **Talking Street** ☎ 212/586-8687 ⊕ www.talkingstreet.com.

SPORTS & THE OUTDOORS

The City of New York's Parks & Recreation division, lists all of the recreational facilities and activities available through New York's Parks Department. For information about athletic facilities in Manhattan as well as a calendar of sporting events, visit the Web site or pick up a copy of *MetroSports* at sporting-goods stores or health clubs. The sports section of *Time Out New York*, sold at most newsstands, lists upcoming events, times, dates, and ticket information.

Parks & Recreation division ☎ 311 in New York City, 212/NEW-YORK or 639-9675 outside New York City ⊕ www.nyc.gov/parks *MetroSports* ⊕ www.metrosportsny.com

BASEBALL

The subway will get you directly to stadiums of both New York–area major-league teams, but the *Yankee Clipper* cruises from Manhattan's east side and from New Jersey to Yankee Stadium on game nights. The round-trip cost is $18. The regular baseball season runs from April through September.

The New York Mets play at Shea Stadium, at the next-to-last stop on the No. 7 train, in Queens. The New York Yankees, having won many a World Series in the 1990s and in 2000, are still licking their wounds after their 2004 curse-breaking loss to the Boston Red Sox. See them play at Yankee Stadium.

Founded in 2001, the minor league Brooklyn Cyclones are named for Coney Island's famous wooden roller coaster. A feeder team for the New York Mets, the team plays its 38 home games at KeySpan Park, next to the Boardwalk, with views of the Atlantic over the right-field wall and views of historic Astroland over the left-field wall. Most people make a day of it, with time at the beach and amusement rides before an evening game. Take the D, F, or Q subway to the end of the line, and walk one block to the right of the original Nathan's Famous hot dog stand.

For a fun, family-oriented experience, check out the Staten Island Yankees, one of New York's minor league teams, which warms up many future New York Yankees players. The stadium, a five-minute walk from the Staten Island Ferry terminal, has magnificent panoramic views of Lower Manhattan and the Statue of Liberty.

🚩 **Brooklyn Cyclones** ⊠ 1904 Surf Ave., at 19th St., Coney Island, Brooklyn ☎ 718/449-8497 ⊕ www.brooklyncyclones.com Ⓜ Subway: D, F, Q to Stillwell Ave. **Shea Stadium** ⊠ Roosevelt Ave. off Grand Central Pkwy., Flushing, Queens ☎ 718/507-8499 ⊕ www.mets.com Ⓜ Subway: 7 to Willets Pt./Shea Stadium. **Staten Island Yankees** ⊠ Richmond County Bank Ballpark at St. George, Staten Island ☎ 718/720-9265 ⊕ www.siyanks.com **Yankee Clipper** ☎ 800/533-3779 ⊕ www.nywaterway.com **Yankee Stadium** ⊠ 161st St. and River Ave., The Bronx ☎ 718/293-6000 Ⓜ Subway: B, D to 167th St., No. 4 to 161st St.-Yankee Stadium.

BASKETBALL

Watching pro basketball at Madison Square Garden is a legendary experience—if you can get a ticket. If the professional games are sold out, try to attend a college game where New York stalwarts Fordham, Hofstra, and St. John's compete against national top 25 teams during invitational tournaments. In addition to schedules for regular games, the Web site also provides listings of special basketball events, such as the Harlem Globetrotters.

The New York Knicks arouse intense hometown passions, which means tickets for home games at Madison Square Garden are hard to come by. The New Jersey Nets play at the Meadowlands in the Continental Airlines Arena. Tickets are generally easy to obtain. The men's basketball season runs from late October through April. The New York Liberty, a member of the Women's NBA, had it's first season in 1997; some of the team's more high-profile players are already legendary. The season runs from Memorial Day weekend through August, with home games played at Madison Square Garden.

🚩 **Madison Square Garden** ⊕ www.thegarden.com **New York Knicks** ☎ 212/465-5867 ⊕ www.nyknicks.com **New Jersey Nets** ☎ box office 201/935-3900, 800/765-6387 ⊕ www.nba.com/nets **New York Liberty** ☎ 877/962-2849 for tickets, 212/564-9622 fan hotline ⊕ www.wnba.com/liberty

BICYCLING

Even in tiny apartments, many locals keep a bicycle for transportation—the intrepid ones swear it's the best (and fastest) way to get around—and for rides on glorious days. A sleek pack of dedicated racers zooms around Central Park at dawn and at dusk daily, and on weekends the parks swarm with recreational cyclists. Central Park has a 6-mi circular drive with a couple of decent climbs. It's closed to automobile traffic from 10 AM to 3 PM (except the southeast portion between 6th Avenue and East 72nd Street) and 7 PM to 10 PM on weekdays, and from 7 PM Friday to 6 AM Monday. On holidays it's closed to automobile traffic from 7 PM the night before until 6 AM the day after.

The bike lane along the Hudson River Park's esplanade parallels the waterfront from West 59th Street south to the esplanade of Battery Park City. The lane also heads north, connecting with the bike path in Riverside Park, the promenade between West 72nd and West 110th streets, and continuing all the way to the George Washington Bridge. From Battery Park it's a quick ride to the Wall Street area, which is deserted on weekends, and over to South Street and a bike lane along the East River.

The 3⅓-mi circular drive in Brooklyn's Prospect Park is closed to cars weekends year-round and from 9 AM to 5 PM and 7 PM to 10 PM weekdays. It has a long, gradual uphill that tops off near the Grand Army Plaza entrance.

🚩 **Bike Rentals** **Bicycle Rentals at Loeb Boathouse** ⊠ Midpark near E. 74th St., Central Park ☎ 212/517-2233 **Hub Station** ⊠ 517 Broome St., at Thompson St., SoHo ☎ 212/965-9334 Ⓜ Subway: A, C, E to Canal St. **Larry's & Jeff's Bicycles Plus** ⊠ 1690 2nd Ave., at E. 87th St., Upper East Side ☎ 212/722-2201 Ⓜ Subway: 4, 5, 6 to 86th St. **Pedal Pusher** ⊠ 1306 2nd Ave., between E. 68th and E. 69th Sts., Upper East Side ☎ 212/288-5592 Ⓜ Subway: 6 to 68th St.-Hunter College. **Toga Bike Shop** ⊠ 110 West End Ave., at W. 64th St., Upper West Side ☎ 212/799-9625 ⊕ www.togabikes.com Ⓜ Subway: 1, 9 to 66th St.

GROUP BIKE RIDES

For organized rides with other cyclists, call or email before you come to New York. Bike New York runs a five-borough bike ride in May. The Five Borough Bicycle Club organizes day and weekend rides.

The New York Cycle Club sponsors weekend rides for every level of ability. Time's Up!, a nonprofit environmental group, leads free recreational rides at least twice a month for cyclists as well as skaters; the Central Park Moonlight Ride, departing from Columbus Circle at 10 PM the first Friday of every month, is a favorite. Transportation Alternatives lists group rides throughout the metropolitan area in its bimonthly email newsletter.

Bike New York ⊠ 891 Amsterdam Ave., at W. 103rd St., Upper West Side ☎ 212/932-2453 ⊕ www.bikenewyork.org **Five Borough Bicycle Club** ⊠ 891 Amsterdam Ave., at W. 103rd St., Upper West Side ☎ 212/932-2300 Ext. 115 ⊕ www.5bbc. org **New York Cycle Club** ⌂ Box 20541, Columbus Circle Station, 10023 ☎ 212/828-5711 ⊕ www.nycc. org **Time's Up!** ☎ 212/802-8222 ⊕ www.times-up. org **Transportation Alternatives** ⌂ 115 W. 30th St., Suite 1207, 10001 ☎ 212/629-8080 ⊕ www. transalt.org

BOATING & KAYAKING

Central Park has rowboats (plus one Venetian gondola for glides in the moonlight) on the 18-acre Central Park Lake. Rent your rowboat at Loeb Boathouse, near East 74th Street, from March through October; gondolas are available only during the summer.

In summer at the Downtown Boathouse you can take a sturdy kayak out for a paddle for free on weekends and weekday evenings. Beginners learn to paddle in the calmer embayment area closest to shore until they feel ready to venture farther out onto open water. More experienced kayakers can partake in the three-hour trips conducted every weekend and on holiday mornings. Sign-ups for these popular tours end at 8 AM. Due to high demand, names are entered into a lottery to see who gets to go out each morning. No reservations are taken in advance. Manhattan Kayak Company runs trips (these are not free) and gives lessons for all levels.

Downtown Boathouse ⊠ Pier 26, N. Moore St. and the Hudson River, TriBeCa ☎ 646/613-0740 daily status, 646/613-0375 information ⊕ www. downtownboathouse.org Ⓜ Subway: 1, 9 to Franklin St. or A, C, E to Canal St. for Pier 26 **Loeb**

Boathouse ☎ 212/517-2233 ⊕ www.centralparknyc. org. **Manhattan Kayak Company** ⊠ Chelsea Piers, Pier 63, W. 23rd St. and the Hudson River, Chelsea ☎ 212/924-1788 ⊕ www.manhattankayak.com Ⓜ Subway: C, E to 23rd St.

FOOTBALL

The football season runs from September through December. The enormously popular New York Giants play at Giants Stadium in the Meadowlands Sports Complex. Most seats for Giants games are sold on a season-ticket basis—and there's a very long waiting list for those. However, single tickets are occasionally available at the stadium box office. The New York Jets also play at Giants Stadium, although at this writing there were plans afoot to build them a stadium on the West Side of Manhattan. Although Jets tickets are not as scarce as those for the Giants, most are snapped up by fans before the season opener.

New York Giants ☎ 201/935-8222 for tickets ⊕ www.giants.com **New York Jets** ☎ 516/560-8200 for tickets, 516/560-8288 for fan club ⊕ www. newyorkjets.com.

ICE-SKATING

The outdoor rink in Rockefeller Center, open from October through early April, is much smaller in real life than it appears on TV and in movies. It's also very busy, so be prepared to wait—there are no advance ticket sales. Although it's also beautiful, especially when Rock Center's enormous Christmas tree towers above it, you pay for the privilege: adult rates including skates start at $16. If you're a self-conscious skater, note that there are usually huge crowds watching.

The city's outdoor rinks, open from roughly November through March, all have their own character. The beautifully situated Wollman Rink offers skating until long after dark beneath the lights of the city. Be prepared for daytime crowds on weekends. The Lasker Rink, at the north end of Central Park, is smaller and usually less crowded than Wollman Rink. Prospect Park's Kate Wollman Rink borders the lake, and has a picture-postcard setting. Chelsea Piers' Sky Rink has two year-round indoor rinks overlooking the Hudson. Rentals are available at all rinks.

F **Kate Wollman Rink** ⊠ Ocean Ave. and Parkside Ave., Prospect Park, Brooklyn ☎ 718/287-6431 **M** Subway: 2, 3 to Grand Army Plaza; B, Q to Prospect Park; F to 15th St./Prospect Park **Lasker Rink** ⊠ Midpark near E. 106th St., Central Park ☎ 212/534-7639 ⊕ www.centralparknyc.org **M** Subway: B, C to 103rd St. **Rockefeller Center** ⊠ 50th St. at 5th Ave., lower plaza, Midtown West ☎ 212/332-7654 ⊕ ww.therinkatrockcenter.com **M** Subway: B, D, F, V to 47th–50th Sts./Rockefeller Center; E, V to 5th Ave.–53rd St. **Sky Rink** ⊠ Pier 61, W. 23rd St. and the Hudson River, Chelsea ☎ 212/336-6100 ⊕ www.chelseapiers.com **M** Subway: C, E to 23rd St. **Wollman Rink** ⊠ North of 6th Ave., between 62nd and 63rd Str, north of park entrance, Central Park ☎ 212/439-6900 ⊕ www.centralparknyc.org

JOGGING

All kinds of New Yorkers jog, some with dogs or babies in tow, so you'll always have company on the regular jogging routes. What's not recommended is to set out on a lonely park path at dusk. Jog when and where everybody else does. On Manhattan streets, roughly 20 north–south blocks make a mile.

In Manhattan, Central Park is the busiest spot, specifically along the 1⅗-mi path circling the Jacqueline Kennedy Onassis Reservoir be sure to ride in a counter-clockwise direction. A runners' lane has been designated along the park roads. A good 1¾-mi route starts at Tavern on the Green along the West Drive, heads south around the bottom of the park to the East Drive, and circles back west on the 72nd Street park road to your starting point; the entire loop road is a hilly 6 mi. Riverside Park, along the Hudson River bank in Manhattan, is glorious at sunset. You can cover 4½ mi by running from West 72nd to 116th Street and back, and the Greenbelt trail extends 4 more miles north to the George Washington Bridge at 181st Street.

Other favorite Manhattan circuits are the Battery Park City esplanade (about 2 mi), which connects to the longer Hudson River Park (about 1½ mi), and the **East River Esplanade** (just over 3 mi from East 59th to East 125th streets). In Brooklyn

try the Brooklyn Heights Promenade (⅓ mi), which faces the Manhattan skyline, or the loop in Prospect Park (3⅓ mi).

STUDENTS IN NEW YORK

New York is home to such major schools as Columbia University, New York University, Fordham University, and the City College of New York. With other colleges scattered throughout the five boroughs, as well as a huge population of public and private high-schoolers, it's no wonder the city is rife with student discounts. Wherever you go, especially museums, sightseeing attractions, and performances, identify yourself as a student up front and ask if a discount is available. However, **be prepared to show your ID** as proof of enrollment and/or age.

A great program for those between the ages of 13 and 18 (or anyone in middle or high school) is High 5 for the Arts. Tickets to all sorts of performances are sold for $5 online, and also at Ticketmaster outlets in the city, including at music stores such as HMV and Tower Records. Tickets are either for a single teen (Friday and weekends) or for a teen and his or her guest of any age (Monday–Thursday). Write to receive a free catalog of events, check it out online, or pick a catalog up at any New York public library or at High 5's offices. These $5 tickets cannot be bought over the phone or at the venue box offices. With the $5 museum pass, a teen can bring a guest of any age to participating museums any day of the week.

F **IDs & Services High 5 for the Arts** ⊠ 1 E. 53rd St., at 5th Ave., Midtown ☎ 212/445-8587 ⊕ www.highfivetix.org.

STA Travel ⊠ 10 Downing St., New York, NY 10014 ☎ 212/627-3111, 800/777-0112 24-hr service center ⊟ 212/627-3387 ⊕ www.sta.com. **Travel Cuts** ⊠ 187 College St., Toronto, Ontario M5T 1P7, Canada ☎ 800/592-2887 in U.S., 416/979-2406 or 866/246-9762 in Canada ⊟ 416/979-8167 ⊕ www.travelcuts.com.

SUBWAY TRAVEL

The 714-mi subway system operates 24 hours a day and serves nearly all the places you're likely to visit. It's cheaper than a cab, and during the workweek it's often faster than either taxis or buses. The trains are clean, well lighted, and air-conditioned. Still, the New York subway is hardly problem-free. Many trains are crowded, and the older ones are noisy. Homeless people sometimes take refuge from the elements by riding the trains, and panhandlers head there for a captive audience. Although trains usually run frequently, especially during rush hours, you never know when some incident somewhere on the line may stall traffic. In addition, subway construction sometimes causes delays or limitation of service, especially on weekends.

Most subway entrances are at street corners and are marked by lampposts with an illuminated Metropolitan Transit Authority (MTA) logo or globe-shape green or red lights—green means the station is open 24 hours and red means the station closes at night (though colors don't always correspond to reality). Subway lines are designated by numbers and letters, such as the 3 line or the A line. Some lines run "express" and skip stops, and others are "locals" and make all stops. Each station entrance has a sign indicating the lines that run through the station. Some entrances are also marked "uptown only" or "downtown only." Before entering subway stations, **read the signs carefully.** One of the most frequent mistakes visitors make is taking the train in the wrong direction. Maps of the full subway system are posted in every train car and usually on the subway platform (though these are sometimes out-of-date). You can usually pick up free maps at station booths.

For the most up-to-date information on subway lines, call the MTA's Travel Information Center or visit its Web site. The Web site HopStop is a good source for figuring out the best line to take to reach your destination. Alternatively, ask a station agent.

FARES & TRANSFERS
Subway fare is the same as bus fare: $2. You can transfer between subway lines an unlimited number of times at any of the numerous stations where lines intersect. If you use a MetroCard (⇨ Public Trans-

portation) to pay your fare, you can also transfer to intersecting MTA bus routes for free. Such transfers generally have time limits of two hours.

PAYING
Pay your subway fare at the turnstile, using a MetroCard bought at the station booth or from a vending machine.

SMOKING
Smoking is not allowed on New York City subways or in subway stations.
🚇 Subway Information **Hopstop** ⊕ www.hopstop. com. **Metropolitan Transit Authority (MTA) Travel Information Line** ☎ 718/330-1234, 718/330-4847 for non-English speakers ⊕ www.mta.nyc.ny.us.

MTA Lost Property Office ☎ 212/712-4500. **MTA Status information hotline** ☎ 718/243-7777, updated hourly.

TAXES
The city charges tax on hotel rooms (13.375%), rental cars (13.625%), and parking in commercial lots or garages (18.625%). An additional fee of $3.50 per unit per day applies to hotel rooms.

SALES TAX
New York City's sales tax of 8.375% applies to almost everything you can buy retail, including restaurant meals. Prescription drugs and nonprepared food bought in grocery stores are tax exempt.

TAXIS & CAR SERVICES
There are several differences between taxis (cabs) and car services, also known as livery cabs. For one thing, a taxi is yellow and a car-service sedan is not. In addition, taxis run on a meter, while car services charge a flat fee. And by law, car services are not allowed to pick up passengers unless you call for one first.

Taxis can be extremely difficult (if not impossible) to find in many parts of Brooklyn, Queens, the Bronx, and Staten Island. As a result, you may have no choice but to call a car service. Always **determine the fee** beforehand when using a car service sedan; a 10%–15% tip is customary above that.

Yellow cabs are in abundance almost everywhere in Manhattan, cruising the streets looking for fares. They are usually easy to hail on the street or from a cab stand in front of major hotels, though finding one at rush hour or in the rain can take some time. Even if you're stuck in a downpour or at the airport, **do not accept a ride from a gypsy cab.** If a cab is not yellow and does not have a numbered aqua-color plastic medallion riveted to the hood, you could be putting yourself in danger by getting into the car.

You can see if a taxi is available by checking its rooftop light; if the center panel is lit and the side panels are dark, the driver is ready to take passengers. Taxi fares cost $2.50 for the first ⅓ mi, 40¢ for each ⅕ mi thereafter, and 20¢ for each minute not in motion. A $1 surcharge is added to rides begun 4–8 PM and a 50¢ surcharge is added between 8 PM and 6 AM.

One taxi can hold a maximum of four passengers (an additional passenger under the age of seven is allowed if the child sits on someone's lap). There is no charge for extra passengers. You must pay any bridge or tunnel tolls incurred during your trip (a driver will usually pay the toll himself to keep moving quickly, but that amount will be added to the fare when the ride is over). Taxi drivers expect a 15% to 20% tip.

To avoid unhappy taxi experiences, **try to know where you want to go and how to get there before you hail a cab.** A few cab drivers are dishonest, and not all know the city as well as they should. Direct your cab driver by the cross streets of your destination (for instance, "5th Avenue and 42nd Street"), rather than the numerical address, which means little to many drivers. Also, speak simply and clearly to make sure the driver has heard you correctly—this will save you time, money, and aggravation. A quick call to your destination will give you cross-street information, as will a glance at a map marked with address numbers. When you leave the cab, **remember to take your receipt.** It includes the cab's medallion number, which can help you track the cabbie down in the event that you lose your possessions in the cab.

🚗 Car Reservations Carmel Car Service ☎ 212/666-6666 or 800/922-7635 ⊕ www.carmelcarservice.com. **London Towncars** ☎ 212/

988-9700 or 800/221-4009 ⊕ www.londontowncars.com. **Tel Aviv Car and Limousine Service** ☎ 212/777-7777 or 800/222-9888 ⊕ www.telavivlimo.com.

TELEPHONES

Avoid making calls from your hotel room, because you may be charged a higher rate than usual for direct-dial calls or a surcharge on credit card calls. Although the near-ubiquity of the cell phone has made them scarcer (and even less reliable) than they used to be, public pay phones can still be found on the street, in subway stations, and in hotels, bars, and restaurants.

Make sure that the pay phone is labeled as a Verizon telephone; the unmarked varieties are notorious change-eaters. A local call costs 50¢. There are also public credit card phones scattered around the city. If you want to consult a directory or make a more leisurely call, pay phones in the lobbies of office buildings or hotels (some of which take credit cards) are a better choice.

The area codes for Manhattan are 212, 646, and 917. For Brooklyn, Queens, the Bronx, and Staten Island, the area codes are 718 and 347. The area codes 917, 347, and 646 are also used for many cell phones and pagers in all five boroughs.

TIME

New York operates on Eastern Standard Time. When it's noon in New York it's 9 AM in Los Angeles, 11 AM in Chicago, 5 PM in London, and 3 AM the following day in Sydney.

TIPPING

The customary tipping rate for taxi drivers is 15%–20%, with a minimum of $2; bellhops are usually given $2 per bag in luxury hotels, $1 per bag elsewhere. Hotel maids should be tipped $2 per day of your stay. A doorman who hails or helps you into a cab can be tipped $1–$2. You should also tip your hotel concierge for services rendered; the size of the tip depends on the difficulty of your request, as well as the quality of the concierge's work. For an ordinary dinner reservation or tour arrangements, $3–$5 should do; if the concierge scores seats at a popular restaurant or show or performs unusual services (getting your laptop repaired, finding a good pet-sitter, etc.), $10 or more is appropriate.

Waiters should be tipped 15%–20%, though at higher-end restaurants, a solid 20% is more the norm. Many restaurants add a gratuity to the bill for parties of six or more. Ask what the percentage is if the menu or bill doesn't state it. Tip $1 per drink you order at the bar, though if at an upscale establishment, those $15 martinis might warrant a $2 tip.

TOURS & PACKAGES

Because everything is prearranged on a prepackaged tour or independent vacation, you spend less time planning—and often get it all at a good price.

BOOKING WITH AN AGENT

Travel agents are excellent resources. But it's a good idea to collect brochures from several agencies, as some agents' suggestions may be influenced by relationships with tour and package firms that reward them for volume sales. If you have a special interest, find an agent with expertise in that area; the American Society of Travel Agents (ASTA; ⇨ Travel Agencies) has a database of specialists worldwide. You can log on to the group's Web site to find an ASTA travel agent in your neighborhood.

Make sure your travel agent knows the accommodations and other services of the place being recommended. Ask about the hotel's location, room size, beds, and whether it has a pool, room service, or programs for children, if you care about these. Has your agent been there in person or sent others whom you can contact?

Do some homework on your own, too: local tourism boards can provide information about lesser-known and small-niche operators, some of which may sell only direct.

BUYER BEWARE

Each year consumers are stranded or lose their money when tour operators—even large ones with excellent reputations—go out of business. So check out the operator. Ask several travel agents about its reputation, and try to **book with a company that has a consumer-protection program.**

(Look for information in the company's brochure.) In the United States, members of the United States Tour Operators Association are required to set aside funds ($1 million) to help eligible customers cover payments and travel arrangements in the event that the company defaults. It's also a good idea to choose a company that participates in the American Society of Travel Agents' Tour Operator Program; ASTA will act as mediator in any disputes between you and your tour operator.

Remember that the more your package or tour includes, the better you can predict the ultimate cost of your vacation. Make sure you know exactly what is covered, and beware of hidden costs. Are taxes, tips, and transfers included? Entertainment and excursions? These can add up.

🔢 Tour-Operator Recommendations **American Society of Travel Agents** (⇨ Travel Agencies). **National Tour Association** (NTA) ✉ 546 E. Main St., Lexington, KY 40508 ☎ 859/226–4444 or 800/682–8886 🖷 859/226–4404 ⊕ www.ntaonline.com. **United States Tour Operators Association** (USTOA) ✉ 275 Madison Ave., Suite 2014, New York, NY 10016 ☎ 212/599–6599 🖷 212/599–6744 ⊕ www.ustoa.com.

TRAIN TRAVEL

For information about traveling by subway within New York City, *see* Subway Travel.

Metro-North Commuter Railroad trains take passengers from Grand Central Terminal to points north of New York City, both in New York State and Connecticut. Amtrak trains from across the United States arrive at Penn Station. For trains from New York City to Long Island and New Jersey, take the Long Island Railroad and New Jersey Transit, respectively; both operate from Penn Station. The PATH trains offer service to Newark and Jersey City. All of these trains generally run on schedule, although occasional delays occur. Smoking is not permitted on any train.

🔢 Train Information **Amtrak** ☎ 800/872–7245 ⊕ www.amtrak.com. **Long Island Railroad** ☎ 718/217–5477 ⊕ www.mta.nyc.ny.us/lirr. **Metro-North Commuter Railroad** ☎ 212/532–4900 ⊕ www.mta.nyc.ny.us/mnr. **New Jersey Transit** ☎ 800/772–

2222 ⊕ www.njtransit.com. **PATH** ☎ 800/234-7284
⊕ www.pathrail.com.
⚏ Train Stations **Grand Central Terminal** ⊠ Park
Ave. and E. 42nd St., Midtown East ☎ 212/340-2210
⊕ www.grandcentralterminal.com. **Penn Station**
⊠ W. 31st to W. 33rd Sts., between 7th and 8th
Aves., Midtown West ☎ 212/630-6401.

TRAVEL AGENCIES

A good travel agent puts your needs first.
Look for an agency that has been in business at least five years, emphasizes customer service, and has someone on staff
who specializes in your destination. In addition, **make sure the agency belongs to a
professional trade organization.** The
American Society of Travel Agents
(ASTA)—the largest and most influential
in the field with more than 20,000 members in some 140 countries—maintains
and enforces a strict code of ethics and
will step in to help mediate any agent-
client disputes involving ASTA members if
necessary. ASTA (whose motto is "Without a travel agent, you're on your own")
also maintains a Web site that includes a
directory of agents. (If a travel agency is
also acting as your tour operator, *see*
Buyer Beware *in* Tours & Packages.)
⚏ Local Agent Referrals **American Society of
Travel Agents (ASTA)** ⊠ 1101 King St., Suite 200,
Alexandria, VA 22314 ☎ 703/739-2782 or 800/965-
2782 24-hr hotline ⎙ 703/684-8319 ⊕ www.
astanet.com. **Association of British Travel Agents**
⊠ 68-71 Newman St., London W1T 3AH ☎ 020/
7637-2444 ⎙ 020/7637-0713 ⊕ www.abta.com. **Association of Canadian Travel Agencies** ⊠ 130 Al-
bert St., Suite 1705, Ottawa, Ontario K1P 5G4 ☎ 613/
237-3657 ⎙ 613/237-7052 ⊕ www.acta.ca. **Australian Federation of Travel Agents** ⊠ Level 3, 309
Pitt St., Sydney, NSW 2000 ☎ 02/9264-3299 or
1300/363-416 ⎙ 02/9264-1085 ⊕ www.afta.com.
au. **Travel Agents' Association of New Zealand**
⊠ Level 5, Tourism and Travel House, 79 Boulcott
St., Box 1888, Wellington 6001 ☎ 04/499-0104
⎙ 04/499-0786 ⊕ www.taanz.org.nz.

VISITOR INFORMATION

Learn more about foreign destinations by
checking government-issued travel advisories and country information. For a
broader picture, consider information
from more than one country.

The Grand Central Partnership (a sort of
civic Good Samaritans' group) has installed a number of unstaffed information
kiosks near Grand Central Terminal.
They're loaded with maps and helpful
brochures on attractions throughout the
city. There are also seasonal outdoor carts
sprinkled throughout the area (there's one
near Vanderbilt Avenue and East 42nd
Street), staffed by friendly, knowledgeable,
multilingual New Yorkers. The 34th Street
Partnership runs a kiosk on the concourse
level at Penn Station (33rd St. and 7th
Ave.); there's even a cart at the Empire
State Building (5th Ave. at 34th St.).

Contact New York City & Company for
brochures, subway and bus maps, Metro-
Cards, a calendar of events, listings of hotels and weekend hotel packages, and
discount coupons for Broadway shows. In
addition to its main center in Times
Square, the bureau also runs kiosks at the
south tip of City Hall Park, in Chinatown
at the intersection of Canal, Walker, and
Baxter Streets, and in Harlem at 163 West
125th Street, near Adam Clayton Powell
Jr. Boulevard. The Downtown Alliance has
information on the area encompassing
City Hall south to Battery Park, and from
the East River to West Street. For a free
booklet listing New York City attractions
and tour packages, contact the New York
State Division of Tourism.
⚏ City Information **Brooklyn Information & Culture Inc. (BRIC)** ⊠ 647 Fulton St., 2nd fl., Brooklyn
11217 ☎ 718/855-7882 ⊕ www.brooklynx.org.
Downtown Alliance ⊠ 120 Broadway, Suite 3340,
between Pine and Thames Sts., Lower Manhattan
10271 ☎ 212/566-6700 ⊕ www.downtownny.com.
Grand Central Partnership ⊕ www.
grandcentralpartnership.org.

NYC & Company Convention & Visitors Bureau
⊠ 810 7th Ave., between W. 52nd and W. 53rd Sts.,
3rd fl., Midtown West ☎ 212/484-1222 ⊕ www.
nycvisit.com. **Times Square Information Center**
⊠ 1560 Broadway, between 46th and 47th Sts.,
Midtown West ☎ 212/768-1560 ⊕ www.
timessquarenyc.org.
⚏ Statewide Information **New York State Division of Tourism** ☎ 518/474-4116 or 800/225-5697
⊕ www.iloveny.state.ny.us.

F Government Advisories **Consular Affairs Bureau of Canada** ☎ 800/267-6788 or 613/944-6788 ⊕ www.voyage.gc.ca. **U.K. Foreign and Commonwealth Office** ⊠ Travel Advice Unit, Consular Division, Old Admiralty Bldg., London SW1A 2PA ☎ 0870/606-0290 or 020/7008-1500 ⊕ www.fco.gov.uk/travel. **Australian Department of Foreign Affairs and Trade** ☎ 300/139-281 travel advice, 02/6261-1299 Consular Travel Advice Faxback Service ⊕ www.dfat.gov.au. **New Zealand Ministry of Foreign Affairs and Trade** ☎ 04/439-8000 ⊕ www.mft.govt.nz.

WALKING

The cheapest, sometimes the fastest, and usually the most interesting way to explore this city is by walking. Because New Yorkers by and large live in apartments rather than in houses, and travel by cab, bus, or subway rather than by private car, they end up walking quite a lot. As a result, street life is a vital part of the local culture. On crowded sidewalks, people gossip, snack, browse, cement business deals, have romantic rendezvous, encounter long-lost friends, and fly into irrational quarrels with strangers. It's a wonderfully democratic hubbub.

As you make your own way, be sure not to stop abruptly in the middle of the sidewalk—move to the side if you need to slow down.

A typical New Yorker walks quickly and focuses intently on dodging cars, buses, bicycle messengers, construction sites, and other pedestrians. Although this might make natives seem hurried and rude, they will often come to the aid of a lost pedestrian, so **don't hesitate to ask a passerby for directions.**

WEB SITES

Do check out the World Wide Web when planning your trip. You'll find everything from weather forecasts to virtual tours of famous cities. Be sure to visit Fodors.com (⊕ www.fodors.com), a complete travel-planning site. You can research prices and book plane tickets, hotel rooms, rental cars, vacation packages, and more. In addition, you can post your pressing questions in the Travel Talk section. Other planning tools include a currency converter and weather reports, and there are loads of links to travel resources.

New York Citysearch supplies comprehensive, searchable events listings to help you find out what's going on around town. Check out Menupages for reasonably up-to-date, printable menus of nearly 4,500 Manhattan restaurants. The Official New York City Web site has plenty of links to agencies, services, and cultural activities. The cable channel New York 1's Web site is frequently updated with the city's breaking stories. To learn about the city in greater depth, go to the New York Public Library's site. The Gothamist blog is a good way to find out what New Yorkers are up to. The *New York Times* keeps online reviews of restaurants and current movies and theater, as well as music, dance, art listings, and show times. To get directions to New York destinations using the bus or subway, consult HopStop.

F Web Addresses **Fodor's.com** ⊕ www.fodors.com. **Gothamist** ⊕ www.gothamist.com. **HopStop** ⊕ www.hopstop.com. **Menupages** ⊕ www.menupages.com. **New York Citysearch** ⊕ www.nycitysearch.com. **New York 1** ⊕ www.ny1.com. **New York Public Library** ⊕ www.nypl.org. *New York Times* ⊕ www.nytoday.com. **Official New York City Web site** ⊕ www.nyc.gov.

Lower Manhattan

Including the Statue of Liberty, Wall Street, Chinatown & SoHo

WORD OF MOUTH

"Museums, ferries, and the view from the Empire State Building all cost you—[the Brooklyn Bridge] doesn't. And the views are spectacular on a clear day. Takes about 45–50 minutes to walk across, depending on how many pictures you stop to take."

—jdavis

"If you're in NYC mid-September, you've GOT TO go to the San Gennaro Feast in Little Italy. Go hungry and just eat your way through all the yummy Italian food. And be sure to sit at one of the little outdoor cafes and drink some espresso and just people watch! It's well worth the price."

—sailorgirl

Updated by
Matthew
Lombardi

NEW YORK LIVES EMPHATICALLY IN THE PRESENT TENSE, but in lower Manhattan you can get a glimpse of the city's past. As you meander the bustling streets, you'll find yourself face to face with vestiges large and small of New York City history.

A ferry ride into the harbor brings you to Ellis Island and the Statue of Liberty, two inspiring testaments to America's ideals and its immigrant culture. On Manhattan's southern tip, the skyscraper-lined canyons of Wall Street and lower Broadway echo with the ghosts of industrialists and robber barons who made their millions here in the late 19th and early 20th centuries. Traveling north past stately City Hall and a cluster of imposing courthouses, you reach Chinatown, where the vibrant street life and the scores of tiny shops are remnants of a time when Manhattan was dominated by ethnic neighborhoods. (Little Italy, bordering Chinatown and virtually swallowed up by it, is a prime example of how many such neighborhoods have all but evaporated.) Above Chinatown and to the west, SoHo has evolved into one of New York's toniest shopping districts, but it too derives its character from the past: the cast-iron buildings and cobblestone streets are reminders of the area's 19th-century role as a warehouse district, and the edgier attitude that distinguishes SoHo's shops from those of Madison Avenue has everything to do with the arts community that flourished here from the 1960s through the 1980s.

Even more than elsewhere in New York, lower Manhattan is an area you can fully appreciate only by walking the streets—which means, among other things, that you'll want to see it on a day when the weather is tolerable. There are numerous museums, but most are surprisingly modest. The history and culture are beneath your feet and towering over your head.

One of the biggest draws for visitors to lower Manhattan is a place known not for what's there but for what isn't: the World Trade Center site. This massive gulf among the financial district's skyscrapers is where, on a sunny autumn morning in 2001, America's position in the world was wrenchingly, brutally redefined. It's become a place of pilgrimage, where people from across the country and around the world bear witness, honor the dead, and watch the site slowly rising from the ashes.

THE STATUE OF LIBERTY & ELLIS ISLAND

A trip to the Statue of Liberty and Ellis Island takes up the better part of a day, and more often than not it requires a good dose of patience to deal with large crowds and rigorous security checks. But it's worth the effort. It's no overstatement to say that these two sights have played defining roles in American culture. They're both well run and eminently satisfying to visit.

Unless time constraints dictate otherwise, it makes sense to see both sights in one trip. Ferries leaving from Battery Park every half hour take you to both islands. (Note that large packages and oversize bags and backpacks aren't permitted on board.) There's no admission fee for either sight, but the ferry ride costs $10. It's worth the additional $1.75 charge to reserve tickets in advance—you'll still have to wait in line, both to pick up the tickets and to board the ferry, but you'll be able to reserve a spot on the Statue of Liberty observatory tour, which will make your experience significantly richer.

The Statue of Liberty

For millions of immigrants, the first glimpse of America was the Statue of Liberty. You get a taste of the thrill they must have experienced as you approach Liberty Island on the ferry from Battery Park and witness the statue grow from a vaguely defined figure on the horizon into a towering, stately colossus. (You're likely to share the boat ride with people from all over the world, which lends an additional dimension to the trip. The statue may be purely a tourist attraction, but the tourists it attracts are a wonderfully diverse group.)

Liberty Enlightening the World, as the statue is officially named, was presented to the United States in 1886 as a gift from France. The 152-foot-tall figure was sculpted by Frederic-Auguste Bartholdi and erected around an iron skeleton engineered by Gustav Eiffel. It stands atop an 89-foot pedestal designed by Richard Morris Hunt, with Emma Lazarus's sonnet "The New Colossus" ("Give me your tired, your poor, your huddled masses . . .") inscribed on a bronze plaque at the base. Over the course of time, the statue has become precisely what its creators dreamed it would be: the single most powerful symbol of American ideals, and as such one of the world's great monumental sculptures.

Inside the statue's pedestal is a museum that's everything it should be: informative, entertaining, and quickly viewed. Highlights include the original flame (which was replaced because of water damage), full-scale replicas of Lady Liberty's face and one of her feet, Bartholdi's alternative designs for the statue, and a model of Eiffel's intricate framework.

You're allowed access to the museum only as part of one of the free tours of the promenade (which surrounds the base of the pedestal) or the observatory (at the pedestal's top). The tours are limited to 3,000 participants a day; to guarantee a place, particularly on the observatory tour, you should order tickets ahead of time—they can be reserved up to 180 days in advance, by phone or over the Internet. Although the narrow, double-helix stairs leading to the statue's crown have been closed to visitors since 9/11, you get a good look at the statue's inner structure on the observatory tour. From the observatory itself there are fine views of the harbor and an up-close (but totally uncompromising) glimpse up Lady Liberty's dress.

If you're on one of the tours, you'll go through a security check more thorough than any airport screening, and you'll have to deposit any bags in a locker. Liberty Island has a pleasant outdoor café for refueling. The only disappointment is the gift shop, which sells trinkets little better than those available from street vendors. ⊠ *Liberty Island, Lower Manhattan* ☎ *212/363–3200, 212/269–5755 ferry information, 866/782–8834 ticket reservations* ⊕ *www.nps.gov/stli, www.statuereservations.com for reservations* ☞ *Free; ferry $10 round-trip* ☉ *Daily 8:30–5; extended hrs in summer.*

Ellis Island

Between 1892 and 1924, approximately 12 million men, women, and children first set foot on U.S. soil at the Ellis Island federal immigration facility. By the time the facility closed in 1954, it had processed ancestors of more than 40% of Americans living today.

The island's main building, now a national monument, reopened in 1990 as the **Ellis Island Immigration Museum**, containing more than 30 galleries of artifacts, photographs, and taped oral histories. The centerpiece of the museum is the white-tile Registry Room (also known as the Great Hall). It feels dignified and cavernous today, but photographs show that it took on a multitude of configurations through the years, always packed with humanity undergoing one form or another of screening. While you're there, take a look out the Registry Room's tall, arched windows and try to imagine what passed through immigrants' minds as they viewed lower Manhattan's skyline to one side and the Statue of Liberty to the other.

Because there's so much to take in, it's a good idea to make use of the museum's interpretive tools. Check at the visitor desk for free film tickets, ranger tour times, and special programs. The audio tour is worth its $6 price: it takes you through the exhibits, providing thorough, engaging commentary interspersed with recordings of immigrants themselves recalling their experiences. Along with the Registry Room, the museum's features include the ground-level Railroad Ticket Office, which has several interactive exhibits and a three-dimensional graphic representation of American immigration patterns; the American Family Immigration Center, where you can search Ellis Island's records for your own ancestors (for a $5 fee); and, outside, the American Immigrant Wall of Honor, where the names of more than 500,000 immigrant Americans are inscribed along a promenade facing the Manhattan skyline. (For $100 you can add a family member's name to the wall.) ⊠ *Lower Manhattan* ☎ *212/363–3200 Ellis Island, 212/883–1986 Wall of Honor information* ⊕ *www.ellisisland. org, www.nps.gov/elis* ⊠ *Free; ferry $10 round-trip* ☉ *Daily 8:30–5:15 extended hrs in summer.*

THE BATTERY & THE FINANCIAL DISTRICT

New York was born on the southern tip of Manhattan. The shore along the harbor was a center of Native American activity before the days of the earliest Dutch settlers, and when the Dutch arrived, this was their base. New York's few vestiges from the Revolutionary War era are found on these streets, dwarfed by the skyscrapers of the financial district—which have in turn taken on a historical air. As you walk along lower Broadway, it can feel like you're living in the world of black-and-white news reels. This is where Amelia Earhart, Joe DiMaggio, and hundreds of other heroes of the day celebrated their triumphs amid a blizzard of tickertape. (You'll see their names imbedded in the sidewalk. For some, fame has withstood the test of time; for others, it's faded with the years.)

As you explore, you may get the sense that this area lives uneasily in the 21st century. It's still one of New York's business centers, but its heyday is tangibly in the past, and what's come since can be an awkward fit. Architectural masterpieces are sometimes occupied at street level by fastfood restaurants and dubious-looking discount stores. (If you're spending the day in lower Manhattan, plan for lunch in Chinatown or SoHo, where dining options are more appealing and more varied.) The hulking buildings where Andrew Carnegie and J. P. Morgan ruled their commercial empires are now condominiums. On Wall Street, several banks have been converted into gyms and hotels, and the New York Stock Exchange has moved part of its operation to New Jersey. The center of the financial universe is now elsewhere—or more accurately everywhere, as the call of the floor trader gets replaced by the click of a mouse.

Numbers in the text correspond to numbers in the margin and on the Lower Manhattan map.

a good walk

At the tip of the island, the **Staten Island Ferry ❸** ⚐ affords a big-picture perspective on Wall Street and the Battery, and you can double the ride's scenic pleasures by taking it at sunset. Just north of the terminal, the white columns and curved brick front of the 1793 **Shrine of St. Elizabeth Ann Seton at Our Lady of the Rosary ❹** are dwarfed by the high-rise behind it. The house was once one of many mansions lining State Street. Across the street from the shrine, the verdant **Battery Park ❺** curves up the west side of the island. It's filled with sculptures and monuments, including the circular **Castle Clinton National Monument ❻**. From Castle Clinton, walk away from the water, following the path running alongside the rose-filled Hope Garden to *The Sphere,* by Fritz Koenig. The damaged bronze sculpture once stood at the center of the World Trade Center plaza. The path ends near **Bowling Green ❼**, an oval greensward at the foot of Broadway that in 1733 became New York's first public park. It provides an excellent view up Broadway of the formidable Canyon of Heroes, site of many a ticker-tape parade. While you're here, duck inside the Cunard Building at 25 Broadway to see the superb ceiling frescoes by Ezra Winter. Now a post office, this Renaissance-style building completed in 1921 once was the booking hall for the great ocean liners owned by Cunard. On the south side of Bowling Green is the beaux-arts **Alexander Hamilton U.S. Custom House ❽**, home of the National Museum of the American Indian.

Follow Whitehall Street (the continuation of Broadway) down the east side of the museum. A left turn onto Bridge Street will bring into focus a block of early New York buildings. As you approach Broad Street, the two-tone Georgian **Fraunces Tavern ❾** will appear on the right, on Pearl Street. Across Pearl Street, the plaza of 85 Broad Street pays homage to urban archaeology with a transparent panel in the sidewalk at the corner of Pearl and Coenties Slip, showing the excavated foundations of the 17th-century Stadt Huys, the Old Dutch City Hall. The course of old Dutch Stone Street is marked in the lobby with a line of brown paving stones.

Next head north on Pearl Street to **Hanover Square ❿**, a quiet tree-lined plaza. Leading south is Stone Street, the oldest paved street in the city.

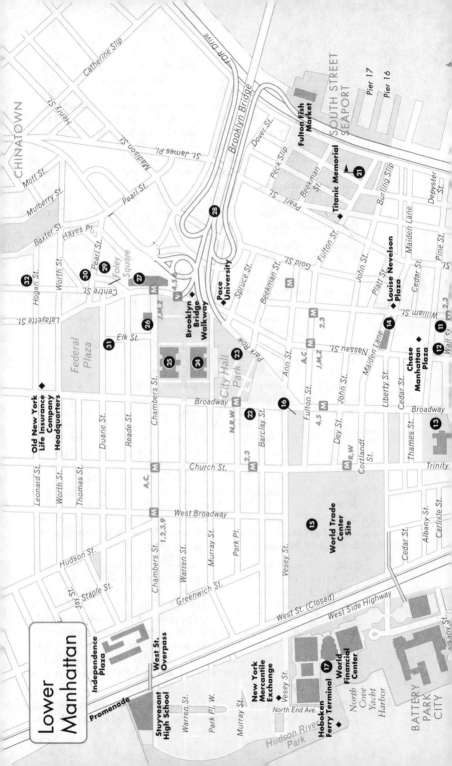

Lower Manhattan

CHINATOWN

Catherine Slip

FDR Drive

Henry St.

Mott St.

Mulberry St.

Baxter St.

St. James Pl.

Madison St.

Pearl St.

Brooklyn Bridge

Dover St.

Fulton Fish Market

SOUTH STREET SEAPORT

Pier 17

Pier 16

Peck Slip

Beekman St.

Titanic Memorial

21

Burling Slip

Depyster St.

Hogan St.

Worth St.

Hayes Pl.

Pearl St.

Foley Square

32

30 **29**

Centre St.

27

28

Pace University

Spruce St.

Gold St.

Fulton St.

John St.

Platt St.

Louise Nevelson Plaza

Maiden Lane

Cedar St.

Pine St.

Lafayette St.

Elk St.

Federal Plaza

31

26

J.M.Z

Brooklyn Bridge Walkway

4,5

Beekman St.

Nassau St.

William St.

14

11

12

Wall St.

2,3

Old New York Life Insurance Company Headquarters

Duane St.

Reade St.

Chambers St.

25 **24**

23

City Hall Park

Park Row

Ann St.

A,C.

J.M.Z

2,3

Maiden Lane

Liberty St.

Cedar St.

Chase Manhattan Plaza

13

Broadway

Leonard St.

Worth St.

Thomas St.

Broadway

22

Barclay St.

Fulton St.

4,5

Dey St.

John St.

Thames St.

Trinity

Church St.

N.R.W

2,3

Cortlandt St.

M R,W

Jay St.

Staple St.

Hudson St.

West Broadway

16

Vesey St.

15

World Trade Center Site

Albany St.

Carlisle St.

Chambers St.

Warren St.

Murray St.

Park Pl.

Greenwich St.

Cedar St.

Vesey St.

West St. (Closed)

West Side Highway

Independence Plaza

West St. Overpass

Promenade

Stuyvesant High School

Warren St.

Park Pl. W.

Murray St.

New York Mercantile Exchange

North End Ave.

North End Ave.

Hoboken Ferry Terminal

17

World Financial Center

North Cove Yacht Harbor

BATTERY PARK CITY

Hudson River Park

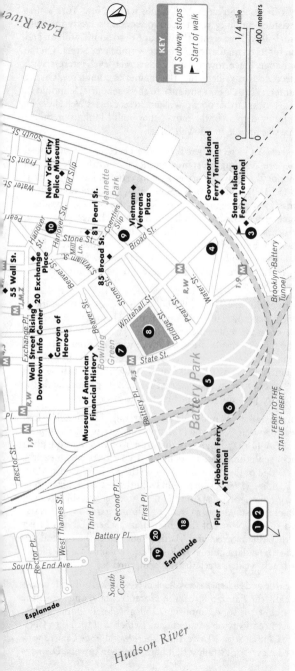

East River

KEY

Ⓜ Subway stops

▲ Start of walk

1/4 mile
400 meters

New York City
Police Museum

Jeanette
Park

Vietnam
Veterans
Plaza

Governors Island
Ferry Terminal

Staten Island
Ferry Terminal

Brooklyn-Battery
Tunnel

Museum of American
Financial History

Wall Street Rising
Downtown Info Center 20 Exchange
Place

Canyon of
Heroes

Battery Park

FERRY TO THE
STATUE OF LIBERTY

Hudson River

South
Cove

Esplanade

Pier A
Hoboken Ferry
Terminal

Battery Pl.

A small alley off Stone Street is Mill Lane, where New York's first Sephardic Jewish community was forced to worship secretly in a mill during the mid-1600s. Turn right off Mill Lane onto South William and walk until you hit its triangular convergence with Beaver Street. On the right, 20 Exchange Place towers and adds street-level interest with weighty art deco doorways depicting the engines of commerce. On the corner to your left is the elegant entrance to the legendary Delmonico's restaurant. Two blocks farther north, William Street crosses **Wall Street** ⓫. For a jaw-dropping display of the money that built Manhattan, take a look at the massive arcade of 55 Wall Street.

One block west on Wall Street, where Broad Street becomes Nassau Street, a statue of George Washington stands on the steps of the **Federal Hall National Memorial** ⓬. Across the street is an investment bank built by J. P. Morgan in 1913. By building only four stories, Morgan was in effect declaring himself above the pressures of Wall Street real estate values. Soon to become part of the New York City Stock Exchange expansion, the building bears pockmarks near the fourth window on the Wall Street side; these were created in 1920 when a bomb that had been placed in a pushcart nearby exploded. The temple-front **New York Stock Exchange (NYSE)** is the central shrine of Wall Street (even though its address is officially on Broad Street).

The focal point at the west end of Wall Street is the brownstone **Trinity Church** ⓭. One block north of the church is tiny Thames Street, where a pair of skyscrapers playfully called the Thames Twins—the Trinity and U.S. Realty buildings—displays early-20th-century attempts to apply Gothic decoration to skyscrapers. Across the street at 120 Broadway, the 1915 Equitable Building rises 30 stories straight from its base with no setback; its overpowering shadow on the street helped persuade the city government to pass the nation's first zoning law.

Four sculpture installations make for an interesting side tour. The first is on Broadway between Cedar and Liberty streets, where the black-glass HSBC Bank USA (1971) heightens the drama of the red-and-silver Isamu Noguchi sculpture *Cube* in its plaza. Two blocks east, near the William Street edge of the plaza surrounding the 65-story Chase Manhattan Bank Building (1960), stands Jean Dubuffet's striking black-and-white *Group of Four Trees*. Just south of the Dubuffet and slightly inset is another Noguchi installation, a circular sculpture garden with his signature carved stones. North of the Chase plaza, where Liberty Street converges with William Street and Maiden Lane under the Federal Reserve Bank, the triangular Louise Nevelson Plaza contains four missilelike pieces of her black-welded-steel abstract sculpture.

The massive, rusticated **Federal Reserve Bank of New York** ⓮, directly across the street, recalls the Palazzo Strozzi in Florence, Italy, and looks the way a bank ought to: solid, imposing, and absolutely impregnable. Walk west past Broadway on Maiden Lane (which will turn into Cortlandt Street) to Church Street. There, the 16-acre **World Trade Center site** ⓯ once contained New York's tallest buildings, the twin towers. Displays along the west side of Church Street list the names of those who were lost on September 11, and tell the history of the towers. Walk south one block to Liberty Street and make a right. The sidewalk and pedestrian bridge (to Tower One of the World Financial Center) on Liberty Street allow pedestrians a close view of the site. From the corner of Liberty and Church streets, walk north three blocks to Fulton Street to visit **St. Paul's Chapel** ⑯ (enter on Broadway). This is the oldest surviving church building in Manhattan. Because of its proximity to the World Trade Center site, the chapel served as a place of rest and refuge for rescue and recovery workers in the year following the September 11 attacks. On September 11, 2002, it opened an exhibit honoring Ground Zero's workers and recalling their efforts in the months following the disaster.

During the twin towers' construction more than a million cubic yards of rock and soil were excavated—then moved across West Street to help reclaim the land that now holds Battery Park City. An impressive feat of urban planning, this complete 92-acre neighborhood houses residences, offices, and several green squares, though it's not a very exciting place to visit. The lovely Hudson River esplanade to the west is the best reason to come here. At the north end of the esplanade, the **World Financial Center (WFC)** ⑰, a four-tower complex designed by Cesar Pelli, rises above the small yacht basin. Just north of the basin is a terminal for ferry service to Hoboken, New Jersey. Beyond the ferry terminal is the south end of Hudson River Park. To the south, the riverside esplanade begins in the residential part of Battery Park City and connects with **Robert F. Wagner Jr. Park** ⑱, home to the **Museum of Jewish Heritage—A Living Memorial to the Holocaust** ⑲. Especially noteworthy among the artwork populating the esplanade are Ned Smyth's columned plaza with chessboards and the South Cove (a collaborative effort), a curved stage set of wooden piers and a steel-frame lookout quietly reminiscent of Lady Liberty's crown. Just across Battery Place from the Holocaust Museum is the **Skyscraper Museum** ⑳, where a history of Manhattan's verticality is waiting to be explored.

TIMING This tour takes about four hours. Visit on a weekday to capture the district's true vitality—but expect to be jostled on the crowded sidewalks if you stand still too long. If you visit on a weekend, on the other hand, in some areas you'll feel like a lone explorer in a canyon of buildings. The perimeter of the World Trade Center site is most crowded on the weekends. The best place to end the day is on the Hudson River, watching the sun set.

What to See

♺ ❽ **Alexander Hamilton U.S. Custom House/National Museum of the American Indian.** The beaux-arts Alexander Hamilton U.S. Custom House (1907) is one of lower Manhattan's finest buildings. From its base, massive granite columns rise to a pediment topped by a double row of statuary. Daniel Chester French, sculptor of Lincoln in the Lincoln Memorial in Washington, D.C., carved the lower statues, which symbolize continents (left to right: Asia, the Americas, Europe, Africa). The upper row represents the major trading cities of the world. Inside, the display of white and color marble couldn't be more remarkable. A semicircular staircase leads to the second floor, where shipping-theme murals by Reginald Marsh completed in 1934 embellish the oval rotunda.

On three sides of the rotunda is the National Museum of the American Indian, a branch of the Washington, D.C.–based Smithsonian Institution. George Gustav Heye, a wealthy New Yorker, amassed most of the museum's collection of more than a million artifacts (only a small fraction of which are on display), including pottery, weaving, and basketry from the southwestern United States; carved jade from the Mexican Olmec and Maya cultures; and contemporary Native American paintings. ⊠ *1 Bowling Green, between State and Whitehall Sts., Lower Manhattan* ☎ *212/514–3700* ⊕ *www.americanindian.si.edu* 🖅 *Free* ☉ *Mon.–Wed. and Fri.–Sun. 10–5, Thurs. 10–8* Ⓜ *Subway: R, W to Whitehall St.*

❺ **Battery Park.** Jutting out as if it were Manhattan's green toe, Battery Park (so named because a battery of 28 cannon was placed along its shore in colonial days to fend off the British) is built on landfill and has gradually grown over the centuries to its present 22 acres. The park's main structure is Castle Clinton National Monument, the takeoff point for ferries to the Statue of Liberty and Ellis Island. The interior of the park is loaded with monuments and statues, some impressive, some downright obscure. Starting near the Staten Island Ferry Terminal, head north along the water's edge to the East Coast Memorial, a statue of a fierce eagle that presides over eight granite slabs inscribed with the names of U.S. servicemen who died in the western Atlantic during World War II. Climb the steps of the East Coast Memorial for a fine view of the main features of New York Harbor; from left to right: Governors Island, a former Coast Guard installation now managed by the National Park Service, a hilly Staten Island in the distance; the Statue of Liberty, on Liberty Island; Ellis Island, gateway to the New World for generations of immigrants; and the old railway terminal in Liberty State Park, on the mainland in Jersey City, New Jersey. On crystal-clear days you can see all the way to Port Elizabeth's cranes, which seem to mimic Lady Liberty's stance.

Continue north past a romantic statue of Giovanni da Verrazano, the Florentine merchant who in 1524 piloted the ship that first sighted New York and its harbor. The Verrazano-Narrows Bridge, between Brooklyn and Staten Island, is visible from here, just beyond Governors Island. It's so long that the curvature of the earth had to be figured into its dimensions. At the park's northernmost edge, Marisol's bronze tribute to the American Merchant Marine in WWII is a dramatic depiction of three sailors trying to rescue a man in the water. Just beyond the sculpture is a white tented ferry terminal to Hoboken, New Jersey. Facing the terminal is Pier A, the last Victorian fireboat pier in the city. The building is undergoing restoration that will eventually transform it into a visitor and shopping center.Its clock tower, erected in 1919, was the nation's first World War I memorial. There are plenty of places to sit and rest in the leafy park, and two tiers of wood benches line the promenade. ⊠ *Broadway and Battery Pl., Lower Manhattan* Ⓜ *Subway: 4, 5 to Bowling Green.*

❼ Bowling Green. This oval greensward at the foot of Broadway became New York's first public park in 1733. On July 9, 1776, a few hours after citizens learned about the signing of the Declaration of Independence, rioters toppled a statue of British king George III that had occupied the spot for 11 years; much of the statue's lead was melted down into bullets. In 1783, when the occupying British forces fled the city, they defiantly hoisted a Union Jack on a greased, uncleated flagpole so it couldn't be lowered; patriot John Van Arsdale drove his own cleats into the pole to replace the flag with the Stars and Stripes. The copper-top subway entrance here is the original one, built in 1904–05.

♨ ❻ Castle Clinton National Monument. This circular red-stone fortress, built in 1811, first stood on an island 200 feet from shore as a defense for New York Harbor. In 1824 it became Castle Garden, an entertainment and concert facility that reached its zenith in 1850 when more than 6,000 people (the capacity of Radio City Music Hall) attended the U.S. debut of the Swedish Nightingale, Jenny Lind. After landfill connected it to the city, Castle Clinton became, in succession, an immigrant processing center, an aquarium, and now a restored fort, museum, and ticket office for ferries to the Statue of Liberty and Ellis Island. Inside the old fort are dioramas of lower Manhattan in 1812, 1886, and 1941. Outside the landward entrance is a statue titled *The Immigrants,* at the beginning of a broad mall that leads back across the park. At the other end of the mall stands the Netherlands Memorial Flagpole, which depicts Dutch traders offering beads to Native Americans in 1626 for the land on which to establish Fort Amsterdam. Inscriptions describe the event in English and Dutch. ✉ *Lower Manhattan* ☎ *212/344–7220 Castle Clinton, 212/269–5755 ferry information* 🎫 *Castle Clinton free; ferry $10 round-trip* ⊘ *Daily 8:30–5, ferry departures daily every 45 min 9:30–3:30; more departures and extended hrs in summer* Ⓜ *Subway: 4, 5 to Bowling Green.*

did you know?

Now in the middle of Battery Park, Castle Clinton was once 300 feet off the southern tip of the island. Originally called the West Battery, it was erected during the War of 1812 to defend the city. (The East Battery sits across the harbor on Governors Island.) As dirt and debris from construction were dumped into the harbor, the island expanded, eventually engulfing the landmark.

⓬ Federal Hall National Memorial. The site of this memorial is rich with both the country's and the city's history. The City Hall here hosted the 1765 Stamp Act Congress and, beginning in 1789, served as the Federal Hall of the new nation. On its balcony, George Washington took his oath as the country's first president. After the capital moved from New York to Philadelphia in 1790, the Federal Hall reverted to New York's City Hall, then was demolished in 1812 when the present City Hall was completed. The current Greek Revival building, built as a U.S. Custom House in 1842, was modeled on the Parthenon. On the steps stands an 1883 statue of George Washington. His likeness was rendered by noted sculptor and presidential kin John Quincy Adams Ward. The hall's interior, which holds a museum with exhibits on New York and Wall Street, is scheduled to reopen in spring 2006 following extensive renovations. ⊠ *26 Wall St., at Nassau St., Lower Manhattan* ☎ *212/825–6888* 🎫 *Free* ⊙ *Weekdays 9–5* Ⓜ *Subway: 4, 5 to Wall St.*

⓮ **Federal Reserve Bank of New York.** Built in 1924 and enlarged in 1935, this neo-Renaissance structure made of sandstone, limestone, and iron-work looks the way a bank ought to: absolutely impregnable. The gold ingots in the subterranean vaults here are worth roughly $140 billion—reputedly a third of the world's gold reserves. Hour-long tours of the bank are conducted five times a day and require reservations made at least five days in advance. They include the gold vault, the trading desk, and "Fed-Works," an interactive multimedia exhibit center where you can make and track hypothetical trades. Computer terminals and displays provide almost as much information as an Economics 101 course—explaining such points as what the Federal Reserve Bank does (besides store gold), what the money supply is, and what causes inflation. ⊠ *33 Liberty St., between William and Nassau Sts., Lower Manhattan* ☎ *212/720–6130* ⊕ *www.newyorkfed.org* 🎫 *Free* ⊙ *1-hr tour by advance reservation, weekdays 9:30–2:30* Ⓜ *Subway: A, C to Fulton St.; 2, 3, 4, 5 to Wall St.*

need a break? The Middle Eastern restaurant **Alfanoose** (⊠ 8 Maiden La. ☎ 212/528–4669) is a modest but heartening example of lower Manhattan recovery: following 9/11, the owner was certain he would have to shut down, but neighborhood officeworkers rallied with the financial backing to keep him in operation. This wasn't simply an act of altruism: the workers couldn't bear to go without the lovingly prepared falafel sandwiches and lamb shawarma.

👆 ⓽ **Fraunces Tavern.** This stately house, with a white-marble portico and cof-fered frieze, is a rare remnant of New York's colonial-era existence. Built in 1719 and converted to a tavern in 1762, it was the meeting place for the Sons of Liberty until the Revolutionary War, and in 1783 George Washington delivered a farewell address here to his officers celebrating the British evacuation of New York. Today a museum occupies the three floors above a restaurant and bar. It contains two fully furnished period rooms—including the Long Room, site of Washington's ad-dress—and other modest displays of 18th- and 19th-century American history. The museum hosts family programs (such as crafts workshops and a scavenger hunt), lectures, and concerts. ⊠ *54 Pearl St., at Broad St., Lower Manhattan* ☎ *212/425–1778* ⊕ *www.frauncestavernmuseum. org* 🎫 *$3* ⊙ *Sept.–June, Tues.–Sat. noon–5; July and Aug., Tues.–Sat. 10–5* Ⓜ *Subway: R, W to Whitehall St.; 4, 5 to Bowling Green.*

⓾ **Hanover Square.** When the East River ran past present-day Pearl Street, this quiet tree-lined plaza stood on the waterfront and was the city's orig-inal printing-house square; on the site of 81 Pearl Street, William Brad-ford established the first printing press in the colonies. The pirate Captain Kidd lived in the neighborhood, and the Italianate sandstone-fronted **India House** (1851–54), a private club, and a restaurant and bar at No. 1, used to house the New York Cotton Exchange. ⊠ *Lower Manhattan.*

Museum of American Financial History. On the site of Alexander Hamilton's law office (today the Standard Oil Building), this one-room museum packs a lot into its limited space, including currency displays, artifacts of the financial market's history, a vintage ticker-tape machine that will print out your name, and well-executed temporary exhibits. ⊠ *28 Broadway, north of Bowling Green, between Exchange Pl. and Beaver St., Lower Manhattan* ☎ *212/908–4110* ⊕ *www.financialhistory.org* ⊠ *$2* ⊘ *Tues.–Sat. 10–4* Ⓜ *Subway: 1, 9, R, W to Rector St.; 4, 5 to Wall St.*

⑲ **Museum of Jewish Heritage—A Living Memorial to the Holocaust.** In a granite hexagon rising 85 feet above Robert F. Wagner Jr. Park at the southern end of Battery Park City, this museum pays tribute to the 6 million Jews who perished in the Holocaust. Kevin Roche and John Dinkeloo, architects, built the museum in the shape of the Star of David, with three floors of exhibits demonstrating the dynamism of 20th-century Jewish culture. You enter through a captivating multiscreen vestibule, perhaps best described as a storytelling gallery, that provides a context for the early-20th-century artifacts displayed on the first floor: elaborate screens hand-painted for the fall harvest festival of Sukkoth, wedding invitations, and tools used by Jewish tradesmen. Also intriguing is the use of original documentary film footage throughout the museum. The second floor details the rise of Nazism, anti-Semitism, and the ravages of the Holocaust. A gallery covers the doomed voyage of the *St. Louis,* a ship of German Jewish refugees that crossed the Atlantic twice in 1939 in search of a safe haven. Signs of hope are on display, as well, including a trumpet that Louis Bannet (the "Dutch Louis Armstrong") played for three years in the Auschwitz-Birkenau inmate orchestra. The third floor covers postwar Jewish life. The east wing contains a theater, memorial garden, resource center, library, more galleries, classrooms, and a café. ⊠ *36 Battery Pl., Battery Park City, Lower Manhattan* ☎ *646/437–4200* ⊕ *www.mjhnyc.org* ⊠ *$10* ⊘ *Thurs., Sun.–Tues. 10–5:45, Wed. 10–8, Fri. and eve of Jewish holidays 10–3* Ⓜ *Subway: 4, 5 to Bowling Green.*

did you know?

Whoever named the streets in Lower Manhattan didn't have much of an imagination. Bridge Street once had a bridge that crossed Broad Street, which was broad enough to have a canal running down its center. Stone Street was the first to get cobblestones, and Pearl Street was paved with mother-of-pearl shells. And yes, Wall Street had a wall that was erected to keep out invaders.

New York City Police Museum. Why are the police called cops? Why does a police badge have eight points? When was fingerprinting first used to solve a crime? Find the answers at this museum dedicated to New York's finest. The force's history from colonial times through the present is traversed with permanent and rotating exhibits, as well as interactive and sometimes chilling displays, including fingerprinting and forensic art stations, a drug-awareness display, and a tactics simulator. The Hall of Heroes honors police officers who have fallen in the line of duty, and a permanent memorial exhibit recognizes the 23 police officers, 13 Port Authority officers, and 343 firefighters who lost their lives on September 11. ✉ *100 Old Slip, near South St., Lower Manhattan* ☎ *212/480–3100* ⊕ *www.nycpolicemuseum.org* 💰 *$5 suggested donation* 🕙 *Tues.–Sat. 10–5, Sun. 11–5* Ⓜ *Subway: R, W to Whitehall St.; 4, 5 to Bowling Green.*

⑱ Robert F. Wagner Jr. Park. This southern link in a chain of parks that stretches from Battery Park to Chambers Street has lawns, walks, garden beds, and benches with a panoramic view of the river and harbor. A stream of runners and rollerbladers flows by on the promenade. ✉ *Between Battery Pl. and Hudson River, Lower Manhattan.*

⑯ St. Paul's Chapel. The oldest (1766) public building in continuous use in Manhattan, this Episcopal house of worship, built of rough Manhattan brownstone, was modeled on London's St. Martin-in-the-Fields (a columned clock tower and steeple were added in 1794). A prayer service here followed George Washington's inauguration as president; Washington's pew is in the north aisle. The gilded crown adorned with plumes above the pulpit is thought to be the city's only vestige of British rule.

St. Paul's and its 18th-century cemetery abut the World Trade Center site. For more than a year following the disaster, the chapel fence served as a shrine for visitors seeking solace. People from around the world left tokens of grief and support, or signed one of the large drop cloths that hung from the fence. After having served as a 24-hour refuge where rescue and recovery workers could eat, pray, rest, and receive counseling, the chapel reopened to the public in fall 2002 with an ongoing exhibit titled "Unwavering Spirit: Hope & Healing at Ground Zero," honoring the workers and recalling their efforts in the months following September 11. ✉ *Broadway and Fulton St., Lower Manhattan* ☎ *212/233–4164* ⊕ *www.saintpaulschapel.org* 🕙 *Mon.–Sat. 10–6, Sun. 9–4* Ⓜ *Subway: 2, 3, 4, 5 to Fulton St.*

❹ Shrine of St. Elizabeth Ann Seton at Our Lady of the Rosary. This redbrick federal-style town house near the Staten Island Ferry terminal provides a rare glimpse at lower Manhattan architecture from an earlier day. With its distinctive portico, shaped to fit the curving street, it exemplifies the mansions that once lined the street. The house was built in 1793 as the home of the wealthy Watson family. Mother Seton and her family lived here from 1801 until the death of her husband in 1803. She joined the Catholic Church in 1805 and went on to found the Sisters of Charity, the first American order of nuns. In 1975 she became the first American-born saint. Masses are held here daily. ✉ *7 State St., near Whitehall St., Lower Manhattan* ☎ *212/269–6865* ⊕ *www.setonshrine-ny.org* Ⓜ *Subway: R, W to Whitehall St.*

⑳ Skyscraper Museum. On the ground floor of a mixed-use building that also holds the Ritz-Carlton Hotel, this small museum celebrates Manhattan's architectural heritage and examines the historical forces and individuals that have shaped its successive skylines. Through exhibitions, lectures, and publications, tall buildings are explored as objects of design, products of technology, sites of construction, investments in real estate, and places of work and residence. The museum's Web site is in many ways more engaging and informative than the museum itself. Among the site's features is "Manhattan Timeformations," which uses computer models and interactive animations to depict the dynamic relationship between skyscrapers and geology, landfill, settlement patterns, real estate cycles, and more. ✉ *39 Battery Pl., Battery Park City, Lower Manhattan* ☎ *212/968–1961* ⊕ *www.skyscraper.org* ✉ *$5* ☽ *Wed.–Sun. noon–6 PM* Ⓜ *Subway: A, C, 2, 3, 4, 5 to Fulton St./Broadway-Nassau.*

☞ ▶ ❸ **Staten Island Ferry.** The best transit deal in town is the Staten Island Ferry, a free 20- to 30-minute ride across New York Harbor providing great views of the Manhattan skyline, the Statue of Liberty, the Verrazano-Narrows Bridge, and the New Jersey coast. Ferries embark on various schedules: every 15 minutes during rush hours, every 20–30 minutes most other times, and every hour on weekend nights and mornings. If you can manage it, catch one of older blue-and-orange ferries, which have outside decks. ✉ *State and South Sts., Lower Manhattan* ☎ *718/390–5253* Ⓜ *Subway: 4, 5 to Bowling Green; 1, 9 to South Ferry.*

frugal fun

About 70,000 people ride the Staten Island Ferry every day, and you should be one of them. Without having to pay a cent, you get great views of the Statue of Liberty, Ellis Island, and the southern tip of Manhattan. You'll pass tug boats, freighters, and cruise ships—a reminder that this is still a working harbor.

⓭ **Trinity Church.** The present Trinity Church, the third on this site since an Anglican parish was established here in 1697, was designed in 1846 by Richard Upjohn. It ranked as the city's tallest building for most of the second half of the 19th century. The three huge bronze doors were designed by Richard Morris Hunt to recall Lorenzo Ghiberti's doors for the Baptistery in Florence, Italy. The church's Gothic revival interior is light and elegant. On the church's north and south sides is a 2½-acre graveyard: Alexander Hamilton is buried beneath a white-stone pyramid, and a monument commemorates Robert Fulton, the inventor of the steamboat (he's buried in the Livingston family vault, with his wife). A museum outlines the church's history, and there's a bookstore and gift shop. A daily tour is given at 2. ✉ *74 Trinity Pl., Broadway at the head of Wall St., Lower Manhattan* ☎ *212/602–0800* ⊕ *www. trinitywallstreet.org* ☽ *Daily 7–6; churchyard Nov.–Apr., daily 7–4, May–Oct. 7–5* Ⓜ *Subway: 4, 5 to Wall St.*

Vietnam Veterans Memorial. At this 14-foot-high, 70-foot-long rectangular memorial (1985), moving passages from news dispatches and the letters of military service people have been etched into a wall of greenish glass. The brick plaza around it is often desolate on weekends. ✉ *End of Coenties Slip between Water and South Sts., Lower Manhattan.*

⓫ **Wall Street.** Named after a wooden wall built across the island in 1653 to defend the Dutch colony against the Native Americans (mostly Algonquins), ⅓-mi-long Wall Street is arguably the most famous thoroughfare in the world—shorthand for the vast, powerful financial community that clusters around the New York and American stock exchanges. "The Street," as it's also widely known, began its financial career with stock traders conducting business along the sidewalks or at tables beneath a sheltering buttonwood tree. Today it's a dizzyingly narrow canyon—look to the east and you'll glimpse a sliver of East River waterfront; look to the west and you'll see the spire of Trinity Church, tightly framed by skyscrapers.

At the intersection with Broad Street stands the New York Stock Exchange, Wall Street's epicenter. The largest securities exchange in the world, it nearly bursts from its neoclassical 1903 building with an august Corinthian entrance—a fitting temple to the almighty dollar. Today's "Big Board" can handle a trillion shares of stock per day. Unfortunately, the exchange isn't open to visitors.

For a clear lesson in the difference between Ionic and Corinthian columns, look at 55 Wall Street. The lower stories were part of an earlier U.S. Custom House, built in 1836–42; it was literally a bullish day on Wall Street when oxen hauled its 16 granite Ionic columns up to the site. When the National City Bank took over the building in 1899, it hired architects McKim, Mead & White to redesign the building and in 1909 added the second tier of columns but made them Corinthian. ⊠ *Lower Manhattan* Ⓜ *Subway: 4, 5 to Wall St.*

need a break? You're not walking in circles or experiencing deja vu—there actually is a Starbucks on every other corner in the financial district. For coffee and a snack of a higher order, head a couple of blocks south of Wall Street to **Financier Patisserie** (⊠ 62 Stone St. ☎ 212/344–5600), on a handsome cobblestone lane just off Hanover Square. The pastries, soups, and sandwiches are all the class of the neighborhood.

Wall Street Rising Downtown Information Center. One block south of the NYSE, this nonprofit organization, whose goal is to revitalize Lower Manhattan from the devastating loss of businesses and residents following the terrorist attack on the World Trade Center, is combination information and neighborhood civic center. ⊠ *25 Broad St., at Exchange Pl., Lower Manhattan* ☎ *212/425–4636* ⊕ *www.downtowninfocenter.org* ⊙ *Weekdays 11–7* Ⓜ *Subway: 4, 5 to Wall St.; J, M, Z to Broad St.*

⓱ **World Financial Center (WFC).** The four towers of this complex, 34–51 stories high and topped with different geometric ornaments, were designed by Cesar Pelli and serve as company headquarters for the likes of American Express and Dow Jones. The sides of the buildings facing the World Trade Center towers were damaged during the September 11 attacks but have been fully restored. The glass-domed Winter Garden atrium is the main attraction here; it's a pleasant open space that's the sight of music and dance performances, as well as a display of architectural plans for the WTC site and an typical selection of mall chain stores. At the south end of the WFC complex, a footbridge connects One WFC to the intersection of Liberty and Washington streets. The windows on the north side of the footbridge provide a good view of the World Trade Center site. ✉ *West St. between Vesey and Liberty Sts., Lower Manhattan* ⊕ *www.worldfinancialcenter.com.*

⑮ World Trade Center site. On September 11, 2001, terrorist hijackers steered two commercial jets into the World Trade Center's 110-story towers, demolishing them and five outlying buildings and killing nearly 3,000 people. Dubbed Ground Zero, the fenced-in 16-acre work site that emerged from the rubble has come to symbolize the personal and historical impact of the attack. In an attempt to grasp the reality of the destruction, to pray, or simply to witness history, visitors come to glimpse the site, clustering at the two-story see-though fence surrounding it. Temporary panels listing the names of those who died in the attacks and recounting the history of the twin towers have been mounted along the fence on the west side of Church Street and the north side of Liberty Street.

The World Trade Center (WTC) was a seven-building, 12-million-square-foot complex resembling a miniature city, with more than 430 companies from 28 countries engaged in a wide variety of commercial activities, including banking and finance, insurance, transportation, import and export, customs brokerage, trade associations, and representation of foreign governments. The daytime population of the WTC included 50,000 employees and 100,000 business and leisure visitors. Underground was a mall with nearly 100 stores and restaurants and a network of subway and other train stations. The twin towers were New York's two tallest buildings, the fourth tallest in the world after Kuala Lumpur's Petronas Towers, Shanghai's Jin Mao Building, and the Sears Tower in Chicago. The two 1,350-foot towers, designed by Minoru Yamasaki and opened in 1973, were more engineering marvel than architectural masterpiece. To some they were an unmitigated design fiasco; to others their brutalist design and sheer magnitude gave them the beauty of modern sculpture, and at night when they were lighted from within, they were indeed beautiful strokes on the Manhattan skyline. Whether they were admired or reviled, the towers endured as a powerful symbol of American ingenuity, success, and dominance in the world marketplace. ✉ *Lower Manhattan* Ⓜ *Subway: R, W to Cortlandt St.*

THE SEAPORT & THE COURTS

New York's role as a great seaport is easiest to understand downtown, with both the Hudson River and East River waterfronts within walking distance. Although the deeper Hudson River came into its own in the steamship era, the more sheltered waters of the East River saw most of the action in the 19th century, during the age of clipper ships. This era is preserved in the South Street Seaport restoration, centered on Fulton Street between Water Street and the East River. Only a few blocks away you can visit another seat of New York history: the City Hall neighborhood, which includes Manhattan's magisterial court and government buildings.

Numbers in the text correspond to numbers in the margin and on the Lower Manhattan map.

a good walk

Begin at the intersection of Water and Fulton streets. Water Street was once the shoreline; the latter thoroughfare was named after the ferry to Brooklyn, which once docked at its foot (the ferry itself was named after its inventor, Robert Fulton [1765–1815]). Extending to the river is the 11-block **South Street Seaport Historic District** ㉑ ▶, which is grounded on 19th-century landfill.

Return to Fulton Street and walk away from the river to Broadway, to St. Paul's Chapel. If you're facing north, forking off to the right is Park Row, which was known as Newspaper Row from the mid-19th to early 20th centuries, when most of the city's 20 or so daily newspapers had offices here. In tribute to that past, a statue of Benjamin Franklin (who was, after all, a printer) stands in front of Pace University, farther east on Park Row. Two blocks north of Fulton Street, on Broadway, is one of the finest skyscrapers in the city, the Gothic **Woolworth Building** ㉒, for which Frank Woolworth paid $13 million—in cash.

Wedged between Broadway and Park Row is triangular **City Hall Park** ㉓, originally the town common, which gives way to a slew of government offices. **City Hall** ㉔, built between 1803 and 1812, is unexpectedly modest. Lurking directly behind it is the **Tweed Courthouse** ㉕, named for the notorious politician William Marcy "Boss" Tweed.

On the north side of Chambers Street, east of the Tweed Courthouse, sits an eight-story beaux-arts château, the 1911 **Surrogate's Court** ㉖, also called the Hall of Records. Across Centre Street from the château is the city government's first skyscraper, the imposing **Municipal Building** ㉗, built in 1914 by McKim, Mead & White. Just steps south of the Municipal Building, a ramp curves up into the pedestrian walkway over the **Brooklyn Bridge** ㉘. The river-and-four-borough views from the bridge are wondrous.

Foley Square, a name that has become synonymous with the New York court system, opens out north of the Municipal Building. On the right, the orderly progression of the Corinthian colonnades of the **U.S. Courthouse** ㉙ and the **New York County Courthouse** ㉚ is a fitting reflection of the epigraph carved in the latter's frieze: THE TRUE ADMINISTRATION OF JUSTICE IS THE FIRMEST PILLAR OF GOOD GOVERNMENT. Turn to look across Foley Square at Federal Plaza, which sprawls in front of the gridlike skyscraper of the Javits Federal Building. The black-glass box to the left houses the U.S. Court of International Trade. South of it, at the corner of Duane and Elk streets, is the site of the **African Burial Ground** ㉛.

Continue north up Centre Street past neoclassical civic office buildings to 100 Centre Street, the **Criminal Courts Building** ㉜, a rather forbidding construction with art moderne details. In contrast, the Civil and Municipal Courthouse (1960), across the way at 111 Centre Street, is an uninspired modern cube, although it, too, has held sensational trials. On the west side of this small square, at 60 Lafayette Street, is the slick black-granite Family Court, built in 1975, with its intriguing angular facade.

Walk west onto Leonard Street, south of the Family Court, and take a look at the ornate Victorian building that runs the length of the block on your left. This is the old New York Life Insurance Company headquarters, an 1870 building that was remodeled and enlarged in 1896 by McKim, Mead & White. The ornate clock tower facing Broadway is occupied by the avant-garde Clocktower Gallery and is used as studio space by artists, who sometimes host exhibitions of their work. The stretch of Broadway south of here is the subject of what is believed to be the oldest photograph of New York. The picture focuses on a paving project—to eliminate the morass of muddy streets—that took place in 1850.

What to See

③① **African Burial Ground.** This grassy corner is part of the original area used to inter the city's earliest African-Americans—an estimated 20,000 were buried here until the cemetery was closed in 1794. The site was discovered during a 1991 construction project, and by an act of Congress it was made into a National Historic Landmark, dedicated to the people who were enslaved in the city between 1626 and Emancipation Day in New York, July 4, 1827. ✉ *Duane and Elk Sts., Lower Manhattan* ☎ *212/ 337–2001* Ⓜ *Subway: 1, 2, 3, 9 to Chambers St.; 4, 5, 6 to Brooklyn Bridge/City Hall.*

★ **②⑧** **Brooklyn Bridge.** "A drive-through cathedral" is how the critic James Wolcott describes one of New York's noblest and most recognized landmarks. Spanning the East River, the Brooklyn Bridge connects Manhattan island to the once-independent city of Brooklyn. Before its opening, Brooklynites had only the Fulton Street Ferry to shuttle them across the river. John Augustus Roebling—a visionary architect, legendary engineer, metaphysical philosopher, and fervid abolitionist—is said to have first conceived of the bridge on an icy winter's day in 1852, when the frozen river prevented him from getting to Brooklyn. Though by no means the first person so inconvenienced, Roebling the bridge builder was perfectly qualified to rectify the matter. Roebling spent the next 30 years designing, raising money for, and building what would be one of the first steel suspension bridges—and what was for several years one of the world's longest. Alas, its construction was fraught with peril. Work began in 1867; two years later Roebling died of gangrene after a wayward ferryboat rammed his foot while he was at work on a pier. His son, Washington, took over the project and was himself permanently crippled—like many others who worked on the bridge underwater, he suffered from the bends, or decompression sickness. With the help of his wife, Emily, Washington nonetheless saw the bridge's construction through to completion.

The long struggle to build the bridge so captured the imagi ..tion of the city that when it opened in 1883 it was promptly crowned the "Eighth Wonder of the World." Its twin Gothic-arch towers, with a span of 1,595½ feet, rise 272 feet from the river below; the bridge's overall length of 6,016 feet made it four times longer than the longest suspension bridge of its day. From roadway to water is about 133 feet, high enough to allow the tallest ships to pass. The roadway is supported by a web of steel cables, hung from the towers and attached to block-long anchorages on either shore.

A walk across the bridge's promenade—a boardwalk elevated above the roadway and shared by pedestrians, in-line skaters, and bicyclists—takes about 40 minutes, from Manhattan's civic center to the heart of Brooklyn Heights. It's well worth traversing for the astounding views. Midtown's jumble of spires and the Manhattan Bridge loom to the north. Mostly modern skyscrapers crowd lower Manhattan, and the tall ships docked at their feet, at South Street Seaport, appear to have sailed in straight from the 19th century. Governors Island sits forlornly in the middle of the harbor, which dramatically sweeps open toward Lady Liberty and, off in the distance, the Verrazano-Narrows Bridge (its towers are more than twice as tall as those of the Brooklyn Bridge). A word of caution to pedestrians: do obey the lane markings on the promenade—pedestrians on the north side, bicyclists on the south—as the latter are moving quickly and will not be pleased if you get in their way. Ⓜ *Subway: 4, 5, 6 to Brooklyn Bridge/City Hall.*

| a new york moment | One of the best ways to see the city's southern tip is to stroll across the boardwalk on the Brooklyn Bridge. You can start in Manhattan at the Brooklyn Bridge/City Hall subway stop, or in Brooklyn Heights at the High Street/Brooklyn Bridge subway stop (a better option, as the skyline is ahead of you the entire time.) Whichever you choose, budget about 40 minutes. |

❷❹ **City Hall.** Reflecting the classical refinement and civility of Enlightenment Europe, New York's decorous City Hall is a diminutive palace with a facade punctuated by arches and columns and a cupola crowned by a statue of Lady Justice. Built between 1803 and 1812, it was originally clad in white marble only on its front and sides. The back was faced in more modest brownstone because city fathers assumed the city would never grow farther north than this. Limestone now covers all four sides. A sweeping marble double staircase leads from the domed rotunda to the second-floor public rooms. The small, Victorian-style **City Council Chamber** in the east wing has mahogany detailing and ornate gilding; the **Board of Estimate Chamber,** to the west, has colonial paintings and church-pew-style seating; and the **Governor's Room** at the head of the stairs, used for ceremonial events, is filled with historic portraits and furniture, including a writing table that George Washington used in 1789 when New York was the U.S. capital. The **Blue Room,** which was traditionally the mayor's office, is on the ground floor and is now used for mayoral press conferences.

Although the building looks genteel, the City Hall politicking that goes on there can be rough and tumble. News crews can often be seen jockeying on the front steps, as they attempt to interview city officials. City Hall is open to the public for tours. ✉ *City Hall Park, Lower Manhattan* ☎ *212/788–6865 tour information* 🎫 *Free* ☉ *Tours by advance (1–2 wks) reservation, weekdays 10, 11, and 2* Ⓜ *Subway: 4, 5, 6 to Brooklyn Bridge/City Hall.*

DOWN BY THE RIVERSIDE

NEW YORK IS A CITY OF ISLANDS, surrounded by ocean, bay, river, and sound. The entire waterfront of the five boroughs measures 578 mi, making it the longest and most diverse of any municipality in the country. Down by the water, the air is salty and fresh, the views exhilarating, the mood peaceful and quiet. Yet downtown, pedestrian-friendly access to the Hudson River didn't come about until 1999, a year after the Hudson River Park Trust was created. The thin ribbon of park currently runs from Battery Park as far north as 59th Street, and is full of joggers, cyclists, and rollerbladers. A trio of piers off Greenwich Village (45 and 46 at Charles Street, and 51 at Jane Street) provide grassy lawns for napping, fields for playing, and a water-theme playground. Greenspace advocates have also spruced up the Empire-Fulton Ferry State Park in Brooklyn's industrial DUMBO neighborhood, which has incredible views of the East River between the Brooklyn and Manhattan bridges.

Though New Yorkers are now spending leisure time by the water, New York grew up as a shipping and shipbuilding town. The Port of New York was first centered near the South Street Seaport on the East River, where the 18th-century streetscape and historic sailing vessels recall the clipper-ship era. Street names suggest the contours of Manhattan before settlers filled in the wetlands: Pearl Street, where mother-of-pearl shells were collected; Water Street; and Front Street. The port then moved to the wider, less turbulent Hudson River, where Robert Fulton launched the first steamboat in 1807. After the opening of the Erie Canal in 1825, which connected it to the Great Lakes and the West for trade, the city became the preeminent port in the country, the gateway to the continent for exports and imports, the "golden door"

for immigrants. In the late 1800s, New York Harbor, crisscrossed with ferries, barges, tugs, canal boats, freighters, and passenger liners, was the busiest in the world. Until the Brooklyn Bridge was completed in 1883, even Manhattanites and Brooklynites couldn't visit each other except by ferries that landed at Fulton Street in lower Manhattan and Fulton Ferry Landing in DUMBO.

On the Hudson River, where older generations once boarded grand ocean liners to make a two-week journey across the Atlantic, New Yorkers are once again using boat travel—this time to commute within their own city. Ferry service provides commuters a transportation method that harkens back to the 1800s. In addition to the 200-plus-capacity boats of New York Waterways, the small, 54-seat New York Water Taxis are serving both rush-hour travelers and tourists.

At the West Side Highway and Christopher Street, walk out on Greenwich Village's popular pier to take in the view back toward the fading vestiges of a Victorian-era waterfront: a panorama of warehouses (many converted to apartments and clubs) and smaller buildings that house cheap hotels and seedy bars. At 14th Street, remember Herman Melville, who worked as a customs inspector nearby. Just south of the Chelsea Piers complex, note the remains of the pier house where the Titanic was scheduled to conclude its maiden voyage. In summer, check out the piers that spring to life with public events—movies, dances, and food festivals.

㉓ City Hall Park. Originally used as a sheep meadow, this green spot was known in colonial times as the Fields or the Common. It went on to become a graveyard for the impoverished, the site of an almshouse, and then the home of the notorious Bridewell jail before it became a park. Even as a park, the locale was far from peaceful: it hosted hangings, riots, and political demonstrations. A bronze statue of patriot Nathan Hale, who was hanged in 1776 as a spy by the British troops occupying New York City, stands facing City Hall. ⊠ *Bordered by Broadway, Park Row, and Chambers St., Lower Manhattan* Ⓜ *Subway: 4, 5, 6 to Brooklyn Bridge/City Hall.*

㉜ Criminal Courts Building. Fans of crime fiction, whether on television, in the movies, or in novels, may recognize this rather grim art deco tower, which is connected by a skywalk (New York's Bridge of Sighs) to the detention center known as the Tombs. In *The Bonfire of the Vanities,* Tom Wolfe wrote a chilling description of this court's menacing atmosphere. ⊠ *100 Centre St., at Hogan St., Lower Manhattan.*

㉗ Municipal Building. Who else but the venerable architecture firm McKim, Mead & White would the city government trust to build its first skyscraper in 1914? The roof section alone is 10 stories high, bristling with towers and peaks and topped by a 25-foot-high gilt statue of Civic Fame. New Yorkers come here to pay parking fines and get marriage licenses (and to get married, in a civil chapel on the second floor). An immense arch straddles Chambers Street (traffic used to flow through here). A gift shop at the left side of the main entrance sells NYC maps, history books, and other souvenirs. ⊠ *1 Centre St., at Chambers St., Lower Manhattan* Ⓜ *Subway: 1, 2, 3, 9, A, C to Chambers St.*

㉚ New York County Courthouse. With its stately columns, pediments, and 100-foot-wide steps, this 1912 classical temple front is yet another spin-off on Rome's Pantheon. It deviates from its classical parent in its hexagonal rotunda, shaped to fit an irregular plot of land. The 1957 courtroom drama *Twelve Angry Men* was filmed here; the courthouse also hosts thousands of marriages a year. ⊠ *60 Centre St., at Foley Sq., Lower Manhattan.*

🔆 ▶ **㉑ South Street Seaport Historic District.** Had it not been declared a historic district in 1967, this charming, cobblestone corner of New York with the city's largest concentration of early-19th-century commercial buildings would likely have been gobbled up by skyscrapers. In the early 1980s the Rouse Company, which had already created Boston's Quincy Market and Baltimore's Harborplace, was hired to restore and adapt the existing buildings, preserving the commercial feel of centuries past. The result is a hybrid of historical district and shopping mall. Many of its streets' 18th-, 19th-, and early-20th-century architectural details recreate the city's historic seafaring era.

At the intersection of Fulton and Water streets, the gateway to the Seaport, stands the **Titanic Memorial,** a small white lighthouse that commemorates the sinking of the RMS *Titanic* in 1912. Beyond it, Fulton Street, cobbled in blocks of Belgian granite, turns into a busy pedestrian mall. Just to the left of Fulton, at 211 Water Street, is **Bowne & Co.**

Stationers, a reconstructed working 19th-century print shop. Continue down Fulton to Front Street, which has wonderfully preserved old brick buildings—some dating from the 1700s. On the south side of Fulton Street is the seaport's architectural centerpiece, **Schermerhorn Row,** a redbrick terrace of Georgian- and federal-style warehouses and counting-houses built in 1811–12. Some upper floors house gallery space, and the ground floors are occupied by upscale shops, bars, and restaurants. Also here is the visitor center and gift shop of the **South Street Seaport Museum** (☎ 212/748–8600 ☉ Apr.–Sept., Fri.–Wed. 10–6, Thurs. 10–8; Oct.–Mar., Wed.–Mon. 10–5), which hosts walking tours, hands-on exhibits, and fantastic creative programs for children, all with a nautical theme. ⊠ *Visitor center 211 Water St., South St. Seaport* ☎ *212/732–7678 events and shopping information* ⊕ *www.southstseaport.org* ☒ *$5 to ships, galleries, walking tours, Maritime Crafts Center, films, and other seaport events* Ⓜ *Subway: A, C, 2, 3, 4, 5 to Fulton St./Broadway Nassau.*

Cross South Street, once known as the Street of Ships, under an elevated stretch of the FDR Drive to **Pier 16,** where historic ships are docked, including the *Pioneer,* a 102-foot schooner built in 1885; the *Peking,* the second-largest sailing bark in existence; the iron-hulled *Wavertree;* and the lightship *Ambrose.* The Pier 16 ticket booth provides information and sells tickets to the museum, ships, tours, and exhibits. Pier 16 also hosts frequent concerts and performances and is the departure point for various cruises, including the **Seaport Music Cruise** (☎ 212/630–8888 ☒ $20 and up), which hosts jazz and blues performances; the Circle Line's **Seaport Liberty Cruise** (☎ 212/563–3200 ☒ $13), a one-hour sightseeing trip; and **"The Beast"** (☎ 212/563–3200 ☒ $16), a 30-minute speedboat ride out to the Statue of Liberty.

To the north is **Pier 17,** a multilevel dockside shopping mall that houses national chain retailers such as Express and Victoria's Secret, among others. Its weathered-wood rear decks make a splendid spot from which to sit and contemplate the river, with views as far north as midtown Manhattan and as far south as the Verazzano-Narrows Bridge.

need a break?	The cuisine at the fast-food stalls on Pier 17's third-floor **Promenade Food Court** is eclectic: Pizza on the Pier, Daikichi Sushi, Simply Seafood, and Salad Mania. But what really makes eating here worthwhile is the spectacular view from the tables in the glass-walled atrium.

㉖ **Surrogate's Court—Hall of Records.** This 1911 building is the most ornate of the City Hall court trio. In true beaux-arts fashion, sculpture and ornament seem to have been added wherever possible to the basic neo-classical structure, yet the overall effect is graceful rather than cluttered. Filmmakers sometimes use its elaborate lobby in opera scenes. A courtroom here was the venue for *Johnson v. Johnson,* where the heirs to the Johnson & Johnson fortune waged their bitter battle. ⊠ *31 Chambers St., at Centre St., Lower Manhattan* Ⓜ *Subway: 4, 5, 6 to Brooklyn Bridge/City Hall.*

㉕ **Tweed Courthouse.** Under the corrupt management of notorious politician William Marcy "Boss" Tweed (1823–78), this Anglo-Italianate gem, one of the finest designs in the City Hall area, took some $12 million and nine years to build (it was finally finished in 1872, but the ensuing public outrage drove Tweed from office). Although it's imposing, with its columned classical pediment outside and seven-story octagonal rotunda inside, almost none of the boatloads of marble that Tweed had shipped from Europe made their way into this building. Today it houses municipal offices; it has also served as a location for several films, most notably *The Verdict*. ⊠ *52 Chambers St., between Broadway and Centre St., Lower Manhattan* Ⓜ *Subway: 4, 5, 6 to Brooklyn Bridge/City Hall.*

㉙ **U.S. Courthouse.** Cass Gilbert built this courthouse in 1936, convinced that it complemented the much finer nearby Woolworth Building, which he had designed three decades earlier. Granite steps climb to a massive columned portico; above this rises a 32-story tower topped by a gilded pyramid, not unlike that with which Gilbert crowned the New York Life building uptown. Julius and Ethel Rosenberg were tried for espionage at this courthouse, and hotel queen Leona Helmsley went on trial here for tax evasion. ⊠ *40 Centre St., at Foley Sq., Lower Manhattan* Ⓜ *Subway: 4, 5, 6 to Brooklyn Bridge/City Hall.*

㉒ **Woolworth Building.** Called the Cathedral of Commerce, this ornate white terra-cotta edifice was, at 792 feet, the world's tallest building when it opened in 1913. The lobby's extravagant Gothic-style details include sculptures set into the portals to the left and right; one represents an elderly F. W. Woolworth pinching his pennies, another depicts the architect, Cass Gilbert, cradling in his arms a model of his creation. Glittering mosaic tiles fill the dome and archways. ⊠ *233 Broadway, between Park Pl. and Barclay St., Lower Manhattan* Ⓜ *Subway: 2, 3 to Park Pl.; N, Q, R, W to City Hall.*

TIMING   You can easily spend a half day at the Seaport, or longer if you browse in shops. Completing the rest of the walking tour takes about 1½ hours. Consider walking across the Brooklyn Bridge in the late afternoon for dramatic contrasts of light.

LITTLE ITALY & CHINATOWN

Mulberry Street is the heart of Little Italy; in fact, at this point it's virtually the entire body. In 1932 an estimated 98% of the inhabitants of this area were of Italian birth or heritage, but since then the growth and expansion of Chinatown to the south have encroached on the Italian neighborhood to such an extent that merchants and community leaders of the Little Italy Restoration Association negotiated with Chinatown to let at least Mulberry remain an all-Italian street. Since the late 1990s, trendy shops and restaurants have sprouted in what were Little Italy's northern reaches, and the area is now known as NoLita (North of *Little Italy*).

In the second half of the 19th century, when Italian immigration peaked, the neighborhood stretched from Houston to Canal streets and the

GANGS OF FIVE POINTS

DEBAUCHERY HAS MADE the very houses prematurely old," novelist Charles Dickens wrote in 1842 after visiting Five Points. Although his prose was a bit purple, historians agree that the description of this former Lower Manhattan neighborhood was accurate.

In the mid-19th century, Five Points was perhaps the city's most notorious neighborhood. This intersection of five streets—Mulberry, Anthony (now Worth), Cross (now Park), Orange (now Baxter), and Little Water (no longer in existence)—had been built over a drainage pond that had been filled in the 1820s. When the buildings began to sink into the mosquito-filled muck, middle-class resident abandoned their homes. Buildings were chopped into tiny apartments that were rented to the poorest of the poor, who at this point happened to be Irish immigrant fleeing famine and newly emancipated slaves.

There's no doubt that Five Points was a dangerous place to live. Newspaper accounts at the time tell of robberies and other violent crimes on a daily basis. And with ward leaders like William Marcy Tweed—better known as "Boss" for his stranglehold on local politics—more concerned with lining their pockets than patrolling the streets, keeping order was left to the club-wielding hooligans portrayed in Martin Scorsese's Gangs of New York.

But the neighborhood, finally razed in the 1880s to make way for Chintatown's Columbus Park, has left a lasting legacy. In the music halls where different ethnic groups begrudgingly met, the Irish jig and the African-American shuffle combined to form a new type fancy footwork called tap dancing.

Bowery to Broadway. During this time residents founded at least three Italian parishes, including the Church of the Transfiguration (which now has masses in Cantonese and Mandarin); they also operated an Italian-language newspaper called *Il Progresso*.

In 1926 immigrants from southern Italy first celebrated the Feast of San Gennaro—a 10-day street fair that still takes place every September. Dedicated to the patron saint of Naples, the festival transforms Mulberry Street into an alfresco eatery, as wall-to-wall vendors sell traditional fried sausages and pastries. The neighborhood is draped in the colors of the Italian flag, and even the parking meters get a fresh coat of red, white, and green paint. The community's other big celebration is the Feast of St. Anthony of Padua in June. These festivals are reminders of how much Little Italy continues to change. If you want the flavor of a truly Italian neighborhood, visit Arthur Avenue in the Bronx—or rent a video of the Martin Scorsese's *Mean Streets*, which was filmed in Little Italy in the early 1970s.

With restaurants serving up steaming bowls of soup and shops overflowing with electronic gadgets, Chinatown attracts busloads of visitors, but it's more than a tourist attraction. Roughly a quarter of the city's

400,000 Chinese residents lives along the neighborhood's tangle of streets. Many of these are immigrants from China, Taiwan, and Hong Kong; in fact, roughly half speak little or no English. Chinatown was once divided from Little Italy by Canal Street, the bustling artery that links the Holland Tunnel (to New Jersey) and the Manhattan Bridge (to Brooklyn). But the neighborhood now spills over its traditional borders into Little Italy to the north and the formerly Jewish Lower East Side to the east. However, due to ever-rising rents in Chinatown proper, newly arrived immigrants are increasingly making their homes in the boroughs of Brooklyn and Queens.

The first Chinese immigrants were primarily railroad workers who came from the West in the 1870s to settle in a limited section of the Lower East Side. For nearly a century anti-immigration laws prohibited most men from having their wives and families join them; the neighborhood became known as a "bachelor society," and for years its population remained static. It was not until the end of World War II, when Chinese immigration quotas were increased, that the neighborhood began the expansion that is evident today.

Except for Wall Street, Chinatown was probably the hardest hit neighborhood in Manhattan following the attacks on the World Trade Center. Partly because of Chinatown's very insular and self-reliant nature, all of its major industries have suffered in the aftermath. To the casual visitor, however, the area still appears to be a lively marketplace crammed with souvenir shops and restaurants in funky pagoda-style buildings and crowded with pedestrians day and night. From fast-food noodles or dumplings to sumptuous Hunan, Szechuan, Cantonese, Mandarin, and Shanghai feasts, every imaginable type of Chinese cuisine is served here. Sidewalk markets burst with stacks of fresh seafood and strangely shaped fruits and vegetables. Food shops proudly display their wares: if America's motto is "A chicken in every pot," then Chinatown's must be "A roast duck in every window."

Numbers in the text correspond to numbers in the margin and on the Little Italy, Chinatown, SoHo & TriBeCa map.

a good walk

Start your tour at the corner of Mott and Prince streets, among the pricey, jewel-box-size boutiques and cafés that form chic NoLita. Mulberry, Mott, and Elizabeth streets between Houston and Kenmare streets are the core of this largely gentrified neighborhood that has weaved itself into the increasingly less visible mix of family-owned Italian, Latino, and Asian businesses. Windows artfully dressed with everything from wrist bags to baby clothes continue to debut, making the area a zestier sort of SoHo. Among these neighborhood debutantes sits the stately dowager, **St. Patrick's Old Cathedral** ❶ ➤, the oldest Roman Catholic church in New York City. Tour the church and walk west on Prince Street to **Mulberry Street** ❷; then walk south to Broome Street. East of Mulberry Street, the building at 375 Broome Street is known for its sheet-metal cornice that bears the face of a distinguished, albeit anonymous, bearded man.

To see the ornate Renaissance revival–style building that was once the **New York City Police Headquarters** ❸, walk west on Broome Street to Centre Street, and south to Grand Street. Next, head east to the corner of Grand and Mulberry streets and stop to get the lay of the land. Facing north (uptown), on your right are a series of multistory houses from the early 19th century, built long before the great flood of immigration hit this neighborhood between 1890 and 1924. Turn and look south along the east side of Mulberry Street to see Little Italy's trademark railroad-apartment tenement buildings.

On the southeast corner of Grand Street, E. Rossi & Co., established in 1902, is an antiquated little shop that sells espresso makers and other essential items for Italian homes. The embroidered postcards of St. Anthony and other religious figures make great souvenirs. Two doors east on Grand Street is Ferrara's, a pastry shop opened in 1892 that ships its creations—cannoli, peasant pie, Italian rum cake—all over the world. Continue south on Mulberry to see another survivor of the pretenement era, the two-story, dormered brick Van Rensselaer House, now Paolucci's Restaurant. Built in 1816, it's a prime example of the Italian federal style.

One block south of Grand Street, on the corner of Hester and Mulberry streets, stands the site of what was once Umberto's Clam House (now Ristorante Da Gennaro), best known as the place where in 1973 mobster Joey Gallo was munching scungilli when he was fatally surprised by a task force of mob hit men. Turn left onto Hester Street to visit yet another Little Italy institution, Puglia, a restaurant where guests sit at long communal tables, sing along with house entertainers, and enjoy southern Italian specialties with quantities of homemade wine. One street west, on Baxter Street about three-quarters of a block toward Canal Street, stands the **San Gennaro Church** ④, which sponsors Little Italy's keynote event, the annual Feast of San Gennaro.

You know you're in Chinatown when you reach the traffic-clogged Canal Street. Its sidewalks are lined with street vendors, and on weekends the crowds move at a snail's pace. For everything from bags of lychee nuts to barrels of dried octopus, stop to browse in the Kam Man Market at 200 Canal Street. A good place to get oriented is the **Museum of Chinese in the Americas (MoCA)** ⑤, in an 1893 schoolhouse at the corner of Bayard and Mulberry streets. Catercorner from the museum is **Columbus Park** ⑥. This gathering spot occupies the area once known as the Five Points, the tough 19th-century slum ruled by Irish gangs that provided the backdrop for Martin Scorsese's film *Gangs of New York*. One block east of Mulberry Street, **Mott Street** ⑦ is another of the neighborhood's main drags. On the corner of Mott and Mosco streets, you can see the mint-green steeple of the **Church of the Transfiguration** ⑧.

Just north of the church is the sign for Pell Street, a narrow lane of wall-to-wall restaurants whose neon signs stretch halfway across the thoroughfare. To the right off Pell is **Doyers Street** ⑨, the site of early-20th-century gang wars. At the end of Doyers is the **Bowery** ⑩. Cross the street to **Kim Lau Square** ⑪, where stands a graceful arch. From Kim Lau Square, continue past Park Row onto St. James Place to find two remnants of this neighborhood's more distant past. On St. James Place is the **First Shearith Israel Graveyard** ⑫, the first Jewish cemetery

Little Italy, Chinatown, SoHo & TriBeCa

W. Houston St.

Prince St.

King St.

Charlton St.

Vandam St.

Spring St.

Dominick St.

Broome St.

Hudson St.

Varick St.

22

Holland Tunnel Entrance

Canal St.

Watts St.

Desbrosses St.

Holland Tunnel Exit

Vestry St.

Laight St.

Hubert St.

Washington St.

Greenwich St.

TRIBECA

N. Moore St.

26

Franklin St.

New York Mercantile Exchange ◆ **25**

Jay St.

Staple St.

24

Harrison St.

West St.

West Side Hwy.

27

◆ **Stuyvesant High School**

Chambers St.

MacDougal St.

Sullivan St.

Ave. of the Americas (Sixth Ave.)

C,E M

1,9

M

A,C,E M

Varick St.

Ericsson Pl.

Hudson St.

1,2,3,9 M

A,C M

Chambers St.

21

SoHo Building ◆

OK Harris ◆

West Broadway

Wooster St.

Greene St.

Broadway

SOHO

Spring St.

20

New Era Building ◆

Broome St.

Mercer St.

Thompson St.

Drawing Center ◆

Grand St.

23

19

◆

Canal St.

Lispenard St.

N,R,W,Q M

Howar

Walker St.

White St.

Franklin St.

Broadway

Leonard St.

West Broadway

Church St.

Worth St.

Thomas St.

Duane St.

Reade St.

Chambers St.

Warren St.

R,W M

Murray St.

14

15

16

0 ⌐⌐⌐⌐⌐⌐⌐⌐⌐⌐ 1/4 mile

0 ⌐⌐⌐⌐⌐⌐⌐⌐⌐⌐ 400 meters

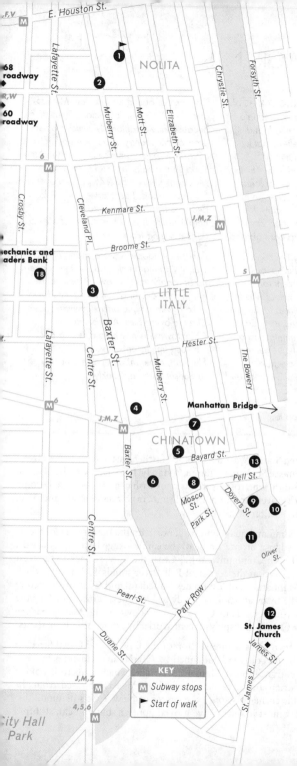

CITY OF IMMIGRANTS

BLACK-AND-WHITE PHOTOGRAPHS of Italians and Russians packed into the waiting rooms at Ellis Island might lead you to believe that it was almost a century ago that most immigrants came to New York City. This is hardly the case. The percentage of foreign-born residents is now 40 percent—an all time high, according to city officials. In fact, close to 3.2 million out of the city's population of 8.1 million was born abroad.

In the late 19th century, most immigrants were from Europe. Today, Europeans make up only about 19 percent for foreign-born residents, the bulk of which are from Latin America, Asia, and the Caribbean. According to census figures from 2000, 13 percent of immigrants are from the Dominican Republic, 9 percent are from China, 6 percent are from Jamaica, 5 percent are from Guyana, and 4 percent are from Mexico. Ecuador, Haiti, Trinidad and Tobago, Colombia, and Russia round out the top ten.

The number of immigrants from Mexico—about 122,600—is especially interesting because they traditionally settle in other parts of the country. A decade earlier, only 32,689 Mexican immigrants lived in New York. That means the total number of Mexicans jumped by 275 percent over a 10-year period. East Harlem, which for decades has been a Puerto Rican neighborhood, now has plenty of Mexican flags hanging from windows.

Other neighborhoods are changing as well. Washington Heights, on the northern tip of Manhattan, is now a Dominican neighborhood. Brighton Beach has been called, with tongue only slightly in cheek, Odessa-by-the-Sea. And because Chinatown has nowhere else to grow, Chinese immigrants have made a home in Flushing, a neighborhood in Queens, and in Sunset Park, in Brooklyn.

in the United States. Walk a half block farther, turn left on James Street, and you can see St. James Church, a stately 1837 Greek revival edifice where Al Smith, who rose from this poor Irish neighborhood to become New York's governor and a 1928 Democratic presidential candidate, once served as altar boy.

Return to Kim Lau Square and walk north up the Bowery to Confucius Plaza, graced by a bronze statue of the Chinese sage bearing his words, "The World Is a Commonwealth." Cross the Bowery back to the west side of the street; at the corner of Pell Street stands 18 Bowery, which is one of Manhattan's oldest homes—a federal and Georgian structure built in 1785 by meat wholesaler Edward Mooney. Farther north up the Bowery, a younger side of Chinatown is shown at the **Asian American Arts Centre** 🄳, which displays recent works by Asian-American artists.

Continue north. At the intersection of the Bowery and Canal Street, a grand arch and colonnade designed by Carrère and Hastings in 1910 mark the entrance to the Manhattan Bridge, which leads to Brooklyn (the pedestrian and bike path over the bridge is accessed from the south). This corner was once the center of New York's diamond district. Today most jewelers have moved uptown, but you can still find some pretty good deals at the shops along the Bowery and the north side of Canal Street.

TIMING Since Little Italy consists of little more than one street, a tour of the area shouldn't take more than one hour. Most attractions are food-related, so plan on visiting around lunchtime. A fun time to visit is during the San Gennaro festival, which runs for two weeks each September, starting the first Thursday after Labor Day. Come on a weekend to see Chinatown at its liveliest; locals crowd the streets from dawn to dusk, along with a slew of tourists. For a more relaxed experience, opt for a weekday. Allowing for stops at the two local museums and a lunch break, a Chinatown tour will take about two additional hours.

What to See

CHINATOWN **Asian American Arts Centre.** This space has impressive contemporary works
⑬ by Asian-American artists, annual folk-art exhibitions during the Chinese New Year, Asian-American dance performances, and videotapes of Asian-American art and events. The center also sells unique art objects from all over Asia. The inconspicuous entrance doesn't have a permanent sign, but the address is posted on a doorway to the right of the entrance to McDonald's. A steep flight of stairs leads up to the third-floor gallery. ⊠ *26 Bowery, between Bayard and Pell Sts., Chinatown* ☎ *212/233–2154* ⊕ *www.artspiral.org* ⊑ *Free* ☉ *Mon.–Wed. and Fri. 12:30–6:30, Thurs. 12:30–7:30* Ⓜ *Subway: N, Q, R, W, 6 to Canal St.*

⑩ **Bowery.** Now a commercial thoroughfare lined with stores selling everything from fanciful light fixtures to secondhand restaurant equipment, this broad boulevard was an agricultural area in the 17th century. Its name derives from *bowerij*, the Dutch word for farm. As the city's growing population moved northward, the Bowery became an elegant avenue lined with taverns and theaters. In the late 1800s the placement of an elevated subway line over the Bowery and the proliferation of saloons and brothels led to its decline; by the early 20th century it had become infamous as a den of crime. Since 1970, efforts to revive the Bowery and neighboring streets has helped disperse some of the neighborhood's indigent population.

⑧ **Church of the Transfiguration.** Built as the English Lutheran Church of Zion in 1801, this imposing Georgian structure changed its name and denomination nine years later, becoming the the Zion Protestant Episcopal Church. When many of its members moved away from the slums of Five Points, the Catholic Church bought the structure in 1853. The first parishioners were Italian and Irish immigrants. Today the church is distinguished by its trilingualism: mass is said in Cantonese, Mandarin, and English. ⊠ *29 Mott St., at Mosco St., Chinatown* ☎ *212/962–5157* ⊕ *www.transfigurationnyc.org* ☉ *Masses weekdays 8 AM and 12:10 PM, Sat. 6 PM, Sun. 9 AM, 10:15 AM, 11:30 AM, 12:45 PM* Ⓜ *Subway: N, Q, R, W, 6 to Canal St.*

⑥ **Columbus Park.** Mornings bring groups of elderly Chinese practicing the graceful movements of tai chi to this shady space. During the afternoons the tables fill for heated games of mah-jongg. In the mid-19th century, the swampy area was known as the **Five Points**—after the intersection of Mulberry Street, Anthony (now Worth) Street, Cross (now Park) Street, Orange (now Baxter) Street, and Little Water Street (no longer in existence)—and was notoriously ruled by dangerous Irish gangs. In the 1880s a neighborhood-improvement campaign brought about the park's creation. Ⓜ *Subway: N, Q, R, W, 6 to Canal St.*

❾ Doyers Street. The "bloody angle"—a sharp turn halfway down this narrow alley—was the site of turn-of-the-20th-century battles between Chinatown's Hip Sing Tong and On Leon Tong, gangs who fought for control over the local gambling and opium trades. Today the street is among Chinatown's most colorful, lined with tea parlors and basement barbershops.

here's where
It may not look like a movie set, and that may be why the corner where Doyers Street spills into Pell Street is irresistible for filmmakers. Tobey McGuire and Kirsten Dunst had a heart-to-heart talk here in *Spider-Man 2*. Woody Allen used it as a location for two of his films, *Alice* and *Small Time Crooks*. It's also seen in *The Believer* and *King of New York*.

⓬ First Shearith Israel Graveyard. Consecrated in 1656 by the country's oldest Jewish congregation, this small burial ground bears the remains of Sephardic Jews (of Spanish-Portuguese extraction) who emigrated from Brazil in the mid-17th century. You can peek through the gates at the ancient headstones here and at the second and third Shearith Israel graveyards on West 11th Street in Greenwich Village and West 21st Street in Chelsea, respectively. ✉ *55 St. James Pl., Chinatown* Ⓜ *Subway: 4, 5, 6 to Brooklyn Bridge/City Hall.*

⓫ Kim Lau Square. Ten streets converge at this labyrinthine intersection crisscrossed at odd angles by pedestrian walkways. Standing on an island in the eye of the storm is the **Kim Lau Arch,** honoring Chinese casualties in American wars. A statue on the square's eastern edge pays tribute to a Quin Dynasty official named Lin Zexu. The 18-foot, 5-inch-tall granite statue reflects Chinatown's growing population of mainland immigrants and their particular national pride: the Fujianese minister is noted for his role in sparking the Opium War by banning the drug. The base of his statue reads: PIONEER IN THE WAR AGAINST DRUGS. On the far end of the square, at the corner of Catherine Street and East Broadway, stands a bank that was built to resemble a pagoda. Ⓜ *Subway: 4, 5, 6 to Brooklyn Bridge/City Hall.*

★ ❼ Mott Street. Broadway's Rogers and Hart immortalized this street in their 1925 hit "Manhattan," waxing poetic about the "sweet pushcarts gently gliding by." That's what Mott Street was like in the late 1880s when Chinese immigrants (mostly men) settled in tenements in a small area that included the lower portion of Mott Street as well as nearby Pell and Doyers streets. It soon became Chinatown's main thoroughfare. Today the busy street overflows with fish and vegetable markets, restaurants, bakeries, and souvenir shops.

need a
break? You can sample crispy pastries, rice dumplings wrapped in banana leaves, yam cakes, and other sweet treats at local favorite **May May Chinese Gourmet Bakery** (⊠ 35 Pell St., off Mott St., Chinatown ☎ 212/267–0733). A colorful flag hangs outside the entrance of the **Chinatown Ice Cream Factory** (⊠ 65 Bayard St., between Mott and Elizabeth Sts., Chinatown ☎ 212/608–4170), where the flavors range from red bean to litchi to green tea. Prepare to eat your scoop on the run since there's no seating.

❺ Museum of Chinese in the Americas (MoCA). On the second floor of an 1893 schoolhouse is the first U.S. museum devoted to preserving the history of the Chinese people. The permanent exhibit—*Where is Home? Chinese in the Americas*—explores the Chinese-American experience through displays of artists' creations, personal and domestic artifacts, and historical documentation. Slippers for binding feet, Chinese musical instruments, a reversible silk gown worn at a Cantonese opera performance, and antique business signs are some of the unique objects on display. Changing exhibits fill a second room. MoCA sponsors workshops, walking tours, lectures, and family events. Its archives (open by appointment only), dedicated to Chinese-American history and culture, include more than 2,000 volumes. ⊠ *70 Mulberry St., at Bayard St., Chinatown* ☎ *212/619–4785* ⊕ *www.moca-nyc.org* ✉ *$3 suggested admission* ☉ *Tues.–Sun. noon–5* Ⓜ *Subway: N, Q, R, W, 6 to Canal St.*

LITTLE ITALY **Mulberry Street.** Crowded with restaurants, cafés, bakeries, imported-
❷ food shops, and souvenir stores, Mulberry Street, between Broome and Canal streets, is where Little Italy lives and breathes. The blocks between Houston and Spring streets fall within the neighborhood of NoLita.

❸ New York City Police Headquarters. This magnificent Renaissance revival structure with baroque embellishments and a striking copper dome served as the headquarters of the New York City Police Department from its construction in 1909 until 1973. The five-story limestone structure was designed to "impress both the officer and the prisoner with the majesty of the law." In 1988 it was converted into a high-price condominium complex. It's known to New Yorkers today as "240 Centre Street," and its big-name residents have included Cindy Crawford, Winona Ryder, and Steffi Graf, among others. ⊠ *240 Centre St., between Broome and Grand Sts., Little Italy* Ⓜ *Subway: N, Q, R, W, 6 to Canal St.*

need a
break? You can savor cannoli and other sweet treats at **Caffe Roma** (⊠ 385 Broome St., at Mulberry St., Little Italy ☎ 212/226–8413), a traditional neighborhood favorite with penny-tile floors and a pressed-tin ceiling. Grab a table outside and watch waiters lure diners into nearby restaurants.

▶ **❶ St. Patrick's Old Cathedral.** The first cornerstone of the original St. Pat's was laid in 1809, making it the city's oldest Roman Catholic church. It was completed in 1815 and completely restored following a fire in 1866. The first American cardinal, John McCloskey, received his red hat in this building. Pierre Toussaint, a former slave who later donated most of his earnings to the poor, was buried in the graveyard. He was reburied at St. Patrick's Cathedral on 5th Avenue in 1983, prior to his veneration by Pope John Paul II. ⊠ *233 Mott St., between Houston and Prince Sts., NoLita* ☎ *212/226–8075* ⊙ *Mon., Tues., Thurs. 8–1 and 3:30–6, Fri. 8–1 and 3:30–9, Sat. 8–1, Sun. 8–4* Ⓜ *Subway: F, V to Broadway–Lafayette St.; R, W to Prince St.*

❹ **San Gennaro Church.** Every September San Gennaro Church—officially known as the Most Precious Blood Church—sponsors the Feast of San Gennaro, the biggest annual event in Little Italy. The 1892 church's richly painted, jewel-box-like interior is worth a glance, especially the replica of the grotto at Lourdes. The church is open for services on weekends. For a visit during the week, see the rector at 109 Mulberry Street. ⊠ *113 Baxter St., near Canal St., Little Italy* ☎ *212/768–9320 festival information, 212/226–6427 church* ⊙ *Masses Sat. 8, 12, 5:30; Sun. 9, 10, noon* Ⓜ *Subway: N, Q, R, W, 6 to Canal St.*

> **a new york moment**
>
> About 1 million people turn out each year for September's Feast of San Gennaro, an 11-day festival that sizzles with the smell of sausage and onions. Held under a canopy of red, white, and green lights strung across Mulberry Street, this is by far the largest of the city's annual street fairs.

SOHO & TRIBECA

Today the names of these two downtown neighborhoods are synonymous with a certain style—an amalgam of black-clad artists, hotshot investors, and media moguls darting between expansive loft apartments, chic boutiques, and packed-to-the-gills restaurants. It's all very urban, very cool, very now. Before the 1970s, though, these two areas were virtual wastelands. SoHo (so named because it is the district South of Houston Street, roughly bounded by Lafayette, Canal Street, and 6th Avenue) was regularly referred to as "Hell's Hundred Acres" because of the many fires that raged through the untended warehouses crowding the area. It was saved by two factors: first, preservationists discovered the world's greatest concentration of cast-iron architecture and fought to prevent demolition; and second, artists discovered the large, cheap, well-lighted spaces that these cavernous structures provide.

All the rage between 1860 and 1890, cast-iron buildings were popular because they did not require massive walls to bear the weight of the upper stories. Since there was no need for load-bearing walls, these buildings had more interior space and larger windows. They were also versatile, with various architectural elements produced from standardized molds to mimic any style—Italianate, Victorian Gothic, Greek Revival, to name but a few visible in SoHo. At first it was technically illegal for artists to live in their loft studios, but so many did that eventually the zoning laws were changed to permit residence.

By 1980 SoHo's trendy galleries, shops, and cafés, together with its marvelous cast-iron buildings and vintage Belgian-block pavements (the 19th-century successor to traditional cobblestones), had made SoHo such a desirable area that only the most successful artists could afford it. Seeking similar space, artists moved downtown to another half-abandoned industrial district, for which a new, SoHo-like name was invented: TriBeCa (the *Tri*angle *Be*low *Ca*nal Street, although in effect it goes no farther south than Murray Street and no farther east than West Broadway). The same scenario has played itself out again, and TriBeCa's rising rents are already beyond the means of most artists, who have moved instead to west Chelsea and the Meatpacking District, Long Island City, areas of Brooklyn, or New Jersey. In SoHo, meanwhile, the arrival of large chain stores such as Pottery Barn and J. Crew has given some blocks the feeling of an outdoor shopping mall.

Numbers in the text correspond to numbers in the margin and on the Little Italy, Chinatown, SoHo & TriBeCa map.

a good walk

Starting at Houston (pronounced *how*-ston) Street, walk south down Broadway, stopping to browse the stores and street vendors between Houston and Prince streets. Within the **Prada** ⓮ ▶ store at 575 Broadway, Dutch architect Rem Koolhaas has created a high-tech setting for the Italian house of fashion. Several art galleries share these blocks as well, most notably at 568 Broadway, which houses a handful of galleries. Just south of Prince Street on the east side of the street, 560 Broadway is home to a dozen or so galleries.

Across Broadway is the charming **Little Singer Building** ⓯, a beaux-arts beauty that outshines all of its neighbors. One block south of the Little Singer Building, between Spring and Broome streets, a cluster of lofts that were originally part of the 1897 New Era Building share an art nouveau copper mansard at No. 495. At the northeast corner of Broadway and Broome Street is the **Haughwout Building** ⓰, a restored classic of the cast-iron genre. At the southeast corner of Broadway and Broome Street, the former Mechanics and Traders Bank at 486 Broadway is a Romanesque and Moorish revival building with half-round brick arches.

If you have youngsters in tow, head east on Grand Street two blocks to the **Children's Museum of the Arts** ⓱, where the interactive exhibits provide a welcome respite from SoHo's mostly grown-up pursuits. Otherwise, walk west on Grand Street three short blocks to discover several of SoHo's better exhibition spaces clustered on the south end of Greene and Wooster streets near Grand and Canal streets. These include Deitch Projects (76 Grand St.), the Drawing Center (35 Wooster St.), and Spencer Brownstone (39 Wooster St.).

From here you may continue north on Wooster Street for Prince Street shops or first head east one block to Greene Street, where cast-iron architecture is at its finest. The block between Canal and Grand streets represents the longest row of cast-iron buildings anywhere. Handsome as they are, these buildings were always commercial, containing stores and light manufacturing firms, principally in the textile trade. (Notice the iron loading docks and the sidewalk vault covers that lead into basement storage areas.) Two standout buildings on Greene Street are the so-called **Queen of Greene Street** 18 and the **King of Greene Street** 19. Even the lampposts on Greene Street are architectural gems: note their turn-of-the-20th-century bishop's-crook style, adorned with various cast-iron curlicues from their bases to their curved tops.

Greene Street between Prince and Spring streets is notable for the SoHo Building (Nos. 104–110); towering 13 stories, it was the neighborhood's tallest building until the SoHo Grand Hotel went up in 1996. At Prince Street, walk one block west to Wooster Street, which between Prince and Spring is a retail paradise. Like a few other SoHo streets, Wooster still has its original Belgian paving stones. Also in this vicinity is one of Manhattan's finest photography galleries, Howard Greenberg (120 Wooster St.) and the Dia Center for the Arts' **New York Earth Room** 20, a must-see reminder of art from SoHo's early days.

From Wooster Street, continue one block west on Prince Street to SoHo's main shopping drag, West Broadway. Although many big-name galleries such as Castelli and Sonnabend have moved uptown, there are still holdouts worth seeing, among them, Franklin Bowles (431 West Broadway) and Nancy Hoffman (429 West Broadway). It's worth taking a detour west on Spring Street four blocks to see the **New York City Fire Museum** 21.

Continue south on West Broadway to the blocks between Spring and Broome streets to one of the area's major art galleries, the immense OK Harris (383 West Broadway). Stay on West Broadway on the west side of the street and proceed south; between Grand and Canal streets stands the **SoHo Grand Hotel** 22. From here, follow West Broadway south past Canal Street, the official boundary between SoHo and TriBeCa. On West Broadway between White and Franklin streets, stop to marvel at the life-size iron Statue of Liberty crown rising above the entrance to 219 West Broadway.

Continuing south on West Broadway to Duane Street, you'll pass Worth Street, once the center of the garment trade and the 19th-century equivalent of today's 7th Avenue. Turn right on Duane Street to Hudson Street and you'll find the calm, shady **Duane Park** 23. Walk one block north on Hudson Street. On the right-hand side is the art deco Western Union Building at No. 60, where 19 subtly shaded colors of brick are laid in undulating patterns.

The area to the west (left), near the Hudson River docks, was once the heart of the wholesale food business. Turn off Hudson Street onto quiet Jay Street and pause at narrow **Staple Street** 24, whose green pedestrian walkway overhead links two warehouses. Also gaze up Harrison Street toward the ornate old New York Mercantile Exchange. If you continue west on Jay Street, you'll pass the loading docks of Bazzini's Nuts and Confections, where the upscale retail shop has peddled nuts, coffee beans, and candies since 1886; there are also a few tables where you can rest and have a snack. The entrance is on Greenwich Street.

Just north of Bazzini's, at the intersection of Harrison and Greenwich streets, is a surprising row of early-19th-century town houses lining the side of Independence Plaza, a huge high-rise apartment complex. The three-story redbrick houses were moved here from various sites in the neighborhood in the early 1970s. Two blocks north on Greenwich Street, at Franklin Street, is the **TriBeCa Film Center** ㉕. Two blocks south of Jay Street on Greenwich Street lies 2½-acre **Washington Market Park** ㉖, a landscaped oasis that has great playground equipment for children. At the corner of the park, turn right on Chambers Street, heading west toward the Hudson River. At the end of the block, cross the overpass across the West Side Highway and you'll find yourself in front of the Stuyvesant High School building. Behind the school lies the north end of the Parks of Battery Park City, which has nearly 30 acres of open spaces, including sculpture installations and an esplanade.

TIMING   To see SoHo and TriBeCa at their liveliest, visit on a Saturday, when the fashion-conscious crowd is joined by smartly dressed uptowners and suburbanites who come down for a little shopping and gallery hopping. If you want to avoid crowds, take this walk during the week. Allow time for browsing in a few galleries and museums, as well as a stop for lunch. Keep in mind that most galleries are closed Sunday and Monday.

What to See

Charlton Street. The city's longest stretch of redbrick town houses preserved from the 1820s and 1830s runs along the north side of this street, which is west of 6th Avenue and south of West Houston Street. The high stoops, paneled front doors, leaded-glass windows, and narrow dormer windows are all intact. While you're here, stroll along the parallel King and Vandam streets for more fine federal houses. This quiet enclave was once an estate called Richmond Hill, whose various residents included George Washington, John and Abigail Adams, and Aaron Burr.

⊙ ⑰ **Children's Museum of the Arts.** In this bi-level space a few blocks from Broadway, children ages 1 to 10 can amuse and educate themselves with various activities, including diving into a pool of colorful balls; play acting in costume; music making with real instruments; and art making, from computer art to old-fashioned painting, sculpting, and collage. ⊠ *182 Lafayette St., between Grand and Broome Sts., SoHo* ☎ *212/941–9198* ⊕ *www.cmany.org* ⊇ *$6, Thurs. 4–6 pay as you wish* ⊙ *Wed., Fri.–Sun. noon–5, Thurs. noon–6* Ⓜ *Subway: 6 to Spring St.*

㉓ **Duane Park.** The city bought this calm, shady triangle from Trinity Church in 1797 for $5. Cheese, butter, and egg warehouses surrounded this oasis for more than a century. ⊠ *Bordered by Hudson, Duane, and Staple Sts., TriBeCa* Ⓜ *Subway: 1, 2, 3, 9, A, C to Chambers St.*

⑯ **Haughwout Building.** Nicknamed the Parthenon of Cast Iron, this five-story, Venetian palazzo–style structure was built in 1857 to house Eder Haughwout's china and glassware business. Each window is framed by Corinthian columns and rounded arches. Inside, the building once contained the world's first commercial passenger elevator, a steam-powered device invented by Elisha Graves Otis. Otis went on to found an elevator empire and made high-rises practical possibilities. ⊠ *488–492 Broadway, at Broome St., SoHo* Ⓜ *Subway: N, Q, R, W to Canal St.*

⑲ **King of Greene Street.** This five-story Renaissance-style 1873 building has a magnificent projecting porch of Corinthian columns and pilasters. Today the King (now painted a brilliant shade of ivory) houses the DBA Gallery and Alice's Antiques. ✉ *72–76 Greene St., between Spring and Broome Sts., SoHo* Ⓜ *Subway: C, E to Spring St.*

🅕 **Little Singer Building.** Ernest Flagg's 1904 masterpiece reveals the final flower of the cast-iron style with a delicate facade covered with curlicues of wrought iron. The central bay windows are recessed, allowing the top floor to arch over like a proscenium. Don't miss the L-shape building's second facade on Prince Street. Its sibling, the Singer Tower, was at one time the tallest building in the world. That structure, at 165 Broadway, was unfortunately razed in 1967. ✉ *561 Broadway, SoHo* Ⓜ *Subway: R, W to Prince St.*

🅤 **New York City Fire Museum.** Real firefighters give the tours at this museum in the former headquarters of Engine 30, a handsome beaux-arts building dating from 1904. The collection of firefighting tools from the 18th, 19th, and 20th centuries includes hand-pulled and horse-drawn engines, pumps, uniforms, and fireboat equipment. Since the 2001 attack on the World Trade Center, when New York's Bravest lost 343 members, the museum has been crowded, especially on weekends. A memorial exhibit with photos, paintings, children's artwork, and found objects all relating to the September 11 attacks is also on view. Guided tours for 12 or more can be made by appointment. ✉ *278 Spring St., near Varick St., SoHo* ☎ *212/691–1303* ⊕ *www.nycfiremuseum.org* ✉ *$5 suggested donation* ☉ *Tues.–Sat. 10–5, Sun. 10–4* Ⓜ *Subway: C, E to Spring St.*

🅥 **New York Earth Room.** Walter de Maria's 1977 avant-garde work consists of 140 tons of gently sculpted soil (22 inches deep) filling 3,600 square feet of space of a second-floor gallery maintained by the Dia Art Foundation. Fans of de Maria's work shouldn't miss his *Broken Kilometer*, a few blocks away at 393 West Broadway. ✉ *141 Wooster St., between W. Houston and Prince Sts., SoHo* ☎ *212/473–8072* ⊕ *www.earthroom.org* ✉ *Free* ☉ *Jan.–mid-June and mid-Sept.–Dec., Wed.–Sun. noon–3 and 3:30–6* Ⓜ *Subway: R, W to Prince St.*

need a break? In one of SoHo's classic buildings, **Space Untitled** (✉ 133 Greene St., south of W. Houston St., SoHo ☎ 212/260–8962) serves caffeine, smoothies, sweets, and sandwiches, as well as wine and beer, in a sprawling gallery space. Diagonally across from Prada, **Dean & DeLuca** (✉ 560 Broadway, at Prince St., SoHo ☎ 212/431–1691), the gourmet food emporium, brews superb coffee and tea and sells yummy pastries at a premium, but it's literally standing room only.

🅓 **Prada.** OMA, the Dutch architecture firm led by Rem Koolhaas, delves into the relations among theory, design, and sheer consumerism at Prada's SoHo store. You may find the technological gizmos and display innovations more fascinating than the latest clothing. A sweeping sine curve of zebrawood dips into a set of oversize steps, creating a continuum from the ground floor to the basement. Metal display cages hung from the ceiling can be rolled along tracks to reconfigure the space; a seamless glass elevator glides between floors. Souped-up dressing rooms have doors that change from clear to opaque; inside, turn slowly in front of a plasma screen to see a video image of how the back of an outfit looks. Strips of video screens elsewhere on the selling floor show arty film clips, and pink resin stripes the shelving areas. And the exposed white spackling? Intentional. ⊠ *575 Broadway, at Prince St., SoHo* ☎ *212/334–8888* ⊕ *www.prada.com* ☉ *Mon.–Sat. 11–7, Sun. noon–6* Ⓜ *Subway: R, W to Prince St.*

⓯ **Queen of Greene Street.** The regal grace of this 1873 cast-iron beauty is exemplified by its dormers, columns, window arches, projecting central bays, and Second Empire–style roof. The Queen received a face-lift in 2003. ⊠ *28–30 Greene St., between Grand and Canal Sts., SoHo* Ⓜ *Subway: N, R, Q, W to Canal St.*

㉒ **SoHo Grand Hotel.** The first major hotel to appear in SoHo since the 1800s, this 15-story stunner pays tribute to the neighborhood's architectural history, particularly the cast-iron historic district. Completed in 1996, Bill Sofield's industrial-chic yet warm decor complements the original 19th-century structure. A 17th-century French stone basin serves as a "dog bar" at the hotel's entrance, signaling that pets are welcome. A staircase—made of translucent bottle glass and iron and suspended from the ceiling by two cables—links the entryway with the second-floor lobby, which has 16-foot-high windows and massive stone columns supporting the paneled mercury mirror ceiling. ⊠ *310 West Broadway, between Canal and Grand Sts., SoHo* ☎ *212/965–3000* Ⓜ *Subway: A, C, E to Canal St.*

㉔ **Staple Street.** Little more than an alley, Staple Street was named for the eggs, butter, cheese, and other staples unloaded here by ships that didn't want to pay duty on any extra cargo. Framed at the end of the alley is the redbrick **New York Mercantile Exchange** (⊠ 6 Harrison St.), with a corner tower topped by a bulbous roof. On the ground floor is the acclaimed French restaurant Chanterelle.

㉕ **TriBeCa Film Center.** Robert De Niro created this complex of editing, screening, and production rooms, where Steven Spielberg, Quincy Jones, and other movie moguls keep offices. Like many of the other stylish and renovated buildings in this area, it's a former factory, the old Coffee Building. On the ground floor is the TriBeCa Grill restaurant, also owned by De Niro. ⊠ *375 Greenwich St., between Franklin and N. Moore Sts., TriBeCa* Ⓜ *Subway: 1, 9 to Franklin St.*

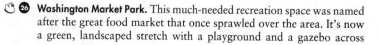

need a break?   For a real New York story, duck into the **Odeon** (⊠ 145 West Broadway, TriBeCa ☎ 212/233–0507), an art deco restaurant-bar. With black-and-red banquettes, chrome mirrors, and neon-lighted clocks, this place has a distinctively slick atmosphere. Come for a drink at the bar or a snack anytime from noon to 2 AM.

☾ ㉖ **Washington Market Park.** This much-needed recreation space was named after the great food market that once sprawled over the area. It's now a green, landscaped stretch with a playground and a gazebo across from a public elementary school. At the corner, a stout little red tower resembles a lighthouse, and iron ship figures are worked into the playground fence—reminders of the neighborhood's long-gone dockside past. ⊠ *Greenwich St. between Chambers and Duane Sts., TriBeCa* Ⓜ *Subway: 1, 2, 3, 9 to Chambers St.*

ART GALLERIES **Ace.** Just west of SoHo proper, Ace is a cavernous space where contemporary artists present large-scale works. Recent shows have included work by Sylvie Fleury, John Armleder, and fashion designer Issey Miyake. ⊠ *275 Hudson St., between Spring and Canal Sts., SoHo* ☎ *212/255–5599* Ⓜ *Subway: C, E to Spring St.*

Art in General. This nonprofit organization often presents group exhibitions organized by guest curators. ⊠ *79 Walker St., between Broadway and Lafayette St., TriBeCa* ☎ *212/219–0473* ⊕ *www.artingeneral. org* Ⓜ *Subway: N, R, Q, W to Canal St.*

Deitch Projects. This energetic enterprise composed of two gallery spaces shows an emerging must-see plucked from the global art scene. Artists on view have included Cecily Brown, Teresita Fernandez, and Shazia Sikhander. ⊠ *76 Grand St., between Greene and Wooster Sts., SoHo* ☎ *212/343–7300* Ⓜ *Subway: C, E to Spring St.* ⊠ *18 Wooster St., at Grand St., SoHo* ☎ *212/343–7300* Ⓜ *Subway: C, E to Spring St.*

Drawing Center. This nonprofit organization focuses on contemporary and historical sketches. Works often push the envelope on what's considered drawing. ⊠ *35 Wooster St., between Broome and Grand Sts., SoHo* ☎ *212/219–2166* ⊕ *www.drawingcenter.org* Ⓜ *Subway: C, E to Spring St.*

Nancy Hoffman. Contemporary painting, sculpture, drawing, prints, and photographic works by an impressive array of international artists are on display here. Gallery artists range from Robert Deese, known for his conceptual shaped canvases, to Yuko Shiraishi, whose abstract oil paintings explore different tones of a single color. ⊠ *429 West Broadway, between Prince and Spring Sts., SoHo* ☎ *212/966–6676* ⊕ *www. nancyhoffmangallery.com* Ⓜ *Subway: R, W to Prince St.*

OK Harris. This SoHo stalwart hosts a wide range of visual arts, from paintings to digitally enhanced photographs to trompe l'oeil reliefs, as well as antiques and collectibles. ⊠ *383 West Broadway, between Spring and Broome Sts., SoHo* ☎ *212/431–3600* ⊕ *www.okharris.com* Ⓜ *Subway: R, W to Prince St.*

East Village & Greenwich Village

Including the Meatpacking District & Lower East Side

2

WORD OF MOUTH

"The villages are great for strolling and dining. So much literary and Beat history. Washington Square Park is loaded with street entertainers, college students, locals, and tourists. St. Mark's Place is filled with funky shops and vendors."

—jdnyc

Updated by
Melisse Gelula

Greenwich Village, between 14th and Houston streets and from Broadway to the Hudson River, is characterized by historical brownstones that
line the grid-defying, often cobbled blocks—and a fey yet formal spirit.
Technically, the West Village, as New Yorkers refer to it, covers just the
area from the Hudson River to 6th Avenue, but this designation is often
used interchangeably with Greenwich Village, the middle section of
"the Village" from 6th Avenue east to Broadway. The Meatpacking District covers a few blocks of the West Village, between the Hudson River
and 9th Avenue, from Little West 12th Street north to West 14th Street.
This burgeoning area is a meat market in the morning, and a metaphor-
ical one at night, when the city's trendiest frequent the equally trendy
restaurants here.

The edgy East Village is bounded by 14th and East Houston streets and
4th Avenue or the Bowery on the west to the East River. It was first founded
by 19th-century immigrants, who also settled the Lower East Side (L.
E.S.), south of Houston. In fact, this entire area was called the Lower
East Side until the 1960s when the East Village separated, becoming its
own neighborhood, with a distinct rock-and-roll attitude. Today, the L.
E.S. is a juxtaposition of old tenements and new tenants, as hipsters have
moved into nearly every nook, remaking the area in their own image.

GREENWICH VILLAGE

Greenwich Village, which New Yorkers invariably speak of simply as
"the Village," enjoyed a raffish reputation for years. The area was originally a rural outpost of the city—a haven for New Yorkers during early-
19th-century smallpox and yellow fever epidemics—and many of its blocks
still look relatively pastoral, with brick town houses and low-rises, tiny
green parks and hidden courtyards, and a crazy-quilt pattern of narrow,
tree-lined streets (some of which follow long-ago cow paths). In the mid-
19th century, however, as the city spread north of 14th Street, the Village became the province of immigrants, bohemians, and students (New
York University [NYU], today the nation's largest private university, was
planted next to Washington Square in 1831). Its politics were radical
and its attitudes tolerant, which is one reason it became a home to such
a large lesbian and gay community.

Several generations of writers and artists have lived and worked here:
in the 19th century, Henry James, Edgar Allan Poe, Mark Twain, Walt
Whitman, and Stephen Crane; at the turn of the 20th century, O. Henry,
Edith Wharton, Theodore Dreiser, and Hart Crane; and during the
1920s and '30s, John Dos Passos, Norman Rockwell, Sinclair Lewis,
John Reed, Eugene O'Neill, Edward Hopper, and Edna St. Vincent Millay. In the late 1940s and early 1950s, the abstract expressionist painters
Franz Kline, Jackson Pollock, Mark Rothko, and Willem de Kooning
congregated here, as did the Beat writers Jack Kerouac, Allen Ginsberg,
and Lawrence Ferlinghetti. The 1960s brought folk musicians and poets,
notably Bob Dylan and Peter, Paul, and Mary.

Today, block for block, the Village is still one of the most vibrant parts
of the city. Well-heeled professionals occupy high-rent apartments and

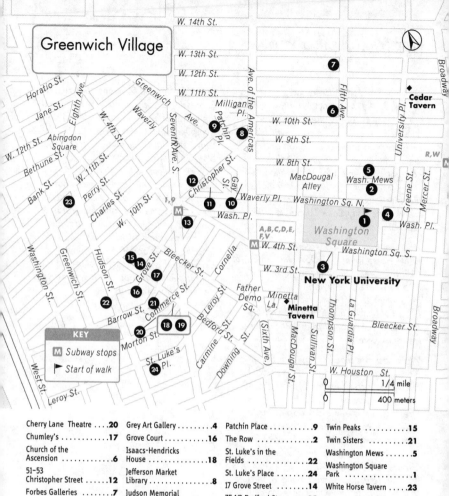

Greenwich Village

W. 14th St.
W. 13th St.
W. 12th St.
W. 11th St.
Horatio St.
Jane St.
Eighth Ave.
W. 4th St.
Greenwich Ave.
Waverly Pl.
Seventh Ave. S.
Milligan Pl.
Patchin Pl.
Ave. of the Americas
W. 10th St.
W. 9th St.
W. 8th St.
Fifth Ave.
University Pl.
Broadway
◆ Cedar Tavern
R, W
A

W. 12th St.
Abingdon Square
Bethune St.
Bank St.
W. 11th St.
Perry St.
Charles St.
Greenwich St.
W. 10th St.
Christopher St.
Gay St.
Waverly Pl.
MacDougal Alley
Wash. Mews
Washington Sq. N.
Greene St.
Mercer St.

Washington St.
Greenwich St.
Hudson St.
Grove St.
Bleecker St.
Wash. Pl.
Cornelia St.
W. 4th St.
W. 3rd St.
Washington Square
New York University
Washington Sq. S.
Washington Sq. S.
Wash. Pl.
A,B,C,D,E, F,V

Barrow St.
Commerce St.
Morton St.
St. Luke's Pl.
Leroy St.
Bedford St.
Leroy St.
Carmine St.
Downing St.
Father Demo Sq.
Minetta La.
Minetta Tavern
(Sixth Ave.)
MacDougal St.
Sullivan St.
Thompson St.
La Guardia Pl.
Bleecker St.
Broadway
W. Houston St.

West St.
Leroy St.

KEY
Ⓜ Subway stops
▶ Start of walk

0 ____ 1/4 mile
0 ____ 400 meters

CloseUp

LITERARY PUB CRAWL

WHERE THERE ARE ACADEMICS, writers, and artists, there are pubs and bars nearby in which to swill the pain of procrastination and lament the limits of creativity. A literary lot has long frequented the West Village's "think tanks" and a tour of a few make for a sophisticated pub crusade rather than crawl. Especially since 10-minute walks separate each.

The most famous '50s watering hole is the **White Horse Tavern** (✉ 567 Hudson St., at 11th St., Greenwich Village ☎ 212/989–3956), where poet Dylan Thomas did not go gently into that good night as much as he drank himself into the state here. He died at 39 of alcoholism in 1953 after a last drink here.

Walk east one block along 11th Street to Bleecker and take a right. It's a good 10-minute walk southeast on Bleecker, past many mediocre NYU bars, to MacDougal Street, which is one block east of Sixth Avenue. Take a left when you reach it. At **Minetta Tavern** (✉ 113 MacDougal St., between Bleecker and W. 3rd Streets, Greenwich Village ☎ 212/475–3850) Italian fare is now served in the venerable Village watering hole that dates to Prohibition. During those years, the tavern was called the Black Rabbit, some say for the scandalous 1890s sex shows held here. In 1923, De Witt Wallace printed his first copies of the simply named Reader's Digest in the basement. Suffice it to say that Wallace and his wife became benefactors of the Met. More recently poets and lit lions, including Nobel Prize–winning poet Seamus Heaney, have been regulars here.

Take a sobering walk north to Washington Square Park, cross it to Washington Square East, and take a left, walking north on University Place, heading for 11th Street. During the '40s and '50s Abstract Expressionist Jackson Pollock, practiced the nondribble method when lifting drink to mouth at the **Cedar Tavern** (✉ 82 University Place, between 11th and 12th Sts., Greenwich Village ☎ 212/929–9089). Willem de Kooning and his wife, Elaine, regularly processed their marital troubles from the captain's-chair barstools during the same time, and rumor has it that beat writer Jack Kerouac, a regular, lost his his drinking privileges here for emptying his bladder in an ashtray. Complete any necessary business of this kind in the traditional WC before waving down a cab for your hotel.

town houses side by side with bohemian, longtime residents—who pay cheap rents thanks to rent-control laws—as well as NYU students. Locals and visitors rub elbows at dozens of small restaurants, cafés spill out onto sidewalks, and a variety of small shops pleases everyone. Except for a few pockets of adult-entertainment shops and divey bars, the Village is as scrubbed as posher neighborhoods.

Numbers in the text correspond to numbers in the margin and on the Greenwich Village map.

a good walk

A walk through the Village covers the sights of the city's preabolitionist and prohibition eras through the Gay Rights movement—and some of the most charmed—and coveted—real estate. At **Washington Square Park** ❶ ☞, the city's central business thoroughfare of 5th Avenue ends, and the student-bohemian feel of the Village begins. Circle the leafy square, but don't expect to find a bench or fountain-side seat that's not occupied by New York University students, professors, pigeon-feeders, or idlers of all ilks.

Walk north through the Washington Arc, and up 5th Avenue, which is lined with austere apartment buildings, then turn left on East 9th Street and walk one block. At Avenue of the Americas (6th Avenue) and 9th Street is **C.O. Bigelow** (No. 414), a 150-year-old apothecary that sells a well-edited selection of hard-to-find or high-end beauty products and remedies.

Cross to the west side of the street for the **Jefferson Market Library** ❽ and clock tower, set on a triangular traffic island. An open gate to the lovingly tended library garden (on the Greenwich Avenue side) is a rare, felicitous find. On the north side of the building, abutting West 10th Street, is **Patchin Place,** a tiny street where Djuna Barnes, Theodore Dreiser, and e. e. cummings, and other authors have lived. Any of the major streets off the triangle will take you into the thick of the Village, where the streets narrow, turn back on themselves (Waverly Place crosses itself at one point) and defy logic. If you continue down West 10th, past Jack's Stir Brew (No. 138), a local coffee spot, and continue west, you'll pass several independently owned shops—still the case in this part of town—set in residential brownstones. At Waverly Place, is Three Lives (No. 154), one of the city's best small bookstores.

Take Waverly one block south to the triangular **Northern Dispensary** ⓫ building at Christopher Street, the symbolic heart of New York's gay and lesbian community. At **51–53 Christopher Street** ⓬, the historic Stonewall riots marked the beginning of the gay rights movement; a block east (back toward 6th Avenue) is the Oscar Wilde bookstore. During the day, this stretch is relatively quiet unless you're here over Gay Pride, the third weekend in June. During the evening, particularly a warm one, however, the whole Village is hopping.

West of 7th Avenue South, the Village turns into a picture-book town of twisting tree-lined streets, quaint houses, and tiny restaurants. Across the busy intersection of 7th Avenue South, is the Village Vanguard, one of many notable music venues in this neighborhood. Here, Christopher

Street continues to the Hudson River, where a landscaped pier with benches marks a stop on the city's riverside path.

Walk south on 7th Avenue and veer southwest on Grove Street, past Marie's Crisis, a piano bar in the house where Thomas Paine died. Try to allow yourself the luxury of getting a bit lost in the area where Grove and Bedford streets intersect, two blocks southwest. These streets still feel very 19th-century New York. One of the few remaining clapboard structures in Manhattan is **17 Grove Street** ⑭. Around the same corner is **Twin Peaks** ⑮, an early-19th-century house that resembles a Swiss chalet. Heading west, Grove Street curves in front of the iron gate of **Grove Court** ⑯, a group of mid-19th-century brick-front residences. One of the most beloved sights in the area is **Chumley's** ⑰, a former speakeasy, at 86 Bedford Street. It still has an unmarked door and book jackets from some of the literary types that frequented here hang on the walls. This landmark eatery is great place to call it quits and get refueled. But it doesn't serve lunch on weekends.

Bleecker Street, on the other hand, always has something cooking. If you take it northwest toward Abingdon Square, you'll find contemporary clothing boutiques, antiques shops, small restaurants—and the popular Magnolia Bakery at the corner of West 11th Street. If you take it southwest, you'll find slew of great Italian pastry shops including Zito's & Sons at No. 259 and Murray's Cheese Shop at No. 254 for goods to go—and a vibe that's Italian. For a bite sitting down, head to Grey Dog's Coffee off Bleecker at No. 33 Carmine Street. It's open from 7 AM until midnight and has great light fare.

TIMING   The walk itself will take you about two hours. However, Greenwich Village lends itself to a leisurely pace, so allow yourself most of a day to explore its backstreets and stop at shops and cafés.

What to See

⑳ **Cherry Lane Theatre.** One of the original off-Broadway houses, this 1817 building was converted into a theater in 1923, thanks to Edna St. Vincent Millay and a group of theater artists. Over the years it has hosted American premieres of works by O'Neill, Beckett, Ionesco, Albee, Pinter, and Mamet. The playhouse still contains the original audience seats. ⊠ *38 Commerce St., at Barrow St., Greenwich Village* ☎ *212/989–2020* ⊕ *www.cherrylanetheatre.com* Ⓜ *Subway: 1, 9 to Houston St.*

★ ⑰ **Chumley's.** A speakeasy during the Prohibition era, this still-secret tavern behind an unmarked door on Bedford Street retains its original ambience with oak booths, a fireplace once used by a blacksmith, and a sawdust-strewn floor. For years Chumley's attracted a literary clientele (John Steinbeck, Ernest Hemingway, Edna Ferber, Simone de Beauvoir, and Jack Kerouac), and the book covers of their publications were proudly displayed (and still appear) on the walls. There's another "secret" entrance in Pamela Court, accessed at 58 Barrow Street around the corner. ⊠ *86 Bedford St., near Barrow St., Greenwich Village* ☎ *212/675–4449* Ⓜ *Subway: 1, 9 to Christopher St./Sheridan Sq.*

⑥ Church of the Ascension. A mural depicting the Ascension of Jesus and stained-glass windows by John LaFarge, as well as a marble altar sculpture by Augustus Saint-Gaudens, are the highlights of this 1841 Gothic Revival–style brownstone church designed by Richard Upjohn. In 1844 President John Tyler married Julia Gardiner here. ⊠ *36–38 5th Ave., at 10th St., Greenwich Village* ☎ *212/254–8620* ⊕ *www.ascensionnyc. org* ⊗ *Mon.–Sat. noon–1* Ⓜ *Subway: R, W to 8th St.*

⑫ 51–53 Christopher Street. On June 27, 1969, a gay bar at this address named the Stonewall Inn was the site of a clash between gay men and women and the New York City police. As the bar's patrons were being forced into police wagons, sympathetic onlookers protested and started fighting back, throwing beer bottles and garbage cans. Protests, addressing the indiscriminate raids on gay bars, lasted for days. Every June the Stonewall Riots are commemorated around the world with Gay Pride parades and celebrations that honor the gay rights movement. A reincarnation named Stonewall is at No. 53. ⊠ *51–53 Christopher St., between Waverly Pl. and 7th Ave. S, Greenwich Village* Ⓜ *Subway: 1, 9 to Christopher St./Sheridan Sq.*

need a break? Taking a break in **Christopher Park** (⊠ Bordered by W. 4th, Grove, and Christopher Sts., Greenwich Village) entails sharing the space with George Segal's life-size sculptures—a lesbian couple sitting on a bench and gay male partners standing and conversing. But even with these perennial occupants, there's usually a greater chance of getting a seat here than in Washington Square Park. It's also a block south of wholesome grocery, Gourmet Garage, at 117 7th Avenue.

⑦ Forbes Galleries. The late publisher Malcolm Forbes's idiosyncratic personal collection fills the ground floor of the limestone Forbes Magazine Building, once the home of Macmillan Publishing. Rotating exhibits are displayed in the large painting gallery and one of two autograph galleries; permanent highlights include U.S. presidential papers, more than 500 intricate toy boats, 10,000 toy soldiers, and some of the oldest Monopoly game sets ever made. ⊠ *62 5th Ave., at 12th St., Greenwich Village* ☎ *212/206–5548* ⊠ *Free* ⊗ *Tues.–Sat. 10–4* Ⓜ *Subway: R, W to 8th St.; F, V to 14th St.*

⑩ Gay Street. A curved, one-block lane lined with small row houses circa 1810, Gay Street is named after the *New York Tribune* editor who lived here with his wife and fellow abolitionist, Lucretia Mott. The black neighborhood was a stop on the Underground Railroad and would later become a strip of speakeasies. In the 1930s this darling thoroughfare and nearby Christopher Street became famous nationwide when Ruth McKenney published her somewhat zany autobiographical stories in the *New Yorker,* based on what happened when she and her sister moved to Greenwich Village from Ohio (they appeared in book form as *My Sister Eileen* in 1938). McKenney wrote in the basement of No. 14. Also on Gay Street, Howdy Doody was designed in the basement of No. 12. ⊠ *Between Christopher St. and Waverly Pl., Greenwich Village* Ⓜ *Subway: 1, 9 to Christopher St./Sheridan Sq.*

④ Grey Art Gallery. New York University's main building has a welcoming street-level space with changing exhibitions usually devoted to contemporary art. *Silver Center* ⊠ *100 Washington Sq. E, between Waverly Pl. and Washington Pl., Greenwich Village* ☎ *212/998–6780* 🖅 *$3 suggested donation* ⊙ *Tues., Thurs., and Fri. 11–6, Wed. 11–8, Sat. 11–5* Ⓜ *Subway: R, W to 8th St.*

⑯ Grove Court. Built between 1853 and 1854, this enclave of brick-front town houses was originally intended as apartments for employees of neighborhood hotels. Grove Court used to be called Mixed Ale Alley because of the neighbors' propensity to pool beverages brought from work. Like the rest of the neighborhood, it now houses more affluent residents. ⊠ *10–12 Grove St., Greenwich Village* Ⓜ *Subway: 1, 9 to Christopher St./Sheridan Sq.*

⑱ Isaacs-Hendricks House. Originally built as a federal-style wood-frame residence in 1799, this immaculate structure is the oldest remaining such house in Greenwich Village. Its first owner, Joshua Isaacs, a wholesale merchant, lost the farmhouse to creditors; the building then belonged to copper supplier Harmon Hendricks. The village landmark was remodeled twice; it received its brick face in 1836, and the third floor was added in 1928. ⊠ *77 Bedford St., at Commerce St., Greenwich Village* Ⓜ *Subway: 1, 9 to Christopher St./Sheridan Sq.*

⑧ Jefferson Market Library. After Frederick Clarke Withers and Calvert Vaux's magnificent, towered courthouse was constructed in 1877, critics variously termed its hodgepodge of styles Venetian, Victorian, or Italian. Villagers, noting the alternating wide bands of red brick and narrow strips of granite, dubbed it the "lean bacon style." The veritable castle in the city was named after the third U.S. president, and the murder trial of architect Standford White took place here. The building was on the verge of demolition when local activists saved it and turned it into a public library in 1967. Inside are handsome interior doorways and a graceful circular stairway. And if the gate is open, the flower garden behind the library is worth a look. ⊠ *425 6th Ave., at 10th St., Greenwich Village* ☎ *212/243–4334* Ⓜ *Subway: A, C, E, F, V to W. 4th St./Washington Sq.*

③ Judson Memorial Church. Designed by celebrated architect Stanford White, this Italian Roman-Renaissance church has long attracted a congregation interested in the arts and community activism. Funded by the Astor family and John D. Rockefeller and constructed in 1892, the yellow-brick and limestone church was built thanks to Edward Judson, who hoped to reach out to the poor immigrants in adjacent Little Italy. The church has stained-glass windows designed by John LaFarge and a 10-story campanile. Inquire at the parish office for weekday access at 243 Thompson Street. ⊠ *55 Washington Sq. S, at Thompson St., Greenwich Village* ☎ *212/477–0351* ⊕ *www.judson.org* ⊙ *Weekdays 10–6* Ⓜ *Subway: A, C, E, F, V to W. 4th St./Washington Sq.*

⑪ Northern Dispensary. Edgar Allan Poe was a frequent patient at the triangular Dispensary, built in 1831 as clinic for indigent Villagers. The Georgian brick building has *one* side on *two* streets (Grove and Christopher streets where they meet) and *two* sides facing *one* street—Waverly

Place, which splits in two directions. A building as odd as Poe's stories. ⊠ *165 Waverly Pl., Greenwich Village* Ⓜ *Subway: 1, 9 to Christopher St./Sheridan Sq.*

⑨ Patchin Place. This little cul-de-sac off West 10th Street between Greenwich and 6th avenues has 10 diminutive 1848 row houses. Around the corner on 6th Avenue is a similar dead-end street, **Milligan Place,** consisting of four small homes completed in 1852. The houses in both quiet enclaves were originally built for the waiters (mostly Basques) who worked at 5th Avenue's high-society Brevoort Hotel, long since demolished. Patchin Place later attracted numerous writers, including Theodore Dreiser, e. e. cummings, Jane Bowles, and Djuna Barnes. Milligan Place eventually became the address for several playwrights, including Eugene O'Neill. Ⓜ *Subway: F, V to 14th St.*

❷ The Row. Built from 1829 through 1839, this series of beautifully preserved Greek Revival town houses along Washington Square North, on the two blocks between University Place and MacDougal Street, once belonged to merchants and bankers, then writers and artists such as John Dos Passos and Edward Hopper. Now the buildings serve as NYU offices and faculty housing. ⊠ *1–13 and 19–26 Washington Sq. N, between University Pl. and MacDougal St., Greenwich Village.*

㉒ St. Luke's in the Fields. The author of "A Visit from St. Nicholas" (" 'Twas the night before Christmas . . ."), Clement Clarke Moore, was the first warden of the Episcopal parish of St. Luke's. When the chapel was constructed in 1822, this part of the city was still the country—in the fields, so to speak. The chapel was the country branch of downtown's Trinity Church. Today St. Luke's Choir, a professional ensemble, and guest choristers perform regularly. The Barrow Street Garden on the chapel grounds is worth visiting in spring and summer. ⊠ *487 Hudson St., between Barrow and Christopher Sts., Greenwich Village* ☎ *212/924–0562* ⊙ *Garden open Tues.–Fri. 8–5 (June–Sept. 8–7), weekends 8–4* Ⓜ *Subway: 1, 9 to Christopher St./Sheridan Sq.*

㉔ St. Luke's Place. Shaded by graceful gingko trees, this street has 15 classic Italianate brownstone and brick town houses (1852–53). Novelist Theodore Dreiser wrote *An American Tragedy* at No. 16, and poet Marianne Moore resided at No. 14. Mayor Jimmy Walker (first elected in 1926) lived at No. 6; the lampposts in front are "mayor's lamps," which were sometimes placed in front of the residences of New York mayors. This block is often used as a film location, too: No. 12 was shown as the Huxtables' home on *The Cosby Show* (although the family lived in Brooklyn), and No. 4 was the setting of the Audrey Hepburn movie *Wait Until Dark.* Before 1890 the playground on the south side of the street was a graveyard where, according to legend, the dauphin of France—the lost son of Louis XVI and Marie Antoinette—is buried. ⊠ *Between Hudson St. and 7th Ave. S, Greenwich Village* Ⓜ *Subway: 1, 9 to Houston St.*

⑭ 17 Grove Street. William Hyde, a prosperous window-sash maker, built this clapboard residence in 1822, and added a workshop out back in 1833 and a third floor in 1870. The building has since served many functions—most interesting of which was as a brothel during the Civil War. It's now the Village's largest remaining wood-frame house. ✉ *17 Grove St., at Bedford St., Greenwich Village* Ⓜ *Subway: 1, 9 to Christopher St./Sheridan Sq.*

⑲ **75½ Bedford Street.** Rising real estate rates inspired the construction of New York City's narrowest house—just 9½ feet wide—in 1873. Built on a lot that was originally a carriage entrance of the Isaacs-Hendricks House next door, this sliver of a building has been home to actor John Barrymore and poet Edna St. Vincent Millay, who wrote the Pulitzer prize–winning *Ballad of the Harp-Weaver* during her tenure here from 1923 to 1924. ✉ *75½ Bedford St., between Commerce and Morton Sts., Greenwich Village* Ⓜ *Subway: 1, 9 to Christopher St./Sheridan Sq.*

⑬ **Sheridan Square.** Once an unused asphalt space, this green triangle was landscaped following an extensive dig by urban archaeologists, who unearthed artifacts dating to the Dutch and Native American eras. ✉ *Bordered by Washington Pl. and W. 4th, Barrow, and Grove Sts., Greenwich Village* Ⓜ *Subway: 1, 9 to Christopher St./Sheridan Sq.*

⑮ **Twin Peaks.** In 1925 financier Otto Kahn gave money to a Village eccentric named Clifford Daily to remodel an 1835 house for artists' use. The building was whimsically altered with stucco, half-timbers, and the addition of a pair of steep roof peaks. The result: an imitation Swiss chalet. ✉ *102 Bedford St., between Grove and Christopher Sts., Greenwich Village* Ⓜ *Subway: 1, 9 to Christopher St./Sheridan Sq.*

need a break? Country-kitsch coffee spot, **Jack's Stir Brew** (✉ 138 W. 10th St., at Greenwich Ave., Greenwich Village ☎ 212/929–0821) doesn't have many tables; locals use it as a morning weigh station, grabbing organic coffee and a fruit-filled muffin from Brooklyn's Blue Sky Bakery on their way to work. You'd be foolish not to follow their lead.

㉑ **Twin Sisters.** These attractive federal-style brick homes connected by a walled garden were said to have been erected by a sea captain for two daughters who loathed each other. Historical record insists that they were built in 1831 and 1832 by a milkman who needed the two houses and an open courtyard for his work. The striking mansard roofs were added in 1873. ✉ *39 and 41 Commerce St., Greenwich Village* Ⓜ *Subway: 1, 9 to Christopher St./Sheridan Sq.*

⑤ **Washington Mews.** This cobblestone private street is lined on one side with the former stables of the houses on the Row on Washington Square North. Writer Walter Lippmann and artist-patron Gertrude Vanderbilt Whitney (founder of the Whitney Museum) once had homes in the mews; today it's mostly owned by NYU. ✉ *Between 5th Ave. and University Pl., Greenwich Village* Ⓜ *Subway: R, W to 8th St.*

★ ☾ ❶ **Washington Square Park.** Earnest-looking NYU students, street musicians, skateboarders, jugglers, chess players, and bench warmers—and those just watching the grand opera of it all—generate a maelstrom of activity in this physical and spiritual heart of the Village. The 9½-acre park had inauspicious beginnings as a cemetery, principally for yellow fever victims—an estimated 10,000–22,000 bodies lie below. In the early 1800s it was a parade ground and the site of public executions; bodies dangled from a conspicuous Hanging Elm that still stands at the northwest corner of the square. The square became the focus of a fashionable residential neighborhood when it was made a public park in 1827. Today, a playground attracts parents with tots in tow, dogs go leash-free inside the popular dog run, and everyone else seems drawn toward the large central fountain where in spring and summer passersby and loungers can cool off in small sprays.

The triumphal **Washington Memorial Arch** stands at the square's north end, marking the start of 5th Avenue, the city's central thoroughfare that's never been marked by understatement. Stanford White designed a wooden version of the Arch, which was built in 1889 to commemorate the 100th anniversary of George Washington's presidential inauguration. It was originally placed about half a block north of its present location. The arch was reproduced in Tuckahoe marble in 1892, and the statues—*Washington at War* on the left, *Washington at Peace* on the right—were added in 1916 and 1918, respectively. The civilian version of Washington is the work of Alexander Stirling Calder, father of the renowned artist Alexander Calder. Bodybuilder Charles Atlas modeled for *Peace*. ⊠ *5th Ave. between Waverly Pl. and 4th St., Greenwich Village* Ⓜ *Subway: A, C, E, F, V to W. 4th St.*

| need a break? | Sandwiches at **Peanut Butter & Co** (⊠ 240 Sullivan St., at W. 3rd St., Greenwich Village ☎ 212/677–3995) may include a simple slathering of smooth or crunchy on white bread, or more complex concoctions with honey, bananas, and even bacon, combinations lifted from the kitchen of childhood. Feel free to ask for yours without the crusts. |

㉓ **White Horse Tavern.** Formerly a speakeasy and a seamen's tavern, the White Horse, dating from 1880, has been popular with artists and writers in recent decades; its best-known customer was Welsh poet Dylan Thomas, who had a room named for him here after his death in 1953. ⊠ *567 Hudson St., at W. 11th St., Greenwich Village* ☎ 212/243–9260 Ⓜ *Subway: 1, 9 to Christopher St./Sheridan Sq.*

MEATPACKING DISTRICT

Until the late 1990s, this area between the Hudson River and 9th Avenue, from Gansevoort Street north to West 14th Street, seemed immune to gentrification due to its industrial function and location far west. But rising rents elsewhere sent entrepreneurs and gallery owners hunting, and once the high-fashion shops, fine art galleries, and adorable bakeries moved in, swinging carcasses and their attendant odors no longer seemed to be much of a deterrent.

Although the overnight beef and poultry movers for which the district is known are still here, as are the transvestite prostitutes who contribute to the area's fringe character, the seeds of chic continue to be sown by new, fashionable folk looking for a real-estate score: trendy restaurateurs and independent retailers, fashion photographers, and their cavalcade, stylists and studio owners. Urbanites and celebrities with their fingers on the pulse followed suit and snatched up the large, unfinished warehouses of abandoned meat-processing plants and automotive stores for renovation as residences.

The main drag for the rapidly multiplying eateries, galleries, shops, and nightclubs is West 14th Street—at the end of which, near the Hudson, Herman Melville was once a customs inspector. The author's grandfather was Revolutionary War hero, General Peter Gansevoort, for whom an 1884 outdoor market (and street) here are named. In 1949 the Gansevoort Meat Center opened. The entrenched meat market continues, dominating the streets weekdays between 5 AM and 9 AM. Thereafter, the sidewalks are hosed down for pedestrians, though an olfactory trace of the trade often lingers into the day, particularly in summer.

a good walk

If you start at West 14th and 8th Avenue, and walk west, you'll notice that as the streets become cobbled, at about 9th Avenue, the shoes traversing them are increasingly well-heeled. (The transsexual protagonist in Off Broadway's *Hedwig and the Angry Inch* suggested it wouldn't be long before the Meating District was renamed MePa, just like many other gentrified city neighborhoods.) Affluent-angled retailers and services line West 14th: the modern Design Within Reach home-furnishings studio (No. 408), hair-cutting extortionist Sally Herschberger (whose cuts cost about $800) at No. 425, and the boutiques of fashion designers Alexander McQueen (No. 417) and Stella McCartney (No. 429). At 10th Avenue is Jeffrey (No. 449), a block-long designer department store. (Consider a quick detour through the shop's exit on West 15th Street to Wooster Projects (No. 418), a pop-art gallery with a huge collection of Warhol, Lichtenstein, and others.)

From Jeffrey's 14th Street entrance, jog back to Washington Street, which has hip shops, such as Dernier Cri (No. 869), tucked under the metal awnings that once supported hanging slabs of meat. One block south at 13th Street is Hogs and Heifers (No. 859), a neighborhood "meet market" and drinking hole infamous for its brassiere-covered bar—and the B-movie *Coyote Ugly,* which was based on it. The next corner at Little West 12th Street is the best place to see The Highline, a 75-year-old elevated railway track (look right or west, toward the Hudson River). It's now being recycled as a park.

Take a left on Little West 12th Street (the *real* West 12th Street is four blocks away) and walk a block to where the street merges with Gansevoort Street, site of an outdoor food market in 1884, and 9th Avenue. Walk up 9th Avenue to the hip Hotel Gansevoort (No. 18), which opened in 2004, with a pooltop bar. Although these mod lodgings contribute to the cultural caché of the neighborhood, the Meatpacking District's newest tenant, Jean-Georges Vongrichten, has forever banished neighborhood's gristly connotations for one that's pure Kobe beef. Take a peek at the sleek Southeast Asian design at Spice Market (No. 403), on the northeast corner of West 13th Street. You can put your name on the list for a seat in lounge, where "upscale street-food" is served, but don't expect to score a table in the dining room without a reservation placed weeks in advance. You can always backtrack to Pastis, chef Keith McNally's (faux) French bistro, at the end of the block. It's open from 9 AM to 2 AM daily—although if it's coming up on 7 PM and you're without a reservation, you're best off walking east to Hudson Street, which is lined with good—just not super trendy—restaurants.

TIMING   The walk itself will take you less than two hours. A little more if you explore the shops.

THE EAST VILLAGE

The progressive East Village—an area bounded by East 14th Street on the north, 4th Avenue or the Bowery on the west, East Houston Street on the south, and the East River on the east—has housed immigrant families since the mid-1800s. Then came a counterculture of hippies and experimental artists, writers, and students in the 1970s; and musicians, artists, and their respective institutions fleeing SoHo's skyrocketing real estate prices in the 1980s. New restaurants, shops, and somewhat cleaner streets arrived in their wave—an influx that drove up rents substantially on some blocks but wasn't pervasive enough to drive out all the neighborhood's original residents. Today an interesting mix has survived, including artistic types and longtime members of various immigrant enclaves, principally Polish, Ukrainian, Slovene, Puerto Rican, Dominican, Japanese, and Filipino groups. With the helpof gentrification, the once sketchy Alphabet City (named for its Avenues A, B, C, and D) now seems like a walk in the park. Good restaurants, stylish bars, and funky shops here are as likely to be patronized by the marginally employed as by young financiers.

Numbers in the text correspond to numbers in the margin and on the East Village & the Lower East Side map.

a good
walk

Begin your walk at **The Strand** ❶ ▶, an enormous secondhand bookstore at Broadway and West 12th Street. Watch the clock at the bookstore (time speeds by inside the stacks) and consider picking up a cheap Strand totebag on your way out, which makes a great souvenir and carryall for the shops ahead. Head south on Broadway, past antiques stores, take a left at **Grace Church** ❷ onto East 10th Street and walk one block. Take a right onto 4th Avenue and walk two blocks south.

At the intersection of 4th Avenue, East 8th Street, and Astor Place, are two traffic islands: On one is the beaux-arts–style entrance to the **Astor Place Subway Station** ❸; on the other stands the **Alamo** ❹, a huge black cube, which is likely to be thronged with skateboarders.

Walk east from the cube, passing the **Cooper Union Foundation Building** ❽ on your right, onto **St. Marks Place** ⑫. Before proceeding down this strip of 8th Street, crowded with shops that cater to the tattooed and pierced, assess whether this is your cup of tea. A kinder, gentler walk one block north on 3rd Avenue, then east (right) on **Stuyvesant Street** ❾

The East Village & the Lower East Side

E. 15th St.

Stuyvesant Town

E. 14th St.

E. 13th St.

E. 12th St.

E. 11th St.

E. 10th St.

E. 9th St.

P.S. 122

Tompkins Square

St. Marks Pl.

Surma

Cooper Square

E. 7th St.

E. 6th St.

EAST VILLAGE

E. 5th St.

E. 4th St.

ALPHABET CITY

E. 3rd St.

E. 2nd St.

Gt. Jones St.

E. 1st St.

Bleecker St.

E. Houston St.

Prince St.

LOWER EAST SIDE

Rivington St.

Spring St.

Delancey St.

0   1/4 mile

0   400 meters

Broadway · Fourth Ave. · Third Ave. · Second Ave. · Stuyvesant St. · First Ave. · Greene St. · Mercer St. · Astor Pl. · Wash. Pl. · Lafayette St. · The Bowery · Broadway · Mulberry St. · Mott St. · Elizabeth St. · Chrystie St. · Eldridge St. · Forsyth St. · Allen St. · Orchard St. · Ludlow St. · Essex St. · Norfolk St. · Suffolk St. · Stanton St. · Ave. A · Ave. B

Taras Shevchenko Pl.

KEY

M Subway stops

▶ Start of walk

R, W · M · L · F, V · B, D, F, V

takes you past the academic St. Mark's Bookstore, down a block of historical redbrick rowhouses, and puts you at **St. Mark's-in-the-Bowery Church** ⑭ on the corner of East 10th Street.

The culturally curious, however, should continue down St. Marks. The best shops are Trash and Vaudeville at No. 4 for seriously edgy outfits, Kim's Underground at No. 6 for music and DVDs, and the Sock Man at No. 27. At 2nd Avenue, take a left and walk two blocks north to the 2nd Avenue Deli (156 2nd Ave., at 10th St.), across from St. Mark's-in-the-Bowery Church. If you took the detour up Stuyvesant Street, you should rejoin the walk at the Deli, where Hollywood-style squares in the sidewalk honor Yiddish stage luminaries—and where you can get an excellent pastrami on rye.

Continue east on East 10th Street toward Alphabet City. Just before Avenue A is the **Russian and Turkish Baths** ⑯, a public bathing house since 1892, where you can spend hours steaming, soaking, and scrubbing yourself (for a modest fee). At Avenue A is **Tompkins Square Park** ⑰, a spot that was once the center of Little Germany in 1904, and is now a respite for the neighborhood's contemporary residents—everyone from the area's homeless to those in renovated tenements paying $2,000 a month in rent.

Walk south on Avenue A, past the century-old Italian bakeries and local boutiques for seven short blocks, and take a right on East 3rd Street. On the north side of the block, between 1st and 2nd avenues, is the Hell's Angels Headquarters, so be sure to not upset any of the motorcycles parked here. Take a left on the Bowery, and walk two blocks south to CBGBs, the birthplace of American punk, where the Ramones, Blondie, and the Talking Heads laid the groundwork for a generation of music. As soon as the sun goes down, there's always a band playing and the beer is cheap. The seriously scruffy setting may not be to everyone's liking, but the T-shirts make a great souvenir, which you can get at CB's 313 Gallery next door to the venerable club.

TIMING   The walk itself will take you less than two hours. A perfect walk to capture the flavor of this diverse neighborhood.

What to See

🅒 ④ **Alamo.** The giant, steel "Cube," as it is locally known, was one of the first abstract sculptures in New York City to be placed in a public space—and intersection. It was created by Bernard Rosenthal in 1967, and is a constant hangout for skateboarders and pierced and studded youth. ⊠ *On traffic island at Astor Pl. and Lafayette St., East Village* Ⓜ *Subway: 6 to Astor Pl.*

Alphabet City. The north–south avenues beyond 1st Avenue are all labeled with letters, not numbers, which give this area its nickname. Alphabet City was once a burned-out area of slums and drug haunts, but some blocks and buildings were gentrified during the height of the East Village art scene in the mid-1980s and again in the late '90s. The reasonably priced restaurants with their bohemian atmosphere on Avenues A, B, and C and the cross streets between them, attract all kinds. A close-knit Puerto Rican community lies east of Avenue A, but amid the Latin shops and groceries Avenue B is now a sort of far-out restaurant row. From the whiff of things, Avenue C looks not far behind. ⊠ *Alphabet City extends from Ave. A to East River, between 14th and E. Houston Sts., East Village.*

❸ Astor Place Subway Station. At the beginning of the 20th century, almost every Interborough Rapid Transit (IRT) subway entrance resembled the ornate cast-iron replica of a beaux arts kiosk that covers the stairway leading to the uptown No. 6 train. Inside, tiles of beavers line the station walls, a reference to the fur trade that contributed to John Jacob Astor's fortune. Milton Glaser, a Cooper Union graduate, designed the station's attractive abstract murals. ⊠ *On traffic island at E. 8th St. and 4th Ave., East Village* Ⓜ *Subway: 6 to Astor Pl.*

❺ Colonnade Row. Marble Corinthian columns front this grand sweep of four Greek Revival mansions (originally nine) constructed in 1833, with stonework by Sing Sing penitentiary prisoners. In their time these once-elegant homes served as residences to millionaires John Jacob Astor and Cornelius Vanderbilt until they moved uptown. Today three houses are occupied on street level by restaurants, while the northernmost building houses the Astor Place Theatre and the *Blue Man Group.* ⊠ *428–434 Lafayette St., between Astor Pl. and E. 4th St., East Village* Ⓜ *Subway: 6 to Astor Pl.*

❽ Cooper Union Foundation Building. This impressive Italianate eight-story brownstone structure overlooks humble Cooper Square, where 3rd and 4th avenues merge into the Bowery. A statue of industrialist Peter Cooper, by Augustus Saint-Gaudens, presides here. Cooper founded this college in 1859 to provide a forum for public opinion—Abraham Lincoln, Mark Twain, and Susan B. Anthony have all delivered speeches here—and free technical education for the working class. The foundation still offers tuition-free education in architecture, art, and engineering. Cooper Union was the first structure to be supported by steel railroad rails—rolled in Cooper's own plant. The Great Hall Gallery is open to the public and presents changing exhibitions during the academic year. ⊠ *7 E. 7th St., at 3rd Ave., East Village* ☎ *212/353–4200 exhibition information, 212/353–4195 events* 🖅 *Free* ☉ *Weekdays 11–7, Sat. noon–5* Ⓜ *Subway: 6 to Astor Pl.*

❷ Grace Church. The finely ornamented octagonal marble spire topping this Episcopal church gives this unattractive stretch of Broadway some soul. The building—a mid-19th-century example of an English Gothic revival church—has excellent Pre-Raphaelite stained-glass windows and was designed (for free) by James Renwick Jr. The church has hosted many society weddings, high and low, including that of P. T. Barnum show member Tom Thumb. ⊠ *802 Broadway, at E. 10th St., East Village* ☎ *212/254–2000* ⊕ *www.gracechurchnyc.org* ☉ *Weekdays noon–1* Ⓜ *Subway: 6 to Astor Pl.; R, W to 8th St.*

❻ Joseph Papp Public Theater. In 1854 John Jacob Astor opened the city's first free public library in this expansive redbrick and brownstone Italian Renaissance–style building. It was renovated in 1967 as the Public Theater to serve as the New York Shakespeare Festival's permanent home. The theater opened its doors with the popular rock musical *Hair*. Under the leadership of the late Joseph Papp, the Public's five playhouses built a reputation for bold and innovative performances; the long-running hit *A Chorus Line* had its first performances here, as have many less commercial plays. Today, director and producer George C. Wolfe heads the Public, which continues to present controversial modern works and imaginative Shakespeare productions here and at Central Park's Delacorte Theater for free during the summer Shakespeare Festival. **Joe's Pub** (☎ 212/539–8777) next door brings such A-list musical and performing artists as Mos Def, Macy Gray, and Sandra Bernhard to its cabaret-style space. ⊠ *425 Lafayette St., between E. 4th St. and Astor Pl., East Village* ☎ *212/260-2400* ⊕ *www.publictheater.org* Ⓜ *Subway: 6 to Astor Pl.; R, W to 8th St.*

⓫ McSorley's Old Ale House. Joseph Mitchell immortalized this spot, which claims to be one of the city's oldest, in the *New Yorker*. McSorley's asserts that it opened in 1854; it didn't admit women until 1970. The mahogany bar, gas lamps, and potbelly stove all hark back to decades past, though it's hard to tell which one. It probably makes no difference: The often crowded saloon attracts many collegiate types enticed by McSorley's own brands of ale, not the history. ⊠ *15 E. 7th St., between 2nd and 3rd Aves., East Village* ☎ *212/473–9148* Ⓜ *Subway: 6 to Astor Pl.*

did you know?

Second Avenue was called the **Yiddish Rialto** in the early part of the 20th century. Eight theaters between Houston and 14th streets showed Yiddish-language musicals, revues, and melodramas. Embedded in the sidewalk in front of the Second Avenue Deli (156 2nd Ave., at 10th St.) are Hollywood-style squares that commemorate the Yiddish stage luminaries.

🖑 ❼ Merchant's House Museum. Built in 1831–32, this redbrick house, combining federal and Greek Revival styles, provides a rare glimpse of family life in the mid-19th century. Retired merchant Seabury Tredwell and his descendants lived here from 1835 right up until it became a museum in 1933. The original furnishings and architectural features remain intact; family memorabilia are also on display. Self-guided tour brochures are always available, and guided tours are given on weekends. Kids tour free. ⊠ *29 E. 4th St., between the Bowery and Lafayette, East Village* ☎ *212/777–1089* ⊕ *www.merchantshouse.com* 🎟 *$8* ◷ *Thurs.–Mon. noon–5* Ⓜ *Subway: 6 to Astor Pl. or Bleecker St.; F, V to Broadway–Lafayette St.; R, W to 8th St.*

⓭ Ottendorfer Branch of the New York Public Library. Eager to improve the lives of fellow German immigrants then heavily populating the East Village, philanthropists Oswald and Anna Ottendorfer commissioned the construction of this library and adjacent German Dispensary (now Stuyvesant Polyclinic), which was designed by William Schickel in 1884. The Dispensary's ornamental terra-cotta, including busts of noted figures in medicine, was a rare design detail in the city at the time. ⊠ *135*

2nd Ave., between St. Marks Pl. and E. 9th St., East Village ☎ *212/ 674–0947* ⊙ *Mon., Wed., Thurs., 10–6, Tues. 1–8, Fri. 1–6* Ⓜ *Subway: 6 to Astor Pl.*

16 **Russian & Turkish Baths.** It's clear from the older Soviet–types devouring blintzes and Baltika beer served in the lobby that this is no 5th Avenue spa. But the three-story public bathhouse, which dates to 1892, isn't about pampering as much as a practical, hearty cleansing. There's a eucalyptus steam room, a redwood sauna, pull-chain showers, and an ice-cold plunge pool (45 degrees), and you're encouraged to alternate cooking in the hot rooms with plunges in the cold pool to stimulate circulation, a bathing cultures staple. Traditional treatments are offered without appointment, such as the detoxifying Platza Oak Leaf ($30), in which a Russian strongman or woman swats your soapy skin with an oak-leaf broom. Except for a few single-sex hours per week, the baths are coed. ✉ *268 E. 10th St., between 1st Ave. and Ave. A, East Village* ☎ *212/ 674–9250* ⊕ *www.russianturkishbaths.com* 🎫 *$25* ⊙ *Mon., Tues., Thurs., and Fri. 11 AM–10 PM, Wed. 9 AM–10 PM, weekends 7:30 AM–10 PM* Ⓜ *Subway: L to 1st Ave.*

need a break?

Pizza at **Two Boots** (✉ 74 Bleecker St., at Elizabeth St., East Village ☎ 212/777–1033), named for Louisiana and Italy, doesn't exactly tout tradition. The individual slices, meant to be eaten on the fly, are named after characters in TV and film, like Emma Peel and Mr. Pink, and represent two of two-dozen imaginatively topped options in the $4 range.

10 **St. George's Ukrainian Catholic Church.** Quite the standout on the block with its copper dome and three brightly colored religious murals on its facade, this ostentatious modern church serves as a central meeting place for the local Ukrainian community. Built in 1977, it took the place of the more modest Greek Revival–style St. George's Ruthenian Church. An annual Ukrainian folk festival is held here in the spring. ✉ *30 E. 7th St., between 2nd and 3rd Aves., East Village* ☎ *212/674–1615* ⊙ *Services: Mon.–Sat. 6:15, 7:45, 8:30, Sun. 7, 8:30, 10, and noon* Ⓜ *Subway: 6 to Astor Pl.*

14 **St. Mark's-in-the-Bowery Church.** This charming 1799 fieldstone country church stands its ground against the monotonous city block system. The area was once Dutch governor Peter Stuyvesant's *bouwerie*, or farm, and the church occupies the former site of his family chapel. St. Mark's is the city's oldest continually used Christian church site, and both Stuyvesant and Commodore Perry are buried here. Over the years St. Mark's has hosted progressive events, mostly in the arts. In the 1920s a pastor injected the Episcopal ritual with Native American chants, Greek folk dancing, and Eastern mantras. William Carlos Williams, Amy Lowell, and Carl Sandburg once read here, and Isadora Duncan, Harry Houdini, and Merce Cunningham also performed here. Today the dancers of Danspace, poets of the Poetry Project, and theater artists in the Ontological Hysteric Theater perform in the main sanctuary, where pews have been removed to accommodate them. ✉ *131 E. 10th St., at*

2nd Ave., East Village ☎ *212/674–6377* Ⓜ *Subway: 6 to Astor Pl.; L to 3rd Ave.*

⑫ **St. Marks Place.** The longtime hub of the edgy East Village, St. Marks Place is the name given to East 8th Street between 3rd Avenue and Avenue A. During the 1950s beatniks such as Allen Ginsberg and Jack Kerouac lived and wrote in the area; the 1960s brought Bill Graham's Fillmore East concerts, the Electric Circus, and hallucinogenic drugs. The black-clad, pink-haired, or shaved-head punks followed, and the imaginatively pierced rockers and heavily made-up goths have replaced them. The blocks between 2nd and 3rd avenues have mostly ethnic restaurants, jewelry stalls, and stores selling incense and vinyl clothing. Despite NYU dorms in the vicinity, even the ubiquitous Gap chain couldn't take root on this raggedy and idiosyncratic street.

At 80 St. Marks Place, near 1st Avenue, is the Pearl Theatre Company, which performs classic plays from around the world. The handprints, footprints, and autographs of such past screen luminaries as Joan Crawford, Ruby Keeler, Joan Blondell, and Myrna Loy are embedded in the sidewalk. At 96–98 St. Marks Place (between 1st Ave. and Ave. A) stands the building that was photographed for the cover of Led Zeppelin's *Physical Graffiti* album. The cafés between 2nd Avenue and Avenue A attract customers late into the night. Ⓜ *Subway: 6 to Astor Pl.*

here's
where

Historical documents notwithstanding, many claim that the New York egg cream hatched at **Gem Spa** (✉ 131 2nd Ave., East Village ☎ 212/995–1866), a 24-hour newsstand, just off St. Marks Place. Cold milk, seltzer, and chocolate syrup combine to make the historically rich beverage, which comes in two sizes: $1.50 for a small, $2 for a large.

★ ⮞ **①** **The Strand.** Serious book lovers make pilgrimages to this secondhand shop with a stock of some 2 million volumes (the store's slogan is "8 Miles of Books"). The stock also includes thousands of collector's items, and barely touched review copies of new books; these sell for 50% off. A separate rare-book room is on the third floor at 826 Broadway, to the immediate north of the main store. Before it moved to its present location in 1956, the Strand, opened by Ben Bass in 1927, was on 4th Avenue's Book Row. A second store is near South Street Seaport. ✉ *828 Broadway, at E. 12th St., East Village* ☎ *212/473–1452* 🕐 *Mon.–Sat. 9:30 AM–10:30 PM, Sun. 11–10:30* Ⓜ *Subway: Union Sq./14th St.*

⑨ **Stuyvesant Street.** This diagonal slicing through the block bounded by 2nd and 3rd avenues and East 9th and 10th streets is unique in Manhattan: it's the oldest street laid out precisely along an east–west axis. (This grid never caught on, and instead a street grid following the island's geographic orientation was adopted.) Among the handsome redbrick row houses are the federal-style**Stuyvesant-Fish House** (✉ 21 Stuyvesant St., East Village Ⓜ Subway: 6 to Astor Pl.), which was built in 1804 as a wedding gift for a great-great-granddaughter of the Dutch governor Peter Stuyvesant, and **Renwick Triangle,** an attractive group of carefully restored one- and two-story brick and brownstone residences originally constructed in 1861.

Surma, the Ukrainian Shop. The exotic stock at this charming little store includes pysanky (Ukrainian Easter eggs) and pysanky-making supplies, as well as Ukrainian books and magazines, musical instruments, and an exhaustive collection of peasant blouses. ✉ *11 E. 7th St., between 2nd and 3rd Aves., East Village* ☎ *212/477–0729* ⊕ *www.surmastore.com* ⊙ *Weekdays 11–6, Sat. 11–4* ⊙ *Closed Mon. in summer.*

⑰ Tompkins Square Park. This leafy spot amid the East Village's crowded tenements is a release valve. The square takes its name from four-time governor Daniel Tompkins, an avid abolitionist and vice president under James Monroe, who once owned this land from 2nd Avenue to the East River. Its history is long and violent: the 1874 Tompkins Square Riot involved some 7,000 unhappy laborers and 1,600 police. In 1988 police followed mayor David Dinkins's orders to clear the park of the many homeless who had set up makeshift homes here, and homeless rights and antigentrification activists fought back with sticks and bottles. The park was reclaimed, nonetheless, and reopened in 1992 with a midnight curfew, still in effect today. The park fills up with locals on mild days year-round, partaking in minipicnics; drum circles; the playground; and, for dog owners, two dog runs. East of the park at 151 Avenue B, near East 9th Street, stands an 1849 four-story white-painted brownstone where renowned jazz musician Charlie Parker lived from 1950 to 1954. The Charlie Parker Jazz Festival packs the park for one day in late August. ✉ *Bordered by Aves. A and B and E. 7th and E. 10th Sts., East Village* Ⓜ *Subway: 6 to Astor Pl.; L to 1st Ave.*

need a break?

At the northwest corner of Thompkins Square Park is **Life Cafe** (✉ 343 E. 10th St., at Ave. B, East Village ☎ 212/477–8791), a hangout featured in the hit Broadway musical *Rent*. This is the Village's answer to chain restaurants—familiar dishes like nachos and burgers here taste homemade.

⑮ Ukrainian Museum. Ceramics, jewelry, hundreds of brilliantly colored Easter eggs, and an extensive collection of Ukrainian costumes and textiles are the highlights of this collection, nurtured by Ukrainian Americans in exile throughout the years of Soviet domination. In 2005 the museum moved to its new home, with a greatly expanded collection of fine arts, folk arts, and photographic documentary archives. ✉ *222 E. 6th St., between 2nd and 3rd Aves., East Village* ☎ *212/228–0110* ⊕ *www.ukrainianmuseum.org* ￭ *$7* ⊙ *Wed.–Sun. 1–5* Ⓜ *Subway: 6 to Astor Pl.; L to 3rd Ave.*

THE LOWER EAST SIDE

The Lower East Side, bounded by the Bowery to the west and East Broadway to the south, which saw waves of American immigration of Europeans and Jews, then Hispanics and Chinese, is now a gentrified enclave, filled with students, young professionals, and artist types, who occupy small apartments in tenement buildings, once belonging to entire families. Popular restaurants, bars, and clubs draw crowds well beyond these

ROCK-AND-ROLL TOUR

FROM GLAM TO PUNK, *the East Village is rock music's beating heart. Start at the northeast corner of St. Marks and Second Avenue, where, at the Gem Spa newstand (131 2nd Ave.), the ground-breaking New York Dolls shot the back of their first album cover in 1973. The Manhattan-based band is credited with spurring punk scenes here and in England. Walk east along St. Marks to No. 19–25, the former site of the Dom Theater and the Electric Circus. Here, in the mid-'60s, Andy Warhol hung out, the Velvet Underground played, and everyone danced until dawn. It closed in '71, one of many happening venues from this era (including Max's Kansas City, just off Union Square, and Fillmore East on 2nd Avenue) that are no more.*

Down the block, at No. 96–98 St. Marks is where Led Zeppelin shot the cover for "Physical Graffiti" in 1974. In the early '70s, a new generation of American punk

rock bands surfaced in conjunction with a seedy bar called CBGBs. To reach it, backtrack to 4th Avenue and turn left. Fourth becomes the Bowery around 5th Street. In 1973, at 315 Bowery, between 1st and 2nd streets, Hilly Kristal opened his country, bluegrass, and blues venue, hence the CBGB acronym. But Kristal changed his tune, when Television, a pop-ish punk band, convinced him to host them, and other unsigned rock bands like the Ramones (from nearby Queens), Blondie, the Talking Heads, and Patti Smith for a night of rock. The decision created an era of music that still garners local nostalgia. In 2003, a stretch of 2nd Street at the Bowery, near CBGBs, was renamed Joey Ramone Place to commemorate the singer's death in 2001.

new locals on the weekends, especially along Ludlow, Orchard, and Clinton streets. And the cycle continues:Latin groceries once displaced for edgy bars such as Arlene Grocery on Stanton, are now meeting a similar fate. Luna Lounge, a popular music venue on Ludlow Street, is being demolished for luxury condos.

Numbers in the text correspond to numbers in the margin and on the East Village & the Lower East Side map.

a good walk

The Lower East Side juxtaposes old and new worlds, tradition and trendiness. Start your walk at Russ & Daughters (179 E. Houston St., between Allen and Orchard Sts.)—a destination for smoked fish, cream cheeses, and bagels since 1914—just steps from the 1st Avenue exit of the F-train. Then head east to Orchard, where you'll turn on Orchard, at the hip American Apparel store, a modern gateway to the historic Orchard Street Garment District strip.

Clothing bargains can be haggled for at a few remaining stores identified by their curbside clothes racks. At No. 157 is Orchard Corset Center, a dated shop still frequented for its bras and brassiere counselor that helps hard-to-fit types, but a younger generation of pricey fashion-furious boutiques such as Frock, across the street at No. 148, are much more common now. Continue south, crossing old Delancy Street (while humming Rogers and Hart's "Manhattan" that references it). To the east, Delancy ends at the Williamsburg Bridge. At Orchard and Broome streets, one block south, the **Lower East Side Tenement Museum** ⑲ brings a bygone era to life with its gallery, excellent gift shop, and docent-led tours of preserved tenements nearby.

☞ Walk two blocks east and take a right onto Essex Street. A block and half south, between Grand and Hester streets, is the Pickle Guys (49 Essex St.). These new-generation kosher picklers are all that remain of the numerous briny shops that once flourished along Essex. (This one gets packed before Passover.) Head north on Essex, back toward Delancy, then walk one block west to Ludlow Street, continuing north along the area's first gentrified stretch, now solidly lined with bars and shops.

At Rivington you can poke around in Toys in Babeland (No. 94), a sex shop for women on the northwest corner, or take the children and head right on Rivington for Economy Candy (No. 108), which is jam packed with barrels and boxes of sugary treats. Continue east past the incongruently modern Hotel on Rivington (No. 107), which was originally billed as the Surface Hotel, for the design magazine formerly aligned with it.

Walk two blocks to Norfolk and take a left. Halfway up the block on your right is the city's oldest synagogue (No. 172), which dates to 1850. It's now the Angel Orensanz Center for the Arts, named for the sculptor who purchased the synagogue when it fell into disrepair. Now the building is mostly a much-coveted wedding reception venue. Walk a half block up to East Houston and take a left, backtracking to the subway. Note the commemorative mural to salsa-music star Cecila Cruz, who died in 2003, across the street. Before you head to your next destination, refuel at the historic Katz's Delicatessen (205 E. Houston St.), at Ludlow Street, an eatery which anchors the area firmly in its immigrant past.

TIMING   The walk itself will take you less than two hours. More if you explore the shops and visit the galleries.

What to See

❷❸ **ABC No Rio.** Founded in 1980, this granddaddy of Lower East Side galleries exhibits art that is political in content and powerful in its imagery. ✉ *156 Rivington St., between Clinton and Suffolk Sts., Lower East Side* ☎ *212/254–3697* ⊕ *www.abcnorio.org* Ⓜ *Subway: F, V to 2nd Ave.*

❷⓿ **ATM Gallery.** Smartly curated shows (by artist William Brady) include new and established artists, from the luminous photos of Benjamin Collier to sculptor-printmaker Peter Gourfain's razor-sharp engravings and Vince Roark's geometric drawings. ✉ *170 Ave. B, between 10th and 11th Sts., East Village* ☎ *212/375–0349* ⊕ *www.ATMGallery.com* ☉ *Tues.–Sun. 11–6* Ⓜ *Subway: 6 to Astor Pl.*

⓵⑧ **Eldridge Street Synagogue.** This was the first Orthodox synagogue erected by the large number of Eastern European Jews who settled on the Lower East Side in the mid- to late 19th century. The lavish Moorish revival–style building has undergone a major restoration. Inside is an exceptional hand-carved ark of Italian walnut, a sculptured wooden balcony, and enormous brass chandeliers. Once the largest Jewish house of worship, it is now the Congregation K'hal Adath Jeshurun and Anshe Lubz. ✉ *12 Eldridge St., between Canal and Division Sts., Lower East Side* 🕾 *212/219–0888* ⊕ *www.eldridgestreet.org* 💲 *$5* 🕒 *Tours Tues.–Thurs. 11:30 and 2:30, Sun. 11–4 on the hr* Ⓜ *Subway: F, V to 2nd Ave.*

★ ㉒ **Gallery Onetwentyeight.** Inside the jewel-box space, artist Kazuko Miyamoto directs crisp and provocative group shows. ✉ *128 Rivington St., between Essex and Norfolk Sts., Lower East Side* 🕾 *212/674–0244* ⊕ *www.galleryonetwentyeight.org* Ⓜ *Subway: F, V to 2nd Ave.*

> **need a break?**
>
> **Teany** (✉ 92 Rivington St., between Orchard and Ludlow Sts., Lower East Side 🕾 212/260–4351) is a hipster's teahouse with vegan-leanings that's owned by the musician Moby. Nearly 100 varieties are served by the pot, which can be taken with tea sandwiches, salads, or vegan desserts. Teany To Go carries the same items next door. Locals rave about **Clinton St. Baking Company and Restaurant** (✉ 4 Clinton St., at E. Houston St., Lower East Side 🕾 646/602–6263), particularly as a place for brunch. There's usually a wait for the scrumptious biscuit sandwiches and pancakes with Maine blueberries, but it can be avoided by visiting on weekdays.

🖑 ⑲ **Lower East Side Tenement Museum.** Step back in time and into the partially restored 1863 tenement building at 97 Orchard Street, where you can squeeze through the apartments of Natalie Gumpertz, a German-Jewish dressmaker (dating from 1878); the Confino family, Sephardic Jews from Kastoria, Turkey, which is now part of Greece (1916); the Rogarshevsky family from Eastern Europe (1918); and Adolph and Rosaria Baldizzi, Catholic immigrants from Sicily (1935). The tour through the Confino family apartment is designed for children, who are greeted by a costumed interpreter playing Victoria Confino. This is America's first urban living-history museum dedicated to the life of immigrants—and one of the city's most underrated and overlooked, since the museum is the actual preserved residences. Walking tours, limited to 10 people, are regularly given. A small gallery at 90 Orchard Street, just off the excellent gift shop, displays photos and videos with interviews of Lower East Side residents past and present. ✉ *90 Orchard St., at Broome St., Lower East Side* 🕾 *212/431–0233* ⊕ *www.tenement.org* 💲 *Tenement and walking tours $13; Confino apartment tour $12* 🕒 *Museum daily 11–5:30; tenement tours Tues.–Sun., call or visit Web site for schedule; Confino apartment tour weekends hrly noon–3; walking tour Apr.–Dec., weekends 1 and 3* Ⓜ *Subway: F, J, M, Z to Delancey/Essex Sts.*

㉑ **Rivington Arms.** A tiny space with a quirky and casual mind-set, this gallery shows pieces such as the photographic-sound works of collective Lansing-Dreiden and portrait paintings by Mathew Cerletty. Owners Mirabelle Marden and Melissa Bent may be moving to more spacious accommodations soon; check the Web site for up-to-date information. ✉ *102 Rivington St., between Essex and Ludlow Sts., Lower East Side* 🕾 *646/654–3213* ⊕ *www.rivingtonarms.com* Ⓜ *Subway: F, V to 2nd Ave.*

Union Square to Murray Hill

WORD OF MOUTH

"[The Empire State Building] is a landmark not to be missed. Take the last elevator up and hit the deck with someone you love—even if it is foggy or overcast. Print tickets online (for the skyride too) and avoid the line."

—DonielleP

"Union Square is a great gathering spot for all sorts of young people, especially in nice weather. There are always skateboarders, break dancers, and other street entertainers."

—jdnyc

www.fodors.com/forums

Updated by
Jacinta
O'Halloran

Take the subway uptown from Union Square and you'll find yourself with a carload of New Yorkers as diverse and contrasting as the neighborhoods—modest, mature Murray Hill; fast, fashionable Flatiron; graceful, grand Gramercy; cool, candid Chelsea; unique, unconventional Union Square—who sit next to each other in this oft overlooked slice of Manhattan. You'll have to get off the train and walk and talk to really feel each neighborhood's vibe because it changes with every turn you take. You can exercise your body at Chelsea Piers and exercise your eyes in Chelsea's gallery scene; get a bellyful at Union Square Farmer's Market and an armload at the trendy stores nearby; daydream at Gramercy Park and pose at the Flatiron Building; swap favorite movie scenes at the Empire State Building, and be composed at the Morgan Library. Pick your pleasure.

MURRAY HILL, FLATIRON DISTRICT & GRAMERCY

The haste and hullabaloo of the city calms considerably as you stroll through the tree-lined neighborhoods of Murray Hill, the Flatiron District, and Gramercy, east of 5th Avenue between 14th and 40th streets. Although its name is fairly unknown, Murray Hill is a charming residential neighborhood—between 34th and 40th streets from 5th Avenue to 3rd Avenue—with some high-profile haunts, including the Morgan Library, the Church of the Incarnation, and King Kong's favorite hangout, the Empire State Building.

A little farther south, the Flatiron District—anchored by Madison Square on the north and Union Square to the south—is one of the city's hottest neighborhoods, bustling with shoppers and lined with trendy stores, restaurants, and hotels. Here stands the photogenic Flatiron Building, Madison Square Park, the Museum of Sex, and an elegant turn-of-the-20th-century skyline.

Gramercy Park, a leafy, dignified, and mostly residential neighborhood, is named for its 1831 gated garden square ringed by historic buildings and pricey hotels. Even though you can't unpack your picnic in this exclusive resident-only park, you can bask in its historic surroundings and literary significance. Gramercy's gems are the Players Club, the National Arts Club, a street named after writer Washington Irving, and the exclusive Gramercy Park.

Numbers in the text correspond to numbers in the margin and on the Murray Hill, Flatiron District & Gramercy map.

a good walk

Begin in Murray Hill at **Sniffen Court** ① ☞ on East 36th Street between Lexington and Third avenues. This charming—yet easily overlooked—enclave is a little reminder that if you walk too fast in this city you might miss a gem. With that in mind, stroll west along the tranquil tree-lined blocks to Madison Avenue. Turn south to see the impressive **Morgan Library** ② but don't let that Starbucks to your right hold your attention too long or you'll miss the **Church of the Incarnation** ③, Murray Hill's landmark Gothic chapel, at 35th Street. Cross the avenue to the **B. Alt-**

man Building/New York Public Library–Science, Industry, and Business Library (SIBL) ❹ on 34th street, and stop. This is a good spot to take in the full height and scale of one of the world's most recognizable silhouettes, the **Empire State Building** ❺. You might want to lower your head as you walk toward this 103-story landmark on 5th Avenue or you'll surely get run over by bargain-mad shoppers rushing to **Macy's** ❻ at 34th and Broadway.

Resist the sigh in your wallet—Macy's is a two-hour walk in its own right—and turn south on 5th Avenue, past the straining photographers outside the Empire State Building. On West 32nd Street a sign declares "6 I LOVE NY T-shirts for $10!"—a steal, and you'll only have to worry about your wardrobe once in the next week. Give thanks for your bargain at the **Marble Collegiate Church** ❼ on 29th Street and again at the **Church of the Transfiguration** ❽ across the avenue. Where 5th Avenue intersects with 27th Street is a discreet building that holds the **Museum of Sex** ❾.

Two blocks farther south on 5th Avenue is **Madison Square Park** ❿, a perfect spot for a brown-bag lunch. A walk through the shady square leads to Madison Avenue, where you can see the gold-top **New York Life Insurance Building** ⓫, which occupies the entire block between East 26th and 27th streets. The limestone beaux-arts courthouse, one block down at East 25th Street, is the **Appellate Division, New York State Supreme Court** ⓬. The lovely **Metropolitan Life Insurance Tower** ⓭, between East 23rd and 24th streets, is another classically inspired spire. On the southern edge of the park is one of New York's most photographed buildings— the 1902 **Flatiron Building** ⓮. This tall and triangular building tapers to the point made by the intersections of 23rd Street, Broadway, and 5th Avenue. It lends its name to the now trendy Flatiron District, which lies to the south between 6th Avenue and Park Avenue South.

From the park, walk east on 23rd Street to lively 3rd Avenue. A walk south will lead you into one of the city's loveliest neighborhoods, Gramercy. A right turn onto East 20th Street and you come upon **Gramercy Park** ⓯, the only private park left in the city. Stroll slowly past the park to soak in the peace and history and then walk south down tree-lined Irving Place to 17th Street. Going west on 17th, you are now within a few minutes of the thriving, pedestrian-friendly **Union Square** ⓰. This square hosts a popular farmers' market and is surrounded by bars and some of the city's most creative restaurants.

TIMING   This ramble from Murray Hill to Union Square will take you 1½–2 hours, with plenty of time to appreciate the views and vibes of your route. Walk off your breakfast and you can stop at the Empire State Building and hopefully beat the lines to buy tickets. Tickets in hand, you can then wander at your ease from Madison Square Park to Gramercy Park to Union Square Park. Have lunch, shop, enjoy the energy and of course the Union Square greenmarket (open all day every Monday, Wednesday, Friday, and Saturday), then catch a train uptown from 14th St./Union Square station to 34th Street and end your day watching the sunset from the Observation Deck of the Empire State Building.

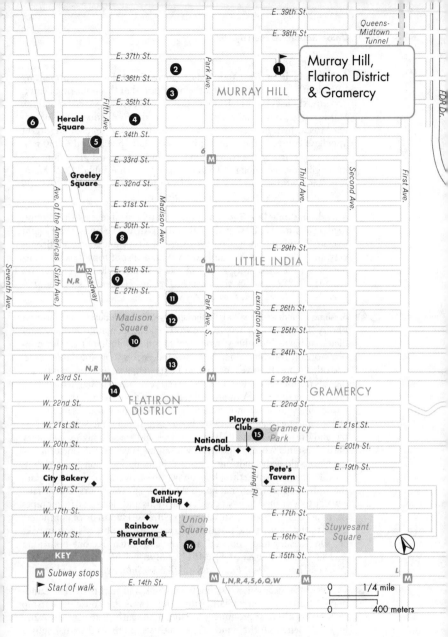

E. 39th St.

E. 38th St.

Queens-Midtown Tunnel

E. 37th St.

2

E. 36th St.

1

Murray Hill, Flatiron District & Gramercy

E. 35th St.

3

MURRAY HILL

6

Herald Square

E. 34th St.

4

5

E. 33rd St.

Ⓜ

Greeley Square

E. 32nd St.

E. 31st St.

E. 30th St.

7

8

E. 29th St.

LITTLE INDIA

Ⓜ

E. 28th St.

9

E. 27th St.

11

E. 26th St.

12

E. 25th St.

Madison Square

10

E. 24th St.

13

E. 23rd St.

Ⓜ N,R

W. 23rd St.

Ⓜ

GRAMERCY

14

W. 22nd St.

E. 22nd St.

FLATIRON DISTRICT

W. 21st St.

Players Club

Gramercy Park

E. 21st St.

15

W. 20th St.

National Arts Club

E. 20th St.

W. 19th St.

Pete's Tavern

E. 19th St.

City Bakery

W. 18th St.

Century Building

E. 18th St.

W. 17th St.

E. 17th St.

Rainbow Shawarma & Falafel

Union Square

Stuyvesant Square

W. 16th St.

E. 16th St.

KEY

16

E. 15th St.

Ⓜ *Subway stops*

▶ *Start of walk*

Ⓜ L,N,R,4,5,6,Q,W

Ⓜ L

Ⓜ L

E. 14th St.

0   1/4 mile

0   400 meters

Park Ave.
Fifth Ave.
Ave. of the Americas (Sixth Ave.)
Seventh Ave.
Madison Ave.
Broadway
Third Ave.
Second Ave.
First Ave.
Lexington Ave.
Park Ave. S.
Irving Pl.
FDR Dr.

What to See

⑫ **Appellate Division, New York State Supreme Court.** Figures representing "Wisdom" and "Justice" flank the main portal of this imposing beaux-arts courthouse, built in 1900 on the eastern edge of Madison Square. Statues of great lawmakers of the past line the roof balustrade, including Moses, Justinian, and Confucius. This is one of the most important appellate courts in the country: it hears 3,000 appeals and 6,000 motions a year. Inside the courtroom is a stunning stained-glass dome set into a gilt-covered ceiling. All sessions are open to the public. ✉ *27 Madison Ave., entrance on E. 25th St., Flatiron District* ☎ *212/340–0400* ⊙ *Weekdays 9–5* Ⓜ *Subway: R, W to 23rd St.*

Arnold Constable Dry Goods Store. Arnold Constable was the Bloomingdale's of its era. Designed by architect Griffith Thomas, this elegant five-story building spans East 19th Street with entrances on both Broadway and 5th Avenue. A double-story mansard roof tops it, white marble covers the Broadway side, and a cast-iron facade hovers over 5th Avenue. ✉ *881–887 Broadway, at E. 19th St., Flatiron District* Ⓜ *Subway: N, Q, R, W, 4, 5, 6 to Union Sq./14th St.*

🐾 ❹ **B. Altman Building/New York Public Library–Science, Industry, and Business Library (SIBL).** In 1906, department storemagnate Benjamin Altman gambled that his fashionable patrons would follow him here from his popular store on 18th Street in fashion row. Indeed, his shopping public came, and other stores followed for a while, but then moved uptown again, leaving this trailblazer behind. In 1996, seven years after the bankruptcy and dismantling of the B. Altman chain, the New York Public Library transferred all scientific, technology, and business materials from its main 42nd Street building to a new state-of-the-art facility here, the **Science, Industry, and Business Library (SIBL).** This sleek and graceful high-tech library heeds Ruskin's words, "Industry without art is brutality," one of many quotations along the undulant upper wall inside the Madison Avenue lobby. Further demonstrating this philosophy is the artwork within Healy Hall, the 33-foot-high atrium that unites the building's two floors. Downstairs a wall of TVs tuned to business-news stations and electronic ticker tapes beam information and instructions to patrons. Hundreds of computers wired to the Internet and research databases are the library's hottest tickets. On Tuesday and Thursday at 2 you can take a free one-hour tour. ✉ *188 Madison Ave., at E. 34th St., Murray Hill* ☎ *212/592–7000* ⊙ *Tues.–Thurs. 10–8, Fri. and Sat. 10–6* Ⓜ *Subway: 6 to 33rd St.*

❸ **Church of the Incarnation.** Dating from 1864, and subtitled "The Landmark Church of Murray Hill," this church was the house of worship to New York's most prominent families in the early 20th century. A fire in 1882 melted all the windows, so they were replaced with English- and American-design stained glass. The north aisle's 23rd Psalm Window is by the Tiffany Glass Works; the south aisle's two Angel windows, dedicated to infants, are by the William Morris Company of London. ✉ *209 Madison Ave., at E. 35th St., Murray Hill* ☎ *212/689–6350* ⊕ *www.churchoftheincarnation.org* ⊙ *Mass Wed. and Fri. 12:05; open Sun. after 11 AM mass* Ⓜ *Subway: 6 to 33rd St.*

⑧ **Church of the Transfiguration.** Known as the Little Church Around the Corner, this Gothic revival structure won its memorable nickname in 1870 after a nearby church refused to bury actor George Holland because those in his profession were thought to be "disreputable." His friends were directed to the "little church around the corner," and the church has been favored by theater-folk since. The south transept's stained-glass window, by John LaFarge, depicts Edwin Booth (brother of Lincoln's assassin) as Hamlet, his most famous role. A lych-gate and quiet garden separates the church from the busy street. Come inside the garden for a lovely view of the Empire State Building. ⊠ *1 E. 29th St., between 5th and Madison Aves., Murray Hill* ☎ *212/684–6770* ⊕ *www. littlechurch.org* ☉ *Mon.–Sat. 8–6, Sun. after 11* AM *mass* Ⓜ *Subway: R, W, 6 to 28th St.*

☾ **⑤** **Empire State Building.** It's no longer the world's tallest building (it currently ranks seventh), but it's one of the world's most recognizable landmarks, and still worth a visit. Its pencil-slim silhouette is an art-deco monument to progress, a symbol for New York City, and a star in some great romantic scenes, on- and off-screen.

Fodor'sChoice
★

Built in 1931 at the peak of the skyscraper craze, this 103-story limestone giant opened after a mere 13 months of construction. The framework rose at an astonishing rate of 4½ stories per week, making the Empire State Building the fastest-rising skyscraper ever built. Many floors were left completely unfinished so tenants could have them custom-designed. But the Great Depression meant most of the building remained empty, causing critics to deem it the "Empty State Building." It's cinematic résumé—the building has appeared in more than 200 movies—means that it remains a fixture of the popular imagination and that many visitors come to relive favorite movie scenes. With luck you'll find yourself at the top of the building with the *Sleepless in Seattle* lookalikes and not the *King Kong* impersonators. Today, millions of visitors fill its hallways and make the pilgrimage to the 86th floor observation deck for the reward of staggering views of the city.

However, getting to the observation deck of this behemoth means standing in three lines (security, tickets, and elevators), taking an elevator to the 80th floor, trekking through hallways to the tower shaft, and then taking a second elevator. You can buy tickets in advance on the building's Web site and avoid at least one long line; for an extra $6 you can rent a headset with an audio tour. The 86th-floor observatory (1,050 feet high) is open to the air (expect heavy winds) and spans the building's circumference. Bring quarters for the high-powered binoculars because the view is one to behold in any weather: on clear days you can see up to 80 mi; on rainy days you can watch the rain travel sideways around the building from the shelter of the enclosed deck; on snowy days you can watch the city's roofs disappear under a blanket of white; and on windy days, hold tight!

It's worth timing your visit for early or late in the day (morning is the least crowded time), when the sun is low on the horizon and the shadows are deep across the city. But at night the city's lights are dazzling.

The French architect Le Corbusier said, "It is a Milky Way come down to earth." Really, both views are a must; one strategy is to go up just before dusk and witness both, as day dims to night.

A major tourist attraction within the Empire State Building is the second-floor **New York Skyride.** A Comedy Central video presentation on the virtues of New York precedes a rough-and-tumble motion-simulator ride above and around some of the city's top attractions, which are projected on a two-story-tall screen. Since it's part helicopter video and part roller-coaster ride, children love it. ☎ *212/279–9777 or 888/759–7433* ⊕ *www.skyride.com* ✉ *$14.50; $26.50 for Skyride and Observatory* ✆ *Daily 10–10.* ✉ *350 5th Ave., at E. 34th St., Murray Hill* ☎ *212/736–3100 or 877/692–8439* ⊕ *www.esbnyc.com* ✉ *$14* ✆ *Daily 9:30 AM–midnight; last elevator up leaves at 11:15 PM* Ⓜ *Subway: B, D, F, N, Q, R, V, W to 34th St./Herald Sq.*

⓮ **Flatiron Building.** When completed in 1902, the Fuller Building, as it was originally known, caused a sensation. Architect Daniel Burnham made ingenious use of the triangular wedge of land and employed a revolutionary steel frame, which allowed for its 20-story, 286-foot height. Covered with a limestone and terra-cotta skin in the Italian Renaissance style, the ship's bowlike structure, appearing to sail intrepidly up 5th Avenue, was the most popular subject of picture postcards at the turn of the 20th century. When it became apparent that the building generated strong winds, ungallant gawkers would loiter at 23rd Street hoping to catch sight of a young lady's billowing skirts. Local traffic cops had to shoo away the male peepers—coining the phrase "23 skiddoo." Today, the building is occupied by publishing houses and stores. You can visit the lobby to look at photos but otherwise the building is best enjoyed from Madison Square, across the street. ✉ *175 5th Ave., bordered by E. 22nd and E. 23rd Sts., 5th Ave., and Broadway, Flatiron District* Ⓜ *Subway: R, W to 23rd St.*

> **need a break?**
>
> **Molly's Shebeen** (✉ 287 3rd Ave., between 22nd and 23rd Sts., Gramercy ☎ 212/889–3361) is a snug Irish pub complete with a friendly Irish staff, log-burning fireplace, and sawdust on the floors. You can enjoy a hearty burger or Shepherd's pie lunch but leave room for dessert—a creamy pint of Guinness.

⓯ **Gramercy Park.** In 1831 Samuel B. Ruggles, an intelligent young real estate developer (he graduated from Yale at age 14), bought and drained a tract of what was largely swamp and created a charming park inspired by London's residential squares. Hoping that exclusivity would create demand, access to the park was limited only to those who bought the surrounding lots. Sixty-six of the city's fashionable elite did just that, and no less than golden keys were provided for them to unlock the park's cast-iron gate. Although no longer golden, keys to the city's only private park are still given only to residents. Passersby can enjoy the carefully maintained landscaping through the 8-foot-high fence.

Lexington Avenue dead-ends here, so vehicles rarely venture near this quiet block. Original 19th-century row houses in Greek Revival, Italianate, Gothic revival, and Victorian Gothic styles surround the park's south and west sides. In the park stands a statue of actor Edwin Booth playing Hamlet; Booth lived at No. 16, which he purchased in 1888 to serve as the **Players Club** (✉ 16 Gramercy Park S, Gramercy Ⓜ Subway: 6 to 23rd St.), an association to elevate the then-lowly status of actors. Stanford White, the architect who renovated the club, was a member, as were many other nonactors. Other members over the years have included Mark Twain (who was once expelled, in error, for nonpayment of dues), John and Lionel Barrymore, Irving Berlin, Winston Churchill, Sir Laurence Olivier, Frank Sinatra, Walter Cronkite, Helen Hayes, and Richard Gere. Women were permitted to join the club in 1989. The club's library holds one of the largest theater collections in America.

The **National Arts Club** (✉ 15 Gramercy Park S, Gramercy) was once the home of Samuel Tilden, a governor of New York and 1876 presidential candidate, who installed steel doors and a tunnel to 19th Street for fear of the mob. Calvert Vaux, codesigner of Central Park, remodeled this building in 1884, conjoining two houses and creating a 40-room mansion. Among its Victorian Gothic decorations are medallions outside portraying Goethe, Dante, Milton, and Benjamin Franklin. The 2,000-member club, founded in 1898 to bring together "art lovers and art workers," moved into the mansion in 1906. Early members included Woodrow Wilson, Dwight Eisenhower, and Theodore Roosevelt; Robert Redford, Ethan Hawke, and Uma Thurman are more recent inductees. Although it's a private club, a number of rooms are open to the public— a great way to get a look around this exclusive property.

The austere gray-brown Friends Meeting House at 28 Gramercy Park South (1859) became the **Brotherhood Synagogue** in 1974, and a narrow plaza just east of the synagogue contains a Holocaust memorial. Dating from 1845, **19 Gramercy Park South** was the home in the 1880s of society doyenne Mrs. Stuyvesant Fish, a fearless iconoclast who shocked Mrs. Astor and Mrs. Vanderbilt when she reduced the time of formal dinner parties from several hours to 50 minutes (gasp!), thus ushering in the modern social era. ✉ *Lexington Ave. between E. 20th and E. 21st Sts., Gramercy* Ⓜ *Subway: 6, R, W to 23rd St.*

need a break?

Friend of a Farmer (✉ 77 Irving Pl., between E. 18th and E. 19th Sts., Gramercy ☎ 212/477–2188) is a two-story local favorite serving organic meats and vegetables, fresh-squeezed juices, and delicious sandwiches on homemade bread. Visit during the week as the buckwheat pancakes have a solid weekend following.

❻ Macy's. Occupying a full city block from 6th to 7th avenues between West 34th and 35th streets, with 11 floors and more than 2 million square feet of selling space, no one contests Macy's claim to be the world's largest store. Opened in 1857 by whaler Rowland Hussey Macy, the red star trademark is taken from his sailor tattoo. Equipped with the world's first modern escalators, Macy's introduced the consumer phenomenon of vertical shopping. You can still ride these narrow wooden steps today. Macy's stayed ahead of its competitors in the 1940s and 1950s, when it sold prefabricated houses, airplanes, and automobiles out of the ninth floor, and when it popularized Scrabble after a Macy's buyer discovered the Brooklyn invention. Today, the store is a must-stop shop for throngs of NYC shoppers but Macy's is perhaps best known for its sponsorship of the Thanksgiving Day Parade, July 4 fireworks, and its Christmas windows. Visit Macy's Flower Show in April when the store is blanketed with banks of tulips, sprouting orchids, and more than 30,000 varieties of flowers and plants to herald Spring. ⊠ *W. 34th St. between 6th and 7th Aves., Murray Hill* ☎ *212/695–4400* ⊕ *www.macys.com* ☉ *Mon.–Sat. 10–8:30, Sun. 11–7* Ⓜ *Subway: B, D, F, N, Q, R, V, W to 34th St./Herald Sq.*

🔟 **Madison Square Park.** The benches of this elegant tree-filled park afford great views of some of the city's oldest and most charming skyscrapers (the Flatiron Building, the Metropolitan Life Insurance Tower, the New York Life Insurance Building, and the Empire State Building) and serves as a perfect vantage point for people-, pigeon-, dog-, or squirrel-watching. Baseball was invented across the Hudson in Hoboken, New Jersey, but the city's first baseball games were played in this 7-acre park circa 1845. On the north end an imposing 1881 statue by Augustus Saint-Gaudens memorializes Civil War naval hero Admiral Farragut. An 1876 statue of Secretary of State William Henry Seward (the Seward of the term "Seward's folly"—as Alaska was originally known) sits in the park's southwest corner, though it's rumored the sculptor placed a reproduction of the statesman's head on a statue of Abraham Lincoln's body. ⊠ *E. 23rd to E. 26th Sts. between 5th and Madison Aves., Flatiron District* Ⓜ *Subway: R, W to 23rd St.*

here's where

On November 4, 1902, publisher William Randolph Hearst arranged for fireworks at Madison Square to celebrate being elected to Congress. The show, however, was poorly planned and a mortar containing 10,000 shells tipped over and caught fire. The ensuing explosion killed 17 people, injured 100, and blew out doors and windows of the buildings surrounding the square.

❼ **Marble Collegiate Church.** Built in 1854 for the congregation organized two centuries earlier by Peter Minuit, the canny Dutchman who bought Manhattan for the equivalent of $24, this impressive church takes its name from the Tuckahoe marble that covers the Romanesque revival facade. The bell in the tower has tolled the death of every president since Martin Van Buren in 1862. Don't miss the Tiffany-design windows depicting Moses and the burning bush. ⊠ *1 W. 29th St., at 5th Ave., Murray Hill* ☎ *212/686–2770* ⊕ *www.marblechurch.org* ☉ *Weekdays 8:30–8:30, Sat. 9–4, Sun. 8–3* Ⓜ *Subway: 6, R, W to 28th St.*

🔞 **Metropolitan Life Insurance Tower.** When it was added in 1909, the 700-foot tower resembling the campanile of St. Mark's in Venice made this 1893 building the world's tallest. The clock's four faces are each three stories high, and their minute hands weigh half a ton each; it chimes on the quarter hour. A skywalk over East 24th Street links the main building to its more austere sibling. The art deco loggias have attracted many film crews—the building has appeared in such films as *After Hours, Radio Days,* and *The Fisher King.* ⊠ *1 Madison Ave., between E. 23rd and E. 24th Sts., Flatiron District* Ⓜ *Subway: R, W, 6 to 23rd St.*

did you know?

The first Macy's Thanksgiving Day Parade in 1924 was called "Macy's Christmas Day Parade" although it took place on Thanksgiving. It included camels, goats, elephants, and donkeys. The Parade is the world's second largest consumer of helium after the U.S. government. Each year, balloons are floated through the parade. Due to a helium shortage in 1958, however, the balloons were brought down Broadway on cranes.

❷ **Morgan Library.** By the end of the 19th century, John Pierpont Morgan was one of New York's wealthiest financiers. To fulfill his desire to match Europe's great libraries, he created this opulent library of cultural treasures: medieval and Renaissance illuminated manuscripts, old-master drawings and prints, rare books, and autographed literary and musical manuscripts. In 1902 Morgan commissioned Charles McKim of McKim, Mead & White to design the Renaissance-style building, which was completed in 1906. Today, the Morgan is a world-class treasury with many of the crowning achievements produced on paper, from the Middle Ages to the 20th century, housed here: letters penned by John Keats and Thomas Jefferson; a summary of the theory of relativity in Einstein's own elegant handwriting; three Gutenberg Bibles; drawings by Dürer, da Vinci, Rubens, Blake, and Rembrandt; the only known manuscript fragment of Milton's *Paradise Lost;* Thoreau's journals; and original manuscripts and letters by Charlotte Brontë, Jane Austen, Thomas Pynchon, and many others. The **East Room** (the main library) has dizzying tiers of handsomely bound rare books, letters, and illuminated manuscripts. The **West Room,** Morgan's personal study, contains a remarkable selection of mostly Italian Renaissance furniture, paintings, and other marvels within its red-damask-lined walls.

Changing exhibitions, drawn from the permanent collection, are often highly distinguished. The library shop is within an 1852 Italianate brownstone, once the home of Morgan's son, J. P. "Jack" Morgan Jr., which is connected to the rest of the library by a graceful glass-roof garden court where lunch and afternoon tea are served. Outside on East 36th Street, the sphinx in the right-hand sculptured panel of the original library's facade was rumored to wear the face of architect Charles McKim. The library is closed for a redesign by architect Renzo Piano. It's scheduled to reopen in 2006 with twice the gallery space, an enlarged auditorium, and a café. ⊠ *29 E. 36th St., at Madison Ave., Murray Hill* ☎ *212/685–0610* ⊕ *www.morganlibrary.org* Ⓜ *Subway: B, D, F, Q, N, R, W to 34th St./Herald Sq.*

❾ **Museum of Sex.** The minimalist design, not-so-cheap admission fee, and studious atmosphere will be a cold shower to those who skimmed over the "museum" part of the name. Ponder the history and cultural significance of sex while staring unabashedly at vintage pornographic photographs, Playboy bunny costumes, S&M paraphernalia, and silent

SO MUCH FUN IT'S SCARY!

ALL THINGS WEIRD AND **WONDERFUL,** all creatures great and squall, all things witty and fantastical, New York City has them all—and on All Hallows Eve they are freaking through the streets in New York's Halloween parade. White-sheeted ghouls feel duller than dead as fishnets and leathers, sequins and feathers, pose and prance along 6th Avenue in this vibrant display of vanity and insanity.

In 1973, maskmaker and puppeteer, Ralph Lee paraded his puppets from house to house visiting friends and family along the winding streets of his Greenwich Village neighborhood. His merry march quickly outgrew its original, intimate route and now, decades later it parades up 6th Avenue, from Spring Street to 22nd Street, attracting 50,000 creatively costumed exhibitionists, artists, dancers, musicians, hundreds of enormous puppets, and more than 2 million spectators. Anyone with a costume can join in, no advance registration required, although the enthusiastic interaction between participants and spectators makes it as much fun to just watch.

The Parade lines up in front of the **HERE Arts Center** on 6th Avenue and Spring Street from 6:30 PM to 8 PM; the walk itself starts at 7 PM, but it takes about two hours to leave the staging area. Get here a few hours early. Costumes are usually handmade, clever, and outrageous, and revelers are happy to strike a pose. The streets are crowded along the route, with the most congestion below 14th Street. You can avoid the crush and take the subway to 23rd Street and walk south to find a good vantage point. Of course the best way to truly experience the parade is to march—if you're not feeling the facepaint, you can volunteer to help carry the puppets. For information, contact ⊕ www.halloween-nyc.com.

– Jacinta O'Halloran

movies. The subject matter ranges from the bawdy humor of Mae West and the development of vaudeville and burlesque to the sex trade and the emergence of AIDS. Evenings bring readings by cutting-edge authors and shows by avant-garde performance artists. For cheap thrills visit the museum's Web site and get a $5 discount on admission. No one under 18 is admitted, unless accompanied by an adult. ⊠ *233 5th Ave., at 27th St., Flatiron District* ☎ *212/689–6337* ⊕ *www.museumofsex.com* ⊠ *$14.50* ☾ *Sun.–Fri. 11–6:30, Sat. 11–8* Ⓜ *Subway: N, R to 28th St.*

⓫ **New York Life Insurance Building.** Cass Gilbert, better known for the Woolworth Building, capped this 1928 building with a gilded octagonal spire that is stunning when illuminated. The soaring lobby's coffered ceilings and ornate bronze doors are equally grand. P. T. Barnum's Hippodrome (1890–1925) formerly occupied this site, and after that Madison Square Garden. ⊠ *51 Madison Ave., between E. 26th and E. 27th Sts., Flatiron District* Ⓜ *Subway: N, R to 28th St.*

❶ **Sniffen Court.** Just two blocks from the Morgan Library, the 10 Romanesque revival former brick carriage houses that line this easily overlooked cul-de-sac were built by Architect John Sniffen in the 1850s. Peer through the locked gate to see the plaques of Greek horsemen hanging on the rear wall at the end of the flagstone paved alley. These were created by sculptor, and former Sniffen-Court resident, Malvina Hoffman. The cover of *The Doors* album *Strange Days* was shot here. ⊠ *150–158 E. 36th St., between Lexington and 3rd Aves., Murray Hill.*

Theodore Roosevelt Birthplace National Historic Site. The 26th U.S. president—the only one from New York City—was born here in 1858. The original 1848 brownstone was demolished in 1916, but this Gothic Revival replica, built in 1923, is a near-perfect reconstruction of the house where Teddy lived until he was 14 years old. Administered by the National Park Service, and decorated with many of its original furnishings, the house has five period rooms, two museum galleries, and a bookstore. Saturday afternoon chamber music concerts take place each fall, winter, and spring. ⊠ *28 E. 20th St., between Broadway and Park Ave. S, Flatiron District* ☎ *212/260–1616* ⊠ *$3* ☉ *Tues.–Sat. 9–5; guided tours 10–4* Ⓜ *Subway: 6, R, W to 23rd St.*

> here's
> where

On September 5th, 1882, more than 10,000 New York City union workers took an unpaid day off to march from City Hall to Union Square in the city's first Labor Day parade. The day was celebrated with picnics, speeches, and concerts. Twelve years later Congress passed an act making the first Monday in September a legal holiday to celebrate workers.

⓰ Union Square. A park, outdoor market, meeting place, and site of rallies and demonstrations, this pocket of green space is the focus of a bustling residential and commercial neighborhood. The name "Union" originally signified that two main roads—Broadway and 4th Avenue—crossed here, but it took on a different meaning in the late 19th and early 20th centuries, when the square became a rallying spot for labor protests; many unions, as well as fringe political parties, moved their headquarters nearby. The park's community role was never more apparent than after the terrorist attacks on September 11, 2001, when the park became the city's primary gathering point for memorial services. Thousands of people nightly lighted candles, created posters and signs, and otherwise gathered for consolation. The 1856 statue of George Washington (Henry Kirke Brown) at the north end of the park serenely overlooked the ceremonies. Other statues in the park include Abraham Lincoln (1866, Henry Kirke Brown) and the Marquis de Lafayette (1875, Frederic Auguste Bartholdi, who also sculpted the Statue of Liberty). A graceful statue of Gandhi (1986, Kantilal B. Patel), usually wreathed with flowers, is now surrounded by its own garden in the southwest corner of the park.

Union Square is at its best on Monday, Wednesday, Friday, and Saturday (8–6), when the largest of the city's 28 **green markets** brings farmers and food purveyors from all over the northeast U.S. Browse the stands of fruit and vegetables, flowers, plants, fresh-baked pies and breads, cheeses, cider, New York State wines, and fish and meat. On the north end, the park's 1932 pavilion is flanked by playgrounds and **Luna Park** (⊠ 1 Union Sq. E ☎ 212/475–8464), an open-air restaurant open from mid-May through October.

New York University dormitories, movie theaters, and cavernous commercial spaces occupy the handsomely restored 19th-century commercial buildings that surround the park. The run of diverse and imaginative architectural styles on the building at 33 Union Square West (the former name, the **Decker Building**, which is visible above the second floor's incised decoration) is, indeed, "fabulous"—it was the home of Andy Warhol's second Factory studio. The redbrick and white-stone **Century Building** (⊠ 33 E. 17th St., Flatiron District), built in 1881, on the square's north side, is now a Barnes & Noble bookstore, which has preserved the building's original cast-iron columns and other architectural details. The building at 17th Street and Union Square East, now housing the New York Film Academy and the Union Square Theatre, was the final home of **Tammany Hall.** This organization, famous in its day as a fairly corrupt yet effective political machine, moved here just at the height of its power in 1929, but by 1943 it went bankrupt and had to sell the building. A block south on Union Square East is the former U.S. Savings Bank, now the Daryl Roth Theater. The southern block is dominated by **The Metronome**, a public artwork and abstract timepiece displayed on the exterior wall of the Virgin Records superstore. The 15 digits display time coming and going relative to midnight. Read time going, from left to right and time coming, from right to left. The center three digits count fractions of seconds to reflect the frantic pace and energy of the city. ⊠ *E. 14th to E. 17th Sts. between Broadway and Park Ave. S, Flatiron District* Ⓜ *Subway: N, Q, R, W, 4, 5, 6 to Union Sq./14th St.*

need a break? City Bakery (⊠ 3 W. 18 St., between 5th Ave. and 6th Ave., Flatiron District ☎ 212/366–1414) serves a tempting array of tarts and pastries as well as lunch and dinner menu. On cool days, warm up with a richmarshmallowy hot chocolate. **Rainbow Falafel & Shawarma** (⊠ 26 E. 17th St., between 5th Ave. and Broadway, Union Sq. ☎ 212/691–8641), a hole-in-the-wall off Union Square has long, but fast-moving lunch lines testifying to its reputation for the best falafel in town. Get there early to beat the lunch-time rush and take your baba ghanoush, falafel, and grape leaves with plenty of extra napkins and grab a seat on one of the many benches in Union Square park.

CHELSEA

This stylish neighborhood has usurped SoHo as the world's art gallery headquarters and replaced Christopher Street in the West Village as New York's Gay central. Extending west of 5th Avenue from 14th to 29th streets, this former warehouse district brims with galleries, studios, dance clubs, bars, and restaurants. Restored historic cast-iron buildings along 6th Avenue house many of America's ubiquitous superstore tenants, who have helped revitalize the area. One-of-a-kind boutiques and pet-pampering salons along 7th, 8th, and 9th avenues are sprinkled among unassuming grocery stores and other remnants of Chelsea's immigrant past. Check out the Cushman Row town houses, dating from the 1820s, between 9th and 10th on 20th Street. If it's art you're seeking, the high-

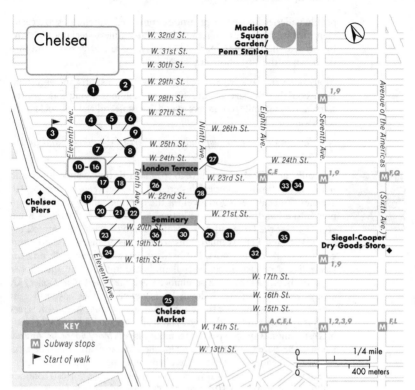

Chelsea

W. 32nd St.
W. 31st St.
W. 30th St.
W. 29th St.
W. 28th St.
W. 27th St.
W. 26th St.
W. 25th St.
W. 24th St.
W. 23rd St.
W. 22nd St.
W. 21st St.
W. 20th St.
W. 19th St.
W. 18th St.
W. 17th St.
W. 16th St.
W. 15th St.
W. 14th St.
W. 13th St.

Madison Square Garden/ Penn Station

Eleventh Ave.
Tenth Ave.
Ninth Ave.
Eighth Ave.
Seventh Ave.
Avenue of the Americas (Sixth Ave.)

London Terrace
Seminary
Chelsea Piers
Chelsea Market

Siegel-Cooper Dry Goods Store

KEY
Ⓜ Subway stops
► Start of walk

1,9
C,E
1,9
F,Q
1,9
A,C,E,L
1,2,3,9
F,L

0   1/4 mile
0   400 meters

profile galleries housed in cavernous converted warehouses are easily identified by their ultracool/cold, glass-and-stainless-steel doors. Many former warehouses, unremarkable by day, pulsate after dark and into the dawn as the city's hottest nightclubs.

Along the water, at 23rd Street, is Chelsea Piers, a sports and entertainment complex the size of four 80-story buildings laying flat. Sports-starved Manhattanites come here to golf, ice-skate, rollerskate, rockclimb, and swim.

Numbers in the text correspond to numbers in the margin and on the Chelsea map.

a good walk

To really "get" Chelsea you have to spend a little time wandering in and out of it's 190-plus galleries clustered mainly between 10th and 11th avenues. You can get a good feel for the thriving gallery scene by popping into a handful of galleries between 26th and 22nd streets. Begin your walk at the large industrial building of 526 West 26th Street, between 10th and 11th avenues. This art mall has big-name and no-name galleries on its many floors. Flit between **Joseph Helman** 3, and the **Clementine** 5 or just check the bulletin board in the lobby and choose impulsively. Across the street at number 524 is the **Robert Miller Gallery** 6, always worth a visit. Walk down 10th Avenue weaving east and west off the avenue as you spot the tell-tale industrial doors. West 24th Street is a busy gallery street with large open spaces housing some of Chelsea's biggest names. A quick visit to the major players **Mary Boone** 14, **Andrea Rosen** 16, **Barbara Gladstone** 10, and **Matthew Marks** 15 and you'll be talking the talk having glimpsed the latest in painting, photography, and sculpture. If you're just getting warmed up to the gallery scene, you can continue walking downtown on 10th veering off to its side streets for serendipitous discoveries—don't miss the **Chelsea Art Museum** 19 on the corner of West 22nd Street and 11th Avenue. However, if you find yourself admiring the creativity of the garbage display outside the **Gagosian** 12 you should take your befuddled self west and head down 8th Avenue from 23rd Street.

23rd Street was once the heart of the entertainment district, lined with theaters, music halls, and beer gardens. One of the more famous reminders of its heyday is the landmark **Chelsea Hotel** 34, between 7th and 8th avenues. The residential heart of Chelsea is between 19th and 23rd streets, from 8th to 10th avenues. To get a quick feel for 8th Avenue, head to 19th Street to see the art moderne **Joyce Theater** 32. Its presence helped attract many good restaurants to the avenue. You've feasted your senses in the galleries now feast your appetite at the **Chelsea Market** 25, a treasure trove of gourmet and specialty stores housed in an industrial building filling the entire block between 9th and 10th avenues on 15th Street.

TIMING You can walk Chelsea in two hours. Art appreciators should plan to spend the day, however, and take time to browse the galleries and stores and have a leisurely lunch. Typical gallery hours are Tuesday–Saturday 10–6. Many galleries are closed the entire month of August, and between Christmas and New Year's.

What to See

B. Altman Dry Goods Store. Built in 1877 with additions in 1887 and 1910, this ornate cast-iron giant originally housed B. Altman Dry Goods until the business moved in 1906 to its imposing quarters at 5th Avenue and 34th Street. ⊠ *621 6th Ave., between W. 18th and W. 19th Sts., Chelsea* Ⓜ *Subway: F, V to 14th St.*

⑲ Chelsea Art Museum. Housed in a former Christmas ornament factory, this museum was created to display a collection of postwar European art and to host traveling exhibitions from European museums. Today, the museum is home to the extensive works of French abstract painter Jean Miotte as well as works by sculptor Pol Bury and *affichiste* (poster designer) Mimmo Rotella. ⊠ *556 W. 22nd St., at 11th Ave., Chelsea* ☎ *212/255–0719* ⊕ *www.chelseaartmuseum.org* 🎟 *$6* ◔ *Tues.–Sat. noon–6, Sun. noon–8.*

㉞ Chelsea Hotel. Constructed of red brick with lacy wrought-iron balconies and a mansard roof, this 11-story neighborhood landmark opened in 1884 as a cooperative apartment house. It became a hotel in 1905, although it has always catered to long-term tenants, with a tradition of broad-mindedness that has attracted many creative types. Its literary roll call of former live-ins includes Mark Twain, Eugene O'Neill, O. Henry, Thomas Wolfe, Tennessee Williams, Vladimir Nabokov, Mary McCarthy, Brendan Behan, Arthur Miller, Dylan Thomas, William S. Burroughs, and Arthur C. Clarke (who wrote the script for *2001: A Space Odyssey* while living here). In 1966 Andy Warhol filmed a group of fellow artists, including Brigid Polk and Nico, in eight rooms; the footage eventually became included in *The Chelsea Girls* (1967). The hotel was also seen on screen in *I Shot Andy Warhol* (1996) and *Sid and Nancy* (1986), a dramatization of the real-life murder of Nancy Spungen, who was stabbed to death here by her boyfriend, punk rocker Sid Vicious. The shabby aura of the hotel is part of its allure. Read the commemorative plaques outside, then check out the eclectic collection of art in the lobby, some donated in lieu of rent by residents down on their luck. In the building's basement, accessible from the street, is the plush lounge Serena. ⊠ *222 W. 23rd St., between 7th and 8th Aves., Chelsea* ☎ *212/243–3700* ⊕ *www.hotelchelsea.com* Ⓜ *Subway: 1, 9, C, E to 23rd St.*

☾ ㉕ Chelsea Market. In the former Nabisco plant, where the first Oreos were baked in 1912, nearly two-dozen food wholesalers flank what is possibly the city's longest interior walkway in a single building—from 9th to 10th avenues. The market's funky industrial design—the awning outside is a tangle of glass and metal and inside a factory pipe has been converted into an indoor waterfall—complements the eclectic assortment of bakers, butchers, florists, and wine merchants inside. Many establishments sell their products to a number of New York restaurants. The wholesale kitchens are on display behind glass so kids can watch cookies, breads, and soups being made. ⊠ *75 9th Ave., between W. 15th and W. 16th Sts., Chelsea* ☎ *212/243–6005* ⊕ *www.chelseamarket.com* ◔ *Daily 8–8* Ⓜ *Subway: A, C, E, L to 14th St.*

Chelsea Piers. Beginning in 1910, the Chelsea Piers were the launching point for a new generation of big ocean liners, including the *Lusitania*, the British liner sunk by a German submarine in 1915. Even the *Titanic* planned to dock here at the end of its ill-fated journey. Decades-long neglect ended with the transformation of the four old buildings along the Hudson River into a 1.7-million-square-foot, state-of-the-art sports and recreation facility, providing a huge variety of activities and several restaurants with river views, including the Chelsea Brewing Company, New York State's largest microbrewery. Private trips on the river via speedboat or yacht can be arranged by **Surfside 3 Marina** (☎ 212/336–7873). ✉ *Piers 59–62 on Hudson River from 17th to 23rd Sts.; entrance at 23rd St., Chelsea* ☎ *212/336–6666* ⊕ *www.chelseapiers.com.*

> **did you know?**
>
> The *Titanic* was scheduled to arrive at Chelsea Piers on April 16, 1912. Fate intervened and the "unsinkable" ship struck an iceberg on April 14 and sank. Of the 2,200 passengers aboard, 675 were rescued by the Cunard liner *Carpathia*, which arrived at Chelsea Piers eight days later.

30 Cushman Row. This string of homes between 9th and 10th avenues represents some of the country's most perfect examples of Greek Revival town houses. Original details include small wreath-encircled attic windows, deeply recessed doorways with brownstone frames, and striking iron balustrades and fences. Note the pineapples, a traditional symbol of welcome, on top of the black iron newels in front of No. 416. ✉ *406–418 W. 20th St., between 9th and 10th Aves., Chelsea* Ⓜ *Subway: C, E to 23rd St.*

26 Empire Diner. This a gleaming stainless-steel hash house from the 1940s couldn't be more out of place among all the brownstones, and that's part of the appeal. Appealing as vinyl booths might be, your best bet is one of the tables outside. ✉ *210 10th Ave., at W. 22nd St., Chelsea* ☎ *212/243–2736* ⊙ *Open 24 hrs.*

29 General Theological Seminary. The secretive grounds of this seminary are usually only discovered by stealth city explorers. The campus, which is hard to see behind the heavy exterior fencing, is accessible through the unremarkable 1960s-era building on 9th Avenue. Inside are administrative offices, a bookstore, and the 240,000-volume **St. Mark's Library**, among the nation's greatest ecclesiastical libraries, with a world-class collection of Latin and English Bibles. When Chelsea developer Clement Clarke Moore divided his estate, he deeded a block-size section to the Episcopal seminary, where he taught Hebrew and Greek. Most of the school was completed in 1883–1902, when the school hired architect Charles Coolidge Haight, who pioneered the English Collegiate Gothic style, to design a campus to rival all other American colleges of the day. It worked. The hushed interior and the elm- and oak-graced lawns "sustain the pastoral illusion better than anything in New York besides Central Park," according to architecture critic Paul Goldberger. ✉ *175 9th Ave., at W. 20th St., Chelsea* ☎ *212/243–5150* ⊕ *www.gts.edu* ⊙ *Grounds weekdays noon–3, Sat. 11–3; call for information on using library* Ⓜ *Subway: C, E to 23rd St.*

You can sit for hours without being disturbed at **Le Gamin** (⊠ 183 9th Ave., at W. 21st St., Chelsea ☎212/243–8864), a rustic French café where soup-bowl-size café au lait, crepes, and salads are de rigueur.

Hugh O'Neill Dry Goods Store. Constructed in 1875, this cast-iron building, originally an emporium, features Corinthian columns and pilasters; its corner towers were once topped with huge bulbous domes. The name of the original tenant is proudly displayed on the pediment. ⊠ 655–671 6th Ave., between W. 20th and W. 21st Sts., Chelsea Ⓜ Subway: N, R, W to 23rd St.

㉘ James N. Wells House. This 1832 2½-story brick house was the home of Clement Clarke Moore's property manager, the man who planned Chelsea. Wells was responsible for the strict housing codes that created the elegant residential neighborhood by prohibiting stables and manure piles and requiring tree planting. ⊠ 401 W. 21st St., between 9th and 10th Aves., Chelsea Ⓜ Subway: C, E to 23rd St.

㉜ Joyce Theater. When the former Elgin movie house built in 1942 was gutted, what emerged in 1982 was this sleek modern theater with art moderne touches. Today it's one of the city's leading modern-dance venues. ⊠ 175 8th Ave., at W. 19th St., Chelsea ☎212/242–0800 ⊕ www.joyce. org Ⓜ Subway: C, E to 23rd St.

㉗ London Terrace. When this 20-story, block-long wall of red and black brick first opened in 1931, it was the largest apartment building in the world complete with state-of-the-art amenities. Creator and real estate mogul Henry Mandel jumped to his death from the top of his dream development when the Great Depression forced him into foreclosure. Today, the desirable 1,665 apartments are home to such stars as Isaac Mizrahi, Deborah Harry, and Annie Leibowitz. ⊠ W. 23rd to W. 24th Sts. between 9th and 10th Aves., Chelsea ⊕ www.londonterrace.com Ⓜ Subway: C, E to 23rd St.

☾ Pier 63. Despite the name, Pier 63 isn't actually a pier. Once owned by the Erie-Lackawanna Railroad, the 320-foot barge once carried freight trains across the Hudson River. It's now open to the public, free of charge so you can come sit by the water and watch locals take a spin in kayaks and outrigger canoes. Docked here is the *Bertha,* a tugboat built in 1925, the *Frying Pan,* a lighthouse boat dating from 1929, and the *John J. Harvey,* a retired fireboat that can still pump 18,000 gallons of water per minute more than 70 years after its first voyage. ⊠ Hudson River at 23rd St., Chelsea ☎ 212/989–6363 ⊕ www.pier63maritime.com ✉ Free.

㉛ St. Peter's Episcopal Church. Built in 1836–38 on a rising tide of enthusiasm for Gothic Revival architecture, St. Peter's is one of New York's first examples of early Gothic Revival, though retaining elements of Greek Revival style. To the left of the church, the brick parish hall is now the home of the Atlantic Theater Company, founded by playwright David Mamet. ⊠ 346 W. 20th St., between 8th and 9th Aves., Chelsea ☎ 212/ 929–2390 ⊕ www.stpeterschelsea.com Ⓜ Subway: C, E to 23rd St.

CHELSEA GALLERIES 101

GOOD ART, BAD ART, EDGY ART, **DOWNRIGHT DISTURBING** ART—it's all here waiting to please and provoke in the contemporary art capital of the world. For the uninitiated, the concentration of more than 250 galleries within a seven-block radius can be overwhelming, and the cool reception upon entering, intimidating. Art galleries are not exactly famous for their customer service skills, but they're free, and you don't need a degree in art appreciation to stare at a canvas. Wear your walking shoes, leave your preconceptions of "art" behind, and don't be intimidated—at the very least your gallery experience will provide some interesting dinnertime talk.

There's no required code of conduct, although most galleries are library-quiet. Don't worry, you won't be laughed at if you mistake the fire extinguisher for a cutting-edge statement and you won't be pressured to buy anything; in fact, if there's a person at reception, they'll most likely be doing their best to ignore you.

Galleries are open free to the public, Tuesday through Saturday from 10 AM to 6 PM. Gallery-hop on a Saturday afternoon—the highest traffic day—if you want company. You can usually find a binder with the artist's résumé, examples of previous work, and exhibit details at the front desk along with reviews if there are any. If not, ask. You should also ask if there's information you can take with you.

You won't be able to see everything in one afternoon so if you have specific interests, plan ahead. You can find gallery information and current exhibit details at ⊕ www.galleryguide.org (you can pick up a free hard copy at any gallery desk). Sift further through your choices by checking the "Art Guide" in Friday's weekend section of the New York Times and the Chelsea Art section of Time Out New York magazine. You can also learn more about the galleries and the genres and artists they represent at ⊕ www.artincontext.org.

— Jacinta O'Halloran

---

need a break? Havana-Chelsea Luncheonette (⊠ 190 8th Ave., between W. 19th and W. 20th Sts., Chelsea ☎ 212/243–9421) dishes out its famous black beans, octopus salad, and belt-popping Cuban sandwich in a no-frills diner.

Siegel-Cooper Dry Goods Store. Built in 1896, much later than its neighbors, this impressive building adorned with glazed terra-cotta encompasses 15½ acres of space, and yet it was built in only five months. In its retail heyday, the store had an immense fountain on its main floor—a circular marble terrace with an enormous white-marble-and-brass replica of *The Republic,* the statue Daniel Chester French displayed at the 1883 Chicago World's Fair—which became a favorite rendezvous point for New Yorkers. During World War I the site was a military hospital. The building's splendid exterior ornamentation contrasts with its otherwise unremarkable brick facade. Today its principal tenants are Bed Bath & Beyond, Filene's Basement, and T. J. Maxx. ⊠ 620 6th Ave., between W. 18th and W. 19th Sts., Chelsea Ⓜ Subway: F, V to 14th St.

ART GALLERIES **Andrea Rosen.** The gallery showcases artists on the cutting edge, such
⑯ as sculptor Andrea Zittel, painter John Currin, and photographer Felix

Gonzalez-Torres. Most every form of artistic expression—from painting to film to performance—is explored here. ✉ *525 W. 24th St., between 10th and 11th Aves., Chelsea* ☎ *212/627–6000* ⊕ *www.andrearosengallery.com* Ⓜ *Subway: C, E to 23rd St.*

⑩ **Barbara Gladstone.** An international roster of artists is cultivated here including sculptor Anish Kapoor, photographer Sharon Lockhart, and painter Lary Pittman. ✉ *515 W. 24th St., between 10th and 11th Aves., Chelsea* ☎ *212/206–9300* ⊕ *www.gladstonegallery.com* Ⓜ *Subway: C, E to 23rd St.*

❼ **Cheim & Read.** This prestigious gallery represents modern painters and photographers such as Louise Bourgeois, and shows work by the late Jean-Michel Basquiat, Andy Warhol, and Diane Arbus. ✉ *547 W. 25th St., between 10th and 11th Aves., Chelsea* ☎ *212/242–7727* ⊕ *www.cheimread.com* Ⓜ *Subway: C, E to 23rd St.*

❺ **Clementine.** Works from artists to keep your eye on—especially painters and photographers—are shown in this intimate Chelsea spot, a favorite of cutting-edge connoisseurs. ✉ *526 W. 26th St., between 10th and 11th Aves., Chelsea* ☎ *212/243–5937* ⊕ *www.clementine-gallery.com* Ⓜ *Subway: C, E to 23rd St.*

FodorsChoice
★

㉔ **David Zwirner.** Proving his finger is on the pulse of contemporary art, Zwirner shows works in all media by such emerging artists as Luc Tuymans, Stan Douglas, Thomas Ruff, Diana Thater, and Yutaka Sone, as well as such contemporary masters as Cy Twombly and Georg Baselitz. ✉ *525 W. 19th St., between 10th and 11th Aves., Chelsea* ☎ *212/727–2070* ⊕ *www.davidzwirner.com* Ⓜ *Subway: C, E to 23rd St.*

need a break? **Petite Abeille** (✉ 107 W. 18th St., near 6th Ave., Chelsea ☎ 212/604–9350) serves tasty café standards in addition to traditional Belgian waffles, chocolates, and cookies. Tintin, the Belgian comic book hero, brightens the walls.

⑫ **Gagosian.** This enterprising modern gallery has two branches in New York City (the other's on the Upper East Side), one in Beverly Hills, and one in London, all presenting works by heavy hitters, such as sculptor Richard Serra and the late pop art icon Roy Lichtenstein. ✉ *555 W. 24th St., at 11th Ave., Chelsea* ☎ *212/741–1111* ⊕ *www.gagosian.com* Ⓜ *Subway: C, E to 23rd St.*

❹ **Galerie Lelong.** This Paris-based gallery presents challenging installations such as Alfred Jaar's 2002 "Lament of the Images" and works by Andy Goldsworthy, Cildo Meireles, and Petah Coyne, among others. ✉ *528 W. 26th St., between 10th and 11th Aves., Chelsea* ☎ *212/315–0470* Ⓜ *Subway: C, E to 23rd St.*

㉝ **Holly Solomon.** Solomon's foresight is legendary—she was an early champion of photographer Robert Mapplethorpe—and now she shows works by artists such as William Wegman and Nick Waplington. ✉ *Room 425, Chelsea Hotel, 222 W. 23rd St., between 7th and 8th Aves., Chelsea* ☎ *212/941–5777* Ⓜ *Subway: C, E to 23rd St.*

㉓ **Jack Shainman.** Both emerging and established artists are shown here. You might find works by Phil Frost, whose imagery is derived from graffiti. The duo of Aziz + Cucher make digital photos of figures with erased features, suggesting body imaging gone awry. ✉ *513 W. 20th St., between 10th and 11th Aves., Chelsea* ☎ *212/645–1701* ⊕ *www.jackshainman.com* Ⓜ *Subway: C, E to 23rd St.*

❷ **JG/Contemporary.** In the northernmost reaches of Chelsea, this gallery always surprises with contemporary artists ranging from the internationally established Dutch painter Karel Appel to Patrick Strzelec, who uses color-cast rubber tubes to define spatial relationships. ✉ *505 W. 28th St., between 10th and 11th Aves., Chelsea* ☎ *212/564–7662* ⊕ *www.jaygrimm.com* Ⓜ *Subway: 1, 9 to 28th St.*

❸ **Joseph Helman.** Contemporary masters such as Claes Oldenburg, Robert Moskowitz, Joe Andoe, and Tom Wesselman are shown here. ✉ *601 W. 26th St., between 10th and 11th Aves., Chelsea* ☎ *212/929–1545* Ⓜ *Subway: C, E to 23rd St.*

❾ **Klotz/Sirmon Gallery.** Fine 19th- and 20th-century photography is the focus of the exhibitions here. Shows range from the modern photo-realistic natural landscapes of Karen Halverson to the more playful portraits of photojournalist Jonathan Torgovnik. Also here are extensive collections from some of history's most important photographers including Josef Sudek, Berenice Abbott, and Eugene de Salignac. ✉ *511 W. 25th St., Suite 701, between 10th and 11th Aves., Chelsea* ☎ *212/741–4764* ⊕ *www.klotzsirmon.com* Ⓜ *Subway: C, E to 23rd St.*

⓭ **Luhring Augustine.** Since 1985 owners Lawrence Luhring and Roland Augustine have worked with established and less well-known artists from Europe, Japan, and America. ✉ *531 W. 24th St., between 10th and 11th Aves., Chelsea* ☎ *212/206–9100* ⊕ *www.luhringaugustine.com* Ⓜ *Subway: C, E to 23rd St.*

㉟ **Marlborough.** With galleries in London, Monaco, and Madrid, the Marlborough empire also operates two of the largest and most influential galleries in New York City. The Chelsea location (the other's in Midtown) shows the latest work of modern artists, with a special interest in sculptural forms, such as the large-scale work of Michele Oka Doner. Red Grooms, Richard Estes, and Fernando Botero are just a few of the 20th-century luminaries represented by Marlborough. ✉ *211 W. 19th St., between 7th and 8th Aves., Chelsea* ☎ *212/463–8634* ⊕ *www.marlboroughgallery.com* Ⓜ *Subway: C, E to 23rd St.*

⓮ **Mary Boone.** A hot SoHo gallery during the 1980s, this venue now resides both in Midtown and in the newer flash point of Chelsea. Boone continues to show established artists such as Barbara Kruger and Eric Fischl, as well as newcomers Tom Sachs and Micha Klein. ✉ *541 W. 24th St., between 10th and 11th Aves., Chelsea* ☎ *212/752–2929* ⊕ *www.maryboonegallery.com* Ⓜ *Subway: C, E to 23rd St.*

⓯ ⓴ **Matthew Marks.** At two Chelsea spaces Marks, one of the most influential art dealers in New York, shows prominent modern artists such as the painters Ellsworth Kelly and Willem de Kooning, as well as up-to-the-minute luminaries such as photographers Andreas Gursky, Inez van Lamsweerde, and Sam Taylor-Wood. ⊠ *522 W. 22nd St., between 10th and 11th Aves., Chelsea* ☎ *212/243–0200* ⊕ *www.matthewmarks.com* Ⓜ *Subway: C, E to 23rd St.* ⊠ *523 W. 24th St., between 10th and 11th Aves., Chelsea* ☎ *212/243–0200* Ⓜ *Subway: C, E to 23rd St.*

⑪ Metro Pictures. The hottest talents in contemporary art shown here include Cindy Sherman, whose provocative and often disturbing photographs have brought her international prominence. ⊠ *519 W. 24th St., between 10th and 11th Aves., Chelsea* ☎ *212/206–7100* Ⓜ *Subway: C, E to 23rd St.*

⑧ Pace Wildenstein. The Midtown specialist in 20th-century art gave up its SoHo location for this enormous space in Chelsea, which can fit the largest sculpture and installations and concentrates on upper echelon artists, sculptors, and photographers. Their roster includes Donald Judd, Elizabeth Murray, Chuck Close, and Sol LeWitt. ⊠ *534 W. 25th St., between 10th and 11th Aves., Chelsea* ☎ *212/929–7000* ⊕ *www. pacewildenstein.com* Ⓜ *Subway: C, E to 23rd St.*

㉑ Paula Cooper. SoHo pioneer Paula Cooper moved to Chelsea in 1996 and enlisted architect Richard Gluckman to transform a warehouse into a dramatic space with tall ceilings and handsome skylights. Now she has two galleries on the same block that showcase the minimalist sculptures of Carl André, the dot paintings of Yayoi Kusama, and the provocative photos of Andres Serrano, among other works. ⊠ *534 W. 21st St., between 10th and 11th Aves., Chelsea* ☎ *212/255–1105* Ⓜ *Subway: C, E to 23rd St.* ⊠ *521 W. 21st St., between 10th and 11th Aves., Chelsea* ☎ *212/255–5247* Ⓜ *Subway: C, E to 23rd St.*

> **need a break?** **Wild Lily Tea Room** (⊠ 511A W. 22nd St., between 10th and 11th Aves., Chelsea ☎ 212/691–2258) is a tranquil Japanese art-cum-food shop with circular koi pool. Teas with poetic names, such as Buddha's Finger and Iron Goddess, are served alongside salads, sandwiches, and desserts.

㊱ Postmasters. A former SoHo gallery, Postmasters shows new and established conceptual artists, with one room devoted to multimedia shows. Recent exhibits have included Claude Wampler's *Pomerania*—a series of photographs, sculptures, video, and drawings examining the artist's relationship with her pet Pomeranian. ⊠ *459 W. 19th St., between 9th and 10th Aves., Chelsea* ☎ *212/727–3323* ⊕ *www.postmastersart.com* Ⓜ *Subway: C, E to 23rd St.*

❻ Robert Miller. Miller, a titan of the New York art world, represents the estates of some of the biggest names in modern painting and photography, such as Joan Mitchell, Robert Mapplethorpe, and Diane Arbus. ⊠ *524 W. 26th St., between 10th and 11th Aves., Chelsea* ☎ *212/366–4774* ⊕ *www.robertmillergallery.com* Ⓜ *Subway: C, E to 23rd St.*

❶ Sean Kelly. Drop in here for works by top contemporary American and European artists including Marina Abramovic, Ann Hamilton, Cathy de Monchaux, and James Casebere. ⊠ *528 W. 29th St., between 10th* *and 11th Aves., Chelsea* ☎ *212/239–1181* ⊕ *www.skny.com* Ⓜ *Subway: 1, 9 to 28th St.*

⑰ Sonnabend. This pioneer of the SoHo art scene continues to show important contemporary artists in its Chelsea space, including Jeff Koons, Ashley Bickerton, and British art duo Gilbert&George. ✉ *536 W. 22nd St., between 10th and 11th Aves., Chelsea* ☎ *212/627–1018* Ⓜ *Subway: C, E to 23rd St.*

㉒ Tanya Bonakdar. This gallery presents such contemporary artists as Uta Barth, whose blurry photos challenge ideas about perception, and Ernesto Neto, a Brazilian artist who has made stunning room-size installations of large nylon sacks filled with spices. ✉ *521 W. 21st St., between 10th and 11th Aves., Chelsea* ☎ *212/414–4144* ⊕ *www. tanyabonakdargallery.com* Ⓜ *Subway: C, E to 23rd St.*

⑱ 303. International cutting-edge artists shown here include photographer Doug Aitken, painter Sue Williams, and installation artist Karen Kilimnik. ✉ *525 W. 22nd St., between 10th and 11th Aves., Chelsea* ☎ *212/255–1121* ⊕ *www.303gallery.com* Ⓜ *Subway: C, E to 23rd St.*

Midtown
Including Times Square & Rockefeller Center

4

Updated by
Mark Sullivan

Don't let the name fool you—this is more than the halfway point between the residential neighborhoods flanking Central Park and the financial center of Wall Street. It's a vibrant area known as much for its
nose-to-the-grindstone business ethic and its shop-'til-you-drop appeal.
Per square foot, Midtown has more major landmarks—Grand Central
Terminal, Rockefeller Center, Times Square, and the United National—
than any other part of the city.

TIMES SQUARE

Whirling in a chaos of flashing lights, honking horns, and shoulder-to-
shoulder crowds, Times Square is the most frenetic part of New York
City. It's a place where you seldom see anyone leaving. Hordes of people arrive every hour by subway, bus, car, or on foot, drawn by its un-
deniable gravitational pull. What brings them here? There's not much
to do—no great shopping, comparatively few notable restaurants, and,
except when they're raising the curtains in the theaters, a dearth of cultural offerings. Simply put, Times Square is a destination in itself.

Like many New York City "squares," Times Square is actually a pair
of triangles, formed by the angle of Broadway slashing across 7th Avenue between West 42nd and 47th streets. Many people walk past this
prestigious piece of real estate and never know it. But Times Square also
refers to the neighborhood. It has been the city's main theater district
since the turn of the 20th century: from West 44th to 51st streets, the
cross streets west of Broadway are lined with some 30 major theaters;
film houses joined the fray beginning in the 1920s.

After World War II, the area began a slow decline, and the once-grand
theaters on 42nd Street switched to second-run and adult movies. But
in the 1990s, when Disney was contemplating a complete renovation
of the decrepit New Amsterdam Theater, the city passed legislation that
sent them all packing. Today you can detect a faint whiff of the glory
days of 42nd Street. Historic theaters like the Selwyn have been revived
(albeit as the American Airlines Theatre), and the Lyric and the Apollo
have been combined (now known as the Ford Center for the Performing Arts). In between are high-price souvenir shops and fast-food restaurants. Many locals avoid the place, arguing that it resembles a shopping
mall. Maybe so, but it's hard to imagine there's a more eye-catching,
heart-racing commercial center anywhere else in the world.

*Numbers in the text correspond to numbers in the margin and on the
Midtown map.*

a good
walk

At the intersection of 7th Avenue and Broadway, the dazzling billboards
of **Times Square** ❶ ► will grab your attention. Zoning actually *requires*
that buildings be decked out with ads, as they have been for nearly a
century. You'll be mesmerized by its usual high-wattage thunder. The
42-foot-tall bottle of Coca-Cola and other crowd-pleasers are gone, but
there are still huge billboards of underwear models, superfast digital displays of world news and stock quotes, on-location broadcasts at television studios, and countless other technologically sophisticated
allurements.

Head two blocks north to the southwest corner of 44th Street. Here you'll probably encounter a crowd of teenagers gawking at the second-floor windows of **MTV Studios** ❷. Across 7th Avenue are the street-level studios of ABC, distinguished by two ribbons of light that flash up the latest headlines. Rockefeller Center may once have been a magnet for media conglomerates, but in the past few years Times Square seems to have been usurping its title. Nearby are the sky-high Reuters headquarters, at the corner of 7th Avenue and 42nd Street, and Condé Nast, at the northwest corner of Broadway and 42nd Street.

Head north to **Duffy Square** ❸, a triangle between West 46th and 47th streets that many people mistakenly refer to as Times Square. It's a bit more open than Times Square, so you get a better look at all the surrounding razzle-dazzle from here. Duffy Square is best known as the home of the TKTS booth. You can score good seats to some of the hottest Broadway shows for half the going rate.

Although people think of Broadway as the heart of the theater scene, few theaters actually line the thoroughfare. (The Winter Garden and the Broadway, both a few blocks north of the area traditionally called Times Square, are the most conspicuous.) In Times Square, the only theaters facing Broadway are the Marquis, in the hotel of the same name between 45th and 46th streets, and the Minskoff, between 44th and 45th streets. Both are rather recent additions to the Great White Way, and rather charmless. To see some of Broadway's grand old dames, head west on 45th Street. Here you can see a bevy of Broadway beauties, including the Booth, the Plymouth, the Royale, the Music Box, and the Imperiale. Farther down the block is the Hirschfeld, recently renamed in honor of the man whose caricatures of theater graced the pages of the *New York Times* for decades. On the southern side of 45th Street you can find the pedestrian-only Shubert Alley, distinguished by colorful posters advertising the latest hit plays and musicals. Its name is no mystery, as Schubert Alley takes you to one of Broadway's most lustrous gems, the **Shubert Theater** ❺. Head west along 44th Street to see its neighbors, the Helen Hayes, the Broadhurst, the Majestic, and the St. James. Tucked among them, at No. 243, is Sardi's, the legendary Broadway watering hole. In movies like *All About Eve*—and in real life—theater folk came here to wait for the reviews to roll off the presses.

Take a left when you reach 8th Avenue, the fringes of a neighborhood called Hell's Kitchen (or Clinton, as real estate agents prefer). On the northwest corner of 8th Avenue and 43rd Street stands the Second Stage Theater, a former four-story former bank that was redesigned by Dutch architect Rem Koolhaas. A block farther, the monolithic Port Authority Bus Terminal dispenses commuters, tourists, and those in search of some excitement onto the street or into the subway running beneath it. Take another left and you're on the most colorful block of the city's most famous thoroughfare, 42nd Street.

There's no doubt where you are, as even the McDonald's is covered with thousands of blinking lights. Dominating the southern side of 42nd Street is **Madame Tussaud's New York** ❼, where you can see life-size wax figures of major celebrities. You can still see several historic theaters—or at least their facades—along the street. The AMC Empire movie theater easily outshines the more recently built Lowes 42nd Street movie theater directly across the street. On the north side of the street you can pass the old Selwyn, now the American Airlines Theater, and the Lyric and the Apollo, combined to make the Ford Center for the Performing Arts (you enter via a slim entrance on 42nd Street—the main facade is on 43rd Street and worth a detour). To see a theater restored to its former glory, without being expanded or combined or converted to another use, head to the southwest corner of 42nd Street and 7th Avenue, to the **New Amsterdam Theater** ⑧.

Back on 7th Avenue, walk two blocks north, then head east on 44th Street. At the corner of 6th Avenue, turn around to see one of the city's quirkier landmarks, an electric sign tallying the national debt. Temporarily turned off during the surpluses on the Clinton years, it's now buzzing again, giving the total national debt and your family's share. Across 6th Avenue you can see the comfortably understated **Algonquin Hotel** ⑪, an old haunt popular among theater folk. The famous bar is a great place to relax after a tour of Times Square.

TIMING   This walk through Times Square and the theater district takes about an hour. Keep in mind that during most of the day and evening, Times Square and 42nd Street can be crowded. To avoid some of the congestion, consider walking around the area between 7 AM and 9 AM, when the city as well as most visitors are just waking up.

What to See

⑪ **Algonquin Hotel.** Considering its history as a haunt of well-known writers and actors, this 1902 hotel is surprisingly unpretentious. Its most famous association is with the Algonquin Round Table, a witty group of literary Manhattanites who gathered in its lobby and dining rooms in the 1920s—a clique that included short-story writer and critic Dorothy Parker, humorist Robert Benchley, playwright George S. Kaufman, journalist and critic Alexander Woolcott, and actress Tallulah Bankhead. One reason they met here was the hotel's proximity to the former offices of the *New Yorker* magazine at 28 West 44th Street (the magazine now resides in the Condé Nast tower on Times Square). Come here for a drink at the cozy bar, dinner and cabaret performances in the intimate Oak Room, or just stroll through the muraled lobby. ⊠ *59 W. 44th St., between 5th and 6th Aves., Midtown West* ☎ *212/840–6800* Ⓜ *Subway: B, D, F, V at 42nd St.*

❸ **Duffy Square.** This triangle of cement at the north end of Times Square is named after Father Francis P. Duffy (1871–1932), known as "the fighting chaplain" because of his bravery during World War I. He later served as pastor of Holy Cross Church on West 42nd Street. There's also a statue of George M. Cohan (1878–1942), the Broadway impresario who penned "Yankee Doodle Dandy." The square is one of the best places for a panoramic view of Times Square's riotous assemblage of signs. At its north end the red-and-white **TKTS** booth sells discounted tickets to Broadway and off-Broadway shows. ⊠ *In traffic island between W. 46th and 47th Sts., Midtown West* Ⓜ *Subway: R, W to 49th St.*

Hell's Kitchen. As the name suggests, the first waves of immigrants in this area stretching from West 30th to 59th streets, and between the Hudson River and 8th Avenue, did not find the living easy. The gritty appellation came either from a gang that ruled the area in the late 1860s, or a nickname cops gave it in the 1870s. Only a few decades ago the rough-and-tumble neighborhood wasn't any more inviting. Today Hell's Kitchen (or Clinton, as real estate agents call it) has been on the up and up since the early 1990s. Along 9th Avenue, sidewalks are lined with perhaps the world's largest assortment of ethnic cafés, restaurants, and groceries. Argentina, Brazil, Indonesia, and Sri Lanka are just some of the countries represented. Each May, the 9th Avenue Food Festival brings tens of thousands of people to the closed street for exotic tasting treats.

need a break?

The delicious and inexpensive baked goods and friendly service at **Amy's Bread** (⊠ 672 9th Ave., at W. 46th St., Hell's Kitchen ☎ 212/977–2670) have quickly made it a New York institution. The prosciutto and black pepper bread is a meal in itself. The pastry masters at **Poseidon Bakery** (⊠ 629 9th Ave., near W. 44th St., Hell's Kitchen ☎ 212/757–6173) have been rolling out beautiful homemade phyllo dough and putting it to delectable use since 1923. Try the *afali,* a bird's nest of pistachios and phyllo dough that's dipped in honey.

❿ International Center of Photography. This leading photography venue doubled its exhibition space when it moved to Midtown in 2001. The expansion included a large bookstore and a small café that's a great place to escape the Midtown crowds. Founded in 1974 by photojournalist Cornell Capa (photographer Robert Capa's brother), the center's exhibits from its permanent collection of 45,000 works often focus on one genre (portraits, architecture, etc.) or the work of a single prominent photographer. ⊠ 1133 6th Ave., at W. 43rd St., Midtown West ☎ 212/857–0000 ⊕ www.icp.org ☎ $10 ☉ Tues.–Thurs. 10–5, Fri. 10–8, weekends 10–6 Ⓜ Subway: B, D, F, V to 42nd St.

☾ ❻ Intrepid Sea-Air-Space Museum. Formerly the USS *Intrepid,* this 900-foot aircraft carrier is serving out its retirement as the centerpiece of Manhattan's only floating museum. An A-12 Blackbird spy plane, a Concorde, lunar landing modules, helicopters, seaplanes, and two-dozen other aircraft are on deck. Docked alongside, and also part of the museum, are the *Growler,* a strategic-missile submarine; the *Edson,* a Vietnam-era destroyer; and several other battle-scarred naval veterans. Children can explore the ships' skinny hallways and winding staircases, as well as manipulating countless knobs, buttons, and wheels. For an extra thrill (and an extra $8), they can try the Navy Flight Simulator and "land" an aircraft onboard. ⊠ Hudson River, Pier 86, 12th Ave. and W. 46th St., Midtown West ☎ 212/245–0072 ⊕ www.intrepidmuseum.org ☎ $17; free to active U.S. military personnel ☉ Apr.–Sept., weekdays 10–5, weekends 10–6; Oct.–Mar., Tues.–Sun. 10–5; last admission 1 hr before closing Ⓜ Subway: A, C, E to 42nd St.; M42 bus to pier.

❼ Madame Tussaud's New York. Go ahead, nuzzle Jennifer Lopez, air-kiss Julia Roberts, and heckle Regis Philbin. You can encounter all three celebs at this display of nearly 200 astoundingly lifelike historical, cultural, and popular characters in wax. The original Madame Tussaud's, which opened in London in 1835, is now England's top tourist draw; the opening of this branch on West 42nd Street confirms Times Square's status as New York's major entertainment destination. The realism of the American celebrities depicted in the "Opening Night Party" room may creep you out: crowded with A-list celebs and a gawking swirl of tourists, you can't tell who's fake anymore—though Woody Allen, grinning alone in a corner, seems to get the last laugh. You can also be filmed on a re-created *American Idol* stage or beside a figure of Al Roker doing the weather on the *Today Show.* ✉ *234 W. 42nd St., between 7th and 8th Aves., Midtown West* ☎ *212/512–9600* ⊕ *www.madame-tussauds.com* ✑ *$28* ☉ *Weekdays 10–9, weekends 10–11* Ⓜ *Subway: A, C, E to 42nd St.*

❷ MTV Studios. No group magnifies the energy of Times Square better than the throngs of teens who gather each afternoon in front of MTV's studios in the heart of the square, hoping to be chosen to be part of the show *Total Request Live. TRL,* as it's popularly known, is filmed live from the second-floor glass windows at West 44th Street and Broadway. Since such well-known performers as Usher and Jessica Simpson make regular rounds here, Times Square has become a mecca for youth. If you want to be in the studio audience, call ahead for tickets. ✉ *1515 Broadway, at 43rd St.* ☎ *212/398–8549* ⊕ *www.mtv.com* Ⓜ *Subway: A, C, E to 42nd St.*

❽ New Amsterdam Theater. The street's most glorious theater, neglected for decades, triumphantly returned to life in 1997 following a breathtaking restoration. Built in 1903 by Herts & Tallant, the art nouveau theater had an innovative cantilevered balcony and was the original home of the Ziegfeld Follies. After years of decay—the flooded orchestra pit was home to an 8-foot tree complete with birds' nests—the theater's new tenant, the Walt Disney Company, had the 1,814-seat art nouveau interior painstakingly restored. Outside, the 1940s-vintage art deco facade dates to the theater's days as a movie house. The stage version of Disney's *The Lion King,* which opened in 1997 to critical accolades and commercial success, is likely to run here for years to come. If you can't get tickets, you can call ahead to join a group tour, which reveal the now-gorgeous theater contrasted with large mounted photographs documenting its prerenovation disrepair. The theater's old, ruined state is captured in the movie *Uncle Vanya on 42nd Street.* ✉ *214 W. 42nd St., between 7th and 8th Aves., Midtown West* ☎ *212/282–2900, 212/282–2952 for information on theater tours* ☉ *Tour schedule varies* ✑ *Tours: $12* Ⓜ *Subway: A, C, E to 42nd St.*

❺ Shubert Theater. Among the most opulent on the Great White Way, this theater has had few tenants over the past few years. It hasn't been vacant, though; a couple of shows—*Chicago, Crazy for You,* and *A Chorus Line*—have dominated the stage since 1975. Other shows that stayed around for a while included 1939's *The Philadelphia Story,*

1956's *Bells Are Ringing,* and 1968's *Promises, Promises.* The theater, dating from 1913, was named for Sam S. Shubert, the eldest of the brothers who made an indelible mark on Broadway. Take a peek at the Renaissance-style interior, covered with gilt everywhere. ⊠ *225 W. 44th St., at Broadway* Ⓜ *Subway: A, C, E to 42nd St.*

need a break? Less than a block from Times Square, **Café Un Deux Trois** (⊠ 123 W. 44th St., at 6th Ave., Midtown West ☎ 212/354–6984) serves up a tasty croque monsieur. The Parisian-style bistro is open until midnight, making it a great place to go after a show.

► ❶ **Times Square.** Before the 1900s, this was New York's horse-trading center, FodorsChoice known as Long Acre Square. Substantial change came with the arrival of the subway and the *New York Times,* then a less prestigious paper, which moved here in exchange for having its name grace the square. On December 31, 1904, the *Times* celebrated the opening of its new headquarters, at Times Tower, with a fireworks show at midnight, thereby starting a New Year's Eve tradition. Now resheathed in marble and called **One Times Square Plaza** (⊠ W. 42nd St. between Broadway and 7th Ave., Midtown West), the building is topped with the world's most famous rooftop pole, down which an illuminated 200-pound ball is lowered each December 31 to the wild enthusiasm of revelers below. In the 1920s the *Times* moved to its present building, a green-copper-roof neo-Gothic behemoth that's half a block away at 229 West 43rd Street. ⊠ *W. 42nd to W. 47th Sts. at Broadway and 7th Ave., Midtown West* Ⓜ *Subway: 1, 2, 3, 9, N, Q, R, W to 42nd St./Times Sq.*

❹ **Times Square Visitors Center.** When it opened in 1925, the Embassy Theater was an exclusive, high-society movie theater; a few years ago the lobby of this landmark theater was transformed into the city's first comprehensive visitor center. Beyond getting general information about the area, you can buy sightseeing and theater tickets, MetroCards, and transit memorabilia; use ATMs; and log onto the Internet for free. There's also a video camera that shoots and e-mails instant photos. Free walking tours of Times Square are given Friday at noon. Perhaps most important, its restrooms are the only facilities in the vicinity open to the nonpaying public. ⊠ *1560 Broadway, between W. 46th and W. 47th Sts., Midtown West* ☎ *212/768–1560* ⊕ *www.timessquarebid.org* ☉ *Daily 8–8* Ⓜ *Subway: 1, 2, 3, 9, N, Q, R, W to 42nd St./Times Sq.*

❾ **Town Hall.** Founded by suffragists in 1921 seeking a venue from which to educate women on political issues (Margaret Sanger was arrested here on November 12, 1921, while speaking about birth control), Town Hall instead quickly became one of the city's premier musical venues when its acoustics were accidentally discovered in its inaugural year. The landmark McKim, Mead & White federal revival building was designed with democracy in mind—there are no box seats and no obstructed views, giving rise to the phrase "not a bad seat in the house." A mix of musicians and entertainers performs here, from world music groups to Garrison Keillor. ⊠ *123 W. 43rd St., between 6th and 7th Aves., Midtown West* ☎ *212/840–2824* Ⓜ *Subway: B, D, F, V to 42nd St.*

GRAND CENTRAL

Grand Central Terminal (*not* Grand Central Station—that refers to the subway stop) is a transportation hub, serving more than half a million commuters each day. But it's also a destination for people intent on shopping, dining, or simply enjoying its grand main concourse. It also serves as a gateway for some of the city's most notable landmarks, such as the Chrysler Building, the New York Public Library, and the United Nations.

New Yorkers take a lot of pride in Grand Central Terminal. Slated for demolition in 1968 (following the monumental Pennsylvania Station, which fell to the wrecking ball in 1964), it was saved by outraged residents. One of the most visible was former first lady Jacqueline Kennedy Onassis, who garnered publicity for the cause by standing outside with a sign protesting plans to replace it with an office tower. Their work led to a preservationist movement that fought for protection of individual buildings and whole neighborhoods and squelched ill-considered city plans, such as one to put a highway through the center of Greenwich Village.

Numbers in the text correspond to numbers in the margin and on the Midtown map.

a good walk

Building buffs won't be able to get enough of this part of the city, as its streets hold examples of every architectural style of the 20th century. Begin at the beaux-arts **Grand Central Terminal** ⑫ ►, one of the city's architectural masterpieces. Up close it's hard to get a good look at the building's fascinating facade, so make sure to glance back when you're walking the two blocks west on 42nd Street to the neighborhood's other beaux-arts gem, the **New York Public Library (NYPL) Humanities and Social Sciences Library** ⑬. Behind this magnificent building rise into the shrubbery and trees of **Bryant Park** ⑭, a perfect place to stop for a break. Benches and tables line the park's perimeter and at the west end are coffee and food kiosks. A well-kept public bathroom is between the park and library, next to West 42nd Street.

Head back toward Grand Central. On the southwest corner of Park Avenue and East 42nd Street is the **Whitney Museum of American Art at Altria** ⑮, the downtown branch of the popular museum. Ask New Yorkers to name their favorite skyscraper, and most will choose the art deco Chrysler Building ⑯ at East 42nd Street and Lexington Avenue. Although the Chrysler Corporation itself moved out long ago, this graceful shaft culminating in a stainless-steel spire still captivates the eye and the imagination. On the south side of East 42nd Street and east one block, the *Daily News* **Building** ⑰, where the newspaper was produced until the spring of 1995, is another art deco tower with a lobby worth visiting. The modern **Ford Foundation Building** ⑱ on the next block encloses a 160-foot-high, ⅓-acre greenhouse that is open to the public.

Climb the steps along East 42nd Street between 1st and 2nd avenues to enter **Tudor City** ⑲, a self-contained complex of a dozen buildings with half-timbering and stained glass. From here you have a great view of the international-style **United Nations Headquarters** ⑳.

PUT IT IN YOUR POCKET

WHEN HE WAS RUNNING FOR MAYOR in 1965, John V. Lindsay came up with an idea that people agreed was a breath of fresh air. With no large tracts of land left in the city, it would have been impossible to build new parks on the scale of Central Park in Manhattan or Prospect Park in Brooklyn. Instead, Lindsay proposed that vacant lots owned by the city be used for "vest-pocket parks." That meant neighborhoods that resembled concrete canyons could have a little bit of green.

After being elected, Lindsay set to work on making these parks a reality. In 1967, the first 10 publicly funded vest-pocket parks were built. Despite the fact that none of them was larger than a quarter of an acre, the puny parks were a huge hit.

At about the same time, privately funded vest-pocket began to spring up. This was partly a result of new zoning ordinances that encouraged building to incorporate "public space" into their plans. Other parks were gifts to the city from philanthropists. One of the first privately funded vest-pocket parks was **Paley Park** (⊠ 3 E. 53rd St., between 5th and Madison Aves., Midtown), which opened in 1967. On a sliver of land once occupied by the Stork Club, this swath of green was funded by William Paley, the founder of CBS. More than a dozen honey locust trees keep the park cool even on the hottest days.

Greenacre Park (⊠ 217–221 E. 51st St., between 2nd and 3rd Aves., Midtown) was a gift of John D. Rockefeller's daughter in 1971. She wanted people to experience "some moments of serenity in this busy world." Despite its size, it's a lush landscape. Water cascades over a 25-foot-tall wall at the rear. Heat lamps mean people gather in the park all year long.

TIMING   This walk takes about 1½ hours. Add additional time if you plan to linger in Grand Central Terminal or the New York Public Library.

What to See

㉒ Beekman Place. This secluded and exclusive two-block-long East Side enclave has an aura of imperturbable calm. Residents of its elegant town houses have included the Rockefellers; Alfred Lunt and Lynn Fontanne; Ethel Barrymore; Irving Berlin; and, of course, Auntie Mame, a character in the well-known Patrick Dennis play (and later movie) of the same name. Steps at East 51st Street lead to an esplanade along the East River. ⊠ *East of 1st Ave. between E. 49th and E. 51st Sts., Midtown East* Ⓜ *Subway: 6 to 51st St./Lexington Ave.; E, V to Lexington–3rd Aves./53rd St.*

⑭ Bryant Park. Midtown's only major green space has become one of the best-loved and most beautiful small parks in the city. Named for the poet and editor William Cullen Bryant (1794–1878), who sits under a dome at the park's eastern edge, the 8-acre park was originally known as Reservoir Square (the adjacent New York Public Library stands on the former site of the city reservoir). America's first World's Fair, the Crystal Palace Exhibition, was held here in 1853–54. Today London plane trees and formal flower beds line the perimeter of its central lawn. In temperate months the park draws thousands of lunching office workers; in summer it hosts live jazz and comedy concerts and sponsors free outdoor film screenings on Monday at dusk. At the east side of the park, near a squatting bronze cast of Gertrude Stein, is the open-air Bryant Park Café, which is open April 15–October 15, and the stylish Bryant Park Grill, which has a rooftop garden. The New York Chess Society sets up public tables near the west-end fountain in good weather (a sign set in the lawn reads SOCIABLE GAMES ARRANGED). In February and early September giant white tents spring up here for the New York fashion shows. On the south side of the park is an old-fashioned carousel where kids can ride fanciful rabbits and frogs instead of horses. ⊠ *6th Ave. between W. 40th and W. 42nd Sts., Midtown West* ☎ *212/768–4242* ⊕ *www.bryantpark.org* ☉ *Oct.–Apr., daily 7–7; May–Sept., weekdays 7 AM–8 PM, weekends 7 AM–11 PM* Ⓜ *Subway: B, D, F, V to 42nd St.; 7 to 5th Ave.*

★ ⑯ **Chrysler Building.** An art deco masterpiece designed by William Van Alen and built between 1928 and 1930, the Chrysler Building is one of New York's most iconic and beloved skyscrapers. It's at its best at dusk, when the stainless-steel spires reflect the sunset, and at night, when its illuminated geometric design looks like the backdrop to a Hollywood musical. The Chrysler Corporation moved out in the mid-1950s, but the building retains its name and many automotive details: gargoyles shaped like car-hood ornaments sprout from the building's upper stories—wings from the 31st floor, eagle heads from the 61st. At 1,048 feet, the building only briefly held the world's-tallest title—for 40 days before the Empire State Building snatched it away. The Chrysler Building has no observation deck, but the dark lobby faced with African marble is worth a visit; the ceiling mural salutes transportation and human endeavor. The 32 Otis elevators are each lined with a different inlay of wood, each of which is from a different part of the world. ⊠ *405 Lexington Ave., at E. 42nd St., Midtown East* Ⓜ *Subway: 4, 5, 6, 7, S to 42nd St./Grand Central.*

Ⓒ ⑰ ***Daily News* Building.** This Raymond Hood–designed art deco tower (1930) has strong vertical lines that make it seem loftier than its 37 stories. The newspaper moved in 1995, but the illuminated, 12-foot-wide globe set into a sunken space beneath a black dome in the lobby continues to revolve. The floor is laid out like a gigantic compass, with bronze lines indicating mileage from New York to international destinations. ⊠ *220 E. 42nd St., between 2nd and 3rd Aves., Midtown East* Ⓜ *Subway: 4, 5, 6, 7, S to 42nd St./Grand Central.*

⑱ **Ford Foundation Building.** Home to one of the largest philanthropic organizations in the world, the Ford Foundation Building, built by Kevin Roche, John Dinkeloo & Associates in 1967, is best known for its glass-wall, 12-story-high atrium, which doubles as a ⅓-acre public greenhouse. Workers whose offices line the interior walls enjoy a placid view of its trees, terraced garden, and still-water pool. ⊠ *320 E. 43rd St., between 1st and 2nd Aves., entrance on 42nd St., Midtown East* ☎ *212/573-5000* Ⓜ *Subway: 4, 5, 6, 7, S to 42nd St./Grand Central.*

need a break? With its myriad food selections, the dining concourse of **Grand Central Terminal** (⊠ E. 42nd St. at Park Ave., Midtown East ☎ 212/935–3960) is a great place to stop for a bite. In the basement-level concourse you can find everything from grill cheese sandwiches to oysters on the half shell.

▶ **⑫** **Grand Central Terminal.** Grand Central is not only the world's largest railway station (76 acres) and the nation's busiest (500,000 commuters and subway riders use it daily), it's also one of the world's greatest public spaces, "justly famous," as critic Tony Hiss has said, "as a crossroads, a noble building . . . and an ingenious piece of engineering." A massive four-year renovation completed in October 1998 restored the 1913 landmark to its original splendor—and then some.

FodorsChoice
★

The south side of East 42nd Street is the best vantage point from which to admire Grand Central's dramatic beaux-arts facade, which is dominated by three 75-foot-high arched windows separated by pairs of fluted columns. At the top are a graceful clock and a crowning sculpture, *Transportation,* which depicts Mercury flanked by Hercules and Minerva. The facade is particularly beautiful at night, when bathed in golden light. Doors on Vanderbilt Avenue and on East 42nd Street lead past gleaming gold- and nickel-plated chandeliers to the cavernous **main concourse.** This majestic space is 200 feet long, 120 feet wide, and 120 feet—roughly 12 stories—high. Overhead, a celestial map of the zodiac constellations covers the robin's egg–blue ceiling (the major stars actually twinkle with fiber-optic lights). A marble staircase modeled after the Garnier stair at the Paris Opera is on the concourse's east end. Climb it to reach Metrazur restaurant. From this perch you can look across the concourse to the top of the opposite staircase, where diners treat themselves to either Cipriani or the mahogany-and-leather setting of Michael Jordan's Steak House. Beyond those two restaurants to the left you can find the Campbell Apartment, an extremely comfortable and stylish cocktail and cigar bar in what was once a rather secretive pied-à-terre.

The Grand Central Market on the east end of the main floor (a street entrance is on Lexington Avenue and East 43rd Street) is a great place to buy fresh fruit, fish, dairy goods, and breads. Dangling from its amazing inverted olive tree are 5,000 glass crystals. Dozens of restaurants (including the mammoth Oyster Bar) and shops, many in spaces long closed to the public, make the downstairs **dining concourse** a destination in its own right.

Despite all its grandeur, Grand Central still functions primarily as a railroad station. Underground, more than 60 ingeniously integrated railroad tracks lead trains upstate and to Connecticut via Metro-North Commuter Rail. The subway connects here as well. The best (and worst) time to visit is at rush hour, when the concourse whirs with the frenzy of commuters dashing every which way. The most popular point for people to meet is at the central information kiosk, topped by a four-faced clock. The **Municipal Arts Society** (⊠ 457 Madison Ave., Midtown East ☎ 212/935–

3960 ⊕ www.mas.org) leads architectural tours of the terminal that begin here on Wednesday at 12:30. A $10 donation is suggested. *Main entrance* ✉ *E. 42nd St. at Park Ave., Midtown East* ☎ *212/935–3960* ⊕ *www.grandcentralterminal.com* Ⓜ *Subway: 4, 5, 6, 7, S to 42nd St./ Grand Central.*

㉑ **Japan Society.** The stylish and serene lobby of the Japan Society has interior bamboo gardens linked by a second-floor waterfall. Works by well-known Japanese artists are exhibited in the second-floor gallery—past shows have included the first-ever retrospective of Yoko Ono's works. ✉ *333 E. 47th St., between 1st and 2nd Aves., Midtown East* ☎ *212/ 832–1155* ⊕ *www.japansociety.org* ✉ *$5* ☉ *Building: weekdays 9:30–5:30; gallery: Tues.–Fri. 11–6, weekends 11–5* Ⓜ *Subway: 6 to 51st St./Lexington Ave.; E, V to Lexington–3rd Aves./53rd St.*

⑬ **New York Public Library (NYPL) Humanities and Social Sciences Library.** This
Fodor'sChoice   1911 masterpiece of beaux-arts design is one of the great research in-
★   stitutions in the world, with 6 million books, 12 million manuscripts, and 2.8 million pictures. But you don't have to crack a book to make it worth visiting: both inside and out, this stunning building, a National Historic Landmark, will take your breath away with its opulence.

Originally financed in large part by a bequest from New York governor Samuel J. Tilden, the library combined the resources of two 19th-century libraries: the Lenox Library and the Astor Library. The latter, founded by John Jacob Astor, was housed in a building downtown that has since been turned into the Joseph Papp Public Theater. Today the library anchors a network of close to 200 local branches throughout the city. You can see unusual behind-the-scenes collections, ranging from 19th- and early-20th-century menus to the personal library of magician Harry Houdini.

The grand entrance is at 5th Avenue just south of 42nd Street, where a pair of **marble lions** guard a flagstone plaza. Mayor Fiorello La Guardia, who said he visited the facility to "read between the lions," dubbed them "Patience" and "Fortitude." (New Yorkers, a notoriously contentious lot, hated them at first, saying they didn't look magisterial enough.) Statues and inscriptions cover the building's white-marble neoclassical facade; in good weather the block-long grand marble staircase is a perfect spot to people-watch.

The library's bronze front doors open into the magnificent marble **Astor Hall,** flanked by a sweeping double staircase. Upstairs on the third floor, the magisterial **Rose Main Reading Room**—297 feet long (almost two full north–south city blocks), 78 feet wide, and just over 51 feet high—is one of the world's grandest library interiors. It has original chandeliers, oak tables, and bronze reading lamps that gleam as if they were new. Gaze up at the ceiling and you can see murals of blue sky and puffy clouds, inspired by Tiepolo and Tintoretto. Exhibitions on photography, typography, literature, bookmaking, and maps are held regularly in the several galleries of the second and third floors. One of the most delightful corners is a third-floor gallery dedicated to the work of cartoonist Charles Addams, who created the creepy characters who inspired *The Addams Family*. Free one-hour tours leave Tuesday–Saturday at 11 and 2 from Astor Hall. There are women's rooms on the ground floor and third floor, and a men's room on the third floor. ⊠ *5th Ave. between E. 40th and E. 42nd Sts., Midtown West* ☎ *212/930–0800, 212/ 869–8089 for exhibit information* ⊕ *www.nypl.org* ☉ *Thurs.–Sat. 10–6, Sun. 1–6, Tues.–Wed. 11–7:30; exhibitions until 6* Ⓜ *Subway: B, D, F, V to 42nd St.*

⑲ Tudor City. Built between 1925 and 1928 to attract middle-income residents, this private "city" on a bluff above East 42nd Street occupies 12 buildings containing 3,000 apartments. Two of the buildings originally had no east-side windows, so the tenants wouldn't be forced to gaze at the slaughterhouses, breweries, and glue factories then crowding the shore of the East River. The terrace at the end of East 43rd Street now affords great views of the United Nations Headquarters and stands at the head of **Sharansky Steps** (named for Natan [Anatoly] Sharansky, the Soviet dissident). The steps run along **Isaiah Wall** (inscribed THEY SHALL BEAT THEIR SWORDS INTO PLOWSHARES); below are **Ralph J. Bunche Park,** named for the African-American former U.N. undersecretary, and **Raoul Wallenberg Walk,** named for the Swedish diplomat and World War II hero who saved many Hungarian Jews from the Nazis. ⊠ *1st and 2nd Aves. from E. 40th to E. 43rd Sts., Midtown East* Ⓜ *Subway: 4, 5, 6, 7 to 42nd St./Grand Central.*

★ ⑳ United Nations Headquarters. Officially an "international zone," not part of the United States, the U.N. Headquarters is a working symbol of global cooperation. The 18-acre riverside tract, now lushly landscaped, was bought and donated by oil magnate John D. Rockefeller Jr. in 1946. The headquarters were built in 1947–53 by an international team led by Wallace Harrison. The slim, 505-foot-tall green-glass **Secretariat Building;** the much smaller, domed **General Assembly Building;** and the **Dag Hammarskjöld Library** (1963) form the complex, before which fly the flags of member nations in alphabetical order, from Afghanistan to Zimbabwe, when the General Assembly is in session (mid-September to mid-December). Architecturally, the U.N. buildings are evocative of Le Corbusier (the influential French modernist was on the team of architects that designed the complex), and their windswept park and plaza remain visionary: there's a beautiful riverside promenade, a rose garden with 1,400 rosebushes, and sculptures donated by member nations.

A 45-minute-long guided tour (given in 20 languages) is the main attraction; it includes the **General Assembly,** the **Security Council Chamber,** the **Trustee Council Chamber,** and the **Economic and Social Council Chamber,** though some rooms may be closed on any given day. Displays on war, nuclear energy, and refugees are also part of the tour; corridors overflow with imaginatively diverse artwork. Free tickets to assemblies are sometimes available on a first-come, first-served basis before sessions begin; pick them up in the General Assembly lobby. The **Delegates Dining Room** (☎ 212/963–7625) is open for a reasonably priced (up to $20) lunch weekdays (jackets required for men; reservations required at least

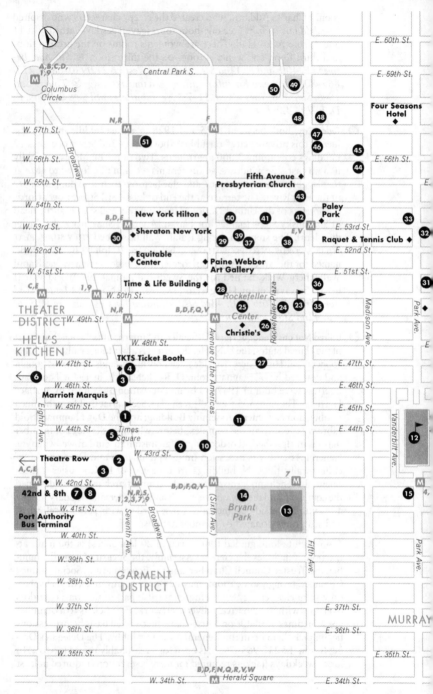

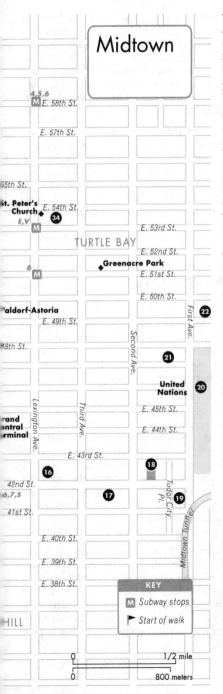

Midtown

one day in advance). The public concourse, one level down from the visitor entrance, has a coffee shop, gift shops, a bookstore, and a post office where you can mail letters with U.N. stamps. *Visitor entrance ✉ 1st Ave. and E. 46th St., Midtown East ☎ 212/963–8687 ⊕ www.un.org 🎟 Tour $11.50 ☞ Children under 5 not admitted ☉ Tours weekdays 9:30–4:45, weekends 10–4:30, no weekend tours Jan. and Feb.; tours in English leave General Assembly lobby every 30 min Ⓜ Subway: 4, 5, 6, 7 to 42nd St./Grand Central.*

🚇 **Whitney Museum of American Art at Altria.** An enormous sculpture garden with outstanding 20th-century sculptures, many of which are simply too big for the Whitney's uptown base, is the centerpiece of the museum's midtown branch. In the adjacent gallery four shows a year show works by living artists. An espresso bar and seating areas make this an agreeable place to rest. *✉ 120 Park Ave., at E. 42nd St., Midtown East ☎ 917/663–2453 ⊕ www.whitney.org 🎟 Free ☉ Sculpture court Mon.–Sat. 7:30 AM–9:30 PM, Sun. and holidays 11–7; gallery Mon.–Wed. and Fri. 11–6, Thurs. 11–7:30. Gallery talks Wed. and Fri. at 1 Ⓜ Subway: 4, 5, 6, 7 to 42nd St./Grand Central.*

ROCKEFELLER CENTER & MIDTOWN SKYSCRAPERS

Athens has its Parthenon and Rome its Colosseum. New York's temples are its steel-and-glass skyscrapers. Many of these massive structures, including the Lever House and the Seagram Building, have been pivotal in the history of modern architecture. At the center of it all are the 19 limestone-and-aluminum buildings that make up Rockefeller Center, one of the world's most recognizable pieces of real estate.

Constructed by John D. Rockefeller between 1931 and 1939, the Rockefeller Center complex—"the greatest urban complex of the 20th century," according to the *AIA Guide to New York City* architecture—occupies nearly 22 acres of prime real estate bordered by 5th and 7th avenues and West 47th and 52nd streets. Its central cluster of buildings consists of smooth shafts of warm-hue limestone, streamlined with glistening aluminum. Interconnected plazas and concourses create a sense of community for the nearly quarter of a million people who use it daily. Restaurants, shops, banks, a post office—all are accommodated within the center, and all parts of the complex are linked by underground passageways.

Rockefeller Center itself is a capital of the communications industry, containing the headquarters of a TV network (NBC), several major publishing companies (McGraw-Hill, Simon & Schuster), and the world's largest news-gathering organization, the Associated Press. And its iconic images—the art deco flourishes of the GE Building, the screaming crowds outside the *Today Show* studios, the gold statue of Prometheus floating above the ice-skating rink—are recognized at a glance by people all over the world.

Numbers in the text correspond to numbers in the margin and on the Midtown map.

a good walk

Begin your tour of the landmarks in and around Rockefeller Center at 5th Avenue between 49th and 50th streets, directly across from Saks Fifth Avenue. The little swath of green in front of you is known as the **Channel Gardens** ㉓ ▶. Journalists gave it that name in 1936, as it lies between almost identical buildings named for Britain and France. A surprising number of gardens are out of view on the rooftops nearby.

At the far end of the Channel Gardens is the sunken **Lower Plaza** ㉔, where the ice-skating rink is dominated by the famous gold-leaf statue of Prometheus. The backdrop to this scene is the 70-story **GE Building** ㉕, originally known as the RCA Building, whose entrance is guarded by a striking figure representing wisdom. The quote above the door—Wisdom and Knowledge Shall Be the Stability of Thy Times—is a tribute to the spirit of the times, as well as to Rockefeller's unshakable self-confidence. The GE Building is home to NBC, but its most famous studios are directly across 49th Street. The *Today Show* **Studios** ㉖ attracts hundreds of people every morning who stand in the pouring rain or blazing sun in hopes of getting their 15 seconds of fame.

Head west on 49th Street past the entrance to the world-famous auction house Christie's. On the west side of 6th Avenue, between West 47th and 51st streets, stand four nearly identical towers that form the Rockefeller Center Extension, part of a mid-1960s expansion. Fox News broadcasts many of its shows from street-level studios on the corner of 6th Avenue and 48th Street (look for the news ticker running around one corner); CNN does the same from the Time-Life Building on 6th Avenue between 50th and 51st streets.

Head north on 6th Avenue. (Street signs may call it the Avenue of the Americas, but New Yorkers *never* do.) As you pass the western entrance to the GE Building, make sure to glance up at the mosaic frieze called *Intelligence Awaking Mankind*. Made from more than 1 million pieces of glass, it portrays radio or television waves enlightening the world. Ahead of you, dominating the northeast corner of 50th Street and 6th Avenue, is one of the most important pieces of art deco architecture, distinguished by the pink-and-blue sign reading **Radio City Music Hall** ㉘. The theater's unusual name, spelled out in huge swirls of neon, comes from the fact that this area was originally known as Radio City. By West 52nd Street you've left Rockefeller's realm, but yet another communications company made sure its headquarters, the towering black **CBS Building** ㉙, stood nearby.

Turn back to 51st Street and walk east. Stop at the corner of Rockefeller Plaza (one of the city's few private streets), where you can see the headquarters of the Associated Press. Above the door is an eye-popping panel called *News,* with heroic-looking reporters and cameramen carrying out their duties with the tools of their trade: notepads, typewriters, and telephones. The sculpture, completed in 1940, was the first large-scale piece cast in stainless steel. Continue east on 51st Street. When you reach 5th Avenue, look to your right. Here is the International Building, guarded by one of the area's great pieces of public art, a huge statue of Atlas carrying the world on his shoulders.

Walk east on 51st Street until you reach Park Avenue. You'll known you've reached it when you spot the dome of **St. Bartholomew's Church** ㉛ on the southeast corner. Head north on Park Avenue, named for the stretch of green that runs down its center. It was more parklike before the street was widened to accommodate more traffic. Two blocks north, just past the monumental brick-and-limestone neo-Renaissance Racquet & Tennis Club dating from 1916, are two prime examples of International Style architecture: the **Seagram Building** ㉜, the only New York building designed by Ludwig Mies van der Rohe, and **Lever House** ㉝. For better or worse, these shiny towers helped usher in the era of glass-block buildings. One long block east on Lexington Avenue, between East 53rd and 54th streets, the luminous silvery shaft of the **Citicorp Center** ㉞ houses thousands more New Yorkers engaged in the daily ritual that built the city—commerce.

TIMING This walk takes about 1½ hours to complete, unless you decide to stop for a tour of NBC Studios. Consider taking this tour in the early morning, when crowds are in front of the *Today Show* studios, or at night, when the neon of Radio City Music Hall is at its most spectacular.

What to See

㉙ **CBS Building.** The only high-rise designed by Eero Saarinen, Black Rock, as this 38-story building is known, was built in 1965. Its dark-gray granite facade actually helps to hold the building up, imparting a sense of towering solidity. ⊠ *51 W. 52nd St., at 6th Ave., Midtown West* Ⓜ *Subway: B, D, F, V to 47th–50th Sts./Rockefeller Center; E, V to 5th Ave./53rd St.*

▶ ㉓ **Channel Gardens.** Separating the British Empire Building to the north from the Maison Française to the south (and thus the "Channel"), this busy promenade of six pools surrounded by seasonal gardens leads the eye from 5th Avenue to the Lower Plaza. The center's horticulturist conceived the gardens and presents around 10 often stunning shows a season. The French building contains, among other shops, the Metropolitan Museum of Art gift shop. ⊠ *5th Ave. between 49th and 50th Sts., Midtown West* Ⓜ *Subway: B, D, F, V to 47th–50th Sts./Rockefeller Center; E, V to 5th Ave./53rd St.*

㉞ **Citicorp Center.** The most striking features of this 1977 design by Hugh Stubbins & Associates are the angled top and the massive "stilts" that support the building. The immense solar-energy collector it was designed to carry was never installed, but the building's unique profile added whimsy to the New York City skyline. At the base of Citicorp Center is a cluster of restaurants and shops. **St. Peter's Church** (☎ 212/935–2200), whose tilted roof is tucked under the Citicorp shadow, is known for its Sunday afternoon jazz vesper service, at 5. ⊠ *Lexington Ave. between E. 53rd and E. 54th Sts., Midtown East* Ⓜ *6 to 51st St./Lexington Ave.; E, V to Lexington–3rd Aves./53rd St.*

ROCKEFELLER VS. RIVERA

A S ROCKEFELLER CENTER neared completion in 1932, John D. Rockefeller Jr. still needed a mural to grace the lobby of the main building. As was the industrialist's taste, the subject of the 63 foot by 17 foot mural was to be grandiose: "human intelligence in control of the forces of nature." He hired an artist known for his grand vision, Mexican painter Diego Rivera.

With its depiction of massive machinery moving mankind forward, Rivera's Man at the Crossroads seemed exactly what Rockefeller wanted. Everything was going fine until someone noticed that near the center of the mural was a portrait of Soviet Premier Vladimir Lenin surrounded by red-kerchiefed workers. Rockefeller, who was building what was essentially a monument to capitalism, was clearly disappointed. When Rivera was accused of willful propagandizing, the artist famously replied that "All art is propaganda."

Rivera refused to remove the offending portrait (although, as an olive branch, he did offer to add an image of Abraham Lincoln). In early 1934, as Rivera was working on the unfinished work, representatives for Rockefeller informed him that his services were no longer required. Within half an hour tarpaper had been hung over the mural. Despite negotiations to move it to the Museum of Modern Art, Rockefeller was determined to get rid of the mural once and for all. Not content to have it painted over, he ordered ax-wielding workers to chip away the entire wall.

Rockefeller ordered the mural replaced by a less offensive one by Jose Maria Sert. (This one, interestingly enough, did include Lincoln.) But Rivera had the last word. He recreated the mural in the Palacio de Bellas Artes in Mexico City, adding a portrait of Rockefeller among the champagne-swilling swells ignoring the plight of the workers.

㉗ Diamond District. The relatively dowdy jewelry shops on West 47th Street between 5th and 6th avenues are just the tip of the iceberg; upstairs, millions of dollars' worth of gems are traded, and skilled artisans cut precious stones. Wheeling and dealing goes on at fever pitch amongst the host of Hasidic Jews in severe black dress, beards, and curled side locks. So thronged is this street during the day that it becomes one of the slowest to navigate on foot in Manhattan. Ⓜ *Subway: B, D, F, V to 47th–50th Sts./Rockefeller Center.*

㉕ GE Building. This 70-story (850-foot-tall) art deco tower, the tallest building in Rockefeller Center, was known as the RCA Building until 1986, when GE acquired its namesake company. (GE also affixed its logo to the top, which many New Yorkers agree ruins its graceful lines). Inside the lobby is a monumental mural by José María Sert, *American Progress.* Sert's 1937 mural depicts the muses of poetry, dance, and music along with those of science, technology, and physical effort. A standing Abraham Lincoln (representing action) and seated Ralph Waldo Emerson (representing thought) are at the center. Sert's mural. Sert's work replaced that of Diego Rivera, which Rockefeller had destroyed because it centered around the likeness of communist leader Vladimir Lenin. Ad-

ditional murals by Sert, and by Frank Brangwyn, an English artist, are
on the north and south corridors of the lobby.

Today the building also known as 30 Rock is the headquarters of the
NBC television network. The two-level, monitor-spiked NBC Experience Store, in the southeast corner of the GE Building, is the departure
point for 70-minute tours of the **NBC Studios.** Ticket information for
other NBC shows is available here as well. There are also tours of
Rockefeller Center, but these do not take you anywhere you can't explore on your own. ⊠ *30 Rockefeller Plaza, between 5th and 6th Aves.
at 48th St., Midtown West* ☎ *212/664–7174* ⊠ *Tour $18* ☞ *Children
under 6 not permitted* ☉ *Tours depart from NBC Experience Store at
street level of GE Bldg. every 15 min Mon.–Sat. 8:30–5:30, Sun.
9:30–4:30* Ⓜ *Subway: B, D, F, V to 47th–50th Sts./Rockefeller Center.*

Marble-lined corridors beneath the GE Building house restaurants in all
price ranges, from the formal Sea Grill to the ubiquitous McDonald's,
as well as numerous shops, a post office, and clean public restrooms (a
rarity in Midtown). To find your way around the concourse, consult the
strategically placed directories or obtain the free "Rockefeller Center
Visitor's Guide" at the **information desk** inside the main entrance.
⊠ *Bounded by Rockefeller Plaza, 6th Ave., and 49th and 50th Sts., Midtown West* ☎ *212/332–6868* ⊕ *www.rockefellercenter.com* Ⓜ *Subway: B, D, F, V to 47th–50th Sts./Rockefeller Center.*

㉝ Lever House. According to the *AIA Guide to New York City,* this gorgeous 1952 skyscraper built for the Lever Brothers soap company is
"where the glass curtain wall began." Gordon Bunshaft, of Skidmore,
Owings & Merrill, designed a sheer, slim glass box that rests on the end
of a one-story-thick shelf balanced on square chrome columns. The whole
building seems to float above the street. Because the tower occupies only
half the air space above the lower floors, its side wall reflects a shimmering image of its neighbors. ⊠ *390 Park Ave., between E. 53rd and
E. 54th Sts., Midtown East* Ⓜ *Subway: 6 to 51st St./Lexington Ave.;
E, V to Lexington–3rd Aves./53rd St.*

 A holiday tradition began in 1931 when workers clearing away the
rubble for Rockefeller Center erected a 20-foot-tall balsam. It was
two years into the Great Depression, and the 4,000 men employed
at the site were grateful to finally be away from the unemployment
lines. The first official tree-lighting ceremony came in 1933.

㉔ Lower Plaza. The gold-leaf statue of the fire-stealing Greek hero
Prometheus, one of the most famous sights in the complex, floats above
the Lower Plaza. A quotation from Aeschylus—PROMETHEUS, TEACHER
IN EVERY ART, BROUGHT THE FIRE THAT HATH PROVED TO MORTALS A MEANS
TO MIGHTY ENDS—is carved into the red-granite wall behind. The sunken
plaza, originally intended to serve as entrance to lower-level retail shops,
was a failure until the now-famous ice-skating rink was installed in 1936.
Skaters line up October through April, and crowds gather above them
on the Esplanade to watch their spins and spills. The rink gives way to
an open-air café the rest of the year. Huge pieces of public art dominate

the plaza during the summer, and in December an enormous twinkling tree towers above. ⊠ *Between 5th and 6th Aves. and W. 49th and W. 50th Sts., Midtown West* ☎ *212/332–7654 for the rink* Ⓜ *Subway: B, D, F, V to 47th–50th Sts./Rockefeller Center.*

㉚ NYC & Company Visitor Information Center. For tourist information, maps, tickets to attractions, souvenirs, and ATMs, stop by this bustling spot. ⊠ *810 7th Ave., between W. 52nd and W. 53rd Sts., Midtown West* ☎ *212/484–1222* ⊕ *www.nycvisit.com* ⊙ *Daily 9–6* Ⓜ *Subway: B, D, E to 7th Ave.*

㉘ Radio City Music Hall. One of the jewels in the crown of Rockefeller Center, this 6,000-seat art deco masterpiece is America's largest indoor theater. Opened in 1932, it astonished the hall's Depression-era patrons with its 60-foot-high foyer, ceiling representing a sunset, and 2-ton chandeliers. The theater originally presented first-run movies in conjunction with live shows featuring the fabled Rockettes chorus line. In 1979 the theater was awarded landmark status. Its year-round schedule now includes major performers, awards presentations, and special events, along with its own Christmas and Easter extravaganzas. A $70 million renovation was completed in 1999 that gladdened critics and the public alike by, among other things, revealing the hall's originally intended gleaming colors. Popular hour-long tours of the theater let you see backstage areas and meet one of the Rockettes. ⊠ *1260 6th Ave., at W. 50th St., Midtown West* ☎ *212/247–4777* ⊕ *www.radiocity.com* ▭ *Tour $17* ⊙ *Mon.–Sat. 11–3, departing every 30 min* Ⓜ *Subway: B, D, F, V to 47th–50th Sts./Rockefeller Center.*

> **need a break?** Café St. Bart's (⊠ Park Ave. and E. 50th St., Midtown East ☎ 212/888–2664) is a charming and tranquil outdoor spot for a relatively inexpensive meal or a glass of wine or beer during the summer. The café serves breakfast and lunch weekdays year-round. Sunday brunches are also served year-round; Sunday dinner is served from April through December.

★ **㉛ St. Bartholomew's Church.** This handsome 1919 limestone-and-brick church, known to locals as St. Bart's, represents a generation of midtown Park Avenue buildings long since replaced by such modernist landmarks as the Seagram and the Lever buildings. The incongruous juxtaposition plays up the church's finest features—a McKim, Mead & White Romanesque portal from an earlier (1904) church and the intricately tiled Byzantine dome. St. Bart's sponsors major music events throughout the year, including the summer's Festival of Sacred Music, with full-length masses and other choral works; an annual Christmas concert; and an organ recital series that showcases the church's 12,422-pipe organ, the city's largest. St. Bart's also runs a popular outdoor café. ⊠ *109 E. 50th St., at Park Ave., Midtown East* ☎ *212/378–0200, 212/378–0248 for concert information* ⊕ *www.stbarts.org* ⊙ *Daily 8–6* Ⓜ *Subway: 6 to 51st St./Lexington Ave.; E, V to Lexington–3rd Aves./53rd St.*

㉜ Seagram Building. Ludwig Mies van der Rohe (1886–1969), a leading interpreter of International Style architecture, built this simple, boxlike bronze-and-glass tower in 1958. The austere facade belies its wit: I-beams, used to hold buildings up, are here attached to the surface, representing the *idea* of support. The Seagram's innovative ground-level plaza, extending out to the sidewalk, has since become a common element in urban skyscraper design. A 52nd Street entrance leads to one of New York's most venerated restaurants, the Four Seasons Grill and Pool Room. Even if you're not dining, peek in to see the Philip Johnson–designed dining room, a modernist masterpiece. Above the Grill Room's bar hangs a frighteningly sharp sculpture installation. ⊠ *375 Park Ave., between E. 52nd and E. 53rd Sts., Midtown East* ⊠ *Free* ☉ *Tours Tues. at 3* Ⓜ *Subway: 6 to 51st St./Lexington Ave.; E, V to Lexington–3rd Aves./53rd St.*

need a break? You have myriad eateries to choose from in Rockefeller Center's underground concourse, including the informal **Cucina & Co.** (⊠ 30 Rockefeller Plaza, between W. 49th St. and W. 50th St., Midtown West ☎ 212/332–7630). This place is packed at lunch, but any other time of the day you'll have no problem snagging a table. Opposite the *Today Show* studios, **Dean & DeLuca** (⊠ 1 Rockefeller Plaza, at W. 49th St., Midtown West ☎ 212/664–1363) serves coffee, pastries, and sandwiches.

26 Today Show Studios. Some of the first TV programs emanated from Rockefeller Center, including the *Today Show,* which is currently broadcast from ground-floor studios at the southwest corner of 49th Street and Rockefeller Plaza. Crowds of perky onlookers gather each morning outside its windows between 7 and 10, hoping for a moment with Al Roker or Katie Couric. To get a place on the rail, get there at least an hour before show airs. And bring a sign—the goofier it is, the better chance you have of getting on the air.

5TH AVENUE & 57TH STREET

Fifth Avenue's gilt-edged character has changed over the past decade as brand-name stores with slick marketing schemes and loud decor have moved in. But sitting amid the gaudiness of the Disney Store and Nike Town you can still find more refined stores such as Bergdorf Goodman, Saks Fifth Avenue, and Tiffany & Co. It may be one of the world's great shopping districts, but 5th Avenue also attracts art lovers, as many of the city's finest museums are nearby, and architecture buffs, who stare up at such landmarks as the Plaza Hotel.

Numbers in the text correspond to numbers in the margin and on the Midtown map.

a good walk Start across the street from Rockefeller Center's Channel Gardens, at the renowned **Saks Fifth Avenue** 🏛 ►, the flagship of the national chain. This elegant emporium, which has never lost its lustre, helped define the modern department store. Across East 50th Street from this cathedral of commerce is the Gothic-style Roman Catholic **St. Patrick's Cathedral** 🏛. From outside, snap one of the city's most photographed views: the ornate spires of St. Pat's against the black-glass curtain of Olympic Tower.

Cartier displays its wares in a jewel-box turn-of-the-20th-century mansion on the southeast corner of 52nd Street and 5th Avenue; similar houses used to line this street, but many of them have been replaced by buildings with far more retail space. Shoppers on 5th Avenue in need of sustenance have long turned to the landmark **"21" Club** ③, which presides over 52nd Street. Next door is the **Museum of Television & Radio** ③, which is as cutting edge as its neighbor is old fashioned. A shortcut through the public garden near the western end of the block takes you to West 53rd Street, which one observer wryly recently dubbed the "Museum Quarter Mile." A trio of galleries make this otherwise undistinguished block a major destination. On the south side of the street is the **Museum of Arts & Design** ③, and directly across is the **American Folk Art Museum** ④. But the lines that wrap around the block are for a museum whose building is a masterpiece in its own right, the **Museum of Modern Art (MoMA)** ④.

Head back to 5th Avenue, where you can see **St. Thomas Church** ④ on the corner. Fifth Avenue Presbyterian Church, a grand brownstone church dating from 1875, sits on the northwest corner of 5th Avenue and 55th Street. On your way north, you'll pass the imposing bulk of the **University Club** ④ at the northwest corner of 54th Street. It shares the block with the Peninsula, one of the city's finer hotels.

Trump Tower ④, on the next block between East 56th and 57th streets, is an apartment and office building named for its self-promoting developer, Donald Trump. It's not hard to find—just look for the tower of tacky pinkish-gold glass. And finally, the jeweler that benefited so much from the cinematic image of Audrey Hepburn standing wistfully outside it, **Tiffany & Co.** ④. Looking much the same as it did in the 1961 movie, Tiffany (*not* Tiffany's) is one of the most photographed spots along the avenue.

When you reach 57th Street, head east. As you pass through the revolving doors of Tourneau (12 E. 57th St.), an audible ticking welcomes you to its four floors of timepieces. The north side of 57th Street has a stellar lineup of boutiques: the English standby Burberrys and the French classics Chanel, Christian Dior, Hermès, and Yves St. Laurent. The fragmented form of the white-glass that's home to Dior lends a lighthearted elegance to the block. The two **Bergdorf Goodman** ④ stores flank 5th Avenue: the extravagant women's boutiques are on the west side of the avenue between 57th and 58th streets, and the men's store is on the east side at 58th Street. Van Cleef & Arpels jewelers is within Bergdorf's West 57th Street corner.

Cross West 58th Street to **Grand Army Plaza** ④, the open space along 5th Avenue between 58th and 60th streets. Appropriately named **The Plaza** ⑤, the famous hotel stands at the western edge of this square. Now return to 57th Street and head west, where the glamour eases off a bit. The large red NO. 9 on the sidewalk, in front of 9 West 57th Street, was designed by Ivan Chermayeff. (If you approach it from the other direction, it resembles an "e," thereby orienting passersby—you're facing east.) Continuing west, you'll pass the Rizzoli Bookstore (No. 31), with a neoclassical-inspired ceiling as elegant as the art books it carries. Across 6th Avenue, you'll know you're in classical-music territory when you peer through the showroom windows at Steinway & Sons (No. 109). Presiding over the southeast corner of 7th Avenue and West 57th Street, **Carnegie Hall** ⑤ has for decades reigned as a premier international concert hall.

TIMING   You can complete this walk in about 1½ hours. Add at least an hour for basic browsing and several more hours for serious shopping. Bear in mind that 5th Avenue is jam-packed with holiday shoppers from Halloween until New Year's. Also add additional time if you plan to visit any of the museums.

What to See

40 American Folk Art Museum. This museum is a work of art itself: an eight-story building designed in 2002 by heralded husband-and-wife team Tod Williams and Billie Tsein. The facade, consisting of 63 hand-cast panels of alloyed bronze, reveals individual textures, sizes, and plays of light. Inside, four gallery floors—dedicated to exhibitions and the collection of arts and decorative objects from the 18th century to the present day—are illuminated by a central skylight. Using multiple paths of circulation, an open atrium, and balconies of clear glass, you are treated to an architectural mix of intimacy and aspiration that echoes the folk art on display. Works include paintings, weather vanes, quilts, pottery, scrimshaw, and folk sculpture such as carousel animals and trade figures. ⊠ *45 W. 53rd St., between 5th and 6th Aves., Midtown West* ☎ *212/ 265–1040* ⊕ *www.folkartmuseum.org* ✉ *$9; free Fri. 5:30 PM–7:30 PM* ☺ *Tues.–Thurs. and weekends 10:30 AM–5:30 PM, Fri. 10:30–7:30* Ⓜ *Subway: E, V to 5th Ave./53rd St.; B, D, E to 7th Ave.; B, D, F, V to 47th–50th Sts./Rockefeller Center.*

48 Bergdorf Goodman. Good taste—at a price—defines this understated department store with dependable service. The seventh floor has room after exquisite room of wonderful linens, tabletop items, and gifts. *Main store* ⊠ *754 5th Ave., between W. 57th and W. 58th Sts., Midtown West* ☎ *212/753–7300* ⊠ *Men's store: 745 5th Ave., at E. 58th St., Midtown East* Ⓜ *Subway: N, R, W to 5th Ave./59th St.*

★ ⑤ **Carnegie Hall.** Musicians the world over have dreamed of playing Carnegie Hall ever since 1891, when none other than Tchaikovsky—direct from Russia—came to conduct his own work on opening night. Designed by William Barnet Tuthill, who was also an amateur cellist, this renowned concert hall was paid for almost entirely by Andrew Carnegie. Outside, the stout, square brown building has a few Moorish-style arches added, almost as an afterthought, to the facade. Inside, the simply decorated 2,804-seat white auditorium is without a doubt one of the world's finest. The hall has attracted the world's leading orchestras and solo and group performers, from Arturo Toscanini and Leonard Bernstein (he made his triumphant debut here in 1943, standing in for New York Philharmonic conductor Bruno Walter) to Duke Ellington, Ella Fitzgerald, Judy Garland, Frank Sinatra, Bob Dylan, the Beatles (playing one of their first U.S. concerts)—and thousands of others. Smaller concerts are held upstairs in the 268-seat Weill Auditorium.

Carnegie Hall was extensively restored in the 1980s; a subsequent mid-1990s renovation removed concrete from beneath the stage's wooden floor, vastly improving the acoustics. The renovation cleared space for the ultra-modern 599-seat Zankel Hall. The work also increased the size of the lobby and added the small **Rose Museum** (✉ 154 W. 57th St., at 7th Ave., Midtown West ☎ 212/247–7800), which is free and open daily 11–4:30 and through intermission during concerts. Just east of the main auditorium, it displays mementos from the hall's illustrious history, such as a Benny Goodman clarinet and Arturo Toscanini's baton. A sensational concert series run by the hall's education department introduces children to classical music through informal sessions with performers, with a low $8 ticket price. You can take a guided one-hour tour of Carnegie Hall, or even rent it if you've always dreamed of singing from its stage. ✉ *W. 57th St. at 7th Ave., Midtown West* ☎ *212/247–7800* ⊕ *www.carnegiehall.org* ✉ *$9* ⊙ *Tours weekdays Oct.–June at 11:30, 2, and 3, performance schedule permitting* Ⓜ *Subway: N, Q, R, W to 5th Ave./57th St.; B, D, E to 7th Ave.*

45 **Dahesh Museum of Art.** Dedicated to European academic art—a 19th-century movement that focused on the idealized human figure and historical, mythological, and religious subjects—this museum is composed of 3,000 works donated by a Lebanese doctor. The museum, on the first three floors of the IBM Building, houses works by such well-known painters as Bonheur, Bouguereau, Gérôme, and Troyon—all painters who have since been upstaged by their contemporaries, the impressionists, but who once claimed greater popularity. The museum has an engaging shop and a café serving lunch and afternoon tea. ✉ *580 Madison Ave., between W. 56th and W. 57th Sts., Midtown East* ☎ *212/759–0606* ⊕ *www.daheshmuseum.org* ✉ *$9* ⊙ *Tues.–Sun. 11–6* Ⓜ *Subway: E, V to Lexington–3rd Aves./53rd St.; E, V to 5th Ave./53rd St.; 6 to 51st St./Lexington Ave.*

need a break? You can relax amid clusters of bamboo in the public atrium of **590 Madison Avenue,** a five-sided, 20-story sheath of dark gray-green granite and glass by Edward Larrabee Barnes. An Alexander Calder mobile hangs in the lobby.

49 **Grand Army Plaza.** The flower beds are attractive, but this square at the southeast corner of Central Park is most certainly the province of tourists and those catering to them. That's not to say a rest here isn't restorative, it's just not as prime a people-watching spot as other public spaces in New York. The **Pulitzer Fountain,** donated by publisher Joseph Pulitzer, dominates the southern portion of the square. Appropriately enough in this prosperous neighborhood, the fountain is crowned by a female figure representing Abundance. To the north prances Augustus Saint-Gaudens's gilded equestrian statue of Civil War general William Tecumseh Sherman. Real horses pull carriages through a southern loop of the park and are available at fixed prices ($34 for 20 minutes or $54 for 45 minutes). Across 60th Street is **Doris C. Freedman Plaza,** with outdoor sculpture courtesy of the Public Art Fund, at the grand Scholars' Gate. Follow the path from this gate direct to the entrance of the Central Park Zoo. The Plaza, the internationally famous hotel, stands at the square's western edge. ✉ *5th Ave. between W. 58th and W. 60th Sts., Midtown West* Ⓜ *Subway: N, R, W to 5th Ave./59th St.*

39 Museum of Arts & Design. This small gallery showcases the decorative arts, displaying works in clay, glass, fabric, wood, metal, paper, and even chocolate by contemporary American and international artisans. Temporary exhibits sit side-by-side with pieces from the permanent collection. The gift shop is irresistible, filled with colorful jewelry and glass. ⊠ *40 W. 53rd St., between 5th and 6th Aves., Midtown West* ☎ *212/956–3535* ⊕ *www.americancraftmuseum.org* ⊠ *$9* ⊗ *Fri.–Wed. 10–6, Thurs. 10–8* Ⓜ *Subway: E, V to 5th Ave./53rd St.; B, D, E to 7th Ave.; B, D, F, V to 47th–50th Sts./Rockefeller Center.*

41 Museum of Modern Art (MoMA).
Fodor'sChoice ★ The masterpieces—Monet's *Water Lilies*, Picasso's *Les Demoiselles d'Avignon*, Van Gogh's *Starry Night*—are still here, but for now the main draw at MoMA is, well, MoMA. A "modernist dream world" is how critics described the museum after its $425 million facelift. Yoshio Taniguchi, the Japanese architect responsible for the six-story structure, said he wanted to "create an environment rather than simply making a building." The massive project nearly doubled the museum's square footage, adding soaring galleries suffused with natural light. The new entrance (accessed from either 53rd or 54th St.) is a 150-foot atrium that leads to the movie theater, cafés, and restaurant. On the second floor, Barnett Newman's *Broken Obelisk* is set in a room that resembles a floating cube. From the popular Abby Aldrich Rockefeller Sculpture Garden, designed by Philip Johnson, a new glass wall lets visitors look directly into the galleries. Note: the museum was an instant success, which means lines are sometimes down the block. Get here before the museum opens for the shortest wait. ⊠ *11 W. 53rd St., between 5th and 6th Aves., Midtown East* ☎ *212/708–9400* ⊕ *www.moma.org* ⊠ *$20* ⊗ *Sat.–Mon. and Wed.–Thurs. 10:30–5:30, Fri. 10:30–8* Ⓜ *Subway: E, V to 5th Ave./53rd St.; B, D, E to 7th Ave.; B, D, F, V to 47th–50th Sts./Rockefeller Center.*

need a break? Restaurateur Pino Luongo's **Tuscan Square** (⊠ 16 W. 51st St., Midtown West ☎ 212/977–7777), a restaurant, wine cellar, espresso bar, and housewares and accessories market, delivers an old-world feel.

38 Museum of Television & Radio.
Fodor'sChoice ★ Three galleries of photographs and artifacts document the history of broadcasting in this 1989 limestone building by Philip Johnson and John Burgee. But the main draw here is the computerized catalog of more than 100,000 television and radio programs. If you want to see a performance of "Turkey Lurkey Time" from the 1969 Tony Awards, for example, simply type in the name of the song, show, or performer into a computer terminal. You can then proceed to a private screening area to watch your selection. People nearby might be watching classic comedies from the '50s, miniseries from the '70s, or news broadcasts from the '90s. ⊠ *25 W. 52nd St., between 5th and 6th Aves., Midtown West* ☎ *212/621–6800* ⊕ *www.mtr.org* ⊠ *$10* ⊗ *Tues.–Wed. and Fri.–Sun. noon–6, Thurs. noon–8* Ⓜ *Subway: E, V to 5th Ave./53rd St.; B, D, F, V to 47th–50th Sts./Rockefeller Center.*

⑤⓪ **The Plaza.** With Grand Army Plaza, 5th Avenue, *and* Central Park at its doorstep, this world-famous hotel claims one of Manhattan's prize real estate corners. A registered historical landmark built in 1907, The Plaza was designed by Henry Hardenbergh, who also built the Dakota apartment building on Central Park West. Here he concocted a birthday-cake effect of highly ornamented white-glazed brick topped with a copper-and-slate mansard roof. The hotel is home to Eloise, the fictional star of Kay Thompson's children's books, and has been featured in many movies, from Alfred Hitchcock's *North by Northwest* to *Plaza Suite*. ⊠ *5th Ave. at W. 59th St., Midtown West* ☎ *212/759–3000* Ⓜ *Subway: N, R, W to 5th Ave./59th St.*

㊱ **St. Patrick's Cathedral.** This Gothic cathedral is one of the city's largest (seating approximately 2,400) and most striking (note the 330-foot spires) churches. Dedicated to the patron saint of the Irish, the 1859 white marble-and-stone structure by architect James Renwick was consecrated in 1879. Additions over the years include the archbishop's house and rectory and the intimate Lady Chapel. The original, predominantly Irish, members of the congregation made a statement when they chose the 5th Avenue location for their church: during the week, most of them came to the neighborhood only as employees of the wealthy. But on Sunday, at least, they could claim a prestigious spot for themselves. Among the statues in the alcoves around the nave is a modern depiction of the first American-born saint, Mother Elizabeth Ann Seton. The steps outside are a convenient, scenic rendezvous spot. Many of the funerals for fallen New York City police and firefighters were held here in the fall of 2001. ⊠ *5th Ave. between E. 50th and E. 51st Sts., Midtown East* ☎ *212/753–2261 rectory* ⊕ *www.ny-archdiocese.org* ⊙ *Daily 8 AM–8:45 PM* Ⓜ *Subway: E, V to 5th Ave./53rd St.*

㊷ **St. Thomas Church.** This Episcopal institution with a grand, darkly brooding French Gothic interior was consecrated on its present site in 1916. The impressive huge stone reredos behind the altar holds the statues of more than 50 apostles, saints, martyrs, missionaries, and other church figures. Lee Lawrie, responsible for Rockefeller Center's massive sculpture of Atlas, created these figures as well as a World War I Memorial near the front door. The church is also known for its men's and boys' choir; choral concerts and organ recitals are regularly scheduled. A Tuesday evening concert series is especially popular. ⊠ *5th Ave. at W. 53rd St., Midtown West* ☎ *212/757–7013* ⊙ *Daily 7–6* Ⓜ *Subway: E, V to 5th Ave.*

▶ ★ **㉟** **Saks Fifth Avenue.** On a breezy day, the 14 American flags fluttering from the block-long facade of Saks's flagship store make for the most patriotic shopping scene in town (the banners have been proudly displayed for years). In 1926, the department store's move from its original Broadway location solidified midtown 5th Avenue's new status as a prestigious retail center. Saks remains a civilized favorite among New York shoppers. The eighth-floor café serves delicious light fare, with a view of Rockefeller Center, and the rooftop pools and gardens of the buildings flanking Channel Gardens. Saks's annual Christmas window displays, on view from late November through the first week of January, are among New York's most festive. ✉ *611 5th Ave., between E. 49th and E. 50th Sts., Midtown East* ☎ *212/753–4000* ⊕ *www. saksfifthavenue.com* Ⓜ *Subway: B, D, F, V to 47th–50th Sts./Rockefeller Center.*

☕ ㊹ **Sony Building.** Designed by Philip Johnson in 1984, the Sony Building's rose-granite columns and its giant-size Chippendale-style pediment made the skyscraper an instant landmark. The first-floor arcade is home to electronics stores, a restaurant, a café, and, to the delight of children, a talking robot. The four-story **Sony Wonder Technology Lab** (✉ E. 56th St. entrance ☎ 212/833–8100 ⊕ www.sonywondertechlab.com ☉ Tues.–Sat. 10–5, Sun. noon–5; last entrance 30 min before closing) is a carnival of interactive exhibits, including a recording studio, and video-game and TV production studios. Admission is free, but call for a reservation to avoid a line. ✉ *550 Madison Ave., between E. 55th and E. 56th Sts., Midtown East* 🎟 *Free* ☉ *Daily 7 AM–11 PM* Ⓜ *Subway: E, V to Lexington–3rd Aves./53rd St.; E, V to 5th Ave./53rd St.; 6 to 51st St./Lexington Ave.*

㊼ **Tiffany & Co.** One of the most famous jewelers in the world and the quintessential New York store, Tiffany & Co. anchors the southeast corner of one of the city's great intersections. The fortresslike art deco entrance and dramatic miniature window displays have been a fixture here since 1940. Founded in 1837 at 237 Broadway, Tiffany slowly made its way uptown in six moves. The store's signature light-blue bags and boxes are perennially in style, especially on gift-giving occasions. ✉ *727 5th Ave., at E. 57th St., Midtown East* ☎ *212/755–8000* ⊕ *www.tiffany. com* Ⓜ *Subway: N, R, W to 5th Ave./59th St.*

here's where ⟩ Tiffany & Co. is immortalized in the 1961 Hollywood classic *Breakfast at Tiffany's,* in which a Givenchy-clad Audrey Hepburn emerges from a yellow cab at dawn to window-shop, coffee and Danish in hand.

㊻ **Trump Tower.** As he has done with other projects, developer Donald Trump named this gaudy 68-story apartment and office building after himself. He also lent his name to everything inside, including a bar, a grill, and an ice cream parlor. The 5th Avenue entrance leads into six-story shopping atrium clad in pinkish-orange marble. (Be careful in wet weather, as the highly polished stone is also quite slippery.) A fountain cascades against one wall, drowning out the clamor of the city, and trees and ivy climb the setbacks outside. ✉ *725 5th Ave., between E. 56th and E. 57th Sts., Midtown East* Ⓜ *Subway: N, R, W to 5th Ave./59th St.; E, V to 5th Ave./53rd St.*

㊲ **"21" Club.** A trademark row of jockey statuettes parades along the wrought-iron balcony of this landmark restaurant, which has a burnished men's-club atmosphere and a great downstairs bar. After a period of decline in the 1980s, when its menu aged along with its wealthy clientele, "21" reinvented itself in the 1990s. Today the power brokers are back, along with the luster of the past. A hidden wine cellar, used during Prohibition, lies beneath a secret passageway. ✉ *21 W. 52nd St., between 5th and 6th Aves., Midtown West* ☎ *212/582–7200* ⊕ *www.21club. com* Ⓜ *Subway: E, V to 5th Ave./53rd St.; B, D, F, V to 47th–50th Sts./Rockefeller Center.*

㊶ University Club. New York's leading turn-of-the-20th-century architects, McKim, Mead & White, designed this 1899 granite palace for an exclusive midtown club of degree-holding men. (The crests of various prestigious universities hang above its windows.) The club's popularity declined as individual universities built their own clubs and as gentlemen's clubs became less important on the New York social scene. Still, the seven-story Renaissance revival building (the facade looks as though it's three stories) is as grand as ever. Architectural critics rate this among Charles McKim's best surviving works. ✉ *1 W. 54th St., at 5th Ave., Midtown West* Ⓜ *Subway: E, V to 5th Ave./53rd St.*

> **frugal fun**
>
> Have kids in tow? The free **Sony Wonder Technology Lab** (✉ 550 Madison Ave., between E. 55th and E. 56th Sts., Midtown East ☎ 212/833–8100 ⊕ www.sonywondertechlab.com ☉ Tues.–Sat. 10–5, Sun. noon–5; last entrance 30 mins before closing) lets them program robots, edit music videos, or take a peek inside the human body. Call ahead, as it is very popular.

ART GALLERIES **David Findlay Jr. Fine Art.** This gallery concentrates on American 19th- and 20th-century painters from Winslow Homer to Robert Richenburg to Andrew Wyeth. ✉ *41 E. 57th St., 11th fl., between 5th and Madison Aves., Midtown East* ☎ *212/486–7660* ⊕ *www.findlayart.com* Ⓜ *Subway: F to 57th St.*

Edwynn Houk. The impressive stable of 20th-century photographers here includes Sally Mann, Lynn Davis, and Elliott Erwitt. The gallery also has prints by masters Edward Weston and Alfred Steiglitz. ✉ *745 5th Ave., between E. 57th and E. 58th Sts., Midtown East* ☎ *212/750–7070* ⊕ *www.houkgallery.com* Ⓜ *Subway: N, R, W to 5th Ave.*

Greenberg Van Doren. This gallery continues to intrigue by exhibiting the works of young artists as well as retrospectives of established masters. Recent shows have included line drawings by David Hockney and Andy Warhol's party pictures from Studio 54. ✉ *730 5th Ave., at E. 57th St., Midtown East* ☎ *212/445–0444* ⊕ *www.agvdgallery.com* Ⓜ *Subway: F to 57th St.*

Marian Goodman. The excellent contemporary art here includes Jeff Wall's staged photographs presented on light boxes, South African artist William Kentridge's video animations, and Rebecca Horn's mechanized sculptures. ✉ *24 W. 57th St., between 5th and 6th Aves., Midtown West* ☎ *212/977–7160* ⊕ *www.mariangoodman.com* Ⓜ *Subway: F to 57th St.*

Marlborough. With its latest branch in Chelsea, Marlborough raises its global visibility up yet another notch. The gallery represents modern artists such as Michele Oka Doner, Magdalena Abakanowicz, and Paula Rego. Look for sculptures by Tom Otterness, whose whimsical bronzes are found in many subway stations. ✉ *40 W. 57th St., between 5th and 6th Aves., Mid-*

town West ☎ *212/541–4900* ⊕ *www.marlboroughgallery.com* Ⓜ *Subway: F to 57th St.*

Pace Wildenstein. The giant gallery—now in Chelsea as well—focuses on such modern and contemporary painters as Julian Schnabel, Mark Rothko, and New York School painter Ad Reinhardt. A recent exhibit examined the work of Saul Steinberg, whose drawings that have appeared in the *New Yorker* for decades. ✉ *32 E. 57th St., between Park and Madison Aves., Midtown East* ☎ *212/421–3292* ⊕ *www.pacewildenstein. com* Ⓜ *Subway: N, R, W to 5th Ave.*

Peter Findlay. Covering 19th- and 20th-century works by European artists, this gallery shows pieces by Mary Cassatt, Paul Klee, and Alberto Giacometti. ✉ *41 E. 57th St., at Madison Ave., Midtown East* ☎ *212/644–4433* ⊕ *www.findlay.com* Ⓜ *Subway: N, R, W to 5th Ave.*

Spanierman. This venerable gallery deals in 19th- and early-20th-century American painting and sculpture. ✉ *45 E. 58th St., between Park and Madison Aves., Midtown East* ☎ *212/832–0208* ⊕ *www.Spanierman. com* Ⓜ *Subway: N, R, W to 5th Ave.*

Tibor de Nagy. Founded in 1950, this reputable gallery shows work by 20th-century artists such as Arthur Dove, Georgia O'Keeffe, Allen Ginsberg, and Trevor Winkfield. ✉ *724 5th Ave., between W. 56th and W. 57th Sts., Midtown West* ☎ *212/262–5050* ⊕ *www.tibordenagy.com* Ⓜ *Subway: F to 57th St.*

Uptown
Including Central Park & Harlem

5

Updated by
Shannon Kelly

Above 57th Street, Midtown melts into the primarily residential neighborhoods of the Upper East Side, the Upper West Side, Morningside Heights, and Harlem. In the middle of it all is New York's playground, Central Park, 843 acres of lakes, trees, hiking and biking paths, sports facilities, and performance spaces. And in these neighborhoods, there's some truth to some of the stereotypes. On the Upper East Side you *are* likely to encounter ladies who lunch weighed down by shopping bags from Bendel's, Fendi, and Manolo Blahnik. Much of the Upper West Side does in fact look like the backdrop for a Woody Allen movie. Harlem is packed to the gills with black history, especially having to do with the 1920s Harlem Renaissance. But the Upper East Side is also peppered with influences from Spanish Harlem, its neighbor to the north and is the home of Museum Mile. The Upper West Side, sandwiched between Central and Riverside parks, is the perfect destination for lazy fair-weather days. And in Harlem, construction at nearly every turn is evidence of its second renaissance, fueled by the young professionals moving north to snatch up reasonably priced brownstones.

THE UPPER EAST SIDE

To many New Yorkers, the words "Upper East Side" connote old money, conservative values, and even snobbery. The neighborhood is certainly the epitome of the high-style, high-society way of life that exists for the privileged in any true cosmopolitan city. Alongside Central Park, between 5th and Lexington avenues, up to about East 96th Street or so, the trappings of wealth are everywhere apparent: well-kept buildings, children in private-school uniforms, nannies wheeling baby carriages, dog walkers, limousines, and doormen in braided livery.

High society wouldn't be high society without a good dose of culture, and the Upper East Side has some of New York's most impressive museums. The Metropolitan Museum of Art, the Guggenheim, the Cooper-Hewitt Museum of Art and Design, and others stretch along "Museum Mile," from 5th Avenue at around 80th Street to 104th Street. The Whitney Museum of American Art on Madison Avenue and the Asia Society Museum on Park Avenue are two world-class museums just off the "Mile."

But like all other New York neighborhoods, this one is diverse, too, and plenty of residents live modestly. The northeast section, which is known as Yorkville, is more affordable and ethnically mixed with a jumble of high and low buildings, old and young people. And east of Lexington Avenue and between the 80s and 90s, young singles reign. On weekend nights, the scene in many bars resembles that of a fraternity and sorority reunion.

Numbers in the text correspond to numbers in the margin and on the Upper East Side & Museum Mile map.

a good
walk

Begin at the corner of 5th Avenue and 60th Street, across from the southeast corner of Central Park, where horse carriages await starry eyed patrons. Walk north up 5th Avenue, following the park. As you take in the grand-dame buildings like the Pierre hotel, at 61st Street, and the exclusive **Knickerbocker Club**, at 62nd, you may feel out of place with-

Upper East Side

E. 105th St.
E. 104th St.
E. 102nd St.
E. 101st St.
E. 100th St.
E. 99th St.
E. 98th St.
E. 97th St.
E. 96th St.
E. 95th St.
E. 94th St.
E. 93rd St.
E. 92nd St.
E. 91st St.
E. 90th St.
E. 89th St.
E. 88th St.
E. 87th St.
E. 86th St.
E. 85th St.
E. 84th St.
E. 83rd St.
E. 82nd St.
E. 81st St.
E. 80th St.
E. 79th St.
E. 78th St.
E. 77th St.
E. 76th St.
E. 75th St.
E. 74th St.
E. 73rd St.
E. 72nd St.
E. 71st St.
E. 70th St.
E. 69th St.
E. 68th St.
E. 67th St.
E. 66th St.
E. 65th St.
E. 64th St.
E. 63rd St.
E. 62nd St.
E. 61st St.
E. 60th St.
E. 59th St.
E. 58th St.

St. Nicholas Russian
Orthodox Cathedral

Ciao Bella
Gelato

Convent
of the
Sacred Heart

Payard

Knickerbocker
Club

Metropolitan
Club

Serendipity 3

Bloomingdale's

YORKVILLE

Roosevelt
Island

Queensboro Bridge

Fifth Ave.
Madison Ave.
Park Ave.
Lexington Ave.
Third Ave.
Second Ave.
First Ave.
York Ave.
East End Ave.
FDR Dr.
East River

CENTRAL PARK

1/4 mile
400 meters

KEY
Ⓜ Subway stops
▶ Start of walk

N,R,W
N,R,W,
4,5,6

out a pastel sweater draped over your shoulders (for that "just-off-the-yacht" look) or a miniature canine in a couture outfit stuffed in a Fendi bag. Even the houses of worship are palatial in this neighborhood—case in point, **Temple Emanu-El** ❻ at East 65th Street. Across the avenue, peer over the stone wall to get a look at the sheep and alpacas at the Central Park Wildlife Center's petting zoo. From 5th Avenue, turn right on East 66th Street, past the house (3 E. 66th St.) where Ulysses S. Grant spent his final years. At 5 East 66th Street is the **Lotos Club** ❼. The large, many-windowed landmark apartment building (45 E. 66th St.) on the northeast corner of Madison Avenue was built from 1906 to 1908. On its ground level is the shop of jeweler-to-the-stars Fred Leighton. Between this point and 68th Street on Madison Avenue, you can window-shop at Versace, Donna Karan, Dolce & Gabbana, Miu Miu, Oscar de la Renta, and Cartier, among others. A detour down 65th Street takes you to nos. 47 and 49, townhouses built in 1908 for Sara Delano Roosevelt and her son, Franklin (after he married Eleanor). Down 66th Street is Andy Warhol's former residence (closed to the public) at no. 57, and on 67th you can see many elegant Federal-style townhouses. Continuing up Madison Avenue, you'll pass the **Whitney Museum of American Art** ⓫ at 75th, and **The Carlyle** ⓬ at 76th, both on your right. Between 78th and 79th Street are a few moderately priced cafés. At 79th Street, walk west. Cross Fifth Avenue and follow street artists selling prints that are placed like breadcrumbs leading to the **Metropolitan Museum of Art** ⓮ at 81st Street. End your walk either with a visit to the museum or a stroll in Central Park (paths just before and just after the museum head into the park). The steps at the Met are a popular place for to take a load off and a good people-watching spot. To get to the **Solomon R. Guggenheim Museum** ⓰, walk north along 5th Avenue to 88th.

TIMING This walk takes roughly an hour at a stroll; much longer you visit the museums along the way. Weekdays, when the museums aren't too crowded, are the best days for this walk. Some shops on Madison Avenue close on Sundays.

What to See

❽ **Americas Society.** This neo-federal town house was one of the first built by McKim, Mead & White on this stretch of Park Avenue from 1909 to 1911. It was commissioned by Percy Rivington Pyne, the grandson of financier Moses Taylor and a notable financier himself. From 1948 to 1963 the mansion housed the Soviet Mission to the United Nations. In 1965 it was turned over to the Americas Society, an organization dedicated to educating U.S. citizens about the rest of the western hemisphere. The society hosts concerts and literary events, and its art gallery presents changing art exhibits. ✉ *680 Park Ave., at 68th St., Upper East Side* ☎ *212/ 249–8950* ⊕ *www.americas-society.org* 🎫 *Free* ☉ *Wed.–Sun. noon–6. Closed between exhibitions* Ⓜ *Subway: 6 to 68th St./Hunter College.*

㉔ **Carl Schurz Park.** Warm weather is the time to visit this park bordering the East River as winds off the river can be frigid in winter. Grab a cone at Temptations (York St., between 90th and 91st Sts.) ice-cream shop and head over to take a look at the mayor's residence, **Gracie Mansion** (⇨ below), at the north end of the park. (The last mayor to live here

BEATING MUSEUM BURNOUT

- Don't try to cram several museums into a day. Instead, do one per day and plan something relaxing afterward to rest tired legs, like a long leisurely lunch.

- Hit major museums on weekdays, when crowds lessen.

- Come to terms with the fact that you can't see all of the Met—probably New York's number-one contributor to burnout—in one visit. The MoMA and the Natural History Museum are other museums that can easily overwhelm. The Whitney and the Guggenheim, on the other hand, are small enough that you can do a thorough tour without major burnout.

- Take a look at floor plans on museum Web sites to decide which collections you want to see before you go.

- We recommend two to three hours, tops, at each museum.

- If you're with a group, consider splitting up so you can all see what you're most interested in, and plan a meetup time.

- Bring water with you.

- Break up art-viewing with coffee- and food breaks. Take advantage of museum cafés.

- Check your bag, or coat in winter months; carrying too much gear contributes to burnout.

- If you're with an infant or young child, call to make sure that strollers aren't prohibited on the day you plan to visit, as they are at the Met on Sundays.

was Rudy Giuliani; Michael Bloomberg apparently prefers his own East 79th Street digs.) Ferryboats depart from the East 90th Street tip of the park to lower Manhattan and up to Yankee Stadium. A path runs along the churning East River, from where you can see the Triborough and Queensboro bridges; Wards, Randall's, and Roosevelt islands; and, on the other side of the river, Astoria, Queens. The view is so tranquil you'd never guess you're directly above the FDR Drive—-apart from the sound of cars whizzing by below. Along the park walkways are raised flower beds, recreation areas, and a playground. Once known as East End Park, the park was renamed in 1911 to honor Carl Schurz (1829–1906), a famous 19th-century German immigrant who served the United States as a minister to Spain, a major general in the Union Army, and asenator from Missouri. During the Hayes administration, Schurz was secretary of the interior; he later moved back to Yorkville and worked as editor of the *New York Evening Post* and *Harper's Weekly*. ✉ *E. 84th to E. 90th St. between East End Ave. and East River, Upper East Side* Ⓜ *Subway: 4, 5, 6 to 86th St.*

 The Carlyle. The mood here is English manor house. The elegant **Café Carlyle** regularly hosts top performers such as Bette Buckley, Elaine Stritch, and Woody Allen (the latter with his New Orleans jazz band). More relaxed **Bemelmans Bar** is known for its murals by Ludwig Bemelmans, the famed illustrator of Madeline, who lived at the Carlyle. Stargazers, take note: this hotel's roster of the rich-and-famous has included George C. Scott, Steve Martin, and Princess Diana. In the early 1960s President John F. Kennedy frequently stayed here; rumor has it he entertained Marilyn Monroe in his rooms. ✉ *35 E. 76th St., at Madison Ave., Upper East Side* ☎ *212/744–1600* ⊕ *www.thecarlyle.com* Ⓜ *Subway: 6 to 77th St.*

need a break?

Classy but unpretentious **Bemelmans Bar** (✉ Carlyle Hotel, 35 E. 76th St., between Madison and Park Aves., Upper East Side ☎ 212/744–1600) is the perfect haunt for a postmuseum or postshopping drink. The bar's repeat patrons have allegedly included Jackie O and Kate Spade. Murals on the wall are by Ludwig Bemelman, the illustrator of the Madeleine children's books.

❹ China Institute Gallery. A pair of stone lions guards the doorway of this pleasant redbrick town house. The institute's gallery is open for two exhibitions each year (usually February–May and September–December) focusing on traditional Chinese art. A recent exhibit displayed artifacts from imperial tombs in Western Han. ✉ *125 E. 65th St., between Lexington and Park Aves., Upper East Side* ☎ *212/744–8181* ⊕ *www.chinainstitute.org* 🎟 *Gallery $5; free Tues. and Thurs. 6–8* ⊙ *Mon.–Sat. 10–5, Tues. and Thurs. 10–8* Ⓜ *Subway: 6 to 68th St./Hunter College.*

㉓ Gracie Mansion. Nothing like the many impressive brick-and-stone mansions of the Upper East Side, the federal-style yellow-frame official residence of the mayor of New York looks like a country manor house, which it was when built in 1799 by wealthy merchant Archibald Gracie. Tours of the interior—which you must schedule in advance—take you through the history of the house and its many objets d'art. The Gracie family entertained many notables here, including Louis-Philippe (later king of France), President John Quincy Adams, the Marquis de Lafayette, Alexander Hamilton, James Fenimore Cooper, Washington Irving, and John Jacob Astor. The city purchased Gracie Mansion in 1887, and after a period of use as the Museum of the City of New York, Mayor Fiorello H. La Guardia made it the official mayor's residence in 1942. Don't expect to find New York City's current mayor Michael Bloomberg here, however; he chose to stay in his own 76th Street town house rather than moving to Gracie Mansion when he took office in 2002. ✉ *Carl Schurz Park, East End Ave. opposite 88th St., Upper East Side* ☎ *212/570–4751* 🎟 *$7* ⊙ *Guided tours Wed. 10–3, starting every hr on the hr; all tours by advance reservation only* Ⓜ *Subway: 4, 5, 6 to 86th St.*

㉒ Henderson Place Historic District. Tucked away off 86th Street, this cozy half-block is a miniature historic district, with 24 Queen Anne–style town houses in excellent condition. The houses were built in the late 1880s for "people of moderate means." Richard Norman Shaw designed the stone-and-brick buildings to be comfortable yet romantic dwellings that combined elements of the Elizabethan manor house with classic Flemish details. Note the lovely bay windows, the turrets marking the corner of each block, and the symmetrical roof gables, pediments, parapets, chimneys, and dormer windows. This is one of those "hidden" New York treasures that most New Yorkers don't even know about. ⊠ *Henderson Pl. and East End Ave., between 86th and 87th St., Upper East Side* Ⓜ *Subway: 4, 5, 6 to 86th St.*

Knickerbocker Club. Built in 1915, this serene marble-trim redbrick and limestone mansion, the third home of the club—originally founded in 1874 by such wheeler-dealers as John Jacob Astor and August Belmont—was designed by Delano and Aldrich. ⊠ *2 E. 62nd St., near 5th Ave., Upper East Side* Ⓜ *Subway: N, R, W to 59th St./Lexington Ave.*

❼ **Lotos Club.** This private club, which attracts devotees of the arts and literature, got its name in 1870 from the poem "The Lotos-Eaters" by Alfred Lord Tennyson. Mark Twain and Andrew Carnegie were among the founding members. Its current home is a handsomely ornate beaux arts mansion originally built in 1900 by Richard Howland Hunt for a member of the Vanderbilt family. ⊠ *5 E. 66th St., between 5th and Madison Aves., Upper East Side* Ⓜ *Subway: 6 to 68th St./Hunter College.*

here's
where

Nathan Hale, of "I have but one life to lose for my country" fame, was likely hanged at a British encampment that was close to the present-day intersection of 66th Street and 3rd Avenue. A plaque on the Banana Republic building on 3rd Avenue (between 65th and 66th Sts.) attests to this.

Metropolitan Club. With a lordly neoclassical edifice, this exclusive club was built in 1891–94 by the grandest producers of such structures—McKim, Mead & White. It was established by J. P. Morgan when a friend of his was refused membership in the Union League Club; its members today include leaders of foreign countries, presidents of major corporations, and former U.S. president Bill Clinton. ⊠ *1 E. 60th St., near 5th Ave., Upper East Side* Ⓜ *Subway: N, R, W to 59th St./Lexington Ave.*

❶ **Roosevelt Island Tramway.** In 1976 the tramway was born as a means to transport Roosevelt Island residents to and from Manhattan. It's the only commuter cable car in North America. The five-minute trip suspends you 3,000 feet in the air. The views—of Queens, the Bronx, and the Queensboro Bridge—are not spectacular, but it's fun, it's cheap, and there are some interesting bits of history to see on Roosevelt Island (⇨ "Roosevelt Island" CloseUp box). ⊠ *Entrance at 2nd Ave. and either 59th St. or 60th St.* ☎ *212/832–4543* ⊠ *$2* ☉ *Sun.–Thurs. 6 AM–2 AM, Fri. and Sat. 6 AM–3:30 AM; leaves every 15 minutes.*

❺ **Seventh Regiment Armory.** The term "National Guard" derives from the Seventh Regiment, which has traditionally consisted of select New York men who volunteered for service. (The Seventh Regiment first used the term in 1824 in honor of the Garde National de Paris.) This huge brick structure, designed by Seventh Regiment veteran Charles W. Clinton in the late 1870s, is still used as an armory and was occupied by the National Guard after the attack on the World Trade Center in September 2001. Parts of the armory that aren't on duty serve various functions: a homeless shelter for women, the Seventh Regiment Mess Restaurant and Bar, and numerous art and antique exhibitions. Both Louis Com-

CloseUp

ROOSEVELT ISLAND

ROOSEVELT ISLAND IS 2-mi-long East River slice of land, parallel to Manhattan proper from East 48th to East 85th streets. The island became a planned mixed-income residential project in the 1970s and is home to some 9,000 people. It's accessible by the Roosevelt Island Tramway from 2nd Avenue and 59th Street.

In the 1800s and early 1900s, Roosevelt Island was a place for society's rejects: criminals and the mentally and physically ill. A penitentiary was built on the island in 1832 (Mae West and William "Boss" Tweed are among those who served time in Blackwell Penitentiary). The New York Lunatic Asylum followed in 1839. The asylum was made famous in 1888 by journalist Nellie Bly, who posed undercover as a patient to expose the inhumane treatment of the mentally ill. The Smallpox Hospital opened on the island in 1856, followed by several more charity houses and hospitals. It's no wonder, then, why the island was renamed Welfare Island in 1921. Some fragments of the asylums, hospitals, and jails once clustered here remain, but the insane were eventually moved to Ward's Island, the criminals to Riker's Island, and most of the hospitals relocated to Manhattan proper.

Points of interest on the island today are a 19th-century lighthouse, designed by James Renwick Jr. (architect of St. Patrick's Cathedral) and Blackwell House (1794), the fifth-oldest wooden house in Manhattan. Walkways follow the island's edge.

---

fort Tiffany and Stanford White designed rooms in its surprisingly residential interior. ✉ *643 Park Ave., between 66th and 67th Sts., Upper East Side* ☎ *212/452–3067, 212/744–4107 restaurant* Ⓜ *Subway: 6 to 68th St./Hunter College.*

did you know? Railroad tracks once ran above ground along Park Avenue. The tracks were covered after World War I and today a manicured median has taken their place.

❻ **Temple Emanu-El.** The world's largest Reform Jewish synagogue seats 2,500 worshippers. Built in 1928–29 of limestone and designed in the Romanesque style with Byzantine influences, the building has Moorish and art deco ornamentation, and its sanctuary is covered with mosaics. A free museum displays artifacts detailing the congregation's history and Jewish life. ✉ *1 E. 65th St., at 5th Ave., Upper East Side* ☎ *212/744–1400* ⊕ *www.emanuelnyc.org* ☉ *Sabbath services Fri. 5:15, Sat. 10:30; weekday services Sun.–Thurs. 5:30. Temple open daily 10–5. Museum open Sun.–Thurs. 10–4:30* Ⓜ *Subway: 6 to 68th St./Hunter College.*

MUSEUMS ❾ **Asia Society and Museum.** The Asian art collection of Mr. and Mrs. John D. Rockefeller III forms the museum's major holdings, which include

South Asian stone and bronze sculptures; art from India, Nepal, Pakistan, and Afghanistan; bronze vessels, ceramics, sculpture, and paintings from China; Korean ceramics; and paintings, wooden sculptures, and ceramics from Japan. Founded in 1956, the society has a regular program of lectures, films, and performances, in addition to changing exhibitions. The gift shop has a great selection of books, jewelry, tea and sake accoutrements and unique gifts. Trees grow in the glassed-in café, which serves an eclectically Asian menu for lunch and dinner. ⊠ *725 Park Ave., at 70th St., Upper East Side* ☎ *212/288–6400* ⊕ *www.asiasociety.org* 🖭 *$10; free Fri. 6–9* ☉ *Tues.–Thurs. and weekends 11–6, Fri. 11–9* Ⓜ *Subway: 6 to 68th St./Hunter College.*

⓲ **Cooper-Hewitt National Design Museum–Smithsonian Institution.** Contemporary and historical design, including drawings, prints, textiles, furniture, metalwork, ceramics, glass, woodwork, and wall coverings, are on display here. Changing exhibitions—which have covered such subjects as jewelry design and the construction of the Disney theme parks—are invariably enlightening and often amusing. In summer, some exhibits make use of the museum's lovely garden. Since 1976, the collection has been housed in the former 64-room mansion of industrialist Andrew Carnegie (1835–1919). The mansion was designed by Babb, Cook & Willard in 1901 on what was then the outskirts of town. This was the year Carnegie became the richest man in the world, and from the first-floor study he administered his extensive philanthropic projects. (Note the low doorways—Carnegie was only 5 foot 2 inches tall.) The core of the museum's collection was assembled in 1897—not by Carnegie—but by the two Hewitt sisters, granddaughters of inventor and industrialist Peter Cooper. The Smithsonian Institution took over the museum in 1967. ⊠ *2 E. 91st St., at 5th Ave., Upper East Side* ☎ *212/849–8400* ⊕ *www.si.edu/ndm* 🖭 *$10* ☉ *Tues.–Thurs. 10–5, Fri. 10–9, Sat. 10–6, Sun. noon–6* Ⓜ *Subway: 4, 5, 6 to 86th St.*

㉑ **El Museo del Barrio.** *El barrio* is Spanish for "the neighborhood," and the museum, focusing on Latin American and Caribbean art, is fittingly located on the edge of East Harlem, where a largely Spanish-speaking, Puerto Rican and Dominican community resides. The 8,000-object permanent collection includes numerous pre-Columbian artifacts, sculpture, photography, film and video, and traditional art from all over Latin America. The collection of 360 *santos*, or saints—carved wooden folk-art figures from Puerto Rico—are a popular attraction. ⊠ *1230 5th Ave., between E. 104th and E. 105th Sts., Upper East Side* ☎ *212/831–7272* ⊕ *www. elmuseo.org* 🖭 *$8* ☉ *Wed.–Sun. 11–5, Thurs. 11–8* Ⓜ *Subway: 6 to 103rd St.*

★ ▶ ⓾ **Frick Collection.** Coke-and-steel baron Henry Clay Frick (1849–1919) amassed this superb art collection far from the soot and smoke of Pittsburgh, where he made his fortune. Édouard Manet's *The Bullfight* (1864) hangs in the Garden Court. Two of the Frick's three Vermeers—*Officer and Laughing Girl* (circa 1658) and *Girl Interrupted at Her Music* (1660–61)—hang by the front staircase. Fra Filippo Lippi's *The Annunciation* (circa 1440) hangs in the Octagon Room. Gainsborough and Reynolds portraits are in the dining room; canvases by Gainsborough,

Constable, Turner, and Gilbert Stuart are in the library; and several Titians (including *Portrait of a Man in a Red Cap,* circa 1516), Holbeins, a Giovanni Bellini (*St. Francis in the Desert,* circa 1480), and an El Greco (*St. Jerome,* circa 1590–1600) are in the "living hall." Nearly 50 additional paintings, as well as much sculpture, decorative arts, and furniture, are in the West and East galleries. Three Rembrandts, including *The Polish Rider* (circa 1655) and *Self-Portrait* (1658), as well as a third Vermeer, *Mistress and Maid* (circa 1665–70), hang in the former; paintings by Whistler, Goya, Van Dyck, Lorrain, and David in the latter. When you're through, the tranquil indoor court with a fountain and glass ceiling is a lovely spot for a respite. The mansion was designed by Thomas Hastings and built in 1913–14. It opened in 1935, but still resembles a gracious private home, albeit one with bona fide masterpieces in almost every room. ⊠ *1 E. 70th St., at 5th Ave., Upper East Side* ☎ *212/288–0700* ⊕ *www.frick.org* 🖾 *$12* ☞ *Children under 10 not admitted; under 16 must be accompanied by adult* ☉ *Tues.–Thurs. 10–6, Fri. 10–9, Sat. 10–6, Sun. 1–6* Ⓜ *Subway: 6 to 68th St./Hunter College.*

⑬ Goethe Institut. In a 1907 beaux arts town house across from the Met, this German cultural center hosts lectures, films, and workshops; its extensive library includes German newspapers and periodicals. Through 2006, the institute's cultural program is TransAtlantic, an exploration of the relationship between Americans and Europeans. ⊠ *1014 5th Ave., between E. 82nd and E. 83rd Sts., Upper East Side* ☎ *212/439–8700* ⊕ *www.goethe.de/newyork* 🖾 *Exhibitions free* ☉ *Library Tues. and Thurs. noon–7, Wed., Fri., and Sat. noon–5. Gallery weekdays 10–5* Ⓜ *Subway: 4, 5, 6 to 86th St.*

⑲ Jewish Museum. One of the largest collections of Judaica in the world, the Jewish Museum explores the development and meaning of Jewish identity and culture over the course of 4,000 years. Housed in a graystone Gothic-style 1908 mansion, the exhibitions draw on the museum's collection of artwork and ceremonial objects, ranging from a 3rd-century Roman burial plaque to 20th-century sculpture by Elie Nadelman. The two-floor permanent exhibition, "Culture and Continuity: The Jewish Journey" displays nearly 800 objects. Special exhibitions focus on Jewish history and art. ⊠ *1109 5th Ave., at E. 92nd St., Upper East Side* ☎ *212/423–3200* ⊕ *www.jewishmuseum.org* 🖾 *$10; Thurs. 5–8 pay what you wish* ☉ *Sun.–Wed. 11–5:45, Thurs. 11–8, Fri. 11–3* Ⓜ *Subway: 6 to 96th St.*

need a break? The ultrapopular **DT-UT** (⊠ 1626 2nd Ave., at E. 84th St., Upper East Side ☎ 212/327–1327) is one of the few *true* coffeeshops in the city, where you can sink into a velvety '70s-era sofa and chain-drink coffee for hours on end (okay, until midnight on weekdays and 2 AM on weekends) without the waitstaff shooting you dirty looks. Plus it's the place that invented indoor s'mores (or so it claims)—marshmallows are toasted over a fondue burner. You can also refuel with soup, sandwiches, quiches, cookies and cakes, or one of 10 kinds of Rice Krispie treats.

⑭ **Metropolitan Museum of Art.** One of the world's greatest museums, the

FodorsChoice Met is also the largest art museum in the western hemisphere—span-

★ ning four blocks and encompassing 2 million square feet. Its permanent
collection of nearly 3 million works of art from all over the world includes objects from the Paleolithic era to modern times.

The Met first opened its doors on March 30, 1880, but the original Victorian Gothic redbrick building by Calvert Vaux has since been encased
in other architecture, which in turn has been encased. The majestic 5th
Avenue facade, designed by Richard Morris Hunt, was built in 1902 of
gray Indiana limestone; later additions eventually surrounded the original building on the sides and back. (You can glimpse part of the museum's
original redbrick facade in a room to the left of the top of the main staircase and on a side wall of the ground-floor European Sculpture Court.)

The 5th Avenue entrance leads into the **Great Hall,** a soaring neoclassical chamber that has been designated a landmark. Past the admission
booths, a wide marble staircase leads up to the **European paintings** galleries, whose 2,500 works include Botticelli's *The Last Communion of
St. Jerome* (circa 1490), El Greco's *View of Toledo* (circa 1590), and
Rembrandt's *Aristotle with a Bust of Homer* (1653). The arcaded **European Sculpture Court** includes Auguste Rodin's giant bronze *The
Burghers of Calais* (1884–95).

The **American Wing,** in the northwest corner, is best approached from
the first floor, where you enter through an airy garden court graced with
Tiffany stained-glass windows, cast-iron staircases by Louis Sullivan, and
a marble federal-style facade taken from the Wall Street branch of the
United States Bank. On the third floor, rooms are decorated in period
furniture—everything from a Shaker retiring room to the living room
of a Frank Lloyd Wright house—and American paintings.

The Met didn't enter the realm of 20th-century art until 1967, allowing the Museum of Modern Art and the Whitney to build their collections with little competition. It has made up for lost time, however, and
in 1987 it opened the three-story **Lila Acheson Wallace Wing.** Pablo Picasso's portrait of Gertrude Stein (1906) is the centerpiece of this collection. The **Iris and B. Gerald Cantor Roof Garden,** above this wing,
open from May to late October, showcases 20th-century sculptures and
has a unique view of Central Park and the Manhattan skyline.

To the left of the Great Hall on the first floor are the **Greek and Roman
galleries.** Grecian urns and mythological marble statuary are displayed
beneath a skylighted, barrel-vaulted stone ceiling. An indoor courtyard
holds Roman sculpture, and on the walls are a collection of rare Roman
wall paintings excavated from the lava of Mt. Vesuvius. The Met's awesome **Egyptian collection,** spanning some 4,000 years, is on the first floor,
directly to the right of the Great Hall. Here you'll find papyrus pages
from the Egyptian Book of the Dead, stone coffins engraved in hieroglyphics, and mummies. The collection's centerpiece is the **Temple of
Dendur,** an entire Roman-period temple (circa 15 BC) donated by the
Egyptian government in thanks for U.S. help in saving ancient monu-

ments. Another spot suitable for contemplation is directly above the Egyptian treasures, in the **Asian galleries**: the Astor Court Chinese garden reproduces a Ming dynasty (1368–1644) scholar's courtyard, complete with water splashing over artfully positioned rocks.

The Gothic sculptures, Byzantine enamels, and full-size baroque choir screen built in 1763, part of the first-floor **Medieval galleries,** might whet your appetite for the thousands of medieval objects displayed at the Cloisters (⇨ below). Straight ahead from the Medieval galleries is the skylighted white space of the **Lehman Wing,** where the large personal collection of late donor Robert Lehman is displayed in rooms resembling those of his West 54th Street town house. The collection's gems are the old-master drawings; Renaissance paintings by Rembrandt, El Greco, Petrus Christus, and Hans Memling; French 18th-century furniture; and 19th-century canvases by Goya, Ingres, and Renoir. To the north of the Medieval galleries is the **Arms & Armor** exhibit, which is full of chain mail, swords, shields, and fancy firearms. On the ground floor, the **Costume Institute** has changing exhibits of clothing and fashion spanning seven centuries that focus on subjects ranging from undergarments to Gianni Versace.

Tours (departing from the Great Hall) covering various sections of the museum begin about every 15 minutes on weekdays, less frequently on weekends. Self-guided audio tours are also available. During evening hours on Friday and Saturday, cocktails are served accompanied by chamber music. It might be easier to induce kids to join you at the museum after they've read *From the Mixed-Up Files of Mrs. Basil E. Frankweiler,* a story of a brother and sister who run away from home and hide out in the museum. ⊠ *5th Ave. at 82nd St., Upper East Side* ☎ *212/535–7710* ⊕ *www.metmuseum.org* ⊠ *$15 suggested donation* ⊙ *Tues.–Thurs. and Sun. 9:30–5:30, Fri. and Sat. 9:30–9* Ⓜ *Subway: 4, 5, 6 to 86th St.*

❷ Mount Vernon Hotel Museum and Garden. On property once owned by Colonel William Stephens Smith, the husband of Abigail Adams, daughter of former president John Adams, this 18th-century carriage house is now owned by the colonial Dames of America and largely restored to look as it did when it served as a bustling day hotel during the early 19th century (a time when the city's population was just beginning to boom). Eight rooms display furniture and artifacts of the federal and empire periods, and an adjoining garden is designed in 18th-century style. ⊠ *421 E. 61st St., between York and 1st Aves., Upper East Side* ☎ *212/838–6878* ⊠ *$5* ⊙ *Tues.–Sun. 11–4* ⊙ *Closed Aug.* Ⓜ *Subway: 4, 5, 6, N, R, W to 59th St./Lexington Ave.*

❸ Museum of American Illustration. This specialized museum was founded in 1901 to "promote and stimulate interest in the art of illustration, past, present, and future." The Society of Illustrators assembles eclectic exhibitions on everything from *New Yorker* cartoons and Norman Rockwell paintings to pictures from *Mad* magazine and children's books. ⊠ *128*

E. 63rd St., between Lexington and Park Aves., Upper East Side ☎ 212/838–2560 ⊕www.societyillustrators.org ⊠Free ⊗Tues. 10–8, Wed.–Fri. 10–5, Sat. noon–4 Ⓜ Subway: F to 63rd St.; 4, 5, 6, N, R, W to 59th St./Lexington Ave.

★ ☾ ⑳ **Museum of the City of New York.** In this huge Georgian mansion built in 1930, city history from the Dutch settlers of Nieuw Amsterdam to the present day are drawn together with period rooms, dioramas, films, prints, paintings, sculpture, and clever displays of memorabilia. An exhibit on Broadway illuminates the history of American theater with costumes, set designs, and period photographs; the noteworthy toy gallery has several meticulously detailed dollhouses. Maps, nautical artifacts, Currier & Ives lithographs, and furniture collections constitute the rest of the museum's permanent displays. Exhibits in 2005 included "Glamour, New York–Style" and "Radicals in the Bronx." The museum hosts New York–centric lectures, films, and walking tours. Weekend programs are especially for kids. ⊠ 1220 5th Ave., at E. 103rd St., Upper East Side ☎ 212/534–1672 ⊕ www.mcny.org ⊠ $7 suggested donation ⊗ Tues.–Sun. 10–5 Ⓜ Subway: 6 to 103rd St.

⑰ **National Academy.** Since its founding in 1825, the Academy has required each member elected to its Museum and School of Fine Arts (the oldest art school in New York) to donate a representative work of art. This criterion produced a strong collection of 19th- and 20th-century American art, as members have included Mary Cassatt, Samuel F. B. Morse, Winslow Homer, Frank Lloyd Wright, Jacob Lawrence, I. M. Pei, Robert Rauschenberg, Maya Lin, Frank Gehry, and Red Grooms. Art and architecture shows highlight both the permanent collection and loan exhibits. The collection's home is a stately 19th-century mansion donated in 1940 by sculptor and academy member Anna Hyatt Huntington. Huntington's bronze, Diana of the Chase (1922), reigns in the academy's foyer. ⊠ 1083 5th Ave., between E. 89th and E. 90th Sts., Upper East Side ☎212/369–4880 ⊕www.nationalacademy.org ⊠$10, pay what you wish Fri. 5–6 ⊗ Wed. and Thurs. noon–5, Fri.–Sun. 11–6 Ⓜ Subway: 4, 5, 6 to 86th St.

> **need a break?**
>
> In an elegant, high-ceiling space below the Neue Galerie, **Café Sabarsky** (⊠ 1048 5th Ave., at E. 86th St., Upper East Side ☎ 212/288–0665) serves Viennese coffee, cakes, strudel, and Sacher torte (Mon. and Wed. 9–6, Thurs.–Sun. 9–9). If you seek something more than a sugar fix, the savory menu includes trout crepes and Hungarian goulash.

⑮ **Neue Galerie New York.** Early-20th-century German and Austrian art and design, as epitomized by Gustav Klimt, Vasily Kandinsky, Paul Klee, Egon Schiele, and Josef Hoffman and other designers from the Wiener Werkstatte, are the focus here. The museum was founded by the late art dealer

Serge Sabarsky and cosmetics heir and art collector Ronald S. Lauder. The two-floor gallery, along with a café serving Viennese pastries and a top-notch design shop, are in a 1914 mansion designed by Carrère and Hastings, which was home to Mrs. Cornelius Vanderbilt III, the top social hostess of the Gilded Age. ⊠ *1048 5th Ave., at E. 86th St., Upper East Side* ☎ *212/628–6200* ⊕ *www.neuegalerie.org* ⊠ *$10* ☞ *Children under 12 not admitted; under 16 must be accompanied by an adult* ☼ *Sat.–Mon. 11–6, Fri. 11–9* Ⓜ *Subway: 4, 5, 6 to 86th St.*

⑯ Solomon R. Guggenheim Museum. Frank Lloyd Wright's landmark museum building is visited as much for its famous architecture as it is for its superlative art. Opened in 1959, shortly after Wright died, the Guggenheim is an icon of modernist architecture, designed specifically to showcase—and complement—modern art. Outside the curvaceous building, Wright's attention to detail is strikingly evident—in the porthole-like windows on its south side, the circular pattern of the sidewalk, and the smoothness of the hand-plastered concrete. Inside, under a 92-foot-high glass dome, a ¼-mi-long ramp spirals down past changing exhibitions. The museum has strong holdings in Vasily Kandinsky, Paul Klee, Marc Chagall, Pablo Picasso, and Robert Mapplethorpe. In its Tower galleries, double-high ceilings accommodate extraordinarily large art pieces, and the Tower's fifth-floor sculpture terrace has a view overlooking Central Park. On permanent display, the museum's Thannhauser Collection is comprised primarily of works by French impressionists and neo-impressionists including Matisse, van Gogh, Toulouse-Lautrec, and Cézanne. Changing exhibitions focus on artists ranging from Norman Rockwell to Jeff Koons. ⊠ *1071 5th Ave., between E. 88th and E. 89th Sts., Upper East Side* ☎ *212/423–3500* ⊕ *www.guggenheim.org* ⊠ *$15* ☼ *Sat.–Wed. 10–5:45, Fri. 10–8* Ⓜ *Subway: 4, 5, 6 to 86th St.*

FodorsChoice
★

need a
break?

The **Whitney Café** (⊠ Whitney Museum, 945 Madison Ave., at E. 75th St., Upper East Side ☎ 212/570–3676) serves up a small selection sandwiches, pastries, and soups. Deep red walls chockablock with framed photos and porthole windows help make it a bit cozier and more interesting than your standard cafeteria.

★ ⑪ Whitney Museum of American Art. This museum grew out of a gallery in the studio of the sculptor and collector Gertrude Vanderbilt Whitney, whose talent and taste were fortuitously accompanied by the wealth of two prominent families. She offered her collection of 20th-century American art to the Met, but they turned it down, so she established an independent museum in 1930. The current minimalist gray-granite building, separated from Madison Avenue by a dry moat, opened in 1966 and was designed by Marcel Breuer, a member of the Bauhaus school. The exterior is much more forbidding than the interior, where exhibitions offer an intelligent survey of 20th-century American works. The fifth floor's eight sleek galleries house "Hopper to Mid-Century," with works by Reginald Marsh, George Bellows, Robert Henri, and Marsden Hartley. Notable pieces include Hopper's *Early Sunday Morning* (1930), Bellows' *Dempsey and Firpo* (1924), and several of Georgia O'Keeffe's dazzling flower paintings. Postwar and contemporary highlights from the permanent collection include paintings and sculpture by such artists as Jackson Pollack, Jim Dine, Jasper Johns, Mark Rothko, Frank Stella, Chuck Close, Cindy Sherman, and Roy Lichtenstein. The museum lobby is home to Alexander Calder's beloved sculpture *Circus* (1926–31) with tiny wire performers swinging from trapezes and walking on tightropes. The famed Whitney Biennial, which showcases the most important developments in American art over the past two years, takes place in even-numbered years. The Whitney also has a branch across from Grand Central Terminal in midtown. The SoundCheck series presents up-and-coming downtown musicians on some Friday nights; tickets are included in the admission price. ✉ *945 Madison Ave., at E. 75th St., Upper East Side* ☎ *212/570–3676* ⊕ *www.whitney.org* 🎟 *$12; Fri. 6–9 pay what you wish* ☉ *Sat.–Thurs. 11–6, Fri. 1–9* Ⓜ *Subway: 6 to 77th St.*

ART GALLERIES   Art galleries, of which there are many on the Upper East Side, are always free. Check *Time Out New York, New York Magazine,* or the *New York Times* Sunday "Arts" section to find out what's showing. Gallery openings often have free food and drink for attendees.

David Findlay. Descend into a warren of rooms to view contemporary, color-soaked paintings by American and French artists. Represented artists include Pierre Lesieur, Roger Mühl, and (for a brightly hued slice of New York streets) Tom Christopher. ✉ *984 Madison Ave., between E. 76th and E. 77th Sts., Upper East Side* ☎ *212/249–2909* ⊕ *www. davidfindlaygalleries.com* 🎟 *Free* ☉ *Mon.–Sat. 10–5* Ⓜ *Subway: 6 to 77th St.*

Hirschl & Adler. Although this gallery has a selection of European works, it's best known for its American paintings, prints, and decorative arts. Among the celebrated 19th- and 20th-century artists whose works are featured are: Thomas Cole, Frederick Church, Childe Hassam, Camille Pissaro, and William Merritt Chase. ✉ *21 E. 70th St., between 5th and Madison Aves., Upper East Side* ☎ *212/535–8810* ⊕ *www. hirschlandadler.com* 🎟 *Free* ☉ *Tues.–Fri. 9:30–5:15, Sat. 9:30–4:45* Ⓜ *Subway: 6 to 68th St./Hunter College.*

Jane Kahan. Besides ceramics by Picasso (one of this gallery's specialties), you'llsee works by 19th- and 20th-century artists such as Fernand Léger, Joan Miró, and Marc Chagall. ✉ *922 Madison Ave., between E. 73rd and E. 74th Sts., Upper East Side* ☎ *212/744–1490* ⊕ *www. janekahan.com* 🎟 *Free* ☉ *Tues.–Sat. 10–6* Ⓜ *Subway: 6 to 77th St.*

Knoedler & Company. Knoedler helped many great American collectors, including industrialist Henry Clay Frick, start their collections. Now its represented artists include 20th-century painters Helen Frankenthaler, Sean Scully, Donald Sultan, and John Walker. ✉ *19 E. 70th St., between 5th and Madison Aves., Upper East Side* ☎ *212/794–0550* ⊕ *www. knoedlergallery.com* 🎟 *Free* ☉ *Tues.–Fri. 9:30–5:30, Sat. 10–5:30* Ⓜ *Subway: 6 to 68th St./Hunter College.*

Leo Castelli. Castelli was one of the most influential dealers of the 20th century. An early supporter of pop, minimalist, and conceptual art, he helped foster the careers of many important artists, including one of his first discoveries, Jasper Johns. The gallery moved here from SoHo and continues to show works by Roy Lichtenstein, Ed Ruscha, Jackson Pollock, and others. ⊠ *18 E. 77th St., between 5th and Madison Aves., Upper East Side* ☎ *212/249–4470* ⊕ *www.castelligallery.com* ✉ *Free* ⊙ *Tues.–Sat. 10–6* Ⓜ *Subway: 6 to 77th St.*

Margo Feiden. Illustrations by the late theatrical caricaturist Al Hirschfeld, who delighted readers of the *New York Times* for more than 60 years, are the draw here. ⊠ *699 Madison Ave., between E. 62nd and E. 63rd Sts., Upper East Side* ☎ *212/677–5330* ⊕ *www.alhirschfeld.com* ✉ *Free* ⊙ *Daily 10–6* Ⓜ *Subway: 4, 5, 6 to 59th St.*

Michael Werner. This German art dealer mounts smart shows of such early-20th-century masters as Otto Freundlich and Francis Picabia in his refined, East Side town house. The emphasis is on sculpture and drawings. ⊠ *4 E. 77th St., between 5th and Madison Aves., Upper East Side* ☎ *212/988–1623* ✉ *Free* ⊙ *Mon.–Sat. 10–6* Ⓜ *Subway: 6 to 77th St.*

Mitchell-Innes & Nash. This sleek spot specializing in contemporary, impressionist, and modern art presents the estates of Willem de Kooning, Tony Smith, and Jack Tworkov. ⊠ *1018 Madison Ave., between 78th and 79th Sts., Upper East Side* ☎ *212/744–7400* ⊕ *www.miandn.com* ✉ *Free* ⊙ *Tues.–Sat. 10–5* Ⓜ *Subway: 6 to 77th St.*

Wildenstein & Co. This branch of the Wildenstein art empire was the first to take root in New York; its reputation for brilliant holdings was cemented by the acquisition of significant private museum-quality collections. Look for French impressionist exhibitions. ⊠ *19 E. 64th St., between 5th and Madison Aves., Upper East Side* ☎ *212/879–0500* ⊕ *www.wildenstein.com* ✉ *Free* ⊙ *Weekdays 10–5* Ⓜ *Subway: 6 to 68th St./Hunter College.*

CENTRAL PARK

Without the Central Park's 843 acres of meandering paths, tranquil lakes, ponds, and open meadows, New Yorkers might be a lot less sane. Every day thousands of joggers, cyclists, in-line skaters, and walkers make their way around this urban oasis. Come summertime the park serves as Manhattan's Riviera, with sun worshippers crowding every available patch of grass. Year-round, the park plays host to equestrians, softball players, ice skaters, roller skaters, rock climbers, croquet and tennis players, bird-watchers, boaters, chess and checkers aficionados, theater- and concert-goers, skateboarders, and more. But nearly everyone occasionally takes the time to escape the rumble of traffic, walk through the trees, and feel, at least for a moment, far from the urban frenzy.

No matter how close to nature New Yorkers feel when reveling in it, Central Park was in fact the first artificially landscaped park in the United States. The design was conceived in 1857 by Frederick Law Olmsted and Calvert Vaux, the founders of the landscape architecture profession in the United States. Their design was one of 33 submitted in a contest arranged by the Central Park Commission. The Greensward Plan, as it was called, combined pastoral, picturesque, and formal elements: open rolling meadows complement fanciful landscapes and grand, formal walkways. The southern portion of the park is more formal and orderly, while the north end is deliberately more wild. The four roads cut through the park from east to west—66th, 79th, 86th, and 96th streets—were designed to carry crosstown traffic beneath the park's hills and tunnels so that park goers would not be disturbed.

The job of constructing the park was monumental. Hundreds of residents were displaced, swamps were drained, and great walls of Manhattan schist were blasted. Thousands of workers were employed to move some 5 million cubic yards of soil and plant thousands of trees and shrubs in a project that lasted 16 years. Today, thanks to the efforts of the Central Park Conservancy, a private, not-for-profit organization, Olmsted and Vaux's green oasis looks better than ever.

In the years following the park's opening in 1859, more than half its visitors arrived by carriage. Today, with a little imagination, you can still experience the park as they did, by hiring a **horse-drawn carriage** at Grand Army Plaza or any other major intersection of Central Park South at 59th Street between 5th Avenue and Columbus Circle. Rates, which are regulated, are $34 for 20 minutes or $54 for 45 minutes for up to four people.

Central Park has one of the lowest crime rates in the city. Still, use common sense and stay within sight of other park visitors, and don't go to the park after dark. Directions, park maps, and event calendars can be obtained from volunteers at two 5th Avenue **information booths,** at East 60th Street and East 72nd Street. ☎*212/408–0266 schedule of park events, 212/360–2727 schedule of walking tours* ⊕ *www.nycgovparks.org.*

did you know?

Along the main Loop and some smaller paths, lampposts are marked with a location code. Posts bear a letter—always "E" (for east) or "W" (for west)—followed by four numbers. The first two numbers tell you the nearest cross street. The second two tell you how far you are from either 5th Avenue or Central Park West (depending on whether it's an "E" or "W" post). So E7803 means you're near 78th Street, 3 posts in from 5th Avenue. For street numbers above 99, the initial "1" is omitted, for example, E0401.

a good walk

Numbers in the text correspond to numbers in the margin and on the Central Park map.

Start at Grand Army Plaza (59th St. and 5th Ave.) and walk more or less parallel to East Drive along **The Pond** ➊ ▶. Just to the north is **Wollman Memorial Rink** ➋ where you can watch skaters cut up the ice from October to April. Beyond the rink, walk uphill past the Dairy, cross the road and veer a bit left to the Literary Walk, flanked at its start by statues of Sir Walter Scott and Rober Burns. A stroll north under a canopy of elms leads to **The Mall** ➓, where it's easy to imagine yourself a 19th-century high-society New Yorker. Near the end of the Mall to your left is Skater's Circle. It's tons of fun to watch the semi-professional skate-

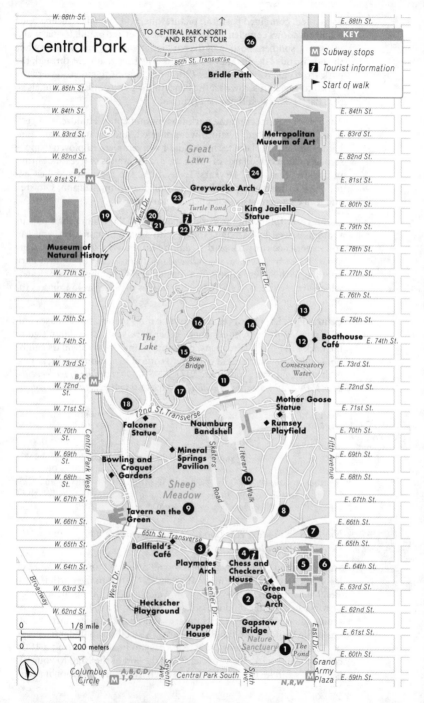

Central Park

TO CENTRAL PARK NORTH
AND REST OF TOUR

KEY
M Subway stops
i Tourist information
▶ Start of walk

W. 88th St.
E. 88th St.

85th St. Transverse

Bridle Path

W. 85th St.
W. 84th St. — E. 84th St.
W. 83rd St. — E. 83rd St.

Metropolitan Museum of Art

W. 82nd St. — E. 82nd St.

Great Lawn

25

W. 81st St. — **M** B,C — E. 81st St.

24

Greywacke Arch

23 — E. 80th St.

Turtle Pond

King Jagiello Statue

W. 79th St. — E. 79th St.

19 — 20 21 — 22 — *West Dr.* — *79th St. Transverse* — *East Dr.*

W. 78th St. — E. 78th St.

W. 77th St. — E. 77th St.

Museum of Natural History

W. 76th St. — E. 76th St.

W. 75th St. — 13 — E. 75th St.

16 — 14

The Lake

12 — **Boathouse Café** — E. 74th St.

W. 74th St.

W. 73rd St. — 15 — *Bow Bridge* — *Conservatory Water* — E. 73rd St.

W. 72nd St. — **M** B,C — 11 — E. 72nd St.

17

18 — *72nd St. Transverse*

W. 71st St. — **Mother Goose Statue** — E. 71st St.

Falconer Statue — **Naumburg Bandshell** — ♦ **Rumsey Playfield** — E. 70th St.

W. 70th St.

W. 69th St. — ♦ **Mineral Springs Pavilion** — E. 69th St.

Bowling and Croquet Gardens

W. 68th St. — E. 68th St.

W. 67th St. — *Sheep Meadow* — E. 67th St.

Tavern on the Green — 9 — *Skaters' Road* — *Literary Walk*

W. 66th St. — 8 — E. 66th St.

7 — E. 65th St.

Ballfield's Café — *65th St. Transverse*

3

W. 64th St. — 4 — **i** — 5 — 6 — E. 64th St.

Playmates Arch — **Chess and Checkers House**

W. 63rd St. — **Green Gap Arch** — E. 63rd St.

2

Heckscher Playground

W. 62nd St. — E. 62nd St.

Puppet House — **Gapstow Bridge**

0 — 1/8 mile — *Nature Sanctuary* — 1 — *The Pond* — E. 60th St.

0 — 200 meters

Columbus Circle — **M** A,B,C,D; 1,9 — *Central Park South* — *Grand Army Plaza* — E. 59th St.

Broadway — *Central Park West* — *West Dr.* — *Center Dr.* — *Seventh Ave.* — *Sixth Ave.* — *Fifth Avenue* — *East Dr.*

M N,R,W

dancers boogie to DJ-spun tunes. At the end of the Mall, walk down the stairs and pass through the tunnel, where you'll emerge at lovely **Bethesda Fountain** ⑪, a popular place to hang out on warm summer days. A path directly west of the fountain forks north and south: go north to stand on the wood-and-cast-iron **Bow Bridge** ⑮, overlooking the Lake. Walk south along the Lake to **Cherry Hill** ⑰ to get a glimpse of the West Side skyline. From here, loop around Lake all the way up to the **Shakespeare Garden** ⑳ and just beyond it, **Belvedere Castle** ㉒. Climb the castle for a view down to the Delacorte Theater stage and the Great Lawn, beyond. From here, walk east along the path and then turn north past **Cleopatra's Needle** ㉔. A left turn brings you to the **Great Lawn** ㉕, usually chock-full on warm days. Make your way across, minding the Frisbees and sidestepping bikini-clad sun-seekers, or settle in for a little R&R yourself before following west-leading paths out to 81st Street and Central Park West, facing the Museum of Natural History.

TIMING   Allow two hours to complete this walk at a leisurely pace. But, if the weather's in your favor, take a half-day to amble along the route, stopping to rest, eat, play, and really enjoy one of New York's most impressive attractions. The circular drive (encompassing West, Center, and East drives) is closed to automobiles weekdays 10 AM–3 PM above 72nd Street and throughout the park is closed 7 PM–10 PM and weekends and holidays. Take side paths at other times. Bike and in-line skate traffic is often heavy and sometimes fast moving, so stay toward the inside when you're walking.

frugal
fun

The **Central Park Conservancy** (☎ 212/360-2726 ⊕ www. centralparknyc.org/thingstodo/walkingtours) gives 9 different free walking tours of the park on Wednesdays, Saturdays, and Sundays. It's the perfect opportunity to explore the Ramble without getting lost, become well-versed in the park's history, or get clued into "hidden" aspects you might otherwise have missed. Most tours are one hour.

What to See

🐦 ⑬ **Alice in Wonderland.** Lewis Carroll's heroine from the immortal *Alice's Adventures in Wonderland* is 11 feet tall and bronzed here, in one of the most popular statues in the park. Alice sits queenlike on a giant mushroom, with the White Rabbit to her left, the Mad Hatter to her right, and the Cheshire cat above in a tree. The statue was donated to the park in 1959 by philanthropist George Delacorte. Sculptor José de Creeft remained true to the John Tenniel's illustrations in the first edition of the book. ⊠ *East of East Dr., just north of Conservatory Water Boathouse, Central Park* Ⓜ *Subway: 6 to 77th St.*

⑥ **The Arsenal.** Built between 1847 and 1851 as a storage facility for munitions, the Arsenal predates the park and is the second-oldest structure within its grounds—the oldest structure is Blockhouse No. 1 (⇨ below). Between 1869 and 1877 it was the early home of the American Museum of Natural History, and is now the headquarters of the Parks and Recreation Department. An upstairs gallery has changing exhibits relating to park and natural-environmental design. Olmsted and Vaux's original plan for Central Park is in a display case on the third floor. ✉ *830 5th Ave., at E. 64th St., Central Park* ☎ *212/360–8111* ✆ *Free* ☉ *Weekdays 9–5* Ⓜ *Subway: 6 to 68th St./Hunter College.*

✋ ⑧ **Balto.** This bronze statue commemorates Balto, a real-life sled dog who led a team of huskies that carried medicine for 60 mi across perilous ice to Nome, Alaska, during a 1925 diphtheria epidemic. The surface of the statue is shiny from being petted by thousands of children. ✉ *East of Center Dr. near Literary Walk and E. 67th St., Central Park* Ⓜ *Subway: 6 to 68th St./Hunter College.*

need a break?

Although the park has plenty of hot dog stands (near park entrances) and a few cafés connected with attractions, food choices are limited. New Yorkers usually pack a snack or picnic lunch for a day in the park. Park goers have practically worn a path from Zabar's, on 80th and Broadway, to the park's 81st Street entrance.

At the **Ballfields Café** (✉ Midpark near W. 63rd St., Central Park), in the redbrick Ballplayers House south of the carousel, kids can order grilled cheese or peanut-butter-and-jelly sandwiches before or after a spin on the carousel. The **Boathouse Café** (✉ Midpark at E. Park Dr., Central Park ☎ 212/517–2233) is an open-air restaurant and bar that serves lunch and dinner. (Not recommended for kids.) An adjacent cafeteria dishes up a good cheap breakfast and lunch. In warm weather, the lake view from the Boathouse's terrace is idyllic. The Moorish-style **Mineral Springs Pavilion** (✉ Midpark near W. 68th St., Central Park) was built as one of the park's four refreshment stands in the late 1860s. The pavilion now houses the Sheep Meadow Cafe, which serves sandwiches, salads, and grilled steak. Behind it are the croquet grounds and lawn-bowling greens.

✋ ㉒ **Belvedere Castle.** Standing regally atop Vista Rock, the second-highest natural point in the park, Belvedere Castle becomes the highest (man-made) point in the park. From here you can see the stage of Delacorte Theater and observe the picnickers and softball players on the Great Lawn. The castle was built in 1872 of the same gray Manhattan schist that thrusts out of the soil in dramatic outcrops throughout the park (you can examine some of this schist, polished and striated by Ice Age glaciers, from the lip of the rock). A typically 19th-century mishmash of styles—Gothic with Romanesque, Chinese, Moorish, and Egyptian motifs—the castle was deliberately kept small so that when it was viewed from across the lake, the lake would seem bigger. (The Ramble, to the south, now obscures the lake's castle view.) Since 1919 it has been a U.S. Weather Bureau station; look for twirling meteorological instruments atop the tower. Inside, the Henry Luce Nature Observatory has nature exhibits, children's workshops, and educational programs. Free discovery kits containing binoculars, bird guides, maps, and sketching materials are available (before 4 PM) in exchange for two pieces of identification. ✉ *Midpark at 79th St. Transverse, Central Park* ☎ *212/772–0210* ✆ *Free* ☉ *Tues.–Sun. 10–5* Ⓜ *Subway: B, C to 81st St.*

⓫ Bethesda Fountain. Few New York views are more romantic than the one

from the top of the magnificent stone staircase that leads down to the ornate, three-tier Bethesda Fountain. The fountain was built to celebrate the opening of the Croton Aqueduct, which brought clean drinking water to New York City. The name Bethesda was taken from biblical pool in Jerusalem that was supposedly given healing powers by an angel, which explains the statue *The Angel of the Waters* rising from the center. (The statue was designed by Emma Stebbins, the first woman to be commissioned for a major work of art in New York City, in 1868.) The four figures around the fountain's base symbolize Temperance, Purity, Health, and Peace. Beyond the terrace stretches the lake, filled with swans and amateur rowboat captains. ⊠ *Midpark at 72nd St. Transverse, Central Park* Ⓜ *Subway: B, C to 72nd St.*

㉙ Blockhouse #1. The oldest building in the park, the Blockhouse was one of three constructed hastily in September of 1814 as a fortification against the British invasion of New York City. The builders were volunteers and worked quickly, as is evident in the unevenness of the stone facade. Only a shell of the blockhouse remains; the interior is not open to visitors. Getting to the blockhouse requires taking winding paths through a heavily wooded area and should not be attempted alone. ⊠ *South of entrance at Adam Clayton Powell Jr. Blvd. and Central Park N, Central Park* Ⓜ *Subway: B, C to Cathedral Pkwy./110th St.*

⓯ Bow Bridge. This splendid cast-iron bridge arches over a neck of the lake between Bethesda Fountain and the Ramble. Stand here to admire the water's mirror image of vintage apartment buildings peeping above the treetops—a quintessential New York image. ⊠ *Midpark north of 72nd St. Transverse, Central Park.*

⓹ Central Park Wildlife Center. Even a leisurely visit to this small but delightful menagerie of more than 130 species will only take about an hour. The Bronx Zoo it isn't—there's no space for such animals as zebras and giraffes to roam, and the biggest specimens here are polar bears. Don't miss the sea lion feedings, possibly the zoo's most popular attraction, daily at 11:30, 2, and 4. Clustered around the central Sea Lion Pool are separate exhibits for each of the Earth's major environments. Penguins and polar bears live at Polar Circle; the highlights of the open-air Temperate Territory are the chattering monkeys; and the Rain Forest contains the flora and fauna of the tropics. ⊠ *Entrance at 5th Ave. and E. 64th St., Central Park* ☎ *212/439–6500* ⊕ *www.centralparkzoo.org* ⊠ *$6* ☞ *No children under 16 admitted without adult* ⊘ *Apr.–Oct., weekdays 10–5, weekends 10–5:30; Nov.–Mar., daily 10–4:30* Ⓜ *Subway: 6 to 68th St./Hunter College; N, R, W to 5th Ave./59th St.; F to Lexington Ave./63rd St.*

⓱ Cherry Hill. Originally a watering area for horses, this circular plaza with a small wrought-iron-and-gilt fountain is a great vantage point for the lake and the West Side skyline. ⊠ *Midpark near 72nd St. Transverse, Central Park.*

㉔ Cleopatra's Needle. This hieroglyphic-covered obelisk that began life in Heliopolis, Egypt, around 1600 BC, has nothing to do with Cleopatra—

it's just New York's nickname for the work. It was eventually carted off to Alexandria by the Romans in 12 BC, and landed here on February 22, 1881, when the khedive of Egypt made it a gift to the city. It stands behind the Metropolitan Museum, on the west side of East Park Drive. A century-plus in New York has done more to ravage the Needle than millennia of globe-trotting, and the hieroglyphics have sadly worn away to a tabula rasa. The copper crabs supporting the huge stone at each corner almost seem squashed by its weight. ⊠ *E. Park Dr. north of 79th St. Transverse, Central Park* Ⓜ *Subway: 6 to 77th St.*

㉗ **Conservatory Garden.** These magnificent formal gardens occupy 6 acres south of the Harlem Meer in Central Park's northeast corner. The conservatory's entrance is marked by elaborate wrought-iron gates that once graced the midtown 5th Avenue mansion of Cornelius Vanderbilt II. The classic Italian–style **Central Garden** has a lawn bordered by yew hedges and cool crab-apple allées. Across the lawn is the large Conservatory Fountain, beyond which a semicircular wisteria-draped pergola rises into the hillside. The French-inspired **North Garden** marshals large numbers of bedding plants into elaborate floral patterns. The three bronze girls dancing in the Untermeyer Fountain are at the heart of a circular bed where 20,000 tulips bloom in spring and 2,000 chrysanthemums herald autumn. Perennials in the English-style **South Garden** surround a statue of characters from the classic children's book *The Secret Garden* by Frances Hodgson Burnett. ⊠ *Near 5th Ave. and E. 105th St., Central Park* ☎ 212/360–2766 ⊠ *Free* ☉ *Daily 8–dusk* Ⓜ *Subway: 6 to 103rd St.*

☝ ⑫ **Conservatory Water.** The sophisticated model boats that sail this Renaissance Revival–style stone basin are raced each Saturday morning at 10, spring through fall. At the north end is the **Alice in Wonderland** statue; on the west side of the pond, a bronze statue of **Hans Christian Andersen,** the Ugly Duckling at his feet, is the site of storytelling hours on summer Saturdays at 11 AM. Model sailboats can be rented from a concession by the boat pond. ⊠ *East side of park, from E. 73rd to E. 75th Sts., Central Park* Ⓜ *Subway: 6 to 77th St.*

❹ **The Dairy.** When it was built in the 19th century—back when the northern border of residential Manhattan was at 38th Street—the Dairy sat amid grazing cows and sold milk by the glass. Today the Swiss-chalet-style Dairy houses the **Central Park Visitor Center,** which has exhibits on the park's history, maps, a park reference library, and information about park events. ⊠ *Midpark south of 65th St. Transverse, Central Park* ☎ 212/794–6564 ☉ *Apr.–Oct., Tues.–Sun. 10–5; Nov.–Mar., Tues.–Sun. 10–4.*

㉓ **Delacorte Theater.** Some of the best things in New York are, indeed, free—including summer "Shakespeare in the Park" performances at this open-air stage. Casts are often studded with Hollywood stars. Meryl Streep, Michelle Pfeiffer, Christopher Walken, Helen Hunt, Morgan Freeman, and Kevin Kline are just a few that have performed here. Tickets are free and are given out starting at 1 PM on the day of each show. What you save in money, you make up for in time—lines are *long.* Plan to line up by mid-morning or earlier if there have been good reviews. It's not unheard of for theatergoers to show up at 7 AM with a breakfast picnic to weather the wait. Each person on line is allowed two tickets for that evening's performance. Same-day tickets are also given away at the Public Theater (425 Lafayette St., East Village) at 1 PM. ⊠ *Midpark near W. 81st St., Central Park* ☎ *212/539–8750 seasonal* ⊕ *www.publictheater. org* ⊙ *Mid-June–Labor Day, Tues.–Sun. 8 PM* Ⓜ *Subway: 6 to 77th St.; B, C to 81st St.*

☾ ❸ **Friedsam Memorial Carousel.** Remarkable for the size of its hand-carved steeds—all 57 are three-quarters the size of real horses—this carousel was built in 1908 and moved here from Coney Island in 1951. Today it's considered one of the finest examples of turn-of-the-20th-century folk art. The carousel's original Wurlitzer organ plays a variety of tunes, from old-time waltzes to polkas. ⊠ *Midpark south of 65th St. Transverse, Central Park* ☎ *212/879–0244* ▤ *$1.25* ⊙ *Apr.–Nov., daily 10–dusk; Dec.–Mar., weekends 10–dusk, weather permitting* Ⓜ *Subway: 1, 9 to 66th Street/Lincoln Center.*

㉕ **Great Lawn.** This 14-acre oval greensward has endured millions of footsteps, thousands of ball games, hundreds of downpours, dozens of concerts, and even the crush attending one papal mass. Yet, it's the stuff of a suburbanite's dream—perfectly tended turf (a mix of rye and Kentucky bluegrass), state-of-the-art drainage systems, automatic sprinklers, and careful horticultural monitoring. The area hums with action on weekends and most summer evenings, when its softball fields and picnicking grounds provide a much-needed outlet for city folk (and city dogs) of all ages. ⊠ *Midpark between 81st and 85th Sts., Central Park.*

㉘ **Harlem Meer.** Those who never venture beyond 96th Street miss out on two of the park's loveliest attractions: the Conservatory Garden and Harlem Meer, an 11-acre sheet of water where, in warmer months, as many as 100 people a day fish for stocked largemouth bass, catfish, golden shiners, and bluegills (catch-and-release only). At the meer's north end is the Victorian-style **Charles A. Dana Discovery Center,** where you can learn about geography, orienteering, ecology, and the history of the upper park. Within walking distance of the center are fortifications from the American Revolution and other historic sites, as well as woodlands, meadows, rocky bluffs, lakes, and streams. Fishing poles are available with identification from mid-April through October. ⊠ *Between 5th and Lenox Aves. at Central Park N, Central Park* ☎ *212/ 860–1370* ⊙ *Discovery Center Tues.–Sun. 10–5* Ⓜ *Subway: 2, 3 to Central Park North/110th St.*

㉖ **Jacqueline Kennedy Onassis Reservoir.** This 106-acre body of water was built in 1862 to provide fresh water to Manhattan residents. Although it still contains 1 billion gallons, it's no longer used for drinking water— the city's main reservoirs are upstate. A 1.58-mi cinder path circling the lake is popular with runners year-round. Please observe local traffic rules and travel counterclockwise. Even if you're not training for the New York Marathon, it's worth visiting the Reservoir for a 360-degree view of surrounding high-rises, which makes for stirring sunsets. In spring and fall the hundreds of trees around the reservoir burst into color, and migrant waterfowl are plentiful. Just remember to look out for the athletes, as they have the right of way. The Reservoir was officially named the Jacqueline Kennedy Onassis Reservoir in 1994 for the former first lady, who frequently jogged in the area and lived nearby. ⊠ *Midpark from 85th to 96th Sts., Central Park.*

⑭ Loeb Boathouse. At the brick neo-Victorian boathouse on the park's 18-acre lake, you can rent a dinghy, take a ride in an authentic Venetian gondola, or pedal off on a rented bicycle. ⊠ *Midpark at E. Park Dr., Central Park* ☎ *212/517–2233* ☞ *Boat rental $10 per hr ($30 deposit); $30 per half-hr for gondola rides; bicycle rental $9–$15 per hr, deposit required* ☉ *Boats and bikes available Mar.–Oct., daily 10–6, weather permitting. Call for gondolier's schedule* Ⓜ *Subway: 6 to 77th St.*

★ ⑩ The Mall. Around the turn of the 20th century, fashionable ladies and gentlemen used to gather to see and be seen on this broad, formal walkway. Today the Mall looks as grand as ever. The south end of its main path, the **Literary Walk,** is covered by the majestic canopy of the largest collection of American elms in North America and lined by statues of authors and artists such as Robert Burns, Shakespeare, and Sir Walter Scott. East of the Mall, behind the Naumburg Bandshell, is the site of **SummerStage,** a free summertime concert series. ⊠ *Midpark between 66th and 72nd Sts., Central Park* Ⓜ *Subway: 6 to 68th St./Hunter College.*

⑲ Naturalists' Walk. Starting at the West 79th Street entrance to the park, this landscaped nature walk (through which you can wind your way toward the **Swedish Cottage,** the **Shakespeare Garden,** and **Belvedere Castle**) has spectacular rock outcrops; a stream that attracts bird life; a woodland area with various native trees; stepping-stone trails; and, thankfully, benches. ⊠ *Off Central Park W between W. 77th and W. 81st Sts., Central Park* Ⓜ *Subway: B, C to 81st St.*

▶ ❶ The Pond. Swans and ducks can sometimes be spotted on the calm waters of the Pond. For an unbeatable view of the city skyline, walk along the shore to **Gapstow Bridge.** From left to right you can see the brown peak-roof Sherry-Netherland Hotel; the black-and-white CBS Building; the rose-color Chippendale-style top of the Sony Building; the black-glass shaft of Trump Tower; and, in front, the green gables of the Plaza hotel. ⊠ *Central Park S and 5th Ave., Central Park* Ⓜ *Subway: N, R, W to 5th Ave.*

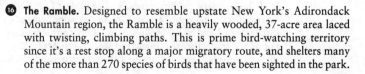

a new york moment

Emerge from the 5th Avenue N/R stop or stand at the corner of 5th and 59th and get hit with the 1-2-3 punch of Central Park with horse-drawn carriages lining its southern border, the majestic Plaza Hotel and Grand Army Plaza fountain, and a view all the way down 5th Avenue to the Empire State Building and beyond.

⑯ The Ramble. Designed to resemble upstate New York's Adirondack Mountain region, the Ramble is a heavily wooded, 37-acre area laced with twisting, climbing paths. This is prime bird-watching territory since it's a rest stop along a major migratory route, and shelters many of the more than 270 species of birds that have been sighted in the park.

The Central Park Conservancy leads walking tours here. Because the Ramble is so dense and isolated, however, it's not a good place to wander alone or at night. ⊠ *Midpark between E. 74th St. and 79th St. Transverse, Central Park* ☎ *212/360–2727 tours.*

㉠ Shakespeare Garden. Inspired by the flora mentioned in the playwright's work, this somewhat hidden garden (between Belvedere Castle and the Swedish Cottage) is well worth a stop. Under the dedicated care of the gardener, something is almost always blooming on the terraced hillside of lush beds. The fantastic spring bulb display beginning in March and June's peak bloom of antique roses are particularly stunning times to visit. The curving paths are furnished with handsome rustic benches, making this park-designated quiet zone a superb spot for a good read or contemplative thought. ⊠ *W. Park Dr. and 79th St. Transverse, Central Park* Ⓜ *Subway: B, C to 81st St.*

❾ Sheep Meadow. A sheep grazing area until 1934, this grassy 15-acre meadow is now a favorite of picnickers and sunbathers. It's a designated quiet zone; the most vigorous sports allowed are kite flying and Frisbee tossing. Just west of the meadow, the famous **Tavern on the Green,** originally the sheepfold, was erected by Boss Tweed in 1870 and is now an overpriced restaurant and the site of many New York weddings. ⊠ *East of West Dr. and north of 65th St. Transverse, Central Park.*

⓲ Strawberry Fields. This memorial to John Lennon, who penned the classic 1967 song "Strawberry Fields Forever," is sometimes called the "international garden of peace." Its curving paths, shrubs, trees, and flower beds donated by many countries create a deliberately informal landscape reminiscent of English parks. Every year on December 8, Beatles fans mark the anniversary of Lennon's death by gathering around the star-shape, black-and-white IMAGINE mosaic set into the pavement. Lennon's 1980 murder took place across the street at the Dakota apartment building, where he lived. ⊠ *W. Park Dr. and W. 72nd St., Central Park* Ⓜ *Subway: B, C to 72nd St.*

☾ ㉑ Swedish Cottage Marionette Theatre. Since 1947, puppet theater has been entertaining pint-size New Yorkers in this 1876 traditional Swedish schoolhouse. The house was imported for the Philadelphia Exhibition and brought to Central Park soon thereafter. At this writing, the show is "Three," which presents the tales "The Three Little Pigs," "The Three Bears," and "The Three Billy Goats Gruff." ⊠ *W. Park Dr. north of 79th St. Transverse, Central Park* ☎*212/988–9093* ☒*$6* ☉ *Shows Oct.–June, Tues.–Fri. 10:30 and noon, Sat. 1; July and Aug., Tues.–Fri. 10:30 and noon. Closed Sun., Mon., and Sept. Reservations required.* Ⓜ *Subway: B, C to 81st St.*

☾ ❼ Tisch Children's Zoo. This minizoo gives kids the opportunity to pet and feed sheep, goats, rabbits, cows, and pigs. The Enchanted Forest is a surreal place filled with "acorns" the size of Saint Bernards, a climbable "spider web," and hoppable "lily pads." Other attractions include a duck pond, children's theater, touch and sound displays, and a water-spray play area. Avoid weekends, when the zoo is packed. ⊠ *Just north of*

Central Park Wildlife Center, Central Park 🖼 *$6; price includes Wildlife Center* ⊙ *Apr.–Oct., weekdays 10–5, weekends 10–5:30; Nov.–Mar., daily 10–4:30* Ⓜ *Subway: 6 to 68th St./Hunter College.*

🌙 ➋ **Wollman Memorial Rink.** Its music blaring out into the tranquillity of the park can be a bit of an intrusion, but you can't deny that this rink dwarfed by billion-dollar Central Park South skyscrapers makes a great setting for a spin on the ice. You can watch skaters from the terrace. ✉ *E. Park Dr. south of 65th St. Transverse, Central Park* ☎ *212/439–6900* 🖼 *$11 Fri.–Sun., $8.50 Mon.–Thurs. Skate rentals $4.75. Lockers $3.75, plus $6.25 refundable deposit* ⊙ *Nov.–Mar., Mon. and Tues. 10–2:30, Wed. and Thurs. 10–10, Fri. and Sat. 10 AM–11 PM, Sun. 10–9, weather permitting* Ⓜ *Subway: N, R, W to 5th Ave.*

THE UPPER WEST SIDE

Never as exclusive as the tony East Side—the primarily residential Upper West Side has a more earthy appeal. Although real estate prices have gone sky high (its restored brownstones and co-op apartments are among the city's most coveted residences), the Upper West Side is still a haven for families. On weekends, stroller-pushing parents cram the sidewalks and shoppers jam the fantastic gourmet food stores and fashion emporiums that line Broadway. In the evenings, Upper West Siders mingle in bars and restaurants along Columbus and Amsterdam avenues. The lively avenues, quiet tree-lined side streets, two flanking parks— Central on the east, Riverside on the west—and leading cultural complexes, such as the American Museum of Natural History and Lincoln Center, all in a relatively compact area, make this a great neighborhood for a relaxing morning or afternoon.

Numbers in the text correspond to numbers in the margin and on the Upper West Side & Morningside Heights map.

a good walk

Begin at **Columbus Circle** ➊ ⏻, at the southwest corner of Central Park. Follow Central Park West up past the gleaming Trump International Hotel & Towers and head west down 64th Street. At the end of the street, across Broadway is **Lincoln Center** ➋. On the next block is the Julliard School of Music. Across the street in the square below Barnes and Noble, there's a farmers market on Thursday and Saturday (8–5), a great place to stop for fruit, homemade pastries, hot chocolate, or apple cider, depending on the season. Head up Columbus Avenue, past ABC studios on your left, and interesting boutiques and restaurants on both sides. Make a right on 71st Street. On the north side of this quiet residential block is low-key Cafe La Fortuna, an old haunt of John Lennon. His former residence, the not-so-low-key **Dakota** ➎ is around the corner, at 72nd Street and Central Park West. Yoko Ono still lives here. Strawberry Fields (⇨ Central Park), a memorial to Lennon, is just inside the park across the street. Continue up Central Park West past the 27-story Italian Baroque San Remo Apartments (between 74th and 75th Sts.), whose twin towers are visible from nearly everywhere in Central Park. (Dustin Hoffman, Paul Simon, and Marilyn Monroe all lived here at

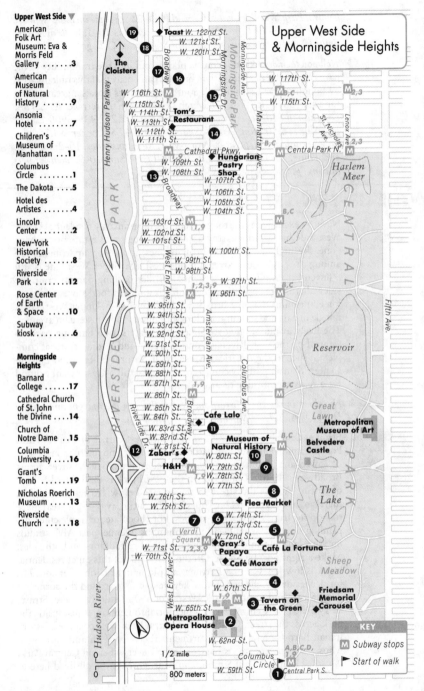

Upper West Side & Morningside Heights

Toast
The Cloisters
Broadway
W. 122nd St.
W. 121st St.
W. 120th St.
Morningside Ave.
Morningside Dr.
Morningside Park
W. 117th St.
W. 116th St.
W. 115th St.
W. 115th St.
Tom's Restaurant
W. 114th St.
W. 113th St
W. 112th St.
W. 111th St.
St. Nicholas Ave.
Lenox Ave.
Manhattan Ave.
Cathedral Pkwy.
W. 109th St.
W. 108th St.
Hungarian Pastry Shop
W. 107th St.
W. 106th St.
W. 105th St.
W. 104th St.
Central Park N.
Harlem Meer
W. 103rd St.
W. 102nd St.
W. 101st St.
W. 100th St.
W. 99th St.
W. 98th St.
W. 97th St.
W. 96th St.
West End Ave.
W. 95th St.
W. 94th St.
W. 93rd St.
W. 92nd St.
W. 91st St.
W. 90th St.
W. 89th St.
W. 88th St.
W. 87th St.
W. 86th St.
W. 85th St.
W. 84th St.
Amsterdam Ave.
Columbus Ave.
Reservoir
Cafe Lalo
W. 83rd St.
W. 82nd St.
W. 81st St.
Museum of Natural History
Great Lawn
Metropolitan Museum of Art
Belvedere Castle
Zabar's
W. 80th St.
W. 79th St.
H&H
W. 78th St.
W. 77th St.
Broadway
Riverside Dr.
W. 76th St.
W. 75th St.
Flea Market
The Lake
Verdi Square
W. 74th St.
W. 73rd St.
Gray's Papaya
Café La Fortuna
W. 72nd St.
W. 71st St.
W. 70th St.
Café Mozart
Sheep Meadow
West End Ave.
W. 67th St.
Tavern on the Green
Friedsam Memorial Carousel
W. 65th St.
Metropolitan Opera House
W. 62nd St.
CENTRAL PARK
Fifth Ave.
Hudson River
Henry Hudson Parkway
RIVERSIDE PARK

1/2 mile
800 meters

Columbus Circle
W. 59th St. Central Park S.

KEY
Ⓜ Subway stops
▶ Start of walk

one time.) Between 76th and 77th streets is the **New-York Historical Society** 8 and three blocks north is the **American Museum of Natural History** 9. Walk down 81st Street to Broadway. Chain stores dominate this section of the Upper West Side, but New York Institutions like Zabar's gourmet market (Broadway above 80th St.) and H&H Bagels (Broadway below 80th St.)—which many consider to be the best bagels in New York—remain. Take a left at 85th Street and walk to Riverside Drive. William Randolph Hearst once occupied the top five floors of the Clarendon Building, at 137 Riverside (between 85th and 86th). Wander down quiet Riverside Drive. Between 83rd and 84th streets, you can access **Riverside Park** 12, where a stroll along the Hudson River will make you feel miles away from Manhattan.

TIMING This walk shouldn't take more than two hours if you don't stop in at the museums. If the weather's bad, skip the walk and nose around the Upper West Side's spectacular museums instead. If you're here on a Sunday, consider hitting the upscale flea market at the southwest corner of West 77th Street and Columbus Avenue (10–5).

What to See

3 **American Folk Art Museum: Eva and Morris Feld Gallery.** The changing exhibitions at this intimate museum (a branch of the American Folk Art Museum on West 53rd Street) include arts and decorative objects from the 18th century to the present day that are culled from all over the Americas. What's on show—folk paintings, textiles, outsider art, dolls, trade signs, weather vanes, and quilts—is frequently an extension of themes highlighted at the main museum. The gift shop has intriguing crafts, books, Christmas ornaments, and cards. ✉ *2 Lincoln Sq., Columbus Ave. between W. 65th and W. 66th Sts., Upper West Side* ☎ *212/595–9533* 💳 *$3 suggested admission* ⏲ *Tues.–Sat. noon–7:30, Sun. noon–5* Ⓜ *Subway: 1, 9 to 66th St./Lincoln Center.*

need a break?

Cute-as-a-button **Cafe Lalo** (✉ 201 W. 83rd St., between Amsterdam and Broadway ☎ 212/496–6031) is the perfect place to stop for a quick *croque monsieur* or chocolate mousse cake. Large windows look out onto a quiet side street. This is where Tom Hanks stood up Meg Ryan in *You've Got Mail.* Weekend brunch hours are beyond busy. Open 24/7, **H & H Bagels** (✉ 2239 Broadway, at W. 80th St., Upper West Side ☎ 212/595–8003) sells—and ships around the world—a dozen varieties of what are arguably the best bagels in New York.

9 Fodor's Choice ★ **American Museum of Natural History.** With 45 exhibition halls and more than 32 million artifacts and specimens, the world's largest and most important museum of natural history can easily occupy you for half a day. Dinosaur mania begins in the barrel-vaulted **Theodore Roosevelt Rotunda,** where a 50-foot-tall skeleton of a barosaurus rears on its hind legs, protecting its fossilized baby from an enormous marauding allosaurus. Three spectacular dinosaur halls on the fourth floor—the **Hall of Saurischian Dinosaurs,** the **Hall of Ornithischian Dinosaurs,** and the **Hall of Vertebrate Origins**—use real fossils and interactive computer stations to present interpretations of how dinosaurs and pterodactyls might

have behaved. In the **Hall of Fossil Mammals,** interactive video monitors featuring museum curators explain what caused the woolly mammoth to vanish from the Earth and why mammals don't have to lay eggs to have babies. The **Hall of Biodiversity** focuses on Earth's wealth of plants and animals; its main attraction is the walk-through "Dzanga-Sangha Rainforest," a life-size diorama complete with the sounds of the African tropics—from bird calls to chain saws. In the revamped **Hall of Meteorites,** the 34-ton *Ahnighito*—the largest meteorite on display in the world—is accompanied by a video on space rocks narrated by Sally Ride, America's first female astronaut. The **Hall of Human Biology and Evolution**'s wondrously detailed dioramas trace human origins and feature a computerized archaeological dig. The popular 94-foot blue whale model swims high above the **Hall of Ocean Life,** a "fully immersive marine environment," complete with shimmering blue lighting and whale song. For a taste of what the museum was like before computers and other high-tech wizardry were introduced, visit the softly lighted **Carl Akeley Hall of African Mammals,** where a small herd of elephants is frozen in time and surrounded by artful early-20th-century dioramas depicting beasts in their habitats.

Attached to the museum is the **Rose Center for Earth and Space** (⇨ below), with various exhibits and the **Hayden Planetarium.** Films on the museum's 40-foot-high, 66-foot-wide **IMAX Theater** (☎ 212/769–5034 show times) screen are usually about nature (climbing Mt. Everest or an underwater journey to the wreck of the *Titanic*) and cost $19, including museum admission. ⊠ *Central Park W at W. 79th St., Upper West Side* ☎ *212/769–5200* ⊕ *www.amnh.org* ☞ *$13 suggested donation, includes admission to Rose Center; museum and planetarium show combination ticket $22. Prices may vary for special exhibitions* ☉ *Daily 10–5:45* Ⓜ *Subway: B, C to 81st St.*

❼ **Ansonia Hotel.** This 1904 beaux arts masterpiece designed by Paul M. Duboy commands its corner of Broadway with as much architectural detail as good taste can stand. Inspiration for the former apartment hotel's turrets, mansard roof, and filigreed-iron balconies came from turn-of-the-20th-century Paris. Suites came without kitchens (and separate quarters for a staff that took care of the food). Designed to be fireproof, it has thick, soundproof walls that make it attractive to musicians; famous denizens of the past include Enrico Caruso, Igor Stravinsky, Arturo Toscanini, Florenz Ziegfeld, Theodore Dreiser, and Babe Ruth. Today, the Ansonia is a condominium apartment building. ⊠ *2109 Broadway, between 73rd and 74th Sts., Upper West Side* Ⓜ *Subway: 1, 2, 3, 9 to 72nd St.*

⓫ **Children's Museum of Manhattan.** In this five-story exploratorium, children ages 1–10 are invited to paint their own masterpieces, float boats down a "stream," and put on shows at a puppet theater. To complement the exhibits, art workshops, science programs, and storytelling sessions are held daily. ⊠ *212 W. 83rd St., between Broadway and Amsterdam Aves., Upper West Side* ☎ *212/721–1234* ⊕ *www.cmom. org* ☞ *$8* ☉ *Wed.–Sun. 10–5* Ⓜ *Subway: 1, 9 to 86th St.*

Wandering leisurely up Central Park West in the 70s and 80s, and down Upper West Side streets just window shopping, stopping into cafés, or eating ice-cream on a stoop makes you feel like a character in a Woody Allen movie—or at least like a regular old New Yorker.

▶ **❶ Columbus Circle.** Broadway, 8th Avenue, Central Park West, and Central Park South all meet at this busy intersection, which gets its name from the 700-ton granite monument capped by a marble statue of Columbus in the middle of the traffic circle. The traffic circle is under construction at this writing, part of the large-scale project to create the monolithic, now-completed **Time Warner Center** that looms over the circle. The 80-story, twin-tower supercomplex designed by skyscraper architect David M. Childs, houses a minimall on the first three floors with a Sephora, Borders, Samsung, Coach, and other shops. The fourth floor has restaurants, including outrageously priced sushi restaurant Masa (a meal for two easily tops $700). Above are luxury condos (in the $45 million range) and the Mandarin Oriental Hotel. Launched in late 2004, **Jazz at Lincoln Center** (✉ Entrance to private escalator on 4th fl. ☎ 212/ 258–9800 ⊕ www.jazzatlincolncenter.org) is the world's first performing-arts center devoted to jazz. The center includes the large Rose Theater concert hall; the Allen Room, with its gorgeous skyline views; Dizzy's Club with a dance floor overlooking Columbus Circle; and the Jazz Hall of Fame with a 24-foot-long video wall showing historic footage of hall-of-fame inductees.

Northeast of the circle, standing guard over the entrance to Central Park, is the **Maine Monument,** whose gleaming equestrian figures perch atop a formidable limestone pedestal. At the monument's foot are horse-drawn cabs awaiting fares through Central Park, and a newsstand in a Victorian-style pavilion. The **Trump International Hotel and Tower** fills the wedge of land between Central Park West and Broadway; it's also home to the self-named Jean-Georges restaurant, where the celebrity chef works his culinary magic.

❺ The Dakota. Most famous for being the home of John Lennon, the Dakota was designed by Henry Hardenbergh, who also built the Plaza Hotel. It was at the Dakota's gate where, in December 1980, a deranged fan shot and killed Lennon as he came home from a recording session. Other celebrity tenants have included Boris Karloff, Rudolf Nureyev, José Ferrer and Rosemary Clooney, Lauren Bacall, Rex Reed, Leonard Bernstein, Gilda Radner, and Connie Chung. When it was completed in 1884, the Dakota was so far uptown that it was jokingly described as being "out in the Dakotas." Indeed, this buff-color château, with picturesque gables and copper turrets, housed some of the West Side's first residents. ✉ 1 W. 72nd St., at Central Park W, Upper West Side Ⓜ Subway: B, C to 72nd St.

❹ Hotel des Artistes. Built in 1918 with an elaborate, mock-Elizabethan lobby, this "studio building," like several others on West 67th Street, was designed with high ceilings and immense windows, making it ideal for artists. Its tenants have included Isadora Duncan, Rudolph Valentino, Norman

CloseUp

FAMOUS FILM SITES

Annie Hall *(1977)*: Alvy waits for Annie in front of the Beekman Theater (2nd Ave., at E. 66th St.). At the end of the movie, Annie and Alvy part ways at 63rd and Columbus.

Breakfast at Tiffany's *(1961)*: Holly Golightly's apartment is at 169 E. 71st Street, between Lexington and 3rd avenues.

Ghostbusters *(1984)*: Dana Barrett's apartment is at 55 Central Park West (between 65th and 66th Sts). Movie magic made it appear taller than its 19 stories. The Columbia University campus appears near the beginning of the movie.

Hannah and Her Sisters *(1986)*: Hannah lives at the Langham (135 Central Park West, between 73rd and 74th Sts.), which was Mia Farrow's own apartment.

Manhattan *(1979)*: The film opens at Elaine's restaurant (2nd Ave., between E. 88th and E. 89th Sts.). Isaac meets his high-school-age girlfriend outside the Dalton School, at 108 East 89th Street.

Rosemary's Baby *(1968)*: Filmed at the Dakota Apartments (Central Park West, at 72nd St.).

West Side Story *(1961)*: The tenements where the film was shot were later torn down to build Lincoln Center.

When Harry Met Sally *(1989)*: The titular characters run into one another at the Shakespeare & Company bookstore (Lexington Ave., at 69th St.). Later they walk through the sunny modern art wing at the Metropolitan Museum of Art.

You've Got Mail *(1998)*: Kathleen's bookshop was Maya Schaper Cheese & Antiques (W. 69th St., at Columbus Ave.). Joe stood her up at Café Lalo (W. 83rd St., between Amsterdam and Broadway) and rescued her at the checkout at Zabar's (Broadway at 80th St.). The final scene is at the Riverside Park 91st Street Garden.

Rockwell, Noël Coward, George Balanchine, and contemporary actors Joel Grey and Richard Thomas; another tenant, Howard Chandler Christy, designed the lush, soft-tone murals in the ground-floor restaurant, Café des Artistes. ⊠ *1 W. 67th St., at Central Park W, Upper West Side* Ⓜ *Subway: 1, 9 to 66th St./Lincoln Center.*

★ ❷ **Lincoln Center.** A unified complex of pale travertine, Lincoln Center (built 1962–68) is the largest performing arts center in the world—so large it can seat nearly 18,000 spectators at one time in its various halls. Here maestro Lorin Maazel conducts Brahms and Beethoven, the American Ballet Theater performs *Swan Lake,* and Tony winner Audra McDonald sings solos and duets—and that's just an average day. The complex's three principal venues are grouped around the central Fountain Plaza: to the left, as you face west, is Philip Johnson's **New York State Theater,** home to the New York City Ballet and the New York City Opera. In the center, brilliantly colored Chagall murals are visible through the arched lobby windows of Wallace Harrison's **Metropolitan Opera House** (⇨ below) home to the Metropolitan Opera. And to the right is Max Abramovitz's **Avery Fisher Hall,** host to the New York Philharmonic Orchestra. A great time to visit the complex is on summer evenings, when hundreds of dancers trot and swing around the plaza during Midsummer Night Swing. One-hour guided tours, given daily, cover the center's history and wealth of artwork.

Lincoln Center encompasses much more than its three core theaters. Its major outdoor venue is **Damrosch Park,** on the south flank of the Met, where summer open-air festivals are often accompanied by free concerts at the **Guggenheim Bandshell.** In chillier months, the Big Apple Circus settles in. Accessible via the walk between the Metropolitan and Avery Fisher is the North Plaza—the best of Lincoln Center's spaces—with a huge Henry Moore sculpture reclining in a reflecting pool. The long lines and glass wall of Eero Saarinen's **Lincoln Center Theater** stand behind the pool. It's home to the **Vivian Beaumont Theater,** officially considered a Broadway house, despite its distance from the theater district. Below it is the smaller **Mitzi E. Newhouse Theater,** where many award-winning plays originate. Next to the Lincoln Center Theater is the **New York Public Library for the Performing Arts** with its extensive collection of books, records, videos, and scores on music, theater, and dance. An overpass leads from this plaza across West 65th Street to the world-renowned **Juilliard School** for music and theater; actors Kevin Spacey, Kevin Kline, Robin Williams, Bebe Neuwirth, Laura Linney, and Patti LuPone studied here. An elevator leads down to street level and **Alice Tully Hall,** home of the Chamber Music Society of Lincoln Center and the New York Film Festival. Or turn left from the overpass and follow the walkway west to Lincoln Center's **Walter Reade Theater,** one of the city's best art-film venues. ⊠ *W. 62nd to W. 66th St. between Broadway and Amsterdam Ave., Upper West Side* ☎ *212/546–2656 general information and performance schedules, 212/875–5350 tour schedule and reservations* ⊕ *www.lincolncenter.org* 🎟 *Tour $12.50* Ⓜ *Subway: 1, 9 to 66th St./Lincoln Center.*

Metropolitan Opera House. In the 1870s the Academy of Music, at 14th Street and Irving Place, was the place for cultured New Yorkers to get their opera. Overcrowding led some wealthy businessmen—Rockefeller and Vanderbilt among them—to fund the new Metropolitan Opera House in 1880, then on Broadway between 39th and 40th streets. This first building was destroyed by fire in 1892 (started by a workman who dropped a cigarette), but was replaced with an even more ornate, baroque structure. The opera house remained there until 1966, when, for want of sufficient space for elaborate productions and such modern conveniences as air-conditioning, a new venue was built at Lincoln Center. The '60s-modern sweeping concrete-and-class facade of today's building, fronted by a plaza and fountain, is a New York icon. It's especially beautiful at night. The old opera house went the way of the old Penn Station, and was demolished in 1967. ⊠ *Lincoln Center, W. 62nd to W. 66th St. between Broadway and Amsterdam Ave., Upper West Side* ☎ *212/362–6000* ⊕ *www.metopera.org.*

❽ New-York Historical Society. The city's oldest museum, founded in 1804, the New-York Historical Society has one of the city's finest research libraries, with a collection of 6 million pieces of art, literature, and memorabilia. Exhibitions shed light on New York's—and America's—history, everyday life, art, and architecture. Highlights of the collection include

George Washington's inaugural chair, 500,000 photographs from the 1850s to the present, original watercolors for John James Audubon's *Birds of America,* the architectural files of McKim, Mead & White, the largest U.S. collection of Louis Comfort Tiffany's lamps, and one of the most in-depth collections of pre-20th-century American paintings in the world, including seminal landscapes by Hudson River School artists Thomas Cole, Asher Durant, and Frederic Church. There are usually four or five changing exhibits on subjects ranging from colonial map-making to Victorian board games. ✉ *2 W. 77th St., at Central Park W, Upper West Side* ☎ *212/873–3400* ⊕ *www.nyhistory.org* ✉ *$10 suggested donation* ⊘ *Tues.–Sun. 10–6* Ⓜ *Subway: B, C to 81st St.*

did you know?

One of the world's largest bible collections is on the Upper West Side. The **American Bible Society Library** (✉ 1865 Broadway, at 61st St. ☎ 212/408–1200) holds nearly 50,000 scriptural items in more than 2,000 languages, including Helen Keller's 10-volume Braille Bible, leaves from a first-edition Gutenberg Bible, and a Torah from China. Tours are by appointment only.

🕐 ⓬ **Riverside Park.** When you spend your days surrounded by cement and skyscrapers, it's easy to forget that an expansive waterfront is just blocks away. Riverside Park—bordering the Hudson from 72nd to 159th streets—dishes out a dose of perspective. The park was laid by Central Park's designers Olmsted and Vaux between 1873 and 1888 and is often, somewhat unfairly, outshone by Olmsted's "other" park. But with its waterfront bike- and walking paths and lesser crowds, Riverside Park holds its own.

From the corner of West 72nd Street and Riverside Drive—where a **statue of Eleanor Roosevelt** stands at the park's entrance—head down the ramp (through an underpass beneath the West Side Highway) to the **79th Street Boat Basin,** a rare spot in Manhattan where you can walk right along the river's edge and watch a flotilla of houseboats bobbing in the water. These boats must sail at least once a year to prove their seaworthiness. Behind the boat basin, the **Rotunda** is home in summer to the Boat Basin Cafe, an open-air spot for a snack and river views. From the Rotunda, head up to the **Promenade,** a broad formal walkway extending a few blocks north from West 80th Street, with a stone parapet overlooking the river.

At the end of the Promenade, a community garden explodes with flowers. To the right, cresting a hill along Riverside Drive at West 89th Street, stands the Civil War **Soldiers' and Sailors' Monument** (1902, designed by Paul M. Duboy), an imposing 96-foot-high circle of white-marble columns. From its base is a view of Riverside Park, the Hudson River, and the New Jersey waterfront. ✉ *W. 72nd to W. 159th Sts. between Riverside Dr. and the Hudson River, Upper West Side* Ⓜ *Subway: 1, 2, 3, 9 to 72nd St.*

⓾ **Rose Center of Earth & Space.** Attached to the Museum of Natural History, the Rose Center is home to the spectacular **Hayden Planetarium,** a 90-foot aluminum-clad sphere that appears to float inside an enormous glass cube. Models of planets, stars, and galaxies dangle overhead, and an elevator whisks you to the top of the sphere and the planetarium's Sky Theater, which "transports" you from galaxy to galaxy as if you were traveling through space. The **Space Shows**, "The Search for Life: Are We Alone?," narrated by Harrison Ford, and "Passport to the Universe," narrated by Tom Hanks, incorporate up-to-the-minute scientific knowledge about the universe in computerized projections generated from a database of more than 2 billion stars. After the show, you descend a spiral walkway that tracks 13 billion years of the universe's evolution. The Rose Center also includes two major exhibits, the **Hall of the Universe**, in which black holes and colliding galaxies are explored, and the **Hall of Planet Earth**, which explains the climate, geology, and evolution of our home planet with the help of more than 100 giant rocks from the ocean floor, glaciers, and active volcanoes. On the first Friday evening of every month the Rose Center turns into a cocktail lounge, with tapas-style dining and live jazz under the "stars" (5:45–8:15). For pure musical entertainment and the latest in high-tech digital animation, **SonicVision** at the Hayden Planetarium is a 35-minute audiovisual roller coaster (think Pink Floyd laser show, with current music) mixed by Moby and featuring music by Radiohead, the Flaming Lips, Cold Play, and David Bowie. ⊠ *Central Park W at W. 79th St., Upper West Side* ☎ *212/769–5200* ⊕ *www.amnh.org/rose* ⊠ *$13 suggested donation, includes admission to Museum of Natural History; museum and planetarium show combination ticket $22; SonicVision $22* ☉ *Sat.–Thurs. 10–5:45, Fri. 10–8:45. Space show Sun.–Thurs. and Sat. 10:30–4:40, Fri. 10:30–7:30. SonicVision Fri. and Sat. at 7:30, 8:30, 9:30, and 10:30* Ⓜ *Subway: B, C to 81st St.*

need a break? The down-at-the-heels decor at **Café La Fortuna** (⊠ 69 W. 71st St., between Columbus Ave. and Central Park W, Upper West Side ☎ 212/724–5846) is actually part of its charm in this ever-more-expensive neighborhood. The tree-filled garden is a quiet place to sip a cappucino and snack on a prosciutto-and-mozzarella sandwich. Photos of the café's most famous patron, John Lennon, adorn the walls.

❻ **Subway kiosk.** This brick-and-terra-cotta building with rounded neo-Dutch molding is one of two remaining control houses from the original subway line (the other is at Bowling Green in lower Manhattan). Built in 1904–05 by the architectural team of Heins and Lafarge, it was the first express station north of 42nd Street. Beneath it is one of the most heavily trafficked subway stations in Manhattan. ⊠ *W. 72nd St. and Broadway, Upper West Side.*

MORNINGSIDE HEIGHTS

Most people think the area north of 106th Street and south of 125th Street on the west side is just part of the Upper West Side. The neighborhood, however, is Morningside Heights, and is largely dominated by Columbia University. Actually, Morningside Heights, on the high ridge north and west of Central Park, was developed in the 19th century partly *because* of Columbia, which relocated here from Midtown in 1897. Idealistically conceived as an American Acropolis, the cluster of academic and religious institutions—Barnard College, St. Luke's Hospital, and St. John the Divine, to name a few—that developed here managed to keep these blocks stable during years when neighborhoods on all sides were collapsing due to the Depression. In the 1980s and 1990s, West Side gentrification reclaimed the area to the south. Within the gates of the Columbia or Barnard campuses or inside the hushed St. John the Divine or Riverside Church, New York City takes on a different character. This is an *uptown* student neighborhood—less hip than the Village, but friendly, fun, and intellectual.

Numbers in the text correspond to numbers in the margin and on the Upper West Side & Morningside Heights map.

a good walk

Begin at 116th Street and Broadway (1, 9 to 116th St./Columbia University). Walk west along 116th Street to Riverside Drive and then head right (north) to **Grant's Tomb** ⑲, one of the most overlooked and underrated sites in the city. From the steps of the tomb, you get an excellent view of Gothic-style **Riverside Church** ⑱. A less-impressive Gothic structure, the Union Theological Seminary, is at Broadway and 122nd Street, on your right as you walk east on 122nd. Across the street is the Manhattan School of Music and across from that, the Jewish Theological Seminary. Head south on Broadway. The block between Broadway and Amsterdam on 120th Street is dominated by redbrick Victorian buildings that house Columbia University's Teachers College, founded in 1887. Enter the **Columbia University** ⑯ campus at 116th Street, on the east side of Broadway. After wandering the truly beautiful campus, take the south exit onto 114th Street, and walk back toward Broadway. Two blocks south, Tom's Restaurant, on your left, should be a familiar sight—the exterior appeared in most episodes of *Seinfeld*. It's also the location mentioned in the Suzanne Vega song, "Tom's Diner." No matter how many times you turn left onto 112th off Broadway, the view of massive **Cathedral Church of St. John the Divine** ⑭, which dead-ends the block, takes your breath away. Don't leave without a peek inside.

TIMING   This walk takes about an hour at an unhurried stride. Fall and spring, when the trees lining the streets are blooming or leaves are turning, are the best seasons for the walk. On Sundays, the bells ring out at Riverside Church, for an extra bit of zen.

What to See

⓱ **Barnard College.** One of the former Seven Sisters women's colleges, Barnard, established in 1889, has steadfastly remained single-sex and independent from Columbia, although its students can take classes there (and vice versa). Note the bear (the college's mascot) on the shield above the main gates at West 117th Street. The brick-and-limestone campus design echoes that of Columbia University. To the right of Barnard Hall, a path leads through the narrow but neatly landscaped campus. Famous Barnard graduates include Suzanne Vega, Laurie Anderson, Martha Stewart, Erica Jong, Zora Neale Hurston, and Joan Rivers. ✉ *Entrance at Broadway and W. 117th St., Morningside Heights* ☎ *212/854-2014* ⊕ *www.barnard.edu* ✆ *Stu-*

dent-led tours Mon.–Sat. at 10:30 and 2:30 when classes are in session Ⓜ *Subway: 1, 9 to 116th St./Columbia University.*

> **need a break?** Columbia-area intellectual hangout **Hungarian Pastry Shop** (✉ 1030 Amsterdam Ave., at W. 111th St., Morningside Heights 🖀 212/866–4230) is a cozy—as in small *and* as in comfortable—place for tasty desserts and coffee. The exterior of **Tom's Restaurant** (✉ 2880 Broadway, at 112th St., Morningside Heights 🖀 212/864–6137) made frequent appearances on the TV show *Seinfeld*. Whether you are excited by its claim to fame or not, this diner is still a good, decently priced place for a New York bite.

🅮 Fodor'sChoice ★ **Cathedral Church of St. John the Divine.** Everything about the cathedral is colossal, from its cavernous 601-foot-long nave, which can hold some 5,000 worshippers, to its 162-foot-tall dome crossing, which could comfortably contain the Statue of Liberty, to its **Great Rose Window**, the largest stained-glass window in the United States, made from more than 10,000 pieces of colored glass. Even though this divine behemoth is unfinished—the transepts and tower are the most noticeably uncompleted elements—it is already the largest Gothic cathedral in the world. To get the full effect of the building's size, approach it from Broadway on West 112th Street. On the wide steps climbing to the Amsterdam Avenue entrance, five portals arch over the entrance doors. The central **Portal of Paradise** depicts St. John witnessing the Transfiguration of Jesus, and 32 biblical characters, all intricately carved in stone. The 3-ton bronze doors below the portal open only twice a year—on Easter and in October for the Feast of St. Francis. The doors have relief castings of scenes from the Old Testament on the left and the New Testament on the right.

The cathedral's first cornerstone was laid in 1892. The original architects were George Heins and Christopher Grant Lafarge, who had beat out 80 other competitors with a Romanesque-Byzantine design. It took nearly 20 years for just the choir and vaulted dome crossing to be completed. When Heins died, the project came under the direction, in 1911, of Ralph Adams Cram, a Gothic Revival purist who insisted on a French Gothic style for the edifice (his work also shaped Princeton University and West Point). The granite of the original Romanesque-Byzantine design is still visible inside at the crossing, where it has yet to be finished with the Gothic limestone facing. Note that the finished arches are pointed—Gothic—while the uncovered two are in the rounded Byzantine style. Although work on the cathedral had continued for nearly 50 years, construction came to a halt during World War II. Work did not resume again until 1979, by which time stonecutting had become something of a lost art in this country; in order to continue building, stonecutters came from Europe to train local craftspeople. As it stands, the cathedral is now about two-thirds complete. In 2002, work was halted again following a fire that damaged the north transept. Though the cathedral remains almost fully functional, the financial burden of the fire put construction on hold.

Inside, the **Saint Saviour Chapel** contains a three-panel bronze altar in white-gold leaf with religious scenes by artist Keith Haring (this was his last work before he died in 1990). The more conventional **baptistry,** to the left of the altar, is an exquisite octagonal chapel with a 15-foot-high marble font and a polychrome sculpted frieze commemorating New York's Dutch heritage. The altar area expresses the cathedral's interfaith tradition and international mission—with menorahs, Shinto vases, and, in the **Chapels of the Seven Tongues** behind the altar, dedications to various ethnic groups. Seventeenth-century Barberini tapestries hang throughout the cathedral.

A precinct of châteaulike Gothic-style buildings, known as the **Cathedral Close,** is behind the cathedral on the south side. In a corner by the Cathedral School is the **Biblical Garden,** with perennials, herbs, and an arbor. Around the bend from here is a rose garden. Back at Amsterdam Avenue, the **Peace Fountain** depicts the struggle of good and evil. The forces of good, embodied in the figure of the archangel Michael, triumph by decapitating Satan, whose head hangs from one side. The fountain is encircled by small, whimsical animal figures cast in bronze from pieces sculpted by children. ⊠ *1047 Amsterdam Ave., at W. 112th St., Morningside Heights* ☎ *212/316–7540, 212/662–2133 box office, 212/ 932–7347 tours* ⊕ *www.stjohndivine.org* ⌑ *Tours $5* ⊙ *Mon.–Sat. 7–6, Sun. 7–7; July and Aug. cathedral closes at 6 on Sun. Tours Tues.–Sat. at 11, Sun. at 1. Sun. services at 8, 9, 9:30, 11, and 6* Ⓜ *Subway: 1, 9 to 110th St./Cathedral Pkwy.*

⑮ Church of Notre Dame. A French neoclassical landmark building (1911), this Roman Catholic church has a grand interior, including a replica of the French grotto of Lourdes behind its altar. It once served a predominantly French community of immigrants, but like the neighborhood, today's congregation is more ethnically diverse, with Irish, German, Italian, African-American, Hispanic, and Filipino members. ⊠ *405 W. 114th St., at Morningside Dr., Morningside Heights* ☎ *212/866–1500* ⊙ *Bldg. open 30 min before and after masses. Masses weekdays at 8 and 12:05, Sat. at 12:05 and 5:30, and Sun. at 8:30, 11:30, and 5:30* Ⓜ *Subway: 1, 9 to 116th St./Columbia University.*

⑯ Columbia University. This wealthy, private, coed Ivy League school was New York's first college when it was founded in 1754. Back then, before American independence, it was called King's College—note the gilded crowns on the black wrought-iron gates at the Amsterdam Avenue entrance—and was in lower Manhattan, near the present-day intersection of Park Place and West Broadway. Famous early graduates were John Jay and Alexander Hamilton.

The herringbone-pattern brick paths of College Walk lead into the open main quadrangle, dominated by the neoclassical **Butler Library** to the south and the rotunda-top **Low Memorial Library** to the north. Butler, built in 1934, holds the bulk of the university's 7 million books. Low was built in 1895–97 by McKim, Mead & White, which laid out the general campus plan when the college moved here in 1897. Modeled on the Roman Pantheon, Low is now mostly offices, but on weekdays you can go inside to see its domed, templelike former Reading Room. Low Library also houses the **visitor center,** where you can pick up a campus guide or arrange a tour. The steps of Low Library, presided over by Daniel Chester French's statue *Alma Mater,* have been a focal point for campus life, not least during the student riots of 1968. The southwest corner of the quad is the site of Lerner Hall, Columbia's distinctly 21st-century **student center**, with a six-story glass atrium and ultramod glass catwalks.

Before Columbia moved here, this land was occupied by the Bloomingdale Insane Asylum, evidenced today only by Buell Hall (1878), a gabled orange-red brick house east of Low Library. North of Buell Hall is the interdenominational **St. Paul's Chapel** (☎ 212/854–1493 ☯ Sept.–May, daily 10 AM–11 PM when classes are in session, with services on Sun.; chapel closes at 5 during school breaks), an exquisite little Byzantine-style dome church with fine tile vaulting inside. It also has a 5,347-pipe organ, a marble terrazzo floor, and stained-glass windows depicting famous Columbia alumni. ✉ *Main entrance at 116th St. and Broadway, Morningside Heights* ☎ 212/854–4900 ⊕ *www.columbia.edu* ☯ *Weekdays 9–5. Tours begin 11 and 2 weekdays from Room 213, Low Library* Ⓜ *Subway: 1, 9 to 116th St./Columbia University.*

> **here's where**
>
> In 1915, the infamous "Typhoid Mary" Mallon was arrested at her place of employment, the Sloan Women's Hospital near Columbia University, where she was working as a cook after city officials had forbidden her from doing so. In her defense, Mallon didn't believe she carried typhoid fever, since she was never sick from it. And despite her notorious legacy, she passed on only 33 cases of the virus, 3 of which resulted in deaths.

⑲ Grant's Tomb. This national monument, the final resting place of Civil War general and two-term president Ulysses S. Grant and his wife Julia Dent Grant, commands a stalwart position overlooking Riverside Park and the Hudson River. Opened in 1897, almost 12 years after Grant's death, it was a more popular sight than the Statue of Liberty until the end of World War I. The towering granite tomb, the largest mausoleum in North America, is engraved with the words LET US HAVE PEACE, recalling Grant's speech to the Republican convention upon his presidential nomination. Under a small white dome, the Grants' twin black-marble coffins are sunk into a deep circular chamber visible from above; mini-galleries to the sides display photographs and Grant memorabilia. ✉ *Riverside Dr. and W. 122nd St., Morningside Heights* ☎ 212/666–1640 ⊕ *www.nps.gov/gegr* 🎫 *Free* ☯ *Daily 9–5; 20-min tours on the hr* Ⓜ *Subway: 1, 9 to 125th St.*

⑬ Nicholas Roerich Museum. An 1898 Upper West Side town house is the site of this small, eccentric museum dedicated to the work of Russian artist Nicholas Roerich, who immigrated to New York in the 1920s and quickly developed an ardent following. Some 200 of his paintings hang here—notably some vast canvases of the Himalayas. He also designed sets for ballets, such as Stravinsky's *Rite of Spring,* photographs of which are also on view. Free chamber music concerts are usually held here on Sunday afternoon at 5. ✉ *319 W. 107th St., between Broadway and Riverside Dr., Morningside Heights* ☎ 212/864–7752 ⊕ *www.*

roerich.org ✉ *By donation* ⊙ *Tues.–Sun. 2–5* Ⓜ *Subway: 1, 9 to 110th St./Cathedral Pkwy.*

⓲ **Riverside Church.** The Riverside Drive–facing edifice of this 1930 Gothic-style church, with elaborate stone carvings modeled on the French cathedral of Chartres, is gorgeous. The other reason to visit the church is to take the elevator to the top of the 22-story, 356-foot tower, with its 74-bell carillon—the heaviest in the world at 200,000 pounds—to get the breathtaking panoramic view of the Hudson River, New Jersey Palisades, and George Washington Bridge from the bell tower. ✉ *490 Riverside Dr., between W. 120th and W. 122 Sts., Morningside Heights* ☎ *212/870–6792* ⊕ *www.theriversidechurchny.org* ✉ *Free* ⊙ *Visitor center Tues. 10:30–5, Wed. 10:30–7, Thurs. and Fri. 10:30–5, Sun. 9:45–10:45 and 12:15–3. Service Sun. at 10:45; call for hrs for tower* Ⓜ *Subway: 1, 9 to 116th St./Columbia University.*

One of the best—and cheapest—ways to see the city is by public bus. For just $2, for example, you can take scenic trip to the Cloisters on the M4 bus. It travels from Madison Avenue right by Grand Central Station up through the Upper East Side, over to Broadway, past Columbia University and through Harlem.

HARLEM

Harlem has been the capital of African-American culture and life for nearly a century, but it didn't start out that way. It was first settled by Dutch farmers; many Jews moved here from the Lower East Side in the late 1800s and by the 19th century, Harlem was a well-to-do suburb. Black New Yorkers began settling here in large numbers in about 1900, moving into a surplus of fine apartment buildings and town houses built by real estate developers for a middle-class white market that never materialized. By the 1920s Harlem had become the most famous black community in the United States.

Harlem's heyday was the Roaring '20s, when a confluence of talent—black novelists, playwrights, musicians, and artists, many of them seeking to escape discrimination and persecution in other parts of the country—gathered here to create what was dubbed the Harlem Renaissance. Whites flocked here for the infamous parties and nightlife, blacks settled in for the opportunity this self-sustaining community represented. But the Depression hit Harlem hard. By the late 1930s it was no longer a hot spot for the downtown set, and many African-American families began moving to Queens and New Jersey.

By the 1960s Harlem's population had dropped dramatically, and many of the Harlemites who remained were disillusioned enough with social injustices to join in civil rights riots. Deteriorating housing, crushing poverty, and petty crime turned the neighborhood into a simmering ghetto. Today, however, Harlem is experiencing a second renaissance. Deserted buildings and yards of rubble still scar certain streets, but shining amid them are old jewels such as the Apollo Theatre, architecturally splendid churches, and

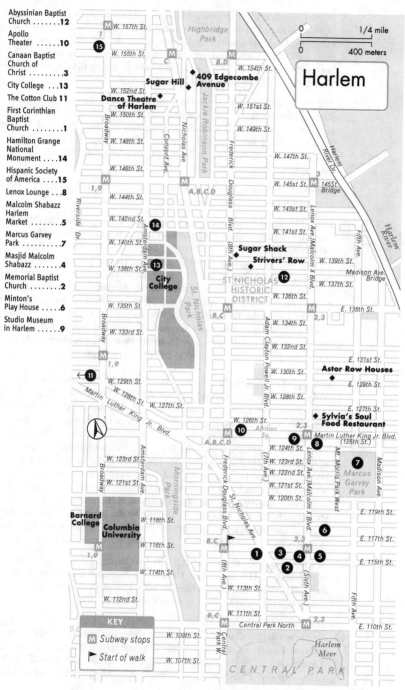

Harlem

cultural magnets like the Studio Museum in Harlem. Black (and, increasingly, white) professionals and young families are restoring many of Harlem's classic brownstone and limestone buildings, bringing new life to the community. Commercial rents have doubled in recent years as the neighborhood became more desirable. Even former President Bill Clinton chose West 125th Street as the site of his official office.

The city's north–south avenues acquire different names in Harlem: 6th Avenue becomes Lenox Avenue or Malcolm X Boulevard, 7th Avenue is Adam Clayton Powell Jr. Boulevard, and 8th Avenue is Frederick Douglass Boulevard; West 125th Street, the major east–west street, is Martin Luther King Jr. Boulevard. People still use the streets' former names, but the street signs use the new ones.

Numbers in the text correspond to numbers in the margin and on the Harlem map.

a good walk

From 116th and 8th Avenue, walk east on 116th Street, passing some of Harlem's most interesting religious institutions: ornate **First Corinthian Baptist Church** ❶ is first, on your right; across 7th Avenue you come to **Canaan Baptist Church of Christ** ❸ and then **Masjid Malcolm Shabazz** ❹ mosque. Straight ahead, across Lenox Avenue/Malcolm X Boulevard on the south side of the street is the **Malcolm Shabazz Harlem Market** ❺, where you can stock up on cowry-shell jewelry, African masks, and caftans at good prices. Go north on Lenox Avenue to 118th Street. On this block is now-defunct **Minton's Playhouse** ❻, the club where bebop was born. Walk east to 5th Avenue and north to **Marcus Garvey Park** ❼. From a vantage point up the steps to the park, you can see all the way way down 5th Avenue to Midtown. Walk around the south and west sides of the park, taking in the well-preserved late-19th-century brownstones of the Mount Morris Historic District. At 124th Street, turn left and then take a right onto Lenox Avenue/Malcolm X Boulevard. Near the corner of 125th Street on your right is the legendary jazz hangout, the **Lenox Lounge** ❽. The hub of present-day Harlem is here, along 125th Street, an in-your-face flurry of activity that resembles an outdoor strip mall. In front of towering stores like Foot Locker and Old Navy, hawkers sell bootleg CDs and DVDs, books, and homemade essential oils in nondescript bottles. One block west, between Lenox Avenue and Adam Clayton Powell Boulevard, is the **Studio Museum in Harlem** ❾ and across the street on the next block is the landmark **Apollo Theater** ❿. The subway (A, B, C, D trains) is at 8th Avenue, but better yet, get the complete Harlem experience with soul food at Sylvia's, on Lenox Avenue and 126th Street.

TIMING The walk takes about an hour and a half without stopping, but dawdling is encouraged. Do the walk in the morning or early afternoon. Blocks that feel perfectly safe during the day when Harlemites are out and about can be equally desolate in cold weather or after dusk.

What to See

⓬ **Abyssinian Baptist Church.** Charlie Parker's funeral was held here. Adam Clayton Powell Jr., the first black U.S. congressman, and his father, Adam Clayton Powell Sr., have both served as pastors here. Fats Waller's father was also a minister. The Gothic-style building opened its doors in

HARLEM'S JAZZ AGE

T WAS IN HARLEM THAT *Billie Holiday got her first singing job, Duke Ellington made his first recording, and Louis Armstrong was propelled to stardom. Jazz was king during the Harlem Renaissance in the 1920s and '30s, and though Chicago and New Orleans may duke it out for the "birthplace of jazz" title, New York was where jazz musicians came to be heard.*

In the 1920s, downtown socialites would flock to Harlem's Cotton Club and Connie's Inn (131st St. and 7th Ave.) to hear "black" music. Both clubs were white-owned and barred blacks from entering, except as performers. (The rules changed years later.) It was at Connie's that New York was introduced to Louis Armstrong. Harlem's most popular nightspot by far, the Cotton Club booked such big names as Fletcher Henderson, Coleman Hawkins, Duke Ellington, Cab Calloway, and Ethel Waters. After shows ended at the paying

clubs, musicians would head to such after-hours places with black patrons as Small's Paradise (229 7th Ave., at 135th St.), Minton's Playhouse, and Basement Brownies, where they'd hammer out new riffs into the wee hours.

Today you can hear great jazz all over the city, but old-time clubs like the Lenox Lounge still hash it out unlike anywhere else. Why? Partly due to history and sense-of-place, and partly due to—as musicians claim—the more easygoing nature of uptown clubs, which tend to have more flexible sets and open jam sessions. You can't go back in time to Harlem's jazz heyday, but you might catch a modern-day jazz great in the making.

1923, but the church was founded in 1808 in lower Manhattan (Worth St.) by a group of parishioners who defected from the segregated First Baptist Church of New York City, making Abyssinian Baptist Church the first African-American Baptist church in New York State. Sermons by pastor Calvin Butts are fiery and the gospel choir is excellent. The Coptic cross on the pulpit was a gift from Haile Selassie, when he was king of Ethiopia. Parishioners take the phrase "Sunday best" to heart, so look the part. Lineups on holiday Sundays can be intense. Expect to arrive at 6:30 AM on Easter Sunday. ✉ *132 Odell Clark Pl. (W. 138th St.), between Adam Clayton Powell Jr. Blvd. (7th Ave.) and Malcolm X Blvd. (Lenox Ave.), Harlem* ☎ *212/862–7474* ⊕ *www.abyssinian.org* ☉ *Sun. services 9 and 11* Ⓜ *Subway: 2, 3 to 135th St.*

🔟 **Apollo Theater.** Since 1934, seemingly nearly every big-time black entertainer has performed here. The careers of Billie Holiday, James Brown, Sarah Vaughan, and Ella Fitzgerald were launched by winning the Apollo's Amateur Night contest. But discovering new talent was not what gained the Apollo its rep; instead the theater was the ultimate venue for established acts—the one that proved an artist had really made it. Crowds were tough and would boo even well-respected acts if they weren't up to snuff. The result was some of the best live performances of all time, by artists like Aretha Franklin, Nat "King" Cole, and Sammy Davis Jr. James Brown's 1962 recording "Live at the Apollo" is thought by many to be the best live recording ever made. Hard to believe that this world-famous slice of Harlem started in 1913 as a whites-only burlesque hall, called Hurtig & Seasom's Burlesque Theater. As more blacks moved to the neighborhood, new owners decided to capitalize on the growing market, and the rest is history. The Apollo fell on hard times in the '70s and went bankrupt in 1978. But it has been back in business since 1983, when the theater was declared a historic landmark. The Apollo's star power is not as great as in its heyday, but Amateur Night is as raucous as ever. Hour-long guided tours are given by appointment. ⊠ *253 W. 125th St., between Adam Clayton Powell Jr. Blvd. (7th Ave.) and Frederick Douglass Blvd. (8th Ave.), Harlem* ☎ *212/531–5301 performances, 212/531–5337 tours* ⊕ *www.apollotheater.com* ⊡ *Tours $11 weekdays, $13 weekends* ⊙ *Tours by appointment. Amateur Night every Wed. at 7:30* Ⓜ *Subway: A, B, C, D to 125th St.*

need a break?

Sylvia's Soul Food Restaurant (⊠ 328 Malcolm X Blvd., between W. 126th and W. 127th Sts., Harlem ☎ 212/996–0660) is the most famous soul-food spot in Harlem—make that in New York. It seated 35 when it opened in 1962, now it seats 450 and takes up half a city block. Southern specialties include giant portions of fried catfish, barbecued pork chops, eggs and fried chicken (for breakfast), and the requisite grits, collard greens, and sweet potatoes on the side.

❸ **Canaan Baptist Church of Christ.** The heavenly gospel music that saturates Sunday-morning services makes up for this church's concrete-box-esque exterior. Tourists (who are there to look, not to participate in the service) are only allowed to enter on Sunday once the parishioners have been seated. Skip that scene and don your Sunday best to attend a service to fully experience the music and one of the Reverend Wyatt Tee Walker's inspirational sermons. Walker worked with Dr. Martin Luther King Jr. in the 1960s and is an internationally known human rights activist. Dr. King delivered his famous "A Knock at Midnight" sermon (penned in 1963) here one month before his assassination in 1968. ⊠ *132. W. 116th St., between Malcolm X Blvd. (Lenox Ave./6th Ave.) and Adam Clayton Powell Jr. Blvd. (7th Ave.), Harlem* ☎ 212/866–0301 ⊙ *Services Sun. at 10:45* AM Ⓜ *Subway: 2, 3 to 116th St.*

⓭ **City College.** The beautiful neo-Gothic stone towers of City College decorate the ridge of Hamilton Heights. The arched schist gates, moss-covered stone, and white terra-cotta trim could easily be part of an Ivy League campus, but the college has always been a public institution. Tuition was actually free until the mid-1970s. Famous alumni include Jonas Salk and Colin Powell. ⊠ *138th St. at Convent Ave., Harlem* ☎ 212/650–7000 ⊕ *www.ccny.cuny.edu* Ⓜ *Subway: 1, 9 to 137th St.*

⓫ **The Cotton Club.** Big-band king Duke Ellington made a name for himself at this elitist club that peaked in the 1930s. Only the wealthiest, most influential New Yorkers could even get into the club—oh, and they had

HARLEM GOSPEL TOURS

THE TYPICAL "GOSPEL TOUR" includes only a 20-minute stop at a church to hear some of the sermon and the gospel music. Then you're off (via bus) to another Harlem sight or to a soul-food brunch. Prices range from $35 to $80. The tours are an expeditious, if not authentic, way to experience a bit of Harlem.

The tours garner mixed reactions from church officials and parishioners. Some see it as an opportunity to broaden horizons and encourage diversity. But others find tours disruptive and complain that tourists take seats away from regular parishioners (churches regularly fill to capacity). If you decide to go on one of these tours, remember that parishioners do not consider the service, or themselves, to be tourist attractions. Also, dress nicely. Harlem church-goers take the term "Sunday best" to heart and are impressively decked out. Be as quiet as possible and avoid taking photos or videos.

For a rich gospel-church experience, do your own tour. The following are some of the Uptown churches with gospel choirs:

Abyssinian Baptist Church (⇨ Harlem) is one of the few churches that does not allow tour groups. Services are at 9 and 11 AM. *Convent Avenue Baptist Church* (✉ 429 W. 145th St., between Convent and St. Nicholas Aves. ☎ 212/234–6767 ⊕ www.conventchurch.org) has services at 8 AM, 11 AM, and 6 PM. *First Corinthian Baptist Church* (⇨ Harlem) has services at 11 AM.

Greater Refuge Temple (✉ 2081 7th Ave., at 124th St. ☎ 212/866–1700) has services at 11 AM. *Memorial Baptist Church* (⇨ Harlem) has services at 10:45 AM. *Riverside Church* (⇨ Harlem) has services at 10:45 AM.

---

to be white, too. Ironically, the club featured some of the most talented black musicians in history, including Cab Calloway and Louis Armstrong. Part of the appeal of the Cotton Club for well-to-do white folks, who would make the pilgrimage from their downtown abodes on weekends, was the thrill: here you could rub elbows with gangsters and celebrities, drink alcohol (during Prohibition), and do it all in the heart of Harlem. The club closed in 1935 and reopened in 1978. Today, the venue has swing dance nights and frequent jazz acts. ✉ 666 W. 125th St., between 129th St. and Riverside Dr., Harlem ☎ 212/663–7980 ⊕ www.cottonclub-newyork.com.

❶ First Corinthian Baptist Church. One of the most ornate structures in Harlem, this church was built in 1913 as the Regent Theatre. The design is based on the Doges' Palace in Venice, evident in the thin columns and arches of the facade. Architect Thomas W. Lamb went on to design a series of Italian Renaissance–style movie theaters, including the Roxy, the Rivoli, and the Regent. ✉ 1912 Adam Clayton Powell Jr. Blvd. (7th Ave.), Harlem ☎ 212/864–9526 ⊘ Services Sun. at 10:45 Ⓜ Subway: 2, 3 to 116th St.

⑭ Hamilton Grange National Memorial. Alexander Hamilton lived in this federal-style house from 1802 to 1804. The pretty row houses and churches that comprise Hamilton Heights were built around the turn of the 20th century on land once owned by Hamilton. The house is crowded between Luke's Episcopal Church and a residential building about 100 yards south of its original location. A statue of the man himself stands outside. ✉ *287 Convent Ave., between W. 141st and 142nd Sts., Harlem* ☎ *212/283–5154* ⬚ *Free* ☉ *Fri.–Sun.9–5* Ⓜ *Subway: 1, 9 to 137th St.*

⑮ Hispanic Society of America. This is the best collection of Spanish art outside the Prado in Madrid, with (primarily 15th- and 16th-century) paintings, sculptures, textiles, and decorative arts from Spain, Portugal, Italy, and South America. There are notable pieces by Goya, El Greco, and Velázquez. An entire room is filled with a collection of antique brass knockers. ✉ *Audubon Terrace, Broadway, between W. 155th and W. 156th Sts., entrance up steps to left, Harlem* ☎ *212/926–2234* ⊕ *www.hispanicsociety.org* ⬚ *By donation* ☉ *Sept.–July, Tues.–Sat. 10–4:30, Sun. 1–4* Ⓜ *Subway: 1 to 157th St.*

⑧ Lenox Lounge. Jazz legends ranging from Billie Holiday to John Coltrane have performed in this art deco masterpiece, opened in 1939. Harlem Renaissance giants James Baldwin and Langston Hughes used to write here, huddled around one of the stylish tables or slumped in one of the corner banquets. Get your jazz on at the vocalist jam sessions in the cozy Zebra Room on Sunday nights (7–11); the cover is $5 and there's a two-drink minimum. ✉ *288 Malcolm X Blvd./Lenox Ave., between W. 125th and W. 124th Sts., Harlem* ☎ *212/427–0253* ⊕ *www.lenoxlounge.com* ☉ *Weekdays 11 AM–4 AM, weekends noon–4 AM* Ⓜ *Subway: 2, 3 to 125th St.*

⑤ Malcolm Shabazz Harlem Market. This colorful indoor-outdoor bazaar, with more than 100 permanent stalls, specializes in imported African products, including Mali mud-cloth coats, skirts, and scarves, as well as West African masks and figurines, herbal soaps, leather bags, and contemporary paintings. Summertime brings a kiosk serving Caribbean and Southern-style dishes. ✉ *52 W. 116th St., between Malcolm X Blvd. and 5th Ave., Harlem* ☎ *212/987–8131* ☉ *Daily 10–7* Ⓜ *Subway: 2, 3 to 116th St.*

did you know? In the decade between 1993 and 2003, Harlem's crime rate dropped 65%, which is more than the crime decrease in famously "safe" neighborhoods Greenwich Village, SoHo, and Gramercy.

⑦ Marcus Garvey Park. The main attraction at this park is the three-tier, 47-foot cast-iron **watchtower** (Julius Kroel, 1856), the only remaining part of a now defunct citywide network used to spot and report fires in the days before the telephone. Originally Mount Morris Park, this rocky plot of land was renamed in 1973 after Marcus Garvey (1887–1940), who preached from nearby street corners and led the back-to-Africa movement. The handsome neoclassical row houses of the **Mount Morris Park Historic District** front the west side of the park and line side streets. ✉ *Interrupts 5th Ave. between W. 120th and W. 124th Sts., Madison Ave. to Mt. Morris Park W, Harlem* ⊕ *www.east-harlem.com/parks mg.htm* Ⓜ *Subway: 2, 3 to 125th St.*

❹ **Masjid Malcolm Shabazz** (Malcolm Shabazz Mosque). Talk about religious conversions. In the mid-'60s the Lenox Casino was transformed into this house of worship that doubles as a community center. Yellow panels were added above the windows to give them arches. A huge green onion dome sits atop the building. Sadly, the spinning golden crescent that once topped the dome has been removed. The mosque was named for El-Hajj Malik El-Shabazz (better known as Malcolm X), who once preached here. Though the mosque was founded on the concept of anti-white racism that Shabazz urged at one point in his life, today the message is one of inclusion, the philosophy that Shabazz adopted near the end of his life. ✉ *102 W. 116th St. at Malcolm X Blvd. (Lenox Ave./6th Ave.), Harlem* ☎ *212/622–2201* Ⓜ *Subway: 2, 3 to 116th St.*

> **need a break?** **Settepani Bakery** (✉ 197 Malcolm X Blvd./Lenox Ave., at 120th St., Harlem ☎ 212/862–5909) is an unexpected oasis of Italy in Harlem. Shiny glass displays are filled with sugary biscotti, pies, and cakes.

❷ **Memorial Baptist Church.** The gospel choir fills the sanctuary with soulful, sorrowful, and often joyous gospel music during a two-hour service each Sunday. You can learn to sing gospel, and study its rhythms and history, by enrolling in a Saturday workshop run by the church. The free sessions are especially popular with busloads of Japanese tourists making the weekend rounds. ✉ *141 W. 115th St., between Malcolm X Blvd. (Lenox Ave./6th Ave.) and Adam Clayton Powell Jr. Blvd. (7th Ave.), Harlem* ☎ *212/663–8830* ⊙ *Services Sun. at 10:45 sharp* Ⓜ *Subway: 2, 3 to 116th St.*

❻ **Minton's Playhouse.** All that remains of this historic jazz club is the exterior sign. Many, including Robert DeNiro, have tried to revive the club, which is know as the birthplace of bebop, but its doors remain closed, its interior gutted. Minton's gave trendsetting musicians like Thelonious Monk, Charlie Christian, and Jimmy Blanton room to experiment with improvisation, mixing elements of blues and swing to create an entirely new genre. ✉ *210 W. 118th St., between 5th Ave. and Lenox Ave./Malcolm X Blvd., Harlem* ☎ No phone.

Strivers' Row. Since 1919, African-American doctors, lawyers, and other professionals have owned these elegant homes designed by such notable architects as Stanford White (his neo-Renaissance creations stand on the north side of West 139th Street). Musicians W. C. Handy ("The St. Louis Blues") and Eubie Blake ("I'm Just Wild About Harry") were among the residents here. Behind each row are service alleys, a rare luxury in Manhattan. The area, now officially known as the St. Nicholas Historic District, got its nickname because less affluent Harlemites felt that its residents were "striving" to become well-to-do. ✉ *W. 138th and W. 139th Sts. between Adam Clayton Powell Jr. and Frederick Douglass Blvds., Harlem* Ⓜ *Subway: B, C to 135th St.*

9 **Studio Museum in Harlem.** African-American, Caribbean, and African art
in the form of paintings, sculpture (in a light-filled garden), and photographs (including historic photographs of Harlem by James Van Der
Zee) are on display at this small museum. The gift shop is full of serious and fun African-American, Caribbean, and African-inspired books,
posters, and jewelry. ⊠ *144 W. 125th St., between Malcolm X and Adam
Clayton Powell Jr. Blvds., Harlem* ☎ *212/864–4500* ⊕ *www.
studiomuseuminharlem.org* ⊠ *$7 suggested donation* ⊙ *Wed.–Fri. and
Sun. noon–6, Sat. 10–6* Ⓜ *Subway: 2, 3 to 125th St.*

Sugar Hill. From the 1920s to the 1950s, Sugar Hill, on a hill overlooking
Colonial Park (now Jackie Robinson Park), was Harlem's high-society
neighborhood. Some of the most affluent and influential African-Americans lived here—to name a few: activist W.E.B. Du Bois; Supreme
Court Justice Thurgood Marshall; NAACP leaders Walter White and
Roy Wilkins (all four of whom lived at 409 Edgecombe Ave.); writers
Langston Hughes and Zora Neale Hurston; and jazz musician Duke Ellington. Despite its wealth of prominent black leaders, Sugar Hill was, and
is, one of the most diverse parts of Harlem. The gradual decline of Sugar
Hill, and Harlem, hit bottom in the '70s and '80s when buildings were
neglected and criminals roamed the streets. Today, although Sugar Hill
hasn't managed reclaimed its old glory, it is benefitting from Harlems
so-called second renaissance. ⊠ *Bounded by 145th and 155th Sts. and
Edgecombe and St. Nicholas Aves.*

NORTH OF HARLEM

The two northernmost neighborhoods in Manhattan—Washington
Heights and Inwood—are primarily residential, but have two of the most
important attractions in the city: the Cloisters and the Dyckman Farmhouse Museum. At the very tip of Manhattan is one of the city's densest and wildest parks, Inwood Park.

The Cloisters. Perched atop a wooded hill in Fort Tryon Park, near Manhattan's northernmost tip, the Cloisters houses the medieval collection
of the Metropolitan Museum of Art in a monasterylike setting. Colon-
naded walks connect authentic French and Spanish monastic cloisters,
a French Romanesque chapel, a 12th-century chapter house, and a Romanesque apse. One entire room is devoted to the extraordinarily detailed 15th- and 16th-century Unicorn Tapestries—a must-see. The
tomb effigies are another highlight. Three gardens shelter more than 250
species of plants similar to those grown during the Middle Ages, including
herbs and medicinals; the Unicorn Garden blooms with flowers and plants
depicted in the tapestries. Concerts of medieval music are held here regularly, and an outdoor café decorated with 15th-century carvings serves
biscotti and espresso (May–October). ⊠ *Fort Tryon Park, Inwood*
☎ *212/923–3700* ⊠ *$15 suggested donation* ⊙ *Mar.–Oct., Tues.–Sun.
9:30–5:15; Nov.–Feb., Tues.–Sun. 9:30–4:45* Ⓜ *Subway: A to 190th St.
Bus: M4 Cloisters–Fort Tryon Park; catch it along Madison Ave. below
W. 110th St., or on Broadway above W. 110th St.*

Dyckman Farmhouse Museum. This gambrel-roof Dutch colonial farmhouse (1784) is the last of its kind in Manhattan. Its six period rooms are furnished with 18th- and 19th-century Dutch and English antiques, and it's surrounded by a ½-acre park with flower and vegetable gardens. ✉ *4881 Broadway, at W. 204th St., Inwood* ☎ *212/304–9422* 💲 *$3 suggested donation* ⊙ *Tues.–Sun. 10–4* Ⓜ *Subway: A to 207th St./Inwood.*

Morris–Jumel Mansion. The oldest surviving private house in Manhattan, this 1765 Palladian-style mansion was once part of a slew of 18th-century homes built by wealthy New Yorkers. It was originally the summer home of British officer Roger Morris. After Morris left for England at the start of the Revolutionary War, George Washington used it as a temporary headquarters (September and October, 1776). In 1810 it was purchased by French merchant Stephen Jumel, whose widow Eliza Bowen married Aaron Burr in the mansion's octagonal parlor in 1834. (They divorced in 1836.) Most of the Empire-style rooms, filled with Georgian, federal, and French Empire furnishings, were decorated by Mrs. Jumel. One room re-creates Washington's war-time office. If you're at the Morris–Jumel Mansion, don't miss **Sylvan Terrace** (✉ Between Jumel Terr. and St. Nicholas Ave.), a tiny strip cobblestone street with pristine row houses that looks much as they did when they were built 1882. ✉ *65 Jumel Terr., at 160th St., east of St. Nicholas Ave., Washington Heights* ☎ *212/923–8008* ⊕ *www.morrisjumel.org* 💲 *$3* ⊙ *Wed.–Sun. 10–4* Ⓜ *Subway: C to 163rd St./Amsterdam Ave.*

Exploring the Outer Boroughs

6

By John
Rambow

WHEN MOST PEOPLE THINK OF NEW YORK, they think of "The City" as Manhattan, with Brooklyn, Queens, the Bronx, and Staten Island as one big peripheral blob—the sticky, brown caramel surrounding the real Big Apple. Although Manhattan Island admittedly contains most of the sights that the city is known for, it's only one of the five boroughs (counties) that make up New York City. More than 80% of New York City's population live outside Manhattan in the so-called "outer boroughs," and if you want to rub shoulders with native New Yorkers, you've got a much better chance here than in Manhattan. Nothing better illustrates the city's ethnic diversity (and divisions) than a subway ride: take the N or R from Queens, through Manhattan, and to Brooklyn, and you can witness the ebb and tide of nations.

You'll also find that the outer boroughs are full of friendly neighborhoods, superb restaurants, and unique museums, parks, and historical sights. And nearly all are within a 45-minute subway ride from Manhattan. The heavy hitters of the Bronx include the New York Botanical Garden, Bronx Zoo, and Yankee Stadium. In Brooklyn, the Brooklyn Academy of Art (BAM), Brooklyn Museum of Art, Brooklyn Botanic Garden, and Coney Island are the main attractions. With such destinations as P.S.1 Contemporary Art Center and the Isamu Noguchi Garden Museum, Queens has become an art-lover's destination. And for a view of the skyline and the Statue of Liberty, nothing beats the 20-minute, free ferry trip to Staten Island.

BROOKLYN

A sibling rivalry has existed between Brooklyn and Manhattan ever since the 1898 unification of Brooklyn with the rest of the city. Hardly Manhattan's wimpy sidekick, Brooklyn is a metropolis in its own right, full of impressive museums, spacious parks, landmark buildings, excellent restaurants, and lively neighborhoods. In fact, it's the most populous of all the boroughs, with nearly 2.5 million residents; even if it were separated from the rest of New York, it would still be among the five largest cities in the United States.

Some of Brooklyn's neighborhoods are as trendy as downtown Manhattan. Some streets in Williamsburg are catwalks of stylish young people, who have built a lively nightlife scene. DUMBO, full of galleries and residential lofts inside former warehouses, is often compared to the SoHo of the past, before major retailers arrived and most artists were priced out. Fort Greene, with the Brooklyn Academy of Music as its anchor, has become a major center for the performing arts. Over in ever-more-gentrified Carroll Gardens, chefs trained at posh Manhattan restaurants have opened their own successful bistros. Brooklyn Heights, Cobble Hill, and Park Slope are favored by young families and professionals drawn by the dignified brownstone- and tree-lined streets, handsome parks, cultural institutions, and the less frenetic pace of life.

The Five Boroughs

PORT
WASHINGTON

Manhasset
Bay

GREAT
NECK

KINGS
POINT

GREAT NECK
ESTATES

NASSAU

LITTLE
NECK

ST. ALBANS

Long Island Sound

Hart I.

City I.

Little Neck Bay

Cross Island Pkwy.

BAYSIDE

Clearview Expwy.

Long Island Expwy.

Grand Central Pkwy.

FLUSHING

Pelham Bay
Park

Eastchester
Bay

Throgs
Neck

Throgs Neck
Bridge

295

Whitestone
Bridge

COLLEGE
POINT

Shea
Stadium

USTA National
Tennis Center

Flushing Meadows–
Corona Park

Roosevelt Ave.

WESTCHESTER

MT. VERNON

Hutchinson
River Parkway

95

695

678

East River

La Guardia
Airport

Northern Blvd.

JACKSON
HEIGHTS

278

Bronx-Pelham
Parkway

THE BRONX

95

Bruckner Expwy

278

HUNTS
POINT

Rikers I.

Grand Central Pkwy.

ASTORIA

YONKERS

New York
Botanical
Garden

Bronx
Park

Bronx Zoo

Cross Bronx Expwy

895

Crotona
Park

Triborough
Bridge

278

LONG
ISLAND
CITY

Fordham
University

Yankee
Stadium

87

Queensboro

Van Cortlandt Park

Grand Concourse

Deegan
Expwy

Harlem R.

MANHATTAN

RIVERDALE

Wave
Hill

The Cloisters

Spuyten
Duyvil

George
Washington
Bridge

Palisades Pkwy.

FORT
LEE

CLIFFSIDE
PARK

Central
Park

Hudson River

WEST
NEW

ENGLEWOOD
CLIFFS

BERGEN

ENGLEWOOD

NEW JERSEY

3 miles

3 km

95

46

80

4

EAST
RUTHERFORD

Meadowlands
Sports Complex

95

0
0

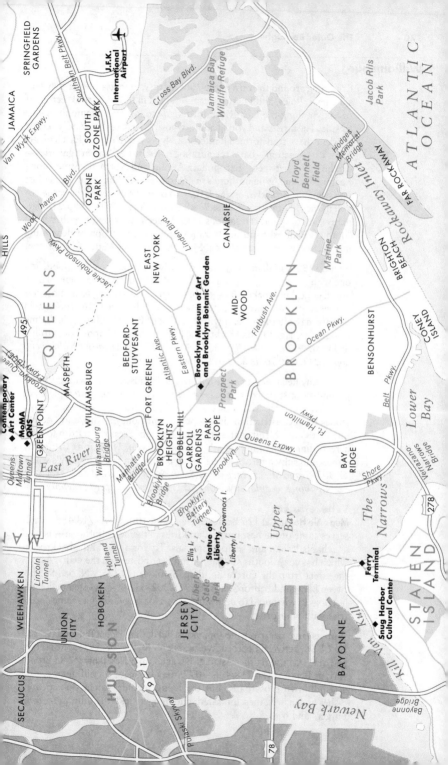

Williamsburg

Beginning around the turn of the 20th century, immigrants—largely Hasidic Jews, Poles, and Puerto Ricans—settled in this industrial section of Brooklyn along the East River, forming autonomous communities side by side. The artists and young adults who are the neighborhood's newest residents have transformed it into Brooklyn's version of the East Village. Most of the action—bars, restaurants, cafés, stores, and art galleries— can be found between Metropolitan Avenue and North 9th Street along Bedford Avenue, Williamsburg's main drag. From Manhattan it takes just one stop into Brooklyn on the L train to be in the center of the scene. To visit the neighborhood's south side, which includes the Williamsburg Bridge, many galleries, and the famous Peter Luger's steak house, either walk south on Bedford from the L train stop (in the direction of decreasing intersecting streets) or take the J, M, or Z train to the Marcy Avenue stop.

Around 1900, Williamsburg was primarily a German neighborhood, and one with nearly 50 breweries and lots of bars and beer gardens. Those are all gone, but **Brooklyn Brewery** has been trying to bring back those traditions in its own way since it opened a plant here in 1996. Tours, held on Saturday afternoon, end with a tasting of Brooklyn brews, including its signature lager. Friday nights, the brewery hosts a happy hour from 6 to 11 PM. ⊠ *79 N. 11th St.* ☎ *718/486–7422* ⊕ *www.brooklynbrewery. com* ▣ *Free* ☉ *Tours Sat. on the hr 1–4.*

At the **City Reliquary,** an unusual streetside museum, the windows of a ground-floor storefront have become an exhibit for forgotten pieces of New York history: weird pieces of trash that washed up from a canal, stones from construction sites, a prize from Coney Island, and "devil's nuts," a kind of fruit that grows in the ocean. Press the button to hear a recording explaining what's in front of you. Directions to nearby streets and subway stops are helpfully painted on the Reliquary's walls. ⊠ *307 Grand St., at Havemeyer St.* Ⓜ *Subway: J, M, Z to Marcy Ave.* ☎ *No phone* ⊕ *dhlabsnyc.com* ▣ *Donations accepted* ☉ *Daily.*

Where to Eat

Mugs Ale House (⊠ 125 Bedford Ave., at N. 10th St. ☎ 718/486–8232) serves some of the best burgers and fries in the neighborhood—as well as reliable Italian and seafood specials. Try for a seat in the backroom, which has cozy booths and lots of fun beer posters on the walls. Across the street from the Girdle Building, **Sparky's** (⊠ 135A N. 5th St., between Berry and Bedford Aves. ☎ 718/302–5151) serves steamed, tasty hot dogs in what used to be a warehouse's loading dock. Get some cheese fries with your order.

With its large size, over-the-top, industrial design, **Planet Thailand** (⊠ 133 N. 7th St., between Bedford Ave. and Berry St. ☎ 718/599–5758) serves pad thai, sushi, and other Asian dishes at cheap prices. **Diner** (⊠ 85 Broadway, at Berry St. ☎ 718/486–3077) may be inside an old diner car on a windblown crossroads, but the menu includes such sophisticated dishes as mussels, mesclun salad, and hanger steak in addition to great burgers and fries.

Peter Luger Steak House (✉ 178 Broadway, at Driggs Ave. ☎ 718/387–7400) brings meat-loving pilgrims from all over the city—and the world. Other steak houses have better lighting, more elegant dining, bigger wine lists, less brusque service, and comfortable chairs instead of wooden benches, but the steak makes it worth it. You probably won't see a menu, but here's all you need to know: shrimp cocktail, beefsteak tomato and onion salad, home fries, creamed spinach, pecan pie, and porterhouse steak—ordered according to how many are in your party. Be sure to make a reservation, and bring lots of cash—Luger's doesn't take plastic.

Shopping

One stop on almost everyone's shopping expeditions to Williamsburg should be the **Girdle Building** (✉ 218 Bedford Ave., at N. 5th St.). No undergarments are made here any more, but the ground floor has become a mall of local shops selling such essentials as books, vintage clothes, cheese, and wine. Taking its cue from its location, the **Girdle Factory** (☎ 718/486–9599) sells vintage lingerie, much of it in sultry designs from the 1950s and '60s. **Bedford Cheese Shop** (☎ 718/599–7588 ⊕ www.bedfordcheeseshop.com) is full of employees who know their merchandise, which includes imported cheese, olives, and chocolate. **Spoonbill & Sugartown Books** (☎ 718/387–7322 ⊕ www.spoonbillbooks.com) carries a large selection of art and design books and magazines, as well as a fair amount of used general titles.

The handknit sweaters, the messenger bags, the candles, and the perfume at the sunny corner boutique **Spacial Etc.** (✉ 199 Bedford Ave. ☎ 718/599–7962 ⊕ www.spacialetc.com) aren't cheap, but they're all wonderfully made and many would be hard to track down elsewhere. **Brooklyn Industries** (✉ 162 Bedford Ave. ☎ 718/486–6464) carries bags, accessories, knits, T-shirts, and other items for men and women: everything's designed for an urban, casual sensibility. **Beacon's Closet** (✉ 88 N. 11th St. ☎ 718/486–0816) is a magnet for the young locals in the neighborhood seeking out vintage clothes and accessories. Most items sell for under $20. The store is across the street from Brooklyn Brewery.

The Arts

Williamsburg's 70-odd galleries are distributed randomly, with no single main drag. Most are open afternoons from Friday through Monday, with many also open on Thursday. The **Williamsburg Gallery Association** (⊕ www.williamsburggalleryassociation.com) Web site has a handy printable map of its nearly 30 members. Also useful is the *Gallery Guide,* a free publication available at many stores and galleries in the neighborhood.

One of the first art galleries to open in Williamsburg, **Pierogi 2000** (✉ 177 N. 9th St., between Bedford and Driggs Aves. ☎ 718/599–2144) is famous for its "Flat Files," a collection of artists' portfolios that travel to other museums and galleries. **Sideshow Gallery** (✉ 319 Bedford Ave., between S. 2nd and S. 3rd Sts. ☎ 718/486–8180) often has artwork hanging from the floor to the ceiling on its walls. **Galapagos** (✉ 70 N. 6th St., between Wythe and Kent Aves. ☎ 718/782–5188 ⊕ www.galapagosartspace.com) is an all-in-one bar, art gallery, performance space, and movie house. Don't be fooled by this former mayo factory's reflecting pool near the front: it's not that deep.

Inside a beautiful 1867 bank building that's in the midst of being restored, the **Williamsburg Art and Historical Center** (WAH; ⊠ 135 Broadway, at Bedford Ave. ☎ 718/486–7372) is a work-in-progress itself. The annual round of exhibits include the Williamsburg Salon winter show, which highlights local artists. Art on view at the **Dollhaus** (⊠ 37 Broadway, between Wythe and Kent Aves. ☎ 718/486–0330 ⊕ www.dollhaus. org) is often self-consciously bizarre. At the cheerfully nonprofessional-looking **Cinders** (⊠ 103 Havemeyer St., between Hope and Grand Sts. ☎ 718/388–2311 ⊕ www.cindersgallery.com), you can buy zines and clothing as well as crafts and art—paintings, silkscreened cloth, and papier-mâché sculptures. **McCaig-Welles** (⊠ 129 Roebling St., Suite B ☎ 718/384–8729) gallery is used for children's art classes as well as displaying art that frequently uses elements of graphic design.

Greenpoint

Since the 1990s, Greenpoint has become a trendy place to live for those priced out of Williamsburg, its more famous (some may say overexposed) neighbor to the south. Until this change, the neighborhood's population was almost entirely Polish, and it retains a highly Eastern European influence in its shops, restaurants, and churches.

A visit to Greenpoint is best combined with one to Williamsburg: take the L train one stop to Bedford Avenue. Walk northeast on Bedford; the numbered cross streets will increase. McCarren Park, which intersects Bedford Avenue at N. 12th Street, marks the unofficial boundary between Greenpoint and Williamsburg. On the way you'll pass the Russian Orthodox Cathedral of the Transfiguration of Our Lord, an onion-domed local landmark built in 1922. Once you've reached the end of the park, turn left onto Manhattan Avenue, the neighborhood's main street, which contains most of its Polish markets, clothing stores, and restaurants. Most of the action on Manhattan is between Driggs and Greenpoint Avenues, especially on Saturday mornings and early afternoons.

Where to Eat

Unlike most places in New York, Greenpoint's Polish restaurants tend to close early, sometimes as early as 7 in winter.

One of the homiest Polish restaurants is **Lomzynianka** (⊠ 646 Manhattan Ave., between Nassau and Norman Aves. ☎ 718/389–9439), which serves its dishes in a narrow space that may have once been someone's living room. Go for the *pierogies,* steamed or fried pockets of dough with such fillings as cheese, meat, or sauerkraut. Resembling a diner, **Christina's** (⊠ 853 Manhattan Ave., between Milton and Noble Sts. ☎ 718/383–4382) is known for its stews, especially its goulash. Already a friendly bar, **Enid's** (⊠ 560 Manhattan Ave., at Driggs Ave. ☎ 718/349–3859) becomes a friendly place for dinner Monday through Thursday and for a classic American brunch on weekend mornings. Come prepared to wait in line for brunch before getting a seat at one of its thrift-store tables.

Brooklyn Heights

"All the advantages of the country, with most of the conveniences of the city," ran the ads for a real estate development that sprang up in the 1820s just across the East River from downtown Manhattan. Brooklyn Heights—named for its enviable hilltop position—was New York's first suburb, linked to the city originally by ferry and later by the Brooklyn Bridge. Feverish construction led by wealthy industrialists and shipping magnates quickly transformed the airy heights into a fashionable upper-middle-class community. It was characterized by radical politics, as in the case of abolitionist Henry Ward Beecher, and had a leisurely, bourgeois air about it.

In the 1940s and '50s, after the subway was built and the neighborhood became accessible, the Heights became a bohemian haven, home to writers that included Carson McCullers, W. H. Auden, Arthur Miller, Truman Capote, Richard Wright, Alfred Kazin, Marianne Moore, and Norman Mailer. Thanks to the vigorous efforts of preservationists in the 1960s, much of the Heights was designated New York's first historic district. Some 600 buildings built in the 19th century, representing a wide range of American building styles, are in excellent condition today. Many of the best line Columbia Heights, a residential street that runs parallel to the Brooklyn Heights Promenade, a paved riverfront path with spectacular Manhattan views.

Numbers in the text correspond to numbers in the margin and on the Brooklyn Heights & DUMBO map.

a good walk

Start with a walk from Manhattan across the Brooklyn Bridge, one of the most beloved city activities. (In Manhattan, the Brooklyn Bridge stop on the 6 train puts you at the foot of the pedestrian bridge path.) It takes 40 minutes to an hour to walk across the bridge and into Brooklyn; stay in the pedestrian lane to avoid the crossing bicyclists. (As you approach Brooklyn, keep an eye for the Watchtower, which is labeled as such. The pale brown building is the world headquarters of the Jehovah's Witnesses religious group, which owns a great deal of other property in Brooklyn Heights.)

To get off the bridge, take the Prospect Street exit (it's in the left lane, and leads down to a set of stairs). Turn left onto Washington Street, and carefully cross Cadman Plaza to Cadman Plaza West. Walk along this road in the direction of Manhattan until you reach the beginning of Middagh Street. Walk a half-block up Middagh to Henry Street. Take a left on Henry and walk two blocks to Orange Street. Turn right; mid-block, on the right side, between Henry and Hicks streets, is the **Plymouth Church of the Pilgrims** ❶, a center of abolitionist sentiment in the years before the Civil War. Continue two blocks up Orange Street and turn left onto **Willow Street** ❷ to see the masterful local architecture between Clark and Pierrepont streets. At the corner of Willow and Pierrepont Sts., turn right and walk up Pierrepont to its end at one of the most famous vistas in all of New York: the **Brooklyn Heights Promenade** ❸. After you've soaked in the views, exit at the north side of the prome-

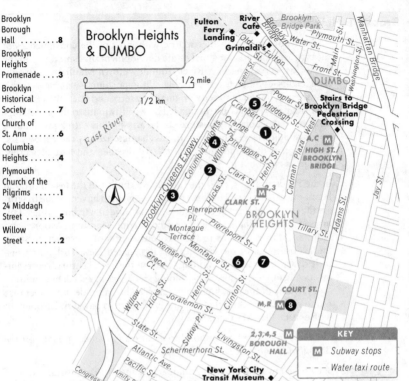

nade and walk along **Columbia Heights** 4 to its intersection with Middagh Street. Turn right and walk a block to the corner of Willow Street: **24 Middagh Street** 5 is the oldest home in the neighborhood. Return to Columbia Heights and walk south to take in its particularly elegant brownstones. At Montague Street, look right to see Nos. 2 and 3 Pierrepont Place, two brick-and-brownstone palaces built in the 1850s. Walk three blocks east on Montague (away from the promenade) to its intersection with Clinton; the **Church of St. Ann and the Holy Trinity** 6 here is a local landmark. Turn left and walk one block on Clinton to Livingston to visit the impressive architecture and exhibits on display at the **Brooklyn Historical Society** 7. Return to Montague and walk one more block along this commercial strip to reach the N and R trains backs to Manhattan. Alternatively, continue on to the **Brooklyn Borough Hall** 8 and the major subway lines there.

TIMING   Allow two to three hours for a leisurely tour of Brooklyn Heights, which combines easily with a visit to DUMBO.

What to See

8 **Brooklyn Borough Hall.** Built in 1848, this Greek Revival landmark is one of Brooklyn's handsomest buildings. The hammered-brass top of the cast-iron cupola was restored by the same French craftsmen who restored

the Statue of Liberty. The stately building is adorned with Tuckahoe marble both inside and out; other highlights are the square rotunda and the two-story beaux arts–style courtroom with plaster columns painted to look like wood. Originally the Brooklyn's city hall, the building lost this function when Brooklyn became part of New York City in 1898. Today the hall serves as the office of Brooklyn's borough president and the location of the **Brooklyn Tourism & Visitors Center** (☎ 718/802–3846), which has historical exhibits and a gift shop as well as many maps and pamphlets covering the borough's attractions. It's open weekdays 10–6. On Tuesday and Saturday a green market sets up on the flagstone plaza in front. ⊠ *209 Joralemon St., at Court St.* ☎ *718/802–3700* ⊕ *www. brooklyn-usa.org* ⊠ *Free* Ⓜ *Subway: 2, 3, 4, 5 to Borough Hall; R, W to Court St.*

Ⓒ ❸ **Brooklyn Heights Promenade.** Stretching from Cranberry Street on the north
Fodor'sChoice to Remsen Street on the south, this ⅓-mi-long esplanade provides en-
★ thralling views of Manhattan. Find a bench and take in the view of the skyline, the Statue of Liberty, Ellis Island, and the Brooklyn Bridge, the impressive steel suspension bridge designed by John Augustus Roebling and completed in 1883. The small island to your left is Governors Island, a former Coast Guard base that's now partially a national park. Below you are the Brooklyn–Queens Expressway and Brooklyn's industrial waterfront of warehouses, piers, and parking lots. At the south end of the promenade, near Montague Street is a small playground. Ⓜ *Subway: 2, 3 to Clark St.; A, C to High St.*

❼ **Brooklyn Historical Society.** Housed in a Queen Anne–style National Landmark building from 1881 that's one of the gems of the neighborhood, the Brooklyn Historical Society displays memorabilia, artifacts, art, and other items relating to the borough, from 17th-century Native American tools to contemporary artworks. Exhibitions here have covered such topics as breweries and other businesses based in Brooklyn. ⊠ *128 Pierrepont St., at Clinton St.* ☎ *718/624–0890* ⊕ *www. brooklynhistory.org* ⊗ *Wed., Thurs., and weekends noon–5, Fri. 10–8.*

❻ **Church of St. Ann and the Holy Trinity.** The 60 stained-glass windows in this Gothic Revival Episcopal church, built in 1847, were the first set to be made and designed in the United States. In addition to services the church is open for visits weekdays from noon to 2. ⊠ *157 Montague St., at Clinton St.* ☎ *718/875–6960.*

❹ **Columbia Heights.** Among the majestic residences on this street, the brownstone grouping of **Nos. 210–220** is often cited as the most graceful in New York. Norman Mailer lives on this street, and from a rear window in **No. 111**, Washington Roebling, who in 1869 succeeded his father as chief engineer for the Brooklyn Bridge, directed the completion of the bridge after a case of the bends left him an invalid. ⊠ *Between Pierrepont and Cranberry Sts.* Ⓜ *Subway: 2, 3 to Clark St.; A, C to High St.*

❶ **Plymouth Church of the Pilgrims.** Thanks to the stirring oratory of Brooklyn's most eminent theologian, Henry Ward Beecher (brother of Harriet Beecher Stowe, author of *Uncle Tom's Cabin*), this house of worship was a center of antislavery sentiment in the years before the Civil War. Several slave auctions, in fact, were held in the church both to gain the slaves' freedom and to publicize the inhumanity of slavery. Because it provided refuge to slaves, the church, which was built in 1849, was known as the Grand Central Terminal of the Underground Railroad in its latter years. The windows of this 1849 church, like those of many others in the neighborhood, were designed by Louis Comfort Tiffany. In the gated courtyard beside the church, a statue of Beecher depicts refugee slaves crouched in hiding behind the base. ⊠ *Orange St. between Henry and Hicks Sts.* ☎ *718/ 624–4743* ⊕ *www.plymouthchurch.org* ☉ *Service Sun. 11 AM; tours by appointment* Ⓜ *Subway: 2, 3 to Clark St.; A, C to High St.*

❺ **24 Middagh Street.** This circa-1829 federal-style clapboard residence is one of the oldest homes in the neighborhood. Peer through a door in the wall on the Willow Street side for a glimpse of the cottage garden and carriage house in the rear. Ⓜ *Subway: 2, 3 to Clark St.; A, C to High St.*

❷ **Willow Street.** One of the prettiest and most architecturally varied blocks in Brooklyn Heights is Willow Street between Clark and Pierrepont streets. At **No. 22** stands Henry Ward Beecher's house—a prim Greek revival brownstone. **Nos. 155–159** are three brick federal row houses that were allegedly stops on the Underground Railroad. Ⓜ *Subway: 2, 3 to Clark St.; A, C to High St.*

Where to Eat

The **Heights Café** (⊠ 84 Montague St., at Hicks St. ☎ 718/625–5555) is a local favorite for American fare. The pan-roasted chicken is especially popular. At **Henry's End** (⊠ 44 Henry St., near Cranberry St. ☎ 718/834–1776) wild game such as elk, buffalo, and quail take center stage; less exotic meats and chicken are also available year-round in the cozy surroundings. **Teresa's** (⊠ 80 Montague St., near Hicks St. ☎ 718/797–3996), like its sister location in the East Village, serves well-prepared Polish and American food. Have a breakfast with the blintzes, pierogi, or kielbasa here, and you won't be ready for lunch for a good long time.

DUMBO

Until the 1970s, the neighborhood Down Under the Manhattan Bridge Overpass was known as Fulton Landing. To the north of Brooklyn Heights and curving east with the river, the area was named after the inventor and engineer Robert Fulton, who in 1814 introduced steamboat ferry service from Brooklyn to Manhattan here. This commuter trip was immortalized in Walt Whitman's poem "Crossing Brooklyn Ferry" (1900).

The transportation hub was also a successful industrial neighborhood, with factories and dry good warehouses, until the Manhattan Bridge was built (from 1889 to 1909). Bridge construction leveled many buildings and eventually made the neighborhood obsolete for pedestrians and buggies. Today, however, the once prosperous area, retitled with the Realtor-friendly name of DUMBO, is enjoying a renaissance. Occupying the formerly industrial spaces are apartment lofts, galleries, bars and restaurants, and home furnishing shops.

☺ **Brooklyn Bridge Park.** The Brooklyn Bridge Park Coalition combined city and state funds to convert this underused patch of prime real estate, which stretches 1.3 mi from the Manhattan Bridge south along the East River to Atlantic Avenue, into a park. The park closes at 5 PM after Labor Day and stays open later in summer, when the outdoor Brooklyn Bridge Park Summer Film Series is held. ⊠ *Entrance at top of Main St.* ⊕ *www.bbpc. net* Ⓜ *Subway: A, C to High St./Brooklyn Bridge; F to York St.*

☺ **Empire-Fulton Ferry State Park.** Adjacent to Brooklyn Bridge Park, this 9-acre park has picnic tables and benches to accompany great views of the nearby bridges and the Manhattan skyline. If you have kids in tow, the large playground, which includes a replica of a boat to crawl around on, provides a welcome spot for tots. The ruins of the Tobacco Inspection Warehouse (circa 1871), now stabilized and part of the park, are sometimes used for band performances and other events. ⊠ *26 New Dock St.* ☎ *718/858–4708* ⊕ *nysparks.state.ny.us* ⊠ *Free* ⊙ *Daily dawn–dusk* Ⓜ *Subway: A, C to High St.; F to York St.*

Fulton Ferry Landing. Old Fulton Street ends at the point at which Robert Fulton's steam-powered ferries carried passengers across the East River before the bridges were built. Brooklyn Ice Cream Factory and New York Water Taxis (www.nywatertaxi.com) are in the middle of the action. ⊠ *At west end of Old Fulton St.* Ⓜ *Subway: A, C to High St./Brooklyn Bridge; F to York St.*

Where to Eat

A classic New York–style pizza parlor, **Grimaldi's Pizzeria** (⊠ 19 Old Fulton St., between Front and Water Sts. ☎ 718/858–4300), near the Brooklyn Bridge, has red-and-white checkered tableclothes, walls filled with autographed photos, and Frank Sinatra crooning on the jukebox. There's better pizza in town, but the experience here is hard to beat. With its exposed brick and pool table in a prominent location, **Superfine** (⊠ 126 Front St., between Jay and Pearl Sts. ☎ 718/243–9005) is as much a highly designed hangout as it is a restaurant. Come here for Mediterranean-influence twists on classic American dishes.

The Arts

Most DUMBO galleries are open afternoons Thursday through Sunday.

The **DUMBO Arts Center** (DAC; ⊠ 30 Washington St., between Water and Plymouth Sts. ☎ 718/694–0831 ⊕ www.dumboartscenter.org) exhibits local artists in its 3,000-square-foot gallery. In fall, its Art Under the Bridge festival brings performances, special exhibits, and other events to locations throughout the neighborhood. The nonprofit **Smack Mellon Studios** (⊠ 92 Plymouth St., at Washington St. ☎ 718/834–8761) specializes in exhibits of local artists, especially those whose art doesn't fit neatly into one category or another. The **5 + 5 Gallery** (⊠ 111 Front St., Suite 210 ☎ 718/488–8383) specializes in contemporary prints.

Shopping

Even if the surrounding streets are empty, **Jacques Torres Chocolate** (⊠ 66 Water St. ☎ 718/875–9772 ⊕ www.mrchocolate.com), a chocolate factory with a small shop and café operated by the French chocolatier, is almost always packed. It's closed on Sunday. One of the better music stores for dance, house, and electronica, **Halcyon** (✉ 57 Pearl St. ☎ 718/260–9299 ⊕ www.halcyonline.com) also sells accessories and DJ gear. The DUMBO outpost of **ABC Carpet & Home** (✉ 20 Jay St. ☎ 718/643–7400) takes up an entire block. Unlike its chaotic headquarters in Manhattan, the sprawling, modern home furnishings shop and showroom is a pleasure to peruse.

Atlantic Avenue

On the busy thoroughfare of Atlantic Avenue, between Court and Clinton streets on the southern border of Brooklyn Heights, are a handful of Middle Eastern restaurants and markets. **Sahadi's** (✉ 187 Atlantic Ave. ☎ 718/624–4550) sells cheap, good-quality dried fruits, nuts, candies, and olives by the pound as well as many other specialty food items. **Damascus Bakery** (✉ 195 Atlantic Ave. ☎ 718/625–7070) is a great place to pick up pita bread—and some killer baklava. Next door, **A Cook's Companion** (✉ 197 Atlantic Ave. ☎ 718/852–6901) carries cookbooks, kitchen gadgets and tools, and lots of paraphernalia for the serious cook.

Farther east on Atlantic, particularly between Hoyt and Bond streets, the leafy street gives way to more than a dozen antique-furniture stores and purveyors of modern housewares. Despite its Dutch-influenced name, **Breukelen** (✉ 369 Atlantic Ave., near Bond St. ☎ 718/246–0024) is stuck anywhere but in the past. On offer are housewares, lamps, modern furniture, and other items in a design-heavy vein. **In Days of Old** (✉ 355–57 Atlantic Ave. ☎ 718/858–4233) looks to Victorian and early 1900s for its stock of antiques.

In among the Atlantic Avenue's housewares are many noteworthy boutiques. **Butter** (✉ 407 Atlantic Ave. ☎ 718/260–9033) was one of the first Brooklyn shops to bring a bit of Manhattan's trend-conscious women's clothes to Atlantic Avenue. At nearby **Jelly** (✉ 389 Atlantic Ave. ☎ 718/858–8214), owned by the sisters who own Butter, it's accessories that take main stage.

To get to the northwest section of this busy stretch, take the subway to the Borough Hall station. To pick up Atlantic Avenue at its southeast edge, take the subway to the Nevins Street station. Both stations are served by a number of subway lines. The blocks between Boerum Place and Smith Street that separate the aforementioned sections is a kind of no-man's-land, looming as it does in the shadow of the Brooklyn House of Detention. Emptied of prisoners in 2004, its fate is currently unknown. A few bail-bond businesses across the street remain for the moment as evidence of its past.

Where to Eat

The cheerful **Brawta Caribbean Cafe** (✉ 347 Atlantic St., near Hoyt St. ☎ 718/855–5515) serves Jamaican specialties. The goat roti is especially tasty, especially when washed down with sorrel, a sweet drink made with hibiscus flowers.

HIP-HOP'S BIRTHPLACE

MAYBE IT'S NOT SO SURPRISING that art forms that depend heavily on competition and audience participation would have developed in New York City, where people spend so much time out of their houses meeting with friends, heading for work, or just looking for something to do.

Most people date modern graffiti's birth to the late 1960s, when a Greek-American boy began writing his nickname and street number, "Taki 183," with a permanent marker on subway cars. Others, primarily teenagers from the poor areas of Manhattan, the Bronx, Brooklyn, and Queens, began to imitate his "tagging." It wasn't too long after that spray paint, with its wealth of colors and looser method of application, became the medium of choice. Spray paint also allowed innovators to start signing their names in the loose "bubble" style that remains prevalent today.

From its start, however, modern graffiti was tied up with petty crime: the ideal "canvas" was the interiors and exteriors of the Metropolitan Transit Authority's trains, and getting to that canvas involved trespassing in the MTA's rail yards, a dangerous place. The spray paint used was generally stolen, both because it was expensive and in some cases illegal for teenagers to buy it. In fact, stealing itself became a graffiti writer's rite of passage.

Rap music and breakdancing's arose at the same time. The DJs who supplied music for South Bronx nightclubs and parties were always trying to create better and better mixes of soul and disco music. One innovation, generally credited to DJ Kool Herc, was to use two turntables with the same record on each and switch repeatedly between the two during their breaks—the section of song in which only bass and percussion are playing. By repeating the break indefinitely, he gave MCs a chance to introduce themselves, get the crowd worked up, and lead everyone in a chant. Soon MCs were delivering full-blown rhymes and verses, and rap music was on its way. Breakdancing's appearance as a distinct form is due to one man: DJ Afrika Bambaataa. During the late '60s, he began organizing teenagers into a group called the Zulu Kings. A gang alternative, the Zulu Kings would breakdance against other groups and against each other during a DJs' breaks, seeing who could move with the most skill and athletic prowess.

By the early 1980s, hip-hop—an umbrella term for rap music, breakdancing, and graffiti writing and the culture around them—was almost mainstream. In its embryonic stages, it was helped along by the art world's embrace. Downtown artists such as Jean-Michel Basquiat and Keith Haring blurred the line between legitimate art and graffiti, tagging and making illegal murals at the same time as dealers and art-lovers were snapping up their work. The new wave band Blondie also helped introduce hip-hop to a wide audience with "Rapture," a 1980 hit song that included a rap namechecking hip-hop artist and impresario Fab Five Freddy.

By this time, New York City had declared war on graffiti artists and their vandalism. By using aggressive cleaning methods and by quickly removing cars that had been "bombed" from service, the city succeeded in reducing the amount of graffiti visible on trains, if not perhaps on the streets themselves.

As the graffiti artist Mare 139 put it in the seminal 1984 hip-hop documentary Style Wars, "We lost the trains, but we gained the world." Hip-hop may have grown up in the lean and mean New York of the 1960s and '70s, but it's now a worldwide phenomemon that brings in about $10 billion dollars a year from its 45 million fans of the music and the lifestyle.

Cobble Hill

On the south side of Atlantic Avenue from Brooklyn Heights, Cobble Hill is a quiet residential area of leafy streets lined with town houses built by 19th-century New York's upper middle class. Court Street is a major drag that runs through the neighborhood. Activity whirls around its cafés, restaurants, bookstores, old-fashioned bakeries, and imported food shops. Smith Street, which runs parallel to Court Street one block east, is somewhat of a restaurant row, augmented by young designers who have set up shop here. The restaurants are some of Brooklyn's best.

Although many of the streets here contain gorgeous houses, the tiny mews called Verandah Place is especially worth a walk through. South of Congress Street and between Henry Street and Clinton Street, Verandah Place has town houses built in the 1850s; the novelist Thomas Wolfe lived for a time at No. 40 in the 1930s. Worth seeking out is the Episcopal **Christ Church and Holy Family** (⊠ 326 Clinton, at Kane St. ☎ 718/624–0083), completed in 1841. The altar, lectern, and other furnishings are by Louis Comfort Tiffany; most of the stained-glass windows he did for the church were lost in a 1939 fire, but a few remain. Richard Upjohn and his son, the church architects, lived down the block at 296 Clinton.

Where to Eat

At the creative American restaurant **Saul** (⊠ 140 Smith St., between Dean and Bergen Sts., Boerum Hill ☎ 718/935–9844), everything on the seasonal menu is well prepared, from such simple dishes as a grilled hanger steak to more involved items like crispy duck confit. One of the best restaurants on Smith Street, the **Grocery** (⊠ 288 Smith St., between Union and Sackett Sts. ☎ 718/596–3335), gets accolades for New American take on such dishes as slowly rendered duck breast. Be sure to make a reservation; it's very popular. Grocery is open for dinner every day but Sunday.

Shopping

Fresh pasta, mozzarella, sausages, olives, and prepared dishes are available at a number of shops, including **Fratelli Ravioli Shop and Café** (⊠ 347 Court St., at Union St. ☎ 718/625–7952). **Sweet Melissa** (⊠ 276 Court St., at Douglass St.) ☎ 718/855–3410), a tiny pastry shop with a few dark-wood booths, serves such sweets as madeleines, dark chocolate–covered graham crackers, and tiny pots of butterscotch pudding, plus finger sandwiches.

Brooklyn Academy of Music (BAM)

Young professionals, families, hipsters, and old-timers live side by side in the brownstone-filled neighborhood of Fort Greene, which is anchored by the Brooklyn Academy of Music (BAM). And with the Mark Morris Dance Center (whose troupe performs at BAM) down the street, the area is now becoming interchangeable with its performing-arts scene.

Attracting lots of downtown Manhattanites as well as locals, BAM's program tends to be a bit more experimental than similar institutions across the river in Manhattan. But even if you're not planning on seeing one of its presentations, it's well worth a glimpse at the facade and the interior of BAM's main building. Built in 1908, the cream-color neo-Italianate building is covered with lots of painted detailing, all of them bright after a 2002 refurbishment.

In addition to the impressive and huge lobby, the BAM building contains an opera house, which seats 2,100, and a movie theater. Nearby is BAM's **Harvey Theater** (⊠ 651 Fulton St.), which is where many of BAM's theatrical works are staged. ⊠ *Peter Jay Sharp Bldg., 30 Lafayette Ave., between Ashland Pl. and St. Felix St.* ☎ *718/636–4100* ⊕ *www. bam.org* Ⓜ *Subway: C to Lafayette Ave.; 2, 3, 4, 5, Q to Atlantic Ave.*

Where to Eat

The **BAMcafé**, serving mostly lighter dishes, is open for dinner Thursday through Saturday and also open two hours before performances at the Harvey Theater and Howard Gilman Opera House. Across the street from BAM, **Thomas Beisl** (⊠ 25 Lafayette Ave., at Ashland Pl. ☎ 718/222–5800) is well acquainted with ensuring its patrons make their show. Viennese specialties here include goulash, sauerbraten, and some wonderfully rich desserts.

It may be a relic of the 1950s, but **Junior's** (⊠ 386 Flatbush Ave. Ext., at DeKalb Ave., Downtown Brooklyn ☎ 718/852–5257) remains a popular destination for locals, especially for its huge, rich cheesecase. The huge menu still has the Jewish specialties that made the restaurant famous, including corned beef, pastrami, and chopped liver sandwiches.

Park Slope

One of Brooklyn's most comfortable places to live, Park Slope contains row after row of immaculate brownstones that date from its turn-of-the-20th-century heyday. At the time, Park Slope had the nation's highest per-capita income. To see some of the neighborhood's most beautiful houses, walk between Seventh Avenue and Prospect Park along any of the streets between Sterling Place and 4th Street.

To get to the north end of the Slope, take the Q to 7th Avenue (at Flatbush Avenue) or the No. 2 or 3 to Grand Army Plaza; to get to the south Slope (roughly between 5th and 15th streets), take the F to 7th Avenue (at 9th Street).

Numbers in the text correspond to numbers in the margin and on the Park Slope & Prospect Park map.

Where to Eat

★ At **Blue Ribbon Brooklyn** (⊠ 280 5th Ave., between Garfield and 1st Sts. ☎ 718/840–0404), the Brooklyn branch of a SoHo original, serves updated, carefully prepared versions of bistro dishes, with an especially strong showing in seafood. At comfortably rustic **al di la** (⊠ 248 5th Ave., at Carroll St. ☎ 718/783–4565), the dining room is furnished with a pressed-tin ceiling and communal bare wooden tables. Plenty of care goes into the authentic Italian dishes, but the entrées are on the small side, so go for an appetizer.

Shopping

Seventh Avenue, between Lincoln and 15th streets, is the neighborhood's main shopping street, with long-established restaurants, groceries, bookstores, shops, cafés, bakeries, churches, and real estate agents (one of the favorite neighborhood pastimes is window shopping for homes). More fun, however, are the restaurants, bars, and gift shops along 5th Avenue.

The Clay Pot (⊠ 162 7th Ave., between Garfield and 1st Sts. ☎ 718/788-6564) is known for original wares and ornaments for the home and for one-of-a-kind wedding bands made by local artisans. The **Community Bookstore and Café** (⊠ 143 7th Ave., at Garfield ☎ 718/783–3075) serves pastries, quiche, and additional light offerings in the lovely, little garden out back or indoors among the bookcases. In addition to an astonishing assortment of imported beers (available by the bottle), **Bierkraft** (⊠ 191 5th Ave., near Union St. ☎ 718/230–7600) also sells cheeses, olives, and some impressively pricey chocolate. **Beacon's Closet** (⊠ 220 5th Ave., between President and Union Sts. ☎ 718/230–1630), like its sister store in Williamsburg, sells vintage clothes, jewelry, and other items at reasonable prices.

Prospect Park

The amenity that gave Park Slope its name, Prospect Park was designed by Frederick Law Olmsted and Calvert Vaux and completed in the late 1880s. It's rumored that the two liked this more naturalistic setting better than their previous creation, Manhattan's Central Park. At 526 acres, Prospect Park is about 60% the size of its more famous cousin. A good way to experience the park is to walk the entirety of its 3.3-mi circular drive and make detours off it as you wish. Joggers, skaters, and bicyclists have the drive to themselves weekdays 9–5 and 7–10 PM April–October and weekends year-round. There are not many vendors selling snacks and beverages in the park, except at the near the Grand Army Plaza entrance.

On weekends and holidays throughout the year, from noon to 5 PM, the red **"Heart of Brooklyn" trolley** circles Prospect Park, leaving Wollman Rink on the hour and hitting the zoo, the Botanic Garden, the Band Shell, and most other sights. Best of all, it's free. ☎ 718/965–8999 events hotline ⊕ www.prospectpark.org.

What to See

Eastern Parkway. The world's first six-lane parkway originates at Grand Army Plaza. When Olmsted and Vaux conceived the avenue's design in 1866, in tandem with their plans for Prospect Park, they wanted it to mimic the grand sweep of the boulevards of Paris and Vienna. Today it continues to play an important role in Brooklyn culture: every Labor Day weekend Eastern Parkway hosts the West Indian American Day Parade, the biggest and liveliest carnival outside the Caribbean. Ⓜ *Subway: 2, 3 to Grand Army Plaza.*

❸ **Grand Army Plaza.** Prospect Park West, Eastern Parkway, and Flatbush and Vanderbilt avenues radiate out from this geographic star. Crossing

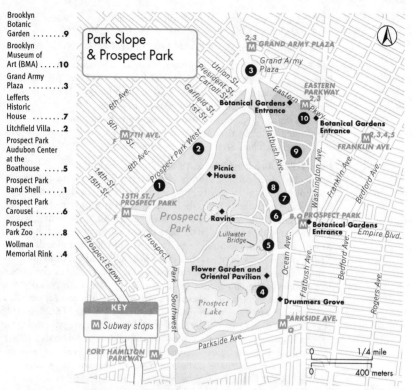

Brooklyn
Botanic
Garden **9**

Brooklyn
Museum of
Art (BMA) **10**

Grand Army
Plaza **3**

Lefferts
Historic
House **7**

Litchfield Villa . . .**2**

Prospect Park
Audubon Center
at the
Boathouse **5**

Prospect Park
Band Shell **1**

Prospect Park
Carousel **6**

Prospect
Park Zoo **8**

Wollman
Memorial Rink . .**4**

the broad streets around here can be dangerous; be careful. At the center of the plaza stands the **Soldiers' and Sailors' Memorial Arch,** honoring Civil War veterans and patterned after the Arc de Triomphe in Paris. Three heroic sculptural groupings adorn the arch: atop, a four-horse chariot by Frederick MacMonnies, so dynamic it seems about to catapult off the arch; to either side, the victorious Union Army and Navy of the Civil War. Inside are bas-reliefs of presidents Abraham Lincoln and Ulysses S. Grant, sculpted by Thomas Eakins and William O'Donovan, respectively. On some warm-weather weekends the top of the arch is accessible. To the northwest of the arch, Neptune and a passel of debauched Tritons leer over the edges of the **Bailey Fountain,** a popular spot for wedding-party photographs. On Saturday year-round, a green market sets up in the plaza; produce, flowers and plants, cheese, and baked goods attract throngs of locals. Ⓜ *Subway: 2, 3 to Grand Army Plaza; Q to 7th Ave.*

Ⓒ ❼ **Lefferts Historic House.** Built in 1783 and moved to Prospect Park in 1918, this gambrel-roof Dutch colonial farmhouse contains a historic house-museum. Rooms are furnished with antiques and period reproductions from the 1820s, the period when the house was last redecorated. The museum hosts all kinds of activities for kids; call for information.

⊠ *Flatbush Ave. north of junction with Park Loop, Prospect Park* ☎ *718/789–2822* ⊕ *www.prospectpark.org* ⊠ *Free* ☉ *Apr.–Nov., Thurs.–Sun. noon–5* Ⓜ *Subway: Q to Prospect Park.*

② **Litchfield Villa.** The most important sight on the western border of Prospect Park, this Italianate mansion, built in 1857 for a prominent railroad magnate, was designed by Alexander Jackson Davis, considered the foremost architect of his day. It has housed the park's headquarters since 1883, but visitors are welcome to step inside and view the domed octagonal rotunda. ⊠ *95 Prospect Park W, at 5th St., Prospect Park* ☎ *718/965–8951* Ⓜ *Subway: F to 7th Ave.*

☝ ⑤ **Prospect Park Audubon Center and Visitor Center at the Boathouse.** Styled after Sansovino's 16th-century Library at St. Mark's in Venice, the impressive boathouse, built in 1904, sits opposite the Lullwater Bridge, creating an idyllic scene on evenings when the lake reflects an exact image of the building. The boathouse now houses the Prospect Park Audubon Center, where you can learn about nature in the park through interactive exhibits, park tours, and educational programs especially for kids. On a nice day, take a ride on the electric boat or rent a pedal boat and head out onto the Lullwater and Prospect Lake. You can also sign up for a bird-watching tour to see some of the 200 species spotted here. The café is always good for a break, and restrooms are also available here. ⊠ *Entrance: Lincoln Rd. or Flatbush Ave. at Empire Blvd., Prospect Park* ☎ *718/287–3400 Audubon Center, 718/282–7789 pedal boats* ⊕ *www.prospectparkaudubon. org* ⊠ *Audubon Center free; electric-boat tours $3; pedal boats $10 per hr* ☉ *Audubon Center: June–Sept., Thurs.–Sun. noon–6; call for program and tour times. Electric-boat tours: Apr.–Oct., Fri.–Sun. 10–4:30, every 30 min. Pedal boats: mid-May–mid-Sept., Thurs.–Sun. noon–6; early May, Thurs.–Sun. noon–5; mid-Sept.–Oct., weekends noon–5* Ⓜ *Subway: 2, 3 to Grand Army Plaza; Q to Prospect Park.*

① **Prospect Park Band Shell.** The Band Shell is the home of the annual **Celebrate Brooklyn Festival,** which from mid-June through the last weekend in August sponsors free films and concerts, which have included African-Caribbean jazz, Nick Cave, the Brooklyn Philharmonic, and the Mark Morris dance company; benefit concerts, which charge admission, also bring big name acts. The crowd either fills the seats or spreads out blankets on the small hill. Food and beverages from Park Slope restaurant Two Boots Brooklyn are available for purchase. ⊠ *Prospect Park W and 9th St., Prospect Park* ☎ *718/965–8999 park hotline, 718/855–7882 Celebrate Brooklyn Festival* ⊕ *www.brooklynx.org/celebrate* ⊠ *$3 suggested donation* Ⓜ *F to 7th Ave.*

☝ ⑥ **Prospect Park Carousel.** Horses, dragon-pulled chariots, and other colorful animals enliven the restored 1912 carousel, handcrafted by master carver Charles Carmel. ⊠ *Flatbush Ave. at Empire Blvd., Prospect Park* ☎ *718/282–7789* ⊠ *$1 per ride* ☉ *July–Labor Day, Thurs.–Sun. noon–6; Labor Day–Oct. and Apr.–June, daily noon–5* Ⓜ *Subway: 2, 3 to Grand Army Plaza; Q to Prospect Park.*

☝ ⑧ **Prospect Park Zoo.** Small and friendly, this children's zoo off the main road of Prospect Park has a number of unusual and endangered species among its 390 inhabitants. The sea-lion pool is a hit with children, as are the indoor exhibits—"Animal Lifestyles," which explains habitats and adaptations, and "Animals in Our Lives," showcasing domesticated and farm animals. An outdoor discovery trail has a simulated prairie-dog burrow, a duck pond, and wallabies in habitat. Family tickets offer deep discounts at $6 (up to four persons). ✉ *450 Flatbush Ave., at Empire Blvd., Prospect Park* ☎ *718/399–7339* ⊕ *www.prospectparkzoo.com* 🏷 *$5* ☉ *Apr.–Oct., weekdays 10–5, weekends 10–5:30; Nov.–Mar., daily 10–4:30; last ticket ½ hr prior to closing* Ⓜ *Subway: Q to Prospect Park.*

🐣 ❹ **Wollman Memorial Rink.** A smaller cousin to Wollman Rink in Central Park, this is one of Prospect Park's most popular destinations. Besides skating in winter, pedal-boat rentals are available here weekends and holidays from April through mid-October. ✉ *Enter park at Ocean Ave. and Parkside Ave., Park Slope* ☎ *718/282–7789* 🏷 *$5, with $5 skate rental; pedal boats $12.50 per hr* ☉ *Mid-Nov.–mid-Mar.; hrs vary, call for specifics* Ⓜ *Subway: 2, 3 to Grand Army Plaza; Q to Prospect Park; F to 15th St./Prospect Park.*

Brooklyn Botanic Garden

★ 🐣 ❾ A major attraction at this 52-acre botanic garden, one of the finest in the country, is the beguiling Japanese Garden—complete with a pond and blazing red *torii* gate, which signifies that a shrine is nearby. The Japanese cherry arbor nearby turns into a breathtaking cloud of pink every spring, and the Cherry Blossom Festival is the park's most popular event. You can also wander through the Cranford Rose Garden (5,000 bushes, 1,200 varieties); the Fragrance Garden, designed especially for the blind; and the Shakespeare Garden, featuring more than 80 plants immortalized by the Bard (including many kinds of roses).

The Steinhardt Conservatory, a complex of handsome greenhouses, holds thriving desert, tropical, temperate, and aquatic vegetation, as well as a display charting the evolution of plants over the past 140 million years. The extraordinary C. V. Starr Bonsai Museum in the Conservatory exhibits about 80 miniature Japanese specimens. Near the conservatory are a café and an outstanding gift shop, with bulbs, plants, and gardening books are well as T-shirts and postcards. Free garden tours are given weekends at 1 PM, except for holiday weekends. Entrances to the garden are on Eastern Parkway, just outside the subway station; on Washington Avenue, behind the Brooklyn Museum of Art; and on Flatbush Avenue at Empire Boulevard. ✉ *1000 Washington Ave., between Flatbush Ave. and Empire Blvd., Prospect Heights* ☎ *718/623–7200* ⊕ *www.bbg.org* 🏷 *$5; free Tues. and Sat. before noon* ☉ *Apr.–Sept., grounds Tues.–Fri. 8–6, weekends 10–6, conservatory daily 10–5:30; Oct.–Mar., grounds Tues.–Fri. 8–4:30, weekends 10–4:30; conservatory 10–4* Ⓜ *Subway: 2, 3 to Eastern Pkwy.; Q to Prospect Park.*

Brooklyn Museum of Art

★ ❿ The Brooklyn Museum of Art (BMA) was founded in 1823 as the Brooklyn Apprentices' Library Association (Walt Whitman was one of its first librarians) and was a pioneer in the collection of non-Western art. With approximately 1.5 million pieces in its permanent collection, from Rodin sculptures to Andean textiles and Assyrian wall reliefs, it ranks as the second-largest art museum in New York—only the Met is larger. As you approach the massive, regal building designed by McKim, Mead & White (1893), look for the allegorical figures of Brooklyn and Manhattan, originally carved by Daniel Chester French for the Manhattan Bridge. The glass-front entranceway and the lobby were designed by Polshek Architects, the same firm that did the Rose Center for Earth and Space at the American Museum of Natural History. Be sure to check out the lively fountain to the left of the entrance.

Beyond the changing exhibitions, highlights include Egyptian Art (third floor), one of the best collections of its kind in the world, and African and Pre-Columbian Art (first floor). In the collection devoted to "American Identity" in the Luce Center for American Art (fifth floor), 350 examples of fine arts and crafts are exhibited thematically rather than chronologically. Although this method can be confusing, many of the pieces, including works by Georgia O'Keeffe, Winslow Homer, John Singer Sargent, Thomas Eakins, and Milton Avery, are still stunners. In early 2005, the Luce Center expanded to allow 1,500 more objects to be shown in the compact Visible Storage/Study Center. On the first Saturday of each month, "First Saturdays" bring a free evening of special programs, including live music, dancing, film screenings, and readings. ⊠ *200 Eastern Pkwy., at Washington Ave., Prospect Heights* ☎ *718/638–5000* ⊕ *www.brooklynmuseum.org* ☞ *$6 suggested donation* ⊙ *Wed.–Fri. 10–5, weekends 11–6; 1st Sat. every month 11–11; call for program schedule* Ⓜ *Subway: 2, 3 to Eastern Pkwy.*

Where to Eat

For great diner fare and uncommonly friendly service, head to **Tom's Restaurant** (⊠ 782 Washington Ave., at Sterling Pl. ☎ 718/636–9738). The family business (since 1937) is closed Sunday and by 4 PM the rest of the week.

Coney Island

Fodor'sChoice
★ Named Konijn Eiland (Rabbit Island) by the Dutch for its wild rabbit population, the Coney Island peninsula on Brooklyn's southern shore has a boardwalk, a 2½-mi-long beach, a legendary amusement park, a baseball stadium, and the city's only aquarium. Coney Island may have declined from its glory days in the early 1900s, but it's still a great place to experience the sounds, smells, and sights of summer: hot dogs, ice cream, and saltwater taffy; suntan lotion; crowds; and old men fishing the sea. And then there's the side shows, the heart-stopping plunge of the king of roller coasters—the Cyclone—and the thwack of bats swung by Brooklyn's own minor league team, the Cyclones. The Coney Island boardwalk remains the hub of the action; amble along it to take in the local color.

Coney Island is at its liveliest on weekends, especially in summer. Allow most of a day for this trip, since it takes at least an hour to get here from Manhattan—take the D, F, or Q subway train to the end of the line.

Astroland......4

Deno's
Wonderwheel
Park..........3

Keyspan Park ... 1

New York
Aquarium......5

Sideshows by the
Seashore and the
Coney Island
Museum.......2

KEY

Ⓜ *Subway stops*

🛈 *Tourist information*

Coney Island

Atlantic Ocean

0   1/4 mile
0   400 meters

👐 ❹ **Astroland.** The world-famous, wood-and-steel Cyclone ($5) is one of the oldest roller coasters still operating (it first rode in 1927); it was moved in 1975 to Astroland, which had first billed itself as a "space-age" theme park. Today a visit is more like stepping into the past than the future, but the rides are still a thrill, as is the Skee-Ball. Farther down the boardwalk, an abandoned Space Needle–like structure, once the Parachute Jump, are testimony to this waning beachside culture. ⊠ *1000 Surf Ave., at W. 10th St., Coney Island* ☎ *718/372–0275* ⊕ *www. astroland.com* ⊗ *Call for seasonal hrs* 🎟 *Free; $2–$5 per ride* Ⓜ *Subway: D, F, Q to Coney Island Stillwell Ave.*

👐 ❸ **Deno's Wonderwheel Park.** You get a new perspective on the island from the Wonder Wheel, which was built in 1920. Though it appears tame, it will still quicken your heart rate. Other rides include the Spook-a-rama, the Thunderbolt, bumper cars, and a number of children's rides. ⊠ *1025 Boardwalk, at W. 12th St., Coney Island* ☎ *718/372–2592* ⊕ *www. wonderwheel.com* ⊗ *Call for seasonal hrs* 🎟 *Free; $5 per ride, 5 rides for $17* Ⓜ *Subway: D, F, Q to Coney Island Stillwell Ave.*

👐 ❶ **Keyspan Park.** Rekindle your Brooklyn baseball memories (or make some new ones) at a Brooklyn Cyclones game. This single A farm team was bought by the Mets in 1999 and moved from St. Catharine's, Ontario, to Brooklyn, bringing professional baseball to the borough for the first time since 1957. ⊠ *1904 Surf Ave., between 17th and 19th Sts., Coney Island* ☎ *718/ 449–8497* ⊕ *www.brooklyncyclones.com* ⊗ *Games June–Sept.; call for schedule* 🎟 *$5–$8* Ⓜ *Subway: D, F, Q to Coney Island Stillwell Ave.*

👐 ❺ **New York Aquarium.** More than 10,000 creatures of the sea make New York City's only aquarium their home. Tropical fish, sea horses, and jellyfish luxuriate in large tanks; otters, walruses, penguins, and seals lounge on a replicated Pacific coast; and a 180,000-gallon seawater complex hosts beluga whales. ⊠ *W. 8th St. and Surf Ave., Coney Island* ☎ *718/ 265–3474* ⊕ *www.nyaquarium.com* 🎟 *$11* ⊗ *Early Apr.–Memorial Day and Labor Day–Oct., weekdays 10–5, weekends 10–5:30; Memorial Day–Labor Day, weekdays 10–6, weekends 10–7; Nov.–early Apr., daily 10–4:30; last ticket sold 45 min before closing* Ⓜ *Subway: D to Coney Island Stillwell Ave. or F, Q West 8th St.*

🔄 ❷ **Sideshows by the Seashore and the Coney Island Museum.** Step right up for a lively circus sideshow, complete with a fire-eater, sword swallower, snake charmer, and contortionist carrying on what was once billed as the "World's Largest Playground." Upstairs from Sideshows, the Museum has historic Coney Island memorabilia and a great deal of tourist information. ✉ *1208 Surf Ave., at W. 12th St., Coney Island* ☎ *718/372–5159 for both* ⊕ *www.coneyisland.com* ✉ *Sideshow $5; museum 99¢* ☉ *Sideshows Memorial Day–Labor Day, Wed.–Fri. 2–8, weekends 1–11; Apr., May, and Sept., weekends 1–8. Museum weekends noon–5. Hrs vary, so call ahead* Ⓜ *Subway: D, F, Q to Coney Island Stillwell Ave.*

Where to Eat

The chewy, deep-fried clams, hot dogs with spicy mustard, and ice-cold lemonade from **Nathan's Famous** (✉ 1310 Surf Ave., at Stillwell Ave. ☎ 718/946–2202) have been nearly inseparable from the Coney Island experience since it opened in 1916. Another branch, on the Boardwalk between Stillwell Avenue and West 12th Street, is open from May through September.

Brighton Beach

East of Coney Island is Brighton Beach, named after Britain's long-standing beach resort. In the early 1900s, Brighton Beach was a resort in its own right, with seaside hotels that catered to rich Manhattan families visiting for the summer. Since the 1970s and '80s, however, Brighton Beach has been known for its 90,000 Soviet emigrés from what are now Russia, Georgia, and Ukraine. On the streets here Russian is the language you'll hear most often. Unlike Coney Island, which most truly comes alive only in summer, Brighton Beach is a vibrant neighborhood year-round.

To get to the heart of "Little Odessa" from Coney Island, walk about a mile east along the boardwalk to Brighton 1st Place, then head up to Brighton Beach Avenue. To get here from Manhattan directly, take the Q train to the Brighton Beach stop; the trip takes about an hour.

Where to Eat

In summer, Brighton Beach's section of the boardwalk, especially between Brighton 3rd St. and 6th St., bustles with restaurants serving traditional Russian dishes—and lots of shots of vodka. **Café Tatiana** (✉ 3152 Brighton 6th St., at the Boardwalk ☎ 718/891–5151), which has a large menu that also includes Continental dishes, is one of the better of these seaside restaurants.

Shopping

The shops, bakeries, markets, and restaurants along Brighton Beach Avenue, the neighborhood's main artery, all cater to the neighborhood's Russian community. This is the place to find knishes with every filling imaginable, borscht, *blinis* (small crepes or pancakes), and cups of dark-roast coffee, plus caviar at prices that can put Manhattan purveyors to shame. Ⓜ *Subway: Q to Brighton Beach.*

M & I International Foods (✉ 249 Brighton Beach Ave., between Brighton 1st Rd. and Brighton 1st Pl. ☎ 718/615–1011) is one the largest food markets on Brighton Beach Avenue. On the ground floor are long counters selling deli foods, smoked fish, meats, and pickled products. Upstairs are baked goods, lots of candy, and a small area with tables and chairs for eating the delicacies you've gathered. **Vintage Food Corp.** (⊠ 287 Brighton Beach Ave., between Brighton 2nd and Brighton 3rd Sts. ☎ 718/759–6674) sells Turkish delight, nuts and fruits, candy, and olives by the pound—and all for reasonable prices.

QUEENS

Home of LaGuardia and John F. Kennedy International airports and many people who commute to Manhattan, Queens is only seen by most visitors from the window of an airplane and cab. Named by the colonists for Queen Catherine of Braganza, wife of Charles II, Queens was largely pro-British through the Revolutionary War. Today it's the largest of the city's five boroughs, accounting for a full third of the city's entire area. Its population of nearly 2,230,000 is the city's most diverse, with 36% of those living in its countless ethnic neighborhoods born on foreign soil. Its inhabitants represent almost all nationalities and speak scores of languages. Queens communities such as Astoria (Greek and Italian), Jackson Heights (Colombian, Mexican, and Indian), Sunnyside (Turkish and Romanian), Woodside (Irish), and Flushing (Korean and Chinese) are fascinating to explore, particularly if you're interested in experiencing some of the city's tastiest—and least expensive—cuisine.

The unusual numbering system used for Queens addresses manages to puzzle even native New Yorkers. Keep in mind that avenues, roads, and drives all run more or less east–west, and streets, places, and lanes run north–south. The first part of a house number refers to the nearest intersection. For instance, 36–01 41st Avenue (different from but *close to* 36–01 41st Drive) is near the intersection of 41st Avenue and 36th Street.

Astoria & Long Island City

Long Island City and Astoria, both just a few minutes from Manhattan, have emerged as the borough's destinations of choice for great museums and superb ethnic dining.

Astoria is like an archaeological site—each layer contains a trace of the area's successive denizens, from moviemakers and Greek immigrants to young artists and professionals. Astoria was named for John Jacob Astor at the behest of an admirer, who was also in the fur trade. Originally German, then Greek, it had earned the nickname Little Athens by the late 1960s. Today a substantial numbers of Asians, Eastern Europeans, Irish, and Latino immigrants reside in Astoria, not to mention a healthy contingent of former Manhattan and Brooklyn residents in search of cheaper rents. Here you can buy kalamata olives and Bulgarian feta cheese from store owners who will tell you where to go for the best spinach pie, or you can sit outside at one of the many pastry shops, drink tall, frothy frappes, and watch the subway's elevated trains roll by.

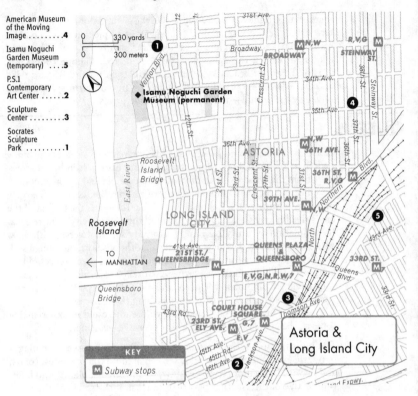

Astoria &
Long Island City

The heart of the Greek community is on Broadway, between 31st and
Steinway streets. Greek pastry shops and coffee shops abound here, and
the elevated subway brings a constant stream of activity. Farther up, 30th
Avenue is another busy thoroughfare with almost every kind of food
store imaginable. The largest Greek Orthodox congregation outside Greece
worships at St. Demetrios Cathedral, off 30th Avenue.

For nearly 25 years, from 1874 until it became part of New York in 1898,
Long Island City really was its own city. At the time an amalgamation
of neighborhoods that included Astoria and Sunnyside, among others,
modern-day Long Island City shrank to become a rectangle formed by
Broadway to the north, 39th Street and Steinway Avenue to the east,
Brooklyn to the south, and the East River to the west., with Astoria beginning at the north side of Broadway. Beginning in the 1960s, artists
began to move to the area for its cheap rent and wide open spaces. Long
Island City has always been an industrial area, and it remains so today.
Its southern sections, however, have continued to get more and more
residential, as recent immigrants as well as young people fleeing the high
rents of Brooklyn and Manhattan seek out apartments with good views
of the sky and easy access to the 7 train, which heads directly into midtown Manhattan.

What to See

④ American Museum of the Moving Image. Crossing the East River to Astoria for the nation's only museum devoted to the art, technology, and history of film, TV, and digital media is a worthwhile pilgrimage. Via artifacts, texts, live demonstrations, and video screenings, the main exhibition, "Behind the Screen," takes you step by step through the process of making movies. Interactive computers allow you to create animation, edit sound effects, dub dialogue, and add sound tracks. The museum's collection of movie memorabilia consists of more than 80,000 items, including the chariot used in *Ben Hur,* the Mohawk bald cap that Robert De Niro wore in *Taxi Driver,* and a model of Regan, possessed by Satan, that was used in *The Exorcist* (Yoda, standing nearby, is far less terrifying). The museum also presents changing exhibits, lectures, and film programs, including retrospectives, Hollywood classics, and contemporary films. The museum shop, full of oddball T-shirts and knick-knacks as well as the requisite film guides and books, is a good place for a nonobvious souvenir or gift. Next door is the imposing Kaufman-Astoria Studios, used for filming movies, commercial, and TV series. ⊠ *35th Ave. at 36th St., Astoria* ☎ *718/784–0077* ⊕ *www.ammi.org* ☜ *$10; free after 4 on Fri.* ☉ *Wed. and Thurs. noon–5, Fri. noon–8, weekends 11–6:30; screenings weekends and Fri. 7:30* Ⓜ *Subway: R, V (weekdays only), R, G (weekends only) to Steinway St.; N, W to Broadway.*

⑤ Isamu Noguchi Garden Museum. The Japanese-American sculptor Isamu Noguchi (1904–88) bought this former photo engraving plant, across the street from his studio at the time, as a place to display his work. The large, peaceful garden and the galleries that border it provide ample room to show more than 250 pieces done in stone, metal, clay, and other materials. On weekends a shuttle bus leaves from in front of Manhattan's Asia Society hourly beginning at 11:30. A round trip costs $10. ⊠ *9–01 33rd Rd., at Vernon Blvd., Long Island City* ☎ *718/204–7088* ⊕ *www.noguchi.org* ☜ *$5* ☉ *Wed.–Fri. 10–5, weekends 11–6* Ⓜ *Subway: N to Broadway, then walk west or take Q104 bus along Broadway to Vernon Blvd.*

★ ② P.S.1 Contemporary Art Center. A pioneer in the "alternative-space" movement, P.S.1 rose from the ruins of an abandoned school in 1976 as a sort of community arts center for the future. Now a partner of the Museum of Modern Art, P.S.1 still focuses on community involvement, with studio spaces for resident artists and educational programs. In summer, its Sunday afternoon outdoor dance parties with fashionable DJs attract a crowd in which everyone looks like an attractive art student. P.S.1's exhibition space is enormous, and every available corner is used—four floors, rooftop spaces, staircases and landings, bathrooms, the boiler room and basement, and outdoor galleries. Exhibitions reflect the center's mission to present experimental and formally innovative contemporary art, from the progressive and interactive to the merely incomprehensible. It's never dull. ⊠ *22–25 Jackson Ave., at 46th Ave., Long Island City* ☎ *718/784–2084* ⊕ *www.ps1.org* ☜ *$5 suggested donation* ☉ *Thurs.–Mon. noon–6* Ⓜ *Subway: 7 to 45 Rd.–Courthouse Sq.; V (weekdays only) or E to 23rd St.–Ely Ave.; G to 21 St.–Van Alst.*

FILMMAKING IN ASTORIA

I N THE 1920S, when Hollywood was still a dusty small town, such stars as Gloria Swanson, Rudolph Valentino, and Claudette Colbert all came out to the Astoria Studio to act in one of the more than 100 movies produced here. Built in 1919 by the film company that would soon become Paramount, "the Big House" was the largest and most important filmmaking studio in the country. Its location was ideal for the time, when filmmakers needed easy access to Broadway's and vaudeville's stars.

By the '30s, the trickle of studios and stars lured to Hollywood and its near-perfect year-round weather had become a full-blown stream. Astoria was able to hold its own for a while longer, creating such films as the Marx Brothers classics The Cocoanuts and Animal Crackers. As the decade went on, Paramount continued to moves its operations west, until finally

shorts were the only films being made at Paramount's eastern branch.

In 1942 the studio was sold to the U.S. Army, and it became the Signal Corps Photographic Center, producing training films and documentaries that include Frank's Capra's classic seven-film series, Why We Fight. The government retained the studio until the early '70s, by which time it had began to fall into disrepair.

Sold to a foundation and then to the city, in 1982 the studio was transferred to real-estate developer George S. Kaufman and his partners, which included Alan King and the late Johnny Carson. Kaufman-Astoria Studio, with six stages, is a thriving operation once again, used for television series (Sesame Street, Law and Order) as well as movies (The Wiz, Hair, The Manchurian Candidate).

❸ **Sculpture Center.** This large museum not far from P.S. 1 is devoted to contemporary sculpture. A former trolley repair shop that was renovated by artist Maya Lin and architect David Hotson, the Sculpture Center exhibits cutting-edge work in its large indoor and outdoor exhibition spaces. Also here are a sculpture library and studios for visiting artists. The museum sometimes closes between exhibition periods; call ahead before visiting. ✉ *44–19 Purves St., at Jackson Ave., Long Island City* ☎ *718/361–1750* ⊕ *www.sculpture-center.org* ✉ *$5 suggested donation* ⊙ *Thurs.–Mon. 11–6* Ⓜ *Subway: 7 to 45 Rd.–Courthouse Sq.; V (weekdays only), E to 23rd St.–Ely Ave.; G to 21st St.–Van Alst.*

👆 ❶ **Socrates Sculpture Park.** In 1985 local artist Mark di Suvero and other residents rallied to transform what had been an abandoned landfill and illegal dump site into this 4½-acre park devoted to public art. The park was named in honor of the philosopher as well as the local Greek community. Today a superb view of the river and Manhattan frames huge, often playful works of art made of scrap metal, old tires, sand, and other recycled materials. You can climb on or walk through a number of the sculptures. ✉ *Vernon Blvd. at Broadway, Long Island City* ☎ *718/956–1819* ⊕ *www.socratessculpturepark.org* ✉ *Free* ⊙ *Daily 10–sunset*

Ⓜ *Subway: N to Broadway, then walk west or take Q104 bus along Broadway to Vernon Blvd.*

Where to Eat

Astoria has emerged as one of the top destinations in Queens for superb ethnic dining. After you're done with the sights, you may want to end your day with dinner at one of Astoria's Greek restaurants (on or near Broadway) or venture to the Middle Eastern restaurants farther out on Steinway Street.

The multilevel ✕ **Karyatis** (✉ 35–03 Broadway, between 35th and 36th Sts., Astoria ☎ 718/204–0666) is among the oldest and most elegant of Queens' neighborhood Greek restaurants. The traditional appetizers, grilled octopus, lamb, grilled fish entrées, and other menu highlights are served by a friendly and professional staff. With live music at night you can make a festive evening of it. **Uncle George's Greek Tavern** (✉ 33-19 Broadway, at 34th St. ☎ 718/626–0593), which looks much more like a diner than a taverns, serves simple preparations of Greek dishes, especially those involving fish.

Jackson Heights

Jackson Heights was primarily farmland until the 1909 opening of the Queensboro Bridge made it appealing to developers. The former Jackson Avenue, which gave the neighborhood it's name, is now Northern Boulevard.

Although South American and immigrants from many other countries live in the area, visitors usually pay calls to the neighborhood for its South Asian shops and restaurants. "Little India," whose center is 74th Street between Roosevelt and 37th avenues, is full of restaurants, jewelry shops, DVD stores, and other businesses catering to the majority of the estimated 110,000 Asian Indians who live in Queens. Pakistanis and Bangladeshis round out the Asian population. To get to this section of Jackson Heights, take the 7 subway train to the 74th Street–Broadway stop.

Where to Eat

Neighborhood folk and Manhattanites alike flock to **Jackson Diner** (✉ 37–47 74th St., between Roosevelt and 37th Aves. ☎ 718/672-1232) for the cheap, spicy, and authentic fare served in generous portions. Popular choices include chicken tandoori, lentil donuts in a tangy broth, and any of the curry dishes, as well as the many vegetarian specialties. Down the block from Jackson Diner, **Delhi Palace** (✉ 37–33 74th St., between Roosevelt and 37th Aves. ☎ 718/507–0666) serves a similar menu of authentic Indian dishes, but many of them are just a bit better—and spicier. The restaurant's daily buffet (around $8), served daily from 11:30 to 4, stands out from the competition.

Shopping

Sahil Sari Palace (✉ 37–39 74th St., between Roosevelt and 37th Aves. ☎ 718/426–9526) is filled with bolts of colorful cloth as well as ready to wear saris and other clothing. **Patel Brothers** (✉ 37–27 74th St., near 37th Ave., Jackson Heights ☎ 718/898–3445), like the other members in this large chain of Indian grocery stores, stocks household goods, produce, and lots of other staples. Especially fun to check out are the ice cream, nuts, and other snacks.

Flushing Meadows–Corona Park

The site of both the 1939 and 1964 World's Fairs, Flushing Meadows–Corona Park puts you within walking distance of some of Queens' major cultural and recreational institutions. It's centerpiece is the Unisphere, which is in front of the Queens Museum of Art. Made entirely of stainless steel, this massive sculpture of Earth is 140 feet high and weighs 380 tons.

The **Queens Museum of Art** shows contemporary works by many interesting local and international artists as well as temporary exhibits on culture, but it's best known for the astonishing Panorama, a nearly 900,000-building model of the five boroughs made for the 1964 World's Fair. The exhibit, brought up to date in 1994, faithfully replicates the city building by building, on a scale of 1 inch per 100 feet. The model's tiny brownstones and skyscrapers are updated periodically to match the real things (a red, white, and blue ribbon now hangs on the World Trade Center). Another permanent exhibit, the Neustadt Museum Collection, brings together Tiffany lamps and windows, many of which were made in nearby Corona, Queens. ⊠ *Flushing Meadows–Corona Park* ☎ *718/592–9700* ⊕ *www.queensmuseum.org* ✉ *$5 suggested donation* ☼ *Sept.–June, Wed.–Fri. 10–5, weekends noon–5; July and Aug., Wed.–Sun. 1–8* Ⓜ *Subway: 7 to Willets Point/Shea Stadium.*

Built in 1964, **Shea Stadium** is named for the lawyer William A. Shea, who was essential in bringing a National League baseball team back to New York. The New York Mets play here from April through September. In addition to its place in sports-making history, Shea Stadium was also the site of a famous Beatles concert in August of 1965. ⊠ *Roosevelt Ave. off Grand Central Pkwy.* ☎ *718/507–8499* ⊕ *www.mets.com* Ⓜ *Subway: 7 to Willets Pt./Shea Stadium.*

The **USTA National Tennis Center,** site of the U.S. Open Tennis Championships, has 42 courts (33 outdoor and 9 indoor, all Deco Turf II) open to the public all year except August and September. Reservations are accepted up to two days in advance, and prices are $20–$50 hourly. ⊠ *Flushing Meadows–Corona Park.* ☎ *718/760–6200* ⊕ *www.usta. com* Ⓜ *Subway: 7 to Willets Pt./Shea Stadium.*

Elsewhere in Queens

Louis Armstrong House. Famed jazz musician Louis Armstrong lived in this three-story house in a working-class neighborhood of Corona Park with his wife, Lucille, from 1943 until his death in 1971. Although the Armstrongs later covered the exterior in brick, it's in the furnishings that their taste really shines through. The 40-minute tour takes you through the large living room, full of mementos and art collected over a lifetime of traveling, the Asian-inspired dining room, and the kitchen, all done up in robin's-egg blue and Lucite. The downstairs bathroom, its walls entirely mirrored and its fixtures plated in gold, is a trip in itself. Amid all this vivid decoration, Louis's den is comparatively drab, with dark wood and a phonograph, ceiling speakers, a bar area, and what were once state-of-the-art reel-to-reel tape recorders. It's here where his spirit shines through most clearly. ⊠ *34–56 107th St., between 37th and 38th Aves., Corona Park* ☎ *718/478–8274* ⊕ *www.satchmo.net* ⊠ *$8* ☉ *Tours hrly Tues.–Fri. 10–4, weekends noon–4* Ⓜ *Subway: 7 to 103rd St.–Corona Plaza.*

Ꚙ **New York Hall of Science.** This top science museum has more than 200 hands-on experiments on subjects ranging from lasers to microbes. Outside, stations on the Science Playground coax youngsters into learning while they're horsing around—a seesaw, for example, becomes a lesson in balance and leverage. ⊠ *111th St. at 46th Ave., Flushing* ☎ *718/699–0005* ⊕ *www.nyscience.org* ⊠ *$11; free Fri. 2–5 and Sun. 10–11, Sept.–June* ☉ *Sept.–June, Mon.–Thurs. 9:30–2, Fri. 9:30–5, weekends 10–6; July and Aug., weekdays 9:30–5, weekends 10–6* Ⓜ *Subway: 7 to 111th St.; walk 3 blocks south.*

Queens Botanical Gardens. Built for the 1939 World's Fair, these 39 acres include gardens of roses and herbs, an arboretum, and plantings especially designed to attract bees and birds. Plans slated for completion in 2006 will bring a new environmentally friendly visitor center that will use solar energy and water-filtering plants in its design. ⊠ *43–50 Main St., Flushing* ☎ *718/886–3800* ⊕ *www.queensbotanical.org* ⊠ *Free* ☉ *Apr.–Oct., Tues.–Fri. 8–6, weekends 8–7; Nov.–Mar., Tues.–Sun. 8–4:30* Ⓜ *Subway: 7 to Main St.–Flushing.*

THE BRONX

New York City's northernmost and only mainland borough (the others are all on islands) was the retreat of wealthy New Yorkers in the 19th century, when the area consisted of a picturesque patchwork of farms, market villages, and country estates. In the 1920s, the Bronx experienced a short-lived golden age: the new elevated subway line attracted an upwardly mobile population, and the Grand Concourse was fashioned as New York City's Champs-Elysées. Although the Bronx has a reputation as a gritty, down-and-out place, the borough is full of vital areas like the Italian neighborhood of Belmont. It has its cultural gems, too—the New York Botanical Garden, the Bronx Zoo, and, of course, Yankee Stadium, home of the celebrated Bronx Bombers.

The good news is that many of New York City's most popular attractions are in the Bronx. The bad news is that while most are within walking distance of each other, you can't possibly see them all in a day. A few, including the New York Botanical Garden and the Bronx Zoo, require at least a half day to see the highlights. You're better off spending a full day so you won't feel rushed. Come back another day to stroll the atmospheric streets of Belmont or to tour Yankee Stadium.

The Bronx Zoo and the New York Botanical Garden are each vast and interesting enough to merit half a day or more. If you want to visit both,

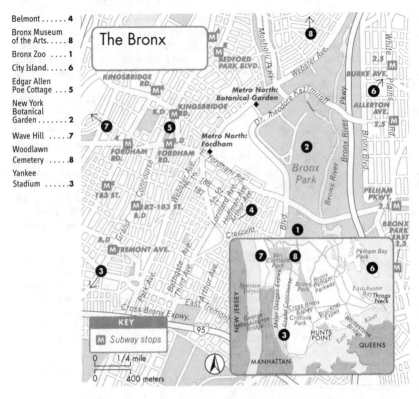

start early and plan on a late lunch or early dinner in Belmont. Saturday is the best day to see the Italian neighborhood at its liveliest; on Sunday most stores are closed. The zoo and the garden are less crowded on weekdays—except Wednesday, when admission to both is free.

The Bronx Zoo

Fodor'sChoice
★

When it opened its gates in 1899, 843 animals were exhibited in small cages and enclosures. Today, this 265-acre zoo is the world's largest. More than 4,500 animals, representing more than 600 species, mostly live in outdoor settings designed to re-create their habitats. You're often separated from them by no more than a moat. One of the zoo's best exhibits is the **Congo Gorilla Forest** ($3) a 6½-acre re-creation of an African rain forest with treetop lookouts, wooded pathways, lush greenery, and 300 animals—including red-river hogs, black-and-white colobus monkeys, and two troops of lowland gorillas.

Planning your trip is important, as it's impossible to see everything here in one day. Try to visit the most popular exhibits, such as Congo Gorilla Forest, early to avoid lines later in the day. Remember that in winter the outdoor exhibitions have fewer animals on view. ✉ *Bronx River Pkwy. and Fordham Rd., Fordham* ☎ *718/367–1010* ⊕ *www.bronxzoo.*

com ✉ *$11; free Wed., donation suggested; extra charge for some exhibits; parking $7* ☉ *Apr.–Oct., weekdays 10–5, weekends 10–5:30; Nov.–Mar., daily 10–4:30; last ticket sold 1 hr before closing* Ⓜ *Subway: 2, 5 to Pelham Pkwy., then walk 3 blocks west to Bronx Pkwy. entrance; Bx11 express bus to zoo entrance.*

New York Botanical Garden

★ ❷ Considered one of the leading botany centers of the world, this 250-acre garden built around the dramatic gorge of the Bronx River is one of the best reasons to make a trip to the Bronx. The garden was founded by Dr. Nathaniel Lord Britton and his wife, Elizabeth. After visiting England's Kew Gardens in 1889, they returned full of fervor to create a similar haven in New York.

On the grounds is the Lorillard Snuff Mill, built by two French Huguenot manufacturers in 1840 to power the grinding of tobacco for snuff. Nearby, the Lorillards grew roses to supply fragrance for their blend. A path along the Bronx River from the mill leads to the garden's 50-acre Forest, the only surviving remnant of the forest that once covered New York City. Outdoor plant collections include the Peggy Rockefeller Rose Garden, with 2,700 bushes of more than 250 varieties; the spectacular Rock Garden, which displays alpine flowers; and the Everett Children's Adventure Garden, 8 acres of plant and science exhibits for children, including a boulder maze, giant animal topiaries, and a plant discovery center. Inside the **Enid A. Haupt Conservatory** (✉ $5), a Victorian-era glass house with 17,000 individual panes, are year-round recreations of misty tropical rain forests and arid African and North American deserts as well as changing exhibitions.

A good way to see the garden is with the **"Garden Passport"** (✉ $13), which gives you access to the Conservatory, Rock Garden, Native Plant Garden, Tram Tour, and Everett Children's Adventure Garden.

The most direct way to the New York Botanical Garden is via **Metro-North** (⊕ www.mta.nyc.ny.us/mnr) from Grand Central Terminal, on the Harlem local line. The Botanical Garden stop is right across from the entrance. Round-trip tickets are $5 to $12, depending on the time of day. A cheaper alternative is to take the B or D train or the No. 4 to Bedford Park Boulevard. From the subway station walk east on Bedford Park Boulevard to the entrance. When you decide to leave the grounds, exit via the main gate near the Great Garden Clock. ✉ *200th St. and Kazimiroff Blvd., Bedford Park* ☎ *718/817–8700* ⊕ *www. nybg.org* ✉ *$3; free Sat. 10–noon and Wed.; parking $7* ☉ *Apr.–Oct., Tues.–Sun. 10–6; Nov.–Mar., Tues.–Sun. 10–5* Ⓜ *Subway: B, D, 4 to Bedford Park Blvd.; Metro-North to Botanical Garden.*

Yankee Stadium

★ ❸ Ever since Babe Ruth hit a home run in the park's inaugural game in 1923, Yankee Stadium has been one of baseball's most revered cathedrals. John Phillip Sousa and the Seventh Regiment Band marked the opening with a fanfare. Many renovations later, the stadium still feels like the place where Lou Gehrig and Micky Mantle performed their heroic deeds. A stadium tour at noon includes glimpses of the field, dugout, and clubhouse. Arrive at least 30 minutes early to buy tickets. If you want to pick up a souvenir, then head to the Yankee's gift store, which is open daily. Better yet, come for a game at the "House That Ruth Built": the Yankees play ball from April through September. On game nights, New York Waterway's *Yankee Clipper* ferry departs for the stadium from Manhattan's east side. For departure information call 800/533–3779; a round-trip ferry ride is $18. ⊠ *161st St. and River Ave., Highbridge* ☎ *718/579–4531 tours, 718/293–6000 box office* ⊕ *www.yankees. com* ⊠ *Tour $12 Sept.–May, $14 June–Aug.* Ⓜ *Subway: B (weekdays only), D to 167th St., No. 4 to 161st St.–Yankee Stadium.*

Where to Eat

Catercorner to Gate 6 of Yankee Stadium and open two hours before and after games, the tiny **Press Café.** (⊠ 114 E. 157th St., between River and Gerard Aves., Highbridge ☎ 718/401–0545) serves delicious salads and pressed Italian-style sandwiches—all for $8 or less. Look for the striped awning and take a seat at one of the seven bar stools or six tables.

Belmont (Arthur Avenue)

❹ Touted as the "Little Italy of the Bronx," Belmont is much more a real, thriving Italian-American community than its Manhattan counterpart, and it's been this way since the late 19th century, when Italians workers were encouraged to move here to help build the Bronx Zoo and other large projects. As the food writer Regina Schrambling puts it, "Arthur Avenue has never catered to fickle tourists, but to passionately loyal shoppers looking for mozzarella so fresh it oozes, for the supplest veal, for fettuccine cut to order, for sausages in a dozen variations."

Don't be surprised to hear people speaking Italian—or Albanian, since the neighborhood has been an enclave for this group since the 1980s. The corner of Arthur Avenue and 187th Street is the heart of this low-key neighborhood—just as Our Lady of Mt. Carmel Roman Catholic Church, at East 187th Street and Belmont Avenue and towering above nearby buildings, is Belmont's spiritual center.

Locals and suburbanites do their shopping on Saturday afternoons, and so should you—you'll find most stores shuttered on Sunday. ⊠ *Bordered by E. Fordham Rd., Southern Blvd., and Crescent and 3rd Aves.* ⊕ *www.arthuravenuebronx.com* Ⓜ *B, D, No. 4 to Fordham Rd., then Bx12 east; No. 2 or 5 to Pelham Pkwy., then Bx12 west; Metro-North to Fordham Rd., then shuttle bus to Belmont.*

Where to Eat

What might be the best restaurant in Belmont, **Roberto's** (⊠ 603 Crescent Ave., at Hughes Ave. ☎ 718/733–9503), serves classic Southern Italian dishes. At **Dominick's** (⊠ 2335 Arthur Ave., at E. 187th St. ☎ 718/733–2807), no-nonsense waiters preside over communal tables in the sparsely decorated dining room. There are no printed menus, but typical Southern Italian items like veal parmigiana, spaghetti with meat sauce, and shrimp scampi are normally available. Stop for a quick lunch at the

Café al Mercato (✉ 2344 Arthur Ave., at E. 187th St. ☎ 718/364–7681), inside the Arthur Avenue Retail Market. Don't pass up the creative pizzas—the tri-color "Italian Flag" is topped with broccoli rabe, artichokes, and sun-dried tomatoes.

Shopping

The covered **Arthur Avenue Retail Market** (✉ 2344 Arthur Ave., at E. 187th St. ☎ 718/367–5686 ⊕ www.arthuravenue.com), in a building sheltering more than a dozen different vendors, was opened by Mayor Fiorello La-Guardia in an effort to get the pushcarts off the crowded streets. Inside you'll find piles of fresh arugula and radicchio, barrels full of olives, and lots of gnocchi *freschi* (fresh) and other pastas. Also sold here are cigars and Italian gifts and kitchenware. The market is open Monday through Saturday 7–6.

The brick ovens at **Madonia Bros. Bakery** (✉ 2348 Arthur Ave., between 187th and Crescent Sts. ☎ 718/295–5573) have been turning out golden-brown loaves since 1918. A ring of salty prosciutto bread makes a great snack. Clams ranging from little necks to cherrystones are iced down in wooden bins in front of **Randazzo's Seafood** (✉ 2327 Arthur Ave., between 187th and Crescent Sts. ☎ 718/367–4139). The front window of **Calandra's Cheese** (✉ 2314 Arthur Ave., between 187th and Crescent Sts. ☎ 718/365–7572) is stuffed with hunks of cheese the size of truck tires. Mozzarella (with salt or without), mascarpone, and scamorza dangle from the rafters.

On bustling 187th Street, **Mount Carmel Wines and Spirits** (✉ 612 E. 187th St., between Arthur and Hughes Aves., Belmont ☎ 718/367–7833) sells a tremendous selection of wines and liqueurs, including limoncello, that sweet, fluorescently yellow drink. **DeLillo Pastry Shop** (✉ 606 E. 187th St., between Arthur and Hughes Aves. ☎ 718/367–8198) serves espresso and gooey pastries as well as superb Italian ices in the warmer months.

Within sight of Our Lady of Mt. Carmel Church, the **Catholic Goods Center** (✉ 630 E. 187 St., between Belmont and Hughes Aves. ☎ 718/733–0250) sells statues, cards, and books, and many other items of a religious nature. **Borgatti's Ravioli & Egg Noodles** (✉ 632 E. 187th St., between Belmont and Hughes Aves. ☎ 718/367–3799) is known for its homemade pastas.

Edgar Allan Poe Cottage

⑤ The poet and his sickly wife, Virginia, sought refuge at this tiny workman's cottage from 1846 to 1849. The family was so impoverished that Poe's mother sometimes wandered along the roadside to pick dandelions for dinner. Virginia died of tuberculosis in 1847, and Poe sought solace in the church chimes at nearby St. John's College Church (now Fordham University); word has it that these haunting sounds inspired one of his most famous poems, "The Bells." ✉ *E. Kingsbridge Rd. and Grand Concourse, Kingsbridge Heights* ☎ *718/881–8900* ⊕ *www.bronxhistoricalsociety.org* 🎫 *$3* ⊙ *Sat. 10–4, Sun. 1–5* Ⓜ *Subway: 4, D to Kingsbridge Rd.*

City Island

6 At the extreme northeast end of the Bronx is a bona fide island of 230 acres. In 1761 a group of local residents planned a port to rival New York's, but when the Revolutionary War intervened, they returned to perennial maritime pursuits such as fishing and boatbuilding. During World War II, the boatyards were put to use building landing craft, and in the years after City Island produced five of the yachts to win the America's Cup.

The last shipyard closed in the early 1980s, but City Island retains its New England fishing-village atmosphere. City Island has as its spine the 1½-mi-long City Island Avenue, which is lined with antiques and gift shops, restaurants, and boat rentals. To reach the island, take the No. 6 subway to Pelham Bay Parkway (the end of the line), which is on the end of the enormous Pelham Bay Park. From there, catch the Bx29 bus.

Where to Eat

Near the bridge to Pelham Bay Park, you'll find one cluster of restaurants; on the other end is another, including **Johnny's Famous Reef Restaurant** (⊠ 2 City Island Ave. ☎ 718/885–2086), where there's a feeding frenzy over the fried fish.

Wave Hill

7 In the mid- to late 19th century, Manhattan millionaires built summer homes in the suburb of Riverdale, where they had stirring views of the New Jersey Palisades. Wave Hill, a former estate dating back to 1843, is now a 28-acre public garden and cultural center. Today the greenhouse and conservatory, plus 18 acres of exquisite herb, wildflower, and aquatic gardens, attract green thumbs from all over the world. Grand beech and oak trees adorn wide lawns, and elegant pergolas are hidden along curving pathways. Additional draws are gardening and crafts workshops, a summertime dance series, changing art exhibitions, and Sunday concerts, which are held in Armor Hall from fall to spring. ⊠ W. 249th St. and Independence Ave., Riverdale ☎ 718/549–3200 ⊕ www.wavehill.org 🖭 Mar.–Nov. $4, Sat. AM and Tues. free; Dec.–Feb. free ☉ Mid-Apr.–May and Aug.–mid-Oct., Tues.–Sun. 9–5:30; June and July, Tues. 9–5:30, Wed. 9–dusk, Thurs.–Sun. 9–5:30; mid-Oct.–mid-Apr., Tues.–Sun. 9–4:30; free garden tours Sun. 2:15 Ⓜ Subway: 1, 9 train to 231st St., then Bx10 bus to 252nd St. and Riverdale Ave.; Metro-North train: Hudson line to Riverdale then 15 min uphill walk.

Woodlawn Cemetery

8 This ornate and star-studded burial ground opened in 1863. Among the 300,000 buried over these 400 acres are R. H. Macy, Fiorello La Guardia and four other former mayors of New York, Robert Moses, financier Jay Gould, Joseph Pulitzer, Elizabeth Cady Stanton, Nellie Bly, Herman Melville, George M. Cohan, Irving Berlin, Duke Ellington, Miles Davis, and Celia Cruz. More impressive than Woodlawn's dead, however, are the elaborate graves and mausoleums that hold them. Stanford White, Louis Comfort Tiffany, and John Russell Pope created many of these markers, which reflect the flamboyant tastes of the late 1800s and often resemble Roman temples and small churches. Maps of the cemetery are available from the guard on duty, and guided tours ($5) are given in the spring and fall. ⊠ *Entrances at 233rd St. and Webster Ave. and at Jerome Ave. north of Bainbridge Ave.* Ⓜ *Subway: 4 to Woodlawn or 2 or 5 to 233rd St.; Metro-North train: Harlem line to Woodlawn* ☎ *718/ 920–0500* ⊕ *www.thewoodlawncemetery.org* ✉ *Free* ☉ *Daily 8:30–5.*

STATEN ISLAND

Numbers in the text correspond to numbers in the margin and on the Staten Island map.

Although Staten Island is a borough of New York City, it is, for many New Yorkers, a distant suburb. Staten Islanders number about 450,000, yet share a space that's 2½ times the size of Manhattan. Locals, many of whom are second- or third-generation residents, feel a strong allegiance to their borough. Its small museums hold unexpected offerings, and its historic villages at Richmondtown and Snug Harbor give a sense of New York's past. Its **Greenbelt** (⊕ www.sigreenbelt.org), a chain of parks, forests, and nature preserves that add up to 2,500 acres, and 35 mi of trails, dwarfs Manhattan's own central plot of green, and the greenspace in most of the rest of the city.

As you make your plans, set aside the better part of a day for Historic Richmondtown, and add on a couple of hours for the Tibetan Museum. If you take the bus, ask the driver about the return schedule. Both Historic Richmondtown and the Tibetan Museum are closed Monday and Tuesday and open afternoons only on weekends. Historic Richmondtown hosts a variety of seasonal events, including "Old Home Day" in October and a Christmas celebration.

Staten Island Ferry

❶ One of Staten Island's biggest attractions for visitors is the phenomenal view of lower Manhattan and the Statue of Liberty afforded by the free 25-minute Staten Island Ferry ride across New York Harbor—the only direct route to Manhattan from the island. On weekdays and weekend afternoons you can catch the ferry at least every half hour. On weekend mornings until 11:30 AM, ferries leave the southern tip of Manhattan at Whitehall Terminal every hour on the half hour; from 11:30 AM until 7:30 PM, they run every half hour. ⊹ *Runs between Manhattan's Whitehall Terminal (Whitehall and South Sts.) and Staten Island's St. George Terminal* ⊕ *www.siferry.com* Ⓜ *Whitehall Terminal: 4 or 5 train to Bowling Green, or R or W train to Whitehall St.*

Historic Richmondtown

☾❷ These 28 buildings, some constructed as early as 1685, others as late as the 19th century, are part of a 100-acre village that was the site of Staten Island's original county seat. Some of the buildings here have been relocated from different spots on the island—all brought together to pro-

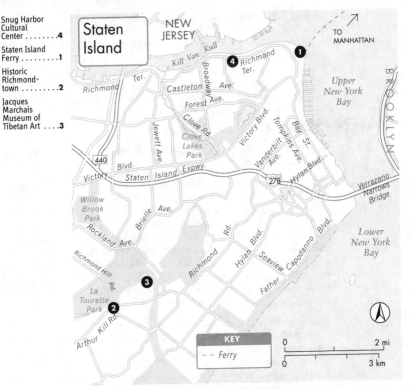

vide a sense of Staten Island's rich history. The Staten Island Historical Society runs the site, and 12 buildings that have been restored are open to the public. Many, such as the Greek revival courthouse, which serves as the **visitor center** in summer, date from the 19th century; other architectural styles on-site range from Dutch colonial to Victorian Gothic revival. The **Staten Island Historical Society Museum,** built in 1848 as the second county clerk's and surrogate's office, now houses furniture, tools, photographs, and other Staten Island artifacts plus changing exhibitions about the island; it serves as the visitor center in winter. **Stephen's General Store,** built in 1837, looks much as it did in the mid-19th century. Adjacent is the late-19th-century **Stephen's House,** which is also filled with artifacts from the period. The **Voorlezer's House,** built in 1695, is one of the oldest buildings on the site; it served as a residence as well as a place of worship and an elementary school.

During special events staff members demonstrate Early American crafts and trades such as printing, tinsmithing, basket making, and fireplace cooking. In summer you might want to make reservations for the traditional dinner (call for details), cooked outdoors and served with utensils of the specific period. Old Home Day in October shows off craftspeople at work; and December brings a monthlong Christmas celebration. A tavern on the historic village grounds hosts a Saturday night concert series showcasing ethnic and folk music; call for details. Take the S74–Richmond Road bus or a car service (which costs about $12) from the ferry terminal. ✉ *441 Clarke Ave., Richmondtown* ☎ *718/351–1611* ⊕ *www.historicrichmondtown.org* 🔲 *$5* ⊙ *July and Aug., Wed.–Sat. 10–5, Sun. 1–5; Sept.–Dec. and Feb.–June, Wed.–Sun. 1–5; early–late Jan., weekends 1–5* Ⓜ *S74 bus to St. Patrick's Pl.*

Where to Eat

For a taste of Historic Richmondtown cuisine, head to the **Parsonage** (✉ 74 Arthur Kill Rd., Richmondtown ☎ 718/351–7879), which serves twists on American classics (pork chops stuffed with prosciutto and mozzarella, filet mignon covered in apple-smoked bacon) in restored 19th-century parish house in the complex.

Jacques Marchais Museum of Tibetan Art

❸ One of the largest private, nonprofit collections of Tibetan and Himalayan sculpture, scrolls, and paintings outside of Tibet is displayed in this museum resembling a Tibetan monastery. The museum often hosts Buddhist monks from across the world, who demonstrate different parts of their faith—the Dalai Lama visited in 1991. Jacques Marchais, a female art dealer, founded the museum in 1945. ✉ *338 Lighthouse Ave., Richmondtown* ☎ *718/987–3500* ⊕ *www.tibetanmuseum.com* 🔲 *$5* ⊙ *Wed.–Sun. 1–5* Ⓜ *S74 bus to Lighthouse Ave. and walk uphill 15 min.*

Snug Harbor Cultural Center

★ ❹ The restored sailor's community of Snug Harbor is Staten Island's most popular attraction. Made up of 26 mostly restored historic buildings, Snug Harbor's center is a row of five columned Greek Revival temples that were built between 1831 and 1880. Also nearby are two small but engaging museums.

Once part of a sprawling farm, the 83-acre hospital and rest home was founded in 1831 at the bequest of wealthy shipowner Robert Richard Randall as a home for "aged, decrepit, and worn-out sailors," and it was used as such until the early 1960s, by which time the number of residents had dropped off greatly. The Trustees, unable to cope with risings costs, began considering tearing the complex down and building again. Their plans were thwarted by the City of New York, who had six buildings designated landmarks and who later bought the entire property from the organization, which relocated to South Carolina.

To get here from the Staten Island Ferry terminal, take the S40 bus 2 mi to the Snug Harbor Road stop—a trip of about seven minutes. Signal the driver as soon as you glimpse the black iron fence along the edge of the property. You can also grab a car service at the ferry terminal (the ride should cost you about $5). ✉ *1000 Richmond Terr., between Snug Harbor Rd. and Tyson Ave., Livingston* ☎ *718/448–2500* ⊕ *www.snug-harbor.org* 🔲 *Cultural Center grounds free* ⊙ *Dawn–dusk; tours weekends at 2, meet at visitor center* Ⓜ *S40 bus to Snug Harbor.*

Snug Harbor's Main Hall—the oldest building on the property and dating from 1833—is home to the **Eleanor Proske Visitors Center,** which has an exhibit on the history of Snug Harbor. ⊠ *Snug Harbor Cultural Center, Bldg. D, Main Hall* ☎ *718/448–2500 Ext. 524* ⊠ *$3* ☉ *Tues.–Sun. 11–5.*

Next to the visitor center is the **Newhouse Center for Contemporary Art.** On display is exhibiting contemporary work, normally within a historical context: older works often sit beside multidisciplinary pieces—in costume, video, mixed-media, and performance, among others—in the expansive space. ⊠ *Snug Harbor Cultural Center, Bldg. D, Main Hall* ☎ *718/448–2500* ⊠ *$3* ☉ *Tues.–Sun. 11–5.*

Next door to the Main Hall is the **John A. Noble Collection,** where an old seaman's dormitory has been transformed into classrooms; a library and archive; a printmaking studio; and galleries displaying maritime-inspired photography, lithographs, and artwork. ⊠ *Snug Harbor Cultural Center, Bldg. D* ☎ *718/447–6490* ⊠ *$3* ☉ *Thurs.–Sun. 1–5.*

Spread over the cultural center grounds is the **Staten Island Botanical Gardens,** which include a perennial garden, a greenhouse, a vineyard, 10 acres of natural marsh habitat, a rose garden, and a sensory garden with fragrant, touchable flowers, and tinkling waterfalls intended for people with vision and hearing impairments. An authentic Chinese Scholars' Garden—hand-created by artisans from China and one of only two in the United States—has reflecting ponds, waterfalls, pavilions, and a teahouse. The Carl Grillo Glass House keeps tropical, desert, and temperate plant environments, and the Connie Gretz Secret Garden is wonderfully child-friendly in design, with castles and moats among the flowers. Buy tickets for the Chinese and Secret gardens at the garden's visitor center, on Cottage Row. ☎ *718/273–8200* ⊕ *www.sibg.org* ⊠ *Free; $5 for Chinese Garden and Secret Garden* ☉ *Daily dawn–dusk; Chinese Garden, Glass House, and Secret Garden Tues.–Sun. 10–5; Nov.–Dec., Tues.–Sun. 10–4.*

☺ The **Staten Island Children's Museum** has five galleries with hands-on exhibitions introducing such topics as nature's food chains, storytelling, and insects. Portia's Playhouse, an interactive children's theater, invites youngsters to step up to the stage and try on costumes. ☎ *718/273–2060* ⊠ *$5* ☉ *During school year, Tues.–Sun. noon–5; in summer Tues.–Sun. 11–5.*

Where to Eat

Adobe Blues (⊠ 63 Lafayette St., off Richmond Terr. ☎ 718/720–2583) is a bar and restaurant that serves up more than 160 beers, 40 types of tequila, and Southwestern fare.

Café Botanica (⊠ Snug Harbor Cultural Center, Cottage Row ☎ 718/720–9737), next to the Staten Island Botanical Garden, serves breakfast and light lunch items daily; its hours are identical to the Chinese Garden nearby.

Where to Eat

WORD OF MOUTH

"The tasting menu [at Gramercy Tavern] was superb. Each dish was exquisitely presented and was absolutely delicious. We were treated like royalty. The wine menu is excellent, as well. We can't wait to go back."

—Leila

"[Joe's Shanghai] is one of my favorite Chinese restaurants. Their steamed crab dumplings are the best! If you go, go during non-rush hour to avoid having to share a table with strangers!"

—Wendy

"Eating at Town is an incredible sensory experience. The sights, sounds, tastes—all amazing. We enjoyed excellent food along with great people-watching in a gorgeous setting."

—Meredith

www.fodors.com/forums

Updated by
Naomi Black,
Adam Kowit,
and Tom Steele

BESIDES SATISFYING A TASTE FOR THE FINER THINGS IN LIFE, restaurants serve Gothamites and our visitors in other crucial ways. They're a vital catalyst for exploring the city (the hunt on Museum Mile for a bite before museum–hopping), a communication device ("Let me tell you about this great little Mexican place way uptown"), and a resource of cocktail-party one-upmanship ("What? You haven't been to Per Se yet?!"). Perhaps most important, restaurants serve as extensions of New Yorkers' usually minute kitchens and nonexistent dining rooms.

Restaurants have consistently demonstrated a savvy sensitivity to the financial times, and a wide array of mid-price restaurants somehow manages to serve high-end food. Quite a few have devised bargain prix-fixe three-course dinners. All in all, though, prices have remained steady.

Still, New York is about extremes, and the metropolis remains a mecca of the monied. So the upswing in thrift-minded diners hasn't stopped new celebrity-chef-driven (and wildly expensive) restaurants such as Thomas Keller's Per Se from opening. Nor has the statewide smoking ban in all indoor public spaces caused more than a mild ripple in restaurant patronage. If anything, more people are dining out as a result of the ban.

So whether you decide to go for a delectable downtown banh mi Vietnamese hero with its surprising counterpoint of flavors and textures, or a prime porterhouse for two with creamed spinach and pommes Lyonnaise at a fancy uptown steak house, note that some of the dishes recommended in the following reviews may not be on the menu you receive when you sit down to eat. Many menus around town are market-driven and seasonal. Use our recommendations as guidelines and you won't be disappointed.

LOWER MANHATTAN

While the Financial District's post–September 11 physical recovery was remarkably speedy, psychologically the turnaround took a while—New Yorkers were understandably slow to return to the neighborhood to make merry. Now back up to speed, the restaurants in this most historic of the city's enclaves are largely busy lunch spots, expense-account dining rooms, and after-work watering holes, with the streets quiet by 9.

American

$$–$$$ ✕ **Delmonico's.** As the oldest continually operating restaurant in New York City, opened in 1837, Delmonico's is steeped in cultural, political, and culinary history. Lobster Newburg and baked Alaska were invented here—and are still served. Inside the stately mahogany-panel dining room, tuck into a 20-ounce boneless rib-eye steak smothered with frizzled onions, dry-aged and spoon tender, and don't forget to order creamed spinach on the side. ⊠ 56 Beaver St., at William St., Lower Manhattan ☎ 212/509–1144 ⚐ Reservations essential ☰ AE, D, DC, MC, V ☺ Closed weekends Ⓜ Subway: 2, 3 to Wall St.; 4, 5 to Bowling Green.

7

In New York, deciding what to eat is as important as deciding what to see and do. The restaurants we list are the cream of the crop in each price category. If you're staying in midtown, note that most restaurants cater to the business crowd and the most practical breakfast and lunch options are the cafeteria-style delis that have both sandwiches and salad bars. The densest cluster of cheap eats is in the East Village. On the street, a hot pretzel from a vendor can come to the rescue between museum visits. To experience the town like a native, make dining a priority, and keep the following things in mind.

Children

Though it is unusual to see children in the dining rooms of Manhattan's most elite restaurants, dining with your youngsters in New York does not have to mean culinary exile. Many of the restaurants reviewed in this chapter are excellent choices for families, and are marked with a ♕ symbol.

Dress

While casual attire is acceptable most of the time, your concept of the term may change while in New York. Think "casual chic." Only a very few of the most formal places still require ties; and only a few dozen require jackets. As a rule, dress at restaurants in midtown and around Wall Street is more conservative than in other, more residential neighborhoods, especially at lunch. Shorts are appropriate only in the most casual spots. Don't be embarrassed to call and ask.

Hours

New Yorkers seem ready to eat at any hour. Many restaurants stay open between lunch and dinner, some offer late-night seating, and still others serve around-the-clock. Restaurants that serve breakfast often do so until noon. Restaurants in the East Village, the Lower East Side, SoHo, TriBeCa, and the Village are likely to remain open late, while midtown spots and those in the theater and financial districts generally close earlier. Unless otherwise noted, the restaurants listed in this guide are open daily for lunch and dinner.

Reservations

At the hottest restaurants reservations need to be made weeks or months in advance, no matter how well-connected the concierge at your hotel is. Tables are especially hard to come by if you want to dine between 7 and 9, or on Friday or Saturday night. Though it is by no means a guarantee, sometimes just showing up at a restaurant that has turned you away on the phone will get you a seat, if you are willing to wait for it. Another good option is to find out if the full menu is served at the bar.

If you change your mind or your plans, cancel your reservation—it's only courteous, plus some of the busiest places have started to charge up to $25 a head for a no-show (they take a credit card number when you reserve). Many restaurants will ask you to call the day before or the morning of your scheduled meal to reconfirm: remember to do so or you could lose out. When you call, double-check that the information listed in these reviews hasn't changed.

Smoking

Smoking is prohibited in all enclosed public spaces in New York City, including restaurants and bars.

Tipping

New Yorkers tip big, maybe because they know they are often demanding. The rules are simple. Never tip the maître d' unless you're out to impress your guests or if you expect to pay another visit soon. In most restaurants, tip the waiter at least 15%–20%. (To figure the amount quickly, just double the tax noted on the check—it's 8.625% of your bill—and, if you like, add a little more.) Bills for parties of six or more sometimes include the tip already. Tip at least $1 per drink at the bar, and $1 for each coat checked.

What It Costs

Entrée prices in general have fallen by a few dollars, and the $60-plus prix-fixe menu has given way to the standard à la carte. Of course, the top-tier restaurants remain impervious to market changes. Beware of the $10 bottle of water poured eagerly for unsuspecting diners.

If you are watching your budget, be sure to ask the price of daily specials recited by the waiter or captain. The charge for specials at some restaurants is noticeably out of line with the other prices on the menu. And of course, always review your bill.

If you eat early or late you may be able to take advantage of a prix fixe deal not offered at peak hours and get more attentive service in the bargain. Most upscale restaurants offer fantastic lunch deals with special menus at cut-rate prices designed to give a true taste of the place.

Credit cards are widely accepted, but many restaurants (particularly smaller ones downtown) accept only cash. If you plan to use a credit card it is a good idea to double-check its acceptability when making reservations or before sitting down to eat.

WHAT IT COSTS				
$$$$	**$$$**	**$$**	**$**	**¢**
AT DINNER over $35	$28–$35	$19–$27	$11–$18	under $10

Prices are per person for a main course at dinner.

Some restaurants are marked with a price range ($$–$$$, for example). This indicates one of two things: either the average cost straddles two categories, or if you order strategically, you can get out for less than most diners spend.

Wine

Although some of the city's top restaurants still include historic French vintages, most sommeliers are now focusing on small-production, lesser-known wineries. Some are even keeping their wine lists purposefully small, so that they can change them frequently to match the season and the menu. Half bottles are becoming more prevalent, and good wines by the glass are everywhere. Don't hesitate to ask for recommendations. Many restaurants with no sommelier on staff designate special people to lend a hand.

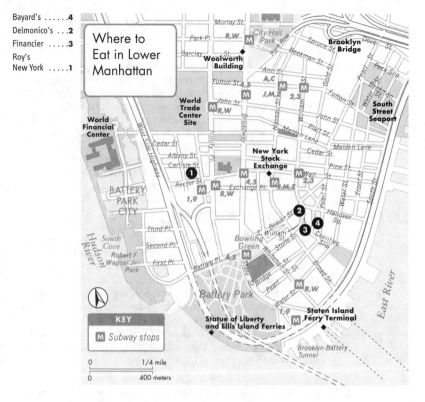

Where to Eat in Lower Manhattan

Cafés

¢–$ ✕ **Financier.** On Manhattan's oldest paved street, a cobblestone alley that dates from the 1600s, sits this small patisserie with great homemade food, especially soup. Celery root with walnut pesto is offered daily, in addition to a special. After a panini, salad, or quiche, settle in with a financier, madeleine, or biscotti and a cup of Illy coffee. If the weather's nice, you can sit outside. ⊠ *62 Stone St., at Pell St., Lower Manhattan* ☎ *212/344–5600* ⚶ *Reservations not accepted* ▤ *AE, MC, V* ☉ *Closed Sun. No dinner Sat.* Ⓜ *Subway: 2, 3, 4, 5 to Wall St.*

Contemporary

$$$–$$$$ ✕ **Bayard's.** Chef Eberhard Müller's austere, classic cooking fits well in this historic, nautical-theme setting. Some of the produce comes direct from his Long Island farm, and is incorporated into seasonal dishes such as roasted monkfish in a savory bacon broth and vegetable risotto with fennel fondue. The restaurant, housed in a stately 1851 Italianate mansion, remains a private club at lunch. At dinner the energy of the subtly lit room exudes a quiet dignity. If you can't get a reservation for a fine meal anywhere on a Saturday night, remember you can probably get in here. ⊠ *1 Hanover Sq., between Pearl and Stone Sts., Lower Man-*

hattan ☎ 212/514–9454 ♣ *Reservations essential* ▭ *AE, D, MC, V* ⊘ *Closed Sun. No lunch* Ⓜ *Subway: 2, 3 to Wall St.*

Pan-Asian

$$–$$$ ✕ **Roy's New York.** Roy's New York guarantees you're getting primo Pacific Ocean fish. The restaurant, part of Hawaii-born pioneering chef Roy Yamaguchi's growing empire of Pacific-Rim eateries, ships in Sandwich Island delicacies such as opakapaka (snapper) and mahimahi a few times a week. For starters, the blackened tuna in spicy soy-mustard butter works well with entrées such as misoyaki butterfish. Roy's stands in high culinary contrast to its largely meat-and-potatoes Wall Street neighbors. ⊠ *130 Washington St., between Albany and Carlisle Sts., Lower Manhattan* ☎ *212/266–6262* ▭ *AE, D, DC, MC, V* ⊘ *No lunch Sat.* Ⓜ *Subway: 1, 9 to Rector St.*

LITTLE ITALY & CHINATOWN

As Chinatown encroaches from the south, Little Italy keeps getting littler, but from a culinary standpoint nobody's grieving the loss of tourist-trap Italian restaurants. Great Italian food, made with fresh seasonal ingredients, now crops up all over Manhattan. Chinatown is known for cheap, authentic food in bare-bones surroundings. But a growing number of restaurants are paying attention to design and presenting menus that show considerable creativity. Shanghai- and Hong Kong–style have replaced Cantonese and Szechuan as the cuisines of choice, and "bubble teas" (hot or cold drinks made from fruit or tea with chewy tapioca pearls) are all the rage.

Cafés

🕙 ¢ ✕ **Saint's Alp Teahouse.** Join the hip Asian youth crowding the small tables at Saint's Alp Teahouse, part of a Hong Kong–based international chain. They're here for bubble tea—frothy, pastel-color, flavored black or green tea speckled with beads of tapioca or sago (they look like tadpoles). Passion-fruit green tea with chewy tapioca is refreshing. You can also order snacks such as spring rolls, dumplings, or sweets. ⊠ *51 Mott St., between Canal and Pell Sts., Chinatown* ☎ *212/766–9889* ♣ *Reservations not accepted* ▭ *No credit cards* Ⓜ *Subway: J, M, Z to Canal St.*

Chinese

🕙 ¢–$$$ ✕ **Ping's Seafood.** Although the original location in Queens still has the most elaborate menu with the most extensive selection of live seafood, the Manhattan location is more accessible both geographically and gastronomically. Helpful menus have pictures of most of the specialties. Among them are Dungeness crab in black bean sauce, crisp fried tofu, silken braised *e-fu* noodles, and Peking duck. Pricier than some other Chinatown haunts, these restaurants are also a notch above in setting and service. ⊠ *22 Mott St., between Bayard and Pell Sts., Chinatown* ☎ *212/602–9988* ♣ *Reservations essential* ▭ *MC, V* Ⓜ *Subway: 6, J, M, Z to Canal St.*

¢–$$ ✕ **Funky Broome.** One of the new generation of Chinese restaurants, Funky Broome looks more like a high-tech Shiseido cosmetics shop than the Hong Kong–style eatery that it is. At night, the place bustles with young, hip neighborhood locals eating Cantonese comfort food like *congee* (rice gruel) topped with assorted meats and vegetables and Sterno-heated mini-woks filled with sizzling stewlike dishes. Funky Broome, a marriage of NoLita cool and Chinatown taste, is an intriguing pit stop while touring the neighborhood. ✉ *176 Mott St., at Broome St., Little Italy* ☎ *212/941–8628* ☰ *AE, MC, V* Ⓜ *Subway: 6 to Spring St.*

🐚 ¢–$$ ✕ **Joe's Shanghai.** Joe opened his first Shanghai restaurant in Queens, but buoyed by the accolades accorded his steamed soup dumplings—magically filled with a rich, fragrant broth and a pork or pork-and-crab-meat mixture—he saw fit to open in Manhattan's Chinatown, and then midtown. There's always a wait, but the line moves fast. Try the crisp turnip shortcakes to start, ropey homemade Shanghai noodles and traditional lion's head—rich pork meatballs braised in brown sauce—to follow. Other more familiar Chinese dishes are also excellent. ✉ *9 Pell St., between the Bowery and Mott St., Chinatown* ☎ *212/233–8888* ☰ *No credit cards* Ⓜ *Subway: 6, J, M, Z, N, Q, R, W to Canal St.*

🐚 ¢–$ ✕ **Dim Sum Go Go.** Dim sum gets a creative spin at this sleek red-and-white spot. Dumplings go beyond steamed shrimp and pork with combos such as duck skin and crab in a spinach wrapper. The stars that mark certain menu items denote the restaurant's specialties, not "hot and spicy." Other entrées include panfried halibut with garlic sauce, and quail on baby bok choy. ✉ *5 E. Broadway, at Chatham Sq., Chinatown* ☎ *212/732–0797* ☰ *AE, MC, V* Ⓜ *Subway: F to East Broadway.*

🐚 ¢–$ ✕ **Great New York Noodletown.** Although the soups and noodles are unbeatable at this no-frills restaurant, what you should order are the window decorations—the hanging lacquered ducks, roasted pork, and crunchy pig. All three are superb, especially if you ask for the pungent garlic-and-ginger sauce on the side. Seasonal specialties such as duck with flowering chives and salt-baked soft-shell crabs are excellent. So is the congee, available with any number of garnishes. Solo diners may end up at a communal table. ✉ *28 Bowery, at Bayard St., Chinatown* ☎ *212/349–0923* ⌕ *Reservations essential* ☰ *No credit cards* Ⓜ *Subway: 6, J, M, Z to Canal St.; B, D to Grand St.*

🐚 ¢–$ ✕ **Jing Fong.** Come to this authentic dim sum palace for a taste of Hong Kong. On weekend mornings people pour onto the escalator to Jing Fong's third-floor dining room. Chinese women push carts to offer *hargow* (steamed shrimp dumplings), *shu mai* (steamed pork dumplings), *chow fun* (wide rice noodles with dried shrimp or beef), and much more. For the adventurous: chicken feet, tripe, and snails. Arrive early for the largest and freshest selection. ✉ *20 Elizabeth St., between Bayard and Canal Sts., Chinatown* ☎ *212/964–5256* ☰ *AE, MC, V* Ⓜ *Subway: 6, J, M, Z, N, Q, R, W to Canal St.*

★ ¢–$ ✕ **Sweet 'n' Tart Café & Restaurant.** You'll be handed four different menus at this multilevel restaurant. One lists dim sum prepared to order; another offers special dishes organized according to principles of Chinese medicine; a third lists more familiar sounding dishes, such as hot-and-sour soup; and the final one lists beverages, curative "teas" (more like soups or fruit shakes, really). The original café, with a more limited menu, is up the street at 76 Mott Street, and some think it has better food. ✉ *20 Mott St., between Chatham Sq. and Pell St., Chinatown* ☎ *212/964–0380* ☰ *AE* Ⓜ *Subway: 6, J, M, Z, N, R, Q, W to Canal St.*

Where to Eat in Little Italy, Chinatown, TriBeCa, SoHo & NoLita

TRIBECA

SoHo Grand Hotel

KEY

Ⓜ Subway stops

Italian

○ ¢–$ ✕ **Bread.** At this stylish little *paninoteca,* owner Luigi Comandatore, a Mercer Kitchen alum, takes advantage of his location, buying top-notch ingredients from neighborhood purveyors such as Di Palo's Fine Foods and Balthazar Bakery to make perfect panini. Italian expats, windows open to the street in summer, and lots of red vino give Bread star lingering quality. ⊠ *20 Spring St., between Elizabeth and Mott Sts., Little Italy* ☎ *212/334–1015* ▭ *AE, D, MC, V* Ⓜ *Subway: 6 to Spring St.*

Malaysian

¢–$ ✕ **Sanur.** Malaysian restaurants are popping up like bamboo shoots in Chinatown, and this dingy subterranean spot is one of the best. Locals crowd the dining room from morning (it opens at 8 AM) to night for the fragrantly spiced food. Indonesian-style chicken, crunchy in a sweet soy sauce; long-simmered beef *rendang*; and whole crabs in a big bowl of spicy curry sauce and vermicelli get hearty nods of approval from anyone who's been to Jakarta or Kuala Lumpur. ⊠ *18 Doyers St., at Pell St., Chinatown* ☎ *212/267–0088* ▭ No credit cards ☉ Closed Mon. Ⓜ *Subway: 6, J, M, Z, N, Q, R, W to Canal St.*

Pizza

★ ○ $–$$ ✕ **Lombardi's.** Brick walls, red-and-white check tablecloths, and the aroma of thin-crust pies emerging from the coal oven set the mood for some of the best pizza in Manhattan. Lombardi's has served pizza since 1905 (though not in the same location), and business has not died down a bit. The mozzarella is always fresh, resulting in an almost greaseless slice, and the toppings, such as homemade meatballs, pancetta, or imported anchovies, are also top quality. ⊠ *32 Spring St., between Mott and Mulberry Sts., Little Italy* ☎*212/941–7994* ▭No credit cards Ⓜ Subway: 6 to Spring St.; F, V to Broadway–Lafayette St.

Vietnamese

¢–$ ✕ **Nha Trang.** You can get a good meal at this inexpensive Vietnamese restaurant if you know how to order. Start with a steaming bowl of spicy sweet-and-sour seafood soup (the small feeds three to four) and shrimp grilled on sugarcane. Follow that up with paper-thin pork chops grilled until crisp and crunchy deep-fried squid on shredded lettuce with a tangy dipping sauce. If the line is long, which it usually is, even with a second location around the corner, you may be asked to sit at a table with strangers. ⊠ *87 Baxter St., between Bayard and Canal Sts., Chinatown* ☎ *212/233–5948* ▭ No credit cards Ⓜ Subway: 6, J, M, Z, N, Q, R, W to Canal St. ⊠ 148 Centre St., at Walker and White St., Chinatown ☎ 212/941–9292.

TRIBECA

This once industrial neighborhood attracts affluent residents seeking spacious lofts. The ground floors of these glamorized former warehouses and factories provide dramatic settings for some of the best restaurants in the city. Residents like Robert De Niro and Harvey Keitel can pop down to their favorite haunts. TriBeCa retains a ghostly, deserted feel at night—part of its charm—but the quiet will be shattered when you walk into one of the many fashionable dining rooms.

American

$$–$$$ ✕ **The Harrison.** Partners Danny Abrams and Jimmy Bradley's formula for the perfect neighborhood eatery, which they perfected at the Red Cat in Chelsea, works like a charm in TriBeCa. The warm, woody room serves as a relaxed backdrop for their interesting wines and many well-exe-cuted dishes such as crispy fried clams with lemon coriander aioli or a skillet calf's liver. Ask for the signature fries, even if they're not on the menu! ⊠ *355 Greenwich St., at Harrison St., TriBeCa* ☎ *212/274–9310* ⌃ *Reservations essential* ⊟ *AE, D, DC, MC, V* ☉ *No lunch* Ⓜ *Subway: 1, 9 to Franklin St.*

American–Casual

↻ **¢–$$** ✕ **Bubby's.** Crowds clamoring for coffee and freshly squeezed juice line up for brunch at this TriBeCa mainstay. The dining room is homey and comfortable with big windows; in summer, neighbors sit at tables out-side with their dogs. For brunch you can order almost anything, including homemade granola, sour cream pancakes with bananas and berries, and *huevos rancheros* with guacamole and grits. Eclectic comfort food—mac-aroni and cheese, southern fried chicken, meat loaf, and Mexican dishes—make up the lunch and dinner menus. ⊠ *120 Hudson St., at N. Moore St., TriBeCa* ☎ *212/219–0666* ⊟ *D, DC, MC, V* Ⓜ *Subway: 1, 9 to Franklin St.*

↻ **$** ✕ **Kitchenette.** This small, comfy restaurant lives up to its name with ta-bles so close together you're likely to make new friends. The dining room feels like a neighbor's breakfast nook, and the food tastes like your mom made it—provided she's a great cook. There are no frills, just solid cook-ing, friendly service, and a long line at peak times. For brunch don't miss the blackberry-cherry pancakes or the pear streusel French toast. ⊠ *80 West Broadway, at Warren St., TriBeCa* ☎ *212/267–6740* ⌃ *Reservations not accepted before 5 PM* ⊟ *AE, D, DC, MC, V* Ⓜ *Subway: 1, 2, 3, 9, A, C to Chambers St.*

Belgian

↻ **$–$$** ✕ **Petite Abeille.** This consistently good but modest chain of Belgian bistros tempts with salads, frites, sandwiches, omelets, and other light fare early in the day. Come evening, sausages, *stoemp* (mashed potatoes and veggies), steak, and stew satisfy. Waffles are always available: both *de Bruxelles* (made fresh and topped with ice cream, whipped cream, and fresh fruit) and the true Belgian waffle, *de Liège* (imported and reheated until the subtle caramelized sugar coating crunches and melts in your mouth). ⊠ *134 West Broadway, between Duane and Thomas Sts., TriBeCa* ☎ *212/791–1360* ⊟ *AE, MC, V* Ⓜ *Subway: 1, 2, 3, 9, A, C to Chambers St.*

Contemporary

$$–$$$ ✕ **Tribeca Grill.** Anchored by the bar, this cavernous brick-wall restau-rant displays art by Robert De Niro Sr., whose movie-actor son is one of restaurateur Drew Nieporent's partners. Chef Stephen Lewandowski oversees the kitchen, but his contemporary American food doesn't seem quite as important to the nightly crowd as does the prospect of sighting somebody famous—a regular occurrence. Still, you can eat well with braised short ribs or the herb-roasted, free-range chicken. ⊠ *375 Greenwich St., at Franklin St., TriBeCa* ☎ *212/941–3900* ⌂ *Reservations essential* ⊟ *AE, D, DC, MC, V* ✆ *No lunch Sat.* Ⓜ *Subway: 1, 9 to Franklin St.*

French

\$\$\$\$ ✕ **Chanterelle.** Soft peach walls, luxuriously spaced tables, and towering floral arrangements set the stage for what is the most understated of New York's fancy French restaurants. Chef David Waltuck's simple, elegant creations include delicious signature grilled seafood sausage that will always be available, but the bulk of the prix-fixe menu is dictated by the season. Roger Dagorn, the restaurant's exceptional sommelier, can help find value in the discriminating, well-chosen wine list. ⊠ *2 Harrison St., at Hudson St., TriBeCa* ☎ *212/966–6960* ⌂ *Reservations essential* ⊟ *AE, D, DC, MC, V* ✆ *Closed Sun. No lunch Mon.* Ⓜ *Subway: 1, 9 to Franklin St.*

\$\$–\$\$\$ ✕ **Montrachet.** Chris Gesualdi 's seasonal three- and five-course menus are still among the best in the city for fine French cuisine. The ever-changing menu might have the succulent frogs' legs with red wine, fricasee of escargots and morel mushrooms, or a truffle-crusted salmon. The distinguished wine list emphasizes smaller regional vineyards. The rooms are warm and intimate, but designed with plenty of space between parties for privacy. ⊠ *239 West Broadway, between Walker and White Sts., TriBeCa* ☎ *212/219–2777* ⌂ *Reservations essential* ⊟ *AE, D, DC, MC, V* ✆ *Closed Sun. No lunch Mon.–Thurs. and Sat.* Ⓜ *Subway: 1, 9 to Franklin St.; A, C to Canal St.*

☾ **\$–\$\$\$**   ✕ **Odeon.** New Yorkers change hangouts faster than they can press speed-dial on their cell phones, but this spot has managed to maintain its quality and flair for 25 years and counting. The neo–art deco room is still packed nightly with revelers. Now, children are also welcome. The pleasant service, relatively low prices, and well-chosen wine list are always in style. The bistro-menu highlights include *frisée aux lardons*, grilled skirt steak, and mussels with *frites*. ⊠ *145 West Broadway, between Duane and Thomas Sts., TriBeCa* ☎ *212/233–0507* ⊟ *AE, D, DC, MC, V* Ⓜ *Subway: 1, 2, 3, 9, A, C to Chambers St.*

Japanese

\$–\$\$\$ ✕ **Nobu.** New York's most famous Japanese restaurant is getting com-
FodorsChoice   petition. Yet what Nobu Matsuhisa started here is still excellent: the paper-
★   thin hamachi spiced up with jalapeño or sea bass topped with black truffle slivers. Put yourself in the hands of the chef by ordering the tasting menu, the *omakase*—specify how much you want to spend (the minimum is \$80 per person) and the kitchen does the rest. Can't get reservations? Try your luck at the first-come, first served sushi bar inside or at Next Door Nobu, with its less-expensive menu. ⊠ *105 Hudson St., at Franklin St., TriBeCa* ☎ *212/219–0500, 212/219–8095 for same-day reservations* ⌂ *Reservations essential* ⊟ *AE, D, DC, MC, V* ✆ *No lunch weekends* Ⓜ *Subway: 1, 9 to Franklin St.* ⊠ *Next Door Nobu* ⊠ *105 Hudson St., at Franklin St., TriBeCa* ☎ *212/334–4445* ✆ *No lunch* Ⓜ *Subway: 1, 9 to Franklin St.*

Seafood

$$–$$$$ ✕ **Fresh.** Fish doesn't get any meatier than it does at Fresh, where you can get oven-roasted monkfish steak and charred "Kobe" tuna (sublimely fatty seared belly flesh). Chef Daniel Angerer continues to reinvent the seafood menu in surprising ways. Halibut cheeks are as tender as the foie gras with which they're paired, and English batter-fried haddock may be the best in the city. Fresh's offerings really are the catches of the day—one of the restaurant's co-owners is also the proprietor of Early Morning Seafood. ⊠ *105 Reade St., between Church St. and West Broadway, TriBeCa* ☎ *212/406–1900* ⊟ *AE, DC, MC, V* ☉ *No lunch weekends* Ⓜ *Subway: 1, 2, 3, 9, A, C to Chambers St.*

SOHO & NOLITA

Old-timers bemoan the fact that SoHo has evolved from red-hot art district to the world's chicest mall—Chanel and Prada have replaced Mary Boone and Gagosian (two seminal galleries that fled to Chelsea). But any way you shop it, the neighborhood still means good eating, whether you feel like a bracing three-tiered iced seafood platter at Balthazar, Jean-Georges Vongerichten cuisine, or hot chocolate at MarieBelle's. NoLita (North of Little Italy), the trendy next-door neighborhood of small shops and restaurants, is reminiscent of a bygone SoHo, with fresh new eateries popping up every month. Expect beautiful crowds dressed in black and service that is refreshingly unpretentious given the clientele.

American

$–$$ ✕ **Rialto.** The shabby-chic dining room with pressed-tin walls, plain wooden chairs, and burgundy banquettes provides a backdrop for seasonal food that is interesting without being fussy, well suited to the noisy space where people-watching can often distract you from your plate. But those who like to eat will have no trouble focusing on such dishes as five-pepper steak *au poivre* in cognac cream sauce or an excellent hamburger. The back garden is a great spot for alfresco summer dining; in winter it's canopied and heated. ⊠ *265 Elizabeth St., between E. Houston and Prince Sts., NoLita* ☎ *212/334–7900* ⊟ *AE, MC, V* Ⓜ *Subway: 6 to Spring St.*

Cafés

★ ☪ ¢–$ ✕ **Le Pain Quotidien.** The concept here and at all Le Pain Quotidiens is good, mostly organic food shared around a communal table. Many other tables for two or more, make for more private dining, but it's interesting to listen to how many languages are being spoken at the big one. Excellent bread, fresh soup and sandwiches, the best croissants, hot chocolate, and café late in big cups keep neighbors coming back again and again. The granola parfait tastes as good as it looks. ⊠ *100 Grand St., at Mercer St., SoHo* ☎ *212/625–9009* ⚖ *Reservations not accepted* ⊟ *AE, DC, MC, V* Ⓜ *Subway: N, R, Q, W to Canal St.*

¢–$ ✕ **Snack.** Misleadingly named Snack serves big Greek flavors in SoHo. Local residents and shop owners come to the sliver of a storefront for toothsome sandwiches, vegetarian souvlaki, and *keftedakia* (veal meatballs with almonds, pine nuts, and prunes in a red wine reduction). Don't expect a greasy gyro shack—Snack is a pretty space. You'll wish there were more than just a handful of chairs. ⊠ *105 Thompson St., between Prince and Spring Sts., SoHo* ☎ *212/925–1040* ⚑ *Reservations not accepted* ▭ *AE, MC, V* Ⓜ *Subway: C, E to Spring St.*

★ ⓒ ¢ ✕ **MarieBelle.** Practically unseen from the front of the chocolate emporium, the back entry to the Cacao Bar opens into a sweet, high-ceiling, 12-table hot chocolate shop. Most people order the Aztec, English-style (that's 63% chocolate mixed with hot water—no cocoa powder here!). The first sip is startlingly rich but not too dense. American-style, made with milk, is sweeter. Variations on the theme include dark and mocha; or you can order coffee and tea. ⊠ *484 Broome St., between West Broadway and Wooster St., SoHo* ☎ *212/925–6999* ⚑ *No reservations accepted* ▭ *AE, D, MC, V* Ⓜ *Subway: A, C, E to Canal St.*

Contemporary

$$–$$$ ✕ **The Mercer Kitchen.** New York celebrity chef Jean-Georges Vongerichten runs this downtown outpost in the basement of the hip Mercer Hotel. The sleek, modern, industrial space sizzles with the energy of the downtown elite, though these days the restaurant draws its share of average Joes checking out the beautiful people. The seasonal menu's organized by preparation area—raw bar, salad bar, pizza oven, rotisserie, pastry oven, and tea bar—with an eclectic mix of possibilities. ⊠ *Mercer Hotel, 99 Prince St., at Mercer St., SoHo* ☎ *212/966–5454* ⚑ *Reservations essential* ▭ *AE, D, DC, MC, V* Ⓜ *Subway: R, W to Prince St.*

$$ ✕ **Savoy.** Chef-owner Peter Hoffman serves a rich mix of dishes inspired by the Mediterranean in this cozy restaurant on a quiet cobblestone corner. Arched wood accents and a blazing fireplace downstairs make the perfect setting for down-to-earth dishes like braised lamb shank with lentils and crispy artichokes and salt-crust baked duck. Upstairs, the original tin ceiling, artwork, and open hearth are equally beautiful. If you order prix fixe in winter, it includes a special grilled dish cooked in the dining-room hearth. The wine list emphasizes small producers. ⊠ *70 Prince St., at Crosby St., SoHo* ☎ *212/219–8570* ▭ *AE, MC, V* ☽ *No lunch Sun.* Ⓜ *Subway: R, W to Prince St.; 6 to Spring St.; F, V to Broadway–Lafayette St.*

$–$$ ✕ **Pfiff.** Compact Pfiff, with its red-vinyl banquettes, custom light fixtures (made by one of the partners, a sculptor), and funky tunes, is one of those rare restaurants you could eat in every night. The affordable menu reads familiar—good salads, sandwiches, pizza, risottos—but the chef gives everything an unexpected, delicious twist. Crème fraîche spiked with cinnamon and nutmeg adds kick to butternut squash soup, and nicely textured peanut-crusted ahi comes with spicy Napa cabbage accents. ⊠ *35 Grand St., at Thompson St., SoHo* ☎ *212/334–6841* ▭ *AE, MC, V* Ⓜ *Subway: 1, 9, A, C, E to Canal St.*

Eclectic

★ ¢–$$$ ✕ **Blue Ribbon.** After more than a decade, Blue Ribbon remains *the* late-night foodie hangout. Join the genial hubbub for some midnight specialness, namely the beef marrow with oxtail marmalade and the renowned raw bar platters. Trust funders, literary types, designers—a good-looking gang fills this dark box of a room until 4 AM. The menu *appears* standard but it's not. Instead of the usual fried calamari, exceptionally tender squid is lightly sautéed with garlic. ⊠ *97 Sullivan St., between Prince and Spring Sts., SoHo* ☎ *212/274–0404* ⚇ *Reservations not accepted* ▭ *AE, DC, MC, V* ⊘ *No lunch* Ⓜ *Subway: C, E, to Spring St.; R, W to Prince St.*

¢–$ ✕ **Rice.** All meals are built on a bowl of rice at this dark and narrow storefront. Choose from an array of rices, such as basmati, brown, Thai black, or Bhutanese red, and create a meal by adding a savory topping such as jerk chicken wings, Thai coconut curry, or Indian chicken curry. The fresh, well-seasoned, budget-price menu affords a satisfying mix of multicultural cuisine and comfort food. ⊠ *227 Mott St., between Prince and Spring Sts., SoHo* ☎ *212/226–5775* ⚇ *Reservations not accepted* ▭ *No credit cards* Ⓜ *Subway: 6 to Spring St.*

Ethiopian

★ $ ✕ **Ghenet.** A rotating exhibit of local, African-inspired art hangs on the walls of this welcoming spot where the food is authentic and delicious. Order one of the combination platters mounded on a platter lined with spongy *injera* flat bread, which is your edible utensil. In addition to the tasty poultry and meat options is a good selection of vegetarian dishes such as rich collard greens with Ethiopian spices, fiery potatoes and cabbage, and carrots in an onion sauce. ⊠ *284 Mulberry St., between E. Houston and Prince Sts., NoLita* ☎ *212/343–1888* ▭ *AE, MC, V* ⊘ *Closed Mon. No dinner Sun.* Ⓜ *Subway: R, W to Prince St.; 6 to Spring St.*

French

$–$$$ ✕ **Balthazar.** This grand brasserie's raw bar may be the best in town, with an outstanding selection of impossibly fresh crustaceans and bivalves. Nightly specials are French dishes that are as classic as the painstakingly accurate reproduction of a Parisian eatery. Steak tartare, steak frites, duck shepherd's pie—it's all good. Breakfast is a civilized affair, with croissants and pains au chocolat coming from the restaurant's own bakery (and you don't need to make reservations). ⊠ *80 Spring St., between Broadway and Crosby St., SoHo* ☎ *212/965–1785* ⚇ *Reservations essential* ▭ *AE, MC, V* Ⓜ *Subway: 6 to Spring St.; N, R to Prince St.*

Italian

$$ ✕ **Peasant.** The crowd at this rustic-yet-hip restaurant is stylishly urban. All of Frank DeCarlo's wonderful peasant food is prepared in a bank of wood- or charcoal-burning ovens, from which the heady aroma of garlic perfumes the room. Don't fill up on the crusty bread and fresh ricotta. Sizzling sardines (crisp on the outside, moist inside) arrive at the table in the terra-cotta pots in which they were baked. Rotisserie lamb is redolent with the scent of fresh herbs. ⊠ *194 Elizabeth St., between Spring and Prince Sts., NoLita* ☎ *212/965–9511* ⚇ *Reservations essential* ▭ *AE, MC, V* ⊘ *Closed Mon. No lunch* Ⓜ *Subway: 6 to Spring St.; R, W to Prince St.*

¢–$ ✕ **Pepe Rosso to Go.** A long list of specials changes daily here, but the menu always includes generously portioned pastas (prepared fresh in the open kitchen), antipasti, salads, entrées, and sandwiches. The gnocchi are as fluffy as can be, and the pesto sauce is fragrant with basil and garlic. Inexpensive wine is available by the glass. Dinner can cost less than $17 at any one of the four "Pepe" restaurants—one of the best Italian values in the city. ✉ *149 Sullivan St., between W. Houston and Prince Sts., SoHo* ☎ 212/677–4555 ⚛ *Reservations not accepted* 🚏 *No credit cards* Ⓜ *Subway: 1, 9 to Houston St.; C, E to Spring St.*

Japanese

$–$$$$ ✕ **Blue Ribbon Sushi.** Sushi, like pizza, attracts opinionated fanatics. Stick to the excellent raw fish and specials here if you're a purist. Others might want to try one of the more experimental rolls: the Blue Ribbon—lobster, shiso, and black caviar—is popular. The dark, intimate nooks, stylized design, and servers with downtown attitude attract a stylish crowd that doesn't mind waiting for a table or for the sake served in traditional wooden boxes. ✉ *119 Sullivan St., between Prince and Spring Sts., SoHo* ☎ *212/343–0404* ⚛ *Reservations not accepted* 🚏 *AE, DC, MC, V* Ⓜ *Subway: C, E to Spring St.; R, W to Prince St.*

¢–$$ ✕ **Honmura An.** At Honmura An, you can watch the art of making buckwheat *soba* noodles at the back of the teak-lined dining room. Like the best restaurants in Tokyo, where the original Honmura An still operates, this one focuses on doing one thing well. The true test of quality is the cold soba, served on square trays with a dipping sauce and a ladle full of cooking water you are expected to slurp as you eat. But everything on the menu is exquisite. ✉ *170 Mercer St., between W. Houston and Prince Sts., SoHo* ☎ *212/334–5253* 🚏 *AE, DC, MC, V* ◷ *Closed Mon. No lunch Tues. and Sun.* Ⓜ *Subway: R, W to Prince St.; 6 to Spring St.; F, V to Broadway–Lafayette St.*

Korean

$–$$ ✕ **Woo Lae Oak.** If you thought Korean food was a cheap bowl of bibimbop, think again: Woo Lae Oak uses traditional flavors to create an elevated cuisine. The food is spicy and flavorful: kimchi burns the lips and prepares the palate for such dishes as *kesalmari* (Dungeness crab wrapped in spinach crepes), and *o ree mari* (duck slices wrapped in miso blini sweetened with date sauce). But fans of tabletop grilling will still be able to get their *bul go gi*. Since this is SoHo, the tables are dark marble slabs and the lighting is low. ✉ *148 Mercer St., between Prince and W. Houston Sts., SoHo* ☎ *212/925–8200* ⚛ *Reservations essential* 🚏 *AE, DC, MC, V* Ⓜ *Subway: R, W to Prince St.*

Latin

¢–$ ✕ **Café Habana.** The simple Cuban-Latin menu at this small neighborhood hangout reflects the friendly, casual atmosphere: Cubano sandwiches, rice and beans, and *camarones al ajillo* (shrimp in garlic sauce), all at budget prices. Just try to get a seat, though: on any given night the sidewalk outside the cheery space with blue booths and pale green Formica tables is littered with belly-baring people waiting to get in. Some fans prefer **Café Habana to Go** around the corner, where the *tortas* and grilled corn are cheap and tasty. ✉ *17 Prince St., at Elizabeth St., NoLita* ☎ *212/625–2001* ⚛ *Reservations not accepted* 🚏 *AE, MC, V* ✉ *229 Elizabeth St., between Houston and Prince Sts., NoLita* ☎ *212/625–2002* 🚏 *AE, MC, V* Ⓜ *Subway: 6 to Spring St.*

Seafood

$–$$ ✕ **Aquagrill.** Aquagrill's friendly staff and extensive all-things-marine menu place it among the best. Chef-owner Jeremy Marshall mans the stove, while his wife, Jennifer, works the host stand. Specialties include roasted Dungeness crab cake napoleon and falafel-crusted salmon served on hummus with tomato and cucumber, not to mention the grilled fresh fish and a rotating selection of East and West Coast oysters. The chocolate tasting plate includes exceptional handmade chocolates. ⊠ *210 Spring St., at 6th Ave., SoHo* ☎ *212/274–0505* ♠ *Reservations essential* ▭ *AE, MC, V* ⊙ *Closed Mon.* Ⓜ *Subway: C, E to Spring St.*

GREENWICH VILLAGE & THE MEATPACKING DISTRICT

One of the most complicated Manhattan neighborhoods to navigate, Greenwich Village has enchanted many a tourist (and frustrated many a cab driver). Cornelia Street is a mini Restaurant Row, and tiny alcoves around the neighborhood have been transformed into serious eateries. To the far west, the Meatpacking District—where you can still see people carting around sides of beef—has blossomed into one of the most chic restaurant destinations in town.

As for the Meatpacking District, by day it's still in part a meatpacking district, but by night, instead of sex clubs and after-hours bars, it has become one of the hottest restaurant destination neighborhoods in town. Celebrities and models and their friends and followers fill the new restaurants, organized with a true Parisian feeling and appearance. This effect was more or less created by trailblazing restaurateur Keith McNally, whose impeccable eye and sensibility drew him to the area to create his Pastis, Balthazar's little brother, which looks more like the Left Bank than a lot of the Left Bank itself these days. Pastis set the visual tone for the nouvelle Meatpacking District in more ways than one.

American

$–$$ ✕ **Home.** Owners David Page and Barbara Shinn have re-created that mythic heartland home in this sliver of a storefront restaurant, where the walls are clapboard and the floorboards wide. Page's Midwestern background sets the menu's tone: perennial favorites include cornmeal-fried oysters, moist roast chicken, and fennel-seed-crusted pork rib chop with sweet potatoes and apples. And what's a home-cooked meal without some creamy chocolate pudding? Brunch is especially nice in the garden on weekends. ⊠ *20 Cornelia St., between Bleecker and W. 4th Sts., Greenwich Village* ☎ *212/243–9579* ▭ *AE, MC, V* Ⓜ *Subway: A, B, C, D, E, F, V to W. 4th St.*

Austrian

$$–$$$ ✕ **Wallsé.** For some, Kurt Gutenbrunner's modern Austrian menu at this neighborhood restaurant with a quasi–Wiener Werkstatt look is everything David Bouley's at Danube is not: soulful, and satisfying, with a strong emphasis on Austrian tradition and an urban New York attitude. It's hard to argue with such dishes as lobster with potato roesti, fennel,

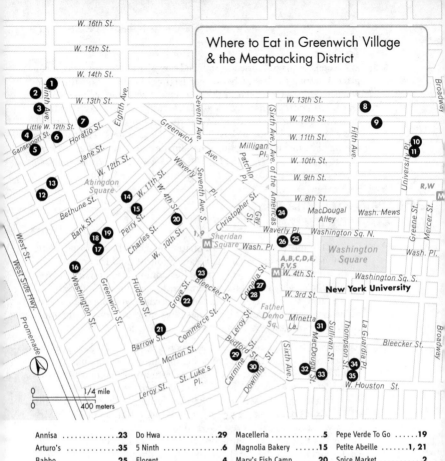

Where to Eat in Greenwich Village & the Meatpacking District

and citrus salad; braised rabbit and spaetzle with mushrooms, and tarragon; and Wiener schnitzel lightened with cucumber-potato salad and lingonberries. ✉ *344 W. 11th St., at Washington St., Greenwich Village* ☎ *212/352–2300* ⚓ *Reservations essential* ▭ *AE, DC, MC, V* ☉ *No lunch Mon.–Sat.* Ⓜ *Subway: A, C, E, L to 14th St.*

Belgian

🍽 **$–$$** ✕ **Petite Abeille.** This consistently good but modest chain of Belgian bistros tempts with salads, frites, sandwiches, omelets, and other light fare early in the day. Come evening, sausages, *stoemp* (mashed potatoes and veggies), steak, and stew satisfy. Waffles are always available: both *de Bruxelles* (made fresh and topped with ice cream, whipped cream, and fresh fruit) and the true Belgian waffle, *de Liège* (imported and reheated until the subtle caramelized sugar coating crunches and melts in your mouth). ✉ *466 Hudson St., at Barrow St., Greenwich Village* ☎ *212/741–6479* ▭ *AE, MC, V* Ⓜ *Subway: 1, 9 to Christopher St.–Sheridan Sq.*

Cafés

¢ ✕ **Caffè Dante.** A longtime Village haunt, this convivial coffee bar on a quiet side street has superlative espresso and knockout tiramisu. The regulars have been coming for years, long before Starbucks made its mark on the city. Sitting at one of the outdoor tables is a bit like going back in time, a reminder of when the Village was the bohemian center of Manhattan. ✉ *79–81 MacDougal St., between W. Houston and Bleecker Sts., Greenwich Village* ☎ *212/982–5275* ⚓ *Reservations not accepted* ▭ *No credit cards* Ⓜ *Subway: 1, 9 to Houston St.; A, B, C, D, E, F, V to W. 4th St.*

¢ ✕ **Caffè Reggio.** In the neighborhood's oldest Italian coffeehouse (established 1927), a huge, antique espresso machine (from 1902) gleams among the tiny, packed tables. How often can you eat pasta or sip a latte under an original painting from the school of Caravaggio? ✉ *119 MacDougal St., between W. 3rd and Bleecker Sts., Greenwich Village* ☎ *212/475–9557* ⚓ *Reservations not accepted* ▭ *No credit cards* Ⓜ *Subway: A, B, C, D, E, F, V to W. 4th St.*

¢ ✕ **Dean & DeLuca.** Known for gourmet goodies, this small local chain is a spin-off of the SoHo gourmet market. Think fast as the line snakes past the upscale gingerbread, cakes, cookies, granola with yogurt parfait, sandwiches, and salads. ✉ *75 University Pl., at E. 11th St., Greenwich Village* ☎ *212/473–1908* ⚓ *Reservations not accepted* ▭ *AE, D, MC, V* Ⓜ *Subway: 4, 5, 6, L, N, Q, R, W to 14th St./Union Sq.*

★ 🍽 ¢ ✕ **Magnolia Bakery.** Sky-high home-style cakes, fabulous cupcakes, puddings, and pies keep this adorable take-out bakery packed into the wee hours. They will even serve you a glass of milk to wash it all down. ✉ *401 Bleecker St., at W. 11th St., Greenwich Village* ☎ *212/462–2572* ▭ *AE, D, DC, MC, V* Ⓜ *Subway: A, C, E to 14th St.; L to 8th Ave.*

Contemporary

$$$–$$$$ ✕ **Gotham Bar & Grill.** A culinary landmark, Gotham Bar & Grill is every
Fodor'sChoice bit as thrilling as it was when it opened in 1984. Celebrated chef Alfred
★ Portale, who made the blueprint for architectural food, builds on a foundation of simple, clean flavors. People come to gorge on transcendent

dishes: no rack of lamb is more tender, no scallop sweeter. A stellar 20,000-bottle cellar provides the perfect accompaniments—at a price. There's also a perfectly splendid three-course $25 prix-fixe lunch from noon to 2:30 weekdays. ⊠ *12 E. 12th St., between 5th Ave. and University Pl., Greenwich Village* ☎ *212/620–4020* ▤ *AE, D, DC, MC, V* ☺ *No lunch weekends* Ⓜ *Subway: L, N, Q, R, W, 4, 5, 6 to 14th St./Union Sq.*

$$–$$$ ✕ **Annisa.** Dining at Annisa is an experience in sweetness and light: chef Anita Lo's ethereal, creative cooking is served in a spare bone-color room. Modern French technique mixes with Asian influences to create seared foie gras with soup dumplings and jicama, and pan-roasted chicken stuffed with pig's feet and truffles. The wine list, created by Roger Dagorn of Chanterelle, features the work of women wine makers and winery owners. From the innovative hors d'oeuvres to the delicate petit fours, Annisa raises the bar on neighborhood dining. ⊠ *13 Barrow St., between 7th Ave. and W. 4th St., Greenwich Village* ☎ *212/741–6699* ▤ *AE, D, DC, MC, V* ☺ *No lunch* Ⓜ *Subway: 1, 9 to Christopher St./Sheridan Sq.*

$$–$$$ ✕ **Blue Hill.** This tasteful, sophisticated chocolate-brown den of a restaurant on a quiet, quaint side street maintains a reputation for excellence and consistency other restaurants can only hope for. Part of the slow food, sustainable agriculture movement, Blue Hill uses ingredients grown or raised around New York, including on a farm at their second restaurant in Pocantico Hills in nearby Westchester. The chefs produce precisely cooked and elegantly constructed food such as lettuce ravioli or poached foie gras with green tomato marmalade, black pepper, and arugula. ⊠ *75 Washington Pl., between Washington Sq. W and 6th Ave., Greenwich Village* ☎ *212/539–1776* ⌕ *Reservations essential* ▤ *AE, DC, MC, V* ☺ *No lunch* Ⓜ *Subway: A, B, C, D, E, F, V to W. 4th St.*

$–$$ **The Spotted Pig.** Part cozy English pub, part laid-back neighborhood hangout, part gatronome's lure, The Spotted Pig showcases the impeccable food of Londoner April Bloomfield (Mario Batali and partners consulted). Pair the tang of the chunky radish, greens, and Parmesan salad with meltingly perfect ricotta gnudi in simple brown butter sauce for a study in contrasts. Shoestring potatoes accompany their namesake blue-cheese burger. Chase it with a glass of foam-dripping Old Speckled Hen cream ale. ⊠ *314 W. 11th St, at Greenwich St., Greenwich Village* ☎ *212/620–0393* ⌕ *Reservations not accepted* ▤ *AE, D, DC, MC, V* ☺ *Closed Mon.* Ⓜ *Subway: A, C, E to 14th St.; L to 8th Ave.*

Eclectic

$$–$$$ ✕ **5 Ninth.** Nestled in a resonant 200-year-old town house, take in the view out the restaurant's front that's so Left-Bank you'll pinch yourself. Chef Zak Pelaccio's fascinating fusions never fail to tantalize. If mackerel is on the menu, seize it—Pelaccio understands mackerel as few chefs do. Steamed loup de mer (branzino) is fall-apart tender, seasoned with coriander, lime, garlic, and the unmistakable sting of Thai chili. Finish with luscious banana pudding and float out into the Parisian night. ⊠ *5 9th Ave., at Gansevoort St., Meatpacking District* ☎ *212/929–9460* ⌕ *Reservations essential* ▤ *AE, MC, V* Ⓜ *Subway: A, C, E, to 14th St.; L to 8th Ave.*

FAST, CHEAP & TASTY

PEANUTS AND PRETZELS ARE RELIABLY GOOD, *but let's face it, sometimes you want more. Good thing Manhattan's street food vendors have taken it up a notch. Beyond the usuals, there are a handful of "destination" food carts that deliver restaurant-quality food at a fraction of the cost and hassle.*

Gyro Truck, on the corner of Wall and Pearl Streets, doles out killer chicken and cheesesteak sandwiches. Nearby is a Sausage Truck with Italian sausage sandwiches and grilled cheesesteaks (Whitehall and Pearl Sts.). Dosa Man fills rice and dal "shells" with heavenly spiced veggies at the southern end of Washington Square Park (4th and Sullivan Sts.). At Daisy Mae's BBQ chili carts (E. 50th St. near 6th Ave.; Broadway and W. 39th St.; 40 Wall St.), be sure to order the chunky Texas chili!

People rave about the goat stew and jerk chicken at Yvonne's Mobile Jamaican Restaurant (E. 71st St. and York Ave.). On weekdays, Hallo Berlin restaurants stock "the 'wurst' pushcart in New York" with bratwurst, Hungarian kielbasa, and other treats, in addition to red cabbage and potato pancakes (5th Avenue and 54th Street). Streetside falafel varies considerably in quality; look no further than Moshe's Falafel, which sells some of the crunchiest fried chickpea balls in town (6th Ave. and W. 46th St.; lunch only). At dinnertime, the well-reputed Taco Truck parks near the corner of W. 96th Street and Broadway. If you want caffeine, the bright orange Mudtruck sells upscale coffee drinks for less than most cafés (at Astor Pl. on 4th Ave.).

So what are you waiting for?

$$-$$$ ✕ **Voyage.** From the front lounge with the digital fireplace to the swank rear dining room (the padded walls make for great tête-à-têtes), Voyage makes you feel like one of the beautiful people without all the fuss. Unusual combinations ahead. For example, crispy Chatham cod gets a rose lentil crust and is plated with cauliflower–sweet pea samosas and a cilantro–coconut broth. ⊠ *117 Perry St., at Greenwich St., West Village* ☎ *212/255–9191* ⊟ *AE, DC, MC, V* ◷ *No lunch Sun.–Fri.* Ⓜ *Subway: 1, 9 to Christopher St./Sheridan Sq.*

$–$$$ ✕ **Blue Ribbon Bakery.** When the owners renovated this space, they uncovered a 100-year-old wood-burning oven. They relined it with volcanic brick, and let it dictate the destiny of their restaurant. The bakery-restaurant has an eclectic menu featuring substantial sandwiches on homemade bread (from the oven, of course), small plates, a legendary bread pudding, and entrées that span the globe. The basement dining room (which has more atmosphere) is dark and intimate; upstairs is a Parisian-style café. ⊠ *35 Downing St., at Bedford St., Greenwich Village* ☎ *212/337–0404* ⊟ *AE, DC, MC, V* Ⓜ *Subway: 1, 9 to Houston St.*

$–$$$ ✕ **Spice Market.** Spice Market is sensual and dazzling. Amid terra-cotta backgrounds, heavy embroidered curtains, and real artifacts from Burma,

Rajasthan (India), and Malaysia, the New York elite gather to eat family style. Chef Jean-Georges Vongerichten elevates southeast Asian street food to new heights as he plays with flavors and textures that will keep you asking the waiters for more information: What exactly was in that? Don't miss the butter garlic lobster or the hot and cold squid salad with spicy slaw and cooling papaya. ⊠ *403 W. 13th St., at 9th Ave., Greenwich Village* ☎ *212/675–2322* ⌕ *Reservations essential* ▤ *AE, D, DC, MC, V* Ⓜ *Subway: A, C, E to 14th St.; L to 8th Ave.*

Fast Food

Ⓒ ¢ ✕ **Gray's Papaya.** It's a stand-up, take-out dive. And, yes, limos do sometimes stop here for the incredibly cheap but good hot dogs. More often than not, though, it's neighbors or commuters who know how good the slim, traditional, juicy all-beef dogs are. Fresh-squeezed orange juice, a strangely tasty creamy banana drink, and the much-touted, healthy papaya juice are available along with more standard drinks—and all 24/7. ⊠ *402 6th Ave., at W. 8th St., Greenwich Village* ☎ *212/260–3532* ⌕ *Reservations not accepted* ▤ *No credit cards* Ⓜ *Subway: A, C, E, F, S, V to W. 4th St.*

French

$$–$$$ ✕ **Jarnac.** At this corner spot with wraparound windows, in a lovely part of the West Village, Maryann Terillo, Jarnac's multifaceted bistro chef, oversees a market-driven menu that usually includes luscious duck and pork rillettes, rib-eye steak Diane, and braised pork cheeks. Terillo's cassoulet of beans with pork, duck confit, and pork sausage is perfection: supple, smooth, and rich without being too oily or—a more frequent problem—too salty. Desserts are all sublime, and the wine list is carefully selected. ⊠ *328 W. 12th St., at Greenwich St., Greenwich Village* ☎ *212/924–3413* ▤ *AE, DC, MC, V* Ⓜ *Subway: A, C, E to 14th St.; L to 8th Ave.*

$–$$ ✕ **Pastis.** A trendy spin-off of Balthazar in SoHo, Pastis looks like it was shipped in tile by nicotine-stained tile from the Left Bank. At night, throngs of whippet-thin cell-phone-slinging boys and girls gather at the bar up front to sip martinis and be seen. French bistro and Provençal fare are front and center, including toothsome steak frites with béarnaise, mussels steamed in Pernod, frisée salad with duck confit, and tasty apple tartelet with phyllo crust. ⊠ *9 9th Ave., at Little W. 12th St., Meatpacking District* ☎ *212/929–4844* ⌕ *Reservations essential* ▤ *AE, DC, MC, V* Ⓜ *Subway: A, C, E to 14th St.; L to 8th Ave.*

$ ✕ **Le Quinze.** This is the casual bistro we all wish we had next door. Sunny in the front, cozy in the back, the tables are a bit tight, but c'est la vie! You might help your neighbors play mini-Scrabble or do a crossword puzzle while owner, former rugby player (rugby paraphernalia is all about), Pascal Escriout looks on. The poached eggs—done the old–fashioned way—are the backbone of a solid eggs Benedict, and the croque monsieur bubbles in all the right places. ⊠ *132 W. Houston St., between MacDougal and Sullivan Sts., Greenwich Village* ☎ *212/475–1515* ▤ *AE* Ⓜ *Subway: 1, 9 to Houston; C, E to Spring.*

¢–$$ ✕ **Florent.** When it's 4 AM and a slice of pizza just won't cut it, head to Florent, the true pioneer of dining in the Meatpacking District. Open 24 hours, this brushed-steel and Formica diner is always a blast—expect loud music, drag queens, and members of every walk of city life. The simple French menu features decent versions of everything you crave—onion soup, mussels steamed in white wine, pâté—and from midnight on, you can also order from a full breakfast menu. ⊠ *69 Gansevoort St., between Greenwich and Washington Sts., Greenwich Village* ☎ *212/989–5779* ▤ *No credit cards* Ⓜ *Subway: A, C, E to 14th St.; L to 8th Ave.*

Italian

$$–$$$ ✕ **Babbo.** After one bite of the ethereal homemade pasta or the tender
FodorsChoice suckling pig, you'll understand why it's so hard to get reservations at
★ Mario Batali's flagship restaurant. A full, complex, yet ultimately satisfying menu includes such high points as spicy lamb sausage and fresh mint "love letters," and rich beef-cheek ravioli. There's something for everyone from simple dishes like succulent whole fish baked in salt to custardy brain ravioli for the adventuresome eater. Service is friendly and helpful. ⊠ *110 Waverly Pl., between MacDougal St. and 6th Ave., Greenwich Village* ☎ *212/777–0303* ⏴ *Reservations essential* ▤ *AE, DC, MC, V* ⊗ *No lunch* Ⓜ *Subway: A, B, C, D, E, F, V to W. 4th St.*

$–$$ ✕ **Barbuto.** In this structural, airy space, you'll be facing either the kitchen or the quiet street on the edge of the Meatpacking District. The Italian bistro food depends on fresh seasonal ingredients that demand an ever-changing menu. Chef Jonathan Waxman shows a deft hand in the kitchen. Homemade, firm duck sausage contrasts nicely with the creamy, lumpy polenta. The peppery, al dente pasta with ragu of boar is light and well seasoned. ⊠ *775 Washington St., between Jane and W. 12th Sts., Greenwich Village* ☎ *212/924–9700* ▤ *AE, D, MC, V* ⊗ *No lunch Sat.* Ⓜ *Subway: A, C, E, L to 14th St.; 1, 9 to Christopher St.–Sheridan Sq.*

$–$$ ✕ **Lupa.** Even the most hard-to-please connoisseurs have a soft spot for Lupa, Mario Batali and Joseph Bastianich's "downscale" Roman trattoria (they also run high-end hits Babbo and Esca). Rough-hewn wood, great Italian wines, and simple preparations with top-quality ingredients define the restaurant. People come repeatedly for dishes such as bucatini with sweet-sausage ragù, house-made salamis and hams, and fried baby artichokes. The front room of the restaurant is seated on a first-come, first-served basis; reservations are taken for the back. ⊠ *170 Thompson St., between Bleecker and W. Houston Sts., Greenwich Village* ☎ *212/982–5089* ▤ *AE, DC, MC, V* Ⓜ *Subway: A, B, C, D, E, F, V to W. 4th St.*

$–$$ ✕ **Vento.** If these walls could talk! The site of one of the city's most notorious sex clubs—gay *and* straight—Vento is as light and breezy as it *was* dark and sleazy. Chef Michael White has devised the perfect menu, going from lightly charred octopus and perfectly moist meatballs in a ruddy gravy to mushroom pizzas with white truffle oil, to grassy sea bream, braised and dappled with mint-coriander pesto. Nice chewy zeppole come in a paper cone, like frîtes. ⊠ *675 Hudson St., at 14th St., Meatpacking District* ☎ *212/699–2400* ▤ *AE, MC, V* Ⓜ *Subway: A, C, E to 14th St.; L to 8th Ave.*

$ ✕ **Macelleria.** Italian for "butcher shop"—the perfect name for an Italian Meatpacking District restaurant—Macelleria's minimalist decor manages to feel simultaneously homey and chic. Start with a meaty *salumi misti,* a platter of prosciutto, salami, olives, and pecorino. Piping hot clams casino are state-of-the-art, with a winey tart lemon gravy. Dry-aged porterhouse for two ($69) sets a standard few could match, yielding such a surprising array of juicy flavors. ⊠ *48 Gansevoort St., between Greenwich and Washington Sts., Meatpacking District* ☎ *212/741–2555* ⊟ *AE, MC, V* Ⓜ *Subway: A, C, E to 14th St.; L to 8th Ave.*

¢–$ ✕ **Pepe Verde to Go.** A long list of specials changes daily here, but the menu always includes generously portioned pastas (prepared fresh in the open kitchen), antipasti, salads, entrées, and sandwiches. The gnocchi nearly float above your plate and the pesto sauce is fragrant with basil and garlic. Inexpensive wine is available by the glass or the bottle. Dinner can cost less than $17 at any one of the four "Pepe" restaurants—among the best Italian values in the city. ⊠ *559 Hudson St., between Perry and W. 11th Sts., Greenwich Village* ☎ *212/255–2221* Ⓜ *Subway: 1, 9 to Christopher St./Sheridan Sq.*

Korean

$–$$ ✕ **Do Hwa.** If anyone in New York is responsible for making Korean food cool, it is the mother-daughter team behind this perennially popular restaurant and its East Village sister, Dok Suni's. Jenny Kwak and her mother, Myung Ja, serve home cooking in the form of *kalbi jim* (braised short ribs), *bibimbop* (a spicy, mix-it-yourself vegetable and rice dish), and other favorites that may not be as pungent as they are in Little Korea but are satisfying nevertheless. ⊠ *55 Carmine St., between Bedford and 7th Ave., Greenwich Village* ☎ *212/414–1224* ⊟ *AE, D, MC, V* Ⓜ *Subway: 1, 9 to Houston St.*

Middle Eastern

★ ¢–$ ✕ **Moustache.** There's always a crowd waiting outside for one of the copper-top tables at this appealing Middle Eastern neighborhood restaurant. The focal point is the pita—the perfect vehicle for the tasty salads, lemony chickpea and spinach, and hearty lentil and bulghur among them. Also delicious is *lahmajun,* spicy ground lamb on a crispy flat crust. For entrées, try the leg of lamb or merguez sausage sandwiches. Although the service can be slow, it's always friendly. ⊠ *90 Bedford St., between Barrow and Grove Sts., Greenwich Village* ☎ *212/229–2220* ⌕ *Reservations not accepted* ⊟ *No credit cards* Ⓜ *Subway: 1, 9 to Christopher St.–Sheridan Sq.*

Pizza

🕑 $–$$$ ✕ **Arturo's.** Few guidebooks list this brick-walled Village landmark, but the jam-packed room and the smell of well-done pies augur a good meal to come. The pizza is terrific, smoky from its roast in a coal-fired oven. Basic pastas as well as seafood, veal, and chicken concoctions with mozzarella and lots of tomato sauce come at giveaway prices. Monday to Thursday, you can call ahead to reserve a table. ⊠ *106 W. Houston St., near Thompson St., Greenwich Village* ☎ *212/677–3820* ⊟ *AE, MC, V* Ⓜ *Subway: 1, 9 to Houston St.; F, V to Broadway–Lafayette St.*

🕑 ¢–$ ✕ **Patsy's Pizzeria.** The original Patsy's opened back in 1933 in East Harlem, when the neighborhood was largely Italian. The pizzeria still serves some of the best slices in New York. The secret is in the thin, crisp, coal-oven-baked crust, with thick sauce and fresh toppings. ⊠ *67 University Pl., between E. 10th and E. 11th Sts., Greenwich Village* ☎ *212/ 533–3500* ⌘ *Reservations not accepted* ▭ *No credit cards* Ⓜ *Subway: L, N, Q, R, W, 4, 5, 6 to 14th St.*

Seafood

$$ ✕ **Mary's Fish Camp.** The neighborhood's second New England fish house (the result of a split between Pearl Oyster Bar's partners) proves you can't have too much of a good thing. Casual Mary's Fish Camp usually has a wait for fried oysters, chowder, moist grilled catches of the day, and, of course, the sweet lobster roll with impeccable frites. A neighborhood favorite is the lobster potpie, which can run out early. ⊠ *64 Charles St., at W. 4th St., Greenwich Village* ☎ *646/486–2185* ⌘ *Reservations not accepted* ▭ *AE, MC, V* ☺ *Closed Sun.* Ⓜ *Subway: 1, 9 to Christopher St.–Sheridan Sq.*

★ **¢–$$** ✕ **Pearl Oyster Bar.** With only 50 seats, chances are there's likely to be a wait for Pearl's fresh seafood: chilled oysters to start, followed by bouillabaisse, a whole fish, or perhaps the famous lobster roll. Locals know to come by for a lazy lunch at the bar, when you can down some Bluepoints and beer in peace. ⊠ *18 Cornelia St., between Bleecker and W. 4th Sts., Greenwich Village* ☎ *212/691–8211* ⌘ *Reservations not accepted* ▭ *MC, V* ☺ *Closed Sun. No lunch Sat.* Ⓜ *Subway: A, B, C, D, E, F, V to W. 4th St.*

Southwestern

☾ **¢–$$** ✕ **Miracle Grill.** The margaritas are fabulous here, and the food reasonably priced and tasty: after all, Bobby Flay got his start—and left his culinary imprint—at the original flagship in the East Village (⇨ see East Village). Appetizers such as cornmeal-crusted catfish soft tacos are crowd pleasers. Entrée portions are huge, and vegetarians will appreciate the grilled or roasted vegetable dishes. ⊠ *415 Bleecker St., between Bank and W. 11th Sts., Greenwich Village* ☎ *212/924–1900* ⌘ *Reservations not accepted* ▭ *AE, MC, V* Ⓜ *Subway: A, C, E, L to 14th St.*

Steak

$$–$$$$ ✕ **Strip House.** With vintage nude photographs and cerise leather banquettes that line the red velvet walls, Strip House is decked out. David Walzog, one of the greatest steak-minded chefs in the country (he also oversees Michael Jordan's—the Steak House NYC), prepares strip steak with an incomparable depth of luscious and beefy flavor. A potato finished in goose fat becomes an exercise in irresistible textures, and truffled creamed spinach is even more resonant. The eight-inch wedge of cheesecake is enough for seven. ⊠ *13 E. 12th St., between 5th Ave. and University Pl., Greenwich Village* ☎ *212/328–0000* ▭ *AE, D, DC, MC, V* ☺ *No lunch* Ⓜ *Subway: L, N, Q, R, W, 4, 5, 6 to 14th St./Union Sq.*

EAST VILLAGE & LOWER EAST SIDE

Once Manhattan's bohemian and immigrant enclave, the East Village has become another high-rent neighborhood. The Lower East Side is undergoing similar changes; however, it's a little edgier and grittier than the East Village—for now, anyway. The influx of deeper pockets is chang-

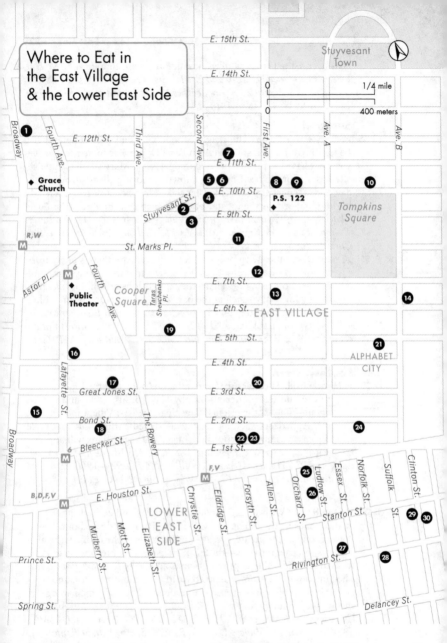

Where to Eat in the East Village & the Lower East Side

ing the restaurant scene, too, in both places. Amid the cheap diners, sushi houses, and tiny Thai restaurants is an army of mid-priced of Italian spots and a growing number of high-end reservations-only eateries. But there's still something for everyone.

American

$$–$$$ ✕ **Prune.** There's just something very right-on about the food at Prune, a cozy treasure of a restaurant serving eclectic, well-executed American food. The choices change with the season, but you might find roasted capon served over garlicky toasted bread, sweetbreads topped with smoky bacon, or roasted marrow bones served with parsley salad. There's usually a wait and the quarters are very cramped, so don't expect to linger at your table. ⊠ *54 E. 1st St., between 1st and 2nd Aves., East Village* ☎ *212/677–6221* ⟁ *Reservations essential* ▤ *AE, MC, V* ⊗ *No lunch weekdays* Ⓜ *Subway: F, V to 2nd Ave.*

Cafés

¢–$ ✕ **Le Gamin.** It's easy to confuse New York for Paris at this hip little haven, where the menu includes all the French café standards: croque monsieur, quiche Lorraine, salade niçoise, crepes (both sweet and savory), and big bowls of café au lait. All the desserts—crème brûlée and tarte tatin, among them—are homemade. Service can be desultory, but the upside is that you're free to lounge for hours. ⊠ *536 E. 5th St., between Aves. A and B, East Village* ☎ *212/254–8409* ▤ *AE* Ⓜ *Subway: F, V to 2nd Ave.*

☾ ¢ ✕ **Kudo Beans.** A light, airy, cheerful spot filled with slackers, students, and the occasional uptowner. They come equally for the Internet connection and for the good upscale food. Kudo carefully selects its offerings: local, renowned Dallis coffee, handmade sandwiches from Bimmy's, and too-good-to-resist organic caramel and chocolate doughnuts from the Donut Plant. You can also create your own smoothie, and there's a menu just for kids. ⊠ *49½ 1st Ave., at 3rd St., East Village* ☎ *212/353–1477* ⟁ *No reservations accepted* ▤ *AE, D, MC, V* Ⓜ *Subway: L to 1st Ave.; F to Houston St.*

☾ ¢ ✕ **Veniero's Pasticceria.** More than a century old, this bustling bakery-café sells every kind of Italian *dolci* (sweet), from cherry-topped cookies to creamy cannoli. A liquor license means you can top off an evening with a nightcap of Kahlua-spiked cappuccino or a dessert wine. ⊠ *342 E. 11th St., near 1st Ave., East Village* ☎ *212/674–7264* ⟁ *Reservations not accepted* ▤ *AE, D, DC, MC, V* Ⓜ *Subway: 6 to Astor Pl.; L to 1st Ave.*

Cajun–Creole

¢–$ ✕ **Great Jones Cafe.** When you pass through the bright-orange door into this small, crowded Cajun joint, known for its jukebox, you'll feel like you're in a honky-tonk. The daily changing menu, posted on the brightly colored walls, always features cornmeal-fried or blackened catfish, gumbo, jambalaya, po'boy sandwiches, and rice. Brunch is also festive, and if the strong coffee isn't enough to wake you up, a Bloody Mary might. ⊠ *54 Great Jones St., between the Bowery and Lafayette St., East Village* ☎ *212/674–9304* ▤ *MC, V* Ⓜ *Subway: R, W to 8th St.; 6, B, D, F, V to Bleecker St.*

BRUNCH IT

SOME MAKE IT A SOCIAL OCCASION, others have a one-on-one date with the Sunday paper. Either way, brunch is an event, a tradition in New York City. Many of the best places, however, don't take reservations. So, line up with the natives and take in the sights as you wait.

If you're on the Upper West Side, try the famous, caught-in-time **Barney Greengrass**, the place to go for bagels and nova (541 Amsterdam Ave., between 86th and 87th Sts.). Families should check out **Homer's World Famous Malt Shop** (487 Amsterdam Ave., between 83rd and 84th Sts.) for its doughnuts and French toast sticks. Bistro **Nice Matin**'s (201 W. 79th St., at Amsterdam Ave.) tables outside are a delight; inside, it's very light and airy. **Sarabeth's** offers more casual yet still sophisticated food, including moist pumpkin muffins and great fresh fruit plates (1295 Madison Ave., between 92nd and 93rd Sts.; 423 Amsterdam Ave., near 80th St.). Upper East Sider **Jo Jo** serves transcendent brunch fare in a sumptuous town house setting. The hip and elegant **Aquavit** (65 E. 55th St., between Madison and Park Aves.) sets out a Swedish smorgasbord every Sunday— it's also great for people-watching. For the ultimate sumptuous (and pricey) hotel buffet—the one that has a bit of everything, including shrimp and a dozen desserts—head to the Essex House's **Café Botanica** (160 Central Park South, between 6th and 7th Aves.).

For what is arguably the best hot chocolate in town (plus homemade marshmallows), go to **City Bakery** (3 W. 18th St., between 5th and 6th Aves.). You can pick from the salad bar and order table-service entrées. Go to **Home** (20 Cornelia St., between Bleecker and W. 4th Sts.) for American basics plus a garden out back. For French

fundamentals—croissants, eggs, and croque monsieur—try **Le Quinze** (132 W. Houston St., between MacDougal and Sullivan Sts.); sit up front for a sunny table.

If you're craving challah French toast, head for **Blue Ribbon Bakery** (35 Downing St., at Bedford St.). **Aquagrill** is elegant without being fussy; order from the classic brunch selections or exotic seafood entrées (210 Spring St., at 6th Ave.). A tasty organic French-Caribbean menu makes cozy **Ivo & Lulu** a destination in its own right (558 Broome St., between Sixth Ave. and Varick St.). **Jerry's** (101 Prince St., between Greene and Mercer Sts.) is a barely dressed-up diner with roots that go back to SoHo's art gallery days. Kids knock knees with models and Apple store aficionados, who come for salads and sandwiches in addition to brunch classics.

In Tribeca, **Bubby's** (120 Hudson St., at N. Moore St.) presents a slightly Southern take on American standards; it's fresh-squeezed citrus juices and buttermilk pancakes draw crowds of all ages. Warm, welcoming, elegant, quiet, and spacious **Capsouto Frères** (451 Washington St., at Watts St.) caters to those who want room to breathe when they eat or who want to talk and— maybe—try the savory soufflés. Quirky and small, the Lower East Side's **Prune** (54 E. 1st St., between 1st and 2nd Aves.) draws brunchers with its legendary Bloody Marys (usually a dozen to choose from) and surprising food combinations. **Miss Mamie's Spoonbread Too** (366 W. 110th St., between Columbus and Manhattan Aves.), not far from Columbia University, is well known for its friendly staff as well as its fried chicken, grits, and cornbread. Former President Clinton dined there, and local politicians are sometimes seen elbow-to-elbow with the students who gather here.

Contemporary

$$-$$$ ✕ **wd-50.** The chef's been called a mad genius. Vongerichten alum
Fodor'sChoice Wylie Dufresne mixes colors, flavors, and textures with a master hand.
★ His staff encourages people to feel at ease trying things like corned duck
on a salty rye crisp finished with purple mustard and horseradish cream,
or foie gras with a grapefruit, basil, and crouton dice and a leaf of
carmelized nori. ✉ *50 Clinton St., between Rivington and Stanton Sts.
Lower East Side* ☎ *212/477–2900* ☰ *AE, D, DC, MC, V* Ⓜ *Subway:
F to Delancey St.; J, M, Z to Essex St.*

¢-$$$ ✕ **Tasting Room.** Ignoring any sense of proportion, this 11-table spot fits
more than 300 different bottles on its American-only wine list. The dozen
wines offered by the glass and the menu change nightly. Owners Colin
and Renée Alevras challenge you to make your own tasting menu with
small ("tastes") and large ("shares") portions. Two examples: their ju-
niper-cured duck breast with roasted carrots, sunchokes, and greens and
the rainbow trout with frisée and marcona almonds. ✉ *72 E. 1st St.,
near 1st Ave., East Village* ☎ *212/358–7831* ☰ *AE, DC, MC, V*
◑ *Closed Sun. and Mon. No lunch* Ⓜ *Subway: F, V to 2nd Ave.*

★ **$-$$** ✕ **71 Clinton Fresh Food.** The name belies the sophisticated experience
that awaits at this off-the-beaten-path fashionista favorite (Calvin
Klein and Michael Kors have eaten here). Food really is the focus—
Jason Neroni's short seasonal menu, and his more expensive tasting
menu, tempt with clean, clever modern dishes. Winter might bring striped
bass with cauliflower and taleggio ravioli in a pine-nut broth or Tas-
manian trout tartare with quail egg. The cramped dining room adds
to the friendly, neighborhood charm of the place. ✉ *71 Clinton St.,
near Rivington St., Lower East Side* ☎ *212/614–6960* ⌨ *Reservations
essential* ☰ *AE, MC, V* ◑ *No lunch* Ⓜ *Subway: F, V to 2nd Ave. J,
M to Essex St.*

Delicatessens

¢-$$ ✕ **Katz's Delicatessen.** Everything and nothing has changed at Katz's since
it first opened in 1888, when the neighborhood was dominated by Jew-
ish immigrants. The rows of Formica tables, the long self-service counter,
and such signs as "send a salami to your boy in the army" are all com-
pletely authentic. What's different are the area's demographics, but all
types still flock here for succulent hand-carved corned beef and pastrami
sandwiches, soul-warming soups, juicy hot dogs, and crisp half-sour pick-
les. ✉ *205 E. Houston St., at Ludlow St., Lower East Side* ☎ *212/254–
2246* ☰ *AE, MC, V* Ⓜ *Subway: F, V to 2nd Ave.*

☾ **¢-$$** ✕ **Second Avenue Deli.** A face-lift may have removed the wrinkles of time,
but the kosher food is as good as ever at this East Village landmark.
The deli's bevy of Jewish classics includes chicken in the pot, matzo-
ball soup, chopped liver, Romanian tenderloin, and *cholent* (a Sabbath
dish of meat, beans, and grain). A better pastrami sandwich you can't
find (don't ask for it lean). A welcome bowl of pickles, sour green tomatoes, and coleslaw satisfies from the start. ✉ *156 2nd Ave., at E. 10th
St., East Village* ☎ *212/677–0606* ☰ *AE, DC, MC, V* Ⓜ *Subway: 6 to
Astor Pl.; F, V to 2nd Ave.*

Dessert

$–$$ ✕ **ChikaLicious Dessert Bar.** It's easy to walk past this small shop with big flavors. Sign on for the three-course prix-fixe dessert, and two women will dole out incomprehensible combinations and irresistibly rich offerings. This is the land of kiwi marinated in lavender soup with yogurt sorbet or warm chocolate tart with pink peppercorn ice cream and red wine sauce. To top things off, they've hired a sommelier to pair wines with each course. ⊠ *203 E. 10th St., between 2nd and 1st Aves., East Village* ☎ *212/995–9511* ⌑ *Reservations not accepted* ⊟ *MC, V* ⊗ *Mon. and Tues.* Ⓜ *Subway: 6 to Astor Pl.; L to 3rd Ave.*

Eclectic

🕐 **$–$$$** ✕ **Schiller's Liquor Bar.** Day and night, it's the kind of hip Lower East Side hang where you'd be equally comfortable as a celebrity of a parent with a baby stroller. The folks at Schiller's have worked hard to make it feel as if it's decades old. Vintage mirrored panels with flecked and peeling silver, forever-in-style subway tiles, a high tin ceiling, and a checkered floor lend an almost Parisian feel. Huevos rancheros, Cuban sandwiches, and steak frites reveal a steady hand in the kitchen. Dollar doughnuts, toasted baguettes with sweet or savory fillings, and a more standard bar menu fill out the list. ⊠ *131 Rivington St., at Norfolk St., Lower East Side* ☎ *212/260–4555* ⊟ *AE, MC, V* Ⓜ *Subway: F to Delancey St.; J, M, Z to Delancey–Essex Sts.*

Italian

$–$$$ ✕ **Il Buco.** The unabashed clutter of vintage kitchen gadgets and tableware harkens back to Il Buco's past as an antiques store. The tables, three of which are communal, are each unique—the effect is a festive, almost romantic country-house atmosphere. Chef Ed Witt uses meats and produce from local farms for the daily entrées and Mediterranean tapaslike appetizers. Book the inspirational wine cellar (with more than 300 varieties) for dinner. ⊠ *47 Bond St., between the Bowery and Lafayette St., East Village* ☎ *212/533–1932* ⊟ *AE, MC, V* ⊗ *No lunch Sun. and Mon.* Ⓜ *Subway: 6 to Bleecker St.; F, V to Broadway–Lafayette St.*

¢–$ ✕ **Gnocco.** The East Village is packed with cheap-and-chic Italian joints. Owners Pierluigi Palazzo and Rossella Tedesco named the place after a regional specialty—deep-fried dough, sort of like wontons, served with salami and prosciutto. Head to the roomy rear canopied garden for savory salads, house-made pastas (tagliatelle with sausage ragù is a winner), pizza, and hearty entrées like sliced beef tenderloin. Homesick expats come here for a dose of comfort. ⊠ *337 E. 10th St., between Aves. A and B, East Village* ☎ *212/677–1913* ⊟ *No credit cards* Ⓜ *Subway: L to 14th St.*

¢–$ ✕ **Il Bagatto.** You have to be a magician (*il bagatto* in Italian) to get a table before 11:30 PM at this hip, inexpensive restaurant, but as the reservationist says in her Italian-accented drawl "you go home, take a shower, relax, everyone else will be tired and drunk, you will come to dinner refreshed and happy." How true. The rich Italian food (try the homemade tagliolini with seafood in a light tomato sauce), and fun, rustic decor make it feel like a party. ⊠ *192 E. 2nd St., between Aves. A and B, East*

Village ☎ *212/228–0977* ⟵ *Reservations essential* ▤ *AE* ⊘ *Closed Mon. and Aug. No lunch* Ⓜ *Subway: F, V to 2nd Ave.*

¢–$ **'inoteca.** The Italian on the menu may be daunting, but the food is not. A wine and sandwich bar, 'inoteca strives for authenticity. Come for the grilled-cheeselike pressed *panini* and the truffle egg toast with asparagus and runny egg *bruschette.* Fresh, unusual salads and antipasti supplement the dozen or so entrées. Or select from their list of tempting, mostly Italian cheeses. At night, there's a din. Daytime's much quieter. ✉ *98 Rivington St., at Ludlow St., Lower East Side* ☎ *212/614–0473* ⟵ *Reservations not accepted* ▤ *AE, MC, V.*

Japanese

$$$–$$$$ ✕ **Jewel Bako.** In a minefield of cheap, often inferior, sushi houses gleams tiny Jewel Bako. In one of the best sushi restaurant in the East Village, this futuristic bamboo tunnel of a dining room is gorgeous, but try to nab a place at the sushi bar and put yourself in the hands of Masato Shimizu (his *omakase* starts at $85). He will serve you only what's best. ✉ *239 E. 5th St., near 2nd Ave., East Village* ☎ *212/979–1012* ⟵ *Reservations essential* ▤ *AE, DC, MC, V* ⊘ *Closed Sun. No lunch* Ⓜ *Subway: 6 to Astor Pl.*

$–$$ ✕ **Bond Street.** The minimalist setting of sleek black tables and taupe screens doesn't seem as chic as it once did, nor does the crowd. But the cooking of the resourceful Linda Rodriguez and the creative sushi of Hiroshi Nakahara have not lost their luster. Try the lobster tempura with yuzu and tomato dressing or rib-eye steak with caramelized shallot teriyaki. As for the sushi bar, you can find a selection of 10 kinds of hamachi and four types of yellowtail. ✉ *6 Bond St., between Broadway and Lafayette St., East Village* ☎ *212/777–2500* ⟵ *Reservations essential* ▤ *AE, MC, V* ⊘ *No lunch* Ⓜ *Subway: 6 to Bleecker St.; F, V to Broadway–Lafayette St.*

¢–$ ✕ **Momofuku Noodle Bar.** It's not authentic, but it sure is good. The chef (a Craft alum) created his own special ramen mixture, with a hint of sake in it to create an haute broth. He uses only the best ingredients throughout the menu—Berkshire pork, free-range chicken, and organic produce (when he can). His modern take on pork buns with cucumber and scallions is not to be missed. A sake card explains what the differences are among the drinks. ✉ *163 1st Ave., between 10th and 11 Sts., East Village* ☎ *212/475–7899* ⟵ *No reservations accepted* ▤ *No credit cards* Ⓜ *L to 1st Ave.*

¢ ✕ **Otafuku.** A tiny hole-in-the-wall with barely any standing room, Otafuku brings Japanese street food to New York. There are only two main items on the menu: *okono miyaki* (an eggy vegetable pancake) and *takoyaki* (unsweetened pancake balls). The flat pancakes come topped with beef, shrimp, pork, or squid. The balls are made in cast-iron molds and sauced with octopus or cheese. Both are topped with a swirl of mayo, special sauce, and a sprinkling of dried bonito (tuna) flakes. ✉ *236 E. 9th St., between 2nd and 3rd Aves., East Village* ☎ *212/353–8503* ⟵ *Reservations not accepted* ▤ *No credit cards* Ⓜ *Subway: 6 to Astor Pl.*

Korean

$ ✕ **Dok Suni's.** Here, and at the restaurant's more upscale Greenwich Village sister, Do Hwa, Korean home cooking marries hip downtown clientele. The combination works to make Korean food more accessible, and a little less pungent, for those on the prowl for good ethnic food. The *bulgogi* (rib eye), bibimbop, and pancakes are favorites. ✉ *119 1st Ave., between E. 7th St. and St. Marks Pl., East Village* ☎ *212/477–9506* ▬ *No credit cards* ⊙ *No lunch* Ⓜ *Subway: 6 to Astor Pl.; F, V to 2nd Ave.*

Latin

¢–$ ✕ **Paladar.** Kitsch 'n' cool Paladar is a party cabana where the drinks are fruity and the pan-Latin dishes are snappy updates of old favorites. Empanadas are filled to bursting with chicken picadillo and a plantain "canoe" is split down the middle and stuffed with a bacalao mash. The bold flavors (and meek prices) are courtesy of chef-heartthrob Aaron Sanchez, the son of restaurateur Zarela Martinez. On weekends, be prepared to perch at the bar and endure your wait with a passion-fruit agua fresca or two. ✉ *161 Ludlow St., between Houston and Stanton Sts., Lower East Side* ☎ *212/473–3535* ▬ *No credit cards* ⊙ *No lunch weekdays* Ⓜ *Subway: F, V to 2nd Ave.*

Mexican

$–$$ ✕ **La Palapa.** Aztec-style pottery inset into the wall, embossed-tin mirrors, and a terra-cotta tile floor provide a cozy setting in which to explore traditional ingredients like *epazote* (an herb), *guajillo* (a chili), and *chayote* (a crunchy vegetable). Revelatory sauces combine ingredients such as chilies, tamarind, and chocolate to create multidimensional flavor. Cod fillet with green pumpkin seed sauce, ancho chili barbecue lamb shank, and an enormous *chiles rellenos* are among several dishes that will ruin you for other Mexican restaurants. ✉ *77 St. Marks Pl., between 1st and 2nd Aves., East Village* ☎ *212/777–2537* ▬ *AE, DC, MC, V* Ⓜ *Subway: 6 to Astor Pl.*

Middle Eastern

★ ¢–$ ✕ **Moustache.** The focal point here is the pita, steam-filled pillows of dough rolled before your eyes and baked in a searingly hot oven. They are the perfect vehicle for the tasty salads—lemony chickpea and spinach, and hearty lentil and bulghur among them. For entrées, try the leg of lamb or merguez sausage sandwiches. Although the service can be slow, it's always friendly. ✉ *265 E. 10th St., between Ave. A and 1st Ave., East Village* ☎ *212/228–2022* ⊛ *Reservations not accepted* ▬ *No credit cards* Ⓜ *Subway: 6 to Astor Pl.; L to 1st Ave.*

Pizza

☺ ¢–$$ ✕ **Pie by the Pound.** At this sparkling, cheery spot, oblong designer pizzas are sold by the pound. Ask the server to cut you as small or as large a wedge as you want. The pies are resourcefully topped, with everything from fried eggs to lemon. Even the plain cheese pie is superb. Don't overlook the irresistible dessert pies as well, such as the nice and sloppy Nutella-ricotta-banana pie. No wonder this place is so popular. ✉ *124 4th Ave., between E. 12th and E. 13th Sts., East Village* ☎ *212/475–4977* ▬ *AE, D, MC, V* Ⓜ *Subway: 4, 5, 6 L, N, Q, R, W to Union Sq./14th St.*

🖑 ¢–$$ ✕ **Serafina.** Mediterranean-hue friezes and an inviting upstairs terrace grace this roomy restaurant. The real draw here is some of Manhattan's most authentic Neopolitan pizza. Beyond the pies are antipasti, salads, pastas including a number of ravioli dishes, and second courses such as veal scaloppine and sea scallops wrapped in zucchini, seared, and sauced with a brandy curry cream. ✉ *393 Lafayette St., at E. 4th St., East Village* ☎ *212/995–9595* 🚘 *AE, DC, MC, V* Ⓜ *Subway: 6 to Bleecker St.; F, V to Broadway–Lafayette St.*

$ ✕ **Una Pizza Napoletana.** Owner Anthony Mangieri raises pizza to an art, simply. Only San Marzano or cherry tomatoes touch his crust. The cheese: fresh buffalo mozzarella. His pizzas need only two minutes in the wood-burning oven. You'll find no slices here; the crisp 12-inch pies are relatively costly but well worth it. ✉ *349 E. 12th St., at 2nd Ave., East Village* ☎ *212/477–9950* 🗋 *Reservations not accepted* 🚘 *No credit cards* 🕑 *Closed Mon.–Wed.* 🍴 *BYOB.*

Southwestern

🖑 ¢–$ ✕ **Miracle Grill.** In fair weather, your long wait for an outdoor table will be rewarded by a seat in a large and pretty garden with a productive peach tree. The margaritas are fabulous and the food reasonably priced and tasty—after all, this is where Bobby Flay got his start. Appetizers such as cornmeal-crusted catfish soft tacos are crowd pleasers. Entrée portions are huge. You'll find one of the East Village's best and most inexpensive brunches in that garden on warm Sundays. ✉ *112 1st Ave., between E. 6th and E. 7th Sts., East Village* ☎ *212/254–2353* 🗋 *Reservations not accepted* 🚘 *AE, MC, V* 🕑 *No lunch weekdays* Ⓜ *Subway: 6 to Astor Pl.*

Thai

¢–$ ✕ **Holy Basil.** It's not often you get to enjoy good Thai food within a clubby setting of dark-wood floors, brick-face walls, huge gilt-framed mirrors, and old-fashioned paintings. The vibrant food—enlivened by chilies, opal basil, and kaffir lime—comes carefully composed in layer-cake form. Taste buds awaken to *Talay Thai* (sautéed seafood with lemongrass, holy basil leaves, galangal, kaffir lime leaves, ground chili pepper, and mushrooms in a white wine sauce). A large and informative wine list is an added bonus. ✉ *149 2nd Ave., between E. 9th and E. 10th Sts., East Village* ☎ *212/460–5557* 🚘 *AE, DC, MC, V* 🕑 *No lunch* Ⓜ *Subway: 6 to Astor Pl.*

Turkish

$–$$ ✕ **Maia.** Said to be the first Turkish *meyhane*, or Turkish "wine house," in Manhattan, Maia is a place to share; the more, the merrier. It's like a Turkish version of dim sum or tapas. Just stick with the cold *meze*, the appetizers—they're the best things on the menu. The waiter brings them, all 20-plus, on a tray, and you can point to what looks good. Belly dancing and music complete the scene some nights. ✉ *98 Ave. B, between 6th and 7th Sts., East Village* ☎ *212/358–1166* 🚘 *D, DC, MC, V* 🕑 *Closed Mon. No lunch* Ⓜ *Subway: L to 1st Ave.*

ETHNIC EATS

YOU CAN TOUR THE WORLD *eating in New York City. Cuisines of all kinds flourish throughout Manhattan, so it becomes even more special that areas like Chinatown and Little Italy (to a lesser extent) remain, adapting to gentrification instead of being overcome by it. As emigrants set down new roots, they bring with them restaurants and traditions that enrich their new neighborhoods.*

The Ukrainian church on East 7th Street (between 2nd and 3rd Aves.) is the epicenter of Eastern European cooking in Manhattan. Nearby, between East 5th Street and East 11th Street along 2nd and 3rd Avenues, a growing crop of Japanese restaurants serves the NYU community. Curry Hill (also known as Little India), the area surrounding the corner of East 27th Street and Lexington Avenue, is rich with South Asian spice shops and restaurants. Offices and warehouses hide some of the restaurants near Koreatown, as some call it (5th and 6th Aves. on W. 32nd St.). On the Upper West Side, a healthy crop of Senegalese and Malian cafés cater to French-speaking African nationals and their American counterparts.

Chinatown no longer dishes out only Cantonese, Szechuan, Hong Kong, and Hunan food. Fujianese, Shanghai, Taiwanese, Uighur, and more northern cuisines find representation as the food demands become more complex. Malaysian and Vietnamese eateries are taking root, too. **Dumpling House** *(118A Eldridge St., between Broome and Grand Sts.), gives the famous Joe's Shanghai a run for its money. The tasty potstickers here run $1–$2 each, so you can afford to supplement them with classic almond cookies from nearby* **Fay Da Bakery** *(83–85 Mott St., near Canal St.).*

Although the best Italian fare does not come from Mulberry St. anymore, a few survivors serve good solid food. Even if you come from uptown, you're a tourist here; but it's worth it for a cannoli at **Ferrara Bakery and Cafe** *(195 Grand St., between Mulberry and Mott Sts.).*

As you sit at the 12-person counter, take a peek behind the white half curtain to watch the Ukrainian ladies preparing goulash, stuffed cabbage, pierogi, blintzes, and more. At **The Stage***'s (128 2nd Ave., between 7th and 8th Sts.) Thursday night homage to corned beef, watch the meat being sliced right in front of you.*

The classic Indian food coming out of **Curry Leaf** *(99 Lexington Ave., at 27th St.) highlights fresh ingredients like the ones that are sold at the owner's grocery down the street at 123 Lexington Avenue. For a visual and aromatic treat, poke around one of the many small stores that sell beautiful spices, fragrant teas, and unusual grains. Try the fresh halvah, too.*

A surprising number of decent Korean restaurants are open either 24/7 or well into the night. The atmosphere may prove wanting, but the food is quite good and is usually hot enough for even hardcore spicy food fanatics. **36 Bar and BBQ** *(5 W. 36th St., near 5th Ave.) is a good beginner's restaurant. It's not traditional, but it gets hipness points.*

Malians, Guineans, and people from the Ivory Coast—along with their American counterparts—frequent the cafés along West 116th Street to get a dose of French news and a taste of home. **La Marmite** *(2264 Frederick Douglass Blvd., at 121st St.) is a few blocks uptown, but it's worth the trek for the debe, lamb chops, and cheb, the Senegalese version of paella.*

MURRAY HILL, FLATIRON DISTRICT & GRAMERCY

Quiet, residential Murray Hill, home to some of the city's most charming boutique hotels, has now become the neighborhood of choice for some of the city's most notable restaurants. Lexington Avenue between 26th and 28th streets is known as Curry Hill for its wall-to-wall subcontinental restaurants and take-out joints. Little Korea is near Herald Square in the West 30s. South of Murray Hill, genteel Gramercy is dotted with fashionable eateries in the neighborhood's stately buildings, especially on lower Madison Avenue. Part of the Flatiron District, Park Avenue South and the streets leading off it may be the city's hottest restaurant district, packed with crowd pleasers like Dos Caminos and top-tier foodie havens such as Gramercy Tavern, Craft, and Bolo.

American

$$$$
Fodor$Choice
★
✕ **Gramercy Tavern.** Danny Meyer's intensely popular restaurant tops many New Yorkers' "favorite restaurant" list. In front, the first-come, first-served tavern presents a somewhat lighter menu than the main dining room. The more formal dining room has a prix-fixe American menu overseen by founding chef and co-owner Tom Colicchio. For $72, choose from seasonal dishes such as roasted monkfish with pancetta, beets, and grapes, or braised lamb shoulder in a minestrone with tiny ricotta ravioli. Meyer's restaurants (which include Tabla, Eleven Madison Park, Blue Smoke, Union Square Cafe, and The Modern, at MoMA) are renowned for their knowledgeable, accommodating service, and Gramercy Tavern sets the gold standard. ⊠ *42 E. 20th St., between Broadway and Park Ave. S, Flatiron District* ☎ *212/477–0777* ⚋ *Reservations essential* ▤ *AE, DC, MC, V* Ⓜ *Subway: 6, R, W to 23rd St.*

$$–$$$$
Fodor$Choice
★
✕ **Craft.** Crafting your ideal meal here is like choosing from a gourmand's well-stocked kitchen—one supervised by the endlessly gifted Tom Colicchio, also chef at Gramercy Tavern. The bounty of simple yet intriguing starters and sides on the menu makes it easy to forget there are also main courses to partner them. Seared scallops, braised veal, seasonal vegetables—just about everything is exceptionally prepared with little fuss. The serene dining room features burnished dark wood, custom tables, a curved leather wall, and a succession of dangling radiant bulbs. ⊠ *43 E. 19th St., between Broadway and Park Ave. S, Flatiron District* ☎ *212/780–0880* ⚋ *Reservations essential* ▤ *AE, D, DC, MC, V* ☉ *No lunch weekends* Ⓜ *Subway: R, W, 6 to 23rd St.*

$$–$$$
✕ **Union Square Cafe.** When he opened Union Square Cafe in 1985, Danny Meyer changed the American restaurant landscape. The combination of upscale food and unpretentious but focused service sparked a revolution. Today chef Michael Romano still draws devotees with his crowd-pleasing menu. Mahogany moldings outline white walls hung with splashy modern paintings; in addition to the three dining areas, there's a long bar ideal for solo diners. The cuisine is American with a thick Italian accent: for example, the signature tuna burger can land on the same table as homemade gnocchi. ⊠ *21 E. 16th St., between 5th Ave.*

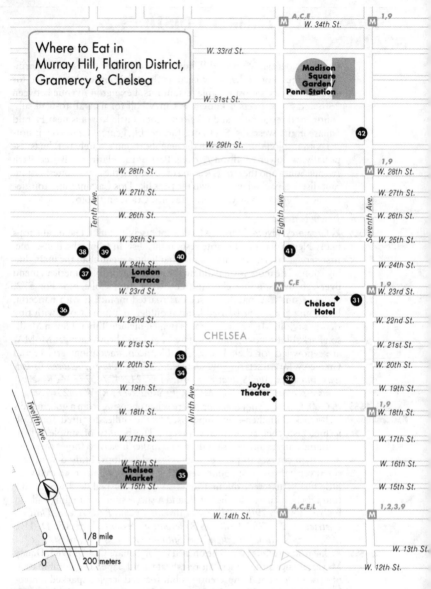

Where to Eat in
Murray Hill, Flatiron District,
Gramercy & Chelsea

A,C,E
W. 34th St.
1,9

W. 33rd St.

Madison
Square
Garden/
Penn Station

W. 31st St.

42

W. 29th St.

1,9
W. 28th St.
W. 28th St.

W. 27th St.

W. 26th St.

W. 25th St.

Tenth Ave.

W. 24th St.
London
Terrace

Eighth Ave.

41

Seventh Ave.

W. 27th St.

W. 26th St.

W. 25th St.

W. 24th St.

C,E

1,9
W. 23rd St.

38 39   40

37

W. 23rd St.

36

W. 22nd St.

CHELSEA

Chelsea
Hotel

31

W. 22nd St.

W. 21st St.

W. 21st St.

W. 20th St.

33

W. 20th St.

34

W. 19th St.

Joyce
Theater

32

W. 19th St.

Ninth Ave.

1,9
W. 18th St.

W. 18th St.

Twelfth Ave.

W. 17th St.

W. 16th St.
Chelsea
Market

35

W. 15th St.

W. 17th St.

W. 16th St.

W. 15th St.

A,C,E,L
W. 14th St.
1,2,3,9

0   1/8 mile

0   200 meters

W. 13th St.

W. 12th St.

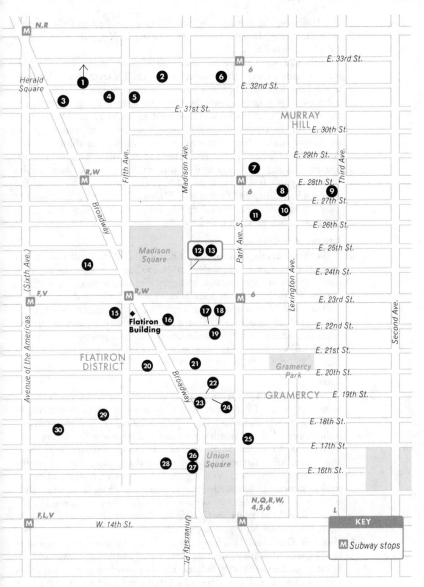

and Union Sq. W, Flatiron District ☎ *212/243–4020* ⌂ *Reservations essential* ▤ *AE, D, DC, MC, V* Ⓜ *Subway: L, N, Q, R, W, 4, 5, 6 to 14th St./Union Sq.*

$$ ✕**Kitchen 22.** Chef and restaurant mogul Charlie Palmer (Aureole, Métrazur) made a clever move when he replaced his restaurant Alva with streamlined Kitchen 22. Where a single entrée once cost about $25, now a three-course prix-fixe costs the same amount. A young, professional crowd willingly waits 45 minutes on weeknights (reservations aren't accepted) for the creative dishes. Choose from five starters and five entrées—say, roasted beet terrine followed by shellfish cassoulet. Homey desserts include the likes of pecan pie and chocolate mousse. The appealing '50s airport-lounge look of teal booths and white plastic chairs is so chic, you'll feel like you should be paying more. ✉ *36 E. 22nd St., between Broadway and Park Ave. S, Flatiron District* ☎ *212/228–4399* ⌂ *Reservations not accepted* ▤ *AE, DC, MC, V* ☽ *Closed Sun. No lunch* Ⓜ *Subway: R, W, 6 to 23rd St.*

American–Casual

¢ ✕**Eisenberg's Sandwich Shop.** Since the 1930s this narrow coffee shop with its timeworn counter and cramped tables has been providing the city with some of the best tuna, chicken, and egg-salad sandwiches. The staff still use the cryptic language of soda jerks, in which "whisky down" means rye toast and "Adam and Eve on a raft" means two eggs on toast. Considering the feeling of mayhem in the place, it's always a pleasant surprise when you actually get your sandwich, quickly and precisely as ordered. ✉*174 5th Ave., between E. 22nd and E. 23rd Sts., Flatiron District* ☎*212/ 675–5096* ▤ *AE* ☽ *Closed Sun.* Ⓜ *Subway: R, W, 6 to 23rd St.*

Cafés

☺ ¢–$ ✕**City Bakery.** This self-service bakery-restaurant has the urban aesthetic to match its name. Chef-owner Maury Rubin's baked goods—giant cookies, flaky croissants, elegant tarts—are unstintingly rich. A major draws is the pricey salad bar, worth every penny—a large selection of impeccably fresh food including whole sides of baked salmon, roasted vegetables, and several Asian-flavored dishes. Much of the produce comes from the nearby farmers' market. In winter, the bakery hosts a hot chocolate festival; in summer it's lemonade time. Weekend brunch includes some tableside service. ✉ *3 W. 18th St., between 5th and 6th Aves., Flatiron District* ☎ *212/366–1414* ▤ *AE, MC, V* ☽ *No dinner* Ⓜ *Subway: L, N, Q, R, W, 4, 5, 6 to 14th St./Union Sq.; F, V to 14th St.*

¢–$ ✕**Le Pain Quotidien.** This international Belgian chain brings its homeland ingredients with it, treating New Yorkers to crusty breads and delicious jams. Best of all is the Belgian chocolate sweetening the café mochas and hot chocolate. For a more substantial meal, take a seat at the long wooden communal table and sample hearty sandwiches like roast beef with caper mayonnaise or roasted turkey with herb dressing. ✉ *38 E. 19th St., between Broadway and Park Ave. S, Flatiron District* ☎ *212/ 673–7900* ▤ *No credit cards* Ⓜ *Subway: R, W, 6 to 23rd St.*

Contemporary

★ $$$$ ✕**Veritas.** What do you do when you own more wine than you can drink? Veritas's wine-collecting owners decided to open a restaurant. Chef Scott

Bryan's prix-fixe contemporary menu runs from such rich, earthy dishes as braised veal with parsnip puree to seared diver scallops with celery root puree and black truffle vinaigrette. A glass of Tokaj and a hazelnut mousse positively sing together. The dining room is distinguished by clean, natural lines, with one wall of Italian tile and another flaunting a collection of hand-blown vases. ⊠ *43 E. 20th St., between Broadway and Park Ave. S, Flatiron District* ☎ *212/353–3700* ⌔ *Reservations essential* ▭ *AE, DC, MC, V* ◴ *No lunch* Ⓜ *Subway: R, W, 6 to 23rd St.*

★ **$$–$$$$** ✕ **Eleven Madison Park.** Like Tabla, this Danny Meyer restaurant occupies the lobby of the landmark Metropolitan Life Building and has views of Madison Square Park. The design incorporates the original art deco fixtures, but the place feels like a modern train station—in a good way. Chef Kerry Heffernan's seasonal menu always includes a delicious braised beef dish (the short ribs are superb), plus skate, squab, lobster, and rarities such as pig's feet, each prepared in his simple, elegant French manner. The bar is exquisite. ⊠ *11 Madison Ave., at E. 24th St., Flatiron District* ☎ *212/889–0905* ⌔ *Reservations essential* ▭ *AE, D, DC, MC, V* ◴ *No lunch Sun.* Ⓜ *Subway: R, W, 6 to 23rd St.*

Eclectic

$$$$ ✕ **Tabla.** In concert with restaurant guru Danny Meyer, chef Floyd Cardoz creates exciting cuisine based on the tastes and traditions of his native India, filtered through his formal European training. Indian ingredients, condiments, and garnishes, such as *kasundi* (tomato sauce), *rawa* (a blend of spices), and *kokum* (dried black plum) garnish familiar fish and meats like skate, lobster, oxtail, and chicken. At the more casual Bread Bar downstairs, you can get in and out faster and for less money while watching fresh naan emerge from the tandoor ovens. ⊠ *11 Madison Ave., at E. 25th St., Flatiron District* ☎ *212/889–0667* ⌔ *Reservations essential* ▭ *AE, D, DC, MC, V* ◴ *No lunch weekends* Ⓜ *Subway: R, W, 6 to 23rd St.*

French

$$$–$$$$ ✕ **Fleur de Sel.** Chef-owner Cyril Renaud, who's danced behind the stoves at such highfalutin restaurants as La Caravelle and Bouley, has settled down nicely in a lovely restaurant of his own. His watercolors adorn the walls and the creative menus. The prix-fixe menu is limited but perfectly tuned to the season and the scale of the dining room. Monkfish is plated with roasted chestnuts and a whiskey lobster jus and crisp *poussin* (baby chicken) is bathed in a rich foie gras sauce. ⊠ *5 E. 20th St., between 5th Ave. and Broadway, Flatiron District* ☎ *212/460–9100* ⌔ *Reservations essential* ▭ *AE, MC, V* Ⓜ *Subway: R, W, 6 to 23rd St.*

$–$$$ ✕ **Artisanal.** This brasserie is a beloved shrine to cheese, the favorite food of chef-owner Terrence Brennan (Picholine) and past-master cheese man Max McCalman. The cheese is pampered and watchfully aged right in the dining room in a temperature-controlled "cave," and it's all over the menu: fondues, gougères, onion soup gratinée, and/or selections from the ever-changing cheese list will leave you simpering and happy. The raw bar is exemplary, and the brasserie fare is thrilling, as is the ample by-the-glass wine list. ⊠ *2 Park Ave., at E. 32nd St., Murray Hill* ☎ *212/725–8585* ▭ *AE, MC, V* Ⓜ *Subway: 6 to 33rd St.*

🌙 **$–$$** ✕ **Les Halles.** Chef Anthony Bourdain is famous not only for his cooking, but for his Food Network programs and best-selling books *Kitchen Confidential, A Cook's Tour,* and his new Les Halles cookbook. But his original restaurant, which recently doubled in size, remains strikingly unpretentious, like a true French bistro–cum–butcher shop. A good bet is steak frites—the fries alone are widely regarded as the best in New York. Other prime choices include crispy duck-leg confit and frisée salad, and firm blood sausage with caramelized apples. ✉ *411 Park Ave. S, between E. 28th and E. 29th Sts., Murray Hill* ☎ *212/679–4111* ⌂ *Reservations essential* ▭ *AE, DC, MC, V* Ⓜ *Subway: 6 to 33rd St.*

Indian

$–$$$ ✕ **Dévi.** Boasting an ecstatically colored interior, with nearly every surface padded and silked, Dévi is almost as beautiful as the amply spiced dishes that co-executive chefs Suvir Saran and Hemant Mathur devise. Set things right with a Maharani—Belvedere vodka with saffron infusion and a splash of orange—then tear into simply humongous shrimp, sizzling out of the tandoori oven. Manchurian cauliflower is happily marinated in spicy ketchup, and lamb chops have never been slathered with more flavors. ✉ *8 E. 18th St., between Broadway and 5th Ave., Flatiron* ☎ *212/691–1300* ▭ *AE, MC, V* Ⓜ *Subway: 4, 5, 6 Q, N, R to Union Sq.*

$–$$$ ✕ **Tamarind.** Many consider Tamarind Manhattan's best Indian restaurant. Forsaking the usual brass, beads, sitar, and darkness, you'll find a lustrous skylighted dining room awash in soothing neutral colors and tantalizing fragrances. The kitchen also departs from tradition, offering multi-regional dishes, some familiar (tandoori chicken, a searing lamb vindaloo), some unique (succulent venison chops in spiced cranberry sauce, she-crab soup with saffron, nutmeg, and ginger juice). The more intriguing a dish sounds, the better it is. Next door is a quaint teahouse/café/takeout shop. ✉ *41–43 E. 22nd St., between Broadway and Park Ave. S, Flatiron District* ☎ *212/674–7400* ⌂ *Reservations essential* ▭ *AE, DC, MC, V* Ⓜ *Subway: N, R, 6 to 23rd St.*

¢ ✕ **Pongal.** One of the city's best inexpensive Indian restaurants is also vegetarian-only and kosher. Its menu is a mix of southern Indian comfort foods (many that would be found on the streets of Bombay) and expertly prepared home-style dishes. Try the spicy, potato-filled samosas or chickpea-battered vegetable *pakoras*. For some home cooking, don't miss the *saag paneer* (fresh curd cheese with spinach) and *kala chana* (seasoned black chickpeas in a rich sauce). ✉ *110 Lexington Ave., between E. 27th and E. 28th Sts., Murray Hill* ☎ *212/696–9458* ▭ *D, DC, MC, V* Ⓜ *Subway: 6 to 28th St.*

Italian

$$–$$$$ ✕ **I Trulli.** Rough-hewn gold walls, a fireplace, a garden for summer dining, and a whitewashed open grill with the traditional beehive shape of early Pugliese houses distinguish this Italian winner from its competitors. The appetizers are certainly enticing—rabbit pâté with pecorino and prosciutto brioche, or grilled baby octopus with fennel-orange supreme salad—and nearly all the pasta is handmade. Main courses include a toothsome rack of lamb with baby artichokes and roasted tomatoes. ✉ *122 E. 27th St., between Lexington Ave. and Park Ave. S, Murray Hill* ☎ *212/481–7372* ⌂ *Reservations essential* ▤ *AE, DC, MC, V* ⊘ *Closed Sun. No lunch Sat.* Ⓜ *Subway: 6 to 28th St.*

$–$$$ ✕ **Beppe.** There are a lot of restaurants claiming to be Tuscan in New York, but chef Cesare Casella's labor of love is one of the few that can wear the mantle. The chef presents a playful menu of Tuscan specialties, such as *farro* cooked risotto-style, and clever concoctions, like semi-boneless quail stuffed with pancetta and sage, roasted and served over Sardinian *fregola* and roasted red peppers. The seasonally changing pastas may be the best part of the satisfying menu. The bright dining room simulates a cheery trattoria. ✉ *45 E. 22nd St., between Broadway and Park Ave. S, Flatiron District* ☎ *212/982–8422* ▤ *AE, DC, MC, V* ⊘ *Closed Sun. No lunch Sat.* Ⓜ *Subway: R, W, 6 to 23rd St.*

Korean

¢–$$ ✕ **Cho Dang Gol.** Situated a few blocks away from the main drag of Little Korea, this restaurant specializes in tofu (*doo-boo* in Korean), and myriad varieties are made on the premises and incorporated into a vast array of traditional Korean dishes of varying heat and spice. Anyone who thinks of tofu as a bland, jiggling substance should try *doo-boo dong-ka-rang-deng*, puffy rounds of tofu filled with shredded vegetables, egg, and ground pork. The staff members don't speak enough English to be of much help. ✉ *55 W. 35th St., between 5th and 6th Aves., Murray Hill* ☎ *212/695–8222* ▤ *AE, DC, MC, V* Ⓜ *Subway: B, D, F, N, Q, R, S, W to 34th St.*

¢–$$ ✕ **Kang Suh.** "Seoul" food at its best is served at this lively, second-floor restaurant. Cook thin slices of ginger-marinated beef (*bul go gui*) or other meats over red-hot coals; top them with hot chilies, bean paste, and pickled cabbage; and wrap them all up with lettuce for a satisfying meal. A crisp oyster-and-scallion pancake, sautéed yam noodles, and other traditional dishes are all expertly prepared. The waitstaff speaks little English, but the menu has lots of pictures, so you can just point and smile. ✉ *32 W. 32nd St., between 5th and 6th Aves., Murray Hill* ☎ *212/947–8482* ▤ *AE, MC, V* Ⓜ *Subway: B, D, F, N, Q, R, S, W to 34th St.*

¢–$ ✕ **Gam Mee Ok.** The deconstructed industrial design, inexpensive menu, and late-night hours attract a young and stylish crowd here. Every item on the very limited menu has a photo to help you order. But all you need to remember to order are oxtail-and-bone-marrow soup—a subtle, satisfying milky-white bowl of soup with rice noodles and beef that you season at your table with Korean sea salt and chopped scallions—and mung bean pancakes, made fresh with scallions, and fried until crisp and chewy. ✉ *43 W. 32nd St., between 5th and 6th Aves., Murray Hill* ☎ *212/695–4113* ⌂ *Reservations not accepted* ▤ *No credit cards* Ⓜ *Subway: B, D, F, N, R, Q, V, W to 34th St.*

¢–$ ✕ **Mandoo Bar.** At this appealing little dumpling shop on Little Korea's main drag, you can watch the ladies making the little oval treats in the window on your way to one of the blond-wood cafeterialike tables in the back. There are plenty of dumplings, or *mandoo,* to choose from, such as broiled shrimp and sea cucumber, Korean kimchi, beef, pork, or leek. Rounding out the menu are noodle and rice dishes and a couple of specialties like *tangsuyook*—fried pork with sweet-and-sour sauce. ⊠ *2 W. 32nd St., between 5th Ave. and Broadway, Murray Hill* ☎ *212/ 279–3075* ☲ *AE, MC, V* Ⓜ *Subway: 6 to 33rd St.*

Mediterranean

$$–$$$ ✕ **Olives.** The New York branch of Boston-based Todd English's grow-ing international Olives empire resides in the capacious lobby of the hip W Hotel on Union Square. His executive chef, Victor LaPlaca, sustains English's penchant for complexity of flavors and ingredients with a level hand. Hand-cut pappardelle is entwined with seven-hour lamb leg meat and mustard cream. A seared tuna loin rests on curried polenta, and is dappled with gingered spinach blood orange vinaigrette. Finish with a vanilla soufflé and you'll float out the bustling lobby sporting quite a grin. ⊠ *201 Park Ave. S, at E. 17th St., Flatiron District* ☎ *212/353– 8345* ⌕ *Reservations essential* ☲ *AE, D, DC, MC, V* Ⓜ *Subway: L, N, Q, R, W, 4, 5, 6 to 14th St./Union Sq.*

Mexican

$–$$$ ✕ **Dos Caminos.** Stephen Hanson, the visionary restaurateur behind a dozen New York restaurants, including Blue Water Grill, has created a sophisticated hit. The array of 150 tequilas will put you in the right frame of mind for anything chefs Ivy Stark and Scott Linquist create. Kobe beef tacos are given searing heat by cascabel chiles, and slow-roasted pork ribs in chipotle barbecue sauce achieve quite a depth of flavor. Be forewarned: the noise level can resemble the climax at a stag party. ⊠ *373 Park Ave. S, between 26th and 27th Sts., Flatiron District* ☎ *212/294–1000* ⌕ *Reser-vations essential* ☲ *AE, DC, MC, V* Ⓜ *Subway: 6 to 28th St.*

Pan-Asian

¢   ✕ **Republic.** Epicureans on a budget flock to this Asian noodle empo-rium that looks like a cross between a downtown art gallery and a Jap-anese school cafeteria. The young waitstaff dressed in black T-shirts and jeans hold remote-control ordering devices to speed the already speedy service. Sit at the long, bluestone bar or at the picnic-style tables and order appetizers such as smoky grilled eggplant and luscious fried won-tons. Entrées are based on noodles or rice. Spicy coconut chicken soup and Vietnamese-style barbecued pork are particularly delicious. ⊠ *37 Union Sq. W, between E. 16th and E. 17th Sts., Flatiron District* ☎ *212/ 627–7172* ☲ *AE, DC, MC, V* Ⓜ *Subway: L, N, Q, R, W, 4, 5, 6 to 14th St./Union Sq.*

Seafood

$–$$$ ✕ **Blue Water Grill.** A copper-and-tile raw bar anchors one end of this warm, sweeping room of indigo, sienna, and yellow. Strong on fresh seafood served neat (chilled whole lobster, shrimp in the rough), the con-stantly changing menu also has international flair—sushi and sashimi, porcini-crusted halibut with pumpkin risotto, lobster and scallop open-faced ravioli—and simple preparations that issue forth from a wood-burning oven. Lobster mashed potatoes are a must. ⊠ *31 Union Sq. W, at E. 16th St., Flatiron District* ☎ *212/675–9500* ⌕ *Reservations es-sential* ☲ *AE, DC, MC, V* Ⓜ *Subway: L, N, Q, R, W, 4, 5, 6 to 14th St./Union Sq.*

Spanish

$$–$$$ ✕ **Bolo.** Although Bolo was already the most vivid and convincing Spanish restaurant in New York, celebrity chef Bobby Flay decided to add tapas to Bolo's menu, making the place even better. Choose—if you can—from over a dozen possibilities, but don't miss the sautéed squid and bacon with garlic oil or white anchovies with tangerine. Another must-try is the roasted rabbit haunch wrapped in serrano ham with yellow pepper risotto. In fact, everything on the menu is marvelous. ⊠ *23 E. 22nd St., between Broadway and Park Ave. S, Flatiron District* ☎ *212/228–2200* ♨ *Reservations essential* 🖃 *AE, MC, V* Ⓜ *Subway: 6 to 23rd St.*

Turkish

$–$$ ✕ **Turkish Kitchen.** This striking multilevel room with crimson walls, chairs with red skirted slipcovers, and colorful kilims is Manhattan's busiest and best Turkish restaurant. For appetizers, choose from the likes of velvety char-grilled eggplant or tender octopus salad, creamy hummus, or poached beef dumplings. The luscious stuffed cabbage is downright irresistible. The restaurant also hosts one of the most alluring Sunday brunch buffets in town, featuring 90 items, Turkish and American—all house-made, including a dozen breads. ⊠ *386 3rd Ave., between E. 27th and E. 28th Sts., Murray Hill* ☎ *212/679–1810* 🖃 *AE, D, DC, MC, V* ☉ *No lunch Sat.* Ⓜ *Subway: 6 to 28th St.*

Vegetarian

$–$$$$ ✕ **Hangawi.** Hangawi, serving "vegetarian mountain Korean cooking," holds a special place in the city's collection of vegetarian restaurants. For the full experience choose the "emperor's menu," a parade of more than 10 courses designed as a complete introduction to this unusual cuisine. Offerings include delicate soups, such as miso broth or pumpkin porridge with marinated wild mountain herbs; and a main-course spread of more than 15 bowls of assorted earthy and/or spicy kimchi. Exotic teas, including one made from a puree of dates, are good accompaniments to the meal. ⊠ *12 E. 32nd St., between 5th and Madison Aves., Murray Hill* ☎ *212/213–0077* ♨ *Reservations essential* 🖃 *AE, DC, MC, V* Ⓜ *Subway: B, D, F, N, R, Q, V, W to 34th St.*

CHELSEA

Soon after the art galleries and gay men surged into the area, Chelsea underwent a residential building boom, bringing a new wave of luxury-condo dwellers to this relentlessly trendy neighborhood. But there has been no congruent influx of great restaurants. Chelsea may not be a white-hot dining destination like, say, its Flatiron neighbor to the east, but you can eat very well if you know where to go.

American

$$$–$$$$ ✕ **The Biltmore Room.** In the most soigné beaux-arts dining room in town, set about with antique marble preserved from the old Biltmore Hotel, feast on brilliant Chef Gary Robins's highly imaginative and deeply delicious fare, like crusty squash blossoms stuffed with Maryland crab and plated with flashy mango-chili sauce and corn-avocado salad, cocoa-dusted venison loin medallions, and Algerian-spiced ruby rack of lamb. The room is a bit crowded, but the gorgeous and quicksilver staff makes everything come together beautifully. ✉ *289 8th Ave., between W. 24th and W. 25th Sts., Chelsea* ☎ *212/807–0111* ▤ *AE, DC, MC, V* ⊙ *No lunch* Ⓜ *Subway: C, E to 23rd St.*

$$–$$$ ✕ **The Red Cat.** Chef-owner Jimmy Bradley oversees this comfortable neighborhood restaurant. Try the seasonal appetizers like sautéed zucchini with almonds and pecorino pan-roasted quail with cremini mushrooms, sausage, golden raisins, and tomato; and fennel-crusted veal sweetbreads with lentils, prosciutto, and pecans. Satisfying entrées include sautéed skate with citrus salad, calf's liver au poivre with Swiss chard–onion pie, and shell steak and golden potatoes with cabernet sauce. The service is friendly and welcoming, and the wine list is reasonably priced. ✉ *227 10th Ave., between W. 23rd and W. 24th Sts., Chelsea* ☎ *212/242–1122* ▤ *AE, DC, MC, V* ⊙ *No lunch* Ⓜ *Subway: C, E to 23rd St.*

$–$$ ✕ **Seven.** In the culinary wasteland around Macy's and Penn Station, there actually are a few serious restaurants. The contemporary American menu runs the gamut from overstuffed sandwiches (at lunch), to seasonal soups, to homemade pastas, to creative entrées such as roasted skate with lobster coral and capers. The decor, like the menu, plays it safe but sophisticated. In another neighborhood this restaurant might not warrant mention, but as an oasis in a desert of fast-food outlets it deserves special mention. ✉ *350 7th Ave., between W. 29th and W. 30th Sts., Chelsea* ☎ *212/967–1919* ▤ *AE, MC, V* Ⓜ *Subway: 1, 9 to 28th St.*

Cafés

¢ ✕ **La Bergamote.** Exemplary French pastries are served in this simple café. Try the buttery pain au chocolat and chewy meringues with a steaming bowl of café au lait. ✉ *169 9th Ave., at W. 20th St., Chelsea* ☎ *212/ 627–9010* ▤ *No credit cards* Ⓜ *Subway: A, C, E, L to 14th St.*

¢ ✕ **Le Gamin.** It's easy to confuse New York for Paris at this hip little haven (one of four in town), where the menu includes all the French-café standards: croque monsieur, quiche Lorraine, salade niçoise, crepes (both sweet and savory), and big bowls of café au lait. Service can be desultory, but the upside is that you're free to lounge for hours. ✉ *183 9th Ave., at W. 21st St., Chelsea* ☎ *212/243–8864* ▤ *AE, MC, V* Ⓜ *Subway: C, E to 23rd St.*

¢ ✕ **Goupil and DeCarlo.** The almond croissants at this small bakery-café rival any baked in France. There's a complete selection of French baked goods, sandwiches (the foot-long baguette stuffed with merguez and potato gratin is satisfying), and a special dish of the day (the likes of beef bourguignonne). ✉ *Chelsea Market, 75 9th Ave., between 15th and 16th Sts., Chelsea* ☎ *212/807–1908* ▤ *MC, V* Ⓜ *Subway: A, C, E, L to 14th St.*

Chinese

¢–$ ✕ **Grand Sichuan International.** This regional Chinese restaurant serves a vast menu of specialties, many of which you won't find anywhere else. The emphasis is on fiery Sichuan (Szechuan) cooking, but Cantonese, Hunan, Shanghai, and even American Chinese food are represented (a handy treatise and guide to Chinese food comes with the menu). Spicy *dan dan* noodles, shredded potatoes in vinegar sauce, crab soup dumplings, minced pork with cellophane noodles or fermented green beans, and sautéed loofah are among the hauntingly delicious dishes. ⊠ *229 9th Ave., at W. 24th St., Chelsea* ☎ *212/620–5200* ▭ *AE, MC, V* Ⓜ *Subway: C, E to 23rd St.*

Eclectic

$$–$$$ ✕ **Sapa.** Proving yet again that she is among the most nuanced and imaginative chefs in the world, chef Patricia Yeo triumphs in a spectacular, shimmering new space. Dishes are French or Vietnamese. Don't miss cocoa and peanut-glazed spareribs with carrot-orange pickle relish, five-vegetable spring roll, sliced duck breast with red curry, pumpkin, and eggplant, and heavenly onion rings with Stilton aioli. Finish with caramelized banana tarte tatin with kumquats "caramel" and chocolate-cinnamon ice cream. ⊠ *43 W. 24th St., between 5th and 6th Aves., Chelsea* ☎ *212/929–1800* ⌂ *Reservations essential* ▭ *AE, MC, V* Ⓜ *Subway: C, E to 23rd St.*

¢–$ ✕ **Wild Lily Tea Room.** A true gem worthy of its setting amid the Chelsea galleries, this tearoom provides endless serenity. The menu describes teas with such eloquence that it could be a book of poetry. Afternoon tea comes complete with dainty finger sandwiches, desserts, and delectable scones with jam and clotted cream, or choose from such savory Asian treats as shu mai dumplings with shrimp, crab, or vegetables; spicy Thai sausage in puff pastry; or an ingenious ginger chicken "hamburger." Similar dishes and more are available for dinner. ⊠ *511A W. 22nd St., between 10th and 11th Aves., Chelsea* ☎ *212/691–2258* ⌂ *Reservations essential* ▭ *AE, MC, V* ☻ *Closed Mon.* Ⓜ *Subway: C, E to 23rd St.*

Italian

$–$$$ ✕ **Bottino.** Chelsea's chic art crowd seems to want good food, good prices, and a good atmosphere at their hangouts. They get it *alla italiana* at this smartly designed, mixed-price west Chelsea restaurant. The menu is straightforward—mixed fry of seafood and vegetables, octopus vinaigrette, grilled Norwegian salmon with salsa verde, and roasted rack of lamb. Service is slow but attractive and friendly. The take-out shop of the same name, next door, has a nice selection of Italian lunch items. ⊠ *246 10th Ave., between W. 24th and W. 25th Sts., Chelsea* ☎ *212/206–6766* ⌂ *Reservations essential* ▭ *AE, D, DC, MC, V* ☻ *No lunch Sun. and Mon.* Ⓜ *Subway: C, E to 23rd St.*

¢–$ ✕ **Pepe Giallo to Go.** The crown of a chain of four tiny Italian eateries, this Chelsea branch is the most spacious and charming of the lot. A long list of specials changes daily, but the menu always includes generously portioned pastas (prepared fresh in the open kitchen), antipasti, salads, entrées, and sandwiches. The gnocchi are as light as little clouds, and the veal scallops are tender. Inexpensive wine is served. Considering dinner can cost less than $17, these restaurants are among the best Italian values in the city. ⊠ *253 10th Ave., at W. 25th St., Chelsea* ☎ *212/242–6055* ▭ *AE, MC, V* Ⓜ *Subway: C, E to 23rd St.*

Mexican

$–$$ ✕ **Rocking Horse.** The modern Mexican interior of this restaurant puts it a cut above the others on the 8th Avenue strip. Riffs on nouvelle Mexican cuisine include chiles rellenos with mushroom-pine nut picadillo, and seared duck breast in herbed pumpkin seed sauce with chayote gratin. Take in the buff gay Chelsea crowd while enjoying a potent margarita and some addictive homemade tortilla chips served in a metal bucket at the bar. ✉ *182 8th Ave., between W. 19th and W. 20th Sts., Chelsea* ☎ *212/463–9511* ▭ *AE, MC, V* Ⓜ *Subway: 1, 9 to 18th St.*

Thai

$–$$ ✕ **The Basil.** It's not often you get to enjoy good Thai food in such a trendy setting. The vibrant food—enlivened by chilies, opal basil, and kaffir lime—comes carefully composed in layer-cake form. Taste buds awaken to the spicy *som tum* and rich *tom kah gai,* not to mention anything in *kaw praw.* A large and informative wine list is an added bonus. ✉ *206 W. 23rd St., between 7th and 8th Aves., Chelsea* ☎ *212/242–1014* ▭ *AE, MC, V* ⊘ *Closed Mon. No lunch* Ⓜ *Subway: C, E to 23rd St.*

MIDTOWN WEST

Big hotels, big businesses, and blockbuster Broadway shows dominate the western half of midtown, and that means plenty of big hungry crowds around the clock. Capitalizing neatly on that fact is an ever-burgeoning plethora of restaurants ranging from inexpensive ethnic eateries and theme restaurants to fine French dining rooms. Be sure to make an informed choice, or you could easily find yourself in a tourist trap. Now that Times Square and the theater district resemble theme parks and Hell's Kitchen has been gentrified (you'll hear it called Clinton), the seedy edge of the area is all but gone. In fact, Times Square is beginning to look more and more like Shinjuku in Tokyo.

American

$$$–$$$$ ✕ **"21" Club.** It's undeniably exciting to hobnob with celebrities and tycoons at this four-story brownstone landmark, a former speakeasy that first opened on December 31, 1929. Chef Erik Blauberg tries—and succeeds—in satisfying everyone, retaining signature dishes like the famous "21" burger, game potpie, and other New American food, while also offering more eclectic fare, such as rotisserie truffle chicken with potato fig gratin. Service is seamless throughout. ✉ *21 W. 52nd St., between 5th and 6th Aves., Midtown West* ☎ *212/582–7200* ⌂ *Reservations essential* ⌂ *Jacket and tie* ▭ *AE, D, DC, MC, V* ⊘ *Closed Sun. No lunch Sat.* Ⓜ *Subway: B, D, F, V to 47–50th Sts./Rockefeller Center.*

$$–$$$$ ✕ **District.** The plush design of this contemporary American restaurant in the Muse Hotel incorporates clever stage references meant to evoke the (theater) district for which it is named. Chef Robert Curran creates quite grown-up food, like gnocchi soufflé with fontina cheese and truffle cream, pepper-crusted venison loin with chestnut, spaetzle, and gin sauce, or brick-pressed garlic chicken with a forest mushroom crepe. A pretheater three-course $48 prix fixe is available. ✉ *130 W. 46th St., between 5th and 6th Aves., Midtown West* ☎ *212/485–2999* ⌂ *Reservations essential* ▭ *AE, D, DC, MC, V* Ⓜ *Subway: R, W to 49th St.*

$$–$$$ ✕ **Beacon.** Chef Waldy Malouf has fully established himself as a past-master of grilling in this multilevel restaurant, where meat, fish, and even vegetables are seared and roasted to a succulent crisp juiciness in enormous wood-fired ovens. Just about everything on the seasonal menu is delectable, but particularly delicious are lamb T-bone, Catskill mountain trout, and dry-aged sirloin with red wine and shallot confit. Although the atmosphere is midtown business, the simple, direct, almost rustic food delights people from all walks of life. ✉ *25 W. 56th St., between 5th and 6th Aves., Midtown West* ☎ *212/332–0500* ▤ *AE, D, MC, V* ⊘ *No lunch weekends* Ⓜ *Subway: R, W to 5th Ave.*

American–Casual

¢ ✕ **Island Burgers and Shakes.** Belly-busting burgers rule at this bright and cheery café with multicolor round tables and funky chairs. Every sandwich can be ordered with grilled chicken instead of the usual beef patty, but true believers stick to the real thing and choose from a staggering variety of toppings. If you're in the mood for even more calories, the tempting selection of shakes is extremely difficult to resist. The only drawback is that there are no french fries—you'll have to settle for "dirty potato chips." ✉ *766 9th Ave., between W. 51st and W. 52nd Sts., Midtown West* ☎ *212/307–7934* ▤ *No credit cards* Ⓜ *Subway: C, E to 50th St.*

Barbecue

☺ $–$$ ✕ **Virgil's Real BBQ.** Neon, wood, and Formica set the scene at this massive roadhouse in the theater district. Start with stuffed jalapeños or—especially—unbelievably succulent BBQ chicken wings. Then, what the hell: go for the "pig out"—a rack of pork ribs, Texas hot links, pulled pork, rack of lamb, chicken, and, of course, more. It's that kind of place. There are also five domestic microbrews on tap and a good list of top beers from around the world. ✉ *152 W. 44th St., between 6th Ave. and Broadway, Midtown West* ☎ *212/921–9494* ✍ *Reservations essential* ▤ *AE, MC, V* Ⓜ *Subway: N, Q, R, S, W, 1, 2, 3, 7, 9 to 42nd St./Times Sq.*

Brazilian

★ $$$$ ✕ **Churrascaria Plataforma.** This sprawling, boisterous shrine to meat, with its all-you-can-eat prix-fixe menu, is best experienced with a group of ravenous friends, preferably teenaged football players. A *caipirinha* (sugarcane liquor and lime) will kick you off nicely, then hit the vast salad bar groaning with vegetables, meats, cheeses, and hot tureens of *feijoada* (beans, pork, greens, and manioc). But restrain yourself—there's an ongoing parade of all manner of grilled meats and poultry, brought to the table on long skewers until you beg for mercy. ✉ *316 W. 49th St., between 8th and 9th Aves., Midtown West* ☎ *212/245–0505* ✍ *Reservations essential* ▤ *AE, DC, MC, V* Ⓜ *Subway: C, E to 50th St.*

Cafés

¢ ✕ **Cupcake Café.** Intensely buttery, magnificently decorated cakes and cupcakes, as well as donuts, pies, coffee cake, and hearty soup, are worth the trek to this funky spot on the western flank of the Port Authority Bus Terminal (a somewhat sketchy area). ✉ *522 9th Ave., at W. 39th*

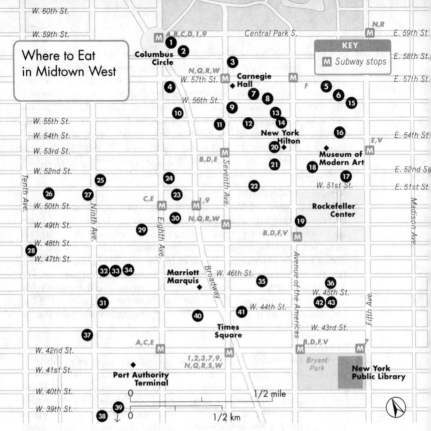

Where to Eat in Midtown West

W. 60th St.

W. 59th St.

Central Park S.

E. 59th St

Ⓜ A,B,C,D,1,9

Columbus Circle

E. 58th St.

N,R Ⓜ

N,Q,R,W Ⓜ

E. 57th St.

W. 57th St.

Carnegie Hall

F

E. 57th St

Ⓜ

W. 56th St.

W. 55th St.

W. 54th St.

New York Hilton

E. 54th St

W. 53rd St.

E,V

W. 52nd St.

B,D,E Ⓜ

Museum of Modern Art

E. 52nd S

Seventh Ave.

E. 51st St

W. 51st St.

Rockefeller Center

W. 50th St.

C,E Ⓜ

Tenth Ave.

Ninth Ave.

Eighth Ave.

Ⓜ 1,9

W. 49th St.

N,Q,R,W Ⓜ

B,D,F,V Ⓜ

W. 48th St.

W. 47th St.

Madison Ave.

Marriott Marquis

W. 46th St.

Broadway

W. 45th St.

W. 44th St.

Avenue of the Americas

Fifth Ave.

Times Square

W. 43rd St.

A,C,E Ⓜ

W. 42nd St.

B,D,F,V Ⓜ

Ⓜ

Bryant Park

New York Public Library

W. 41st St.

1,2,3,7,9, N,Q,R,S,W Ⓜ

Port Authority Terminal

W. 40th St.

W. 39th St.

0   1/2 mile

0   1/2 km

St., Midtown West ☎ *212/465–1530* ▭ *No credit cards* Ⓜ *Subway: A, C, E to 42nd St.*

Chinese

$–$$$ ✕ **Joe's Shanghai.** Joe opened his first Shanghai restaurant in Queens, but, buoyed by the accolades accorded his steamed soup dumplings—magically filled with a rich, fragrant broth and a pork or pork-and-crab-meat mixture—he saw fit to open in Manhattan's Chinatown, and then here in midtown. Menu highlights include turnip shortcakes and dried bean curd salad to start, and succulent braised pork shoulder, ropey home-made Shanghai noodles, and traditional lion's head—rich pork meat-balls braised in brown sauce—to follow. ✉ *24 W. 56th St., between 5th and 6th Aves., Midtown West* ☎ *212/333–3868* ▭ *AE, DC, MC, V* Ⓜ *Subway: F to 57th St.*

¢–$$ ✕ **Grand Sichuan International.** This regional Chinese restaurant serves a vast menu of specialties you probably won't find anywhere else. The emphasis is on fiery Sichuan (Szechuan) cooking, but Cantonese, Hunan, Shanghai, and even American Chinese food are represented (a handy treatise and guide on Chinese food comes with the menu). Spicy dan dan noodles, shredded potatoes in vinegar sauce, crab soup dumplings, minced pork with cellophane noodles or fermented green beans, and sautéed loofah are among the hauntingly delicious dishes. ✉ *745 9th Ave., between W. 50th and W. 51st Sts., Midtown West* ☎ *212/582–2288* ▭ *AE, MC, V* Ⓜ *Subway: C, E to 50th St.*

Contemporary

$$$$ ✕ **Town.** It's difficult to decide which is more soigné in this bi-level restaurant: the design, the food, or the crowd. Ubiquitous architect David Rockwell has created a contemporary restaurant with a truly in-ternational feel. Geoffrey Zakarian's cooking is every bit as sophisti-cated as the environment. The prix-fixe menu offers such dishes as Escargot risotto, cod in porcini puree, quail baked over lusty marcona almonds with griddled foie gras, and tender duck steak with buckwheat pilaf. All are intricate exercises in culinary craft. ✉ *15 W. 56th St., be-tween 5th and 6th Aves., Midtown West* ☎ *212/582–4445* ✍ *Reser-vations essential* ▭ *AE, D, DC, MC, V* Ⓜ *Subway: F to 57th St.*

Continental

$$–$$$$ ✕ **Petrossian.** After a massive restoration to the edifice of the historic Alwyn Court Building, Petrossian now closely resembles a haute Parisian restaurant. In addition to the luxurious caviars and silky smoked salmon, Chef Michael Lipp will pan roast a wild sturgeon that gave you her eggs, or roast sea scallops and plate them with seared foie gras. For dessert, lighten up with candied ginger panna cotta. The café next door serves a selection of creative treats—plus caviar, of course. ✉ *182 W. 58th St., at 7th Ave., Midtown West* ☎ *212/245–2214* ✍ *Reservations essen-tial* ▭ *AE, DC, MC, V* Ⓜ *Subway: F, N, R, Q, W to 57th St.*

Cuban

$–$$$ ✕ **Victor's Café.** The heady aroma of authentic Cuban cooking greets you as you enter this Technicolor restaurant, a neighborhood fixture since 1963. The high-back booths and rattan chairs evoke golden-age movies set in Old Havana. Better than average, the food is a contemporary transcription of Cuban, Puerto Rican, and Latin dishes, such as hearty adobo, paella, adobo-rubbed prime steak, and suckling pig marinated and roasted on a plantain leaf. The staff couldn't be friendlier. ⊠ *236 W. 52nd St., between Broadway and 8th Ave., Midtown West* 🕾 *212/ 586–7714* 🖃 *AE, DC, MC, V* Ⓜ *Subway: C, E to 50th St.*

Delicatessens

$–$$ ✕ **Carnegie Deli.** Although not what it once was, this no-nonsense deli is still a favorite with out-of-towners. The portions are so huge you feel like a child in some surreal culinary fairy tale. The matzo balls could eat Chicago, the knishes hang off the edge of the plates, and some combination sandwiches are so tall they have to be held together with bamboo skewers. Don't miss the cheesecake, to our palates the best (and, of course, biggest) in the city. ⊠ *854 7th Ave., at W. 55th St., Midtown West* 🕾 *212/757–2245* 🖃 *No credit cards* Ⓜ *Subway: B, D, C, E to 7th Ave.; N, R, Q, W to 57th St.*

Ethiopian

¢–$ ✕ **Meskerem.** The tasty Ethiopian delicacies offered in this Hell's Kitchen storefront include *kitfo* (spiced ground steak), which you can order raw, rare, or well-done, and *yebeg alecha,* tender pieces of lamb marinated in Ethiopian butter flavored with curry, rosemary, and an herb called *kosart,* and then sautéed with fresh ginger and a bit more curry. The vegetarian combination, served on *injera* (a yeasty flat bread used as a utensil to sop up the food) is a seriously good deal. ⊠ *468 W. 47th St., near 10th Ave., Midtown West* 🕾 *212/664–0520* 🖃 *AE, DC, MC, V* Ⓜ *Subway: C, E to 50th St.*

French

$$$$ ✕ **Alain Ducasse.** Created by France's most copiously decorated chef, this shrine to French cuisine is an exercise in unbridled luxury. If you manage to reserve a table in the hushed 65-seat dining room, it's yours for the entire evening, and you'll need the time to navigate through some of the most luscious food in town. Let sommelier André Compeyre partner your dishes with exquisite wines. ⊠ *Essex House, 155 W. 58th St., between 6th and 7th Aves., Midtown West* 🕾 *212/265–7300* ⌕ *Reservations essential* 🏛 *Jacket and tie* 🖃 *AE, D, DC, MC, V* ☻ *Closed Sun. No lunch* Ⓜ *Subway: B, D, C, E to 7th Ave.; N, R, Q, W to 57th St.*

$$$$ ✕ **Le Bernardin.** Owner Maguy LeCoze presides over the plush, teak-panel
Fodor's Choice dining room at this trend-setting French seafood restaurant, and chef-
★ partner Eric Ripert works magic with anything that swims—preferring at times not to cook it at all. Deceptively simple dishes such as poached lobster in rich coconut-ginger soup or crispy spiced black bass in a Peking duck bouillon are typical of his style. There's no beating Le Bernardin for thrilling French cuisine, seafood or otherwise, coupled with some of the finest desserts in town. ⊠ *155 W. 51st St., between 6th and 7th Aves., Midtown West* 🕾 *212/489–1515* ⌕ *Reservations essential* 🏛 *Jacket required* 🖃 *AE, DC, MC, V* ☻ *Closed Sun. No lunch Sat.* Ⓜ *Subway: R, W to 49th St.; B, D, F, V to 47th–50th Sts.*

$$–$$$ ✕ **db bistro moderne.** Daniel Boulud's "casual bistro" (it's neither, actually) consists of two elegantly appointed rooms. The menu is organized by the French names of seasonal ingredients—lobster (*homard*), tuna (*thon*), and mushroom (*champignon*), *par exemple*. Within each category, appetizers and main courses are listed. There has been quite a fuss made over the $29 hamburger, available at lunch and dinner. But considering it is gloriously stuffed with braised short ribs, foie gras, and black truffles, it's almost a bargain. ⊠ *55 W. 44th St., between 5th and 6th Aves., Midtown West* ☎ *212/391–5353* ⌂ *Reservations essential* ▭ *AE, MC, V* ⊘ *No lunch Sun.* Ⓜ *Subway: B, D, F, V to 42nd Sts.*

$$–$$$ ╳ **Triomphe.** You have to pretty sure of yourself to name your restaurant Triomphe, but indeed the team behind this jewel box in the Iroquois Hotel has triumphed. The intimate dining room is pleasing but unfussy, and chef Steve Zobel's focused menu is bold and ambitious yet understated. Appetizers include such lusciousness as pan-seared sea scallops with porcini mushroom foie gras butter, and entrées are the likes of lamb rack with foie gras–stuffed prunes (known as French kisses). ⊠ *49 W. 44th St., between 5th and 6th Aves., Midtown West* ☎ *212/ 453–4233* ⌂ *Reservations essential* ▭ *AE, D, MC, V* ⊘ *Closed Sun. No lunch Sat.* Ⓜ *Subway: B, D, F, V to 47th–50th Sts.*

$–$$$ ╳ **Seppi's.** With a prime location just steps from Carnegie Hall and City Center, reasonable prices, and a 2 AM closing time, this luscious French bistro attracts a devoted clientele, including more than a few celebrities. Tender tarte flambée (Alsatian pizza) is carved into manageable finger-length rectangles, escargots are given their classic—and rapidly vanishing—presentation, and steak au poivre is as good as it gets, with deeply beefy gravy. All this and much more—including 15 desserts— are served until closing. ⊠ *123 W. 56th St., between 6th and 7th Aves., Midtown West* ☎ *212/453–4233* ⌂ *Reservations suggested* ▭ *AE, D, MC, V* ⊘ *No lunch Sat.* Ⓜ *Subway: B, D, E to 7th Ave., F, N, Q, R, W to 57th St.*

¢–$$ ╳ **Marseille.** A fetching brasserie outfitted with dark cherry leather banquettes beautifully showcases the soulful Mediterranean–North African cooking of Andy D'Amico. Begin with mezes (think tapas), like juicy *merguez* sausages or white anchovies rolled into pinwheels with *piquillo* peppers. Grilled octopus is deeply flavored, and bouillabaisse is classically prepared, with four North Atlantic fillets and a nice garlicky rouille on the side. Service is skillful. The place is often mobbed before and after theater, usually restful from 8 to 10:30, but always intensely delicious. ⊠ *630 9th Ave., at W. 44th St., Midtown West* ☎ *212/333– 3410* ⌂ *Reservations essential* ▭ *AE, D, MC, V* Ⓜ *Subway: A, C, E to 42nd St.*

German

¢–$ ╳ **Hallo Berlin.** When nothing but bratwurst will do, lunge for this Hell's Kitchen café. In addition to more than 10 varieties of "brats," accompanied by traditional German side dishes such as sauerkraut, spaetzle, or particularly addictive panfried potatoes. The atmosphere is low-budget Berlin beer garden, and the low, low prices match the lack of pretension. There are other authentic dishes on the menu, but none can compete with a sausage paired with a cold pint of German beer. ⊠ *402 W. 51st St., between 9th and 10th Aves., Midtown West* ☎ *212/541– 6248* ▭ *No credit cards* ⊘ *No lunch Sun.* Ⓜ *Subway: C, E to 50th St.*

Greek

$$–$$$$ ✕ **Estiatorio Milos.** This dramatic, dazzling restaurant flaunts white-washed walls, table umbrellas, and sultry European diners. Classic spreads—*tzatziki* (yogurt–cucumber), *tarama* (smoked carp roe–olive oil–lemon), and *scordalia* (almonds–garlic)—make a delicious appetizer. If you're feeling flush, select from the glimmering display of fresh Mediterranean seafood flown in every day. Your choice will be weighed (fair warning: you pay by the pound), grilled whole, and filleted tableside. For dessert, don't pass up thick Greek-style goat's milk yogurt with thyme honey. ✉ *125 W. 55th St., between 6th and 7th Aves., Midtown West* ☎ *212/245–7400* ♿ *Reservations essential* 🚪 *AE, D, MC, V* Ⓜ *Subway: F, N, R, Q, W to 57th St.*

$$–$$$ ✕ **Molyvos.** Fresh ingredients, lusty flavors, fine olive oil, and fragrant herbs emerge from Jim Botsacos's marvelous kitchen at this upscale taverna. Start with a bang: *saganaki* (fried *kefalotiri* cheese), or a lump crab cake aching with flavor. Seasonal entrées include traditional Greek dishes, such as a perfected moussaka, lamb *yuvetsi* (marinated lamb shanks braised in a clay pot), and cabbage *dolmades* (cabbage stuffed with ground lamb in a lemon-dill sauce). The baklava will make you completely rethink that poor abused dessert. ✉ *871 7th Ave., between W. 55th and W. 56th Sts., Midtown West* ☎ *212/582–7500* ♿ *Reservations essential* 🚪 *AE, D, DC, MC, V* Ⓜ *Subway: F, N, R, Q, W to 57th St.*

Italian

$$–$$$$ ✕ **Abboccato.** Making a delightful attempt to convey the wide regional Italian palate in its near entirety, Abboccato is the third marvelous restaurant to be opened by the Livanos family (after Oceana and Molyvos). There are some highly unusual—in this country—dishes, like Umbrian quail, boned and stuffed with mortadella, formed into a ball, breaded, and fried. The richest possible carbonara sauce features creamy duck eggs and duck prosciutto. Finish with satiny panna cotta, dotted with pomegranate seeds and juice. ✉ *136 W. 55th St., between 6th and 7th Aves., Midtown West* ☎ *212/265–4000* ♿ *Reservations essential* 🚪 *AE, DC, MC, V* Ⓜ *Subway: N, R to 57th St.*

$$–$$$$ ✕ **Osteria del Circo.** Opened by the sons of celebrity restaurateur Sirio Maccioni, this less-formal restaurant celebrates the Tuscan cooking of their Mamma Egi. The contemporary menu offers a wide selection and includes some traditional Tuscan specialties, such as Egi's ricotta-and-spinach-filled ravioli, tossed in butter and sage and gratinéed with imported Parmesan, and a stew of prawns, cuttlefish, octopus, monkfish, clams, and mussels. Don't miss the fanciful Circo desserts, especially the filled *bomboloncini* donuts. ✉ *120 W. 55th St., between 6th and 7th Aves., Midtown West* ☎ *212/265–3636* ♿ *Reservations essential* 🚪 *AE, DC, MC, V* ☉ *No lunch Sun.* Ⓜ *Subway: F, N, R, Q, W to 57th St.*

$$–$$$$ ✕ **San Domenico.** A dedicated ambassador of authentic Italian cuisine, dapper owner Tony May presides over his lush dining room, where gauzy drapes swathe the wraparound windows that gaze onto Central Park. Don't miss chef Odette Fada's signature truffle-butter-dribbled ravioli pocketing a quivering egg yolk filling. Reconstituted salt cod is whipped into submission with house olive oil, and served with polenta *crostini*. Goat—in line to be the hot "new" ingredient on next year's menus—is done three delicious ways: pureed, fried, and braised on the bone. ✉ *240 Central Park S, between Broadway and 7th Ave., Midtown West* ☎ *212/265–5959* ⌕ *Reservations essential* ⌂ *Jacket required* 🖃 *AE, DC, MC, V* ⊘ *No lunch weekends* Ⓜ *Subway: A, B, C, D, 1, 2 to 59th St.–Columbus Circle.*

$–$$$$ ✕ **Baldoria.** It's impossible to get into Frank Pellegrino's restaurant Rao's, an institution in Harlem, so try Frank Jr.'s theater district edition. The bi-level restaurant is almost 10 times the size of Rao's, but the atmosphere is still homey and personal. Seared octopus is plated with broccoli rabe, cippolini onions, and balsamic reduction. Fluffy gnocchi are dappled with a ground veal, pork, and beef tomato sauce. And the lemon chicken in a red vinegar, oregano, and garlic sauce is even tastier than Dad's uptown. ✉ *249 W. 49th St., between Broadway and 8th Ave., Midtown West* ☎ *212/582–0460* ⌕ *Reservations essential* 🖃 *AE, D, MC, V* ⊘ *No lunch weekends* Ⓜ *Subway: C, E to 50th St.*

🐣 **$–$$$$** ✕ **Carmine's.** Savvy New Yorkers line up early for the affordable family-style meals (read: massive portions to share) at this large, busy eatery. There are no reservations taken for parties of fewer than six people after 7 PM, but those who wait are rewarded with mountains of such popular, toothsome items as fried calamari, linguine with white clam sauce, chicken parmigiana, and veal saltimbocca. You'll inevitably order too much, but most of the food tastes just as wonderful the next day. ✉ *200 W. 44th St., between Broadway and 8th Ave., Midtown West* ☎ *212/221–3800* 🖃 *AE, D, DC, MC, V* Ⓜ *Subway: N, Q, R, S, W, 1, 2, 3, 7 to 42nd St./Times Sq.*

$$–$$$ ✕ **Barbetta.** Operated by the same family since it opened in 1906, Barbetta offers a uniquely authentic Piedmontese experience in a throwback of a dining room that evokes the tired, old-world charm of Turin. The vast menu highlights dishes from the restaurant's past, as well as traditional Piedmontese cooking. Pasta, like the eggy tajarin, and risotto stand out. A beautiful garden affords a lovely summertime setting. Incidentally, Barbetta claims to be the first restaurant in New York to serve white truffles, in 1962. ✉ *321 W. 46th St., between 8th and 9th Aves., Midtown West* ☎ *212/246–9171* 🖃 *AE, D, DC, MC, V* ⊘ *Closed Sun. and Mon.* Ⓜ *Subway: A, C, E to 42nd St.*

$$–$$$ ✕ **Becco.** An ingenious concept makes Becco a prime Restaurant Row choice for time-constrained theatergoers. There are two pricing scenarios: one includes an all-you-can-eat selection of antipasti and three pastas served hot out of pans that waiters circulate around the dining room; the other adds a generous entrée. The selection changes daily but often includes gnocchi, fresh ravioli, and something in a cream sauce. The entrées include braised veal shank, rack of lamb, and various fish. ✉ *355 W. 46th St., between 8th and 9th Aves., Midtown West* ☎ *212/397–7597* ⌕ *Reservations essential* 🖃 *AE, DC, MC, V* Ⓜ *Subway: A, C, E to 42nd St.*

$–$$$ ✕ **Acqua Pazza.** Endlessly chic and sexy, Acqua Pazza attracts all sorts of clever people. The kitchen has widened its focus from a nearly all-seafood menu to include meat and poultry, as well as some highly imaginative pastas, like espresso-flavor tagliolini with rock shrimp and porcini mushrooms. For a Milanese presentation, a large veal rib chop is flattened, breaded, and plated with fluttery arugula, tomatoes, and buffalo moz-zarella—quite a delicious bargain at $24. The wine list is especially user-friendly. ⊠ *36 W. 52nd St., between 5th and 6th Aves., Midtown West* ☎ *212/582–6900* ◬ *Reservations essential* ▤ *AE, D, DC, MC, V* Ⓜ *Subway: B, D, F, V to 47th–50th Sts., Rockefeller Center.*

$–$$$ ✕ **Azalea.** Cheek-by-jowl with the giant Gershwin Theater, gracefully appointed Azalea presents the cuisines of Parma (meats, milks, and cheeses) and the Amalfi Coast (seafood and citruses). Short rigatoni are stuffed with beautifully seasoned ground veal, dribbled with a white truf-fle cream, and finished with toasted walnuts. Thick slices of roasted duck breast are fanned around a fat disk of grilled polenta. Finish jubilantly with warm beignets filled with lemon crème anglaise drizzled with honey and bittersweet chocolate syrup. ⊠ *224 W. 51st St., between Broad-way and 8th Ave., Midtown West* ☎ *212/262–0105* ▤ *AE, D, DC, MC, V* Ⓜ *Subway: R, W to 49th St.*

✕ 🕙 $–$$$ ✕ **Il Gattopardo.** As sleek and poised as the leopard it is named for, this Southern Italian newcomer attracts plenty of soigné regulars. Rare and juicy beef–veal meatballs swathed and braised in savoy cabbage leaves are a marvelous signature dish and a must. Tender house-made pastas are imaginatively sauced. Thick veal scallops are bundled around egg-plant and caciocavallo cheese for great depth of flavor. Finish with Si-cilian cassata, steeped in semifreddo: Christmas in your mouth! ⊠ *33 W. 54th St., between 5th and 6th Aves., Midtown West* ☎ *212/246–0412* ▤ *AE, DC, MC, V* Ⓜ *Subway: N, Q, R, B, to 57th St.*

$–$$$ ✕ **Remi.** A Venetian sensibility pervades this stylish restaurant, with its skylit atrium, blue-and-white stripe banquettes, Venetian glass chande-liers, and a soaring room-length mural of the city of canals. And its Vene-tian cuisine is equally stylish: fresh sardines make a lovely beginning, with their contrasting toasted pine nut and golden raisin sauce, and you can't go wrong with the luscious pastas, expertly prepared rack of lamb, or any of the wonderful desserts. ⊠ *145 W. 53rd St., between 6th and 7th Aves., Midtown West* ☎ *212/581–4242* ◬ *Reservations essential* ▤ *AE, DC, MC, V* ⊙ *No lunch weekends* Ⓜ *Subway: E, V to 5th Ave.–53rd St.*

¢–$ ✕ **Mangia.** Office workers looking for out-of-the-ordinary takeout come here for sandwiches and salads that include fresh mozzarella, prosci-utto, focaccia, grilled eggplant, and sun-dried tomatoes. In the sit-down restaurant upstairs, small pizzas and pastas are a regular feature, and special dishes might include grilled herb-crusted tilapia with tomato pesto or veal Milanese. The restaurant offers one of the most reasonably priced lunches in midtown. ⊠ *50 W. 57th St., between 5th and 6th Aves., Midtown West* ☎ *212/582–5882* ▤ *AE, D, DC, MC, V* ⊙ *Closed weekends. No dinner* Ⓜ *Subway: F to 57th St.*

Japanese

$$$$ ✕ **Sugiyama.** Acquaint yourself with the Japanese style of eating known as *kaiseki*, a meal of small portions presented in a ritualized order, at this charming prix-fixe-only restaurant. First timers should order the *omakase* (chef's tasting) to appreciate the true breadth of the genre. It may start with a wild mountain plum floating in a glassy cube of gelatin, and proceed to a gurgling pot of blowfish or to sweet lobster to be cooked on a hot stone. The experience is exhilarating. ⊠ *251 W. 55th St., between Broadway and 8th Ave., Midtown West* ☎ *212/956–0670* ▤ *AE, D, MC, V* ✆ *Closed Sun. and Mon. No lunch* Ⓜ *Subway: A, B, C, D, 1, 2, 3, 9 to 59th St.–Columbus Circle.*

Kosher

$–$$$ ✕ **Le Marais.** The appetizing display of meats and terrines at the entrance, the bare wood floors, tables covered with butcher paper, the French wall posters, and maroon banquettes will remind you of a Parisian bistro. Yet the clientele (mostly male) is strictly kosher (as is the food), and they don't speak French. Start with pan-seared sweetbreads with wild mushrooms, and follow with perfect steak au poivre. The accompanying fries are perfect. ⊠ *150 W. 46th St., between 6th and 7th Aves., Midtown West* ☎ *212/869–0900* ▤ *AE, MC, V* ✆ *Closed Sat. No dinner Fri.* Ⓜ *Subway: R, W to 49th St.*

Mediterranean

$$–$$$ ✕ **Josephs Citarella.** Cozily ensconced in a luxurious four-story space, the restaurant now showcases the pan-culinary wiles of chef Bill Yosses, Citarella's brilliant former pastry chef who also soars in the savory arena. Citarella's stores around Manhattan are cherished for their wrigglingly fresh fish, and the restaurant offers gorgeous seafood preparations, but Yosses has a deft touch with meat as well, like his breaded veal chop fluttered with arugula and cherry tomatoes. And he still makes some of the best soufflés in town. ⊠ *1240 6th Ave., at 49th St., Midtown West* ☎ *212/332–1515* ⌖ *Reservations essential* ▤ *AE, D, DC, MC, V* Ⓜ *Subway: B, D, F, V to 47th–50th Sts./Rockefeller Center.*

Russian

$$$–$$$$ ✕ **Firebird.** Eight dining rooms full of objets d'art and period antiques lie within these two brownstones resembling a pre-Revolutionary St. Petersburg mansion. Staples of the regional cuisine range from caviar and *zakuska* (assorted Russian hors d'oeuvres) to porcini-crusted monkfish, hot-smoked salmon with saffron orzo and herb salad, and beet borscht with duck, beef, smoked pork, and mushroom pirogi. Great desserts (an assortment of Russian cookies steals the show) and an extraordinary vodka selection are giddy indulgences. ⊠ *365 W. 46th St., between 8th and 9th Aves., Midtown West* ☎ *212/586–0244* ⌖ *Reservations essential* ▤ *AE, DC, MC, V* ✆ *Closed Mon. No lunch Sun.* Ⓜ *Subway: A, C, E to 42nd St.*

$$–$$$ ✕ **Esca.** Mario Batali's Esca, Italian for "bait," lures diners in with delectable raw preparations called *cruda*—tilefish with orange and Sardinian oil or pink snapper with a sprinkle of crunchy red clay salt—and hooks them with such entrées as whole, salt-crusted *branzino* (sea bass), or *bucatini* pasta with spicy baby octopus. Batali's partner, Joe Bastianich, is in charge of the wine cellar, so expect an adventurous list of esoteric Italian bottles. ⊠ *402 W. 43rd St., at 9th Ave., Midtown West* ☎ *212/564–7272* ⌖ *Reservations essential* ▤ *AE, DC, MC, V* ✆ *No lunch Sun.* Ⓜ *Subway: A, C, E to 42nd St.*

Steak

$$$$ ✕ **Uncle Jack's Steakhouse.** Surpassing even its celebrated flagship restaurant in Bayside, Queens, Uncle Jack's soars directly into the pantheon of the best steakhouses in Manhattan. As in most great steak houses, you can feel the testosterone throbbing all through the place. The space is vast and gorgeously appointed, and service is swift and focused. USDA Prime steaks are dry-aged for 21 days. Australian lobster tails are so enormous they have to be served carved, yet the flesh is meltingly tender. ⊠ *440 9th Ave., between 34th and 35th Sts., Midtown West* ☎ *212/244–0005* ⌂ *Reservations essential* ☰ *AE, DC, MC, V* ☉ *Closed Sun. No lunch weekends* Ⓜ *Subway: A, C, E to 34th St.*

$$–$$$$ ✕ **Ben Benson's Steak House.** Among the most venerable steak houses around, Ben Benson's feels like a clubby hunting lodge. The gracefully choreographed, intensely focused staff will bring you only the finest dry-aged USDA-graded prime meats and only the freshest seafood, all classically prepared, teeming with familiar and beloved flavors. All the trimmings are ravishing, too: perfect creamed spinach, sizzling onion rings, and decadent hash-browns are essential. Power lunches were practically invented here; just being in the place makes you feel important. ⊠ *123 W. 52nd St., between 6th and 7th Aves., Midtown West* ☎ *212/581–8888* ⌂ *Reservations essential* ☰ *AE, DC, MC, V* ☉ *No lunch Sat. and Sun.* Ⓜ *Subway: B, D, F, V to 47th–50th Sts./Rockefeller Center.*

$–$$$$ ✕ **Palm West.** They may have added tablecloths, but it would take more than that to hide the brusque, no-nonsense nature of this West Side branch of the legendary steak house. The steak is always impeccable, and the lobsters are so big—4 pounds and up—there may not be room at the table for such classic side dishes as rich creamed spinach. The "half and half" side combination of cottage-fried potatoes and fried onions is particularly addictive. ⊠ *250 W. 50th St., between Broadway and 8th Ave., Midtown West* ☎ *212/333–7256* ⌂ *Reservations essential* ☰ *AE, DC, MC, V* ☉ *No lunch weekends* Ⓜ *Subway: F, N, R, Q, W to 57th St.*

MIDTOWN EAST

Power brokers like to seal their deals over lunch on the East Side, so that means more than a few suits and ties at the restaurants during the day. At night the streets are relatively deserted, but the restaurants are filled with people celebrating success over some of the finest, most expensive, and most formal food in town.

American

$$$$ ✕ **Four Seasons.** The landmark Seagram Building houses one of America's most famous restaurants. The stark Grill Room, birthplace of the power lunch, has one of the best bars in New York. Illuminated trees and a gurgling Carrara marble pool characterize the more romantic Pool Room. The menu changes seasonally; there's a $55 prix-fixe pretheater dinner; otherwise, the menu is among the priciest in town. You can't go wrong with Dover sole, truffled bison, or crispy duck, which features a tableside final preparation. ⊠ *99 E. 52nd St., between Park and Lexington Aves., Midtown East* ☎ *212/754–9494* ⌂ *Reservations essen-*

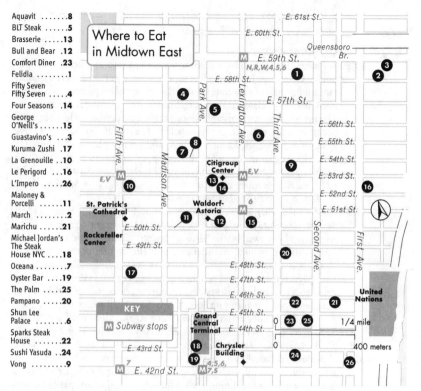

Where to Eat in Midtown East

KEY

Ⓜ Subway stops

tial 🏛 *Jacket required* 🖃 *AE, DC, MC, V* ⊘ *Closed Sun. No lunch Sat.* Ⓜ *Subway: E, F, 6 to 51st St.–Lexington Ave.*

American-Casual

¢–$ ✕ **Comfort Diner.** If you're in search of a quick, casual, and satisfying meal, true to its name, Comfort Diner is more than happy to oblige, with a menu of such deeply American fare as buffalo wings, Caesar salad, grilled chicken club sandwich, macaroni and cheese, meat loaf, and burgers. The pies and cakes are baked fresh daily. The chrome and terrazzo may look a bit faded, but at least the price is right. Prepare to wait on line for the popular weekend brunch. ⊠ *214 E. 45th St., between 2nd and 3rd Aves., Midtown East* 🕾 *212/867–4555* 🗏 *Reservations not accepted* 🖃 *D, DC, MC, V* Ⓜ *Subway: S, 4, 5, 6, 7 to 42nd St.–Grand Central.*

Chinese

$–$$$ ✕ **Shun Lee Palace.** If you want inexpensive Cantonese food without pretensions, head to Chinatown; but if you prefer to be pampered and don't mind spending a lot of money, this is the place. The cuisine is absolutely classic Chinese. Beijing pan-fried dumplings make a good starter, and rack of lamb Szechuan style is a popular entrée. Beijing duck is sure to please. ⊠ *155 E. 55th St., between Lexington and 3rd Aves., Midtown*

East ☎ 212/371–8844 ⚛ *Reservations essential* ▤ *AE, DC, MC, V*
Ⓜ *Subway: N, R, W, 4, 5, 6 to 59th St.–Lexington Ave.*

Contemporary

$$$$ ✕ **March.** This romantic restaurant is tucked into an enchanting town house. Co-owner Joseph Scalice supervises the polished service and the intriguing wine list that complement the cuisine of his partner, chef Wayne Nish, master of classical French technique with a strong Asian influence. The prix-fixe menu is organized into tasting categories. Select any number of courses, then choose from a list of seasonal dishes, such as five-spice salmon with wild mushrooms, and luxury plates, like duck foie gras with Indian spices and port wine apple and raisin puree. ✉ *405 E. 58th St., between 1st Ave. and Sutton Pl., Midtown East* ☎ *212/754–6272* ⚛ *Reservations essential* ▤ *AE, DC, MC, V* Ⓜ *Subway: N, R, W, 4, 5, 6 to 59th St.–Lexington Ave.*

$$–$$$$ ✕ **Fifty Seven Fifty Seven.** I. M. Pei's strikingly sleek Four Seasons Hotel houses this restaurant and a sophisticated adjacent bar. Even locals come in to be wowed by the 22-foot coffered ceilings, inlaid maple floors, onyx-studded bronze chandeliers, and the contemporary American menu. Creative interpretations such as creamless mushroom bisque with pistachio essence and poached quail eggs, or wild salmon with oven-dried zucchini and tomato-bacon vinaigrette, or barbecued braised pork belly with pickled autumn vegetables will enthrall weary palates. ✉ *57 E. 57th St., between Madison and Park Aves., Midtown East* ☎ *212/ 758–5757* ⚛ *Reservations essential* ▤ *AE, DC, MC, V* Ⓜ *Subway: N, R, W, 4, 5, 6 to 59th St.–Lexington Ave.*

$$–$$$$ ✕ **Maloney & Porcelli.** Known for generous portions of whimsical American food, this comfortable restaurant (named for the owner's lawyers) is ideal when you're dining with a hungry crowd of people (especially men) who can't decide where to eat. Lunge for a huge, juicy crackling pork shank served on a bed of poppy-seed sauerkraut with a Mason jar of tangy, homemade "Firecracker" jalapeño-spiced apple sauce. "Drunken doughnuts," served warm with three small pots of liqueur-flavor jam, are one of the fun desserts. ✉ *37 E. 50th St., between Madison and Park Aves., Midtown East* ☎ *212/750–2233* ⚛ *Reservations essential* ▤ *AE, DC, MC, V* Ⓜ *Subway: 6 to 51st St.–Lexington Ave.*

Eclectic

🔥 $$–$$$$ ✕ **Guastavino's.** Under the Queensboro Bridge lies this famously soaring space that flaunts the pristine tile work of Raphael Guastavino, and now the marvelous cooking of celebrity chef Michael Lomonaco. Begin with a selection of East and West Coast oysters and marvel at the differences, then have a generous quivering slab of seared foie gras with apple chutney. All the fish entrées are superlative, but roasted chicken also achieves perfection. Finish with lusty butterscotch bread pudding. ✉ *409 E. 59th St., between 1st Ave. and York Ave., Midtown East* ☎ *212/ 980–2455* ▤ *AE, DC, MC, V* Ⓜ *Subway: N, R, W, 4, 5, 6 to 59th St.–Lexington Ave.*

French

$$$$ ✕ **La Grenouille.** This is such a quintessential Manhattan French restaurant that it almost feels like a retro theme restaurant. It's also one of

the few remaining in town. The menu presents a $87 menu of three courses (with tempting supplements that fatten your bill). Choices include lobster-tarragon ravioli to start, followed by grilled Dover sole with mustard sauce, or sautéed frogs' legs Provencale. This isn't just about having memorable food—it's about having a wonderful experience. ⊠ *3 E. 52nd St., between 5th and Madison Aves., Midtown East* ☎ *212/752–1495* ☜ *Reservations essential* 🖃 *AE, DC, MC, V* ⊗ *Closed Sun.* Ⓜ *Subway: E, V to 5th Ave.–53rd St.*

$$$$ ✕ **Le Perigord.** Owner Georges Briguet has presided over his beautiful kingdom of high-end French cuisine for more than three decades, and he's the very definition of bonhomie; chef Joel Benjamin has pedigree and considerable flair. Start with succulent smoked salmon with a corn muffin, sour cream, and salmon roe. One of the restaurant's signature dishes, turbot with a comté cheese crust in champagne sauce, is alone worth a visit—or two. Don't forget to order a soufflé at the beginning of your meal. ⊠ *405 E. 52nd St., between FDR Dr. and 1st Ave., Midtown East* ☎ *212/755–6244* ☜ *Reservations essential* 🏛 *Jacket and tie* 🖃 *AE, DC, MC, V* ⊗ *No lunch weekends* Ⓜ *Subway: 6 to 51st St.*

$–$$$ ✕ **Brasserie.** This midtown ultramodern brasserie has an unmistakably downtown vibe. Architects Diller & Scofidio have created quite an otherworldly environment. The contemporary brasserie fare—served from morning to late night—is perfectly scrumptious. Order from the ample raw bar, dive into frisée aux lardons or blue crab bisque, and move on to bouillabaisse with lobster, scallops, clams, shrimp, and sea bass. Save room for dessert—it's special here. ⊠ *100 E. 53rd St., between Lexington and Park Aves., Midtown East* ☎ *212/751–4840* ☜ *Reservations essential* 🖃 *AE, D, DC, MC, V* Ⓜ *Subway: 6 to 51st St.*

Italian

$$–$$$$ ✕ **Felidia.** Manhattanites frequent this *ristorante* as much for the winning enthusiasm of owner/cookbook author/Public Television chef Lidia Bastianich as for the food. The menu emphasizes authentic regional Italian cuisines, with a bow to dishes from Bastianich's homeland, Istria, on the Adriatic. Sit in an attractive front room with a wooden bar, a rustic room beyond, or in the elegant second-floor dining room. Order risotto, fresh homemade pasta, or roasted whole fish, and choose from a wine list representing Italy's finest vineyards. ⊠ *243 E. 58th St., between 2nd and 3rd Aves., Midtown East* ☎ *212/758–1479* ☜ *Reservations essential* 🏛 *Jacket required* 🖃 *AE, DC, MC, V* ⊗ *Closed Sun. No lunch Sat.* Ⓜ *Subway: N, R, W, 4, 5, 6 to 59th St.–Lexington Ave.*

$–$$$ ✕ **L'Impero.** Rather than flaunt its proximity to the United Nations by offering a view, L'Impero instead provides a comfortable escape. Scott Conant's Italian cooking is respectful of the cuisine's fine traditions, yet quite resourceful. Not to be missed: unforgettable braised rabbit risotto flickered generously with black truffles (the only entrée on the menu over $30). Another signature is moist roasted baby goat wound with artichoke and mounded on a potato "groestle" (pancake). Finish with a lovely cheese course and warm pumpkin bread pudding-polenta. ⊠ *45 Tudor City Pl., between W. 42nd and W. 43rd Sts., Midtown East* ☎ *212/599–5045* 🖃 *AE, DC, MC, V* ⊗ *Closed Sun. No lunch Sat.* Ⓜ *Subway: S, 4, 5, 6, 7 to 42nd St.–Grand Central.*

Japanese

★ **$$–$$$$** ✕ **Kuruma Zushi.** Only a small sign in Japanese indicates the location of this extraordinary restaurant that serves only sushi and sashimi. Bypass the tables, sit at the sushi bar, and put yourself in the hands of Toshihiro Uezu, the owner and chef. Among the selections are hard-to-find fish that Uezu imports directly from Japan. The most quietly attentive, pampering service staff in the city completes the wildly expensive experience. ✉ *7 E. 47th St., 2nd fl., between 5th and Madison Aves., Midtown East* ☎ *212/317–2802* ◬ *Reservations essential* ▭ *AE, MC, V* ⊗ *Closed Sun.* Ⓜ *Subway: 4, 5, 6, 7 to 42nd St.–Grand Central.*

$–$$$ ✕ **Sushi Yasuda.** The sleek bamboo-lined space in which chef Maomichi Yasuda works his aquatic sorcery is as elegant as his food. Whether he's using fish flown in daily from Japan or the creamiest sea urchin, Yasuda makes sushi so fresh and delicate it melts in your mouth. A number of special appetizers change daily (crispy fried eel backbone is a surprising treat), and a fine selection of sake and beer complements the lovely food. ✉ *204 E. 43rd St., between 2nd and 3rd Aves., Midtown East* ☎ *212/972–1001* ▭ *AE, D, MC, V* ⊗ *Closed Sun. No lunch Sat. Closed for dinner 2nd and 4th Sat. of each month* Ⓜ *Subway: 4, 5, 6, 7 to 42nd St.–Grand Central.*

Mexican

★ **$$** ✕ **Pampano.** Richard Sandoval, who gave New Yorkers the great Maya uptown, here turns his attention to Mexican seafood. Start with a tart, meaningful Margarita, or choose from about 50 tequilas available by the snifter. An addictive smoked swordfish is served with freshly fried tortilla chips you could well spoil your appetite. Continue with a sampling of three highly complex ceviches, then go for pompano sautéed with chorizo, cactus leaves, requeson cheese, and garlic-chile guajillo sauce. ✉ *209 E. 49th St., at 3rd Ave., Midtown East* ☎ *212/751–4545* ◬ *Reservations essential* ▭ *AE, DC, MC, V* ⊗ *No lunch weekends* Ⓜ *Subway: 6 to 51st St.–Lexington Ave.*

Pan-Asian

$–$$$$ ✕ **Vong.** Jean-Georges Vongerichten's intensely delicious French–Thai menu changes seasonally, but reliable standbys include chicken and coconut soup with *galangal* (a gingerlike root) and shiitake mushrooms (one of the best soups in town); braised rabbit and carrot curry, and grilled beef and noodles in a tangy ginger broth. A good strategy for two or more: Order set preordained assortments of five appetizers ($21 per person) and five terrific desserts ($14), including a spiced peach tarte tatin. ✉ *200 E. 54th St., at 3rd Ave., Midtown East* ☎ *212/486–9592* ◬ *Reservations essential* ▭ *AE, DC, MC, V* ⊗ *No lunch weekends* Ⓜ *Subway: 6 to 51st St./Lexington Ave.; E, V, to Lexington–3rd Aves./53rd St.*

Scandinavian

★ **$$$$** ✕ **Aquavit.** The dearly beloved restaurant relocated a block northeast to an even more Scandinavian space, leaving the famous waterfall behind. There's a café, lounge, bar, and 80-seat dining room, all decorated with more precise brush strokes. Emboldened by the move, celebrity chef Marcus Samuelsson is doing his best cooking ever. Don't miss the ingenious herring preparations—four of them, served in glass bowls with Carlsberg beer and aquavit. Duck breast never had it so good, lemon-cured and partnered by sultry potato–duck leg hash. ⊠ *65 E. 55th St., between Madison and Park Aves., Midtown East* ☎ *212/307–7311* ⌕ *Reservations essential* ⊟ *AE, DC, MC, V* ⊘ *No lunch Sat., except in café* Ⓜ *Subway: E, V to 5th Ave.–53rd St.*

Seafood

$$$$ ✕ **Oceana.** With all the dignity and hushed importance of the state room of a luxury ocean liner, Oceana is as nautical as it gets on land. Deeply gifted Chef Cornelius Gallagher's ever-changing menus are not without distinctive whimsy. Thus, blue marlin—not often encountered in these parts—is served rare with phyllo hugging it and accented with Swiss chard and glazed peaches. Halibut is brushed with melted espresso butter and plated with corn, pine nuts, and mustard greens in a pool of hot basil corn milk. ⊠ *55 E. 54th St., between Madison and Park Aves., Midtown East* ☎ *212/759–5941* ⊟ *AE, D, DC, MC, V* Ⓜ *Subway: 6, 7 to 51st St.*

$$–$$$ ✕ **Oyster Bar.** Nestled deep in the belly of Grand Central Station, the Oyster Bar has been a worthy seafood destination for over nine decades. Sit at the counter and slurp an assortment of bracingly fresh oysters, or a steaming bowl of clam chowder, and wash it down with an ice-cold brew. Or experience the forgotten pleasure of fresh, unadorned seafood such as lobster with drawn butter or matjes herring in season. Avoid anything that sounds newfangled. ⊠ *Grand Central Station, dining concourse, 42nd St. and Vanderbilt Ave., Midtown East* ☎ *212/490–6650* ⌕ *Reservations essential* ⊟ *AE, D, MC, V* ⊘ *Closed Sun.* Ⓜ *Subway: S, 4, 5, 6, 7 to 42nd St.–Grand Central.*

Spanish

$–$$$ ✕ **Marichu.** All bricks and beams, this Basque restaurant is just steps from the United Nations. A fascinating list of Spanish wines nicely complements the refined cuisine, which is particularly strong on seafood. Feast on piquillo peppers stuffed with a puree of salt cod. Other preparations, such as sautéed monkfish in a parsley and garlic sauce with clams and shrimps, are fresh and boldly seasoned. Finish with *leche frita*—fried milk delicacies with caramel sauce. ⊠ *342 E. 46th St., between 1st and 2nd Aves., Midtown East* ☎ *212/370–1866* ⌕ *Reservations essential* ⊟ *AE, DC, MC, V* ⊘ *No lunch weekends* Ⓜ *Subway: S, 4, 5, 6, 7 to 42nd St.–Grand Central.*

Steak

$$–$$$$ ✕ **BLT Steak.** Chef Laurent Tourondel sets a new steak house standard in this classy space all decked out in beige and suede and resined black tables. The no-muss, no-fuss menu is nonetheless large, and so are the portions of supple crab cakes and luscious ruby tuna tartare. A veal chop is crusted with rosemary and Parmesan, which imbue the veal with more flavor than veal ever has. The quintessential BLT includes Kobe beef, foie gras, bacon, and tomato in a split ciabatta. Sides and desserts are all superior. ⊠ *106 E. 57th St., between Lexington and Park Aves., Midtown East* ☎ *212/752–7470* ⌕ *Reservations essential* ⊟ *AE, DC, MC, V* Ⓜ *Subway: 4, 5, 6, N, R to 59th St.*

Steak

$$–$$$$ ✕ **Bull and Bear.** Among the most masculine spaces in Manhattan, the sheer puissance in the air of the bar and dining room is palpable. This is the only kitchen on the Eastern seaboard that has access to Certified Angus Beef Prime, which comprises less than one percent of all American beef. Go with a 24-ounce porterhouse, and you'll have two days of absolute succulence. All the sides are terrific, especially hash browns sizzling away in a six-inch cast iron skillet. ✉ *Waldorf Astoria, 570 Lexington Ave., at 49th St., Midtown East* ☎ *212/872–4900* ⌕ *Reservations essential* ▤ *AE, DC, MC, V* Ⓜ *Subway: 6 to 51st St.*

$$–$$$$ ✕ **George O'Neill's.** This butch steak house is kick-back comfortable, all chocolate leather banquettes and cranberry tablecloths. Rev up your appetite with fresh selections from the exemplary raw bar (a full array of shrimp, lobster, crabmeat, oysters, and clams is just $22 per person), and/or burly five-onion soup with a puff pastry dome, then set your inner caveman upon one of steakmeister Neal Myers's dry-aged prime steaks. Especially rewarding is the two-inch-thick bone-in rib steak. You'll be gnawing that bone at home by midnight. ✉ *145 E. 50th St., between Lexington and 3rd Aves., Midtown East* ☎ *212/888–1220* ⌕ *Reservations essential* ▤ *AE, DC, MC, V* Ⓜ *Subway: 4, 5 to 51st St.*

$$–$$$$ ✕ **Michael Jordan's The Steak House NYC.** Don't be dissuaded by the fact that this place is technically part of a chain: there's nowhere like it. This handsomely appointed space overlooks one of the most famous interiors in America. Few chefs in Manhattan know steak as well as David Walzog. Start with inch-square logs of toasted bread brushed with garlic butter resting on a creamy pool of hot Gorgonzola fondue. Follow with pristine oysters, then lunge for a prime dry-aged rib eye. Finish with luscious 5-inch 1,000-layer chocolate cake. ✉ *Grand Central Terminal, West Balcony, 23 Vanderbilt Ave., between 43rd and 44th Sts., Midtown East* ☎ *212/655–2300* ⌕ *Reservations essential* ▤ *AE, DC, MC, V* Ⓜ *Subway: 4, 5, 6, 7 to 42nd St. Grand Central Station.*

$$–$$$$ ✕ **Sparks Steak House.** Magnums of wines that cost more than most people earn in a week festoon the large dining rooms of this classic New York steak house. Although seafood is given fair play on the menu, Sparks is about dry-aged steak. The lamb chops and veal chops are also noteworthy. Classic sides of hash browns, creamed (or not) spinach, mushrooms, onions, and broccoli are all you need to complete the experience. ✉ *210 E. 46th St., between 2nd and 3rd Aves., Midtown East* ☎ *212/ 687–4855* ⌕ *Reservations essential* ▤ *AE, D, DC, MC, V* ☾ *Closed Sun. No lunch Sat.* Ⓜ *Subway: S, 4, 5, 6, 7 to 42nd St.–Grand Central.*

$–$$$$ ✕ **The Palm.** They may have added tablecloths, but it would take more than that to hide the brusque, no-nonsense nature of this legendary steak house. The steak is always impeccable, and lobsters are so big there may not be room at the table for such classic side dishes as rich creamed spinach. Overflow from the restaurant caused the owners to open Palm Too, a slightly less raffish version of the original, across the street, and another edition across town. ✉ *837 2nd Ave., between E. 44th and E. 45th Sts., Midtown East* ☎ *212/687–2953* ⌕ *Reservations essential* ▤ *AE, DC, MC, V* ☾ *Closed Sun. No lunch Sat.* ✉ *Palm Too, 840 2nd Ave., between E. 44th and E. 45th Sts., Midtown East* ☎ *212/697–5198* Ⓜ *Subway: S, 4, 5, 6, 7 to 42nd St.–Grand Central.*

UPPER EAST SIDE

Long viewed as an enclave of the privileged, the Upper East Side has plenty of elegant restaurants to serve ladies who lunch and bankers who look forward to a late-night meal and single malt at the end of the day. However, the eastern and northern reaches of the area have some quite affordable spots, too. Whether you want to celebrate a special occasion or have simply worked up an appetite after a long museum visit, you're sure to find something appropriate for almost any budget.

American

$–$$$ ✕ **Lenox.** This small neighborhood restaurant keeps a clubby low pro-file; nevertheless, insiders know it's a serious place to dine. Although the menu changes seasonally, such items as shrimp cocktail, oysters, crisp-skinned Atlantic salmon, and pan-roasted chicken are mainstays, as are "Tiers of Taste"—think American tapas. Thanks to congenial and charming host Tony Fortuna, the red-color dining room is always comfortable. The lounge is often crowded with well-heeled locals. ⊠ *1278 3rd Ave., between E. 73rd and E. 74th Sts., Upper East Side* ☎ *212/772–0404* ⊟ *AE, D, MC, V* Ⓜ *Subway: 6 to 77th St.*

Cafés

¢–$ ✕ **Toraya.** A traditional and serene Japanese tearoom, Toraya is tucked into a row of town houses off 5th Avenue. Along with green tea, you can try some of the seasonal *wagashi*, a sweet bean-paste cake often shaped like flowers or leaves. A lunch menu includes such creative items as a salad of shiitake mushrooms, bacon, and *mochi* (lightly fried rice cakes), and a smoked turkey sandwich with miso and wasabi mayonnaise. Takeout is also available. ⊠ *17 E. 71st St., between 5th and Madison Aves., Upper East Side* ☎ *212/861–1700* ⊟ *AE, DC, MC, V* ⊙ *Closed Sun. No dinner* Ⓜ *Subway: 6 to 68th St./Hunter College.*

Contemporary

$$$$ ✕ **Aureole.** Celebrity chef Charlie Palmer's protégé Dante Boccuzzi is in charge of the kitchen at Palmer's top-rated restaurant. Several distinct flavors work their way into single dishes such as grilled quail and leeks with port–pomegranate vinaigrette and frisée and amaranth salad, or butter-poached lobster with Meyer lemon and Jerusalem artichokes. Desserts, too, are breathtaking. The town-house setting on two floors has striking floral displays. For a romantic evening, reserve a table on the ground floor. ⊠ *34 E. 61st St., between Madison and Park Aves., Upper East Side* ☎ *212/319–1660* ◬ *Reservations essential* ⊟ *AE, DC, MC, V* ⊙ *Closed Sun. No lunch Sat.* Ⓜ *Subway: N, R, W to 5th Ave.*

$$$–$$$$ ✕ **Mark's Restaurant.** Dignified yet relaxed, staid yet festive, Mark's excels in every way. Andrew Chase's market-driven menu always features his signature slow-poached salmon, which is neither slow nor poached—a fillet is immersed in olive oil at 200 degrees for 20 minutes, with insanely delicious results. No less tasty is a tender, juicy herb-roasted veal chop. There are perfectly prepared daily pasta and risotto options as well. Service is focused and prompt. ⊠ *25 E. 77th St., at Madison Ave., Upper East Side* ☎ *212/879–1864* ◬ *Reservations essential* ⊟ *AE, DC, MC, V* Ⓜ *Subway: 6 to 77th St.*

Where to Eat
on the Upper
East Side

$$–$$$ ✕ **Etats-Unis.** The open kitchen and shelves lined with cookbooks should
tell you that the food is the primary focus at this small restaurant. The
menu changes daily, but dishes lean toward the traditional, with some
modern combinations to liven things up. Good examples are roasted
boneless chicken stuffed with mascarpone and rosemary on truffled polenta or charcoal-grilled rack of lamb with olive tapenade and fresh mint.
The same dinner menu is available across the street at The Bar@Etats-
Unis. ⊠ 242 E. 81st St., between 2nd and 3rd Aves., Upper East Side
☎ 212/517–8826 ⊟ AE, DC, MC, V ⊠ Bar@Etats-Unis, 247 E. 81st
St., Upper East Side ☎ 212/396–9928 ⊟ AE, DC, MC, V Ⓜ Subway:
6 to 77th St.

$$–$$$ ✕ **Park Avenue Cafe.** Folk art, antique toys, and sheaves of dried wheat
decorate this inviting New American restaurant. Chef Neil Murphy's
presentations are imaginative and extraordinarily delicious—such as duck
breast, duck meat loaf, and foie gras dumplings, or "filet mignon" of
lobster with lobster risotto. The desserts are enticing visual masterpieces, like the thin chocolate cube filled with espresso mousse, presented
with equal flair by the exuberant waitstaff. ⊠ 100 E. 63rd St., between
Park and Lexington Aves., Upper East Side ☎ 212/644–1900 ⌕ Reservations essential ⊟ AE, DC, MC, V Ⓜ Subway: N, R, W, 4, 5, 6 to
59th St.–Lexington Ave.

French

$$$$
Fodor'sChoice
★

✕ **Daniel.** Celebrity chef Daniel Boulud has created one of the most memorable dining experiences in Manhattan today. The prix-fixe–only menu is predominantly French, with such modern classics as roasted venison loin with braised red cabbage and a sweet potato–apple gratin. Equally impressive is the professional service and primarily French wine list. Don't forget the decadent desserts and overflowing cheese trolley. For a more casual evening, you can reserve a table in the lounge area, where entrées range from $36 to $50. ✉ *60 E. 65th St., between Madison and Park Aves., Upper East Side* ☎ *212/288–0033* ⚑ *Reservations essential* 🍴*Jacket required* ▤*AE, DC, MC, V* ⊙*Closed Sun. No lunch* Ⓜ *Subway: 6 to 68th St.–Hunter College.*

★ **$$$–$$$$**
✕ **Dumonet.** Quite a succession of lusciousness awaits you at this sumptuously appointed space in the Carlyle Hotel, as dignified as the international crowd that loves to come here. Service is attentive, but comfortable, and the classic French menu has more than a few modern touches. Some extraordinary wines are available by the glass. Begin with pike quenelles with lobster sauce. The squab is far larger than usual, and many times tastier. Don't miss the Grand Marnier soufflé. ✉ *Madison Ave. at E. 76th St., Upper East Side* ☎ *212/744–1600* ⚑ *Reservations essential* ▤ *AE, DC, MC, V* Ⓜ *Subway: 6 to 77th St.* ⊙ *No lunch Sun.*

★ **$$–$$$$**
✕ **Café Boulud.** Both the food and service are top-notch at Daniel Boulud's conservative (but not overly stuffy) bistro in the Surrey Hotel. The menu is divided into four short parts: under *La Tradition* you'll find such classic French dishes as slow-cooked halibut with summer beans and heirloom tomatoes; *Le Potager* tempts with goat cheese ravioli; *La Saison* follows the rhythms of the season and really shines in early autumn; and *Le Voyage* is where the kitchen reinterprets the myriad cuisines of the world. ✉ *20 E. 76th St., between 5th and Madison Aves., Upper East Side* ☎ *212/772–2600* ⚑ *Reservations essential* ▤ *AE, DC, MC, V* ⊙ *No lunch weekends* Ⓜ *Subway: 6 to 77th St.*

$$–$$$$
✕ **Orsay.** It's hard to believe that this elegant, sedate brasserie was once the socialite hangout Mortimers—gone are the party favors, the minihamburgers, and the snooty staff. Instead, it's a serious French restaurant featuring a menu that includes a list of whimsical tartares and an array of house-smoked items. Traditional brasserie fare such as steak frites as well as more creative options like Thai bouillabaisse with ginger and lemongrass are skillfully executed. A reasonably priced wine list and professional service complete the dining experience. ✉ *1057 Lexington Ave., at E. 75th St., Upper East Side* ☎ *212/517–6400* ⚑ *Reservations essential* ▤ *AE, D, MC, V* Ⓜ *Subway: 6 to 77th St.*

$–$$$$
✕ **Jo Jo.** After a million-dollar face-lift, this gorgeous town-house restaurant feels much roomier even when it's packed, as it usually is. It's the flagship restaurant in the glittering empire of chef Jean-Georges Vongerichten (Jean-Georges, Vong, The Mercer Kitchen, V Steak House). The food combines classic cooking techniques with infused oils and reductions. Foie gras is married to quince in a terrine with warm lentil salad, and rack of lamb is dusted with seven spices and offered with cucumber mint relish. ✉ *160 E. 64th St., between Lexington and 3rd Aves.,*

Upper East Side ☎ *212/223–5656* ⌕ *Reservations essential* ▤ *AE, MC, V* Ⓜ *Subway: 6 to 68th St./Hunter College.*

$$–$$$ ✕ **Payard Pâtisserie & Bistro.** Pastry chef François Payard is the force behind this combination bistro and pastry shop, festooned by bosomy, exuberant lanterns. Snazzy people come here in droves, and you'll quickly discover why. Start with an insanely rich and delicious cheese soufflé with Parmesan cream sauce. All-the-rage veal cheeks are almost as thick with flavor as they are texturally dense, in a near-bordelaise sauce that will leave you sticky-lipped with glee. Payard's tarts, soufflés, and other French pastries are truly memorable. ⊠ *1032 Lexington Ave., between E. 73rd and E. 74th Sts., Upper East Side* ☎ *212/717–5252* ⌕ *Reservations essential* ▤ *AE, MC, V* ⊙ *Closed Sun.* Ⓜ *Subway: 6 to 77th St.*

Italian

¢–$$ ✕ **Luca.** This casual spot happens to serve some of the best Northern Italian food on the Upper East Side, including fresh pastas like pappardelle with duck ragù and ravioli filled with spinach and ricotta. Main courses—including potato-crusted salmon with caper sauce on sautéed vegetables and chicken breast *rollatini* stuffed with goat cheese and pesto—leave regulars satisfied. Chef-owner Luca Marcato wanders the clean, sparse restaurant when he's not performing Italian sorcery in the kitchen. ⊠ *1712 1st Ave., between E. 88th and E. 89th Sts., Upper East Side* ☎ *212/987–9260* ▤ *MC, V* ⊙ *No lunch* Ⓜ *Subway: 4, 5, 6 to 86th St.*

Japanese

$$$–$$$$ ✕ **Kai.** One flight up from a glamorous stretch of Madison Avenue you'll find serenity and sheer culinary bliss in this jewel box. Three prix-fixe menus consisting of 5 to 10 small courses of chef Hitoshi Kagawa's premium Japanese fare—like lily bulb soup with eel dumpling and pristine sashimi—are paired with exceptional teas and/or sakes. Many of the teas are available for sale in the elegant shop downstairs. All this indulgence comes at a price, but you'll leave feeling restored. ⊠ *822 Madison Ave., between 68th and 69th Sts., Upper East Side* ☎ *212/988–7277* ▤ *AE, D, MC, V* ⊙ *Closed Sun. and Mon.* Ⓜ *Subway: 6 to 68th St./Hunter College.*

$–$$$$ ✕ **Sushi of Gari.** Options at this popular sushi restaurant range from the ordinary (Alaska maki, California roll) to such exotic items as salmon with guacamole, broiled whole squid with teriyaki sauce, and meltingly delicious lightly fried cream cheese dumpling. Japanese noodles (udon or soba) and meat dishes such as teriyaki and negimaki (scallions rolled in thinly sliced beef) are all well prepared. Reservations are strongly recommended. ⊠ *402 E. 78th St., at 1st Ave., Upper East Side* ☎ *212/517–5340* ▤ *AE, D, MC, V* ⊙ *Closed Mon. No lunch* Ⓜ *Subway: 6 to 77th St.*

Mexican

★ $–$$ ✕ **Maya.** The upscale hacienda appearance of this justifiably popular restaurant showcases some of the best Mexican food in the city. Begin with a delicious fresh mango margarita, then tuck into intensely delicious roasted corn soup, poblano pepper stuffed with seafood and

PIZZA PIZZA

PIZZA, OR RATHER, *the best pizza, is a controversial topic in New York City. It sparks debates more fervent than many political issues, and that's saying a lot in a city that votes democratic but has a Republican mayor.*

For many years, the list of contenders was small but distinguished. A few shops sold good, fresh thin- to medium-crust pies with mozzarella and red sauce. Taxis started showing up outside of **Patsy's** *East Harlem doors (2287 1st Ave., between 117th and 118th Sts.) practically since the day it opened.* **John's** *(233 Bleecker St., at Carmine St.) staked out the territory downtown along with* **Arturo's** *(106 W. Houston St., at Thompson St.) and* **Lombardi's** *(32 Spring St., between Mott and Mulberry Sts.).*

Now, however, the debate has become ever more complex, with restaurants serving excellent rustic or ethnic versions

of our beloved pie. The questions remain the same. Which crust is best? Thinner or thicker? Chewy or crispy? Do cheeses other than mozzarella work as well? Is the sauce homemade? Is it made in a wood-fired brick oven?

At **Una Pizza Napoletana** *(349 E. 12th St., at 2nd Ave.), the owner uses San Marzano or cherry tomatoes, real buffalo mozzarella, and fresh basil. At* **Peasant** *(194 Elizabeth St., between Spring and Prince Sts.), it's their rustic, oblong irregular three-cheese bianca with mortadella that's one of the city's treasures.*

Hungering for a sweet pizza? **Pie by the Pound** *(124 4th Ave., between E. 12th and E. 13th Sts.) offers a Nutella version with or without bananas. Kids love* **Two Boots Restaurant** *(37 Ave. A, between E. 2nd and E. 3rd Sts.) as much for the funky Day of the Dead decor as for the food.*

Gouda cheese, and smoky butterflied beef tenderloin marinated in lime or ancho chili-crusted striped bass. Finish with crepes dribbled with goat milk *dulce de leche* and you'll leave wearing a great big grin. ✉ *1191 1st Ave., between E. 64th and E. 65th Sts., Upper East Side* ☎ *212/585–1818* ⌂ *Reservations essential* ▭ *AE, DC, MC, V* ⊘ *No lunch* Ⓜ *Subway: 6 to 68th St.–Hunter College.*

$–$$ ✗ **Zócalo.** Explore the unusual menu while enjoying a first-class margarita and chunky guacamole or stinging ceviche. Among the frolicsome and inventive entrées are crispy whole (boneless) red snapper and slow-cooked pork ribs with chipotle barbecue sauce and onion rings. There are also such classics as quesadillas and enchiladas. Burnt-orange and blue walls add zest to the attractive main dining room, although it can get a bit crowded. ✉ *174 E. 82nd St., between Lexington and 3rd Aves., Upper East Side* ☎ *212/717–7772* ⌂ *Reservations essential* ▭ *AE, DC, MC, V* ⊘ *No lunch* Ⓜ *Subway: 4, 5, 6 to 86th St.*

Pizza

¢–$$ ✗ **Serafina Fabulous Pizza.** Mediterranean-hue friezes, a most inviting upstairs terrace, and a steady stream of models and celebrities grace this very Italian café. Scene aside, the real draw here is some of Manhattan's most authentic Neopolitan pizza—they even filter the water for the pizza dough to make it closely resemble the water in Naples! Beyond the pies are antipasti, salads, pastas including a number of ravioli dishes, and second courses like veal scaloppine with lemon and capers. ⊠ *1022 Madison Ave., at E. 79th St., Upper East Side* ☎ *212/734–2676* ▤ *AE, DC, MC, V* Ⓜ *Subway: 6 to 77th St.* ⊠ *29 E. 61st St., between Madison and Park Aves., Upper East Side* ☎ *212/702–9898* Ⓜ *Subway: N, R, W, 4, 5, 6 to 59th St.–Lexington Ave.*

Seafood

$–$$ ✕ **Atlantic Grill.** It may be one of Manhattan's most popular dining rooms, but oddly, few people outside of New York have heard of this seafood restaurant. The combination of friendly service, fair prices, and reliably fresh fish means the large dining room is usually filled to capacity. Traditional appetizers are joined by sushi and sashimi starters. Straight-ahead entrées like roasted organic Scottish salmon and crab cakes usually make better choices than rococo concoctions like barbecue-glazed mahimahi. ⊠ *1341 3rd Ave., between E. 76th and E. 77th Sts., Upper East Side* ☎ *212/988–9200* ◬ *Reservations essential* ▤ *AE, MC, V* Ⓜ *Subway: 6 to 77th St.*

Vietnamese

¢–$ ✕ **Saigon Grill.** Serving some of the best Vietnamese food in Manhattan, this is also quite affordable. The appetizers are so delicious you might never make it to the entrées—standout starters include the shrimp summer roll, chicken satay, and barbecued spareribs with plum sauce. Main courses like basil prawns and grilled marinated pork chops with lemongrass are also worth a try. The sparse dining room is nothing special to look at, but the waiters are both speedy and polite. ⊠ *1700 2nd Ave., at E. 88th St., Upper East Side* ☎ *212/996–4600* ◬ *Reservations not accepted* ▤ *AE, D, DC, MC, V* Ⓜ *Subway: 6 to 86th St.*

UPPER WEST SIDE & HARLEM

Considering the fact that Lincoln Center's theaters can seat more than 18,000 audience members at one time, you would certainly expect the Upper West Side to be jammed with competitive, wonderful restaurants catering to all tastes and budgets. The main avenues are indeed lined with restaurants, but many of them are mediocre; they survive by catering to a local population that has neither the time nor the inclination to cook at home. Progress is being made, with the opening of the Time Warner Center in 2004, which houses a handful of New York's most high-end restaurants, and with the steady gentrification uptown into Harlem, where there are plenty of great cheap offerings beyond a slice of pizza.

American–Casual

$–$$ ✕ **Sarabeth's.** Lining up for brunch here is as much an Upper West Side tradition as taking a sunny Sunday afternoon stroll in nearby Riverside Park. Locals love the bric-a-brac-filled restaurant for unbeatable morningtime dishes like lemon ricotta pancakes, as well as for the comfort-

KEY

M *Subway stops*

W. 98th St.

W. 97th St.

W. 96th St.

W. 95th St.

W. 94th St.

W. 93rd St.

W. 92nd St.

W. 91st St.

W. 90th St.

W. 89th St.

W. 88th St.

W. 87th St.

W. 86th St.

W. 85th St.

W. 84th St.

W. 83rd St.

W. 82nd St.

W. 81st St.

W. 80th St.

W. 79th St.

W. 78th St.

W. 77th St.

W. 76th St.

W. 75th St.

W. 74th St.

W. 73rd St.

W. 72nd St.

W. 71st St.

W. 70th St.

W. 69th St.

W. 68th St.

W. 67th St.

W. 66th St.

W. 65th St.

W. 64th St.

W. 63rd St.

W. 62nd St.

W. 59th St.

W. 58th St.

W. 57th St.

1,2,3,9

B,C

B,C

B,C

B,C

1,9

1,9

1,9

1,2,3,9

1,9

A,B,C,D,
1,9

Broadway

West End Ave.

Amsterdam Ave.

Columbus Ave.

Central Park W.

Riverside Park

Riverside Dr.

West End Ave.

Broadway

Central Park

Central Park

American
Museum
of Natural
History

The Dakota

Lincoln
Center

Columbus
Circle

Central Park S.

0   1/4 mile

0   400 meters

Where to Eat on
the Upper West Side
& in Harlem

CloseUp

THE BAGEL PILGRIMAGE

MAGINE IT: *fresh bagels, still warm in a paper bag. Add maybe a little cream cheese and lox on the side. A coffee and the weekend paper. Back in the day, there were no nine-grain honey, sundried tomato, or blueberry bagels, let alone maple raisin walnut cream cheese. Purists insist on plain, poppy, sesame, and salt, the flavors that were available when bagel making was in its heyday.*

Size matters, too. For anyone who remembers, the original New York bagels weighed about half as much as their modern day counterparts. What's lost in these outsize—some might say mutant—versions is the close relationship of the crispy exterior to its chewy interior. A good bagel should not be sugary. Which brings us to ingredients: high-gluten flour, yeast, salt, and a little malt for sweetness and tang.

Absolute Bagels *(2788 Broadway, between 107th and 108th Sts.) uses malt*

and makes minis that come closest to the bagels of yore; their big ones are good, too. ***H&H Bagels'*** *(2239 Broadway, at W. 80th St.; 639 W. 46th St., at 12th Ave.) hefties taste much sweeter (due to a lot more sugar), but they have an almost cultlike following even though there's no place to sit.* ***Murray's*** *makes good big hand-rolled bagels, as does* ***Ess-a-Bagel*** *(359 1st Ave., at E. 21st St.; 831 3rd Ave., between E. 50th and 51st Sts.). Murray's has a better bite; it's a little denser, more toothsome. Ess-a-Bagel's are a bit lighter.*

ing dinners. The afternoon tea includes buttery scones with Sarabeth's signature jams, savory nibbles, and outstanding baked goods. ✉ 423 *Amsterdam Ave., between W. 80th and W. 81st Sts., Upper West Side* ☎ *212/496–6280* ▭ *AE, DC, MC, V* Ⓜ *Subway: 1, 9 to 79th St.*

¢–$ ✕ **Barney Greengrass.** At this Old-New-York-Jewish landmark, brusque waiters send out stellar smoked salmon, sturgeon, and whitefish to a happy crowd packed to the gills at small Formica tables. Split a fish platter with bagels, cream cheese, and other fixings, or get your fish with scrambled eggs. If you're still hungry, go for a plate of scrumptious cheese blintzes or the to-die-for chopped liver. Beware: the weekend brunch wait can exceed an hour. ✉ *541 Amsterdam Ave., between W. 86th and W. 87th Sts., Upper West Side* ☎ *212/724–4707* ⌦ *Reservations not accepted* ▭ *No credit cards* ⊘ *Closed Mon.* Ⓜ *Subway: 1, 9 to 86th St.*

¢–$ ✕ **Big Nick's.** This cramped neighborhood diner is decorated with photographs of the celebrities who've visited, but the primary draw is the burgers, which are huge and juicy. The tomelike menu lists every conceivable burger topping, from avocado and bacon to Greek tsatsiki sauce. The classic Bistro Burger has mushrooms, cheddar, and fried onions on toasted challah bread. Nick's is open later than most burger joints—until 5 AM. ✉ *2175 Broadway, between 76th and 77th Sts., Upper West Side* ☎ *AE, MC, V* Ⓜ *Subway: 1, 2, 3, 9 to 72nd St.*

¢–$ ✕**Kitchenette.** Many a hungry Columbia student arriving intent on a meal has gotten waylaid by the gooey cakes, cookies, and other goodies displayed at the bakery counter of this country kitchen, amid decorative old signs and cookware. Those who hold out are rewarded with good, solid cooking, like turkey meat loaf or rich baked cheese macaroni at dinner, or gingerbread French toast and thick-cut bacon at brunch. ✉ *1272 Amsterdam Ave., between 122nd and 123rd Sts., Morningside Heights* ☎ *212/531–7600* ⊟ *AE, DC, MC, V* Ⓜ *Subway: 1, 9 to 125th St.*

Cafés

¢–$ ✕**Cafe Lalo.** The plentiful pastries, floor-to-ceiling French windows, and vintage posters attract enough people to make seating a squeeze, but the Parisian setting and decadent cakes, pies, tarts, and cheesecakes are worth it. Somehow a camera crew fit in here to film Tom Hanks and Meg Ryan parleying in *You've Got Mail*. ✉ *201 W. 83rd St., between Broadway and Amsterdam Ave., Upper West Side* ☎ *212/496–6031* ⚐ *Reservations not accepted* ⊟ *No credit cards* Ⓜ *Subway: 1, 9 to 86th St.*

¢ ✕**Columbus Bakery.** Aside from the addictive cookies, muffins, and other baked goods, Columbus Bakery carries fresh, homemade sandwiches, soups, salads, and frittatas. It's great for a pit stop after exploring Central Park or the nearby Museum of Natural History. If you can snag a table outdoors, the seating area is lovely for sipping a cappuccino (or a glass of wine) and watching the neighborhood's endless parade of oversize baby strollers and pedigree dogs. ✉ *474 Columbus Ave., between 82nd and 83rd Sts., Upper West Side* ☎ *212/724–6880* ⚐ *Reservations not accepted* ⊟ *AE, MC, V* Ⓜ *Subway: B, C to 81st St.*

Chinese

$–$$$ ✕**Shun Lee West.** For Chinese food without pretensions, head to Chinatown; but if you'd rather be pampered and are willing to pay for it, this is the place. The dramatically lighted dining room, accented by images of white dragons and monkeys, serves classic dishes like crispy prawns with XO sauce and rack of lamb Szechuan style. Less expensive Shun Lee Café next door has some of the best dim sum around. ✉ *43 W. 65th St., between Columbus Ave. and Central Park W, Upper West Side* ☎ *212/595–8895* ⚐ *Reservations essential* ⊟ *AE, D, DC, MC, V* Ⓜ *Subway: 1, 9 to 66th St.–Lincoln Center.*

¢–$ ✕**Ollie's.** This no-frills Chinese chain is a blessing for locals and Lincoln Center patrons in search of a quick budget meal. The best dishes are the noodle soups (with dumplings, vegetables, and meat), ribs, and the dim sum prepared by speedy chefs. The portions are generous, but don't expect any culinary revelations. ✉ *1991 Broadway, at W. 67th St., Upper West Side* ☎ *212/595–8181* ⚐ *Reservations not accepted* ⊟ *AE, MC, V* Ⓜ *Subway: 1, 9 to 66th St.–Lincoln Center* ✉ *2315 Broadway, at W. 86th St., Upper West Side* ☎ *212/362–3111* Ⓜ *Subway: 1, 9 to 66th St.–Lincoln Center* ✉ *2957 Broadway, at W. 116th St., Morningside Heights* ☎ *212/932–3300* Ⓜ *Subway: 1, 9 to 116th St.*

Contemporary

$$$$ ✕ **Asiate.** The view alone is reason enough to visit Asiate's pristine dining room, perched on the 35th floor of the Time Warner Center in the Mandarin Oriental Hotel. Artfully positioned tables draw the eyes to the great floor-to-ceiling window, which looks onto the expanse of Central Park and midtown; at night, the crystalline lighting reflects in the glass to haunting effect. Efficient service and mostly successful French-Asian dishes (like cod with foie gras miso sauce) do not break the spell. ⊠ *80 Columbus Circle at 60th St., Time Warner Center, 35th fl., Upper West Side* ☎ *212/805–8881* ⌲ *Reservations essential* ▤ *AE, D, DC, MC, V* Ⓜ *Subway: A, B, C, D, 1, 9 to 59th St.–Columbus Circle.*

$$$$
Fodor'sChoice
★
✕ **Per Se.** Thomas Keller, who gave the world butter-poached lobster and the Napa Valley's The French Laundry restaurant, has given New York Per Se, which serves his witty, magical creations to fifteen lucky tables. Come with an open mind and open wallet, and discover his inventive combinations of flavors reduced to their essences. Waiters can (and may) recite the provenance of the tiniest turnip. For reservations, call exactly two months in advance; hit redial, repeat. ⊠ *10 Columbus Circle at Time Warner Center, 4th fl., Upper West Side* ☎ *212/823–9335* ⌲ *Reservations essential* 🏛 *Jackets required* ⊘ *No lunch Mon.–Thurs.* ▤ *AE, MC, V* Ⓜ *Subway: A, B, C, D, 1, 9 to 59th St.–Columbus Circle.*

$$–$$$$ ✕ **Ouest.** Celebrity chef Tom Valenti's contemporary American restaurant, which paved the way for fine cooking on the Upper West Side when it opened in 2001, still reigns supreme with intense flavors that rock, whether you order stick-to-the-ribs fare like braised lamb shanks or grilled meats, or go lighter with roasted sturgeon, chanterelles, and truffled rice. If that's not enough, the $24 multi-course Sunday brunch is a caloric orgy that will make you an instant convert. ⊠ *2315 Broadway, between W. 83rd and W. 84th Sts., Upper West Side* ☎ *212/580–8700* ⌲ *Reservations essential* ▤ *AE, D, DC MC, V* ⊘ *No lunch Sat.* Ⓜ *Subway: 1, 9 to 86th St.*

$$–$$$$ ✕ **Tavern on the Green.** The food and service may be erratic, but people throng nonetheless (by foot, by taxi, even by horse and carriage) to this fantastical maze of dining rooms in Central Park. In good weather (May through October), there's a lovely garden area under a canopy of lighted trees. Foodwise, simple dishes are best bets, like prime rib—or skip the grub and grab a drink at the charming upstairs bar. ⊠ *In Central Park at W. 67th St., Upper West Side* ☎ *212/873–3200* ⌲ *Reservations essential* ▤ *AE, D, DC, MC, V* Ⓜ *Subway: 1, 9 to 66th St.–Lincoln Center.*

★ **$$–$$$** ✕ **Café Gray.** Four-star chef Gray Kunz, creator of the culinary temple Lespinasse (now closed), has shifted his talents to preparing a more reasonably priced menu of top-notch Asian-accented French dishes, like braised short ribs with grits and meaux mustard sauce. You can watch them being made in the open kitchen running the length of the dining room, or head to the lively bar area, which serves the full menu plus other tidbits also worth trying. ⊠ *10 Columbus Circle at Time Warner Center, 3rd fl., Upper West Side* ☎ *212/823–6338* ⌲ *Reservations essential* ▤ *AE, DC, MC, V* Ⓜ *Subway: A, B, C, D, 1, 9 to 59th St.–Columbus Circle.*

Continental

$$$–$$$$ ✕ **Café des Artistes.** Howard Chandler Christy's murals of naked nymphs at play grace the walls of this thoroughly romantic restaurant, which opened in 1917 (to add to the romance). Although the haute French cuisine may no longer be among New York's best, the menu always has some stunners, like pan-roasted squab with chanterelles and garlic flan over a potato cake. Desserts like hot fudge napoleon or a perfect apple strudel are champions. The prix-fixe dinner is $45. ✉ *1 W. 67th St., at Central Park W, Upper West Side* ☎ *212/877–3500* ⚑ *Reservations essential* ▤ *AE, DC, MC, V* Ⓜ *Subway: 1, 9 to 66th St.–Lincoln Center.*

Creole

$–$$ ✕ **Bayou.** Harlem is still known for its casual soul-food spots, but trendy restaurants like Bayou are beginning to move in, too. The modern Creole menu includes classics like crawfish étouffée, as well as more inventive choices like a grilled pork chop with green peppercorn demi-glace. Bayou's dining room has a pressed-tin ceiling and brass lamps, an accommodating waitstaff, and even a small wine list. ✉ *308 Lenox Ave., between W. 125th and W. 126th Sts., Harlem* ☎ *212/426–3800* ▤ *AE, MC, V* Ⓜ *Subway: 2, 3 to 125th St.*

French

$$$$ ✕ **Jean Georges.** This culinary temple focuses wholly on *chef celebre* Jean-
Fodor'sChoice Georges Vongerichten's spectacular creations. Some approach the lim-
★ its of the taste universe, like trout sashimi with trout eggs, lemon foam, dill, and horseradish. Others are models of simplicity, like young garlic soup with frogs' legs. Exceedingly personalized service and a well-selected wine list contribute to an unforgettable meal. (For Jean Georges on a budget, try the $20 lunch at **Nougatine** in the front area.) ✉ *1 Central Park W, at W. 59th St., Upper West Side* ☎ *212/299–3900* ⚑ *Reservations essential* 🛈 *Jacket required* ▤ *AE, DC, MC, V* ✪ *Closed Sun.* Ⓜ *Subway: A, B, C, D, 1, 9 to 59th St.–Columbus Circle.*

★ **$$$–$$$$** ✕ **Picholine.** With an elegant, mellow dining room painted in soft colors and accented by gorgeous dried flowers, Picholine is made for special occasions. Whatever you order, allow fromager Max McCalman to discuss his celebrated cart of cheeses, which ripen to glorious maturity in a "cave" in the back. Terrance Brennan's Mediterranean-accented French cuisine is considered among the best in Manhattan: top dishes include Maine lobster with caramelized endive and vanilla brown butter, and daily Scottish game. ✉ *35 W. 64th St., between Broadway and Central Park W, Upper West Side* ☎ *212/724–8585* ⚑ *Reservations essential* ▤ *AE, DC, MC, V* ✪ *No lunch Sun. and Mon.* Ⓜ *Subway: 1, 9 to 66th St.–Lincoln Center.*

$–$$$ ✕ **Café Luxembourg.** The old soul of the Lincoln-Center neighborhood seems to inhabit the tiled and mirrored walls of this lively, friendly bistro, where West End Avenue regulars are greeted with kisses, and musicians and audience members pack the room after a concert. The menu (served until 11:45) includes classic bistro dishes like steak au poivre and hamburgers alongside more contemporary spins like rack of lamb with tomato-orange relish. ✉ *200 W. 70th St., between Amsterdam and*

West End Aves., Upper West Side ☎ *212/873–7411* ⬧ *Reservations essential* ▭ *AE, DC, MC, V* Ⓜ *Subway: 1, 2, 3, 9 to 72nd St.*

Greek

★ **$–$$** ✕ **Onera.** This intimate town house restaurant (a foyer-size bar leads to a clean white- and navy-walled dining room) feels like a tastefully decorated home, especially when the young, personable chef Michael Psilakis wanders in to advise on his creative menu of Greek-inspired dishes. The many mouthwatering categories, including raw meze, pasta, game, seafood, and offal (like tender braised tongue in porcini broth), drive indecisive diners toward the $45 five-course tasting menu, a bargain. ✉ *222 W. 79th St., between Broadway and Amsterdam Ave., Upper West Side* ☎ *212/873–0200* ▭ *MC, V* Ⓜ *Subway: 1, 9 to 79th St.*

Indian

¢–$$ **Mughlai.** Standing well above the neighborhood's just-average offerings, Mughlai serves excellent Indian food in a pleasant glass-enclosed setting. The slightly higher-than-average prices reflect noticeably fresher ingredients, and less greasy, more expertly prepared dishes than you'll find elsewhere. Order one of the well-prepared classics, like chicken tikka masala; or grab a round of samosas and wait a little longer for succulent meats and vegetables to come out of the tandoori oven. ✉ *320 Columbus Ave., at 75th St., Upper West Side* ☎ *212/724–6363* ▭ *AE, DC, MC, V* ☽ *No lunch* Ⓜ *Subway: B, C to 72nd St.*

Italian

$–$$$$ ✕ **Carmine's.** This family-friendly restaurant serves truly huge portions of garlicky Italian-American food, like linguine with clam sauce, chicken parmigiana, and lobster fra diavolo. The dining room has dark woodwork and black-and-white tiles; outdoor seating is available in the front. Although it's impossible not to order too much, everything tastes just as satisfying the next day. ✉ *2450 Broadway, between W. 90th and W. 91st Sts., Upper West Side* ☎ *212/362–2200* ▭ *AE, DC, MC, V* Ⓜ *Subway: 1, 2, 3, 9 to 96th St.*

$$ ✕ **'Cesca.** Chef Tom Valenti's foray into Southern Italian cuisine provides intense, comforting-yet-sophisticated flavors in a rambling but stylish space. The shrimp raviolini has urban sophistication, but true Italophiles might opt for a heady bowl of tripe with red wine and pancetta. Desserts are excellent, but for a really authentic finish, try one of the amari, Italian bitters: this place easily has the best selection of them in New York, if not the country. ✉ *164 W. 75th St., at Amsterdam Ave., Upper West Side* ☎ *212/787–6300* ▭ *AE, D, DC, MC, V* ☽ *No lunch* Ⓜ *Subway: 1, 2, 3, 9 to 72nd St.*

¢–$$ ✕ **Nonna.** Grandma would have to cook for weeks to prepare all the rustic Italian dishes served at this farmhouse-inspired, family trattoria. You could make a meal just from the vast antipasti menu, which ranges from simple marinated mushrooms to baked clams and arancini (fried risotto balls). The menu rolls on with spaghetti carbonara and chicken under a brick. When everyone's full, sit back with a classic negroni, and digest! ✉ *520 Columbus Ave., at 85th St., Upper West Side* ☎ *212/579–3194* ▭ *AE, MC, V* Ⓜ *Subway: 1, 9 to 86th St.*

¢–$ ✕ **Gennaro.** A small space and excellent food equal long waits at this neighborhood restaurant, but an expansion has helped ease the crush. The pleasant dining room has brick walls and tables covered with white tablecloths. Start with the huge antipasto platter filled with hot and cold vegetables, prosciutto, fresh mozzarella, and shrimp, and then move on to the pastas or entrées like lemony roasted Cornish hen or red-wine braised lamb shank. ⊠ *665 Amsterdam Ave., between W. 92nd and W. 93rd Sts., Upper West Side* ☎ *212/665–5348* ⌲ *Reservations not accepted* ▭ *No credit cards* ⊘ *No lunch* Ⓜ *Subway: 1, 2, 3, 9 to 96th St.*

Latin

¢–$ ✕ **Café con Leche.** The Cuban and Dominican food here is inexpensive and satisfying. The counter area in front is perfect for enjoying a filling pressed sandwich and a café con leche. The menu also has numerous rice dishes and hefty entrées like *cerdo guisado* (pork stew). ⊠ *424 Amsterdam Ave., between W. 80th and W. 81st Sts., Upper West Side* ☎ *212/595–7000* ▭ *AE, MC, V* Ⓜ *Subway: 1, 9 to 86th St.* ⊠ *726 Amsterdam Ave., between W. 95th and W. 96th Sts., Upper West Side* ☎ *212/678–7000* Ⓜ *Subway: 1, 2, 3, 9 to 96th St.*

Mexican

¢–$ ✕ **Gabriela's.** For authentic Mexican cuisine at rock-bottom prices, this noisy, festive, kid-friendly cantina is the way to go. Top choices include tacos with roast pork and tamales stuffed with mushrooms and vegetables. The house specialty is a whole rotisserie chicken, served moist and spicy with rice, beans, and plantains and your choice of four mole sauces. ⊠ *685 Amsterdam Ave., at W. 93rd St., Upper West Side* ☎ *212/961–0574* Ⓜ *Subway: 1, 2, 3, 9 to 96th St.*

Pizza

¢–$ ✕ **Patsy's Pizzeria.** Not quite on par with the original Patsy's (which opened in 1933 in then-Italian East Harlem and continues to serve great pies from its coal oven), this outpost nevertheless serves some of the best pizza on the Upper West Side. The crust is thin, the sauce is thick, the cheese is bubbling, and the toppings are fresh. ⊠ *61 W. 74th St., between Columbus Ave. and Central Park W, Upper West Side* ☎ *212/579–3000* ▭ *No credit cards* Ⓜ *Subway: B, C to 72nd St.*

Seafood

$–$$ ✕ **Ocean Grill.** Known for its expansive raw bar, this stylish seafood spot is consistently packed with couples who look grateful that the babysitter didn't cancel. The drinks are generous, the prices are reasonable, and the fish is impeccably fresh. Best bets beyond the raw bar are the selection of sushi rolls and simple grilled entrées, such as tuna, salmon, and swordfish, although there are also more elaborate creations. ⊠ *384 Columbus Ave., between W. 78th and W. 79th Sts., Upper West Side* ☎ *212/579–2300* ▭ *AE, D, DC, MC, V* Ⓜ *Subway: B, C to 81st St.*

Vietnamese

¢–$ ✕ **Saigon Grill.** Some of New York's best is served at lightening speed at this affordable no-atmosphere restaurant, which packs in families and students alike thrilled to have found Chinatown-quality food uptown.

The appetizers are so delicious you might never make it to the entrées—standout starters include the shrimp summer roll, chicken satay, and barbecued spareribs with plum sauce. Main courses include basil shrimp and grilled marinated pork chops. ✉ *620 Amsterdam, at W. 90th St., Upper West Side* ☎ *212/875–9072* ⌨ *Reservations not accepted* ▭ *AE, D, DC, MC, V* Ⓜ *Subway: 1, 9 to 86th St.*

The Performing Arts

8

WORD OF MOUTH

"*Phantom* is an excellent, classic musical. It has wonderful music and a good storyline. If it is your first time in NYC, then it is a good choice."

—Susan56

"Last night I had the privilege of seeing the new ballet by Susan Stroman at Lincoln Center. It was so heartbreakingly beautiful that I think I stopped breathing at one point. No one in the packed house spoke, fidgeted, or had a cell phone go off. The first time in my life I have been left speechless."

—bugswife1

By Lynne Arany **THE PERFORMING ARTS CAPITAL** of American, New York attracts celebrated artists from around the world. But the city's own artistic resources are what make the performing arts here so special. Thousands of great actors, singers, dancers, musicians, and other artists populate the city, infusing New York's cultural scene with unparalleled levels of creative energy. And discerning patrons drive the arts scene as they strive to keep up with the latest—from flocking to a concert hall to hear a world-class soprano deliver a flawless performance to crowding in a cramped basement bookstore to support young writers nervously stumbling over their own prose.

New York has somewhere between 200 and 250 legitimate theaters, and many more ad hoc venues—parks, churches, universities, museums, lofts, galleries, streets, rooftops, and even parking lots. The city also keeps up a revolving door of festivals and special events: summer jazz, one-act-play marathons, international film series, and musical celebrations from the classical to the avant-garde, to name just a few. It's this unrivaled wealth of culture and art that many New Yorkers cite as the reason why they're here.

Getting Tickets

Scoring tickets to shows and concerts is fairly easy—especially if you have some flexibility with dates and times. The only way to ensure you'll get the seats you want, on the day that you want, at the price you want, is to purchase tickets in advance—and that might be months ahead for a hit show. In general, you'll find that tickets are more readily available for evening performances from Tuesday through Thursday and matinees on Wednesday. Tickets for Friday and Saturday evenings and for weekend matinees are tougher to secure.

What do tickets sell for, anyway? For the most part, the top ticket price for Broadway musicals is about $100; the best seats for Broadway plays can run as high as $90. Off-Broadway show tickets average about $50, while off-off-Broadway shows can be as low as $10. Tickets to an opera start at about $25 for the nosebleed seats and soar to more than $200 for those in the orchestra. Classical music concerts range from $25 to $90, depending on the venue. Dance performances are usually $15 to $50.

HOW TO BUY THEM   For Broadway shows, off-Broadway shows, and other big-ticket events, you can order tickets well in advance through **Telecharge** (☎ 212/239–6200 ⊕ www.telecharge.com) and **Ticketmaster** (☎ 212/307–4100 ⊕ www.ticketmaster.com). For off-Broadway shows, try **SmartTix** (☎ 212/868–4444 ⊕ www.smarttix.com) or **Ticket Central** (✉ 416 W. 42nd St., between 9th and 10th Aves., Midtown West ☎ 212/279–4200 ⊕ www.ticketcentral.org Ⓜ Subway: A, C, E to 42nd St.)

For opera, classical music, and dance performances, you should call the box office or order tickets from the venue's Web site. Some people prefer to purchase tickets at the box office, where they can see where they will be sitting on the seating chart. Brokers can get you last-minute seats, but these go for much more than the price on the ticket.

WHAT'S GOING ON

WITH SO MUCH to choose from, you might want to consult the critics—and in New York, there's one on every corner. From the journalists serving up their picks and pans at the newsstands and on television, to the opinionated cabbie who whisks you off to your next destination, there's plenty to go by.

There are many publications with arts and cultural coverage, but **Time Out New York** (⊕ www.timeoutny.com) provides the broadest of choices. Readings, lectures, and poetry slams that barely merit mention elsewhere get full attention. The **Village Voice**, (⊕ www.villagevoice.com), a weekly tabloid that comes out on Wednesday, has extensive arts listings as well.

In **New York** (⊕ www.newyorkmetro.com), check out the section called "The Week" for more the hot tickets. The **New Yorker** (⊕ www.newyorker.com), long known for its "Goings On About Town" listings, contains limited, yet ruthlessly succinct, reviews of the arts. Although they complain about the arts coverage in the **New York Times** (⊕ www.nytimes.com), everyone picks up a copy on Friday for its two-section "Weekend" overview. The Sunday "Arts and Leisure" section has longer articles on everything from rock to opera, plus a survey of cultural events for the coming week.

For unbiased briefs on individual performing arts events in all five boroughs—dance, music, theater, and family-friendly fare—contact **NYC/ONSTAGE** (☎ 212/768–1818). Run by the Theater Development Fund, the 24-hour service provides reliable information about performances in English and Spanish. You can easily select events by date as well as by type. If you want to purchase tickets, it patches you through to the appropriate company.

THEATER

Broadway—not the Statue of Liberty or even the Empire State Building—is the city's number one tourist attraction. The renovation and restoration of some of the city's oldest and grandest theaters on and near 42nd Street has drawn New Yorkers' attention again to Times Square. But to fully experience theater in New York, you'll also want to consider the many offerings outside of this hearty center. From splashy musical to austere performance piece, from the Battery to the Bronx, New York has shows for every taste and budget—on just about any night (or day) of the week.

So what to see, and where? For Broadway, off-Broadway, off-off Broadway, and unique performance art turn to *Time Out New York*; check the *New York Times* and the back pages of *New York* magazine for comprehensive up-to-the-minute Broadway coverage.

Broadway

To most people, New York theater is Broadway, meaning the region roughly bounded by West 41st and West 52nd streets, between 6th and 9th avenues. The names of the many theaters read like a roll call of American theater history: Edwin Booth, the Barrymores (Ethel, John, and Lionel), Eugene O'Neill, George Gershwin, Alfred Lunt and Lynn Fontanne, Helen Hayes, Richard Rodgers, Neil Simon, and now renowned theatrical illustrator Al Hirschfeld (after whom the Martin Beck was renamed in 2003).

Among the 40-odd Broadway theaters are some old playhouses as interesting for their history as for their current offerings. The handsomely renovated Selwyn is now known as the **American Airlines Theatre** (⊠ 227 W. 42nd St., between 7th and 8th Aves., Midtown West ☎ 212/719–1300 Ⓜ Subway: A, C, E to 42nd St.). After various reincarnations as a burlesque hall and pornographic movie house, this Venetian-style theater is now home to the Roundabout Theatre Company, which is acclaimed for its revivals of classic musicals and plays, such as a star-studded production of *12 Angry Men.* The lavish **Hilton Theatre** (⊠ 213 W. 43rd St., between 7th and 8th Aves., Midtown West ☎ 212/207–4100 Ⓜ Subway: A, C, E to 42nd St.) is an 1,839-seat house that combines two classic auditoriums, the Lyric and the Apollo. It incorporates architectural elements from both, adding state-of-the-art sound and lighting equipment.

Disney refurbished the art-nouveau **New Amsterdam Theater** (⊠ 214 W. 42nd St., between 7th and 8th Aves., Midtown West ☎ 212/282–2907 Ⓜ Subway: A, C, E to 42nd St.), where Eddie Cantor, Will Rogers, Fanny Brice, and the Ziegfeld Follies once drew crowds. Today it's the long-running den of *The Lion King.* The **St. James** (⊠ 246 W. 44th St., between Broadway and 8th Ave., Midtown West ☎ 212/269–6300 Ⓜ Subway: A, C, E to 42nd St.), current home of Mel Brooks's juggernaut *The Producers,* is where Lauren Bacall was an usherette in the '40s and where a little show called *Oklahoma!* changed musicals forever.

Off-Broadway Theaters

The best theater can often be found far from Times Square. Off- and off-off-Broadway houses are where you can find showcases for emerging playwrights, classic plays performed with new twists, and crowd-pleasers like *Blue Man Group* and *Stomp.* The venues themselves are often found in clusters around the city—in Greenwich Village, the East Village, and the Lower East Side, as well as in Brooklyn neighborhoods like DUMBO and Williamsburg.

At the cozy 178-seat theater belonging to the **Classic Stage Company** (⊠ 136 E. 13th St., between 3rd and 4th Aves., East Village ☎ 212/677–4210 ⊕ www.classicstage.org Ⓜ Subway: 4, 5, 6, L, N, R, Q, W to Union Sq.) you can see revivals of older works—such as Chekhov's *Three Sisters*—that still have relevance today. The **Ensemble Studio Theatre** (⊠ 549 W. 52nd St., between 10th and 11th Aves., Midtown West ☎ 212/247–4982 ⊕ www.ensemblestudiotheatre.org Ⓜ Subway: C, E to 50th St.) develops new American plays. Each spring it presents a monthlong festival of new one-acts by prominent playwrights. With the help of its resident acting troupe, **Jean Cocteau Repertory** (⊠ Bouwerie Lane Theatre, 330 the Bowery, at Bond St., East Village ☎ 212/677–0060, 212/279–4200 Tickets ⊕ www.jeancocteaurep.org Ⓜ Subway: B, D, F, V to

LAST-MINUTE TICKETS

FOR TICKETS at 25% to 50% off the usual price, head to TKTS (E Duffy Sq., W. 47th St. and Broadway, Midtown West m Subway: N, R, W to 49th St.; 1, 9 to 50th St. b South St. Seaport, at Front and John Sts., Lower Manhattan m Subway: 2, 3 to Fulton St.). There's usually a good selection of shows available, but don't expect to see the latest hits. The kiosks accept cash and traveler's checks—no credit cards. The Times Square location is open Monday– Saturday 3–8 and Sunday 11–7:30, as well as Wednesday and Saturday at 10–2 for matinee shows. South Street Seaport hours are Monday–Saturday 11–6 and Sunday 11–3:30.

Online deals can be found at **TheaterMania** (⊕ www.theatermania.com) and **Playbill** (⊕ www.playbill.com). You can subscribe to weekly e-mail notices or just log-in and troll their sites for Broadway and off-Broadway offers. For discounted tickets you'll need to print the page and present it at the box office.

For long-running shows, including popular hits like Phantom of the Opera, numerous vendors offer discount ticket vouchers. Exchange them at the box office for an actual ticket. The **Broadway Ticket Center** (✉ 1560 Broadway, between W. 46th and W. 47th Sts., Midtown West ☎ No phone Ⓜ Subway: R, W to 49th St.), inside the Times Square Visitors Center, is open Monday–Saturday 9–6 and Sunday 10–3.

Need to see the hottest show, no matter what it costs? **Continental Guest Services** (☎ 212/944–8910 ⊕ www.intercharge. com) is one of the best-known ticket brokers in Manhattan. Be warned: tickets can be double the usual price. Order "VIP tickets" from **Broadway Inner Circle** (☎ 866/847–8587 ⊕ www. broadwayinnercircle.com).

Broadway–Lafayette St.; 6 to Bleecker St.) revives classics by playwrights such as Genet, Moliere, Beckett, and Brecht.

The Public Theater (✉ 425 Lafayette St., south of Astor Pl., East Village ☎ 212/260–2400 ⊕ www.publictheater.org Ⓜ Subway: 6 to Astor Pl.; R, W to 8th St.) presents new, innovative theater. Productions of *Bring In 'Da Noise, Bring In 'Da Funk, A Chorus Line,* and *Hair* that began here all went on to successful Broadway runs. In summer you won't want ★ to miss the annual Shakespeare in the Park performances. **Manhattan Theatre Club (MTC)** (✉ Biltmore Theatre, 261 W. 47th St., between Broadway and 8th Aves., Midtown West ☎ 212/239–6200 ⊕ www.mtc-nyc.org Ⓜ Subway: R, W to 49th St.) presents challenging new plays and revivals in the magnificently restored 650-seat Biltmore Theatre. Playwrights Terrence McNally, Richard Greenberg, Elaine May, Craig Lucas, Athol Fugard, August Wilson, and A. R. Gurney were all produced here. Make sure to call ahead, as most of the tickets go to subscribers.

The New York Theater Workshop (✉ 79 E. 4th St., between 2nd and 3rd Aves., East Village ☎ 212/460–5475 ⊕ www.nytw.org Ⓜ Subway: F, V to 2nd Ave.; B, D, F, V to Broadway–Lafayette St.; 6 to Bleecker St.) produces new work by playwrights such as Paul Rudnick, Tony Kushner, and Claudia Shear. Jonathan Larson's musical, *Rent,* debuted here in 1996 three months before moving to Broadway. **Playwrights Horizons** (✉ 416 W. 42nd St., between 9th and 10th Aves., Midtown West ☎ 212/564–1235, 212/279–4200 tickets ⊕ www.playwrightshorizons.org Ⓜ Subway: 1, 2, 3, 7, 9, N, Q, R, W to 42nd St./Times Sq.) produces promising new works, including Pulitzer Prize winners such as Wendy Wasserstein's *The Heidi Chronicles* and Stephen Sondheim's *Sunday in the Park with George.*

Signature Theatre Company (✉ Peter Norton Space, 555 W. 42nd St., between 10th and 11th Aves., Midtown West ☎ 212/244–7529 ⊕ www.signaturetheatre.org Ⓜ Subway: 1, 2, 3, 7, 9, N, Q, R, W to 42nd St./Times Sq.) devotes each season to works by a single playwright; past luminaries have included Lanford Wilson and Sam Shepard. The **Vineyard Theatre** (✉ 108 E. 15th St., between Park Ave. S and Irving Pl., Gramercy ☎ 212/353–0303 ⊕ www.vineyardtheatre.org Ⓜ Subway: 4, 5, 6, L, N, R to 14th St./Union Sq.), one of the best-regarded off-Broadway companies, knows how to pick a winner. Its productions of Paula Vogel's *How I Learned to Drive* and Edward Albee's *Three Tall Women* both won Pulitzers; *Avenue Q* began here and went on to Broadway.

Elsewhere in the City

The following theaters host works that are often startling in their originality. You won't find anything resembling this on Broadway.

The **Brooklyn Academy of Music** (✉ Peter Jay Sharp Bldg., 30 Lafayette Ave., between Ashland Pl. and St. Felix St., Fort Greene, Brooklyn ☎ 718/636–4100 ⊕ www.bam.org Ⓜ Subway: C to Lafayette Ave.; 2, 3, 4, 5, Q to Atlantic Ave.) has built its considerable reputation on its annual Next Wave Festival, which stages avant-garde works. **Galapagos Art Space** (✉ 70 N. 6th St., between Kent and Wythe Aves., Williamsburg Brooklyn ☎ 718/384–4586 ⊕ www.galapagosartspace.com Ⓜ Subway: L to Bedford Ave.) has firmly established itself as an integral part of Brooklyn's arts scene. On its two stages (in what was once a mayonnaise factory) theatrical hijinks run the gamut from puppet musicals to bawdy burlesque. **HERE Arts Center** (✉ 145 6th Ave., between Spring and Broome Sts., SoHo ☎ 212/868–4444 tickets ⊕ www.here.org Ⓜ Subway: C, E to Spring St.), home to Eve Ensler's 1997 *The Vagina Monologues,* has three theaters, and art gallery, and a café.

The Kitchen (✉ 512 W. 19th St., between 10th and 11th Aves., Chelsea ☎ 212/255–5793 ⊕ www.thekitchen.org Ⓜ Subway: C, E to 23rd St.) is the place for performance art. Ellen Stewart, also known as La Mama, was the moving force behind **La Mama E.T.C.** (✉ 74A E. 4th St., between Bowery and 2nd Ave., East Village ☎ 212/475–7710 ⊕ www.lamama.org Ⓜ Subway: F, V to 2nd Ave.; B, D, F, V to Broadway–Lafayette St.; 6 to Bleecker St.). What was a tiny performance space in 1961 has grown to include two theaters and a club. Productions include everything from African fables to new-wave operas. Past triumphs have included the original productions of *Godspell* and *Torch Song Trilogy.* **P.S.122** (✉ 150 1st Ave., at E. 9th St., East Village ☎ 212/477–5288 ⊕ www.ps122.

org Ⓜ Subway: 6 to Astor Pl.), housed in a former public school, has served as an incubator for talent like Spalding Gray and Laurie Anderson.

St. Ann's Warehouse (✉ 38 Water St., between Main and Dock Sts., DUMBO Brooklyn ☎ 718/254–8779 ⊕ www.stannswarehouse.org Ⓜ Subway: A, C to High St.; F to York St.) hosts everything from puppet operas to the Wooster Group's latest theatrical productions. A four-theater cultural complex is home to **Theater for the New City** (✉ 155 1st Ave., between E. 9th and E. 10th Sts., East Village ☎ 212/254–1109 ⊕ www.theaterforthenewcity.net Ⓜ Subway: 6 to Astor Pl.). It puts on 30–40 new American plays each year, including works by Moises Kaufman and Mabou Mines.

Theater for Children

★ ☺ The **New Victory Theater** (✉ 209 W. 42nd St., between 7th and 8th Aves., Midtown West ☎ 212/239–6200 ⊕ www.newvictory.org Ⓜ Subway: 1, 2, 3, 7, 9, N, Q, R, W to 42nd St./Times Sq.) presents plays, music, and dance performances, and even minicircuses in a magnificently restored century-old theater. The 500-seat venue attracts top-notch
☺ shows enjoyed by children and their parents. The **Paper Bag Players** (✉ Kaye Playhouse, E. 68th St., between Park and Lexington Aves., Upper East Side ☎ 212/772–4448 ⊕ www.paperbagplayers.org Ⓜ Subway: 6 to 68th St./Hunter College), the country's oldest children's theater, stages original plays for youngsters under 10.

☺ **Tada!** (✉ 120 W. 28th St., between 6th and 7th Aves., Chelsea ☎ 212/252–1619 ⊕ www.tadatheater.com Ⓜ Subway: 1, 9 to 28th St.) is a popular children's theater group that presents vibrant musical theater pieces.

☺ **Theatreworks/USA** (✉ Auditorium at Equitable Tower, 787 7th Ave., between 51st and 52nd Sts., Midtown West ☎ 212/647–1100 Ⓜ Subway: 1, 9 to 79th St.) mounts original productions based on well-known children's books. Popular shows have included *The Adventures of Curious George* and *Junie B. Jones*.

The Circus

☺ New York's wonderful **Big Apple Circus** (✉ Lincoln Center Plaza, Upper West Side ☎ 212/721–6500 or 800/922–3772 ⊕ www.bigapplecircus.org) is a must-see. It entertains kids and their families both in New York and in shows around the country. The world-renowned **Cirque du Soleil** (⊕ www.cirquedusoleil.com) visits New York with some regularity. Cirque offers sophisticated productions—and pricey tickets to go with them—but their acrobatics and atmosphere always amaze.

Puppet Shows

☺ **Puppet Playhouse** (✉ Asphalt Green, 555 E. 90th St., between York and East End Aves., Upper East Side ☎ 212/369–8890 ⊕ www.asphaltgreen.org Ⓜ Subway: 4, 5, 6 to 86th St.) presents original shows every Saturday; hand puppets, marionettes, rod puppets, or shadow puppets
☺ could all make an appearance. Finely detailed wooden marionettes and hand puppets are on the bill at **Puppetworks** (✉ 338 6th Ave., at 4th St., Park Slope, Brooklyn ☎ 718/965–3391 ⊕ www.puppetworks.org) Familiar childhood tales like *Little Red Riding Hood* and *Peter and the Wolf* come to life in this 75-seat neighborhood theater.

The **Swedish Cottage Marionette Theater** (✉ Swedish Cottage, W. Park Dr., north of W. 79th St., Central Park ☎ 212/988–9093 ⊕ www. centralparknyc.org Ⓜ Subway: B, C to 79th St.) entertains children year-round. The charming wooden 100-seat state-of-the-art playhouse (originally brought here from Sweden in 1876) presents classics like *Hansel and Gretel, Cinderella,* and *Jack and the Beanstalk.* Latino arts and culture are celebrated with a very sly sense of humor at the bilingual **Teatro SEA @ Los Kabayitos Puppet & Children's Theater** (✉ Clemente Soto Vélez Cultural & Educational Center, 107 Suffolk St., between Delancey and Rivington Sts., Lower East Side ☎ 212/260–4080 Ext.14 ⊕ www.sea-ny.org Ⓜ Subway: F to Delancey St.; J, M, Z to Essex St.). All shows in this 50-seat venue are presented in English and Spanish, and you're likely to see the *Three Little Pigs* dancing to salsa music.

MUSIC

"Gentlemen," conductor Serge Koussevitzky once told the assembled Boston Symphony Orchestra, "maybe it's good enough for Cleveland or Cincinnati, but it's not good enough for New York." In a nutshell he described New York's central position in the musical world. New York possesses the country's oldest symphony orchestra (the New York Philharmonic) as well as three renowned conservatories (the Juilliard School, the Manhattan School of Music, and Mannes College of Music). For more than a century, the best orchestras have made this a principal stop on their tours. The city is also a mecca for an astonishing variety of musicians playing everything from klezmer to Senegalese percussion.

Concert Halls

The **Brooklyn Academy of Music (BAM)** (✉ 30 Lafayette Ave., between Ashland Pl. and St. Felix St., Fort Greene, Brooklyn ☎ 718/636–4100 ⊕ www.bam.org Ⓜ Subway: C to Lafayette Ave.; 2, 3, 4, 5, Q to Atlantic Ave.) has two spaces with extraordinary acoustics: the 2,100-seat Howard Gilman Opera House and the smaller Harvey Theater. Both host contemporary and experimental works by renowned artists such as Philip Glass, Laurie Anderson, and Robert Wilson. BAM is the home of the **Brooklyn Philharmonic** (☎ 718/488–5700 ⊕ www. brooklynphilharmonic.org), with a reputation for having the city's most adventurous symphonic programming.

Fodor'sChoice ★ **Carnegie Hall** (✉ 881 7th Ave., at W. 57th St., Midtown West ☎ 212/247–7800 ⊕ www.carnegiehall.org Ⓜ Subway: N, Q, R, W to 57th St.; B, D, E to 7th Ave.) is one of the best places to hear classical music. The world's top orchestras sound their best because of the incomparable acoustics of the 2,804-seat **Stern Auditorium.** So do smaller ensembles and soloists such as soprano Renée Fleming. The subterranean **Zankel Hall,** which also has excellent acoustics, attracts performers such as the Kronos Quartet and Youssou N'Dour. Many young talents make their New York debuts in the **Weill Recital Hall.**

Lincoln Center for the Performing Arts (✉ W. 62nd to W. 66th Sts., Broadway to Amsterdam Ave., Upper West Side ☎ 212/546–2656 ⊕ www.

lincolncenter.org Ⓜ Subway: 1, 9 to 66th St./Lincoln Center) is the city's musical nerve center, especially when it comes to classical music. Intimate **Alice Tully Hall,** Lincoln Center's "little white box," is considered to be as acoustically perfect as a concert hall can get. The massive **Avery Fisher Hall** hosts the world's great musicians. The concert hall is home to the **New York Philharmonic** (☏212/875–5656 ⊕newyorkphilharmonic.org), one of the world's finest symphony orchestras. Lorin Maazel conducts performances from late September to early June. In addition, the orchestra occasionally schedules bargain-price weeknight "rush hour" performances at 6:45 PM and "Saturday matinee" concerts at 2 PM; Orchestra rehearsals at 9:45 AM are open to the public on selected weekday mornings (usually Wednesday or Thursday)for $15.

Other Venues

Aaron Davis Hall at City College (✉ Convent Ave., between W. 133rd and 135th Sts., Harlem ☏212/650–6900 ⊕www.aarondavishall.org Ⓜ Subway: 1, 9 to 137th St.) is an uptown venue for jazz and world music, hosting groups like the Abbey Lincoln Quartet. **The Cloisters** (✉Fort Tryon Park, Morningside Heights ☏212/923–3700 information, 212/650–2290 tickets ⊕ www.metmuseum.org Ⓜ Subway: A to 190th St.) offers matinee performances of sacred and secular music from the Middle Ages, all of which take place within the authentic ambience of a 12th-century Spanish chapel. **Frederick P. Rose Hall** (✉ Columbus Circle, at W. 60th St., Upper West Side ☏ 212/258–9800 ⊕ www.jalc.org) is the superb new home of **Jazz at Lincoln Center,** featuring the Lincoln Center Jazz Orchestra under the direction of Wynton Marsalis. The space overlooking Central Park contains two concert halls: the Rose Theater (seating 1,100–1,220 people) and the Allen Room (seating 300–600 people).

The **Knitting Factory** (✉ 74 Leonard St., between Broadway and Church Sts., TriBeCa ☏212/219–3055 ⊕www.knittingfactory.com Ⓜ Subway: 1, 9 to Franklin St.) is a funky, three-story complex that hosts a wide range of downtown musicians. The emphasis is on jazz of all types. **Merkin Concert Hall** (✉ Kaufman Center at Goodman House, 129 W. 67th St., between Broadway and Amsterdam Ave., Upper West Side ☏ 212/501–3330 ⊕ www.kaufman-center.org/ Ⓜ Subway: 1, 9 to 66th St./Lincoln Center) presents chamber pieces, but it's also a fine spot for jazz and other types of music. The **Metropolitan Museum of Art** (✉ 1000 5th Ave., at E. 82nd St., Upper East Side ☏ 212/570–3949 ⊕ www.metmuseum. org Ⓜ Subway: 4, 5, 6 to 86th St.) has three stages—the Temple of Dendur; the Grace Rainey Rogers Auditorium; and the Medieval Sculpture Hall—with concerts by leading classical and jazz musicians. Other than Friday and Saturday evenings, when the museum is open late, access is through the street-level entrance at East 83rd Street and 5th Avenue.

The **Miller Theatre** (✉ Columbia University, Broadway at W. 116th St., Morningside Heights ☏212/854–1633 ⊕www.millertheatre.com Ⓜ Subway: 1, 9 to 116th St.) presents a varied program of cutting-edge jazz, classical, and modern music. **Symphony Space** (✉ 2537 Broadway, at W. 95th St., Upper West Side ☏212/864–5400 ⊕ www.symphonyspace.org Ⓜ Subway: 1, 2, 3, 9 to 96th St.) presents a fine range of chamber, new music, folk, and pop music in its Peter Jay Sharp Theatre. **The Town Hall** (✉ 123 W. 43rd St., between 6th and 7th Aves., Midtown West ☎ 212/840–2824 ⊕ www.the-townhall-nyc.org Ⓜ Subway: 1, 2, 9, N, R, A, C, E to Times Sq.) hosts eclectic programs of jazz and world music.

Well-known soloists and chamber music groups perform in Kaufmann Concert Hall at the **Tisch Center for the Arts** (✉ 92nd St. Y, 1395 Lexington Ave., at E. 92nd St., Upper East Side ☎ 212/996–1100 ⊕ www.92ndsty.org Ⓜ Subway: 1, 9 to 96th St.). The **Tribeca Performing Arts Center** (✉ 199 Chambers St., at Greenwich St., TriBeCa ☎ 212/220–1460 ⊕ www.tribecapac.org Ⓜ Subway: A, C, E to Chambers St.) has an eclectic music program, but the long-running "Highlights in Jazz" concert series is the main event.

OPERA

The greatest singers in the world all clamor to test their mettle at the Metropolitan Opera, where they can work alongside internationally admired directors and designers. The Met's lavish productions are far from cheap, unless you buy standing-room tickets. Another opera company next door—the New York City Opera—is known for nurturing up-and-coming talent and staging new and obscure works.

Major Companies

Fodor'sChoice
★
The titan of American opera companies, the **Metropolitan Opera** (✉ W. 62nd to W. 66th Sts., Broadway to Amsterdam Ave., Upper West Side ☎ 212/362–6000 ⊕ www.metopera.org Ⓜ Subway: 1, 9 to 66th St./Lincoln Center) brings the world's leading singers to its massive stage at Lincoln Center from October to April. Under the direction of James Levine, the company's music director and principal conductor, the orchestra rivals the world's finest symphonies. All performances, including those sung in English, are unobtrusively subtitled on small screens on the back of the seat in front of you. As for standing room, the Met is the rare venue that makes these tickets available in advance. They go on sale at their box office Saturday at 10 AM for the following week, and usually cost $15 to $20.

Although not as famous as its next-door neighbor, the **New York City Opera** (✉ W. 62nd to W. 66th Sts., Broadway to Amsterdam Ave., Upper West Side ☎ 212/870–5570 ⊕ www.nycopera.com Ⓜ Subway: 1, 9 to 66th St./Lincoln Center) draws a crowd to its performances at the New York State Theater. Founded in 1943, the company is known as well for its innovative and diverse repertory. Under the leadership of artistic director Paul Kellogg, City Opera stages rarely seen baroque operas such as *Acis and Galatea* and *Rinaldo,* adventurous new works such as Jack Beeson's *Lizzie Borden,* and beloved classics such as *La Bohème, Carmen,* and the like. Placido Domingo and Beverly Sills began their careers at City Opera; a new generation of great voices is following in their footsteps. City Opera performs September to November and March to April. All performances of foreign-language operas have supertitles— line-by-line English translations—displayed above the stage.

Smaller Companies

🕙 In New York, small opera companies can be very, very good. The **Amato Opera Theatre** (✉ 319 Bowery, at E. 2nd St., East Village ☏ 212/228–8200 ⊕ www.amato.org Ⓜ Subway: B, D, F, V to Broadway–Lafayette St.; 6 to Bleecker St.; F, V to 2nd Ave.), which claims to be the world's smallest opera house, is a well-established showcase for rising singers and performs classics by Verdi, Mozart, and others. To top it off, it has reasonable prices. "Opera-in-Brief" matinees are tailored to children. Originally known as the Henry Street Chamber Opera, the **Gotham Chamber Opera** (✉ Harry de Jur Playhouse, 466 Grand St., at Pitt St., Lower East Side ☏ 212/868–4460 ⊕ www.gothamchamberopera.org Ⓜ Subway: F to Delancey St.; J, M, Z to Essex St.) presents small-scale chamber works. Featuring American premieres of little-known works (such as Handel's *Arianna in Creta*), the 350-seat Georgian Revival theater makes a fine home to pieces from the Baroque era to the present. The **New York Gilbert & Sullivan Players** (☏ 212/769–1000 ⊕ www.nygasp.org) present lively productions of operettas such as *The Pirates of Penzance* and *The Mikado* plus rarities like Sullivan's last completed work, *The Rose of Persia*.

DANCE

In a city that seems never to stop moving, dance is a thriving art form. Ballet aficionados are well-served in the grand performing arts centers, while those in search of something different will find it in all corners of the city, including more experimental venues downtown.

Ballet

The **American Ballet Theatre** (☏ 212/477–3030 ⊕ www.abt.org) is renowned for its brilliant renditions of the great 19th-century classics (*Swan Lake, Giselle, The Sleeping Beauty,* and *La Bayardère*) as well as its more modern repertoire, including works by such 20th-century masters as George Balanchine, Jerome Robbins, and Agnes de Mille. Since its founding in 1940, the company has nurtured some of the great dancers, including Mikhail Baryshnikov, Natalia Makarova, Rudolf Nureyev, Gelsey Kirkland, and Cynthia Gregory. The ballet has two New York seasons—eight weeks beginning in May at its home in the Metropolitan Opera House and two weeks in the fall (usually October) at City Center.

★ 🕙 With more than 90 dancers, the **New York City Ballet** (☏ 212/870–5570 ⊕ www.nycballet.com), has an unmatched repertoire of 20th-century works. Its fall season, which runs from mid-November through December, includes the beloved annual production of George Balanchine's *The Nutcracker*. Its spring season runs from April through June. The company continues to stress the works themselves rather than individual performers, although that hasn't stopped a number of principal dancers (such as Kyra Nichols, Darci Kistler, Damian Woetzel, and Jock Soto) from earning kudos. The company performs in Lincoln Center's New York State Theater. Family-friendly Saturday matinees are offered throughout the regular season.

Modern Dance

The world's most innovative dance companies perform in New York throughout the year, especially in fall and spring, showcasing the thrilling work of such legendary choreographers as Martha Graham, Merce Cunningham, Alvin Ailey, Mark Morris, and Paul Taylor.

The **Brooklyn Academy of Music** (✉ 30 Lafayette Ave., between Ashland Pl. and St. Felix St., Fort Greene, Brooklyn ☎ 718/636–4100 ⊕ www. bam.org Ⓜ Subway: C to Lafayette Ave.; 2, 3, 4, 5, Q to Atlantic Ave.) hosts an assortment of such innovative troupes as German choreographer Pina Bausch's dance-theater company. You can also catch the clever **Mark Morris Dance Group** (⊕ www.mmdg.org) here. At **City Center** (✉ 131 W. 55th St., between 6th and 7th Aves., Midtown West ☎ 212/581–1212 ⊕ www.citycenter.org Ⓜ Subway: N, R, Q, W to 57th St./7th Ave.; F to 57th St./6th Ave.), marvelous modern dance troupes such as **Alvin Ailey American Dance Theater** (www.alvinailey.org) and **Paul Taylor Dance Company** (www.ptdc.org) hold sway. **Dance Theater Workshop** (✉ 219 W. 19th St., between 7th and 8th Aves., Chelsea ☎ 212/924–0077 ⊕ www.dtw. org Ⓜ Subway: 1, 9 to 23rd St.) serves as a laboratory for new choreographers. Performances here are enhanced by a wonderfully renovated space.

★

Danspace Project (✉ 131 E. 10th St., at 2nd Ave., East Village ☎ 212/674–8194 ⊕ www.danspaceproject.org Ⓜ Subway: 6 to Astor Pl.), founded to foster the work of independent choreographers such as Bill T. Jones, sponsors a series of avant-garde performances that runs from September through June. In a former art deco movie house in Chelsea, the 500-seat **Joyce Theater** (✉ 175 8th Ave., at W. 19th St., Chelsea ☎ 212/242–0800 ⊕ www.joyce.org Ⓜ Subway: A, C, E to 14th St.; L to 8th Ave.) presents contemporary dance ranging from tap to ballet. **David Parsons** (www. parsonsdance.org) is a regular on the line-up. The Joyce is also known for its special family matinees. The **Joyce SoHo** (✉ 155 Mercer St., between Houston and Prince Sts., SoHo ☎ 212/431–9233 Ⓜ Subway: R, W to Prince St.) hosts performances by an array of up-and-coming choreographers. The **Harkness Dance Project** (✉ The Duke on 42nd St., 229 W. 42nd St., between 8th and 9th Aves., Midtown West ☎ 212/415–5500 ⊕ www.92ndsty.org Ⓜ Subway: A, C, E to 42nd St.) presents contemporary dance troupes at the cutting edge (and at very reasonable prices).

★ ♻

Performing Arts Centers

Fodor'sChoice
★

America's oldest performing arts center, the **Brooklyn Academy of Music** (✉ Peter Jay Sharp Bldg., 30 Lafayette Ave., between Ashland Pl. and St. Felix St., Fort Greene Brooklyn ☎ 718/636–4100 ⊕ www.bam.org Ⓜ Subway: C to Lafayette Ave.; 2, 3, 4, 5, Q to Atlantic Ave.), has been around since in 1859. BAM has a reputation for daring and innovative dance, music, opera, and theater productions, as well as a renowned film series, BAMcinématek. The main performance spaces are the 2,100-seat Howard Gilman Opera House (which the Brooklyn Philharmonic calls home), a white-brick Renaissance Revival palace built in 1908 and now spectacularly restored, and the 874-seat Harvey Theater, a 1904 theater a block away at 651 Fulton Street. BAM's annual Next Wave Festival in fall draws a global audience for its cutting-edge productions. Year-round you can grab a bite—or a meal—at the BAMcafé, which becomes a cabaret venue Thursday through Saturday nights. The **BAMbus** (Whitney Museum of American Art at Altria ⊠ 120 Park Ave., at E. 42nd St., Midtown East ☎ 718/636–4100) provides round-trip transportation from Manhattan one hour prior to a performance. Reservations are required.

Carnegie Hall (⊠ 881 7th Ave., at W. 57th St., Midtown West ☎ 212/247–7800 ⊕ www.carnegiehall.org Ⓜ Subway: N, Q, R, W to 57th St.; B, D, E to 7th Ave.) is one of the world's most famous concert halls. Virtually every important musician of the 20th century performed in this century-old Italian Renaissance–style building, often at the peak of his or her creative powers. Tchaikovsky conducted the opening night concert on May 5, 1891, Leonard Bernstein had his famous debut here, and Vladimir Horowitz made his historic return to the concert stage here, as well. Performances are given in the grand 2,804-seat Isaac Stern Auditorium, the Weill Recital Hall (where many young talents make their New York debuts), as well as the new, intimate, and acoustically superb Judy and Arthur Zankel Hall on the lower level. Although the emphasis is on classical music, Carnegie Hall also hosts jazz, pop, cabaret, and folk music concerts.

City Center (⊠ 131 W. 55th St., between 6th and 7th Aves., Midtown West ☎ 212/581–1212 ⊕ www.citycenter.org Ⓜ Subway: N, R, Q, W to 57th St./7th Ave.; F to 57th St./6th Ave.) has a neo-Moorish look (no surprise, as it was built in 1923 by the Ancient and Accepted Order of the Mystic Shrine). Saved from demolition in 1943 by Mayor Fiorello LaGuardia, it's the primary New York performance space for major dance troupes such as the Martha Graham Dance Company and Alvin Ailey American Dance Theater, and hosts annual appearance by the American Ballet Theatre and the Paul Taylor Dance Group. The lush 2,750-seat theater is also home to a number of productions and programs of the Manhattan Theatre Club.

★ **Lincoln Center for the Performing Arts** (⊠ W. 62nd to W. 66th Sts., Broadway to Amsterdam Ave., Upper West Side ☎ 212/546–2656 ⊕ www.lincolncenter.org Ⓜ Subway: 1, 9 to 66th St./Lincoln Center) is a 16-acre complex comprised of the Metropolitan Opera House, the New York State Theater (home of the New York City Opera and the American Ballet Theatre), Avery Fisher Hall (home of the New York Philharmonic), Alice Tully Hall, the Vivian Beaumont Theater, the Mitzi E. Newhouse Theater, the New York Public Library for the Performing Arts, and the Walter Reade Theater. The predominately travertine-clad buildings were designed by a multiple of architects, all of whom applied a relatively classical aesthetic to the angular modern structures. Philharmonic Hall (now Avery Fisher), designed by Max Abramovitz, broke ground first, opening in 1962. The hall's improved acoustics came with a Philip Johnson and John Burgee renovation in 1976. The Met, with its Austrian-crystal chandeliers and Marc Chagall paintings, premiered in 1966. Eero Saarinen was the architect for the two finely scaled theaters, the Beaumont (a Broadway house) and the Newhouse (an off-Broadway house).

By the 1990s the huge open plaza surrounding the famous fountain had become a well-used performance space of its own. The **Midsummer Night Swing** (☎ 212/875–5766) is a monthlong dance party that runs three or four nights each week starting in late June on the central plaza. Dancers swing, hustle, polka, merengue, salsa, tango, and more to the beat of a live band. The **Lincoln Center Festival** (☎ 212/875–5928) runs for three weeks, usually in July. The programs include classical and contemporary music concerts, dance, film, and theater works. Lincoln Center's longest running classical series is the August **Mostly Mozart Festival** (☎ 212/875–5399), featuring the music of Mozart and other classical favorites.

The **Skirball Center for the Performing Arts at NYU** (✉ 566 LaGuardia Pl., Washington Sq. Park S, Greenwich Village ☎ 212/992–8484 ⊕ www. skirballcenter.nyu.edu Ⓜ Subway: A, B, C, D, E, F, V to W. 4th St./Washington Sq.), in the Kimmel Center for University Life, is a sleekly designed 879-seat space for music, dance, and theater. Recent performers include the Parsons Dance Company, the Eos Orchestra, and Ballet Hispanico.

Symphony Space (✉ 2537 Broadway, at W. 95th St., Upper West Side ☎ 212/864–5400 ⊕ www.symphonyspace.org Ⓜ Subway: 1, 2, 3, 9 to 96th St.) presents a rich program of contemporary dance, chamber, folk, and new music, film, and spoken word events. Its 760-seat Peter Jay Sharp Theatre adjoins the 176-seat Leonard Nimoy Thalia Theatre.

FILM & TELEVISION

Film

On any given week New York City theaters screen all the major new releases, classics renowned and obscure, foreign films, small independent flicks, hard-to-find documentaries, and cutting-edge video and experimental works. The theaters themselves run the gamut from sleek multiplexes with massive screens and rows of stadium seating to shoe-box-size screening rooms with room for a few dozen people.

Getting Tickets

New York may be the global capital of cineasts, so sold-out shows are common. It's a good idea to purchase tickets in advance. A good rule of thumb, unless your pick has been out for at least a week or two, is to get to the box office at least an hour ahead of show time. If you're seeing a blockbuster, you'll need even more lead time. If you do arrive around show time, you may have to hunt for the few remaining seats.

Oddly enough, no one phone or online ticket service handles advance ticket purchase for all of the city's screens. For chains, and even many independent houses, you'll need to contact one of the following to purchase tickets ahead with a credit card: **Fandango** (☎ 800/555–8355 ⊕ www.fandango.com) handles Landmark, Loew's, and Regal theaters. Tickets for the remaining chains, including United Artists and Clearview, may be purchased from **AOLMovieFone** (☎ 212/777–3456 ⊕ www.moviefone.com). There's usually a service charge of $1 to $2

TRIBECA FILM FESTIVAL

Not surprisingly, film festivals abound in New York City. But none has the razzle-dazzle of a relative newcomer, The Tribeca Film Festival. Born of the aftermath of the World Trade Center disaster, the festival—brainchild of producer Jane Rosenthal and actor Robert De Niro—was meant to not only boost the devastated economy of Lower Manhattan, but also to celebrate the city's preeminence as a filmmaking capital.

Seeking to capture the excitement and power of film, Rosenthal and De Niro put together a rich assortment of major-studio premieres (the latest installment in the Star Wars series was the surprise starter for 2002), independent films, documentaries, shorts, and restored classics. The low cost—$10 to most screenings—makes it affordable for everyone. To keep things lively, there were panel discussions, outdoor concerts, and even a street fair. Local residents and merchants gave the project their wholehearted support, and with the assistance of more than 1,300 volunteers (and many corporate sponsors) the first annual Tribeca Film Festival was a rousing success. It attracted a remarkable 150,000 in its first year.

In just a few years, the Tribeca Film Festival has grown into a 10-day event covering two weekends in April or May. About 250 films from more than 40 different countries, many of them world premieres, are screened in a variety of venues below Canal Street. The impressive panels of jurors are chosen from a wealth of arts luminaries, among them film star Glenn Close and architect Richard Meier. Illuminating panel discussions with writers, directors, actors, directors, producers, cinematographers, get past the glamor and glitz and focus on the nitty-gritty of filmmaking.

Each year sees a special theme. In 2003 a series of the "10 most influential African-American films of the 20th Century" celebrated the Black Filmmaker Foundation's 25th anniversary. Martin Scorsese's "Restoration Film Series" has become an audience feature. Outdoor events—like the Family Outdoor Street Fair (with live music, puppet shows, and a "garden of kites") and the Tribeca Drive-in Theater (with screenings of old favorites like West Side Story on Pier 25 overlooking the Hudson River—contribute to the special neighborhood atmosphere that pervades the festival. For more information, go to www.tribecafilmfestival.org.

for phone or online orders. Note that tickets for some smaller venues—usually independent theaters—may be purchased through that venue's Web site.

Tickets to most theaters in New York are $9.50 to $10.50. Although there are no bargain matinees in Manhattan, discounts for seniors and children are usually available. For quick access to show times and locations, try the ticket services listed above or the *New York Times* ⊕ www.nytimes.com. *Time Out New York* ⊕ www.timeoutny.com is especially good for its "Alternatives & Revivals" listings.

First-Run Movies

Wherever you are in New York City, you usually don't have to walk far to find a movie theater showing recent releases. And "first-run" in New York is as much about documentaries and foreign films as it's about commercial blockbusters.

Foreign and independent films are screened at the **Angelika Film Center** (✉ 18 W. Houston St., at Mercer St., Greenwich Village ☎ 212/995–2000 ⊕ www.angelikafilmcenter.com Ⓜ Subway: B, D, F, V to Broadway/Lafayette St.; 6 to Bleecker St.). It's incredibly popular, despite its tunnel-like theaters and truncated screens. The upstairs café has food that's a cut above your average multiplex. **Cinema Village** (✉ 22 E. 12th St., between University Pl. and 5th Ave., Greenwich Village ☎ 212/924–3363 Ⓜ Subway: 4, 5, 6, L, N, Q, R, W to 14th St./Union Sq.) has three tiny screening rooms (with surprisingly good sight lines) that show a smart selection of documentaries and foreign films. Within a sleekly renovated space that was once a vaudeville theater, **Landmark's Sunshine Cinema** (✉ 143 E. Houston St., between 1st and 2nd Aves., Lower East Side ☎ 212/358–7709 ⊕ www.landmarktheatres.com Ⓜ Subway: F, V to 2nd Ave.) has seven decent-size screens showing independent films.

A comfortable, modern multiplex with good-size screens, **Lincoln Plaza Cinemas** (✉ 1886 Broadway, at 62nd St., Upper West Side ☎ 212/757–2280 Ⓜ Subway: 1, 9 to 66th St.) is especially big on foreign-language film. Just off Central Park, **The Paris** (✉ 4 W. 58th St., between 5th and 6th Aves., Midtown West ☎ 212/688–3800 Ⓜ Subway: F to 57th St.) is a rare single-screen showcase for new movies, usually those with a limited release.

Movie lovers adore the **Quad Cinema** (✉ 34 W. 13th St., between 5th and 6th Aves., Greenwich Village ☎212/255–8800 ⊕www.quadcinema.com Ⓜ Subway: 4, 5, 6, L, N, Q, R, W to 14th St./Union Sq.), which plays first-run art and foreign films on four very small screens. The **Village East Cinemas** (✉181–189 2nd Ave., at E. 12th St., East Village ☎212/529–6799 Ⓜ Subway: 6 to Astor Pl.) is housed in a restored Yiddish theater. Catch a film that's screening on the ground floor and check out the Moorish-style decor.

★ To experience the last of the old-fashioned movie palaces, head to the **Ziegfeld** (✉ 141 W. 54th St., between 6th and 7th Aves., Midtown West ☎ 212/765–7600 Ⓜ Subway: N, R, W, Q to 57th St.). Its crimson decor, good sight lines, and solid sound system make it a special place to view the latest blockbusters; grand-opening galas often take place here as well.

Alternative Spaces, Revival Films & Festivals

New Yorkers have such a ravenous appetite for celluloid that even barely publicized independent projects can expect a full house, as can revivals of obscure movies and foreign film festivals. Besides traditional movie houses, these gems frequently screen at museums, cultural societies, and other performance spaces, such as the Brooklyn Academy of Music, the Film Society of Lincoln Center, the Museum of Modern Art, Scandinavia House, the French Institute, and even branches of the New York Public Library.

Fodor'sChoice In addition to premiering new releases, **Film Forum** (✉ 209 W. Houston
★ St., between 6th Ave. and Varick St., Greenwich Village ☎ 212/727–8110 ⊕ www.filmforum.com Ⓜ Subway: 1, 9 to Houston St.), a non-profit theater with three small screening rooms, hosts ongoing series of movies by directors such as Samuel Fuller, festivals of genres like film noir or silent films, and newly restored prints of classic works. The café serves unbelievable brownies.

The **American Museum of the Moving Image** (✉ 35th Ave. at 36th St., Astoria, Queens ☎ 718/784–0077 ⊕ www.ammi.org Ⓜ Subway: R, V [weekdays only], or G, R [weekends only] to Steinway St.) presents special series, such as a Martin Scorsese marathon. Admission is free to museum patrons; films are shown Friday to Sunday evenings and Saturday and Sunday afternoons. Dedicated to preserving and exhibiting independent and avant-garde film, **Anthology Film Archives** (✉ 32 2nd Ave., at E. 2nd St., East Village ☎ 212/505–5181 ⊕ www.anthologyfilmarchives.org Ⓜ Subway: F to 2nd Ave.) consists of two small screening rooms in a renovated courthouse. This is a good place for obscure and hard-to-find films. The Essential Cinema series delves into the works of filmmakers like Stan Brakhage, Robert Bresson, and more. Part of the Brooklyn Academy of Music, the four-screen **BAM Rose Cinemas** (✉ 30 Lafayette Ave., between Ashland Pl. and St. Felix St., Fort Greene ☎ 718/636–4100 ⊕ www.bam.org Ⓜ Subway: C to Lafayette Ave.; 2, 3, 4, 5, Q to Atlantic Ave.) offers first-run foreign-language and popular independent films. BAMcinématek is an eclectic repertory series.

The **Museum of Modern Art (MoMA)** (✉ 11 W. 53rd St., between 5th and 6th Aves., Midtown East ☎ 212/708–9400 ⊕ www.moma.org Ⓜ Subway: E, V to 5th Ave./53rd St.; B, D, E to 7th Ave.; B, D, F, V to 47th–50th Sts./Rockefeller Center) is once again in the pair of Roy and Niuta Titus screening rooms. It has some of the most engaging international repertory you'll find anywhere. Movie tickets are available at the museum only; they are free if you have purchased museum admission. Run by the Film Society of Lincoln Center, the comfortable, 268-★ seat modern auditorium of the **Walter Reade Theater** (✉ Lincoln Center, 165 W. 65th St., between Broadway and Amsterdam Ave., Upper West Side ☎ 212/875–5600 ⊕ www.filmlinc.com Ⓜ Subway: 1, 9 to 66th St./Lincoln Center) has what may be the best sight lines in town. It presents series devoted to "the best in world cinema" that run the gamut from silents (with occasional live organ accompaniment) and documentaries to retrospectives and recent releases, often on the same theme or from the same country. Purchase tickets at the box office or online up to four weeks in advance.

New York's leading annual film event is the **New York Film Festival** (☎ 212/875–5050 ⊕ www.filmlinc.com Ⓜ Subway: 1, 9 to 66th St./Lincoln Center), sponsored by the Film Society of Lincoln Center every September and October. Screenings are announced more than a month in advance and sell out quickly. Venues are Lincoln Center's Alice Tully Hall (with opening and closing night extravaganzas in Avery Fisher Hall) and the Walter Reade Theater. The festival's program includes many movies never before seen in the United States. Each March, the Film Society of Lincoln Center joins forces with the Museum of Modern Art to produce **New Directors–New Films** (☎ 212/875–5050 ⊕ www.filmlinc. com), giving up-and-coming directors their moment to flicker.

Film for Children

Several museums sponsor special programs aimed at families and children, including the Museum of Modern Art, the Museum of Television and Radio, and the American Museum of the Moving Image. Children marvel at the amazing nature and science films shown on the huge screen in the **IMAX Theater** (✉ Central Park W and W. 79th St., Upper West Side ☎ 212/769–5034 ⊕ www.amnh.org Ⓜ Subway: B, C to 79th St.) at the American Museum of Natural History. At the **Loews Lincoln Square Theater** (✉ 1998 Broadway, at W. 68th St., Upper West Side ☎ 212/336–5020 Ⓜ Subway: 1, 9 to 66th St.) audience members strap on high-tech headgear for the specially created 3-D films.

★ Each March, the two-week-long **New York International Children's Film Festival** (☎ 212/349–0330 ⊕ www.gkids.com) screens 60 new films and videos for ages 3–18 at venues around the city. The **SonyWonder Technology Lab** (✉ 550 Madison Ave., between E. 55th and E. 56th Sts., Midtown East ☎ 212/833–7858 weekdays ⊕ www.sonywondertechlab. com Ⓜ Subway: E, V to 53rd St.), an interactive experience that uses multimedia presentations to demystify technology, shows free films for kids. Selections range from G-rated holiday classics to PG-13 thrillers. Children under 17 must be accompanied by an adult. Call ahead for reserved tickets.

Television

Tickets to tapings of television shows are free, but can be difficult to come by on short notice. For the most popular shows, like *The Late Show with David Letterman,* the best you can do is send in a postcard requesting tickets. Other shows accept requests by e-mail, phone, or online. In most cases, same-day standby tickets are available to people willing to wait in line for several hours, sometimes starting at 5 or 6 AM, depending on how hot the show is, or the wattage of the celebrity involved.

The Daily Show with Jon Stewart. With a knowing smirk, the amiable Jon Stewart pokes fun at news headlines on this half-hour cable show. The program tapes from Monday through Thursday, and free tickets can be obtained by calling the studio. Those under 18 may not attend. ⊠ *513 W. 54th St., between 10th and 11th Sts., Midtown West* ☎ *212/586–2477* Ⓜ *Subway: C, E to 50th St.*

It's Showtime at the Apollo. One of Harlem's most renowned landmarks hosts this raucous talent search where competitors must display both talent and nerves of steel. Tickets to tapings are free, but you must send a self-addressed stamped envelope in advance. ⊠ *Tickets, 3 Park Ave., 40th fl., between E. 33rd and 34th Sts., 10016* ☎ *212/889–3532.*

Late Night with Conan O'Brien. This late night popular variety show targets hip viewers and attracts consistently interesting guests. Standby tickets are available from Tuesday through Friday after 9 AM at the 49th Street side of 30 Rockefeller Plaza. Call the **Ticket Information Line** (☎ 212/664–3056) for advance reservations. No one under 16 may attend. ⊠ *NBC Studios, 30 Rockefeller Plaza, between W. 49th and W. 50th Sts., Midtown West, 10112* Ⓜ *Subway: B, D, F, V to 47th–50th Sts./Rockefeller Center.*

The Late Show with David Letterman. David Letterman has a famously quirky manner that makes his show capable of real surprises. Call 212/247–6497 at 11 AM on tape days for standby tickets. You can sign up for cancellation tickets online or write for reservations: the request must be on a postcard—for two tickets—and the wait may be as much as a year. No one under 18 may attend. ⊠ *Late Show Tickets, c/o Ed Sullivan Theater, 1697 Broadway, between 53rd and 54th Sts., Midtown West, 10019* ☎ *212/975–1003* ⊕ *www.cbs.com* Ⓜ *Subway: 1, 9, C, E to 50th St.*

Live! with Regis and Kelly. The sparks fly on this morning program, which books an eclectic roster of guests. Standby tickets become available weekdays at 7 AM at the **ABC studio** (⊠ 71 Lincoln Sq., between W. 67th St. and Columbus Ave., Upper West Side). Otherwise, write for tickets a full year in advance. Children under 10 may not attend. ⓕ *Live! Tickets, Ansonia Station, Box 230777, 10023* ☎ *212/456–3537* Ⓜ *Subway: 1, 9 to 66th St./Lincoln Center.*

MTV Studios. If you're between the ages of 18 and 24 you can be an audience member of **Total Request Live (TRL)** with host Carson Daly. This hugely popular show is taped weekdays at 4 PM on the second floor of the high-energy MTV studios in Times Square. For advance reservations, e-mail or call the TRL hotline. ⊠ *1515 Broadway, at 43rd St., Midtown West* ☎ *212/398–8549* Ⓜ *Subway: 1, 2, 3, 9, N, R, Q, W to 42nd St./Times Sq.*

Saturday Night Live. Probably the most influential comedy variety show in the history of television, *SNL* continues to captivate audiences. Standby tickets are distributed on a first-come, first-served basis at 7 AM on the day of the show at the West 50th Street entrance to 30 Rockefeller Plaza. You may receive tickets for a dress rehearsal (7 PM arrival time) or the live show (10 PM arrival time). Submit requests for advance tickets by mail in August; your card is then entered in ticket lotteries. You will be notified one to two weeks in advance if you're selected. No one under 16 may attend. ⊠ *NBC Studios, Saturday Night Live, 30 Rockefeller Plaza, between 5th and 6th Aves., Midtown West, 10112* ☎ *212/664–4444* Ⓜ *Subway: B, D, F, V to 47th–50th Sts./Rockefeller Center.*

Today. The king of morning talk news airs weekdays from 7 AM to 10 AM in the glass-enclosed, ground-level NBC studio at the corner of West

49th Street and Rockefeller Plaza. You may well be spotted on TV by friends back home standing behind anchors Katie Couric and Matt Lauer. ☒ *Rockefeller Plaza between W. 48th and W. 49th Sts., Midtown West* Ⓜ *Subway: B, D, F, V to 47th–50th Sts./Rockefeller Center.*

The View. The Emmy-winning chitchat and celebrity gossip show has been an unqualified hit since it launched in 1997. Join Star Jones Reynolds, Meredith Vieira, Joy Behar, Elisabeth Hasselbeck, and, occasionally, Barbara Walters herself for an often outrageous hour of live television. Ticket requests (postcards only) must be sent four to six months in advance; you may also request tickets online. No one under 18 will be admitted. ☒ *Tickets, The View, 320 W. 66th St., at West End Ave., Upper West Side, 10023* ⊕ *www.abc.com.*

READINGS & LECTURES

Literary figures great and small share their work at dozens of readings held each week in New York. From formal venues like the New York Public Library, where you might hear well-known panelists comment on local architecture, to the very casual Nuyorican Poets Café, where obscure writers show up for an open-mike night, you'll find New Yorkers sharing their thoughts, insight, and their most creative work.

Time Out New York has the most comprehensive listing of reading and lectures; also check out the *New York Press* and the *Village Voice.* Admission most of these events are usually under $15, although it might go up to $25 for certain luminaries. At small venues they are often free.

Series & Special Events

The **Center for Architecture** (☒ 536 LaGuardia Pl., between W. 3rd and Bleecker Sts., Greenwich Village ☎ 212/683–0023 ⊕ www.aiany.org Ⓜ Subway: A, C, E, B, D, F, V to W. 4th St.), a glass-faced gallery, hosts lively discussions (often accompanied by films or other visuals) on topics like cutting-edge architecture in Mexico City or visionary American architects of the 1930s. In its home in City Center, the **Manhattan Theatre Club** (☒ 131 W. 55th St., between 6th and 7th Aves., Midtown West ☎ 212/581–1212 ⊕ www.mtc-nyc.org Ⓜ Subway: F to 57th St.) sponsors Writers in Performance, a program of dramatic readings and roundtable discussions that showcase novelists, poets, and playwrights from the United States and abroad.

In the historic Villard Houses, the nonprofit **Municipal Art Society** (☒ Urban Center, 457 Madison Ave., at E. 51st St., Midtown East ☎ 212/935–3960 ⊕ www.mas.org Ⓜ Subway: 6 to 51st St.; E, F to 53rd St.; B, D, F, V to 47th–50th Sts./Rockefeller Center) is dedicated to preserving New York's architectural treasures. As well as leading the city's most interesting walking tours, it presents a free lecture series at noon on Thursday. Well-known authors speak on topics ranging from subway ornamentation to houses of worship. Many branches of the **New York Public Library** (☒ 5th Ave. at 42nd St., Midtown West ☎ 212/869–8089 ⊕ www.nypl.org Ⓜ Subway: B, D, F, V to 42nd St.) present lectures and reading events. Most branches have monthly calendars on hand.

★ Authors, poets, and playwrights, as well as political pundits, industry
leaders, take the stage at the **92nd St. Y** (✉ 1395 Lexington Ave., at E. 92nd St., Upper East Side ☎ 212/415–5500
⊕ www.92ndsty.org Ⓜ Subway: 6 to 96th St.). The **Makor/Steinhardt
Center** (✉ 35 W. 67th St., between Central Park W and Columbus
Ave., Upper West Side ☎ 212/601–1000 ⊕ www.makor.org Ⓜ Subway:
1, 9 to 66th St./Lincoln Center), part of the 92nd St. Y, is a sleek cultural arts center with excellent literary events geared toward people in
their twenties and thirties. **Symphony Space** (✉ 2537 Broadway, at W.
95th St., Upper West Side ☎ 212/864–5400 ⊕ www.symphonyspace.
org Ⓜ Subway: 1, 2, 3, 9 to 96th St.) hosts literary events including the
famed "Selected Shorts" series of stories read by prominent actors and
broadcast on National Public Radio.

Fiction & Poetry Readings

★ "Poetry Czar" Bob Holman's **Bowery Poetry Club** (✉ 308 Bowery, at
Bleecker St., Lower East Side ☎ 212/614–0505 ⊕ www.bowerypoetry.
com Ⓜ Subway: B, D, F, V to Broadway–Lafayette St.; 6 to Bleecker
St.) serves up coffee and knishes along with its ingenious poetry events.
Expect every permutation of the spoken word—and art and music, too.
The **Cornelia Street Café** (✉ 29 Cornelia St., between W. 4th and Bleecker
Sts., Greenwich Village ☎ 212/989–9319 ⊕ www.poetz.com Ⓜ Sub-
way: A, C, E, B, D, F, V to W. 4th St./Washington Sq.) is a good bet for
original poetry and fiction readings.

Dixon Place (✉ 258 Bowery, between Houston and Prince Sts., Lower
East Side ☎ 212/219–0736 ⊕ www.dixonplace.org Ⓜ Subway: F, V to
2nd Ave.), "NYC's laboratory for performance," hosts readings of fiction, science fiction, and poetry, plus the celebrated "Performance
Works-in-Progress" series that showcases theater and performance art
pieces. One of the most influential and avant-garde series around town
is "Line Reading," which explores how the visual arts and literature in-
terrelate. Readings are held at 6:30 on Tuesday evenings at the **Drawing Center** (✉ 35 Wooster St., between Grand and Broome Sts., SoHo
☎ 212/219–2166 ⊕ www.drawingcenter.org Ⓜ Subway: R, W to Prince
St.), an art space in SoHo.

★ Amid its collection of 45,000 titles, the **Housing Works Used Book Café**
(✉ 126 Crosby St., between Houston and Prince Sts, SoHo ☎ 212/334–
3324 ⊕ www.housingworks.org/usedbookcafe Ⓜ Subway: R, W to
Prince St.; B, D, F, V to Broadway–Lafayette St.; 6 to Bleecker St.) sponsors readings—often by breakout local authors or from books on social
issues—and a monthly acoustic music series called "Live from Home."
Events at this cozy store and café benefit homeless people with HIV/AIDS.
The Kitchen (✉ 512 W. 19th St., between 10th and 11th Aves., Chelsea
☎ 212/255–5793 ⊕ www.thekitchen.org Ⓜ Subway: C, E to 23rd St.)
presents readings from the edges of the world of arts and literature.

The **Lesbian, Gay, Bisexual & Transgender Community Center** (✉ 208 W.
13th St., between 6th and 7th Aves., West Village ☎ 212/620–7310
⊕ www.gaycenter.org Ⓜ Subway: F, V to 14th St.) sponsors "In Our
Own Write," a series of readings by up-and-coming gay writers, as well

as "Second Tuesdays," which features more established writers. The **Nuyorican Poets Café** (✉ 236 E. 3rd St., between Aves. B and C, East Village ☎ 212/505–8183 ⊕ www.nuyorican.org Ⓜ Subway: F, V to 2nd Ave.) schedules daily readings, open-mike events, screenplay readings, and hosts the granddaddy of the current spoken word scene, the "Friday Night Poetry Slam."

Nightlife

9

WORD OF MOUTH

"Listening to jazz at the [Village Vanguard] was like going back in time to the days of John Coltrane."

—jeninnyc

"What always impresses me about New York is the endless array of themed bars. Upscale, divey, rock and roll, lounges—the list goes on."

—dan1900

Updated by
Stella Fiore,
Adam Kowit,
Robin
Rothman, and
Lisa Marie
Rovito

EVERY NIGHT OF THE WEEK you'll find New Yorkers going out on the town. Nobody here waits for the weekend—in fact, many people prefer to party during the week when there's actually room to belly up to the bar. But don't assume that you'll have the place to yourself. If word gets out that a hot band is playing in a bar on a Tuesday, or if a well-known DJ takes over a dance club on a Thursday, you can be assured these places will be packed like it's Saturday night.

The nightlife scene is still largely downtown—in drab-by-day dives in the East Village, classic jazz joints in the West Village, and the Meatpacking District's see-and-be-seen boîtes—but you don't have to go below 14th Street to have a good time. Midtown, especially around Hell's Kitchen is developing a reputation, and there are still plenty of preppy hangouts on the Upper East and Upper West sides. And across the East River, Brooklyn has become the place for artists, hipsters, and rock-and-roll fans.

There are enough committed club crawlers to support venues for almost every idiosyncratic taste. But keep in mind that *when* you go is just as important as *where* you go. A spot is only hot when it's hopping—a club that is packed at 11 might empty out by midnight, and a bar that raged last night completely empty tonight. These days, night prowlers are more loyal to floating parties, DJs, and club promoters than to any specific addresses.

For the totally hip, **Paper** magazine has a good list of the roving parties and the best of the fashionable crowd's hangouts. **Time Out New York** provides a comprehensive weekly listing of amusements by category. The **Village Voice,** a free weekly newspaper, probably has more club ads than any other rag in the world. Also check out the **New York Press,** which has pages and pages of nightlife listings. The **New York Times** has listings of cabaret shows. Flyers about and passes to coming events are stacked in the entry at **Tower Records** (⌧ 692 Broadway, at 4th St., East Village ☎ 212/505–1500 ⌧ 1961 Broadway, at W. 66th St., Upper West Side ☎ 212/799–2500). You may also get good tips from a suitably au courant hotel concierge. Keep in mind that events change almost weekly, and venues have the life span of a tsetse fly, so phone ahead to make sure your target hasn't closed or turned into a polka hall (although that might be fun, too).

Most clubs charge a cover, which can range from $5 to $25 or more, depending on the venue and the night. And take cash, because many places don't accept credit cards. (Nothing will enrage the people behind you in line like whipping out the plastic). Remember to dress properly, something that is easily accomplished by wearing black and leaving your sneakers at home. Smoking is prohibited in all enclosed public places in New York City, including restaurants and bars. Some bars have gardens or fully enclosed smoking rooms for those who wish to light up, but in most places you will have to step outside.

CLUBS & ENTERTAINMENT

Quintessential New York

These are the crème de la crème of New York's nightlife venues, distinguished by an unbeatable locale, a unique style, a hip vibe, or a combination of the three. Reservations are essential. Admission can be steep—cover charges for big-name acts go as high as $100—but in many cases you can snag a spot at the bar if you show up several hours before showtime.

Fodor'sChoice
★
The Carlyle. The hotel's discreetly sophisticated Café Carlyle hosts such top performers such as Bette Buckley, Elaine Stritch, Barbara Cook, and Ute Lemper. Stop by on a Monday night and take in Woody Allen, who swings on the clarinet with his New Orleans Jazz Band. Bemelmans Bar, with murals by the author of the Madeline books, features a rotating cast of pianist-singers. ⊠ *35 E. 76th St., between Madison and Park Aves., Upper East Side* ☎ *212/744–1600* Ⓜ *Subway: 6 to 77th St.*

Four Seasons. New York City (and American) history is made here in Philip Johnson's landmarked temple of modern design. Watch for politicos and media moguls in the Grill Room, or enjoy the changing foliage in the romantic pool room. ⊠ *99 E. 52nd St., between Park and Lexington Aves., Midtown East* ☎ *212/754–9494* Ⓜ *Subway: E, V to Lexington Ave./53rd St.; 6 to 51st St.*

Lever House. This spot on the garden level of one of the city's most stylish office buildings was an instant hit, drawing a younger and faster crowd than its closest competition, the Four Seasons. People flock here to see and be seen in a futuristic, honeycombed setting where just about everybody looks like they're somebody. ⊠ *390 Park Ave., at 53rd St., Midtown East* ☎ *212/888–2700* Ⓜ *Subway: E, V to Lexington Ave./53rd St.; 6 to 51st St.*

Oak Room. One of the great classic cabaret venues, the Oak Room is formal (jackets are mandatory; ties are the norm). You might find the hopelessly romantic singer Andrea Marcovicci, among other top-notch performers, crooning here. ⊠ *Algonquin Hotel, 59 W. 44th St., near 6th Ave., Midtown West* ☎ *212/840–6800* Ⓜ *Subway: B, D, F, V to 42nd St.*

Rainbow Room. Heavenly views top the bill of fare at this romantic institution on the 65th floor, where a revolving dance floor and 12-piece orchestra ensure high spirits, even on a cloudy night. ⊠ *30 Rockefeller Plaza, between 5th and 6th Aves., Midtown West* ☎ *212/632–5000* Ⓜ *Subway: B, D, F, V to 47th–50th Sts./Rockefeller Center.*

Rise. Ensconced on the 14th floor of the Ritz-Carlton New York, this swank lounge has stunning views of the harbor and the Statue of Liberty. In summer you can sit outside and watch the sun set over America. ⊠ *2 West St., at Battery Pl., Battery Park* ☎ *917/790–2626* Ⓜ *Subway: 1, 9 to Rector St.*

River Café. If you're looking for an eminently romantic locale, head out to this restaurant hidden at the foot of the Brooklyn Bridge. The bar has smashing views of the downtown Manhattan skyline across the East

River, and after cocktails you can enjoy a splendid meal. ✉ *1 Water St., near Old Fulton St., DUMBO, Brooklyn* ☎ *718/522–5200* Ⓜ *Subway: F to York St.; A, C to High St.*

"21" Club. Famous for its clubby atmosphere even before it became a setting in *All About Eve,* this New York classic still has a conservative air that evokes a sense of connections, power, and prestige. ✉ *21 W. 52nd St., between 5th and 6th Aves., Midtown West* ☎ *212/582–7200* Ⓜ *Subway: B, D, F, V to 47–50th Sts./Rockefeller Center.*

Dance Clubs & DJ Venues

The city's hottest clubs aren't just places to hit the dance floor. Revelers come to socialize with friends, to find romance, to show off their newest outfits, or to be photographed rubbing shoulders with stars. Some clubs are cavernous spaces filled with a churning sea of bodies. Others are like small get-togethers in a basement belonging to a friend of a friend of a friend. Parties—dance and otherwise—with DJs, salsa bands, and themes ranging from '60s bossa-nova nights to soul-and-drag galas have been known to crop up at such places as Irving Plaza and Opaline. Be aware that weeknight parties don't make allowances for early-morning risers: the crowd often doesn't arrive until well after midnight.

Apt. Music is the priority at this polished club, where some of the world's top DJs—those who elevate record-spinning to a high art—ply their trade in a tiny, luminous basement room. At the restaurant upstairs you can order tapas or sip a cocktail while reclining on a double bed. ✉ *419 W. 13th St., between 9th Ave. and Washington St., Meatpacking District* ☎ *212/414–4245* Ⓜ *Subway: A, C, E to 14th St.; L to 8th Ave.*

Avalon. This deconsecrated church, which gained notoriety during the '90s as the Limelight, has been reborn yet again. The owners run successful clubs of the same name in Boston and Los Angeles, so it looks like the hallowed space will have a successful afterlife. The complete interior makeover (the cages with dancing girls are gone, replaced by VIP balconies) and the A-list DJs don't hurt either. Sunday night the place is full of sweaty, shirtless gay men. ✉ *660 6th Ave., at 20th St., Chelsea* ☎ *212/807–7780* Ⓜ *Subway: F, V to 23rd St.*

Canal Room. Polished wood floors, elegant potted palms, and stylish Barcelona chairs distinguish this intimate club. Musicians perform here several times a month (the Roots and Tony Bennett are two recent acts), but they also come just to enjoy themselves. The owners' record business connections, a spectacular speaker system, and DJs who keep the crowds moving has drawn the likes of Mariah Carey, Missy Elliott, and Sean "Puffy" Combs. ✉ *285 West Broadway, at Canal St., TriBeCa* ☎ *212/941–8100* Ⓜ *Subway: A, C, E to Canal St.*

China Club. This symbol of high-living excess has relocated from its original Upper West Side location to an 8,000-square-foot bi-level space in newly hip Hell's Kitchen, with the exclusionary velvet ropes still in place. ✉ *268 W. 47th St., between Broadway and 8th Ave., Midtown West* ☎ *212/398–3800* Ⓜ *Subway: R, W to 49th St.*

Cielo. A relatively mature crowd gravitates to this small, super-fashionable Meatpacking District destination to sip cocktails and groove to soulful house music on the sunken dance floor. ☒ *18 Little W. 12th St., between 9th Ave. and Washington St., Meatpacking District* ☎ *212/645–5700* Ⓜ *Subway: A, C, E to 14th St.*

Fodor'sChoice **Club Shelter.** This warehouselike space is the home to some of the best dancing in the city, which is no surprise, as it takes its name and its low-key attitude from a long-running after-hours party that was once found at the old TriBeCa club Vinyl. ☒ *20 W. 39th St., between 5th and 6th Aves., Midtown West* ☎ *212/719–4479* Ⓜ *Subway: B, D, F, V to 42nd St.*

★ **Coral Room.** Silver-finned mermaids in seashell bikinis swim with tropical fish in a lagoon-size tank behind the main bar at this club where glamour and fun flourish. The VIP room is outfitted with portholes for watching the action on the coral-walled dance floor. ☒ *512 W. 29th St., between 10th and 11th Aves., Chelsea* ☎ *212/244–1965* Ⓜ *Subway: A, C, E to 34th St.*

Crobar. Well-heeled professionals and nightlife scenesters alike flock to this high-gloss megaclub. Enter through an art gallery, descend into a packed cocktail lounge, then proceed through a luminous white tunnel with curved walls to the cavernous dance floor. ☒ *530 W. 28th St., between 10th and 11th Aves., Chelsea* ☎ *212/629–9000* Ⓜ *Subway: 1, 9 to 28th St.*

Culture Club. From the Pacman illustration on the outside awning to the interior murals of Adam Ant and the cast from *The Breakfast Club*, if you're desperately seeking a dose of '80s nostalgia, this is your place. ☒ *179 Varick St., between Charlton and King Sts., SoHo* ☎ *212/243–1999* Ⓜ *Subway: 1, 9 to Houston St.*

Discotheque. This top nightclub is known for its excellent sound system and the top DJs, like Junior Vasquez and Hex Hector, who play hip-hop and house for a young crowd of enthusiastic dancers. ☒ *17 W. 19th St., between 5th and 6th Aves., Chelsea* ☎ *212/352–9999* Ⓜ *Subway: F, V to 14th St.*

★ **Exit.** This extravagant multilevel club has everything from a massive dance floor to an outdoor patio. A-list DJs spin for an enthusiastic crowd that often includes a hip-hop star or two. ☒ *610 W. 56th St., between 11th and 12th Aves., Midtown West* ☎ *212/582–8282* Ⓜ *Subway: 1, 9, A, B, C, D to 59th St.*

Plaid. Resembling an upper-middle-class living room (albeit a very large living room), this downtown club has upholstered couches and patterned wallpaper. Rock bands threaten eardrums here on occasion; the rest of the time the modest dance floor thumps with hip-hop, house, and R&B. ☒ *76 E. 13th St., between Broadway and 4th Ave., East Village* ☎ *212/388–1060* Ⓜ *Subway: 4, 5, 6, L, N, Q, R, W to 14th St./Union Sq.*

Roxy. Most nights this huge hall is a standard bridge-and-tunnel magnet, mostly attracting those who live in other New York boroughs and in New Jersey and occasionally drawing a mixed rave crowd. Gay men rule the roost on Saturday, and Wednesday is roller-disco night. Call ahead for special events. ☒ *515 W. 18th St., between 10th and 11th Aves., Chelsea* ☎ *212/645–5157* Ⓜ *Subway: A, C, E to 14th St.*

Sapphire. The party gets started late at this lively Lower East Side hangout, but the DJ keeps the diverse crowd going with deep house, soul, funk, and Latin music. Ultrafriendly patrons might drag you onto the floor to strut your stuff. Drinks are half price before 10 PM. ✉ *249 Eldridge St., between E. Houston and Stanton Sts., Lower East Side* ☎ 212/777–5153 Ⓜ *Subway: F, V to 2nd Ave.*

Show. The atmosphere at this lush, cabaret-style nightspot varies depending on which promoter is running things, but it tends to draw young hipsters, professional basketball players, and wayward pop stars (Britney Spears once did a striptease on stage). ✉ *135 W. 41st St., between 6th Ave. and Broadway, Midtown West* ☎ 212/278–0988 Ⓜ *Subway: B, D, F, V to 42nd St.*

Spirit. This raver's paradise, a branch of a popular Dublin dance club, is massive (the dance floor alone is 10,000 square feet). And because of its New Age roots, on Saturday nights you can stop by the club's holistic healing center for an astrological consultation or a soothing massage. ✉ *530 W. 27th St., between 10th and 11th Aves., Chelsea* ☎ 212/ 268—9477 Ⓜ *Subway: 1, 9 to 28th St.*

Subtonic. Experimental DJs present thought-provoking sound collages and electro-acoustic collaborations several nights a week in this basement bar, downstairs from the live music venue Tonic. The building was once a kosher winery, so you can enjoy the music from a comfortable seat inside a massive wine barrel. ✉ *107 Norfolk St., between Delancey and Rivington Sts., Lower East Side* ☎ 212/358–7501 Ⓜ *Subway: F, J, M to Delancey St.*

Webster Hall. Five types of music are played on the four floors of this fave among New York University students and out-of-towners looking for the most bang for their buck. The barely clad go-go dancers certainly work hard for the crowd. On Friday there's an amateur striptease contest for those with more nerve than cash. ✉ *125 E. 11th St., between 3rd and 4th Aves., East Village* ☎ 212/353–1600 Ⓜ *Subway: 4, 5, 6, L, N, Q, R, W to 14th St./Union Sq.*

Jazz Clubs

With more than a dozen jazz nightclubs, Greenwich Village is still New York's jazz mecca, although many others are strewn around town. Cover charges can be steep, and it's common for a venue to present multiple sets each evening. Jazz at Lincoln Center now grooves at a complex on Columbus Circle. The West 59th Street facility includes two auditoriums, a jazz café, rehearsal studios, classrooms, and a Jazz Hall of Fame.

Arthur's Tavern. Unless there's a festival in town, you won't find many big names jamming here. But you will find nightly performances, without a cover charge, amid the dark-wood ambience of old Greenwich Village. The acts tend to be bluesier and funkier for the late shows. ✉ *57 Grove St., between 7th Ave. S and Bleecker St., Greenwich Village* ☎ 212/675–6879 Ⓜ *Subway: 1, 9 to Christopher St.*

Birdland. This place gets its name from saxophone great Charlie Parker, so expect serious, up-and-coming groups. The dining room serves moderately priced American fare with a Cajun accent. If you sit at the bar your cover charge includes a drink. ✉ *315 W. 44th St., between 8th and 9th Aves., Midtown West* ☎ 212/581–3080 Ⓜ *Subway: 1, 2, 3, 9, 7, N, Q, R, W to 42nd St./Times Sq.*

★ **Blue Note.** Considered by many to be the jazz capital of the world, the Blue Note could see on an average month Spyro Gyra, Ron Carter, and Jon Hendricks. Expect a steep cover charge except on Monday, when record labels promote their artists' recent releases for an average ticket price of less than $20. ⊠ *131 W. 3rd St., near 6th Ave., Greenwich Village* ☎ *212/475–8592* Ⓜ *Subway: A, C, E, F, V to W. 4th St.*

Cajun. Mardi Gras masks and beads conjure up the spirit of New Orleans at this Chelsea restaurant. There's music nine times a week (that's nightly plus a champagne brunch on Sunday and a lunchtime combo on Wednesday). ⊠ *129 8th Ave., at 16th St., Chelsea* ☎ *212/691–6174* Ⓜ *Subway: A, C, E to 14th St.; L to 8th Ave.*

Garage Restaurant & Café. There's no cover at this bi-level Village hot spot, where you can hear live jazz seven nights a week; a fireplace sets the mood upstairs. ⊠ *99 7th Ave. S, between Bleecker St. and Christopher St., Greenwich Village* ☎ *212/645–0600* Ⓜ *Subway: 1, 9 to Christopher St./Sheridan Sq.*

Iridium. This cozy club is a sure bet for big-name talent. It has good sight lines, and the sound system was designed with the help of Les Paul, the inventor of the solid-body electric guitar, who takes the stage on Monday night. ⊠ *1650 Broadway, at W. 51st St., Midtown West* ☎ *212/582–2121* Ⓜ *Subway: 1, 9 to 50th St.; R, W to 49th St.*

Ⓒ **Jazz Standard.** This sizable underground room draws the top names in the business. Part of Danny Meyer's Southern-food restaurant Blue Smoke, it's one of the few spots where you can get dry-rubbed ribs to go with your bebop. Bring the kids for the Jazz Standard Youth Orchestra concerts every Sunday afternoon. ⊠ *116 E. 27th St., between Park and Lexington Aves., Murray Hill* ☎ *212/576–2232* Ⓜ *Subway: 6 to 28th St.*

Knickerbocker. Piano-and-bass duets are on the menu at this old-fashioned steak house. Think red meat and good jazz. ⊠ *33 University Pl., at E. 9th St., Greenwich Village* ☎ *212/228–8490* Ⓜ *Subway: R, W to 8th St.*

Lenox Lounge. This art deco lounge opened in the 1930s and currently hosts jazz ensembles, blues acts, and jam sessions in the Zebra Room. The restaurant in front serves great food to go with the soulful music. ⊠ *288 Malcolm X Blvd., between W. 124th and W. 125th Sts., Harlem* ☎ *212/427–0253* Ⓜ *Subway: 2, 3 to 125th St.*

Smoke. If you can't wait until after dark to get your riffs on, head uptown to this lounge near Columbia University, where the music starts as early as 6 PM. Performers include some of the top names in the business, including turban-wearing organist Dr. Lonnie Smith and the drummer Jimmy Cobb (who laid down the beat on Miles Davis's seminal album *Kind of Blue*). ⊠ *2751 Broadway, between W. 105th and W. 106th Sts., Upper West Side* ☎ *212/864–6662* Ⓜ *Subway: 1, 9 to 103rd St.*

Sweet Rhythm. This sleek West Village nightspot occupies the former Sweet Basil space. On Sunday nights the Frank & Joe show keeps old-timers happy with its vintage swing. Every Monday, an ensemble from the New School University's famed jazz and contemporary music program takes the stage. College students with ID get in for free. ⊠ *88 7th Ave. S, between Bleecker and Grove Sts., Greenwich Village* ☎ *212/255–3626* Ⓜ *Subway: 1, 9 to Christopher St./Sheridan Sq.*

Fodor'sChoice   **Village Vanguard.** This prototypical jazz club, tucked into a cellar in Green-
★   wich Village, has been the haunt of legends like Thelonious Monk.
Today you might hear jams from the likes of Wynton Marsalis and Roy
Hargrove, among others. ⊠ *178 7th Ave. S, between W. 11th and Perry
Sts., Greenwich Village* ☎ *212/255–4037* Ⓜ *Subway: A, C, E to 14th
St.; L to 8th Ave.*

Zinc Bar. This tiny underground spot presents a forward-thinking mix
of jazz and world music. You can hear African music on Friday, Brazilian jazz on Saturday and Sunday nights, and a range of creative sounds
throughout the week. ⊠ *90 W. Houston St., at LaGuardia Pl., Greenwich Village* ☎ *212/477–8337* Ⓜ *Subway: 6 to Bleecker St.; A, C, E,
B, D, F, V to W. 4th St.*

Rock Clubs

If you love rock music, you've come to the right place. New York continues to give birth to some of the most compelling rock performers.
(Witness the recent meteoric rise of local bands like Scissor Sisters and
the Yeah Yeah Yeahs.) Catch a rising star at one of the small clubs on
the Lower East Side and in Brooklyn or check out the stellar schedules
at the city's mid-size venues, where more established groups deliver the
goods night after night. Buy tickets in advance whenever possible; bands
that are obscure to the rest of the country frequently play here to sold-
out crowds.

Arlene's Grocery. On Monday night, crowds pack into this converted con-
venience store for Rock and Roll Karaoke, where they live out their rock-
star dreams by singing favorite punk anthems onstage with a live band.
Other nights are hit-or-miss. ⊠ *95 Stanton St., between Ludlow and Orchard Sts., Lower East Side* ☎ *212/358–1633* Ⓜ *Subway: F, V to 2nd Ave.*

Bitter End. This Greenwich Village standby has served up its share of talent; Billy Joel, David Crosby, and Dr. John are among the stars who have
played here. These days you're more likely to find lesser-known musicians playing blues, rock, funk, and jazz. ⊠ *147 Bleecker St., between
Thompson St. and LaGuardia Pl., Greenwich Village* ☎ *212/673–7030*
Ⓜ *Subway: A, C, E, B, D, F, V to W. 4th St.*

Fodor'sChoice   **Bowery Ballroom.** This theater with art deco accents is the city's top mid-
★   size concert venue. Packing in the crowds for a two-night stand is a rite
of passage for musicians on their way to stardom, including Franz Fer-
dinand, Neko Case, and Bright Eyes. You can grab one of the tables on
the balcony or stand on the main floor. There's a comfortable bar in the
basement. ⊠ *6 Delancey St., near the Bowery, Lower East Side* ☎ *212/
533–2111* Ⓜ *Subway: F, J, M to Delancey St.*

CBGB & OMFUG. American punk rock and New Wave—think the Ramones, Blondie, the Talking Heads—were born in this long, black tunnel of a club. (CBGB T-shirts, on sale here, are must-have items for
teenagers who never even heard of these groups.) Today you're more
likely to hear obscure garage and hardcore bands. Next door, at **CB's
313 Gallery,** a quieter (and older) crowd enjoys mostly acoustic music.
⊠ *315 Bowery, at Bleecker St., East Village* ☎ *212/982–4052* Ⓜ *Subway: B, D, F, V to Broadway–Lafayette St.; 6 to Bleecker St.*

Continental. A favorite haunt of NYU students, this dive is loud, cheap, and lots of fun in a delightfully sophomoric way. Deliberately trashy local bands keep things from getting too serious. ⊠ *25 3rd Ave., at St. Marks Pl., East Village* ☎ *212/529–6924* Ⓜ *Subway: 6 to Astor Pl.*

Don Hill's. At this downtown favorite, you'll find a mixed crowd of gays and straight folk who gather to dance to '80s and New Wave music. The long-running TISWAS party is a good place to check out rock bands. ⊠ *511 Greenwich St., at Spring St., SoHo* ☎ *212/219–2850* Ⓜ *Subway: C, E to Spring St.*

★ **Irving Plaza.** This two-story venue has a near-monopoly on the hottest bills in town, from Erasure to Norah Jones. The good sound system and ample sight lines don't hurt, either. The space is nothing to look at, just a couple of bars and a balcony, but people don't come for the atmosphere. ⊠ *17 Irving Pl., at E. 15th St., Gramercy* ☎ *212/777–6800* ✢ *Subway: 4, 5, 6, L, N, Q, R, W to 14th St./Union Sq.*

★ **Knitting Factory.** This art-rock club is one of the city's most enjoyable performance spaces—the 400-capacity room never gets overcrowded, the sound system is superb, and the front-room bar is a convivial retreat when your eardrums need a break. indie-rock darlings, Japanese hardcore legends, and avant-garde noise bands are common sights on the main stage; quieter and more obscure performers prevail in the two smaller rooms on the lower levels. ⊠ *74 Leonard St., between Broadway and Church St., TriBeCa* ☎ *212/219–3055* Ⓜ *Subway: 1, 9 to Franklin St.*

Luna Lounge. Local musicians audition at this Ludlow Street staple in hopes of snagging a coveted opening-band slot at the more prestigious Mercury Lounge around the corner. In short, this is your best bet for finding quality rock for free. Stand-up comics take over the stage every Monday. ⊠ *171 Ludlow St., between E. Houston and Stanton Sts., Lower East Side* ☎ *212/260–2323* Ⓜ *Subway: F, V to 2nd Ave.*

Maxwells. If that concert at the Bowery Ballroom is already sold out—or if you just hate crowds—consider a trip to this small New Jersey club. Bands headed to New York perform here for audiences that are less jaded than their big-city counterparts. Go early and enjoy the splendid comfort food at the attached restaurant. PATH trains zip you across the river to Hoboken. ⊠ *1039 Washington St., at 11th St., Hoboken, NJ* ☎ *201/798–0406.*

Mercury Lounge. You'll have to squeeze past all the sardine-packed hipsters in the front bar to reach the stage, but it's worth it. This top-quality venue specializes in bands about to hit the big time. The Yeah Yeah Yeahs played their first show here, opening for the White Stripes. ⊠ *217 E. Houston St., between Ludlow and Essex Sts., Lower East Side* ☎ *212/260–4700* Ⓜ *Subway: F, V to 2nd Ave.*

Northsix. At this spacious Brooklyn club, near the end of Williamsburg's hip North 6th Street, you can take in an indie-rock show while sitting on the gymnasium-style bleachers that dominate the room. ⊠ *66 N. 6th St., between Wythe and Kent Aves., Williamsburg, Brooklyn* ☎ *718/599–5103* Ⓜ *Subway: L to Bedford Ave.*

Rothko. A relative newcomer to the scene, this club books an eclectic mix of music. Come here for your fix of underground hip-hop, electronica, dance music, and rock—a typical monthly lineup might include Northern State, DJ Spooky, and Jean Grae. This place hosts what may be the the city's only hip-hop karaoke night. ⊠ *116 Suffolk St., at Rivington St., Lower East Side* ☎ *No phone* Ⓜ *Subway: F, V to 2nd Ave.*

Sin-é. Back in the early '90s, when this club was in the East Village, it was the center of the city's acoustic rock scene (the late Jeff Buckley was a regular). In its present incarnation, however, it draws quadruple bills of great underground rock nearly every night. ⊠ *150 Attorney St., at Stanton St., Lower East Side* ☎ *212/388–0077* Ⓜ *Subway: F, J, M, Z to Delancey St.*

Southpaw. Folk-rock and pop for refined tastes are on the bill at this Park Slope hangout. You can enjoy your show in comfort, thanks to an elevated area of sleek tables and cushioned benches. If you feel like dancing, stand up front near the stage. ⊠ *125 5th Ave., between St. Johns Pl. and Sterling Pl., Park Slope, Brooklyn* ☎ *718/230–0236* Ⓜ *Subway: M, R to Union St.*

Tonic. This former kosher winery on the Lower East Side presents innovative rock, jazz, and avant-garde music. At Subtonic, the bar in the basement, you can listen to some of the world's most respected DJs without paying a cover. ⊠ *107 Norfolk St., between Delancey and Rivington Sts., Lower East Side* ☎ *212/358–7501* Ⓜ *Subway: F, J, M to Delancey St.*

TriBeCa. Once known for its blues acts, this downtown club books the music's distant descendants—contemporary jam bands that in previous days would have been found at the defunct club Wetlands or, to go back a bit farther, San Francisco's Haight-Ashbury neighborhood. Did you pack your patchouli oil? ⊠ *16 Warren St., between Broadway and Church St., TriBeCa* ☎ *212/766–1070* Ⓜ *Subway: R, W to City Hall.*

World Music Venues

A former mayor once called New York a "gorgeous mosaic" for the rich ethnic mix of its inhabitants, and the music in some of its clubs reflects that. Brazilian, Celtic, and of course Latin—salsa, samba, merengue—revel in the ever-present energy of the streets.

Connolly's. This tri-level Irish pub with a *Cheers*-like atmosphere often hosts the Irish rock-and-roots hybrid Black 47 (named for the year of the Great Famine) on Saturday night. ⊠ *121 W. 45th St., between Broadway and 6th Ave., Midtown West* ☎ *212/597–5126* Ⓜ *Subway: B, D, F, V to 42nd St.*

Copacabana. The granddaddy of Manhattan dance clubs (it has been open almost continuously since 1940) hosts music and dancing on three levels. From the disco on the lower level to the salsa and merengue performers in the main ballroom, few other clubs can compare. ⊠ *560 W. 34th St., at 11th Ave., Midtown West* ☎ *212/239–2672* Ⓜ *Subway: A, C, E to 34th St.*

☺ **Satalla.** This self-proclaimed "temple of world music" earns its title by presenting top-rated Brazilian, Jamaican, and African musicians, as well as folk singers, Asian throat-singers, and groups of Brooklyn kids playing Romanian music. Most Sunday afternoons you'll hear kid-friendly klezmer bands. ✉ *37 W. 26th St., between Broadway and 6th Ave., Chelsea* ☎ *212/576–1155* Ⓜ *Subway: F, V to 23rd St.*

SOB's. The initials stand for Sounds of Brazil at *the* place for reggae, zydeco, African, and especially Latin tunes and salsa rhythms. The decor is à la Tropicana; the favored drink, a *caipirinha*, a mixture of Brazilian sugarcane liquor and lime. Dinner is served as well. ✉ *204 Varick St., at W. Houston St., SoHo* ☎ *212/243–4940* Ⓜ *Subway: 1, 9 to Houston St.*

Acoustic & Blues Venues

B. B. King Blues Club & Grill. It ain't no Mississippi juke joint. This lavish Times Square club is vast and shiny and host to a range of musicians from Bo Diddley to Peter Frampton. Every so often the relentlessly touring owner stops by as well. ✉ *237 W. 42nd St., between 7th and 8th Aves., Midtown West* ☎ *212/997–4144* Ⓜ *Subway: 1, 2, 3, 7, N, Q, R, W to 42nd St./Times Sq.*

Hogs & Heifers Uptown. The sibling of the similarly named downtown bar draws a slightly preppier but equally inebriated crowd. During the week, country, blues, and rockabilly music are free; on Friday and Saturday there's a cover charge. ✉ *1843 1st Ave., between E. 95th and E. 96th Sts., Upper East Side* ☎ *212/722–8635* Ⓜ *Subway: 6 to 96th St.*

Fodor'sChoice
★ **Living Room.** Singer-songwriters—some solo, some with their bands—are what you'll find at this casually classy club. Enjoy the sweet music while seated at a candlelit table. ✉ *154 Ludlow St., between Stanton and Rivington Sts., Lower East Side* ☎ *212/533–7235* Ⓜ *F, V to 2nd Ave.*

Rodeo Bar. There's never a cover at this Texas-style roadhouse, complete with barn-wood siding and a Tex-Mex menu that's heavy on the barbecue. The music is American roots—country, rock, rockabilly, swing, bluegrass, and blues. ✉ *375 3rd Ave., at 27th St., Murray Hill* ☎ *212/683–6500* Ⓜ *Subway: 6 to 28th St.*

Sidewalk Café. This old-school haunt is the headquarters of the irreverent antifolk scene that spawned the Moldy Peaches. It hosts regular singer-songwriter showcases and "antihootenannies" where anyone can grab the microphone. ✉ *94 Ave. A, at E. 6th St., East Village* ☎ *212/473–7373* Ⓜ *F, V to 2nd Ave.*

Terra Blues. A second-story haven for blues lovers, this cozy Greenwich Village club is surprisingly short on NYU students and rowdy folk. It must be the candlelit tables. Great national and local acts grace the stage 365 days a year. ✉ *149 Bleecker St., between Thompson and La-Guardia Sts., Greenwich Village* ☎ *212/777–7776* Ⓜ *Subway: B, D, F, V to Broadway–Lafayette St.; 6 to Bleecker St.*

Comedy Clubs

Neurotic New York comedy is known the world over, and a few minutes watching these Woody Allen types might just make your own problems seem laughable. Expect to pay about $15 per person on a weekend, sometimes topped off by a drink minimum. Reservations are usually necessary. Only those skilled in the art of repartee should sit in the front; everyone else should hide in a corner or risk being relentlessly heckled.

Caroline's on Broadway. This high-gloss club presents established names as well as comedians on the edge of stardom. Janeane Garofalo, Bill Bellamy, Colin Quinn, and Gilbert Gottfried have headlined. ⊠ *1626 Broadway, between W. 49th and W. 50th Sts., Midtown West* ☎ *212/ 757–4100* Ⓜ *Subway: 1, 9 to 50th St.*

★ **Chicago City Limits.** This crew has been doing improvisational comedy for a long time. The shows, heavy on audience participation, seldom fail to whip visitors into a laughing frenzy. ⊠ *318 W. 53rd St., between 8th and 9th Aves., Midtown West* ☎ *212/888–5233* Ⓜ *Subway: C, E to 50th St.*

Comedy Cellar. Laughter fills this space beneath the Olive Tree Café. The bill is a good barometer of who's hot. ⊠ *117 MacDougal St., between W. 3rd and Bleecker Sts., Greenwich Village* ☎ *212/254–3480* Ⓜ *Subway: A, C, E, B, D, F, V to W. 4th St.*

Comic Strip Live. The atmosphere here is strictly corner bar ("More comfortable than a nice pair of corduroys," says the manager). The stage is brilliantly lighted but minuscule; the bill is unpredictable but worth checking out. ⊠ *1568 2nd Ave., between E. 81st and 82nd Sts., Upper East Side* ☎ *212/861–9386* Ⓜ *Subway: 4, 5, 6 to 86th St.*

Dangerfield's. Since 1969 this has been an important showcase for prime comic talent. Prices are reasonable ($12.50 during the week and $15–$20 on the weekends, with no drink minimum). ⊠ *1118 1st Ave., between E. 61st and E. 62nd Sts., Upper East Side* ☎ *212/593–1650* Ⓜ *Subway: 4, 5, 6, N, R, W to 59th St.*

Gotham Comedy Club. Housed in a landmark building, this club—complete with a turn-of-the-20th-century chandelier and copper bars— showcases popular headliners such as Chris Rock and David Brenner. Once a month there's a Latino comedy show. ⊠ *34 W. 22nd St., between 5th and 6th Aves., Flatiron District* ☎ *212/367–9000* Ⓜ *Subway: F, V to 23rd St.*

Luna Lounge. On Monday night the back room at this watering hole hosts no-name stand-ups as well as big-name stars such as Janeane Garofalo. ⊠ *171 Ludlow St., between E. Houston and Stanton Sts., Lower East Side* ☎ *212/260–2323* Ⓜ *Subway: F, V to 2nd Ave.*

★ **Upright Citizens Brigade Theatre.** Sketch comedy, audience-initiated improv, and even classes are available at this venue. ⊠ *307 W. 26th St., between 8th and 9th Aves., Chelsea* ☎ *212/366–9176* Ⓜ *Subway: C, E to 23rd St.*

Cabaret & Performance Spaces

Cabaret takes many forms in New York, from a lone crooner at the piano to a full-fledged song-and-dance revue. Some nightspots have stages; almost all have a cover and a minimum food and/or drink charge. In addition to the Carlyle and the Oak Room (⇨ Quintessential New York), here are some of the best venues.

Danny's Skylight Room. Housed in Danny's Grand Sea Palace, this fixture on Restaurant Row presents a little bit of everything: jazz performers, crooners, and ivory ticklers. The porcelain-voiced treasure Blossom Dearie calls this room home Saturday and Sunday evening. ⊠ *346 W.*

BURLESQUE IS MORE

I N RECENT YEARS, *a not so new activity has returned to the New York City nightlife scene—burlesque. The phenomenon is something more (as well as something less) than the elaborate Ziegfeld and Minsky Brother revues of the '20s and '30s and the stripped-down striptease acts of the '50s, which eventually gave way to go-go dancers and strippers of the '60s and '70s and lap dancers of the '80s and '90s. The latter are still around, of course, but the new burlesque is something altogether different.*

While not exactly family-friendly, many of today's shows are self-consciously feminist, organized and run by women. What's missing, though, are the bright lights and the glamour. There'll probably never be another performer as big as Sally Rand or Gypsy Rose Lee, but the movement's stars carry on in their own underground way.

If your trip is timed right, the **New York Burlesque Festival** *(⊕ www. thenewyorkburlesquefestival.com) is a must for fans of this adult art form. This three-day event attracts more than 40 performers from all around the world to several snazzy rooms around the Bog Apple.*

Aficionados recommend heading to the **Cutting Room** *(✉ 19 W. 24th St., between Broadway and 6th Ave., Chelsea ☎ 212/691-1900) on Saturday night. Le Scandal, the troupe behind the fabled Blue Angel Cabaret, runs the show here, offering a bit of belly dancing, sword swallowing, fan dancing, and, of course, lots of skin. High profile attendees have included Demi Moore, Wesley Snipes, and Drew Barrymore (who joined the show). When the World Famous Pontani Sisters aren't taking their sexy sibling act on national and international tours, these tattooed tootsies can be found at the Cutting Room.*

On Saturday nights, at the **Slipper Room** *(✉ 167 Orchard St., at Stanton St., Lower East Side ☎ 212/253-7246) you'll find two troupes worth seeing. The glitter-laden Dazzle Dancers are a former street ensemble that was known for its performances in Tompkins Square Park. The heavily spangled group of men and women usually end their shows wearing nothing but smiles. Ixion takes its plots straight from the annals of Greek mythology, turning epic tales erotic adventures. You'll also frequently find Ixion at Brooklyn's* **Galapagos Art Space** *(✉ 70 N. 6th St., Williamsburg ☎ 718/384-4586) for Monday Evening Burlesque.*

46th St., between 8th and 9th Aves., Midtown West ☎ *212/265–8133* Ⓜ *Subway: A, C, E to 50th St.*

Don't Tell Mama. Composer-lyricist hopefuls and established talents show their stuff until 4 AM at this convivial theater-district cabaret. Extroverts will be tempted by the piano bar's open-mike policy. In the club's two rooms you might find singers, comedians, or female impersonators. ✉ *343 W. 46th St., between 8th and 9th Aves., Midtown West* ☎ *212/ 757–0788* Ⓜ *Subway: 1, 2, 3, 7, 9, N, Q, R, W to 42nd St./Times Sq.*

The Duplex. Since 1951 this music-scene veteran on busy Sheridan Square has hosted young singers on the rise, comedians polishing their acts, and Broadway performers dropping by after a show. No matter who's performing, the largely gay audience hoots and hollers in support. Plays and rock bands round out the entertainment. ✉ *61 Christopher St., at 7th Ave. S, Greenwich Village* ☎ *212/255–5438* Ⓜ *Subway: 1, 9 to Christopher St.*

Feinstein's at the Regency. That the world-touring Michael Feinstein performs here only once a year (usually in winter) and still gets a venue named after him speaks volumes about the charismatic cabaret star. This space presents some of the top names in the business. ✉ *540 Park Ave., at E. 61st St., Upper East Side* ☎ *212/339–4095* Ⓜ *Subway: 4, 5, 6, N, R, W to 59th St.*

★ **Joe's Pub.** Wood paneling, red-velvet walls, and comfy sofas make a lush setting for top-notch performers and the A-list celebrities who come to see them. There's not a bad seat in the house, but if you want to sit, arrive at least a half hour early and enjoy the Italian dinner menu. ✉ *425 Lafayette St., between E. 4th St. and Astor Pl., East Village* ☎ *212/539– 8770* Ⓜ *Subway: 6 to Astor Pl.*

Laurie Beechman Theater. This polished theater below the attractive West Bank Café is often home to moonlighting musical-comedy triple threats (actor-singer-dancers). ✉ *407 W. 42nd St., between 8th and 9th Aves., Midtown West* ☎ *212/695–6909* Ⓜ *Subway: 1, 2, 3, 7, 9, N, Q, R, W to 42nd St./Times Sq.*

Rose's Turn. This unpretentious, unpolished landmark cabaret draws a lively, friendly crowd that enjoys singers, sketch-comedy groups, and various other performers. Downstairs at the piano bar you can join the bartenders singing "I Feel Pretty." ✉ *55 Grove St., near Bleecker St. and 7th Ave. S, Greenwich Village* ☎ *212/366–5438* Ⓜ *Subway: 1, 9 to Christopher St.*

BARS

New York has no shortage of places to wet your whistle. You'll find a glut of mahogany-panel taverns in Greenwich Village; chic lounges in SoHo and TriBeCa; yuppie hangouts on the Upper West and Upper East sides; and hipster bars on the Lower East Side. Most pubs and taverns have a wide draught selection, while bars and lounges often have a special drink menus with concoctions no one would ever think up on their own. A single martini of the increasingly creative variety can send your tab into double digits. If velvet ropes or shoulder-to-shoulder crowds ever rub you the wrong way, feel free to move on and find a more comfortable spot, because there's always another one nearby. The city's liquor law allows bars to stay open until 4 AM.

Lower Manhattan, SoHo & TriBeCa

Bar 89. This bi-level lounge has the most entertaining bathrooms in town: the high-tech doors of unoccupied stalls are transparent, but (ideally) turn opaque when you step inside. Like the neighborhood, the crowd at the perennially popular spot is hip and monied, but the help manages to be remarkably friendly. ⊠ *89 Mercer St., between Spring and Broome Sts., SoHo* ☎ *212/274–0989* Ⓜ *Subway: 6 to Spring St.*

Bridge Café. Just a hop away from South Street Seaport, this busy little restaurant flanking the Brooklyn Bridge is a world apart from that touristy district. The bar is one of the oldest in Manhattan (dating from 1794). Though the space is small, the selection is huge: choose from over 100 domestic wines and 75 single-malt scotches. ⊠ *279 Water St., at Dover St., Lower Manhattan* ☎ *212/227–3344* Ⓜ *Subway: A, C, 2, 3, 4, 5, 6 to Fulton St./Broadway-Nassau.*

Broome Street Bar. A local hangout since 1972, when the neighborhood was known as the cast-iron district, this casual corner has a fine selection of draught beers and a full diner-style menu. ⊠ *363 West Broadway, at Broome St., SoHo* ☎ *212/925–2086* Ⓜ *Subway: C, E to Spring St.*

Double Happiness. On a block where the boundary between Little Italy and Chinatown blurs, a stairwell descends into a former speakeasy where couples converse in nooks beneath a low ceiling. Drinks are as diverse as a green-tea martini and tap beer. The music is often classic rock or old-school hip-hop. ⊠ *173 Mott St., between Broome and Grand Sts., Chinatown* ☎ *212/941–1282* Ⓜ *Subway: F to Delancey St.; 6 to Spring St.*

Fanelli's. Linger over the *New York Times* at this down-to-earth neighborhood bar and restaurant, which harks back to 1847. ⊠ *94 Prince St., at Mercer St., SoHo* ☎ *212/226–9412* Ⓜ *Subway: R, W to Prince St.*

Lucky Strike. Now that the supermodels party elsewhere, this ultracool bistro is the domain of hipsters who pose at the cozy back tables. DJs play reggae, R&B, and hip-hop on crowded weekend nights. ⊠ *59 Grand St., between West Broadway and Wooster St., SoHo* ☎ *212/941–0772* Ⓜ *Subway: R, W, A, C, E, 1, 9 to Canal St.*

Lush. One of TriBeCa's hottest lounges, this modern-looking space has a cool banquette running the length of its loftlike room, as well as a couple of round chambers where you may spot a celebrity or two. ⊠ *110 Duane St., between Church St. and Broadway, TriBeCa* ☎ *212/766–1275* Ⓜ *Subway: A, C, 1, 2, 3 to Chambers St.*

★ **MercBar.** A chic local crowd and Europeans in the know come to this dark, nondescript bar for the wonderful martinis. Its street number is barely visible—look for the French doors, which stay open in summer. ⊠ *151 Mercer St., between Prince and W. Houston Sts., SoHo* ☎ *212/966–2727* Ⓜ *Subway: R, N, W to Prince St.*

Naked Lunch. Dazzlingly popular, this William S. Burroughs–inspired haunt is frequented by celebrities and other beautiful people. On weekends the crowd dances to old-school '80s hits late into the night. ⊠ *17 Thompson St., at Grand St., SoHo* ☎ *212/343–0828* Ⓜ *Subway: A, C, E, 1, 9 to Canal St.*

Pravda. Cocktails are the rule at this Eastern European-style bar. Choose from more than 70 brands of vodka, including house infusions, and nearly as many types of martinis. The cellarlike space, with an atmospheric vaulted ceiling, is illuminated with candles. Reserve a table for the Russian-inspired fare, especially on weekends. ⊠ *281 Lafayette St., between Prince and Houston Sts., SoHo* ☎ *212/226–4944* Ⓜ *Subway: B, D, F, V to Broadway–Lafayette St.; 6 to Bleecker St.*

Raoul's. One of the first trendy spots in SoHo, this arty French restaurant has yet to lose its touch. Expect a chic bar scene filled with model-pretty men and women, and an intriguing fortune-teller upstairs. ⊠ *180 Prince St., between Sullivan and Thompson Sts., SoHo* ☎ *212/966–3518* Ⓜ *Subway: C, E to Spring St.*

The Room. It can get rather cozy in this minimalist but comfortable spot where the selection of 70 bottled beers and over 20 wines by the glass draws a friendly mix of locals as well as an international crowd. Alternative rock music is played low enough to have a conversation. ⊠ *144 Sullivan St., between W. Houston and Prince Sts., SoHo* ☎ *212/477–2102* Ⓜ *Subway: C, E to Spring St.*

Thom Bar. This lounge inside the 60 Thompson boutique hotel is the perfect place to splurge, fireside, on a litchi martini. Pick a weeknight if you want to have a relaxed drink among the elegant patrons who make up the clientele. ⊠ *60 Thompson St., between Spring and Broome Sts., SoHo* ☎ *212/219–3200* Ⓜ *Subway: C, E to Spring St.*

Chelsea, the Meatpacking District & Greenwich Village

Bongo. Like its namesake, this bar is small but cool. The decor harkens back to a time when Beat poets recited poetry as a cool cat tapped out a syncopated rhythm on the drum. There are a boomerang-shaped coffee table, mod couches, and a crowd that's as stylish as the surroundings. ⊠ *299 10th Ave., between 27th and 28th Sts., Chelsea* ☎ *212/947–3654* Ⓜ *Subway: 1, 9 to 28th St.*

Bright Bar. A modest but stylish storefront watering hole with a healthy sense of humor (the decor includes playful Lite-Brite sculptures), Bright Bar is a beacon in a neighborhood of austere art galleries. ⊠ *297 10th Ave., at W. 27th St., Chelsea* ☎ *212/279–9706* Ⓜ *Subway: 1, 9 to 28th St.*

Café Loup. This restaurant is something of a neighborhood institution, and its cozy, unpretentious bar serves some of the best margaritas in the city. (The secret is fresh fruit juices.) A literary crowd chats as jazz tunes play overhead. ⊠ *105 W. 13th St., between 6th and 7th Aves., Greenwich Village* ☎ *212/255–4746* Ⓜ *Subway: F, V to 14th St.*

Cedar Tavern. A block or two from its original location, this old-fashioned tavern was a favorite haunt back of abstract expressionists back in the 1950s. College students and blue-collar workers enjoy the faded ambience, though the tin ceiling and 150-year-old back bar are offset by a more modern and open feel upstairs. ⊠ *82 University Pl., between W. 11th and W. 12th Sts., Greenwich Village* ☎ *212/741–9754* Ⓜ *Subway: 4, 5, 6, N, R, Q, W to 14th St./Union Sq.*

★ **Chumley's.** There's no sign to help you find this place—they took it down during its days as a speakeasy—but when you reach the corner of Bedford and Barrow, you're very close (just head a little north on Barrow and duck into the doorway on the east side of the street). A fireplace warms the relaxed dining room, where the burgers are hearty and the clientele collegiate. ✉ *86 Bedford St., between Barrow and Grove Sts., Greenwich Village* ☎ *212/675–4449* Ⓜ *Subway: 1, 9 to Christopher St./Sheridan Sq.*

Cibar. Descend into the warm pink-and-peach basement to find this candlelit martini lounge. Nightly DJs play an eclectic mix of music; the bamboo garden is quieter. ✉ *56 Irving Pl., between W. 17th and W. 18th Sts., Greenwich Village* ☎ *212/460–5656* Ⓜ *Subway: 4, 5, 6, N, R, Q, W to 14th St./Union Sq.*

★ **Cornelia Street Café.** Share a bottle of merlot at a street-side table on a quaint West Village lane. Downstairs you can groove to live jazz, catch a poetry reading, or take in the "Entertaining Science" evenings hosted by the Nobel laureate chemist Roald Hoffmann. ✉ *29 Cornelia St., between W. 4th and Bleecker Sts., Greenwich Village* ☎ *212/989–9319* Ⓜ *Subway: A, C, E, B, D, F, V to W. 4th St./Washington Sq.*

Corner Bistro. Opened in 1961, this neighborhood saloon serves the best hamburgers in town. The cozy place is so inviting and the professional crowd so friendly, you might think you're in a small town. ✉ *331 W. 4th St., at 8th Ave., Greenwich Village* ☎ *212/242–9502* Ⓜ *Subway: A, C, E to 14th St.; L to 8th Ave.*

★ **Flatiron Lounge.** Soft lighting and smart leather banquettes distinguish this art-deco hideout where guest mixologists, a seasonal drink menu, and owner Julie Reiner's daily "flights" of fanciful mini-martinis elevate bartending to an art form. ✉ *37 W. 19th St., between 5th and 6th Aves., Chelsea* ☎ *212/727–7741* Ⓜ *Subway: F, V to 23rd St.*

40/40. Rap superstar Jay-Z opened this upscale sports bar with more flat-screen TVs than an episode of MTV's "Cribs." The chic crowd is equally telegenic. ✉ *6 W. 25th St., at Broadway, Chelsea* ☎ *212/832–4040* Ⓜ *Subway: R, W to 23rd St.*

Half King. Writer Sebastian Junger (*The Perfect Storm*) is one of the owners of this mellow pub, which draws a friendly crowd of media types and stragglers from nearby Chelsea galleries for its Monday night readings, gallery exhibits, and Irish-American menu. ✉ *505 W. 23rd St., between 10th and 11th Aves., Chelsea* ☎ *212/462–4300* Ⓜ *Subway: C, E to 23rd St.*

Hogs & Heifers. This raucous place is all about the saucy barkeeps berating men over their megaphones and baiting women to get up on the bar and dance (and add their bras to the collection on the wall). Celebrities drop in to get their names in the gossip columns. ✉ *859 Washington St., at W. 13th St., Greenwich Village* ☎ *212/929–0655* Ⓜ *Subway: A, C, E to 14th St.; L to 8th Ave.*

La Bottega. Vintage Italian posters, international magazines, and a kiosk selling fresh flowers set the stage at the Maritime Hotel's European-style restaurant and bar. In the winter, bring your drink out to the lobby and nestle in front of the fireplace. ✉ *363 W. 16th St., at 9th Ave., Chelsea* ☎ *212/242–4300* Ⓜ *Subway: A, C, E to 14th St.; L to 8th Ave.*

Madame X. The bordello atmosphere here is enhanced by blood-red walls and a sexy crowd. Madame X is across West Houston Street from SoHo, which means it has an attractive clientele, but less attitude. The garden is a pleasure in warm weather. ⊠ *94 W. Houston St., between LaGuardia Pl. and Thompson St., Greenwich Village* ☎ *212/539–0808* Ⓜ *Subway: 1, 9 to Houston St.*

★ **Ono.** The O Bar at Ono, Hotel Gansevoort's trendy Japanese restaurant, must be seen to be believed. Designed by Jeffrey Beers International, the elegant touches include gold-leaf brick walls and a fiber-optic "waterfall" chandelier. Sip on sake in one of the two lounges or the stylish outdoor garden. ⊠ *18 9th Ave., at W. 13th St., Meatpacking District* ☎ *212/660–6766* Ⓜ *Subway: A, C, E to 14th St.; L to 8th Ave.*

The Park. This former taxi garage has been transformed into a dreamy California mansion: wander from the penthouse, complete with fireplace and hot tub, to the Asian-theme Red Room and you may feel like a bicoastal millionaire. A reservation is required on the weekends. ⊠ *118 10th Ave., between W. 17th and W. 18th Sts., Chelsea* ☎ *212/352–3313* Ⓜ *Subway: A, C, E to 14th St.; L to 8th Ave.*

Peculier Pub. A selection of nearly 500 beers from 43 countries, including Peru, Vietnam, and Holland, is the draw at this heart-of-the-Village pub. If you're hungry, you can also order some grub. ⊠ *145 Bleecker St., at LaGuardia Pl., Greenwich Village* ☎ *212/353–1327* Ⓜ *Subway: A, C, E, B, D, F, V to W. 4th St./Washington Sq.*

Shag. White carpet (shag, of course) lines the walls at this shoebox-size spot. The vibe is L.A.–pool-party-meets-groovy-bachelor-pad, set to an '80s soundtrack. ⊠ *11 Abingdon Sq., at Bleecker St. and 8th Ave., Greenwich Village* ☎ *212/242–0220* Ⓜ *Subway: A, C, E to 14th St.; L to 8th Ave.*

Serena. This remarkably stylish subterranean lounge, painted an eye-popping shade of pink, draws a chic crowd. The addictive bar snacks are the work of the bar's original owner, caterer Serena Bass. ⊠ *Chelsea Hotel, 222 W. 23rd St., between 7th and 8th Aves., Chelsea* ☎ *212/255–4646* Ⓜ *Subway: C, E to 23rd St.*

Fodor'sChoice ★ **Spice Market.** Asian street fare served with a Jean-Georges twist accompanies Spice Market's equally exotic cocktails. An open space with slowly-rotating fans, intricately carved woodwork, and sheer flowing curtains lends an aura of calm to this hot celebrity hangout. ⊠ *403 W. 13th St., at 9th Ave., Meatpacking District* ☎ *212/675–2322* Ⓜ *Subway: A, C, E to 14th St.; L to 8th Ave.*

Star Bar. If you don't spot your favorite celebrity on the street, head to Star Bar; Howie Keck's fluorescent portraits of Hollywood's jet set cover the walls. The pop culture haven has a psychedelic vibe and is studded with stars galore—the cosmic kind. A DJ keeps toes tapping on weekends. ⊠ *4 West 22nd St., between 5th and 6th Aves., Chelsea* ☎ *646/230–1444* Ⓜ *Subway: F, V to 23rd St.*

Tortilla Flats. The back room is a tribute to the stars of Las Vegas, from Martin and Lewis to Siegfried and Roy, but the real action is in the main room, where a rambunctious crowd packs the tight quarters for games (bingo on Monday and Tuesday, hula-hooping on Wednesday), tequila, and Mexican food. The Flats is a prime bachelorette-party destination. ⊠ *767 Washington St., at W. 12th St., Greenwich Village* ☎ *212/243–1053* Ⓜ *Subway: A, C, E to 14th St.; L to 8th Ave.*

White Horse Tavern. According to (dubious) New York legend, Dylan Thomas drank himself to death in this historic tavern founded in 1880.

THEME DREAMS

Those who relish sitting beneath a hair dryer will feel right at home at **Beauty Bar** (✉ 231 E. 14th St., between 2nd and 3rd Aves., East Village ☎ 212/539–1389 Ⓜ Subway: 4, 5, 6, L, N, R to 14th St./Union Sq.). There's even a manicurist on call. Put your tray tables in their full upright position at **Idlewild** (✉ 145 E. Houston St., between Forsyth and Eldridge Sts., Lower East Side ☎ 212/477–5005), where you can relax in real airplane seats. High tech geeks dig **Remote**

(✉ 327 Bowery, between E. 2nd and E. 3rd Sts., East Village ☎ 212/228–0228), where patrons control the video cameras. Try a more old-fashioned form of communication on the English phone booths at **Telephone Bar** (✉ 149 2nd Ave., between E. 9th and E. 10th Sts., East Village ☎ 212/529–5000).

From April to October try to snag a seat at one of the sidewalk tables. ✉ *567 Hudson St., at W. 11th St., Greenwich Village* ☎ *212/989–3956* Ⓜ *Subway: 1, 9 to Christopher St./Sheridan Sq.*

Lower East Side & East Village Through East 20s

B Bar. Long lines of people peer through venetian blinds at the stylish downtown crowd within this trendy bar and grill. If the bouncer says there's a private party going on, more likely than not it's his way of turning you away nicely. Dress your best if you want a seat in the covered outdoor space, a far cry from this spot's former gas station days. ✉ *358 Bowery, at E. 4th St., East Village* ☎ *212/475–2220* Ⓜ *Subway: 6 to Astor Pl.*

Beauty Bar. Grab a seat in a barber chair or under a dryer at this madeover hair salon. During happy hour, the manicurist will do your nails. The DJ spins rock during the week and soul on Saturday nights. ✉ *231 E. 14th St., between 2nd and 3rd Aves., East Village* ☎ *212/539–1389* Ⓜ *Subway: 4, 5, 6, L, N, R to 14th St./Union Sq.*

Cloister Café. With one of Manhattan's largest and leafiest outdoor gardens, the Cloister is a perfect perch for lingering over a drink. Be warned: the frozen margaritas are not very good. ✉ *238 E. 9th St., between 2nd and 3rd Aves., East Village* ☎ *212/777–9128* Ⓜ *Subway: 6 to Astor Pl.*

Coyote Ugly. At this grimy dive the raucous patrons wailing along with the Lynyrd Skynyrd on the jukebox. The attractive female bartenders are an ironic twist on the bar's name. ✉ *153 1st Ave., between E. 9th and E. 10th Sts., East Village* ☎ *212/477–4431* Ⓜ *Subway: 6 to Astor Pl.*

Good World Bar & Grill. On an isolated street in Chinatown is this glass-fronted bar full of artists, writers, and their subjects, as well as cool music, a catwalk-ready staff, and—believe it or not—tasty Swedish specialties like gravlax, herring, and meatballs. ✉ *3 Orchard St., between Canal and Division Sts., Lower East Side* ☎ *212/925–9975* Ⓜ *Subway: F to East Broadway.*

Local 138. If you're looking for a neighborly spot to catch the Yankees, Knicks, or the World Cup, head to this cozy, low-lighted pub. The friendly bartenders and relaxed customers are a nice change of pace from the typical Ludlow Street scene. ⊠ *138 Ludlow St., between Stanton and Rivington Sts., Lower East Side* ☎ *212/477–0280* Ⓜ *Subway: F, V to 2nd Ave.*

Lucky Cheng's. Although locals deride its mediocre Asian fare, Lucky Cheng's is famous for the drag queens who cavort with the tourists singing karoake in the lounge downstairs. ⊠ *24 1st Ave., between E. 1st and E. 2nd Sts., East Village* ☎ *212/473–0516* Ⓜ *Subway: F, V to 2nd Ave.*

Fodor'sChoice **Luna Park.** This open-air café near the northern end of Union Square is
★ a great place for a romantic date on a summer evening. Arrive before the nine-to-five crowd to secure a seat beneath the strings of white lights. ⊠ *Union Sq. between Broadway and Park Ave. S, Flatiron District* ☎ *212/475–8464* Ⓜ *Subway: 4, 5, 6, N, R, Q, W to 14th St./Union Sq.*

Max Fish. This crowded, kitschy palace on a gentrified Lower East Side strip has one of the most eclectic jukeboxes in town, a pool table and pinball machine in the back, and a young crowd that comes for the live music. ⊠ *178 Ludlow St., between E. Houston and Stanton Sts., Lower East Side* ☎ *212/529–3959* Ⓜ *Subway: F, V to 2nd Ave.*

McSorley's Old Ale House. One of New York's oldest saloons (it claims to have opened in 1854) and immortalized by *New Yorker* writer Joseph Mitchell, this is a must-see for beer lovers, even if only two kinds of brew are served: McSorley's light and McSorley's dark. Go early to avoid the lines that stretch down the block on Friday and Saturday night. ⊠ *15 E. 7th St., between 2nd and 3rd Aves., East Village* ☎ *212/473–9148* Ⓜ *Subway: 6 to Astor Pl.*

Old Town Bar & Restaurant. This proudly unpretentious watering hole is heavy on the mahogany and redolent of old New York—it's been around since 1892. Make sure to try the top-notch tavern fare. ⊠ *45 E. 18th St., between Broadway and Park Ave. S, Flatiron District* ☎ *212/529– 6732* Ⓜ *Subway: 4, 5, 6, N, Q, R, W to 14th St./Union Sq.*

Otto's Shrunken Head. A bamboo bar with fish lamps floating overhead sets the mood at this South Seas–inspired tiki bar. Otto's sells beef jerky to chew on as you play the pinball machine, pose inside the photo booth, or jive to the DJ or band playing anything from '50s to New Wave. ⊠ *538 E. 14th St., between Aves. A and B, East Village* ☎ *212/228–2240* Ⓜ *Subway: L to 1st Ave.; 4, 5, 6, N, R, Q, W to 14th St./Union Sq.*

Pete's Tavern. This saloon is famous as the place where O. Henry is alleged to have written *The Gift of the Magi* (at the second booth as you come). These days it's crowded with locals enjoying a beer or a burger. ⊠ *129 E. 18th St., at Irving Pl., Gramercy* ☎ *212/473–7676* Ⓜ *Subway: 4, 5, 6, N, R, Q, W to 14th St./Union Sq.*

Remote. The tables in the upstairs lounge have video screens on them, and you control the cameras that scan the room. For a technology that's designed to work over long distances, the effect, strangely enough, is to bring people closer together. Perhaps there are just more show-offs in New York City than elsewhere. ⊠ *327 Bowery, between E. 2nd and E. 3rd Sts., East Village* ☎ *212/228–0228* Ⓜ *Subway: B, D, F, V to Broadway–Lafayette St.; 6 to Bleecker St.*

CUT THE BLARNEY

With its rich Irish heritage, New York City is far from hurting for authentic Irish pubs. It seems like every corner has its own Blarney Stone. But three establishments in particular merit mention. Offering a simple selection of its own light and dark beers, **McSorley's Old Ale House** (⊠ 15 E. 7th St., between 2nd and 3rd Aves., East Village ☎ 212/473–9148) is also one of the New York City's oldest standing bars, Irish or otherwise. **P. J. Clarke's** (⊠ 915 3rd Ave., at E. 55th St., Midtown East

☎ 212/317–1616), however, is the city's most famous Irish pub. Scenes from the 1945 film Lost Weekend were filmed on the premises. The three-level **Connolly's** (⊠ 121 W. 45th St., between Broadway and 6th Ave., Midtown West ☎ 212/597–5126 Ⓜ Subway: B, D, F, V to 42nd St.) often hosts bands from the old country.

Telephone Bar. Bright red telephone booths imported from England and a polite, attractive college crowd mark this pub, which has great tap brews and killer mashed potatoes. ⊠ 149 2nd Ave., between E. 9th and E. 10th Sts., East Village ☎ 212/529–5000 Ⓜ Subway: 6 to Astor Pl.

Temple Bar. This unmarked haunt is famous for its martinis and romantic atmosphere. Look for the painted iguana skeleton on the facade, and walk past the slim bar to the back where, in near-total darkness, you can lounge on a plush banquette surrounded by velvet drapes. ⊠ 332 Lafayette St., between Bleecker and E. Houston Sts., East Village ☎ 212/925–4242 Ⓜ Subway: B, D, F, V to Broadway–Lafayette St.; 6 to Bleecker St.

Midtown & the Theater District

Algonquin Hotel. This venerable bar plays up its history as the home of the Algonquin Roundtable, a literary clique that included sharp-tongued Dorothy Parker. The clubby, oak-panel lobby and overstuffed easy chairs encourage lolling over cocktails and conversation. ⊠ 59 W. 44th St., between 5th and 6th Aves., Midtown West ☎ 212/840–6800 Ⓜ Subway: B, D, F, Q to 42nd St.

FodorśChoice ★ **Campbell Apartment.** One of Manhattan's more beautiful rooms, this restored space inside Grand Central Terminal dates to the 1920s, when it was the private office of an executive named John W. Campbell. He knew how to live, and you can enjoy his good taste from an overstuffed chair. ⊠ 15 Vanderbilt Ave. entrance, Midtown East ☎ 212/953–0409 Ⓜ Subway: 4, 5, 6, 7, S to 42nd St./Grand Central.

Cellar Bar. This stylish boîte inside the Bryant Park Hotel is distinguished by a tiled arched ceiling. One of the more spectacular spaces in Midtown, it attracts an attractive crowd from the fashion industry. A DJ with a taste for classic R&B keeps the crowd on its toes. ⊠ 40 W. 40th St., between 5th and 6th Aves., Midtown West ☎ 212/642–2260 Ⓜ Subway: B, D, F, V to 42nd St.

Divine Bar. Zebra-stripe barstools downstairs and jewel-tone velvet couches upstairs make this bar unusually chic for Midtown. The selection of tapas is complemented by 55 beers from around the world. There are 70 wines by the glass, and the frequently updated wine list includes such hard-to-come-by vintages as Robert Mondavi's Opus One. ⊠ *244 E. 51st St., between 2nd and 3rd Aves., Midtown East* ☎ *212/319–9463* Ⓜ *Subway: 6 to 51st St.*

ESPN Zone. When there's a play-off game, expect a line at the door of this multistory sports bar. With one 16-foot and two 14-foot video screens, plus scores of high-definition TVs, there isn't a bad seat in the house. Try the sports-theme video games on the top floor, or dig into the kitchen's full menu. ⊠ *1472 Broadway, at 42nd St., Midtown West* ☎ *212/921– 3776* Ⓜ *Subway: 1, 2, 3, 9, N, R, Q, W to 42nd St./Times Square.*

Hudson Bar. This swank establishment combines the exclusive feeling of a hot club with the excellent taste of a top hotel. Slip in between the beautiful people mingling under the hand-painted ceiling. The room is illuminated by lights in the glass floor. ⊠ *356 W. 58th St., between 8th and 9th Aves., Midtown West* ☎ *212/554–6303* Ⓜ *Subway: 1, 9, A, B, C, D to 59th St.*

Joe Allen. At this old reliable on Restaurant Row, celebrated in the musical version of *All About Eve*, everybody's en route to or from a show. The posters that adorn the "flop wall" are from Broadway musicals that bombed. ⊠ *326 W. 46th St., between 8th and 9th Aves., Midtown West* ☎ *212/581–6464* Ⓜ *Subway: A, C, E to 42nd St.*

Keens Steakhouse. Just around the corner from Madison Square Garden, this restaurant from 1885 is stocked with more than 200 single-malt scotches. Take a look at the ceilings, which are lined with thousands of clay pipes that once belonged to patrons. ⊠ *72 W. 36th St., between 5th and 6th Aves., Midtown West* ☎ *212/947–3636* Ⓜ *Subway: B, D, F, N, R, Q, V, W to 34th St.*

King Cole Bar. A famed Maxfield Parrish mural is a welcome sight at this classic Midtown meeting place, which happens to be the birthplace of the Bloody Mary. ⊠ *St. Regis Hotel, 2 E. 55th St., near 5th Ave., Midtown East* ☎ *212/753–4500* Ⓜ *Subway: E, V to 5th Ave./53rd St.*

K. Housed above an Indian restaurant, this stylish lounge is outfitted with intricately carved chairs and cozy banquettes. Couples sit close together as turbaned business executives stir their drinks. The K stands for Kama Sutra, making this quite the place for an exotic cocktail. ⊠ *30 W. 52nd St., between 5th and 6th Aves., Midtown West* ☎ *212/ 265–6665* Ⓜ *Subway: E, V to 5th Ave./53rd St.*

Monkey Bar. Once a fabled spot where the likes of Tennessee Williams and Tallulah Bankhead gathered, this lounge was restored in the '90s. Despite the simian light fixtures, there's very little barbarism in the mild-mannered banker types who shoot back scotch here. ⊠ *60 E. 54th St., between Park and Madison Aves., Midtown East* ☎ *212/838–2600* Ⓜ *Subway: E, V to Lexington Ave./53rd St.; 6 to 51st St.*

Morgans Bar. This dark, perpetually hip lounge in the basement of Ian Schrager's namesake boutique hotel draws supermodels and their kin. The after-work crowd of trendy Manhattanites can be overwhelming. Late night DJs turn up the volume. ⊠ *237 Madison Ave., between E.*

37th and E. 38th Sts., Midtown East ☎ 212/726–7600 Ⓜ Subway: 4, 5, 6, 7, S to 42nd St./Grand Central.

Morrell Wine Bar and Café. Run by the wine purveyors next door, this vibrant bar has one of the city's best selections of wine by the glass. In summer you can sip your viognier at outdoor tables in the heart of Rockefeller Center. ✉ 1 Rockefeller Center, W. 49th St. between 5th and 6th Aves., Midtown West ☎ 212/262–7700 Ⓜ Subway: B, D, F, V to 47th–50th Sts./Rockefeller Center.

Pen Top Bar & Lounge. Take a break from 5th Avenue shopping at this glass-lined penthouse bar on the 23rd floor. Drinks are pricey but the views are impressive, especially from the rooftop terraces. ✉ Peninsula Hotel, 700 5th Ave., at W. 55th St., Midtown West ☎ 212/956–2888 Ⓜ Subway: E, V to 5th Ave./53rd St.

P. J. Clarke's. Mirrors and polished wood adorn New York's most famous Irish bar, where scenes from the 1945 movie Lost Weekend were shot. The after-work crowd that unwinds here seems to appreciate the old-fashioned flair. ✉ 915 3rd Ave., at E. 55th St., Midtown East ☎ 212/317–1616 Ⓜ Subway: 4, 5, 6 to 59th St.

Fodor'sChoice
★
Royalton. Philippe Starck's minimalistic hotel has two places to drink—the large lobby bar furnished with armchairs and chaise longues and the banquette-lined Round Bar. In a circular room to your right as you enter, it's the place to sip vodka and champagne. The entrance to the hotel is difficult to find (look for the curved silver railings). ✉ 44 W. 44th St., between 5th and 6th Aves., Midtown West ☎ 212/869–4400 Ⓜ Subway: B, D, F, V to 42nd St.

Sardi's. "The theater is certainly not what it was," said a forlorn feline in the musical Cats, and the same could be said for this Broadway institution. Still, theater fans should make time for a drink in one of the red-leather booths, which are surrounded by caricatures of stars past and present. ✉ 234 W. 44th St., between Broadway and 8th Ave., Midtown West ☎ 212/221–8440 Ⓜ Subway: A, C, E to 42nd St.

Single Room Occupancy. Nearly impossible to find (look for the green light and ring the bell), this beer and wine bar has a sleek interior outfitted with such luxurious touches as fresh flowers. The friendly staff makes everyone feel welcome. ✉ 360 W. 53rd St., between 8th and 9th Ave., Midtown West ☎ 212/765–6299 Ⓜ Subway: C, E to 53rd St.

Top of the Tower. There are lounges at higher altitudes, but this one on the 26th floor feels halfway to heaven. The atmosphere is elegant and subdued. There's piano music every night save Monday. ✉ Beekman Tower, 3 Mitchell Pl., near 1st Ave. at E. 49th St., Midtown East ☎ 212/355–7300 Ⓜ Subway: 6 to 51st St./Lexington Ave.; E, V to Lexington Ave./53rd St.

Water Club. You're not sailing on the East River, although you might feel as if you are, when you step onto the pleasing outdoor deck at the Water Club. This is a special-occasion place—especially for those who've already been to all the landlocked ones in town. A fireplace warms the downstairs bar, and there's piano music every night save Sunday. ✉ 500 E. 30th St., at FDR Dr., Midtown East ☎ 212/683–3333 Ⓜ Subway: 6 to 28th St.

Whiskey Park. At the noted nightlife impresario Rande Gerber's sleek, dark-wood lounge, visiting business executives and wayward Wall Street

DIVE IN

When dressing up has got you down and casual—really casual—is what you crave, it's time to find one of New York's dive bars. At **American Trash** (✉ 1471 1st Ave., between E. 76th and E. 77th Sts., Upper East Side ☎ 212/988–9008), stuff found in the garbage has been transformed into decor. At **Hogs & Heifers** (✉ 859 Washington St., at W. 13th St., Greenwich Village ☎ 212/929–0655 Ⓜ Subway: A, C, E to 14th St.; L to 8th Ave.) has no pretense of propriety.

Women with no intentions of dancing for the crowd may find the atmosphere tough to take. In that same vein, but slightly less intense, **Coyote Ugly** (✉ 153 1st Ave., between E. 9th and E. 10th Sts., East Village ☎ 212/477–4431) puts the hotties behind the bar, rather than on top of it.

types unwind with local sports games and sips of scotch. The candle-lighted outpost is across the street from Central Park. ✉ 100 Central Park S, at 6th Ave., Midtown West ☎ 212/307–9222 Ⓜ Subway: F to 57th St.

Upper East Side

American Trash. The name refers to the decor—bicycle tires, golf clubs, and other cast-offs cover the walls and ceiling. Eight plasma TVs, three video games, a rock-and-roll jukebox, and a pool table keep the neighborhood crowd busy. Some nights local bands play classic rock. ✉ 1471 1st Ave., between E. 76th and E. 77th Sts., Upper East Side ☎ 212/988–9008 Ⓜ Subway: 6 to 77th St.

Auction House. There's a loosely enforced dress code (no baseball hats, no sneakers) at this lounge with high ceilings and candlelight, so the neighborhood crowd is a little better in appearance, and behavior, than at many other bars. ✉ 300 E. 89th St., between 1st and 2nd Aves., Upper East Side ☎ 212/427–4458 Ⓜ Subway: 4, 5, 6 to 86th St.

Big Easy. Decorated with Bourbon Street memorabilia, this sprawling party spot puts you in a Mardi Gras mood with $2 drinks from 11 PM to midnight. With pool tables, dart boards, and weekend DJs, there's no shortage of ways for the young, energetic crowd to while away the evening. ✉ 1768 2nd Ave., between E. 92nd and E. 93rd Sts., Upper East Side ☎ 212/348–0879 Ⓜ Subway: 6 to 96th St.

Guastavino's. High-vaulted ceilings give this upscale restaurant and bar beneath the Queensborough Bridge a feeling of grandeur. Expect mellow music and double-digit drink prices. ✉ 409 E. 59th St., between 1st and York Aves., Upper East Side ☎ 212/980–2455 Ⓜ Subway: 4, 5, 6, N, R to Lexington Ave./59th St.

Metropolitan Museum of Art. On Friday and Saturday evening until 8 or 9, unwind to the sounds of a string quartet at the Great Hall's Balcony Bar. In summer be sure to visit the bar on the Iris and B. Gerald Cantor Roof Garden for a view of Central Park and the skyline that's as stunning as anything in the museum's vast collections. ⊠ *1000 5th Ave., at E. 82nd St., Upper East Side* ☎ *212/879–5500* Ⓜ *Subway: 4, 5, 6 to 86th St.*

Session 73. Live music sets this sizable restaurant and bar apart from others in the neighborhood. Young locals groove to the nightly mix of funk, R&B, and blues. If the songs don't set your heart racing, there's always the generous assortment of tequilas and beers on tap. ⊠ *1359 1st Ave., at E. 73rd St., Upper East Side* ☎ *212/517–4445* Ⓜ *Subway: 6 to 77th St.*

Upper West Side

★ **Burton Lounge.** Bar-hopping is expected at this bi-level establishment, since it has three spaces competing for your attention. Upstairs, a subdued sports bar sits alongside a lounge where you can kick back in front of the fireplace. Downstairs, at the Kama Lounge, a DJ romances the crowd, although the throw pillows, gushing fountains, ornate lamps, and stone walls certainly don't hurt. It's located across from the Museum of Natural History. ⊠ *380 Columbus Ave., Upper West Side* ☎ *212/724–9888* Ⓜ *Subway: B, C to 81st St.*

Café des Artistes. At this restaurant known for its glorious art-nouveau murals, there's a small, warm bar where interesting strangers tell their life stories and the house drink is pear champagne. It's one of the city's special hideaways. ⊠ *1 W. 67th St., between Central Park W and Columbus Ave., Upper West Side* ☎ *212/877–3500* Ⓜ *Subway: 1, 9 to 66th St.*

Gabriel's. This highly regarded Northern Italian restaurant has a 35-foot curved mahogany bar and a stupendous selection of grappas. The atmosphere couldn't be warmer. ⊠ *11 W. 60th St., between Broadway and Columbus Ave., Upper West Side* ☎ *212/956–4600* Ⓜ *Subway: A, B, C, D, 1, 9 to 59th St.*

Hi-Life. Padded black walls, large round mirrors, and an L-shape bar give this spot the look of a 1940s movie. Settle into a banquette and watch the budding neighborhood bons vivants in action. ⊠ *477 Amsterdam Ave., at W. 83rd St., Upper West Side* ☎ *212/787–7199* Ⓜ *Subway: 1, 9 to 86th St.*

Peter's. A staple of the Upper West Side scene since the early 1980s, this vast, noisy establishment, adorned with copies of the frescoes at Pompeii, hosts a pretheater crowd. Patrons range from their late 20s to their early 40s. ⊠ *182 Columbus Ave., between W. 68th and W. 69th Sts., Upper West Side* ☎ *212/877–4747* Ⓜ *Subway: B, C to 72nd St.*

Shark Bar. The classy bar at this soul-food (and soul-music) restaurant fills with eye candy every night. Rapper LL Kool J has been known to stop by, and it's very popular among young black executives, music industry bigwigs, and professional athletes. ⊠ *307 Amsterdam Ave., between W. 74th and W. 75th Sts., Upper West Side* ☎ *212/874–8500* Ⓜ *Subway: 1, 2, 3, 9 to 72nd St.*

Brooklyn

Barbes. Named for a Parisian neighborhood brimming with North African record shops, this simple but inviting little bar draws local writers as well as more far-flung visitors, such as the noted roots, jazz, folk, and world-music musicians that crowd its tiny back room. Stop by on a Monday night for free movies. ✉ *376 9th St., at 6th Ave., Park Slope* ☎ *718/965-9177* Ⓜ *Subway: F to 7th Ave.*

Brooklyn Brewery. No jacket is required at Brooklyn's working brewery. Happy hour means $3 beers—try the popular Brooklyn Lager or one of the seasonal brews. Beer buffs can join a guided tour on Saturday afternoon. ✉ *79 N. 11th St., between Berry St. and Wythe Ave., Williamsburg* ☎ *718/486-7422* Ⓜ *Subway: L to Bedford Ave.; G to Nassau Ave.*

Brooklyn Social. Take care not to walk past this former men's social club. The inconspicuous storefront—no sign, dark windows—recalls its members-only nights. Inside, a local crowd carouses amid vintage club memorabilia while a jukebox plays Rubén González piano tunes one minute, Bjork singles the next. Shoot pool, order a killer panini, or just admire the bartender's dapper outfit (and mixing skills). ✉ *335 Smith St., between President and Carroll Sts., Carroll Gardens* ☎ *718/858-7758* Ⓜ *Subway: F, G to Carroll St.*

Floyd, NY. New York's only bocce bar is a spacious, softly-lighted den of jukebox bluegrass, vintage loveseats, patterned tin walls, and friendly bartenders. Order the tasty beercheese (a blend of cheddar cheese, beer, and spices) with your game of foosball or bocce. There's no bowling alley clatter here, just the soft hum of coffee shop conversation. ✉ *131 Atlantic Ave., between Clinton and Henry Sts., Cobble Hill* ☎ *718/858-5810* Ⓜ *Subway: F, G to Bergen St.; R to Court St.*

★ **Galapagos.** Artists, hipsters, and visiting Europeans file past a shallow pool filled with water dyed black to reflect the atmospheric exposed brick walls. An elevated stage in this former mayonnaise factory is the place to see dance troupes, theater performances, and live bands; Monday night there's an old-fashioned burlesque show. Ocularis hosts its popular Sunday-night independent-film series here. ✉ *70 N. 6th St., between Wythe and Kent Aves., Williamsburg* ☎ *718/782-5188* Ⓜ *Subway: L to Bedford Ave.*

Pete's Candy Store. Williamsburg's beloved outpost has a retro feel, a friendly crowd, and great cocktails. The back room is smaller than a subway car, but it's the nightly stop for some of the city's best free music (Norah Jones once graced this stage). Brainy hipsters start off their Monday nights with spelling bees, Tuesday night locals turn out for bingo, and the trivia contests on Wednesday draws folks from the entire metropolitan area. ✉ *709 Lorimer St., between Frost and Richardson Sts., Williamsburg* ☎ *718/302-3770* Ⓜ *Subway: L to Lorimer St.*

Superfine. The pool table takes center stage for the young, hip crowd at this sprawling restaurant and bar located at the base of the Manhattan Bridge. Rotating artwork, exposed brick walls lined with tall windows, sunken second-hand chairs and mellow music make for a distinctively DUMBO scene. ✉ *126 Front St., between Jay and Pearl Sts., DUMBO* ☎ *718/243-9005* Ⓜ *Subway: F to York St.*

GAY & LESBIAN

Any night of the week, gay men and lesbians can find plenty to keep them occupied. For the latest listings of nightlife options, check out gay publications such as *HX*, *Next*, *MetroSource*, and the *New York Blade*, as well as *Paper* and *Time Out New York*. *GO NYC* is good source for lesbian happenings.

Some venues always have a mixed crowd, while others are exclusively for gay men or lesbians. Some clubs have one night a week where they roll out the red carpet for gay men or lesbians. We sort it out for you below.

Dance Clubs & Parties

Avalon. Housed in a converted church, this club's Sunday night party throbs with techno beats, big-name DJs on two dance floors, and lots of sweaty men. As with other big venues, there's a sizable cover. ⊠ *660 6th Ave., at 20th St., Chelsea* ☎ 212/807–7780 Ⓜ *Subway: F, V to 23rd St.*

Beige. Gay men in fashion and advertising predominate at this long-running Tuesday get-together. An occasional celebrity or two keeps it lively. Dress up, or look as if you don't have to. ⊠ *B Bar, 358 Bowery, at E. 4th St., East Village* ☎ 212/475–2220 Ⓜ *Subway: 6 to Astor Pl.*

Big Apple Ranch. Country-western and other dance styles are in full swing at this venue, with half-hour two-step lessons at 8 PM, line dancing at 8:30 PM, and then a down-home dance party. Another room has salsa, meringue, and hustle. ⊠ *Dance Manhattan, 39 W. 19th St., 5th fl., between 5th and 6th Aves., Chelsea* ☎ 212/358–5752 Ⓜ *Subway: F, V to 23rd St.*

Escuelita. One of the city's biggest Latin clubs, Escuelita has a diverse crowd, campy drag shows, and loud music ranging from hip-hop to salsa. ⊠ *301 W. 39th St., at 8th Ave., Midtown West* ☎ 212/631–0588 Ⓜ *Subway: A, C, E, to 42nd St.*

LoverGirlNYC. This Saturday night women's dance party at Club Shelter has two floors of house, salsa, hip-hop, and R&B. Men are welcome, but pay a higher cover. ⊠ *20 W. 39th St., between 5th and 6th Aves., Midtown* ☎ 212/252–3397 Ⓜ *Subway: B, D, F, V to 42nd St.*

1984. Madonna still reigns supreme on Friday night at Pyramid, a two-story bar with an always-packed dance floor where DJs play '80s pop for a hip, young, and enthusiastic mixed crowd. ⊠ *Pyramid, Ave. A, between 6th and 7th Sts., East Village* ☎ 212/473–7184 Ⓜ *Subway: 6 to Astor Pl.*

The Rambles. It's not a coincidence that this late-night party on Sunday is named for a cruisy part of Central Park. Go-go boys and sets by eclectic DJs help draw a crowd of fashion-conscious men. Line up for the open vodka bar from 10 to 11 PM. ⊠ *The Park, 118 10th Ave., at 18th St., Chelsea* ☎ 212/352–3313 Ⓜ *Subway: A, C, E to 14th St.*

Lounges

Barracuda. The comfy couches in back are one big plus at this hangout where hilarious, unpredictable send-ups of game shows draw a mostly male crowd. ⊠ *275 W. 22nd St., between 7th and 8th Aves., Chelsea* ☎ 212/645–8613 Ⓜ *Subway: C, E to 23rd St.*

Girlsroom. With a funky young clientele, go-go girls, drink specials, and a cozy lounge, this little Lower East Side dance club packs everything you need for a night out, whether you're after mellow conversation or something racier. ⊠ *210 Rivington St., between Pitt and Ridge Sts.,*

Lower East Side ☎ 212/677–6149 Ⓜ *Subway: F, J, M, Z to to Delancy St.–Essex Station.*

Hell. This groovy lounge with crystal chandeliers and red drapes attracts a trendy crowd of straight and gay yuppies, fashionistas, and downtowners. The drinks are expensive but creative. ⊠ *59 Gansevoort St., between Washington and Greenwich Sts., Meatpacking District* ☎ 212/727–1666 Ⓜ *Subway: A, C, E, L to 8th Ave.*

Starlight. The East Village goes fashionable at this lounge packed with hip, stylish boys. The narrow banquette-lined bar in front can become a tight squeeze; head to the back room, which often hosts cabaret and stand-up comedy. Starlette, on Sunday, is one of the most popular lesbian nights in town. ⊠ *167 Ave. A, between 10th and 11th Sts., East Village* ☎ 212/475–2172 Ⓜ *Subway: L to 1st Ave.*

Therapy. With slate floors, wood-panel walls, and a small stone-filled pond, this lounge's decor is as diverse as its mostly male clientele, which ranges from twentysomething hipsters to professionals. An appetizing menu of small dishes is available. ⊠ *348 W. 52nd. St., between 8th and 9th Ave., Midtown West* ☎ 212/397–1700 Ⓜ *Subway: C, E to 50th St.*

XL. The owners reported poured $2.5 million into this stylish multilevel lounge, but all eyes are on the bare-chested bartenders. Check out the fish tanks in the bathroom. ⊠ *357 W. 16th St., between 8th and 9th Aves., Chelsea* ☎ 212/995–1400 Ⓜ *Subway: A, C, E to 14th St.; L to 8th Ave.*

Neighborhood Bars

Cubby Hole. Early in the evening the crowd is mixed at this neighborhood institution where Madonna and Rosie used to hang out. Later on the room belongs to the women. ⊠ *281 W. 12th St., at W. 4th St., Greenwich Village* ☎ 212/243–9041 Ⓜ *Subway: A, C, E to 14th St.; L to 8th Ave.*

Henrietta Hudson. The nightly parties at this laid-back bar attract young professional women, out-of-towners, and longtime regulars. ⊠ *438 Hudson St., at Morton St., Greenwich Village* ☎ 212/924–3347 Ⓜ *Subway: 1, 9 to Christopher St./ Sheridan Sq.*

The Hole. At this graffiti-sprayed bar, the loud music and cheap drinks keep the mood a little trashy. Friday's Mad Clams party brings in the lesbian crowd. ⊠ *29 2nd Ave., between 1st and 2nd Sts., East Village* ☎ 212/437–9406 Ⓜ *Subway: F, V to 2nd Ave.*

The Phoenix. With a pool table, pinball machine, and an outstanding, constantly updated jukebox, this neighborhood bar is packed almost every night of the week with gay men. The $1 beers on Wednesday are always popular. ⊠ *447 E. 13th St., at Ave. A, East Village* ☎ 212/477–9979 Ⓜ *Subway: L to 1st Ave.*

The Slide. In this underground space, a long wooden bar and vaguely Victorian furnishings are a nice contrast with the raunchy go-go boys. Upstairs are performances by drag queens and cult bands. ⊠ *356 Bowery, near 4th St., East Village* ☎ 212/420–8885 Ⓜ *Subway: F, V to 2nd Ave.*

Stonewall. With its odd assortment of down-to-earth locals and tourists snapping pictures, the scene here is definitely democratic. ⊠ *53 Christopher St., near 7th Ave. S, Greenwich Village* ☎ 212/463–0950 Ⓜ *Subway: 1, 9 to Christopher St./ Sheridan Sq.*

Piano Bars

Brandy's Piano Bar. A singing waitstaff warms up the mixed crowd at this classy lounge, getting everyone in the mood to belt out their favorite tunes. ⊠ *235 E. 84th St., between 2nd and 3rd Aves., Upper East Side* ☎ *212/650–1944* Ⓜ *Subway: 4, 5, 6 to 86th St.*

Marie's Crisis. Everyone seems to know all the words to songs you've never even heard of, but after a few drinks you'll be standing around the piano and making lots of new friends. ⊠ *59 Grove St., at 7th Ave., Greenwich Village* ☎ *212/243–9323* Ⓜ *Subway: 1, 9 to Christopher St./ Sheridan Sq.*

The Monster. A longtime meeting place in the West Village, the Monster has a piano bar upstairs and a disco downstairs. It's mostly men, but women won't feel out of place. ⊠ *80 Grove St., between W. 4th St. and 7th Ave. S, Greenwich Village* ☎ *212/924–3558* Ⓜ *Subway: 1, 9 to Christopher St./ Sheridan Sq.*

The Townhouse. Older, well-off men from the Upper East Side as well as their admirers populate the bars of this brownstone, which sometimes has a piano player. ⊠ *236 E. 58th St., between 2nd and 3rd Aves., Midtown East* ☎ *212/754–4649* Ⓜ *Subway: 4, 5, 6, N, R, W to 59th St.*

10 Shopping

WORD OF MOUTH

"Go to Tiffany's upper floors. Tourists rarely go up there, so sales people are eager to let you try on extremely expensive and beautiful jewelry. It's like a small museum."

—NYCdreamer

"We explored SoHo where my daughter found the unusual and alternative vinyl records she was looking for, as well as the consignment, art, and other funky stores."

—BuzzyJ

"Well, you have to walk up Madison Avenue . . . just to experience it."

—tinaerrico

www.fodors.com/forums

By Sarah Gold
and Jennifer
Paull

TRUE TO ITS NATURE, New York shops on a grand scale, from the glossy couture houses along Madison Avenue to the quirky spots downtown. No matter which threshold you cross, shopping here is an event. For every bursting department store, there's an echoing, minimalist boutique; for every nationally familiar brand, there's a local favorite. The foremost American and international designers stake their flagship stores here; meanwhile, small neighborhood shops guarantee a reservoir of both the down-to-earth and the unexpected. National chains often make their New York stores something special, with unique sales environments and merchandise.

One of Manhattan's biggest shopping lures is the bargain—a temptation fueled by Century 21, H&M, and other discount divas. Hawkers of not-so-real Rolex watches and Kate Spade bags are stationed at street corners, even on Madison Avenue, and Canal Street is lined with counterfeit Gucci logos and Burberry plaid. There are uptown thrift shops where socialites send their castoffs, and downtown spots where the fashion crowd turns in last week's supertrendy must-haves. And of course, thousands of eyes train on the cycles of sales.

SALES

Even a temporary New Yorker loves a bargain. Seasonal and holiday sales are a way of life for NYC consumers, and local publications are larded with sales-oriented ads and listings. Be sure to check out *New York* magazine's "Sales and Bargains" column, which often lists sales in manufacturers' showrooms that are not otherwise promoted publicly, and *Time Out New York*'s "Shoptalk" page, which includes sales. The *Village Voice* is also a good source for tip-off ads. Web sites such as Daily Candy (www.dailycandy.com) and Manhattan User's Guide (www.manhattanusersguide.com) regularly list sales, too. (⇨ For info on sample sales, which can net you even deeper discounts, *see* the "Sample Sales" CloseUp box.)

If it's not a sale period, you can always get a bargain fix at **Woodbury Common** (☎ 845/928–4000), a giant outlet village in Central Valley, New York, where businesses such as Brooks Brothers, Donna Karan, and Williams-Sonoma offer deep discounts. **Shortline Coach USA** (☎ 800/631–8405) buses shuttle from New York City to the outlet a dozen times a day.

SHOPPING NEIGHBORHOODS

Malls are not the New York shopper's natural habitat. Stores tend to cluster in a few main neighborhoods, which makes shopping a good way to get to know the area. However, in spring 2004 **The Shops at Columbus Circle** arrived to challenge the conventional wisdom. This three-floor shopping center in the Time Warner building has amped-up branches of such mall standbys as Williams-Sonoma and J. Crew. But overall, it's more fun to save the chain stores for home, and seek out the shops that are unique to New York, or at least unique to the world's shopping cap-

CloseUp

SAMPLE SALES

F A SEASONAL SALE *makes New Yorkers' eyes gleam, a sample sale throws the city's shoppers into a frenzy. With so many designer flagships and corporate headquarters in town, merchandise fallout periodically leads to tremendous deals. Sample sales typically comprise leftover, already discounted stock, sample designs, and show models. Location adds a bit of an illicit thrill to the event—sales are held in hotels, warehouses, or loft spaces. Clothes incredible and unfortunate jam a motley assortment of racks, tables, and bins. Generally, there is a makeshift communal dressing room but mirrors are scarce. Veteran sample-sale shoppers come prepared for wriggling in the aisles; some wear skirts, tights, and tank tops for modest quick-changes. Two rules of thumb: grab first and inspect later, and call in advance to find out what methods of payment are accepted.*

The level of publicity and regularity of sales vary. The print and online versions of publications like New York *and* Time Out New York *magazines are always worth checking for sample sale tip-offs. High season for sales is August–September and February–March, but these days an off-loading of goods can happen year-round. One of the ultimate experiences is the Barneys Warehouse Sale, held in February and August in Chelsea. Other luscious sales range from the Vera Wang bridal-gown sale (early winter) to TSE cashmere (spring and late fall). If you're interested in specific designers, call their shops and inquire—you may get lucky.*

itals. If you head off in search of an outlying store, you may end up discovering something else—new boutiques are constantly springing up, even on previously deserted streets. Below are the shopping highlights in each neighborhood. Addresses for shops can be found in the store listings later in the chapter.

SoHo

Once an abandoned warehouse district, then lined with artists' studios and galleries, the cobbled streets of SoHo are now packed with high-rent boutiques and national chains. Big fashion guns such as **Louis Vuitton, Chanel, Burberry,** and **Prada** have established themselves, raising local retail a notch above the secondary-line designer outposts, such as **D&G, DKNY,** and **Miu Miu.** Adornment advances further in a flock of makeup stores, including **Shu Uemura, M.A.C.,** and French import **Sephora.** Much to the distress of longtime residents, the mall element (**Victoria's Secret, Old Navy, J. Crew,** and many more) has a firm foothold; however, you can still find many unique shops, especially for housewares and clothing. Some well-known stops include **Dean & DeLuca,** a gourmet food emporium, and **Moss,** full of museum-quality designed home furnishings and gadgets. There are the two Kates as well: **Kate's Paperie,** for stationery and other paper products, and **Kate Spade,** for handbags and accessories. On Lafayette Street below East Houston Street, a fashionable strip includes shops outside the mainstream, dealing in urban streetwear and vintage 20th-century furniture. Many SoHo stores are open seven days a week.

NoLita

FodorsChoice
★

This Nabokovian nickname, shorthand for "*N*orth of *Li*ttle I*taly,*" describes a neighborhood that has taken the commercial baton from SoHo and run with it. Like SoHo, NoLita has gone from a locals-only area with businesses thin on the ground to a crowded weekend shopping destination, though its stores remain mostly one-of-a-kind. NoLita's parallel north–south spines are Elizabeth, Mott, and Mulberry streets, between East Houston and Kenmare streets. Tiny boutiques continue to jostle each other in pursuit of real estate. A cache of stylish shops—such as **Mayle, Tory by TRB, Lyell, Seize sur Vingt,** and the various **Calypso**s—will start your sartorial engines running. Deals can be found at some of the best branches of **INA.** Accessories are hardly neglected: **Jamin Puech** provides swish purses, and such spots as **Lace** and **Hollywould** play to women's shoe cravings. **Sigerson Morrison** covers both bases with smart shoes and handbags. Meanwhile, **Me + Ro, Objets du Désir,** and **Femmegems** beckon with jewelry.

Lower East Side & the East Village

Once home to millions of Jewish immigrants from Russia and Eastern Europe, the Lower East Side has traditionally been New Yorkers' bargain beat. The center of it all is Orchard Street. The spirit of "Have I got a bargain for you!" still fills the narrow street crammed with tiny, no-nonsense clothing and lingerie stores and open stalls. A lot of the merchandise here is of dubious quality, but there are some finds to be made. Increasingly, these scrappy vendors are giving way to edgy boutiques, like **Frock,** where models and stylists hunt for one-of-a-kind vintage dresses and shoes. Among the Orchard Street veterans, essential stops include **Fine & Klein** for handbags and **Klein's of Monticello** for deals on dressy clothes. Many shops on or near Orchard Street sell candy, nuts, dried fruit, and Israeli sweets. Note that many Orchard Street stores are closed Saturday in observance of the Jewish Sabbath. Ludlow Street, one block east of Orchard, is buzzing with little storefronts selling hipster gear such as electric guitars, vintage '60s and '70s furniture, and clothing and accessories from local designers; check out **TG-170** for downtown womenswear and messenger bags. To the north, the East Village offers diverse, offbeat specialty stops, plenty of collectible kitsch, and some great vintage-clothing boutiques, especially along East 7th and East 9th streets. East 9th Street between 2nd Avenue and Avenue A merits a ramble for its variety: an herbalist, a couple of gown boutiques, a few music specialists, and casual new threads at spots like Meg and A. Cheng.

Manhattan Shopping Neighborhoods

Randalls Island

HARLEM

Columbia University

W. 116th St.
Morningside Park
E. 110th St.
E. 106h St.
Riverside Dr.
Broadway
Amsterdam Ave.
AW.96th St.
Madison Ave.
Lexington Ave.
5th Ave.
E. 96th St.

UPPER WEST SIDE

UPPER EAST SIDE

Gracie Mansion

Riverside Park
W. 86th St.
Central Park
E. 86th St.
Metropolitan Museum of Art
E. 79th St.
Columbus Ave.
Central Park West
West End Ave.
Park Ave.
American Museum of Natural History
E. 72nd St.
W. 72nd St.

Hudson River

Broadway
Amsterdam Ave.
MADISON. AVENUE
E. 65th St.

FDR Dr.
Roosevelt Island

QUEENS

Lincoln Center

Time Warner Center

W. 57th St.
57TH STREET
E. 59th St.
E. 57th St.
Queensboro Bridge

5TH. AVENUE

Rockefeller Center
E. 50th St.
Grand Central Terminal
United Nations

11th Ave.
10th Ave.
9th Ave.
8th Ave.
Times Square
E. 42nd St.
Madison Ave.
5th Ave.
3rd Ave.
2nd Ave.
1st Ave.

W. 42nd St.

Lincoln Tunnel

Port Authority Bus Terminal

Queens-Midtown Tunnel

Javits Convention Center

W. 34th St.
Madison Square Garden
Empire State Building

East River

CHELSEA
W. 23rd St.
FLATIRON DISTRICT
E. 23rd St.

7th Ave.
Ave. of the Americas

Union Sq.
W. 14th St.
E. 14th St.

MEATPACKING DISTRICT

EAST VILLAGE

Washington Sq.

GREENWICH VILLAGE

Hudson River

E. Houston St.

NOLITA
LOWER EAST SIDE

Williamsburg Bridge

West Side Hwy.
W. Houston St.
SOHO
Canal St.

TRI-BECA
CHINA-TOWN

Manhattan Bridge

W. Broadway
West St.
Chambers St.

Brooklyn Bridge

NEW JERSEY

Holland Tunnel

World Trade Center Site

South Street Seaport

BROOKLYN

Battery Park
Brooklyn-Battery Tunnel

Chelsea & the Flatiron District

Fifth Avenue south of 23rd Street, along with the streets fanning east and west, nurses a mix of the hip, such as **Intermix** and **Paul Smith**, and the hard-core, such as the mega-discounter **Loehmann's** on 7th Avenue. Broadway has a smattering of stores dear to New Yorkers' hearts, including the richly overstuffed **ABC Carpet & Home** and the comprehensive **Paragon Sporting Goods**. In the teens on 6th Avenue is a cluster of superstores, including the colossal Bed Bath & Beyond. Several blocks west, between 10th and 11th avenues, a few intrepid retailers, such as the cutting-edge **Comme des Garçons** and **Balenciaga**, took root amid the flourishing art galleries in what was until recently the desolate fringe of Chelsea.

The Meatpacking District

Until the late 1990s, the area between West 14th Street and Gansevoort (on the north-south) and Hudson Street and 11th Avenue (on the east-west) was primarily the domain of suppliers to the city's steak houses. Now, however, many of the old warehouses, some of which still sport meat hooks, house ultrachic fashion boutiques and homewares shops, as well as galleries, nightclubs, and restaurants-of-the-moment. High-fashion temple **Jeffrey** was the first shop to put the area on the map, followed by **Stella McCartney** and **Alexander McQueen**. More recently, **Christian Louboutin** and **Henry Beguelin** have joined the fray with their opulent, must-have accessories. Eclectic boutiques are continually popping up here; many of them, like bespoke womenswear designer Jussara Lee, have limited but extremely high-quality merchandise.

5th Avenue

Fifth Avenue from Rockefeller Center to Central Park South still wavers between the money-is-no-object crowd and an influx of more accessible stores. The flag-bedecked **Saks Fifth Avenue** faces **Rockefeller Center,** which harbors branches of Banana Republic and **J. Crew** as well as smaller specialty shops, both along the outdoor promenade and in the underground marketplace. The perennial favorites will eat up a lot of shoe leather: **Cartier** jewelers and **Salvatore Ferragamo**, at 52nd Street; **Takashimaya**, at 54th Street; **Henri Bendel**, at 56th Street; **Tiffany** and **Bulgari** jewelers, at 57th Street; and **Bergdorf Goodman** at 58th Street. The landmark **F.A.O. Schwarz** toy store is back after a major overhaul, with its "toy soldier" doorman ushering in hordes of kids. Exclusive design houses such as **Versace, Prada, Bottega Veneta,** and **Gucci** are a stone's throw from the über-chain Gap and a souped-up branch of good old **Brooks Brothers. Zara, Mexx,** and Swedish retailer **H&M** add affordable designer knockoffs to the mix.

57th Street

Despite the tougher economic climate, luxury houses have reclaimed more 57th Street frontage. **Louis Vuitton** wraps the northeast corner of 5th Avenue, with **Yves Saint Laurent** as its neighbor. The angular, white-glass Louis Vuitton Moët Hennesy headquarters, on the north side of East

ATTENTION FOODIES!

L**OOSEN YOUR BELTS,** as Manhattan has more destinations for food lovers than ever before. Start early to cover downtown by lunchtime. Begin in Chinatown, at **Kam-Man** (✉ 200 Canal St., at Mott St., Chinatown ☎ 212/571–0330), packed with dried squid, steamed bread, edible birds' nests, and dried shark fins. Next stop: **Mott Street** (below Grand Street), where markets and stalls sell ginger root, vegetables, meat, and live fish. Take another dip into the briny deep with a taste of herring or salmon at **Russ & Daughters** (✉ 179 E. Houston St., between Allan and Orchard Sts., Lower East Side ☎ 212/475–4880). Then zip over to Broadway where the brilliantly white **Dean & DeLuca** (✉ 560 Broadway, at Prince St., SoHo ☎ 212/226–6800) artfully displays intriguing produce and prepared food such as horned melons and stuffed quail; gleaming racks of cookware are in back. For more affordable kitchen gear, try **Broadway Panhandler** (✉ 477 Broome St., between Greene and Wooster Sts., SoHo ☎ 212/966–3434), where Calphalon, Le Creuset, and other professional-level makers are priced lower than retail.

A food corridor is developing on Bleecker Street, with Amy's Bread, Wild Edibles (seafood), and **Murray's Cheese** (✉ 254 Bleecker St., between 6th and 7th Aves., Greenwich Village ☎ 212/243–3289). At Murray's, you can taste cheddars and triple crèmes carried exclusively here, and gaze at ripening cheese in the aging rooms in back.

Monday, Wednesday, Friday, and Saturday, farmers and other food producers arrive at dawn at the **Union Square Greenmarket** bearing organic produce, flowers, homemade bread, preserves, fish, and seasonal fare. A square block of foodie heaven, **Chelsea**

Market (✉ 75 9th Ave., between W. 15th and W. 16th Sts., Chelsea ☎ 212/243–6005) is home to butchers, bakers, and a dozen other specialty food purveyors.

Macy's Cellar (✉ 151 W. 34th St., between 6th and 7th Aves., Midtown West ☎ 212/695–4400), inside Macy's, is a great place to rummage through kitchen gadgets. Farther north at **Zabar's** (✉ 2245 Broadway, at W. 81st St., Upper West Side ☎ 212/787–2000), grab a loaf of the fabled bread, examine the smoked fish and cheeses, and climb upstairs to the well-priced kitchenware section.

The East Side has plenty of stores to focus on. If you're passing through Grand Central Terminal, duck into the **Grand Central Market** area to check out the vendors of spices, cheese (from the Village's Murray's Cheese Shop), pasta, and other specialties. At **Bridge Kitchenware** (✉ 214 E. 52nd St., between 2nd and 3rd Aves., Midtown East ☎ 212/688–4220), a dusty, unpretentious hideaway, you can scoop up tiny ramekins and countless doodads. Farther uptown, **Kitchen Arts & Letters** (✉ 1435 Lexington Ave., between E. 93rd and E. 94th Sts., Upper East Side ☎ 212/876–5550) has thousands of cookbooks and other titles on food and wine. For a fitting conclusion, head back down to **Payard Pâtisserie & Bistro** (✉ 1032 Lexington Ave., between E. 73rd and E. 74th Sts., Upper East Side ☎ 212/717–5252), a glossy, Parisian-perfect patisserie where you can sample impeccable pastries and pick up succulent pâtes de fruits (fruit jellies).

57th Street between 5th and Madison avenues, houses **Christian Dior** and **Bliss**, the SoHo-born superspa. These glamazons are surrounded by big-name art galleries and other swank flagships such as **Burberry** and **Chanel**. The block isn't limited to top-echelon shopping, however; a **Nike-Town** sits cheek by jowl with the couture houses. To the west of 5th Avenue are a few less monolithic shops, such as **Smythson of Bond Street**.

Madison Avenue

FodorsChoice
★ Madison Avenue from East 57th to about East 79th streets can satisfy almost any couture craving. **Giorgio Armani, Dolce & Gabbana, Valentino, Gianni Versace, Alessandro Dell'Acqua**, Gianfranco Ferre, and **Prada** are among the avenue's Italian compatriots. French houses assert themselves with **Yves Saint Laurent Rive Gauche, Hermès, Jean Paul Gaultier**, and a pair of **Chanel** specialty boutiques. New York's hometown designer Donna Karan posts both **DKNY** and **Donna Karan** collections. Many of these stores occupy much larger spaces than traditional, one-level Madison boutiques; still, some smaller shops, such as perfumer **Bond 09**, are able to squeeze in. The full-fledged department store **Barneys** fits right in with its recherché roll call. Madison Avenue isn't just a fashion funnel, however; a couple of marvelous bookstores, several outstanding antiques dealers, a branch of the foodie haven Dean & Deluca, and numerous art galleries are here as well.

DEPARTMENT STORES

Most of these stores keep regular hours on weekdays and are open late (until 8 or 9) at least one night a week. Many have personal shoppers who can walk you through the store at no charge, as well as concierges who will answer all manner of questions. Some have restaurants or cafés that offer decent meals and pick-me-up snacks.

FodorsChoice
★ **Barneys New York.** Barneys continues to provide fashionistas with irresistible objects of desire at its uptown flagship store. The extensive menswear selection has introduced a handful of edgier designers, though made-to-measure is always available. The women's department showcases cachet designers of all stripes, from the subdued lines of Armani and Jil Sander to the irrepressible Alaïa and Zac Posen. The shoe selection trots out Prada boots and strappy Blahniks; the makeup department will keep you in Kiehl's. Expanded versions of the less expensive Co-op department occupy the old Barneys' warehouse space on West 18th Street and a niche on Wooster Street. ☒ *660 Madison Ave., between E. 60th and E. 61st Sts., Upper East Side* ☎ *212/826–8900* Ⓜ *Subway: N, R, W, 4, 5, 6 to 59th St./Lexington Ave.* ☒ *Barneys Co-op, 236 W. 18th St., between 7th and 8th Aves., Chelsea* ☎ *212/716–8817* Ⓜ *Subway: A, C, E to 14th St.* ☒ *116 Wooster St., between Prince and Spring Sts., SoHo* ☎ *212/965–9964* Ⓜ *Subway: R, W to Prince St.*

Bergdorf Goodman. Good taste reigns in an elegant and understated setting, but remember that elegant doesn't necessarily mean sedate. Bergdorf's carries some brilliant lines, such as John Galliano's sensational couture and Philip Treacy's dramatic hats. In the basement Level of Beauty, find a seat at the manicure bar (no appointments) for a bit of impromptu pampering. The home department has rooms full of wonderful linens, tableware, and gifts. Across the street is another entire store devoted to menswear: made-to-measure shirts, custom suits, designer lines by the likes of Ralph Lauren and Gucci, and scads of accessories, from hip flasks to silk scarves. ⊠ *754 5th Ave., between W. 57th and W. 58th Sts., Midtown West* ✉ *Men's store, 745 5th Ave., at 58th St., Midtown East* ☎*212/ 753–7300* Ⓜ *Subway: N, R, W to 5th Ave./59th St.*

Bloomingdale's. Only a few stores occupy an entire city block; the uptown branch of this New York institution is one of them. The main floor here is a stupefying maze of cosmetic counters, mirrors, and perfumespraying salespeople; once you get past this, though, you can find good buys on designer clothes, bedding, and housewares. The downtown location is smaller, and has a smaller, higher-end selection of merchandise, so you can focus your search for that Michael Kors handbag or pricey pair of stilettos. ⊠ *1000 3rd Ave., main entrance at E. 59th St. and Lexington Ave., Midtown East* ☎ *212/705–2000* Ⓜ *Subway: N, R, W, 4, 5, 6 to 59th St./Lexington Ave.* ✉ *504 Broadway, between Spring and Broome Sts., SoHo* ☎ *212/729–5900* Ⓜ *R, W to Prince St.*

Century 21. For many New Yorkers, this downtown fixture—right across the street from the World Trade Center site—remains the mother lode of discount shopping. The four floors here are crammed with everything from Gucci sunglasses to half-price cashmere sweaters to Ralph Lauren towels, though you may have to weed through racks of less-fabulous stuff to find it. The best bets in the men's department are shoes and the designer briefs; the full floor of designer womenswear can yield some real treasures, such as a Calvin Klein leather trench for less than $600 or a sweeping crinoline skirt from John Paul Gaultier. Since lines for the communal dressing rooms can be prohibitively long, you might want to wear a bodysuit under your clothes for quick, between-the-racks try-ons. ⊠ *22 Cortlandt St., between Broadway and Church St., Lower Manhattan* ☎ *212/227–9092* Ⓜ *Subway: R, W to Cortlandt St.*

Henri Bendel. Behind the graceful Lalique windows you can discover more than the usual fashion suspects. Bendel's dedication to the unusual begins on the ground-floor cosmetic area, filled with lines like Vincent Longo, and percolates through the floors of women's clothing and accessories. Designers such as Yeohlee, Catherine Malandrino, Rebecca Taylor, and Diane von Furstenberg have room to breathe here; the staircase mezzanine is a minitrove of great handbags and gloves. Shoe lovers will be disappointed here, though: there's no true footwear department. ⊠ *712 5th Ave., between W. 55th and W. 56th Sts., Midtown West* ☎ *212/247– 1100* Ⓜ *Subway: E, V to 5th Ave./53rd St.*

Lord & Taylor. Comfortably conservative and never overwhelming, Lord & Taylor is a stronghold of classic American designer clothes. Instead of unpronounceable labels, you can find Dana Buchman, Jones New York, and a lot of casual wear. It also has a large selection of reasonably priced full-length gowns. ⊠ *424 5th Ave., between W. 38th and W. 39th Sts., Midtown West* ☎ *212/391–3344* Ⓜ *Subway: B, D, F, N, Q, R, V, W to 34th St./Herald Sq.*

Macy's. Macy's headquarters store claims to be the largest retail store in America; expect to lose your bearings at least once. Fashion-wise, there's a concentration on the mainstream rather than the luxe. One strong suit is denim, with everything from Hilfiger and Calvin Klein to Earl Jeans and Paper Denim & Cloth. There's also a reliably good selection of American designs from Ralph Lauren, Tommy Hilfiger, and Nautica. For cooking gear and housewares, the Cellar nearly outdoes Zabar's. ⊠ *Herald Sq., 151 W. 34th St., between 6th and 7th Aves., Midtown West* ☎ *212/ 695–4400* Ⓜ *Subway: B, D, F, N, Q, R, V, W to 34th St./Herald Sq.*

Pearl River Mart. If you want to redecorate your entire apartment with a Chinese theme for less than $1,000, this is the place to do it. Every Asian-style furnishing, houseware, and trinket can be found here, from bamboo rice streamers and ceramic tea sets to paper lanterns and grinning wooden Buddha statues. On the main floor, under a ceiling festooned with dragon kites and rice-paper parasols, you can buy kimono-style robes, pajamas, and embroidered satin slippers for the whole family. There's also a dry-goods section, where you can load up on packages of ginger candy, jasmine tea, and cellophane noodles. ⊠ *477 Broadway, between Broome and Grand Sts., SoHo* ☎ *212/431–4770* Ⓜ *Subway: N, R, Q, W to Canal St.*

Saks Fifth Avenue. A fashion-only department store, Saks sells an astonishing array of apparel. The choice of American and European designers is impressive without being esoteric—the women's selection includes Gucci, Narciso Rodriguez, and Marc Jacobs, plus devastating ball gowns galore. The footwear collections are gratifyingly broad, from Ferragamo to Nine West. In the men's department, sportswear stars such as John Varvatos counterbalance formal wear and current trends. ⊠ *611 5th Ave., between E. 49th and E. 50th Sts., Midtown East* ☎ *212/753–4000* Ⓜ *Subway: E, V to 5th Ave./53rd St.*

Takashimaya New York. This pristine branch of Japan's largest department store carries stylish accessories and fine household items, all of which reflect a combination of Eastern and Western designs. In the Tea Box downstairs, you can have a *bento* box lunch in the serene, softly lighted tearoom or stock up on green tea. The florist-cum-front-window-display provides a refreshing mini botanical garden. ⊠ *693 5th Ave., between E. 54th and E. 55th Sts., Midtown East* ☎ *212/350–0100* Ⓜ *Subway: E, V to 5th Ave./53rd St.*

SPECIALTY SHOPS

Many specialty stores have several branches in the city; in these cases, we have listed the locations in the busier shopping neighborhoods.

Antiques

Antiquing is a fine art in Manhattan. Goods include everything from rarefied museum-quality to wacky and affordable. Premier shopping areas are on Madison Avenue north of 57th Street, and East 60th Street between 2nd and 3rd avenues, where more than 20 shops, dealing in everything from 18th-century French furniture to art deco lighting fixtures, cluster on one block. Around West 11th and 12th streets between University Place and Broadway, a tantalizing array of settees, bedsteads, and rocking chairs can be seen in the windows of about two dozen dealers, many of whom have TO THE TRADE signs on their doors; a card from your architect or decorator, however, may get you inside. Finally, for 20th-century furniture and fixtures, head south of West Houston Street, especially along Lafayette Street. Most dealers are closed Sunday.

Manhattan Art & Antiques Center. Art-nouveau perfume bottles and samovars, samurai swords, pewter pitchers, and much more fill 100-plus galleries. The level of quality is not, as a rule, up to that of Madison Avenue, but then neither are the prices. ⊠ *1050 2nd Ave., between E. 55th and E. 56th Sts., Midtown East* ☎ *212/355–4400* Ⓜ *Subway: N, R, W, 4, 5, 6 to 59th St./Lexington Ave.*

American & English

Florian Papp. The shine of gilt—on ormolu clocks, chaise longues, and marble-top tables—lures casual customers in, but this store has an unassailed reputation among knowledgeable collectors. ⊠ *962 Madison Ave., between E. 75th and E. 76th Sts., Upper East Side* ☎ *212/288–6770* Ⓜ *Subway: 6 to 77th St.*

Israel Sack Inc. This is widely considered one of the best places in the country for 17th-, 18th-, and early-19th-century American furniture. Although the store is reputed to be very expensive, there's actually plenty of furniture for less than $25,000. ⊠ *730 5th Ave., between W. 56th and W. 57th Sts., Midtown West* ☎ *212/399–6562* Ⓜ *Subway: F, N, R, Q, W to 57th St.*

Kentshire Galleries. Pristine furniture is displayed in room settings on eight floors here, with an emphasis on formal English pieces from the 18th and 19th centuries, particularly the Georgian and Regency periods. Their collection of period and estate jewelry is a showstopper, from Edwardian pearl earrings to vintage gold watches from Van Cleef & Arpels. ⊠ *37 E. 12th St., between University Pl. and Broadway, Greenwich Village* ☎ *212/673–6644* Ⓜ *Subway: 4, 5, 6, L, N, R, Q, W to 14th St./Union Sq.*

Leigh Keno American Antiques. Twins Leigh and Leslie Keno set an auction record in the American antiques field by paying $2.75 million for a hairy paw–foot Philadelphia wing chair. They have a good eye and an interesting inventory; gaze up at a tall case clock or down at the delicate legs of a tea table. It's best to make an appointment. ⊠ *127 E. 69th St., between Park and Lexington Aves., Upper East Side* ☎ *212/734–2381* Ⓜ *Subway: 6 to 77th St.*

Newel Art Galleries. Near the East Side's interior-design district, this huge collection roams from the Renaissance to the 20th century. The non-furniture finds, from figureheads to bell jars, make for prime conversation pieces. ⊠ *425 E. 53rd St., between 1st Ave. and Sutton Pl., Midtown East* ☎ *212/758–1970* Ⓜ *Subway: 6 to 51st St./Lexington Ave.; E, V to Lexington–3rd Aves./53rd St.*

Steve Miller American Folk Art. This appointment-only gallery is run by one of the country's premier folk-art dealers, the author of *The Art of* *the Weathervane.* ✉ *17 E. 96th St., between Madison and 5th Aves., Upper East Side* ☎ *212/348–5219* Ⓜ *Subway: 6 to 96th St.*

Woodard & Greenstein. Americana, antique quilts and rugs, and 19th-century country furniture are among the specialties of this prestigious dealer. ✉ *506 E. 74th St., between York Ave. and FDR Dr., Upper East Side* ☎ *212/794–9404* Ⓜ *Subway: 6 to 77th St.*

Asian

Chinese Porcelain Company. Though the name of this prestigious shop indicates one of its specialties, its stock covers more ground, ranging from lacquerware to Khmer sculpture to 18th-century French furniture. ✉ *475 Park Ave., at E. 58th St., Midtown East* ☎ *212/838–7744* Ⓜ *Subway: N, R, W to 5th Ave.*

Flying Cranes Antiques. Here you can find a well-regarded collection of rare, museum-quality pieces from the Meiji period, the time known as Japan's Golden Age. Items include ceramics, cloisonné, metalwork, carvings, ikebana baskets, and Samurai swords and fittings. ✉ *Manhattan Art and Antiques Center, 1050 2nd Ave., between E. 55th and E. 56th Sts., Midtown East* ☎ *212/223–4600* Ⓜ *Subway: N, R, W, 4, 5, 6 to 59th St./Lexington Ave.*

Jacques Carcangues, Inc. Carrying goods from Japan to India, this SoHo gallery offers an eclectic array of objects, from pillboxes to 18th-century Burmese Buddhas. At this writing, the store planned a move to 21 Greene Street. ✉ *106 Spring St., at Mercer St., SoHo* ☎ *212/925–8110* Ⓜ *Subway: R, W to Prince St.*

Old Japan. This little Village shop specializes in antique textiles and kimonos. You can also find furniture, such as chests and low tables, plus small items such as 100-year-old sake bottles, bamboo baskets, and sewing boxes (which can double as jewelry boxes). Contemporary gift items are also available. ✉ *382 Bleecker St., between Perry and Charles Sts., Greenwich Village* ☎ *212/633–0922* Ⓜ *Subway: 1, 9 to Christopher St.–Sheridan Sq.*

European

Newel Art Galleries and Florian Papp, covered under American and English antiques, and the Chinese Porcelain Company, listed under Asian antiques, also carry European pieces.

Barry Friedman Ltd. Having championed 20th-century art for decades, Barry Friedman now turns to contemporary decorative objects, such as art glass by Dale Chihuly. Vintage and contemporary photographs are also available. ✉ *32 E. 67th St., between Park and Madison Aves., Upper East Side* ☎ *212/794–8950* Ⓜ *Subway: 6 to 68th St.–Hunter College.*

DeLorenzo. Come here for the sinuous curves and highly polished surfaces of French art deco furniture and accessories. ✉ *956 Madison Ave., between E. 75th and E. 76th Sts., Upper East Side* ☎ *212/249–7575* Ⓜ *Subway: 6 to 77th St.*

Didier Aaron. This esteemed gallery specializes in superb 18th- and 19th-century French decorative arts and paintings. ✉ *32 E. 67th St., between Park and Madison Aves., Upper East Side* ☎ *212/988–5248* Ⓜ *Subway: 6 to 68th St.–Hunter College.*

L'Antiquaire & The Connoisseur, Inc. Proprietor Helen Fioratti has written a guide to French antiques, but she's equally knowledgeable about her Italian and Spanish furniture and decorative objects from the 15th through the 18th centuries, as well as the medieval arts. ⊠ *36 E. 73rd St., between Madison and Park Aves., Upper East Side* ☎ *212/517–9176* Ⓜ *Subway: 6 to 77th St.*

Leo Kaplan Ltd. The impeccable items here include art nouveau glass and pottery, porcelain from 18th-century England, antique and modern paperweights, and Russian artwork. ⊠ *114 E. 57th St., between Park and Lexington Aves., Upper East Side* ☎ *212/249–6766* Ⓜ *Subway: N, R, W, 4, 5, 6 to 59th St./Lexington Ave.*

Les Pierre Antiques. Pierre Deux popularized French Provincial through reproductions; come here for a strong selection of the real thing. ⊠ *369 Bleecker St., at Charles St., Greenwich Village* ☎ *212/243–7740* Ⓜ *Subway: 1, 9 to Christopher St./Sheridan Sq.*

20th-Century Furniture & Memorabilia

Las Venus. Step into this kitsch palace and you'll feel as though a time machine has zapped you back to the groovy '70s. Look for bubble lamps, lots of brocade, and Knoll knockoffs. ⊠ *163 Ludlow St., between E. Houston and Stanton Sts., Lower East Side* ☎ *212/982–0608* Ⓜ *Subway: F, V to 2nd Ave.*

Lost City Arts. In addition to mod furniture, like pod and Eames chairs, and industrial memorabilia, such as neon gas-station clocks, Lost City can help you relive the Machine Age with an in-house, retro-modern line of furniture. ⊠ *18 Cooper Sq., at E. 5th St., East Village* ☎ *212/375–0500* Ⓜ *Subway: 6 to Astor Pl.*

Beauty

Bond 09. Created by the same fragrance team as Creed, this new line of scents purports to evoke the New York City experience. Perfumes are named after neighborhoods: "Central Park," a men's fragrance, is woodsy and "green"; the feminine "Park Avenue" is regal and sophisticated, with hints of iris and rose. The downtown shop, with its airy space and wood-panel "tea library," is a lovely place to linger. ⊠ *9 Bond St., between Lafayette St. and Broadway, East Village* ☎ *212/228–1940* Ⓜ *Subway: 6 to Bleecker St.* ⊠ *897 Madison Ave., between E. 72nd and E. 73rd Sts., Upper East Side* ☎ *212/794–4480* Ⓜ *Subway: 6 to 68th St./Hunter College* ⊠ *680 Madison Ave., between E. 61st and E. 62nd Sts., Upper East Side* ☎ *212/838–2780* Ⓜ *Subway: N, R, W, 4, 5, 6 to 59th St./Lexington Ave.*

Floris of London. Floral English toiletries beloved of the British royals fill this re-creation of the cozy London original. If you love lathering, look for the wooden bowls of shaving or bath soap. ⊠ *703 Madison Ave., between E. 62nd and E. 63rd Sts., Upper East Side* ☎ *212/935–9100* Ⓜ *Subway: 6 to 68th St./Hunter College.*

Jo Malone. Consider this extra incentive to visit the landmark Flatiron Building. Unisex scents such as lime blossom and vetiver can be worn alone or, in the Malone style, layered. Since Malone uses colognes, not perfumes, it's not overpowering. You can also book one of the famed massage-based facials. (The uptown branch offers all the scents, but not the facial.) ✉ *949 Broadway, at 5th Ave., Flatiron District* ☎ *212/ 673–2220* Ⓜ *Subway: R, W to 23rd St.* ✉ *946 Madison Ave., between E. 74th and E. 75th Sts., Upper East Side* ☎ *212/472–0074* Ⓜ *Subway: 6 to 77th St.*

Fodor'sChoice **Kiehl's Since 1851.** At this favored haunt of top models and stylists, white-★ smocked assistants can help you choose among the lotions and potions, all of which are packaged in deceptively simple-looking bottles and jars. Some of the products, such as the pineapple-papaya facial scrub and the super-rich Creme de Corps, have attained near cult status among beautyphiles, and have prices to match. ✉ *109 3rd Ave., at E. 13th St., East Village* ☎ *212/677–3171* Ⓜ *Subway: 4, 5, 6, L, N, R, Q, W to 14th St./Union Sq.*

L'Artisan Parfumeur. This tiny, hole-in-the-wall shop may look unassuming—but the line of gorgeous, limited-edition scents sold here is nothing to sneeze at. Some fragrances, like the myrrh-and-vetiver-infused Timbuktu, conjure exotic locales; others, like the rosy, feminine La Chasse aux Papillons ("Chasing the Butterflies"), or the manly Mechant Loup ("Big Bad Wolf") evoke nostalgic whimsy. ✉ *68 Thompson St., between Spring and Broome Sts. SoHo* ☎ *212/334–1500* Ⓜ *Subway: R, W to Prince St.*

Lush. Some of these products are so fresh, you need to keep them in the fridge. Most of the soaps, facial treatments, and lotions have vegetal ingredients and very few preservatives. The "bath bombs," in such flavors as Honey Bee and Ginger Man, dissolve to release essential oils and moisturizers when dropped into a bath. ✉ *1293 Broadway, at W. 34th St., Midtown West* ☎ *212/564–9120* Ⓜ *Subway: B, D, F, N, Q, R, V, W to 34th St./Herald Sq.*

M.A.C. Fashion hounds pile into these boutiques, both for the basics (foundation and concealer for a huge range of skin tones) and the far-out (eye shadow colors like "electric eel" and "chrome yellow"). Salespeople can offer expert advice—many of them also work as professional makeup artists. ✉ *113 Spring St., between Mercer and Greene Sts., SoHo* ☎ *212/ 334–4641* Ⓜ *Subway: C, E to Spring St.* ✉ *1 E. 22nd St., between 5th Ave. and Broadway, Flatiron District* ☎ *212/677–6611* Ⓜ *Subway: F, V, R, W to 23rd St.* ✉ *202 W. 125th St., at Adam Clayton Blvd., Harlem* ☎ *212/665–0676* Ⓜ *Subway: A, B, C, D to 125th St.*

Make Up For Ever. The makeup from this Paris-based boutique does not hew to the natural look. The products are pigment-rich and boldly colored; liquid eyeliner could be bright green as well as dark brown, mascara pearly white as well as black. The staff applications help nonprofessionals navigate the spectrum for everyday wear. ✉ *409 West Broadway, between Prince and Spring Sts., SoHo* ☎ *212/941–9337* Ⓜ *Subway: C, E to Spring St.*

★ **Santa Maria Novella.** A heavy, iron-barred door leads to a hushed, scented inner sanctum of products from this medieval Florentine pharmacy. Many of the colognes, creams, and soaps are intriguingly archaic, such as the iris toothpaste, the "carta d'Armenia" (scented papers that perfume a room when burned), and the "vinegar of the seven thieves" (a variant on smelling salts). Everything is packaged in bottles and jars with antique apothecary labels. ✉ *285 Lafayette St., between E. Houston and Prince Sts., SoHo* ☎ *212/925–0001* Ⓜ *N, R to Prince St.*

Shu Uemura. Top-of-the-line Japanese skincare products, makeup, and tools distinguish this downtown spot; among the bestsellers are the Balancing Cleansing Oil, the professional-grade eyelash curl, and lip glosses in such yummy flavors as orange sorbet and lemonade. One clever touch: there are four light simulators, which allow you to test makeup colors under officelike and simulated outdoor lighting. ✉ *121 Greene St., between Prince and W. Houston Sts., SoHo* ☎ *212/979–5500* Ⓜ *Subway: R, W to Prince St.*

Books

Manhattan supports dozens of bookstores, small and large, chain and independent. A few of the city's landmark independent stores have been in flux. At this writing, for instance, Gotham Book Mart was still on the lookout for a new space, while Coliseum Books had settled on a new location at 11 West 42nd Street.

Children's Books

Books of Wonder. A friendly staff can help select gifts for all reading levels from the extensive stock of children's books here; Oziana is a specialty. An outpost of the Cupcake Café gives browsers a second wind. ✉ *16 W. 18th St., between 5th and 6th Aves., Chelsea* ☎ *212/989–3270* Ⓜ *Subway: F, V to 14th St.*

Foreign Language

Librairie de France/Libreria Hispanica. This store offers one of the country's largest selections of foreign-language books, videos, and periodicals, mostly in French and Spanish. You can also find dozens of dictionaries, phrase books, and other learning materials. ✉ *610 5th Ave., Rockefeller Center Promenade, Midtown West* ☎ *212/581–8810* Ⓜ *Subway: B, D, F, V to 47th–50th Sts./Rockefeller Center.*

Gay & Lesbian

Oscar Wilde Bookshop. Opened in 1967, this was the first gay and lesbian bookstore in the city and is now the oldest existing one in the country, having weathered a close brush with closure in 2003. It's just steps from the site of the Stonewall riots. The shelves hold everything from cultural studies and biographies to fiction and first editions by the likes of Djuna Barnes and Paul Monette. ✉ *15 Christopher St., between 6th and 7th Aves., Greenwich Village* ☎ *212/255–8097* Ⓜ *Subway: 1, 9 to Christopher St./Sheridan Sq.*

General Interest

Biography Bookshop. Published diaries, letters, biographies, and autobiographies fill this neighborly store; there's also a careful selection of general nonfiction, fiction, guidebooks, and children's books. The sale tables outside have deals on everything from Graham Greene to Chuck Palahniuk. ✉ *400 Bleecker St., at W. 11th St., Greenwich Village* ☎ *212/807–8655* Ⓜ *Subway: 1, 9 to Christopher St./Sheridan Sq.*

 Crawford Doyle Booksellers. You're as likely to see an old edition of Wodehouse as a best seller in the window of this shop. There's a thoughtful selection of fiction, nonfiction, biographies, etc., plus some rare books on the tight-fit balcony. Salespeople offer their opinions *and* ask for yours. ✉ *1082 Madison Ave., between E. 81st and E. 82nd Sts., Upper East Side* ☎ *212/288–6300* Ⓜ *Subway: 4, 5, 6 to 86th St.*

Gotham Book Mart. The late Frances Steloff opened this store in 1920 with just $200 in her pocket, half of it on loan. But she helped launch James Joyce's *Ulysses*, D. H. Lawrence, and Henry Miller and is now legendary among bibliophiles—as is her bookstore. There's a wealth of signed editions of deliciously macabre Edward Gorey books. ✉ *16 E. 46th St., between 5th and Madison Aves., Midtown East* ☎ *212/719–4448* Ⓜ *Subway: B, D, F, V to 47th–50th Sts./Rockefeller Center.*

Lenox Hill Bookstore. Narrow in shape but not in spirit, this shop carries many copies of books signed by their authors and often hosts readings. ✉ *1018 Lexington Ave., between E. 72nd and E. 73rd Sts., Upper East Side* ☎ *212/472–7170* Ⓜ *Subway: 6 to 77th St.*

★ **McNally Robinson.** McNally makes a happy counterpart to the nearby Housing Works bookstore; both places have that welcoming vibe. Check the tables up front for hot-off-the-press novels, nonfiction, and manifestos. Downstairs you'll find fiction arranged by the authors' region of origin, a great way to learn more about, say, Asian or South American writing. (Salman Rushdie gets grouped with the "global nomads.") ✉ *50 Prince St., between Lafayette and Mulberry Sts., SoHo* ☎ *212/274–1160* Ⓜ *Subway: R, W to Prince St.*

Partners & Crime. Imported British paperbacks, helpful staff, a rental library, and whodunits galore—new, out-of-print, and first editions—make this a must-browse for fans. Revered mystery writers give readings here. Check out the "radio mystery hour" on the first Saturday of every month. ✉ *44 Greenwich Ave., between 6th and 7th Aves., Greenwich Village* ☎ *212/243–0440* Ⓜ *Subway: F, V, 1, 2, 3, 9 to 14th St.*

Posman Books. Good to know of if you're about to embark on a long train ride out of Grand Central, the last remaining Posman store in the city carries mostly best sellers and new releases, often at a discount. ✉ *9 Grand Central Terminal, at Vanderbilt Ave. and E. 42nd St., Midtown East* ☎ *212/983–1111* Ⓜ *Subway: 4, 5, 6, 7 to 42nd St./Grand Central Terminal.*

★ **St. Mark's Bookshop.** Extending far beyond the *New York Times* bestseller list, this store carries a truly eclectic reading collection. On the main floor, critical theory books are right up front and across from the new fiction titles—perhaps the only place where you can find Jacques Derrida facing off against T. C. Boyle. Cultural and critical theory books are right up front; it also has a rich store of literature, literary journals, and even a rack of self-published booklets. ✉ *31 3rd Ave., at 9th St., East Village* ☎ *212/260–7853* Ⓜ *Subway: 6 to Astor Pl.*

Shakespeare & Co. Booksellers. The stock here represents what's happening in just about every field of publishing today: students can grab a last-minute Gertrude Stein for their literature class, then rummage through the homages to cult pop-culture figures. Late hours at this location (until midnight on Friday and Saturday, 11 PM the rest of the week) are a plus. ✉ *939 Lexington Ave., between E. 68th and E. 69th Sts., Upper East Side* ☎ *212/570–0201* Ⓜ *Subway: 6 to 68th St./Hunter College*

✉ *137 E. 23rd St., at Lexington Ave., Gramercy* ☎ *212/505–2021* Ⓜ *Subway: 6 to 23rd St.* ✉ *716 Broadway, at Washington Pl., Greenwich Village* ☎ *212/529–1330* Ⓜ *Subway: R, W to 8th St.* ✉ *1 Whitehall St., at Beaver St., Lower Manhattan* ☎ *212/742–7025* Ⓜ *Subway: 4, 5 to Bowling Green.*

The Strand. The Broadway branch proudly claims to have "10 miles of books"; craning your neck among the tall-as-trees stacks will likely net you something from the mix of new and old. Rare books are next door, at 826 Broadway, on the third floor. The Fulton Street branch is near South Street Seaport; it's decidedly less overwhelming. ✉ *828 Broadway, at E. 12th St., East Village* ☎ *212/473–1452* Ⓜ *Subway: L, N, Q, R, W, 4, 5, 6 to 14th St./Union Sq.* ✉ *95 Fulton St., between Gold and William Sts., Lower Manhattan* ☎ *212/732–6070* Ⓜ *Subway: A, C, J, M, Z, 1, 2, 4, 5 to Fulton St./Broadway-Nassau.*

★ **Three Lives & Co.** Three Lives has one of the city's best book selections. The display tables and counters highlight the latest literary fiction and serious nonfiction, classics, quirky gift books, and gorgeously illustrated tomes. The staff members' literary knowledge is formidable, and they can help you find most any book—even if it's not carried in the store. ✉ *154 W. 10th St., at Waverly Pl., Greenwich Village* ☎ *212/ 741–2069* Ⓜ *Subway: 1, 9 to Christopher St./Sheridan Sq.*

Music

Colony Music. Siphoning energy from Times Square, this place keeps its neon blinking until at least midnight every night. Inspired by the Broadway musical or concert you've just seen? Snap up the sheet music, CD, or karaoke set here. ✉ *1619 Broadway, at W. 49th St., Midtown West* ☎ *212/265–2050* Ⓜ *Subway: R, W to 49th St.*

Joseph Patelson Music House. A huge collection of scores (some 47,000 pieces of sheet music for piano, organ, strings, woodwind and brass, and chambers and ensembles) has long made this a mecca for music lovers; fittingly, it's right by Carnegie Hall. ✉ *160 W. 56th St., between 6th and 7th Aves., Midtown West* ☎ *212/582–5840* Ⓜ *Subway: F, N, R, Q, W to 57th St.*

Rare & Used Books

Crawford Doyle Booksellers and the Strand, covered under General Interest, also carry rare and used titles.

Argosy Bookstore. This sedate landmark, established in 1921, keeps a scholarly stock of books and autographs. It's also a great place to look for low-price maps and prints. ✉ *116 E. 59th St., between Park and Lexington Aves., Midtown East* ☎ *212/753–4455* Ⓜ *Subway: N, R, W, 4, 5, 6 to 59th St./Lexington Ave.*

Bauman Rare Books. This successful Philadelphia firm offers New Yorkers the most impossible-to-get titles, first editions, and fine leather sets. The Madison Avenue store is by far the larger of the two. ✉ *535 Madison Ave., between E. 54th and E. 55th Sts., Midtown East* ☎ *212/751– 0011* ✉ *Waldorf-Astoria, lobby level, 301 Park Ave., at E. 50th St., Midtown East* ☎ *212/759–8300* Ⓜ *Subway: E, V, 6 to 51st./Lexington Ave.*

★ **Housing Works Used Book Cafe.** If the jostling sidewalks of SoHo have you on edge, head one-block east of Broadway to this sanctuary of a used bookstore. There's lots of room to browse here, and chairs where you can relax and flip through your finds (for some of the heftier art books, you might want to grab a table at the café in back). ⊠ *126 Crosby St., between E. Houston and Prince Sts., NoLita* ☎ *212/334–3324* Ⓜ *Subway: R, W to Prince St.*

J. N. Bartfield. A legend in the field offers old and antiquarian books distinguished by binding, author, edition, or content. ⊠ *30 W. 57th St., between 5th and 6th Aves., 3rd fl., Midtown West* ☎ *212/245–8890* Ⓜ *Subway: F, N, R, Q, W to 57th St.; N, R, W to 5th Ave.*

Skyline Books and Records, Inc. Come here for out-of-print and unusual books in all fields. The store handles literary first editions, as well as a small handful of jazz records. ⊠ *13 W. 18th St., between 5th and 6th Aves., Chelsea* ☎ *212/675–4773* Ⓜ *Subway: 4, 5, 6, N, R, Q, W to 14th St./Union Sq.*

Westrider Rare & Used Books. This wonderfully crammed space is a bibliophile's lifesaver in the otherwise sparse Upper West Side. Squeeze in among the stacks of art books and fiction; clamber up the steep stairway and you'll find all sorts of rare books. ⊠ *2246 Broadway, between W. 80th and W. 81st Sts., Upper West Side* ☎ *212/362–0706* Ⓜ *Subway: 4, 5, 6 to 86th St.*

Theater

Drama Book Shop. If you're looking for a script, be it a lesser-known Russian translation or a Broadway hit, chances are you can find it here. The range of books spans film, music, dance, TV, and biographies. The shop hosts lots of in-store events, too, such as free writing seminars and talks with well-known playwrights. ⊠ *250 W. 40th St., between 7th and 8th Aves., Midtown West* ☎ *212/944–0595* Ⓜ *Subway: A, C, E to 42nd St./Port Authority.*

Cameras & Electronics

Apple Store SoHo. This former post office is now home base for e-mail-generation hipsters. Though you'll have to elbow through a crowd, this is the place to check out Mac minis, iPods, and digital moviemaking equipment. Head up the glass staircase for software, a demo area, and a troubleshooting desk. ⊠ *103 Prince St., at Greene St., SoHo* ☎ *212/226–3126* Ⓜ *Subway: R, W to Prince St.*

Fodor'sChoice **B&H Photo Video and Pro Audio.** As baskets of purchases trundle along
★ on tracks overhead, you can plunge into the excellent selection of imaging, audio, video, and lighting equipment. The staff willingly give advice and compare merchandise. Low prices, good customer service, and a liberal returns policy make this a favorite with pros and amateurs alike. Be sure to leave a few extra minutes for the checkout procedure; also, keep in mind that the store is closed Friday evening through Saturday. ⊠ *420 9th Ave., between W. 33rd and W. 34th Sts., Midtown West* ☎ *212/ 444–5000* Ⓜ *Subway: A, C, E, 1, 2, 3 to 34th St./Penn Station.*

J&R Music World. Just south of City Hall, J&R has emerged as the city's most competitively priced one-stop electronics outlet, with an enormous selection of video equipment, computers, stereos, and cameras. The staff is hands-on and superknowledgable; many of them are A/V wizards who've worked here since the early 1990s. Home-office supplies are at No. 17, computers at No. 15, small appliances at No. 27. ⊠ *23 Park Row, between Beekman and Ann Sts., Lower Manhattan* ☎ *212/ 238–9000* Ⓜ *Subway: 4, 5, 6 to Brooklyn Bridge/City Hall.*

SONY Style. This equipment and music store comes in a glossy package, with imaginative window displays and a downstairs demonstration area for the integrated systems. The latest stereo and entertainment systems, video cameras, and portable CD and mp3 players preen on the shelves. ⊠ *550 Madison Ave., at E. 55th St., Midtown East* ☎ *212/833– 8800* Ⓜ *Subway: E, V, 6 to 51st./Lexington Ave.*

Willoughby's. Having started more than 100 years ago as a camera store, Willoughby's now includes DVD players, scanners, and other electronics alongside digital cameras, manual models, and point-and-shoots. ⊠ *136 W. 32nd St., between 6th and 7th Aves., Midtown West* ☎ *212/ 564–1600* Ⓜ *Subway: A, C, E, 1, 2, 3 to 34th St./Penn Station.*

CDs, Tapes & Records

The city's best record stores provide browsers with a window to New York's groovier subcultures. The East Village is especially good for dance tracks and used music.

Academy Records & CDs. You can walk into Academy with just $15 and walk out happy. The new and used CDs, DVDs, and records are well organized, low-priced, and in good condition; sometimes they've never even been opened. ⊠ *12 W. 18th St., between 5th and 6th Aves., Chelsea* ☎ *212/ 242–3000* Ⓜ *Subway: 4, 5, 6, N, R, Q, W to 14th St./Union Sq.*

Bleecker Bob's Golden Oldies Record Shop. One of the oldest independent record stores in town, this pleasingly shabby-looking shop with its old-fashioned neon sign sells punk, jazz, metal, and reggae, plus good old rock on vinyl until the wee hours. ⊠ *118 W. 3rd St., at MacDougal St., Greenwich Village* ☎ *212/475–9677* Ⓜ *Subway: A, C, E, F, V to W. 4th St./Washington Sq.*

Footlight Records. Stop here to browse through New York's largest selection of old and new musicals and movie sound tracks (hello Judy Garland!). There's also a great selection of big-band jazz and American popular standards, and some hilariously odd choices—like compilations from porno soundtracks, and a (perhaps thankfully) little-known album by Jack Palance. It's closed Monday. ⊠ *113 E. 12th St., between 3rd and 4th Aves., East Village* ☎ *212/533–1572* Ⓜ *Subway: L, N, Q, R, W, 4, 5, 6 to 14th St./Union Sq.*

House of Oldies. The specialty here is records made between 1950 and the late 1980s—45s and 78s, as well as LPs. There are more than a million titles, and friendly owner Bob Abramson seems to know them all. ⊠ *35 Carmine St., between Bleecker St. and 6th Ave., Greenwich Village* ☎ *212/ 243–0500* Ⓜ *Subway: A, C, E, F, V to W. 4th St./Washington Sq.*

Jazz Record Center. Long-lost Ellingtons and other rare pressings come to light here; the jazz-record specialist also stocks collectibles. ⊠ *236*

W. 26th St., between 7th and 8th Aves., 8th fl., Chelsea ☎ 212/675–4480 Ⓜ *Subway: 1, 9 to 28th St.*

J&R Music World. This store has a huge selection of pop music and videos, as well as Latin, jazz, and classical, with good prices on major releases. You can even buy music by telephone. ✉ *23 Park Row, between Beekman and Ann Sts., Lower Manhattan* ☎ 212/238–9000 Ⓜ *Subway: 4, 5, 6 to Brooklyn Bridge/City Hall.*

Kim's Video & Music. Scruffy and eclectic, Kim's crystallizes the downtown music scene. Its top-20 list is a long, long way from the Top 40; instead, there's a mix of electronica, jazz, lounge, and experimental. ✉ *6 St. Marks Pl., between 2nd and 3rd Aves., East Village* ☎ 212/598–9985 Ⓜ *Subway: 6 to Astor Pl.* ✉ *144 Bleecker St., between Thompson St. and La Guardia Pl., Greenwich Village* Ⓜ *Subway: A, C, E, F, V to W. 4th St./Washington Sq.* ☎ 212/260–1010 ✉ *2906 Broadway, between W. 113th and W. 114th Sts., Morningside Heights* ☎ 212/864–5321 Ⓜ *Subway: 1, 9 to 116th St.*

★ **Other Music.** Across the way from Tower Records, both spatially and spiritually, this spot carries hard-to-find genres on CD and vinyl, from Japanese electronica and Krautrock to acid folk and Americana. There's also a great selection of used CDs, including seminal punk classics from the Clash and the Stooges. ✉ *15 E. 4th St., between Lafayette St. and Broadway, East Village* ☎ 212/477–8150 Ⓜ *Subway: 6 to Astor Pl.*

Tower Records. Uptown, patrons discuss jazz; downtown, many customers are multipierced and rainbow-haired. ✉ *692 Broadway, at E. 4th St., East Village* ☎ 212/505–1500 ✉ *1961 Broadway, at W. 66th St., Upper West Side* ☎ 212/799–2500 ✉ *725 5th Ave., basement level of Trump Tower, between E. 56th and E. 57th Sts., Midtown East* ☎ 212/838–8110 ✉ *20 E. 4th St., at Lafayette St., East Village* ☎ 212/228–7317.

Virgin Megastore. A Megastore in each major square: Times and Union. Rows upon rows of CDs, videos, books, and DVDs, and still room for live band appearances. ✉ *1540 Broadway, between W. 45th and W. 46th Sts., Midtown West* ☎ 212/921–1020 ✉ *52 E. 14th St., at Broadway, East Village* ☎ 212/598–4666.

Westrider Records & Music. One of the city's best rare-record stores, it stocks some 90,000 out-of-print and rare LPs. ✉ *233 W. 72nd St., between Broadway and West End Ave., Upper West Side* ☎ 212/874–1588 Ⓜ *Subway: 1, 2, 3, 9 to 72nd St.*

Chocolate

Chocolate Bar. Sweets from some of New York's finest "chocolate chefs" fill the cases here. Along with its signature and "retro" chocolate bars (the latter include such flavors as caramel apple and coconut cream pie) are an array of filled chocolate bonbons and a café counter where you can get a steaming cup of cocoa. It's open until 10 PM most nights. ✉ *48 8th Ave., between Horatio and Jane Sts., Greenwich Village* ☎ 212/366–1541 Ⓜ *Subway: A, C, E to 14th St.*

Elk Candy Co. This slice of old Yorkville carries European treats such as Mozartkugeln along with specialty chocolates and wonderful marzipan.

✉ *1628 2nd Ave., between E. 84th and E. 85th Sts., Upper East Side* ☎ *212/650–1177* Ⓜ *Subway: 4, 5, 6 to 86th St.*

Jacques Torres Chocolate Haven. Visit the cafe and shop here and you'll literally be surrounded by chocolate. The glass-walled space is in the heart of Torres's chocolate factory, so you can watch the goodies being made while you sip a richly spiced cocoa. Signature taste: the "wicked" chocolate, laced with cinnamon and chili pepper. ✉ *350 Hudson St., at King St., SoHo* ☎ *212/414–2462.*

Kee's Chocolates. Walking into this small store, you might get a whiff of warm chocolate or spy a few smeared spatulas in the back, attesting to the candy's homemade origin. Yet what's in the case looks preternaturally perfect: dark chocolates filled with *yuzu* (a Japanese citrus), covered with freshly crushed pistachios, or flavored with lemongrass and mint. ✉ *80 Thompson St., between Broome and Grand Sts., SoHo* ☎ *212/ 334–3284* Ⓜ *Subway: A, C to Spring St.*

★ **La Maison du Chocolat.** Stop in at this chocolatier's small tea salon to dive into a cup of thick, heavenly hot chocolate. The Paris-based outfit sells handmade truffles, chocolates, and pastries that could lull you into a chocolate stupor. ✉ *1018 Madison Ave., between E. 78th and 79th Sts., Upper East Side* ☎ *212/744–7117* Ⓜ *Subway: 6 to 77th St.* ✉ *30 Rockefeller Center, between 5th and 6th Aves., Midtown West* ☎ *212/ 265–9404* Ⓜ *Subway: B, D, F, V to 47th–50th St./Rockefeller Center.*

Li-Lac Chocolates. This adorable nook has been feeding the Village's sweet tooth since 1923. You can buy dark-chocolate-dipped marzipan acorns here by the pound, as well as such specialty items as chocolate-molded Statues of Liberty. If you can't get downtown, try a hand-dipped treat at their stand in the Grand Central Market at Grand Central Terminal. ✉ *40 8th Ave., at Jane St. Greenwich Village* ☎ *212/ 242–7374* Ⓜ *Subway: 1, 9 to Christopher St./Sheridan Sq.*

Lunettes et Chocolat. Eyeglasses and candy? The better to see your chocolate with, my dear. Gaze at the rows of dashing frames by New Yorker favorite Selima and various designer shades for as long as you can withstand the beckoning smell of cocoa. Then melt for the chocolates, with their delectable ganache, praline, and cream-based fillings. ✉ *25 Prince St., between Elizabeth and Mott Sts., NoLita* ☎ *212/925–8800* Ⓜ *Subway: R, W to Prince St.*

★ **Marie Belle.** The handmade chocolates here are nothing less than works of art. Square truffles and bonbons—which come in such flavors as Earl Grey tea, cappuccino, passion fruit, saffron, lemon milk, and lavender—are painted with edible dyes so each resembles a miniature painting, and packaged in decorative leather boxes. Tins of aromatic tea leaves and Aztec hot chocolate are also available. ✉ *484 Broome St., between West Broadway and Wooster St., SoHo* ☎ *212/925–6999* Ⓜ *Subway: R, W to Prince St.*

Richart Design et Chocolat. This French shop is worth its weight in cacao beans. The sophisticated chocolates are mostly dark, the ganaches and fillings are intense, and many are imprinted with intricate and colorful patterns. ✉ *7 E. 55th St., between 5th and Madison Aves., Midtown East* ☎ *212/371–9369* Ⓜ *Subway: N, R, W to 5th Ave./59th St.*

Teuscher Chocolates of Switzerland. Fabulous chocolates (try the champagne truffles) made in Switzerland are flown in weekly for sale in these jewel-box shops, newly decorated each season. ✉ *620 5th Ave., in Rockefeller Center, Midtown West* ☎ *212/246–4416* Ⓜ *Subway: E, V to 5th Ave./53rd St.* ✉ *25 E. 61st St., between Madison and Park Aves., Upper East Side* ☎ *212/751–8482* Ⓜ *Subway: N, R, W, 4, 5, 6 to 59th St./Lexington Ave.*

★ **Vosges Haut Chocolat.** This chandeliered salon takes chocolate couture to a new level. The creations are internationally themed: the Budapest bonbons combine dark chocolate and Hungarian paprika, the Black Pearls contain wasabi, and the Aboriginal collection uses such esoteric ingredients as wattleseed and ryeberry. The vibe here is unabashedly arty: films are projected on a section of white wall, T-shirts obsessively repeat the word chocolate, and silk-covered handbags are printed with a cocoa-pod design. ✉ *132 Spring St., between Greene and Wooster Sts., SoHo* ☎ *212/625–2929* Ⓜ *Subway: R, W to Prince St.*

Clothing

Children's Clothing

Bonpoint. The sophistication here lies in the beautiful designs and impeccable workmanship—velvet-tipped coats with matching caps and hand-embroidered jumpers and blouses. ✉ *1269 Madison Ave., at E. 91st St., Upper East Side* ☎ *212/722–7720* Ⓜ *Subway: 4, 5, 6 to 86th St.* ✉ *811 Madison Ave., at E. 68th St., Upper East Side* ☎ *212/879–0900* Ⓜ *Subway: 6 to 68th St./Hunter College.*

Bu and the Duck. Vintage-inspired children's clothing, shoes, and toys distinguish this shop. The Italian-made, two-toned spectator boots might make you wish your own feet were tiny again. ✉ *106 Franklin St., at Church St., TriBeCa* ☎ *212/431–9226* Ⓜ *Subway: 1, 9 to Franklin St.*

Calypso Enfant et Bébé. Sailor-stripe tops, polka-dot PJs, lovely party dresses . . . you may find yourself dressing vicariously through your children. ✉ *426 Broome St., between Lafayette and Crosby Sts., No-Lita* ☎ *212/966–3234* Ⓜ *Subway: 6 to Spring St.*

Flora and Henri. The padded twill coats, slate-blue pleated skirts, and pin-dot cotton dresses here are cute but not overly so. They'll stand up to wear and tear; witness the sturdy Italian-made shoes. ✉ *943 Madison Ave., between E. 74th and E. 75th Sts., Upper East Side* ☎ *212/249–1695* Ⓜ *Subway: 6 to E. 77th St.*

Infinity. Mothers gossip near the dressing rooms as their daughters try on slinky Les Tout Petits dresses, Miss Sixty Jeans, and cheeky tees with slogans like "chicks ahoy." The aggressively trendy and the rather sweet meet in a welter of preteen accessories. ✉ *1116 Madison Ave., at E. 83rd St., Upper East Side* ☎ *212/517–4232* Ⓜ *Subway: 4, 5, 6 to 86th St.*

Les Petits Chapelais. Designed and made in France, these kids' clothes are adorable but also practical. Corduroy outfits have details like embroidered flowers and contrasting cuffs; soft fleecy jackets are reversible, and sweaters have easy-zip-up fronts and hoodies. ✉ *142 Sullivan St., between Prince and W. Houston Sts., SoHo* ☎ *212/505–1927* Ⓜ *Subway: C, E to Spring St.*

Lilliput. At both locations, which are across the street from each other, kids can up their coolness quotient with Paul Smith sweaters, sequined party dresses, and denimwear by Diesel. The difference is that the shop at No. 265 carries it all up to size 8, whereas the original shop goes up to teens. ✉ *240 Lafayette St., between Prince and Spring Sts., SoHo* ☎ *212/965–9201* Ⓜ *Subway: R, W to Prince St.* ✉ *265 Lafayette St., between Prince and Spring Sts., SoHo* ☎ *212/965–9567* Ⓜ *Subway: 6 to Spring St.*

Little Eric. Hip adult styles—Camper knockoffs, brogues—play footsie alongside the familiar loafers and Mary Janes. ✉ *1118 Madison Ave., at E. 83rd St., Upper East Side* ☎ *212/717–1513* Ⓜ *Subway: 4, 5, 6 to 86th St.*

Morris Bros. This gold mine of boys' and girls' active wear carries Bear down jackets, mesh shorts, Quiksilver swim trunks, and stacks of Levi's. ✉ *2322 Broadway, at W. 84th St., Upper West Side* ☎ *212/724–9000* Ⓜ *Subway: 1, 9 to 86th St.*

Oilily. Stylized flowers, stripes, and animal shapes splash across these brightly colored play and school clothes. ✉ *820 Madison Ave., between E. 68th and E. 69th Sts., Upper East Side* ☎ *212/772–8686* Ⓜ *Subway: 6 to 68th St./Hunter College.*

Petit Bateau. Fine cotton is spun into comfortable underwear, play clothes, and pajamas; T-shirts come in dozens of colors and to every specification, with V-necks, round necks, snap-fronts, and more. ✉ *1094 Madison Ave., at E. 82nd St., Upper East Side* ☎ *212/988–8884* Ⓜ *Subway: 4, 5, 6 to 86th St.*

Pipsqueak. Some clothes play to kid appeal, like the sweaters knit with iguanas or ladybugs, and others reveal what's on the adults' minds (tees emblazoned with "hellraiser"). ✉ *248 Mott St., between Prince and E. Houston Sts., NoLita* ☎ *212/226–8824* Ⓜ *Subway: R, W to Prince St.*

Shoofly. Children's shoes and accessories are the name of the game here; you can choose from Mary Janes, wing tips, and Dolce & Gabbana fur-lined booties along with pom-pom hats, brightly patterned socks, and jewelry. ✉ *42 Hudson St., between Thomas and Duane Sts., TriBeCa* ☎ *212/406–3270* Ⓜ *Subway: 1, 9 to Franklin St.*

Space Kiddets. The funky (Elvis-print rompers, onesies made from old concert tees) mixes with the old-school (retro cowboy-print pants, brightly colored clogs) at this casual, trendsetting store. ✉ *46 E. 21st St., between Broadway and Park Ave., Flatiron District* ☎ *212/420–9878* Ⓜ *Subway: 6 to 23rd St.*

Z'Baby Company. Outfit the eight-and-unders for dress-up or play with overalls, tulle-skirted party dresses, even motorcycle jackets. ✉ *100 W. 72nd St., at Columbus Ave., Upper West Side* ☎ *212/579–2229* Ⓜ *Subway: 1, 2, 3, 9 to 72nd St.* ✉ *996 Lexington Ave., at E. 72nd St., Upper East Side* ☎ *212/472–2229* Ⓜ *Subway: 6 to 68th St.*

Discount Clothing

Find Outlet. These outlets are like year-round sample sales. Both locations stock up-and-coming and established designer merchandise for 50%–80% off the original price. It's easy to make finds on a regular basis, like Paul & Joe silk chiffon tops or Twinkle sweaters, as the stock is replenished daily. For a wider selection visit the Chelsea shop; it's open only Thursday through Sunday, however. ✉ *229 Mott St., between Prince and Spring Sts., NoLita* ☎ *212/226–5167* Ⓜ *Subway: 6 to*

Spring St. ✉ *361 W. 17th St., between 8th and 9th Aves., Chelsea* ☎ *212/243–3177* Ⓜ *Subway: A, C, E to 14th St.*

Klein's of Monticello. One of the most genteel stores in the Lower East Side (no fluorescent lighting!), Klein's has authentic labels—Malo cashmere sweaters and separates from MaxMara, Les Copains, Etro, and Piazza Sempione—normally for 20%–30% off. ✉ *105 Orchard St., at Delancey St., Lower East Side* ☎ *212/966–1453* Ⓜ *Subway: F, J, M, Z to Delancey St./Essex St.*

Loehmann's. Label searchers can turn up $40 Polo/Ralph Lauren chinos and Donna Karan and Yves Saint Laurent suits in the men's department here on a regular basis. Head up to the "back room" on the top floor for the best women's designers, but you may need to make a repeat visit or two before emerging victorious. ✉ *101 7th Ave., at W. 16th St., Chelsea* ☎ *212/352–0856* Ⓜ *Subway: 1, 2, 3, 9 to 14th St.*

Men's & Women's Clothing

Alessandro Dell'Acqua. Sexiness with a soft touch has become this designer's forte. Chiffon and silk jersey drape and cling in the right places, and the sweaters and polos fit just so. ✉ *818 Madison Ave., between E. 68th and E. 69th Sts., Upper East Side* ☎ *212/253–6861* Ⓜ *Subway: 6 to E. 68th St.*

A.P.C. This hip French boutique proves to be deceptively simple. Watch your step on the uneven wooden floorboards while choosing narrow gabardine and corduroy suits or dark denim jeans and jackets, some with a hint of military. ✉ *131 Mercer St., between Prince and Spring Sts., SoHo* ☎ *212/966–9685* Ⓜ *Subway: 6 to Spring St.; R, W to Prince St.*

Bagutta Life. With its stash of European designers—including Blumarine, Valentino, Dior, Rochas, and the black, body-skimming women's creations of Azzedine Alaïa—downtowners can have all the temptations of Madison Avenue. Other accoutrements, such as shagreen-covered furniture, take a correspondingly high road. ✉ *76 Greene St., between Spring and Broome Sts., SoHo* ☎ *212/925–5216* Ⓜ *Subway: R, W to Prince St.*

Barbour. The company's waxed jackets are built to withstand raw British weather—or any other kind. The tweeds, moleskin pants, lambswool sweaters, and tattersall shirts invariably call up images of country rambles, trusty hunting dog not included. ✉ *1047 Madison Ave., at E. 80th St., Upper East Side* ☎ *212/570–2600* Ⓜ *Subway: 6 to 77th St.*

A Bathing Ape. Known simply as "BAPE" to devotees, this exclusive label has a cult following in its native Tokyo. Though the shop's opened with fanfare in 2005, it's hard to see at first glance what the fuss is all about. A small selection of camouflage gear and limited-edition T-shirts are placed throughout the minimalist space; the real scene-stealers, though, are the flashy retro-style sneakers in neon colors. ✉ *91 Greene St., between Prince and Spring Sts., SoHo* ☎ *212/925–0222* Ⓜ *Subway: R, W to Prince St.*

Brooks Brothers. The clothes at this classic American haberdasher are, as ever, traditional, comfortable, and fairly priced. A modernizing trend has resulted not only in slightly modified styles, but also in a foray into digital tailoring. At the Madison Avenue store, you can step into a computer scanner to get precisely measured for a custom shirt or suit. Summer seersucker, navy blue blazers, and the peerless oxford shirts have

CloseUp

COOL LOCAL CHAINS

FOLLOWING ARE THE BEST *of the local chain stores, the places New Yorkers head to in a fashion pinch.*

INA. *Although you may spot something vintage, like a 1960s Yves Saint Laurent velvet bolero, most clothing at these small boutiques harks back only a few seasons, and in some cases, it's never been worn. The Mott Street location racks up menswear; the other three stores carry women's resale.* ⊠ 101 Thompson St., between Prince and Spring Sts., SoHo ☎ 212/941–4757 ⊠ 21 Prince St., between Elizabeth and Mott Sts., NoLita ☎ 212/334–9048 ⊠ 262 Mott St., between Prince and E. Houston Sts., NoLita ☎ 212/334–2210 ⊠ 208 E. 73rd St., between 2nd and 3rd Aves., Upper East Side ☎ 212/249–0014.

Ricky's. *Shopping at any one of these wacky stores is a uniquely New York experience. The loud and fun drugstores attract an eclectic, mostly young crowd who come just as often for the crazy-color wigs or fishnet stockings as they do for the body glitter and Neutrogena soap. Every fall the stores turn into Halloween central, with a huge assortment of feather boas, sequined masks, spray-on hair color, and spangled false eyelashes. The NoLita branch, called Ricky's Naturals, specializes in products made with essential oils and organic ingredients.* ⊠ 590 Broadway, at Prince St., SoHo ☎ 212/226–5552 ⊠ 235 Mulberry St., NoLita ☎ 212/925–6750 ⊠ 7 E. 14th St., Union Sq. ☎ 212/691–7930 ⊠ 718 Broadway, at Astor Pl., East Village ☎ 212/979–5232 ⊠ 466 6th Ave., at W. 12th St., Greenwich Village ☎ 212/924–3401 ⊠ 44 E. 8th St., between Broadway and University Pl., Greenwich Village ☎ 212/254–5247 ⊠ 1412 Broadway, at W. 38th St., Midtown West ☎ 212/768–1175

⊠ 988 8th Ave., at W. 59th St., Midtown West ☎ 212/957–8343 ⊠ 1189 1st Ave., at E. 64th St., Upper East Side ☎ 212/879–8361 ⊠ 1380 3rd Ave., between E. 78th and E. 79th Sts., Upper East Side ☎ 212/737–7723.

Scoop. *Chic without trying too hard, these clothes will help you fit in with the too-cool-to-dress-up crowd. Look for lots of jeans (limited-edition Levi's, Citizens of Humanity, Chip & Pepper), along with slinky tops for girls and vintage-looking tees and rugby shirts for guys. The SoHo branch is for women only.* ⊠ 1273–1277 3rd Ave., between E. 73rd and E. 74th Sts., Upper East Side ☎ 212/535–5577 ⊠ 430 W. 14th St., at Washington St., Meatpacking District ☎ 212/929–1244 men's shop, 212/691–1905 women's ⊠ 532 Broadway, at Spring St., SoHo ☎ 212/925–2886.

Searle. *Mostly strung along the East Side, these stores have a devoted following for their coats: pea coats, long wool coats, shearlings, leather, or even llama hair. There are plenty of other designer things to layer, too, from cowl-neck sweaters to fitted tees.* ⊠ 1051 3rd Ave., at E. 62nd St., Upper East Side ☎ 212/838–5990 ⊠ 609 Madison Ave., at E. 58th St., Midtown East ☎ 212/753–9021 ⊠ 805 Madison Ave., between E. 67th and E. 68th Sts., Upper East Side ☎ 212/628–6665 ⊠ 1296 3rd Ave., between E. 74th and E. 75th Sts., Upper East Side ☎ 212/717–5200 ⊠ 1035 Madison Ave., at E. 79th St., Upper East Side ☎ 212/717–4022 ⊠ 1124 Madison Ave., at E. 84th St., Upper East Side ☎ 212/988–7318 ⊠ 156 5th Ave., between W. 20th and W. 21st Sts., Flatiron District ☎ 212/924–4330.

been staples for generations. The women's selection has variations thereof. ⊠ *666 5th Ave., at W. 53rd St., Midtown West* ☎ *212/261–9440* Ⓜ *Subway: E, V to 5th Ave./53rd St.* ⊠ *346 Madison Ave., at E. 44th St., Midtown East* ☎ *212/682–8800* Ⓜ *Subway: S, 4, 5, 6, 7 to 42nd St./Grand Central* ⊠ *1 Church St., at Liberty St., Lower Manhattan* ☎ *212/267–2400* Ⓜ *Subway: R, W to Cortlandt St.*

Burberry. The signature plaid is hardly square these days, as bikinis, leather pants, and messenger-style bags join the traditional gabardine trench coats. The flagship store on East 57th Street is the mother lode; the SoHo branch has an abbreviated assortment. ⊠ *9 E. 57th St., between 5th and Madison Aves., Midtown West* ☎ *212/407–7100* Ⓜ *Subway: N, R, W to 5th Ave./59th St.* ⊠ *131 Spring St., between Greene and Wooster Sts., SoHo* ☎ *212/925–9300* Ⓜ *Subway: R, W to Prince St.*

Calvin Klein. Though the namesake designer has bowed out, the label keeps channeling his particular style. This stark flagship store emphasizes the luxe end of the clothing line. Men's suits tend to be soft around the edges; women's evening gowns are often a fluid pouring of silk. There are also shoes, accessories, housewares, and makeup. ⊠ *654 Madison Ave., at E. 60th St., Upper East Side* ☎ *212/292–9000* Ⓜ *Subway: N, R, W, 4, 5, 6 to 59th St./Lexington Ave.*

Christian Dior. The New York outpost of one of France's most venerable fashion houses makes its home in the dazzlingly modern LVMH tower. The designs bring elements of everything from raceways to skate punks to haute couture. If you're not in the market for an investment gown, peruse the glam accessories, like the latest stirrup bag. The Dior menswear boutique is just next door; the rocking cigarette-thin suits are often pilfered by women. ⊠ *21 E. 57th St., at Madison Ave., Midtown East* ☎ *212/931–2950* Ⓜ *Subway: E, V to 5th Ave./53rd St.* ⊠ *Men's store, 21 E. 57th St., Midtown East* ☎ *212/207–8448* Ⓜ *Subway: E, V to 5th Ave./53rd St.*

Christopher Fischer. Featherweight cashmere sweaters, wraps, and throws in Easter-egg colors have made Fischer the darling of Hamptonites. His shop also carries luggage and leather accessories by Henry Beguelin, and such homewares as flokati pillows and wooden bowls from South Africa. ⊠ *80 Wooster St., SoHo* ☎ *212/965–9009* Ⓜ *Subway: R, W to Prince St.*

Comme des Garçons. The designs in this stark, white, swoopy space consistently push the fashion envelope with brash patterns, unlikely juxtapositions (tulle and neoprene), and cuts that are meant to be thought-provoking, not flattering. Architecture students come just for the interior design. ⊠ *520 W. 22nd St., between 10th and 11th Aves., Chelsea* ☎ *212/604–9200* Ⓜ *Subway: C, E to 23rd St.*

Costume National. Although entering this dramatically murky shop may seem intimidating (the black-wall space evokes a sort of futuristic tomb), the sexy, slim-cut leather coats and sheer black shirts for both men and women are chic and beautifully made. ⊠ *108 Wooster St., between Prince and Spring Sts., SoHo* ☎ *212/431–1530* Ⓜ *Subway: C, E to Spring St.*

DDC Lab. The super-hip offerings at this shop's new location include bomber jackets and pleated skirts in paper-thin leather, plus brazenly colored PF Flyers sneakers for men. The overdyed denim comes in hues of supersaturated purple and acid green; you can even by canisters of special laundry powder to wash it with. ✉ *427 W. 14th St., at Washington St., Meatpacking District* ☎ *212/414–5801* Ⓜ *Subway: A, C, E to 14th St.*

D&G. This outpost for the secondary Dolce & Gabbana line sells less pricey, but still over-the-top Italian designs to a young crowd. This isn't the place to shop for basics—the jeans and separates are all trimmed with embroidery, sequins, lace inserts, and neon-colored patent leather accents—but the clothes are nothing if not fun. ✉ *434 West Broadway, between Prince and Spring Sts., SoHo* ☎ *212/965–8000* Ⓜ *Subway: C, E to Spring St.*

Diesel. The display windows styled like washing machines at the Lexington Avenue superstore will tip you off to Diesel's industrial edge. They give their mainstay, denim, various finishes, from a dusty-looking indigo to superfaded. **Diesel Style Lab** carries a secondary line with futuristic leanings in graphic prints and souped-up fabrics. The **Diesel Denim Gallery** will even launder your purchase for you. ✉ *770 Lexington Ave., at E. 60th St., Upper East Side* ☎ *212/308–0055* Ⓜ *Subway: N, R, W, 4, 5, 6 to 59th St./Lexington Ave.* ✉ *1 Union Sq. W, at 14th St.* ☎ *646/336–8552* Ⓜ *Subway: L, N, Q, R, W, 4, 5, 6 to 14th St./Union Sq.* ✉ *Diesel Style Lab, 416 West Broadway, between Prince and Spring Sts., SoHo* ☎ *212/343–3863* Ⓜ *Subway: C, E to Spring St.* ✉ *Diesel Denim Gallery, 68 Greene St., between Spring and Broome Sts., SoHo* ☎ *212/966–5593* Ⓜ *Subway: C, E to Spring St.*

DKNY. Not only does DKNY embrace the lifestyle store concept, but it's a lifestyle with a relatively short attention span. New merchandise arrives frequently, so there's always something new to wish for. Cocktail-party ensembles, chunky-knit sweaters, and knockaround denim vie for notice; the "pure" line is reserved for all-natural fibers. A scattering of vintage pieces, such as leather bomber jackets or 1930s jet jewelry, ensures that you can have something no one else has. Scout out the non-wearables, too; the candles, toiletries, and home accessories are unfailingly cool. Then you can belly up to the juice bar, log on to an in-store iMac, or listen to a featured CD. ✉ *655 Madison Ave., at E. 60th St., Upper East Side* ☎ *212/223–3569* Ⓜ *Subway: N, R, W, 4, 5, 6 to 59th St./Lexington Ave.* ✉ *420 West Broadway, between Prince and Spring Sts., SoHo* ☎ *646/613–1100* Ⓜ *Subway: C, E to Spring St.*

Dolce & Gabbana. It's easy to feel like an Italian movie star amid these extravagant (in every sense) clothes. Pinstripes are a favorite; for women, they could be paired with something sheer, furred, or leopard-print, while for men they elongate the sharp suits. ✉ *825 Madison Ave., between E. 68th and E. 69th Sts., Upper East Side* ☎ *212/249–4100* Ⓜ *Subway: 6 to 68th St./Hunter College.*

Donna Karan. Collections may pendulum from raw-edged to refined, but the luxurious materials remain a constant. Cashmere jersey, silk, and deerskin are drawn into carefully un-precious pieces. A Zen garden lets you relieve sticker shock. ✉ *819 Madison Ave., between E. 68th and E. 69th Sts., Upper East Side* ☎ *212/861–1001* Ⓜ *Subway: 6 to 68th St./Hunter College.*

Emporio Armani. At this "middle child" of the Armani trio, the clothes are dressy without quite being formal, often in cream, muted blues, and the ever-cool shades of soot. ⊠ *601 Madison Ave., between E. 57th and E. 58th Sts., Midtown East* ☎ *212/317–0800* Ⓜ *Subway: N, R, W, 4, 5, 6 to 59th St./Lexington Ave.* ⊠ *410 West Broadway, at Spring St., SoHo* ☎ *646/613–8099* Ⓜ *Subway: C, E to Spring St.*

Etro. There are echoes of 19th-century luxury in Etro's clothing, along with a strong whiff of the exotic and a dash of levity. Trademark paisleys sprawl over richly covered suits, dresses, and lustrous pillows. ⊠ *720 Madison Ave., between E. 63rd and E. 64th Sts., Upper East Side* ☎ *212/317–9096* Ⓜ *Subway: 6 to 68th St./Hunter College.*

Façonnable. This French company has a lock on the Euro-conservative look. The women's sportswear leans on the men's pillars: tailored end-on-end shirts in bold stripes or pastels, argyle sweaters, double-breasted coats. The men's Italian-made suits may be expensive, but the craftsmanship and canvas fronting will allow them to withstand years of dry cleaning. ⊠ *636 5th Ave., at W. 51st St., Midtown West* ☎ *212/319–0111* Ⓜ *Subway: E, V to 5th Ave./53rd St.*

Gianni Versace. The five-story flagship store, in a restored turn-of-the-20th-century landmark building on 5th Avenue, hums with colored neon lights. Although the sometimes outrageous designs and colors of Versace clothes might not be to everyone's taste (or budget), they're never boring. A second five-story store has a steely, modern take; it focuses on higher-end clothes and accessories. ⊠ *647 5th Ave., near E. 51st St., Midtown East* ☎ *212/317–0224* Ⓜ *Subway: E, V to 5th Ave./53rd St.* ⊠ *815 Madison Ave., between E. 68th and E. 69th Sts., Upper East Side* ☎ *212/744–6868* Ⓜ *Subway: 6 to 68th St./Hunter College.*

Giorgio Armani. Armani managed to beat out Calvin Klein on the exterior-minimalism front; inside, the space has a museumlike quality, reinforced by the refined clothes. Suits for men and women have a telltale perfect drape, and women's might be accessorized with a broad, striking, beaded necklace. ⊠ *760 Madison Ave., between E. 65th and E. 66th Sts., Upper East Side* ☎ *212/988–9191* Ⓜ *Subway: 6 to 68th St./Hunter College.*

Gucci. With a female designer in place, the clothing is a tad less aggressively sexy than in the Tom Ford era. Skintight pants might be paired with a blousey jacket; lace tops leave a little more to the imagination. The accessories, like wraparound shades and studded or snakeskin shoes, continue to spark consumer frenzies. ⊠ *685 5th Ave., between 54th and 55th Sts., Midtown East* ☎ *212/826–2600* Ⓜ *Subway: N, R, W to 5th Ave./59th St.* ⊠ *840 Madison Ave., between E. 69th and E. 70th Sts., Upper East Side* ☎ *212/717–2619* Ⓜ *Subway: 6 to 68th St./Hunter College.*

Guess? The denim here seizes on all kinds of trends at once: wide legs and tight low-riders, preshredded hems and pockets, rhinestones, studs, cutoffs, and whatever else takes teenagers' fancy. ⊠ *537 Broadway, between Prince and Spring Sts., SoHo* ☎ *212/226–9545* Ⓜ *Subway: R, W to Prince St.*

Helmut Lang. Lang's men's and women's lines—mostly in black, white, and gray, with the occasional touch of bright orange or yellow—are tough distillations of his skinny-pants aesthetic. Black, mirror-ended walls slice

NATIONAL CHAINS

American Apparel. Huge with the teenage set for its line of colorful "sweatshop free" T-shirts and undies. ✉ 121 Spring St., between Mercer and Greene Sts., SoHo ☎ 212/226–4880 ✉ 183 Houston St., at Orchard St., Lower East Side ✉ 373 6th Ave., between 63rd and 64th Sts., Greenwich Village ☎ 646/336–6515 ✉ 1090 3rd Ave., at 64th St., Upper East Side ☎ 212/772–7462.

A/X: Armani Exchange. Affordable basics and dark-washed jeans make it possible for most people to own an Armani . . . something. ✉ 568 Broadway, at Prince St., SoHo ☎ 212/431–6000 ✉ 645 5th Ave., at E. 51st St., Midtown East ☎ 212/980–3037 ✉ 129 5th Ave., between W. 19th and W. 20th Sts., Flatiron District ☎ 212/254–7230 ✉ 10 Columbus Circle, at W. 59th St., Midtown West ☎ 212/823–9321.

Barnes & Noble. The biggest bookstore presence in the city. ✉ 396 6th Ave., at W. 8th St., Greenwich Village ☎ 212/674–8780 ✉ 33 E. 17th St., at Union Sq., Flatiron District ☎ 212/253–0810 ✉ 4 Astor Pl., at Lafayette St., East Village ☎ 212/420–1322 ✉ 600 5th Ave., at W. 48th St., Midtown West ☎ 212/765–0592 ✉ 1972 Broadway, at W. 66th St., Upper West Side ☎ 212/595–6859 ✉ 2289 Broadway, at W. 82nd St., Upper West Side ☎ 212/362–8835 ✉ 240 E. 86th St., between 2nd and 3rd Aves., Upper East Side ☎ 212/794–1962.

Borders. The second-biggest bookstore presence in the city. ✉ 461 Park Ave., at E. 57th St., Midtown East ☎ 212/980–6785 ✉ 550 2nd Ave., at E. 32nd St., Murray Hill ☎ 212/685–3938 ✉ 100 Broadway, at Wall St., Lower Manhattan ☎ 212/964–1988 ✉ 10 Columbus Circle, Upper West Side ☎ 212/823–9775.

Club Monaco. Manageable prices, neutral palettes, and mild designer knockoffs.

✉ 121 Prince St., between Wooster and Greene Sts., SoHo ☎ 212/533–8930 ✉ 2376 Broadway, at W. 87th St., Upper West Side ☎ 212/579–2587 ✉ 160 5th Ave., at W. 21st St., Flatiron District ☎ 212/352–0936 ✉ 6 W. 57th St., between 5th and 6th Aves., Midtown West ☎ 212/459–9863 ✉ 1111 3rd Ave., at E. 65th St., Upper East Side ☎ 212/355–2949 ✉ 520 Broadway, between Broome and Spring Sts., SoHo ☎ 212/941–1511.

Coach. Classic glove-tanned leather goes into handbags, briefcases, wallets, shoes, and dozens of other accessories. ✉ 2321 Broadway, at W. 84th St., Upper West Side ☎ 212/799–1624 ✉ 3 W. 57th St., between 5th and 6th Aves., Midtown West ☎ 212/754–0041 ✉ 620 5th Ave., at Rockefeller Center, Midtown West ☎ 212/245–4148 ✉ 342 Madison Ave., at E. 44th St., Midtown East ☎ 212/599–4777 ✉ 143 Prince St., at West Broadway, SoHo ☎ 212/473–6925 ✉ 79 5th Ave., at E. 16th St., Flatiron District ☎ 212/675–6403 ✉ 10 Columbus Circle, at W. 59th St., Midtown West ☎ 212/581–4115.

Crate & Barrel. A carefully coordinated selection of modern housewares and doodads for every imaginable room. ✉ 650 Madison Ave., at E. 59th St., Upper East Side ☎ 212/308–0011 ✉ 611 Broadway, at W. Houston, SoHo ☎ 212/308–0011.

FACE Stockholm. Pretty pastel and neutral makeup, brazenly colored nail polish (emerald green, sky blue), and juicy red glosses. ✉ 110 Prince St., at Greene St., SoHo ☎ 212/966–9110 ✉ 1263 Madison Ave., between E. 90th and E. 91st Sts., Upper East Side ☎ 212/987–1411 ✉ 226 Columbus Ave., between W. 70th and W. 71st Sts., Upper West Side ☎ 212/769–1420 ✉ 10 Columbus

Circle, at W. 59th St., Midtown West
☎ 212/823–9415.

Fresh. *Sounds good enough to eat: a brown-sugar skin-care line, pomegranate hair conditioner, pear-cassis cologne.* ✉ 57 Spring St., between Lafayette and Mulberry Sts., SoHo ☎ 212/925–0099 ✉ 1367 3rd Ave., at E. 78th St., Upper East Side ☎ 212/585–3400 ✉ 388 Bleecker St., between Perry and W. 11th Sts., Greenwich Village ☎ 917/408–1850.

H&M. *Swarm the racks for up-to-the-minute trends at unbelievably low prices.* ✉ 640 5th Ave., at W. 51st. St. ☎ 212/489–0390 ✉ 1328 Broadway, at W. 34th St., Midtown West ☎ 646/473–1165 ✉ 731 Lexington Ave., at E. 58th St., Midtown East ☎ 212/935–6781 ✉ 558 Broadway, between Prince and Spring Sts., SoHo ☎ 212/343–2722 ✉ 515 Broadway, between Spring and Broome Sts., SoHo ☎ 212/965–8975 ✉ 125 W. 125 St., between Lenox Ave. and Adam Clayton Powell Jr. Blvd., Harlem ☎ 212/665–8300.

J. Crew. *Get turned out for a job interview, a first day at school, or a week in the Adirondacks.* ✉ 99 Prince St., between Mercer and Greene Sts., SoHo ☎ 212/966–2739 ✉ 203 Front St., at Fulton St., Lower Manhattan ☎ 212/385–3500 ✉ 91 5th Ave., between E. 16th and E. 17th Sts., Flatiron District ☎ 212/255–4848 ✉ 30 Rockefeller Plaza, W. 50th St., between 5th and 6th Aves., Midtown West ☎ 212/765–4227 ✉ 347 Madison Ave., at E. 45th St., Midtown East ☎ 212/949–0570 ✉ 10 Columbus Circle, at W. 59th St., Midtown West ☎ 212/823–9302.

L'Occitane. *Provençal all the way, with extra-mild orange blossom, rosemary, and lavender soaps, shampoos, and creams.* ✉ 92 Prince St., at Mercer St., SoHo ☎ 212/219–3310 ✉ 1046 Madison

Ave., at E. 80th St., Upper East Side ☎ 212/639–9185 ✉ 412 Lexington Ave., at E. 43rd St., Midtown East ☎ 212/557–6754 ✉ 247 Bleecker St., at Leroy St., Greenwich Village ☎ 212/367–8428 ✉ 10 Columbus Circle, at W. 59th St., Midtown West ☎ 212/333–4880.

Sephora. *An alphabetical wall of perfumes and a comprehensive makeup selection ranging from Urban Decay to Nars to hard-to-find names such as Peter Thomas Roth.* ✉ 555 Broadway, between Prince and Spring Sts., SoHo ☎ 212/625–1309 ✉ 119 5th Ave., at E. 19th St., Flatiron District ☎ 212/674–3570 ✉ 1500 Broadway, at W. 44th St., Midtown West ☎ 212/944–8168 ✉ 130 W. 34th St., between 7th Ave. and Broadway, Midtown West ☎ 212/629–9135 ✉ 10 Columbus Circle, at W. 59th St., Midtown West ☎ 212/823–9383.

Urban Outfitters. *Fashions change a few times a semester in this hipster emporium.* ✉ 162 2nd Ave., between E. 10th and E. 11th Sts., East Village ☎ 212/375–1277 ✉ 374 6th Ave., at Waverly Pl., Greenwich Village ☎ 212/677–9350 ✉ 582 6th Ave., at W. 14th St., Greenwich Village ☎ 646/638–1646 ✉ 628 Broadway, between Bleecker and E. Houston Sts., East Village ☎ 212/475–0009 ✉ 2081 Broadway, at W. 72nd St., Upper West Side ☎ 212/579–3912.

Zara. *The tags covered with prices in international currencies all boil down to one thing: inexpensive clothes and accessories for the office or a night out.* ✉ 689 5th Ave., at E. 54th St. ☎ 212/371–2555 ✉ 750 Lexington Ave., between E. 59th and E. 60th Sts., Midtown East ☎ 212/754–1120 ✉ 101 5th Ave., between E. 17th and E. 18th Sts., Flatiron District ☎ 212/741–0555 ✉ 580 Broadway, between Prince and E. Houston Sts., SoHo ☎ 212/343–1725.

up the space, which is punctuated by the digital ticker tape designed by artist Jenny Holzer. Cross the street to sniff a unisex scent at Lang's even more spare perfume boutique. ⊠ *80 Greene St., between Spring and Broome Sts., SoHo* ☎ *212/925–7214* Ⓜ *Subway: C, E to Spring St.*

Hermès. Sweep up and down the curving stairway in this contemporary flagship while on the prowl for the classic, distinctively patterned silk scarves and neckties, the coveted Kelly and Birkin handbags, or the beautifully simple separates. True to its equestrian roots, Hermès still stocks saddles and dressage items. ⊠ *691 Madison Ave., at E. 62nd St., Upper East Side* ☎ *212/751–3181* Ⓜ *Subway: N, R, W, 4, 5, 6 to 59th St./Lexington Ave.*

Hugo Boss. While Hugo Boss is known for its menswear, women will have no trouble occupying themselves. Choose a business-meeting wool suit, then cut a dash with something leather or a wild striped shirt. ⊠ *717 5th Ave., at E. 56th St., Midtown East* ☎ *212/485–1800* Ⓜ *Subway: F to 57th St.* ⊠ *10 Columbus Circle, at W. 59th St., Midtown West* ☎ *212/485–1900* Ⓜ *Subway: 1, 9, A, C, B, D to Columbus Circle.*

Írma. This unprepossessing nook with its squeaky plank floors is actually home to some of the most hard-to-find designers in the city. Besides carrying a good selection of Vivienne Westwood, it stockpiles whisper-light cashmere tees by Fifi, leather trenches by Histoire, and vintage Belstaff motorcycle boots. ⊠ *378 Bleecker St., Greenwich Village* ☎ *212/206–7475* Ⓜ *Subway: A, C, E, F, V to W. 4th St./Washington Sq.*

Issey Miyake. Pleats of a Fortuny-like tightness are the Miyake signature—but instead of Fortuny's silks, these clothes are in polyester or ultra-high-tech textiles, often forming sculptural shapes. **Pleats Please** carries a line with simpler silhouettes, from tunics to long dresses. ⊠ *992 Madison Ave., between E. 76th and E. 77th Sts., Upper East Side* ☎ *212/439–7822* Ⓜ *Subway: 6 to 77th St.* ⊠ *119 Hudson St., at N. Moore St., TriBeCa* ☎ *212/226–0100* Ⓜ *Subway: 1, 9 to Franklin St.* ⊠ *Pleats Please, 128 Wooster St., at Prince St., SoHo* ☎ *212/226–3600* Ⓜ *Subway: R, W to Prince St.*

Jean Paul Gaultier. The powder-pink padded walls give the impression of a style sanctum—but the calm certainly doesn't extend to the clothes. Look for nomad-inspired layers, deconstructed pinstripe suits, and sexy takes on the striped sailor shirt for both sexes. ⊠ *759 Madison Ave., between E. 66th and E. 65th Sts., Upper East Side* ☎ *212/249–0235* Ⓜ *Subway: 6 to 68th St./Hunter College.*

Jeffrey. The Meatpacking District really arrived when this Atlanta-based mini-Barneys opened its doors. You can find an incredible array of designer shoes—Valentino, Lanvin, and red-soled Christian Louboutin are some of the bestsellers—plus überlabels like Marni, Gucci, and Collette Dinnigan. ⊠ *449 W. 14th St., between 9th and 10th Aves., Meatpacking District* ☎ *212/206–1272* Ⓜ *Subway: A, C, E, L to 14th St./8th Ave.*

Jil Sander. A herringbone coat or a bit of neon trim is about as unruly as this label gets. The designs are unflappable, whether for shirtdresses or boxy jackets, and the colors urban. ⊠ *11 E. 57th St., between 5th and Madison Aves., Midtown East* ☎ *212/838–6100* Ⓜ *Subway: F to 57th St.*

Marc Jacobs. The ladylike designs filling this shop's SoHo branch are made with luxurious fabrics: silk, cashmere, wool bouclé, and tweeds ranging from the demure to the flamboyant (think teal-color houndstooth).

The details, though—oversize buttons, circular patch pockets, or military-style grommet belts—add a sartorial wink. The Bleecker Street spaces carry more casual clothes; look for slouchy pants and cotton sweaters in sherbet colors, or suede sneakers and scalloped-leather pumps in the accessories boutique next door. ⊠ *163 Mercer St., between W. Houston and Prince Sts., SoHo* ☎ *212/343–1490* Ⓜ *Subway: R, W to Prince St.* ⊠ *Accessories boutique: 385 Bleecker St., at Perry St., Greenwich Village* ☎ *212/924–6126* Ⓜ *Subway: 1, 9 to Christopher St./Sheridan Sq.* ⊠ *403–405 Bleecker St., at W. 11th St., Greenwich Village* ☎ *212/924–0026* Ⓜ *Subway: 1, 9 to Christopher St./Sheridan Sq.*

Nicole Farhi. The designer's New York store represents the convergence of her many design talents and endeavors—men's and women's apparel, home furnishings, and restaurants. On entering the store, you can look from the walkway to the inviting tables below. The clothing can be engrossing, especially the knits. The housewares, also downstairs, mix modern and vintage. ⊠ *10 E. 60th St., between 5th and Madison Aves., Upper East Side* ☎ *212/223–8811* Ⓜ *Subway: N, R, W to 5th Ave./59th St.*

Nom de Guerre. Brave the narrow staircase at this basement-level hipster hideaway to find racks filled with vintage T-shirts, military-inspired jackets and pants, limited edition sneakers, and haute-street denim by Rogan and Red Label. There's an Army-Navyish vibe, with camo-green dressing room curtains and a concrete floor, but the staff is militant only about style and fit. ⊠ *640 Broadway, at Bleecker St., Greenwich Village* ☎ *212/253–2891* Ⓜ *Subway: F, V to Broadway–Lafayette.*

Patricia Field. If you loved Carrie Bradshaw's wilder outfits on *Sex and the City,* this is the place for you. As well as designing costumes for the show, Field has been a longtime purveyor of flamboyant club-kid gear. Her basement-level emporium is chock-a-block with teeny kilts, lamé, marabou, pleather, and vinyl, as well as wigs in every color, and stiletto heels in some very large sizes. ⊠ *382 West Broadway, between Spring and Broome Sts., SoHo* ☎ *212/966–4066* Ⓜ *Subway: C, E to Spring St.*

Paul Frank. The flat visage of Julius the monkey, the original Paul Frank character, plasters vinyl wallets, flannel PJs, skateboards, and, of course, T-shirts. Also look for tees evoking such formative elements of '80s youth as corn dogs and break dancing. ⊠ *195 Mulberry St., at Kenmare St., NoLita* ☎ *212/965–5079* Ⓜ *Subway: 6 to Spring St.*

Phat Farm/Baby Phat. Hip-hop impresario Russell Simmons's logo-heavy parkas, sweatshirts, and oversize polos and jeans have remained consistently popular among New York funk-soul brothers. Wife Kimora Lee's Baby Phat womenswear line, which is heavy on body-hugging jeans and tops, shares the same space. ⊠ *129 Prince St., between West Broadway and Wooster St., SoHo* ☎ *212/533–7428* Ⓜ *Subway: R, W to Prince St.*

Polo/Ralph Lauren. One of New York's most distinctive shopping experiences, Lauren's flagship store is in the turn-of-the-20th-century Rhinelander mansion. Clothes range from summer-in-the-Hamptons madras to exquisite silk gowns and Purple Label men's suits. **Polo Sport** (⊠ *888 Madison Ave., at 72nd St., Upper East Side* ☎ *212/434–8000* Ⓜ *Subway: 6 to 68th St./Hunter College* ⊠ *381 West Broadway, between Spring and Broome Sts., SoHo* ☎ *212/625–1660* Ⓜ *Subway: R, W to Prince St.*) carries casual clothes and sports gear, from puffy anoraks to wick-away tanks. The Village branch of **Ralph Lauren** (✉ 380 Bleecker St., at Perry St., Greenwich Village ☎ 212/645–5513 Ⓜ Subway: 1, 9 to Christopher St./Sheridan Sq.), on the other hand, is a small, tightly packed boutique. It stocks items for women (and dogs) only, pulling together sequin-slicked skirts, sturdy cable knits and tweeds, and the odd bit of vintage. ✉ *867 Madison Ave., at E. 72nd St., Upper East Side* ☎ *212/606–2100* Ⓜ *Subway: 6 to 68th St./Hunter College.*

Prada. Prada's gossamer silks, slick black suits, and luxe shoes and leather goods are among the all-time great Italian fashion coups. The uptown stores pulse with pale "verdolino" green walls (remember this if you start questioning your skin tone). The 57th Street branch carries just the shoes, bags, and other accessories. The SoHo location, an ultramodern space designed by Rem Koolhaas, incorporates so many technological innovations that it was written up in *Popular Science.* The dressing-room gadgets alone include liquid crystal displays, changeable lighting, and scanners that link you to the store's database. ✉ *724 5th Ave., between W. 56th and W. 57th Sts., Midtown West* ☎ *212/664–0010* Ⓜ *Subway: Q, W to 5th Ave./60th St.* ✉ *45 E. 57th St., between Madison and Park Aves., Midtown East* ☎ *212/308–2332* Ⓜ *Subway: E, V to 5th Ave./53rd St.* ✉ *841 Madison Ave., at E. 70th St., Upper East Side* ☎ *212/327–4200* Ⓜ *Subway: 6 to 68th St./Hunter College* ✉ *575 Broadway, at Prince St., SoHo* ☎ *212/334–8888* Ⓜ *Subway: R, W to Prince St.*

R by 45rpm. Japanese interpretations of Western styles, from pea coats to bandannas, are marked by their attention to detail. Look for hand-stressed denim. ✉ *169 Mercer St., between W. Houston and Prince Sts., SoHo* ☎ *917/237–0045.*

Reiss. The first American outpost of this U.K.-based chain carries chic, casual-but-tailored clothes with beautiful details. Women's blouses and skirts have delicate pleats and contrast-stitched embroidery; halter dresses have swirly, summery prints. Men's slouchy pants are complemented by shrunken blazers, military-cut shirts, and trim leather jackets. The prices are slightly higher than those at similar chain shops (French Connection, Club Monaco). ✉ *387 West Broadway, between Spring and Broome Sts. SoHo* ☎ *212/925–5707* Ⓜ *Subway: R, W to Prince St.*

Roberto Cavalli. Rock-star style (at rock-star prices) delivers denim decked with fur, feathers, prints, even shredded silk overlays. ✉ *711 Madison Ave., at E. 63rd St., Upper East Side* ☎ *212/755–7722* Ⓜ *Subway: N, R, W to 5th Ave./59th St.*

Seize sur Vingt. In bringing a contemporary sensibility to custom tailoring, this store realized an ideal fusion. Brighten a men's wool suit or cotton moleskin flat-front pants with a checked or striped shirt; all can be made to order. Women are also the beneficiaries of their crisp button-downs and single-pleat trousers. ✉ *243 Elizabeth St., between Prince and E. Houston Sts., NoLita* ☎ *212/343–0476* Ⓜ *Subway: R, W to Prince St.*

Seven New York. Björk-worthy levels of experimental fashion are achieved at this boutique; check out the designs of such cutting-edge designers as Imitation of Christ, Cosmic Wonder, Preen, and Obesity and Speed. ✉ *180 Orchard St., between E. Houston and Stanton Sts., Lower East Side* ☎ *646/654–0156* Ⓜ *Subway: F, V to 2nd Ave.*

Shanghai Tang. Slide into a loose crepe de chine or velvet Tang jacket, silk pajamas, or a form-fitting cheongsam dress; these modern adaptations of Chinese styles come in soft colors or eye-popping lime and fuschia. ✉ *714 Madison Ave., between E. 63rd and E. 64th Sts., Upper East Side* ☎ *212/888–0111* Ⓜ *Subway: N, R, W to 5th Ave./59th St.*

Thomas Pink. Impeccably tailored shirts are the hallmark of this Jermyn Street transplant. The majority of the men's and women's styles—which come in a candy-shop array of stripes, tattersall checks, and ginghams—have spread collars and French cuffs, but there are also more casual buttondowns for men and three-quarter-sleeve blouses for women. ✉ *520 Madison Ave., at E. 53rd St., Midtown East* ☎ *212/838–1928* Ⓜ *Subway: N, R, W to 5th Ave./59th St.* ✉ *1155 6th Ave., at E. 44th St., Midtown East* ☎ *212/840–9663* Ⓜ *Subway: B, D, F, V to 42nd St.* ✉ *10 Columbus Circle, at W. 59th St., Midtown West* ☎ *212/823–9650* Ⓜ *Subway: 1, 9, A, C, B, D to Columbus Circle.*

Tommy Hilfiger. With their patriotic red, white, and blue logos, bright colors and casual, outdoorsy look, these clothes have a recognizably American style. This store takes a more upscale tack with tailored suits for men, smart sweater sets and pencil skirts for women, and broadcloth shirts for both. ✉ *372 West Broadway, at Broome St., SoHo* ☎ *917/237–0774* Ⓜ *Subway: R, W to Prince St.*

Trash and Vaudeville. Goths, punks, and other nightcrawlers have favored this standby for years. You might hear the Ramones on the sound system while you browse through bondage-inspired pants and skirts covered in straps, buckles, and other hardware; striped stovepipe pants; vinyl corsets; and crinolines painted with flames. ✉ *4 St. Marks Pl., between 2nd and 3rd Aves., East Village* ☎ *212/982–3590* Ⓜ *Subway: 6 to Astor Pl.*

Triple 5 Soul. Headquarters for urban, hip-hop gear, this Brooklyn-based label's shop has graffiti murals on the walls and experimental beats playing on the stereo. The label's signature cargo pants, parkas, shoulder bags, and hoodies—many incorporating camo and high-tech fabrics—fill the racks. ✉ *290 Lafayette St., between Prince and Houston Sts., Greenwich Village* ☎ *212/431–2404* Ⓜ *Subway: B, D, F, V to Broadway–Lafayette St.*

TSE. The soft delicacy of the cashmere here doesn't stop at the fabric; TSE's designs are hopelessly refined. ✉ *827 Madison Ave., at E. 69th St., Upper East Side* ☎ *212/472–7790* Ⓜ *Subway: 6 to 68th St./Hunter College.*

Valentino. The mix here is at once audacious and beautifully cut; the fur or feather trimmings, low necklines, and opulent fabrics are about as close as you can get to celluloid glamour. No one does a better red. ✉ *747 Madison Ave., at E. 65th St., Upper East Side* ☎ *212/772–6969* Ⓜ *Subway: 6 to 68th St./Hunter College.*

Yohji Yamamoto. Although almost entirely in black and white, these clothes aren't as severe as they seem. Whimsical details, like giant polka dots, shirts with drawstring hems, and slouchy, rolled trouser cuffs, add a dash of levity. ✉ *103 Grand St., at Mercer St., SoHo* ☎ *212/966–9066* Ⓜ *Subway: J, M, N, Q, R, W, Z, 6 to Canal St.*

Yves Saint Laurent Rive Gauche. Tom Ford's successor, Stephano Pilati, is lightening up the fabled French house; think seduction instead of sexpot, with ruffles, wide belts, and safari-style jackets. ✉ *855 Madison*

Ave., between E. 70th and E. 71st Sts., Upper East Side ☎ *212/988-3821* Ⓜ *Subway: 6 to 68th St./Hunter College* ✉ *3 E. 57th St., between 5th and Madison Aves., Midtown East* ☎ *212/980-2970* Ⓜ *Subway: N, R, W to 5th Ave./59th St.*

Men's Clothing

Agnès b. Homme. This French designer's love for the movies makes it easy to come out looking a little Godard around the edges. Turtleneck sweaters, lean black suits, and black leather porkpie hats demand the sangfroid of Belmondo. ✉ *79 Greene St., between Broome and Spring Sts., SoHo* ☎ *212/925-4339* Ⓜ *Subway: 6 to Spring St.*

Duncan Quinn. Shooting for nothing less than "sartorial splendor," this designer provides everything from chalkstripe suits to cuff links in a shop not much bigger than its silk pocket squares. Only a few of each style of shirt are made, so the odds are slim that you can see someone else in your blue, violet, or orange button-down with contrast-color undercuffs. ✉ *8 Spring St., between Elizabeth and Bowery Sts., NoLita* ☎ *212/226-7030* Ⓜ *Subway: 6 to Spring St.*

Dunhill. Corporate brass come here for finely tailored clothing, both ready-made and custom-ordered, and smoking accessories; the walk-in humidor upstairs stores top-quality tobacco and cigars. ✉ *711 5th Ave., between E. 56th and E. 55th Sts., Midtown East* ☎ *212/753-9292* Ⓜ *Subway: F to 57th St.*

John Varvatos. After years with Calvin Klein and Ralph Lauren, Varvatos set off on his own and quickly racked up design awards. There's a casual insouciance in his soft-shouldered, unconstructed suits, cotton crewneck shirts, and jeans in leather, velvet, or denim. ✉ *149 Mercer St., between W. Houston and Prince Sts., SoHo* ☎ *212/965-0700* Ⓜ *Subway: R, W to Prince St.*

Paul Smith. Dark mahogany Victorian cases complement the dandyish British styles they hold. Embroidered vests, brightly striped socks, scarves, and shirts, and tongue-in-cheek cuff links leaven the classic, dark, double-back-vent suits. Ashtrays, photography books, cordial glasses, and other such oddments beg for a toff bachelor pad. ✉ *108 5th Ave., at E. 16th St., Flatiron District* ☎ *212/627-9770* Ⓜ *Subway: F, V to 14th St.*

Sean. These snug shops carry low-key, well-priced, and comfortable apparel from France—wool and cotton painter's coats, very-narrow-wale corduroy pants, and a respectable collection of suits and dress shirts. ✉ *132 Thompson St., between W. Houston and Prince Sts., SoHo* ☎ *212/598-5980* Ⓜ *Subway: R, W to Prince St.* ✉ *224 Columbus Ave., between W. 70th and W. 71st Sts., Upper West Side* ☎ *212/769-1489* Ⓜ *Subway: B, C to 72nd St.*

Vilebrequin. Allow St-Tropez to influence your swimsuit; these striped, floral, and solid-color French-made trunks come in sunny hues. Waterproof pocket inserts keep your essentials safe from beachcombers. Many styles come in boys' sizes, too. ✉ *1070 Madison Ave., at E. 81st St., Upper East Side* ☎ *212/650-0353* Ⓜ *Subway: 6 to 77th St.* ✉ *436 West Broadway, between Prince and Spring Sts., SoHo* ☎ *212/431-0673* Ⓜ *Subway: R, W to Prince St.*

Vintage & Resale Clothing

In addition to the selections below, *see* Lyell *in* Women's Clothing, *below.*

Allan & Suzi. The proprietors, whom you'll no doubt find behind the counter, are the godfather and -mother of fashion collecting. Their wacky shop preserves 1980s shoulder pads and 1940s gowns for posterity (or sale). ✉ *416 Amsterdam Ave., between W. 79th and W. 80th Sts., Upper West Side* ☎ *212/724–7445* Ⓜ *Subway: 1, 2, 3, 9 to 72nd St.*

Cheap Jack's. Three floors are jammed with almost everything you could wish for: track suits, bomber jackets, early 1980s madras shirts, old prom dresses, and fur-trimmed wool ladies' suits with the eau-de-mothball stamp of authenticity. The name's not quite accurate, though—some of the stuff here is pricey. ✉ *841 Broadway, between E. 13th and E. 14th Sts., Greenwich Village* ☎ *212/995–0403* Ⓜ *Subway: L, N, Q, R, W, 4, 5, 6 to 14th St./Union Sq.*

Fisch for the Hip. These resale racks are evenly split between men's and women's clothes, with a well-edited selection throughout. You could find last season's Catherine Malandrino chiffon dress with its tags intact, or a Zegna jacket for under $300. Look for multiple discounts on such wardrobe warhorses as little black dresses. ✉ *153 W. 18th St., between 6th and 7th Aves., Chelsea* ☎ *212/633–9053* Ⓜ *Subway: F, V, 1, 2, 3, 9 to 14th St.*

Frock. Models and stylists frequent this tiny shop for vintage womenswear from the 1960s, '70s, and '80s. The store carries pieces from such new-wave, mid-'80s designers as Thierry Mugler, Stephen Sprouse, and Claude Montana, not to mention pumps and lizard clutch purses from Ferragamo, Bruno Magli, and Charles Jourdan. ✉ *148 Orchard St., between Stanton and Rivington Sts., Lower East Side* ☎ *212/594–5380* Ⓜ *Subway: F, J, M, Z to Delancey St./Essex St.*

New York Vintage. No patience to search through the Chelsea flea market? Ransack the racks of womenswear in this narrow space across the way, where the prime picks have been winnowed out for you. The 1930s chiffon blouses, '50s circle skirts, and '60s cocktail dresses are well kept; there's a good selection of handbags and pumps, too. ✉ *117 W. 25th St., between 6th and 7th Aves., Chelsea* ☎ *212/647–1107* Ⓜ *Subway: 1, 9 to 28th St.*

★ **Resurrection.** With original Courrèges, Puccis, and foxy boots, this store is a retro-chic gold mine. It's also responsible for the vintage selection at Henri Bendel's uptown. ✉ *217 Mott St., between Prince and Spring Sts., NoLita* ☎ *212/625–1374* Ⓜ *Subway: 6 to Spring St.*

Screaming Mimi's. Vintage 1960s and 1970s clothes and retro-wear include everything from djellabas to soccer shirts to prom dresses. You can also find a selection huge tinted sunglasses, in case you feel like channeling Yoko Ono or one of the Olsen twins. ✉ *382 Lafayette St., between 4th and Great Jones Sts., East Village* ☎ *212/677–6464* Ⓜ *Subway: F, V to Broadway–Lafayette St.*

What Comes Around Goes Around. Thanks to the staff's sharp eyes, the denim and leather racks here are reliably choice. You can also find such hip-again items as rabbit-fur jackets, decorative belt buckles, and some terrific vintage rock concert T-shirts. If the idea of forking out $100 for an Alice Cooper number pains you, just remember: unlike the copies everyone else is wearing, you'll be sporting the real deal. ⊠ *351 West Broadway, between Grand and Broome Sts., SoHo* ☎ *212/343–9303* Ⓜ *Subway: J, M, N, Q, R, W, Z, 6 to Canal St.*

Women's Clothing

Agnès b. With this quintessentially French line you can look like a Parisienne schoolgirl—in snap-front tops, slender pants, sweet floral prints— or like her chic *maman* in tailored dark suits and leather jackets. ⊠ *103 Greene St., between Prince and Spring Sts., SoHo* ☎ *212/431–4649* Ⓜ *Subway: R, W to Prince St.* ⊠ *13 E. 16th St., between 5th Ave. and Union Sq. W, Flatiron District* ☎ *212/741–2585* Ⓜ *Subway: F, V to 14th St.* ⊠ *1063 Madison Ave., between E. 80th and E. 81st Sts., Upper East Side* ☎ *212/570–9333* Ⓜ *Subway: 6 to 77th St.*

Alexander McQueen. No matter how flouncy McQueen's ensembles become, they retain idiosyncratic, unsettling elements. Delicate, floaty dresses might be cross-hatched with bright-red boning; intricate, brocade skirts and jackets could be juxtaposed with stiff leather corsets. ⊠ *417 W. 14th St., between 9th and 10th Aves., Meatpacking District* ☎ *212/645–1797* Ⓜ *Subway: A, C, E to 14th St.*

Alicia Mugetti. Silks and velvets are layered, softly shaped, and sometimes hand-painted. ⊠ *999 Madison Ave., between E. 77th and E. 78th Sts., Upper East Side* ☎ *212/794–6186* Ⓜ *Subway: 6 to 77th St.*

Anna Sui. The violet-and-black salon, hung with Beardsley prints and alterna-rock posters, is the ideal setting for Sui's bohemian, flapper- and rocker-influenced designs. ⊠ *113 Greene St., between Prince and Spring Sts., SoHo* ☎ *212/941–8406* Ⓜ *Subway: R, W to Prince St.*

Anne Fontaine. The white blouses here might make you swear off plain oxford shirts forever. Rows of snowy tops, most in cotton poplin or organdy, are jazzed up with lacings, embroidery, or ruching. Some shirts are executed in black, and a few warm-weather choices come in watercolory floral prints. ⊠ *93 Greene St., between Prince and Spring Sts., SoHo* ☎ *212/343–3154* Ⓜ *Subway: R, W to Prince St.* ⊠ *687 Madison Ave., between E. 62nd and E. 61st Sts., Upper East Side* ☎ *212/688–4362* Ⓜ *Subway: N, R, 4, 5, 6 to 59th St.*

Balenciaga. Nicolas Ghesquière, a recent *amour fou* in the fashion world, took a page from the neighboring galleries for the first U.S. store. His clothing's not always the most wearable, but always stimulating. You might luck onto a reissue from the (Cristobal) Balenciaga archives, made up in modern fabrics. ⊠ *54 W. 22nd St., between 10th and 11th Aves., Chelsea* ☎ *212/206–0872* Ⓜ *Subway: C, E to 23rd St.*

Barbara Bui. Though these designs have a youthful, slightly trendy edge—skinny pants are made for tucking into boots; draped blouses and safari-style jackets hang close to the body—their elegance and soft lines flatter women of all ages. ⊠ *115–117 Wooster St., between Prince and Spring Sts., SoHo* ☎ *212/625–1938* Ⓜ *Subway: R, W to Prince St.*

BCBG. If flirtation's your sport, you'll find your sportswear here: fluttering skirts, beaded camisoles, chiffon dresses, and leather pants fill the racks. The accessories section has satin evening clutches and strappy sandals. ⊠ *120 Wooster St., between Prince and Spring Sts., SoHo* ☎ *212/625–2723* Ⓜ *Subway: R, W to Prince St.* ⊠ *770 Madison Ave., at E.*

66th St., Upper East Side ☎ *212/717–4225* Ⓜ *Subway: 6 to 68th St./Hunter College.*

Betsey Johnson. The SoHo store departs from the traditional (if such a word can be applied) hot-pink interior; instead its walls are sunny yellow with painted roses, and there's a bordello-red lounge area in back. Besides the quirkily printed dresses, available in all stores, there's a slinky upscale line. This is not the place for natural fibers—it's ruled by rayon, stretch, and the occasional faux fur. ✉ *138 Wooster St., between Prince and W. Houston Sts., SoHo* ☎ *212/995–5048* Ⓜ *Subway: R, W to Prince St.* ✉ *251 E. 60th St., between 2nd and 3rd Aves., Upper East Side* ☎ *212/319–7699* Ⓜ *Subway: N, R, W, 4, 5, 6 to 59th St./Lexington Ave.* ✉ *248 Columbus Ave., between W. 71st and W. 72nd Sts., Upper West Side* ☎ *212/362–3364* Ⓜ *Subway: 1, 2, 3, 9 to 72nd St.* ✉ *1060 Madison Ave., between E. 80th and E. 81st Sts., Upper East Side* ☎ *212/734–1257* Ⓜ *Subway: 6 to 77th St.*

Bond 07. The clothing by edgy designers might draw you into this store, but the accessories will keep you browsing for an hour: Selima two-tone glasses (with prescription lenses if you need them), inventive handbags, leopard-print cowboy hats, gloves, and even Jean Paul Gaultier striped umbrellas are all here. ✉ *7 Bond St., between Lafayette St. and Broadway, East Village* ☎ *212/677–8487* Ⓜ *Subway: 6 to Astor Pl.*

Calypso. Spring for something with a tropical vibe, like a sweeping, ruffled skirt in guava-color silk, an embroidered kurta-style top, or a fringed shawl. The jewelry offshoot at 252 Mott Street can doll you up in equally colorful semiprecious stones or shells. Search out a deal at the 405 Broome Street outlet branch or troll the vintage next door at 407. ✉ *424 Broome St., at Crosby St., SoHo* ☎ *212/274–0449* Ⓜ *Subway: 6 to Spring St.* ✉ *280 Mott St., between E. Houston and Prince Sts., NoLita* ☎ *212/965–0990* Ⓜ *Subway: 6 to Bleecker St.* ✉ *935 Madison Ave., at E. 74th St., Upper East Side* ☎ *212/535–4100* Ⓜ *Subway: 6 to 77th St.* ✉ *Bijoux, 252 Mott St., between Prince and E. Houston Sts., NoLita* ☎ *212/334–9730* Ⓜ *Subway: R, W to Prince St.* ✉ *Outlet, 405 Broome St., between Lafayette and Centre Sts., NoLita* ☎ *212/343–0450* Ⓜ *Subway: 6 to Spring St.* ✉ *Vintage, 407 Broome St., between Lafayette and Centre Sts., NoLita* ☎ *212/941–9700* Ⓜ *Subway: 6 to Spring St.*

Carolina Herrera. This couture deserves a truly outstanding occasion; the beading and sequinning work are stunning. Expect anything from demure, shimmering bands of decoration to knockout swaths of beaded lace. ✉ *954 Madison Ave., at E. 75th St., Upper East Side* ☎ *212/249–6552* Ⓜ *Subway: 6 to 77th St.*

Catherine Malandrino. Designs here evoke the flapper-era: frothy chiffon dresses with embroidered empire waists, beaded necklines, and tiny matching fur stoles let you pretend you're Daisy Buchanan. ✉ *468 Broome St., at Greene St., SoHo* ☎ *212/925–6765* Ⓜ *Subway: 6 to Spring St.* ✉ *652 Hudson St., Meatpacking District* ☎ *212/929–8710* Ⓜ *Subway: A, C, E to 14th St.*

Chanel. The midtown flagship has often been compared to a Chanel suit—slim, elegant, and timeless. Inside wait the famed suits themselves, along with other pillars of Chanel style: chic little black dresses and evening gowns, chain-handled bags, and yards of pearls. Frédéric Fekkai's five-story, Provence-saturated salon perches upstairs. Downtown's branch concentrates on more contemporary forays, including ski gear, while Madison's boutique is dedicated to shoes, handbags, and other accessories. ⊠ *139 Spring St., at Wooster St., SoHo* ☎ *212/334–0055* Ⓜ *Subway: C, E to Spring St.* ⊠ *15 E. 57th St., between 5th and Madison Aves., Midtown East* ☎ *212/355–5050* Ⓜ *Subway: N, R, W to 5th Ave./59th St.* ⊠ *737 Madison Ave., at E. 64th St., Upper East Side* ☎ *212/535–5505* Ⓜ *Subway: 6 to 68th St./Hunter College.*

★ **Charles Nolan.** Formerly an exclusive designer for Saks, Nolan opened this shop in winter of 2005. The craftsmanship of the pieces here is impeccable: colorful quilted jackets have decorative stitching; body-skimming skirts are beautifully cut; and silken trousers have a creamy drape. There are also a few whimsical styles, such as the black wool coat covered in Puli-like cords. ⊠ *30 Gansevoort St., at Hudson St., Meatpacking District* ☎ *212/924–4888* Ⓜ *Subway: A, C, E to 14th St.*

Chloé. Phoebe Philo's devil-may-care baggy trousers, hobo bags, and clingy chiffon numbers may induce you to roll out some Philo dough. ⊠ *850 Madison Ave., at E. 70th St., Upper East Side* ☎ *212/717–8220* Ⓜ *Subway: 6 to 68th St./Hunter College.*

Cynthia Rowley. As one half of the *Swell* team, you can expect this designer to be a party-outfit pro. She delivers with such flirty picks as bow-top pumps, swingy, swirly halter dresses with heart-shape appliqués, and handbags with small inset mirrors, ideal for checking your lipstick. The *Swell* books are on hand too, natch. ⊠ *376 Bleecker St., between Charles and Perry, Greenwich Village* ☎ *212/242–3803* Ⓜ *Subway: 1, 9 to Christopher St./Sheridan Sq.*

Destination. The model pigs guarding this store fit right in with the Meatpacking District. Inside are clothes and accessories (some for men, too) that marry handmade and sophisticated styles. Heike Javick fitted tweed skirts hang next to Nicholas K striped sweaters, with jeans made from pieced-together denim flowers. Up front, there's a collection of dramatic hats and scarves. ⊠ *32–36 Little West 12th St., between Greenwich and Washington Sts., Meatpacking District* ☎ *212/727–2031* Ⓜ *Subway: 1, 9 to Christopher St./Sheridan Sq.*

Emanuel Ungaro. The vibrant shocking pink of the stairway will keep you alert as you browse through swell ladies-who-lunch daytime suits and grande dame, sometimes bead-encrusted, evening wear. ⊠ *792 Madison Ave., at E. 67th St., Upper East Side* ☎ *212/249–4090* Ⓜ *Subway: 6 to 68th St./Hunter College.*

Erica Tanov. Full-skirt slip dresses in soft florals, airy tunics, and ticking-stripe tops balance ease and polish. The designer's also known for her tissue-thin cotton sleepwear and children's clothes. ⊠ *204 Elizabeth St., between Prince and Spring Sts., NoLita* ☎ *212/334–8020* Ⓜ *Subway: 6 to Spring St.*

Herve Leger. Shimmy into something clingy by the man who brought the world the "bandage" dress. Even when you're covered neck to wrists, these looks manage to be come-hither. ⊠ *744 Madison Ave., between E. 64th and E. 65th Sts., Upper East Side* ☎ *212/794–7008* Ⓜ *Subway: 6 to 68th St./Hunter College.*

Intermix. Aimed at those who like to pair denim with silk, chiffon, or just plain revealing tops, this boutique gathers together a solid mid- to high-range lineup, plus a just-enough layout of shoes and accessories. ⊠ *125 5th Ave., between E. 19th and E. 20th Sts., Flatiron District* ☎ *212/533–9720* Ⓜ *Subway: R, W to 23rd St.* ⊠ *210 Columbus Ave., between W. 69th and W. 70th Sts., Upper West Side* ☎ *212/769–9116* Ⓜ *Subway: 1, 2, 3, 9 to 72nd St.* ⊠ *1003 Madison Ave., between E. 77th and E. 78th Sts., Upper East Side* ☎ *212/249–7858* Ⓜ *Subway: 6 to 77th St.*

★ **Kirna Zabête.** A heavy-hitting lineup of cachet designers—Balenciaga, Viktor & Rolf, Behnaz Sarafour, Clements Ribiero—is managed with an exceptionally cheerful flair. Step downstairs for Burberry dog coats and e.vil tees to announce your true colors ("Little Miss Drama"). ⊠ *96 Greene St., between Spring and Prince Sts., SoHo* ☎ *212/941–9656* Ⓜ *Subway: R, W to Prince St.*

Liz Lange Maternity. By using lots of stretch fabrics, even stretch leather, this designer can conjure up maternity versions of the latest trends. ⊠ *958 Madison Ave., between E. 75th and E. 76th Sts., Upper East Side* ☎ *212/879–2191* Ⓜ *Subway: 6 to 77th St.*

Lyell. True vintage meets vintage-inspired. From the enticing few racks, you might slip into a jet-beaded top (old) or a draped silk dress (new) that would do well for dancing to Benny Goodman. Don't miss the vintage shoe selection, ranged in rows on the floor. ⊠ *173 Elizabeth St., between Spring and Kenmare Sts., NoLita* ☎ *212/966–8484* Ⓜ *Subway: 6 to Spring St.*

Malia Mills. Fit fanatics have met their match here. Bikini tops and bottoms are sold separately: halters, bandeaus, and triangle tops, boy-cut, side-tie, and low-ride bottoms, in any combination; a few one-pieces are here, too. If you've got a warm-weather honeymoon coming up, you could go for a bikini with "Just Married" across your bum. ⊠ *199 Mulberry St., between Spring and Kenmare Sts., NoLita* ☎ *212/625–2311* Ⓜ *Subway: 6 to Spring St.* ⊠ *1031 Lexington Ave., at E. 74th St., Upper East Side* ☎ *212/517–7485* Ⓜ *Subway: 6 to E. 77th St.*

Marina Rinaldi. These plus-size tailored suits, hip-slung belts, and sweeping coats know just how to flatter. ⊠ *800 Madison Ave., between E. 67th and E. 68th Sts., Upper East Side* ☎ *212/734–4333* Ⓜ *Subway: 6 to 68th St./Hunter College.*

Marni. Weaving among the suspended garments in Marni's first U.S. store, you may fall prey to a hemp-cloth duster jacket, brightly striped cotton trousers, or a coyly creased floral blouse. ⊠ *161 Mercer St., between W. Houston and Prince Sts., SoHo* ☎ *212/343–3912.*

Max Mara. Think subtle colors and plush fabrics—straight skirts in cashmere or heathered wool, tuxedo-style evening jackets, and several choices of wool and cashmere camel overcoats. ⊠ *813 Madison Ave., at E. 68th St., Upper East Side* ☎ *212/879–6100* Ⓜ *Subway: 6 to 68th St./Hunter College* ⊠ *450 West Broadway, between Prince and Spring Sts., SoHo* ☎ *212/674–1817* Ⓜ *Subway: C, E to Spring St.*

Mayle. This boutique basks in the ineffable vapor of cool. Designer Jane Mayle whips up close-fitting knit tops, lanky pants, and retro-inflected dresses that always look effortless, never overdone. ⊠ *242 Elizabeth St., between E. Houston and Prince Sts., NoLita* ☎ *212/625–0406* Ⓜ *Subway: 6 to Bleecker St.*

Michael Kors. In his deft reworkings of American classics, Kors gives sportswear the luxury treatment, as with sorbet-color cashmere pullovers. A haute-hippie element is creeping in, too, with keyhole necks, hobo bags, and floppy hats. ☒ *974 Madison Ave., at E. 76th St., Upper East Side* ☎ *212/452–4685* Ⓜ *Subway: 6 to 77th St.*

Miu Miu. Prada front woman Miuccia Prada established a secondary line (bearing her childhood nickname, Miu Miu) to showcase her more experimental ideas. Look for Prada-esque styles in more daring colors and cuts, such as orange-and-brown short-shorts, lurex sweaters, brocade coats in pink and scarlet, and aqua wedge shoes. ☒ *100 Prince St., between Mercer and Greene Sts., SoHo* ☎ *212/334–5156* Ⓜ *Subway: R, W to Prince St.* ☒ *831 Madison Ave., at E. 69th St., Upper East Side* ☎ *212/249–9660* Ⓜ *Subway: 6 to 68th St./Hunter College.*

Morgane Le Fay. The clothes here used to have a sort of billowy, Stevie Nicks quality, but though they're still Renaissance-inspired, the designs are more streamlined. Silk organza gowns have empire waists and crinkly skirts; fitted velvet jackets have covered buttons. ☒ *746 Madison Ave., between E. 64th and E. 65th Sts., Upper East Side* ☎ *212/879–9700* Ⓜ *Subway: 6 to 68th St./Hunter College* ☒ *67 Wooster St., between Broome and Spring Sts., SoHo* ☎ *212/219–7672* Ⓜ *Subway: C, E to Spring St.*

Nanette Lepore. "Girly" may well be the description that comes to mind as you browse through this cheerful shop; skirts are pleated and adorned with bows, jackets are enhanced by embroidery and floral appliqués; fur shrugs have tiny sleeves. ☒ *423 Broome St., between Lafayette and Crosby Sts., NoLita* ☎ *212/219–8265* Ⓜ *Subway: 6 to Spring St.*

O.M.O. Norma Kamali. A fashion fixture from the 1980s has a newly modern, though still '80s-influenced, line. Her luminously white store carries bold black-and-white-patterned bathing suits, slinky separates in velvet and jersey, and poofy "sleeping bag coats." You can also choose from a selection of skincare products and fragrances. ☒ *11 W. 56th St., between 5th and 6th Aves., Midtown West* ☎ *212/957–9797* Ⓜ *Subway: E, V to 5th Ave./53rd St.*

Oscar de la Renta. The ladylike yet lighthearted runway designs of this upper-crust favorite got their first U.S. store here. Skirts swing, ruffles billow, embroidery brightens up tweed, and even a tennis dress looks like something you could go dancing in. ☒ *772 Madison Ave., at E. 66th St., Upper East Side* ☎ *212/288–5810* Ⓜ *Subway: 6 to E. 68th St.*

Philosophy di Alberta Ferretti. The designer's eye for delicate detailing is evident in the perforated hemlines, embroidered stitching, and sprinklings of beads across gauzy fabrics or soft knits. ☒ *452 West Broadway, between W. Houston and Prince Sts., SoHo* ☎ *212/460–5500* Ⓜ *Subway: F, V to Broadway–Lafayette St.*

Rebecca Taylor. Follow the dandelion fluff painted on the walls around racks of lace-overlay dresses and silk-piped trousers. Appliqués and embroideries add fillips of craftiness. ☒ *260 Mott St., between Prince and Spring Sts., NoLita* ☎ *212/966–0406* Ⓜ *Subway: 6 to Spring St.*

Sonia Rykiel. Paris's "queen of knitwear" sets off strong colors such as fuchsia or orange with, *naturellement,* black. ☒ *849 Madison Ave., between E. 70th and E. 71st Sts., Upper East Side* ☎ *212/396–3060* Ⓜ *Subway: 6 to 68th St./Hunter College.*

Stella McCartney. A devout vegetarian setting up shop in the Meatpacking District may seem odd, but it's further proof that chic trumps many other considerations. You could put together an outfit of head-to-toe satin or chiffon, but it's more in keeping to mix it with shredded denim or a pair of knee-high ultrasuede cowboy boots (since leather is verboten, shoes and accessories come in satin, canvas, and synthetics). The dressing rooms are so beautiful you might just want to move in. ✉ *429 W. 14th St., at Washington St., Meatpacking District* ☎ *212/255–1556* Ⓜ *Subway: A, C, E to 14th St.*

Tracy Feith. *Mr.* Feith makes the most of feminine curves with vibrant dresses and separates. Necklines on tees scoop wide and low, skirts flirt with flounces and yokes, and the sexy printed silk dresses are light as a feather. Peer into the cases for a bauble or two. ✉ *209 Mulberry St., between Spring and Kenmare Sts., NoLita* ☎ *212/334–3097* Ⓜ *Subway: 6 to Spring St.*

TG-170. Chiffon Jill Stuart camisoles, pea coats, and a terrific assortment of one-of-a-kind Swiss Freitag messenger bags (made from colorful reused trucking tarps) can be found at this downtown spot. ✉ *170 Ludlow St., between E. Houston and Stanton Sts., Lower East Side* ☎ *212/995–8660* Ⓜ *Subway: F, J, M, Z to Delancey St./Essex St.*

Tory by TRB. Bright orange lacquer zings through this space, which, in a reversal of the usual flow, brings uptown downtown. Orange joins navy, flamingo pink, and mossy green on espadrilles, printed cotton blouses, and zip-backed cashmere turtlenecks. ✉ *257 Elizabeth St., between E. Houston and Prince Sts., NoLita* ☎ *212/334–3000* Ⓜ *Subway: R, W to Prince St.*

Vera Wang. The made-to-order bridal and evening wear glows with satin, beading, and embroidery. Periodic pret-a-porter sales offer the dresses for a (relative) song. ✉ *991 Madison Ave., at E. 77th St., Upper East Side* ☎ *212/628–3400* Ⓜ *Subway: 6 to 77th St.*

Vivienne Tam. Tam is known for her playful "China chic" take on familiar Asian images. Cold-weather creations in emerald-and-ruby–color silk are embroidered with dragons and flowers; the warm weather clothes are pale and floaty. ✉ *99 Greene St., between Prince and Spring Sts., SoHo* ☎ *212/966–2398* Ⓜ *Subway: R, W to Prince St.*

Home Decor

FodorsChoice ★ **ABC Carpet & Home.** ABC seems to cover most of the furnishings alphabet; over several floors it encompasses everything from rustic furniture to 19th-century repros, refinished Chinese chests and Vitra chairs, not to mention that loose category "country French." The ground floor teems with a treasure-attic's worth of accessories. ✉ *888 Broadway, at E. 19th St., Flatiron District* ☎ *212/473–3000* Ⓜ *Subway: L, N, Q, R, W, 4, 5, 6 to 14th St./Union Sq.*

Armani Casa. In keeping with the Armani aesthetic, these minimalist furniture and homewares have a subdued color scheme (cream, black, a crimson accent here and there). You might find lacquered ebony-stain boxes, square-cut porcelain bowls and plates, or silky linens and pillows. ✉ *97 Greene St., between Prince and Spring Sts., SoHo* ☎ *212/334–1271* Ⓜ *Subway: R, W to Prince St.*

Avventura. Glory in Italian design in all its streamlined beauty here. Tabletop items and mouth-blown glass accessories are all stunning. ✉ *463 Amsterdam Ave., at W. 82nd St., Upper West Side* 🖀 *212/769–2510* Ⓜ *Subway: 1, 9 to 86th St.*

★ **Bellora.** Fine linens for bath and bedroom have been the trademark of this Italian family business since the late 19th century. High-thread-count sheets, duvets, and pillowcases come in soothing color combinations: beachy stripes in pale blue and cream; springtime checks in celadon and rose. There are baffled cotton towels and robes, too, and a line of linen sprays and body lotions to keep everything (including you) smelling lovely. ✉ *156 Wooster St., at W. Houston St., SoHo* 🖀 *212/228–6651* Ⓜ *Subway: R, W to Prince St.; B, D, F, V to Broadway–Lafayette.*

Bodum. "Give Up Bad Design For Good" is the motto at this Danish kitchen- and homewares chain, and the huge selection of affordable coffeemakers, kettles, pots, and dishes, all in brushed steel, glass, and Pyrex, make it seem attainable. The front of the huge store space has a café; the back has table linens and natty office supplies. ✉ *413–415 W. 14th St., between 9th and 10th Aves., Meatpacking District* 🖀 *212/367–9125* Ⓜ *Subway: A, C, E to 14th St.*

Carol Boyes. Whimsical metal tableware fills the shop of this South African designer. Cutlery, vases, dishes, and candlesticks made from pewter, aluminum, or stainless steel take the shapes of snailshell whorls or supine human bodies. Beaded South African goods like purses, napkin rings, and figurines add splashes of color. ✉ *118 Prince St., between Greene and Wooster Sts., SoHo* 🖀 *212/334–3556* Ⓜ *Subway: R, W to Prince St.*

Cath Kidston. Unflaggingly cheery, this British import pushes the retro red, white, and blue for all kinds of houseware essentials and impulses. Pink-and-crimson roses bloom on tote bags, tablecloths, and chintz cushions; polka-dots spatter powder blue and cherry egg cups, bedding, and dog bowls. ✉ *201 Mulberry St., between Spring and Kenmare Sts., NoLita* 🖀 *212/343–0223* Ⓜ *Subway: 6 to Spring St.*

c.i.t.e. Plastic bubble chairs, wavy-looking Holmegaard glassware, bulbous chrome table lamps, and dishes in bright-orange or lime-green enamel are among the fun finds here. ✉ *120 Wooster St., between Prince and Spring Sts., SoHo* 🖀 *212/431–7272* Ⓜ *Subway: R, W to Prince St.*

Clio. Take a shortcut to find the accessories you've seen in the shelter mags. This boutique sets its table with delicate Czech glass vases, bone china with raised dots, and colorful handblown glass bottles. ✉ *92 Thompson St., between Prince and Spring Sts., SoHo* 🖀 *212/966–8991* Ⓜ *Subway: C, E to Spring St.*

Design Within Reach. "An interesting plainness is the most difficult and precious thing to achieve" reads one of the quotes discreetly placed on the walls here. You can get a lot closer to Mies van der Rohe's ideal with these tasteful mid-20th century pieces, such as Noguchi's paper column lamps and Le Corbusier's steel-frame sofa, plus contemporary furnishings in the same spirit, such as Jesús Gasca's beech "globus" chair. ✉ *408 W. 14th St., at 9th Ave., Meatpacking District* 🖀 *212/242–9449* Ⓜ *Subway: A, C, E to 14th St.* ✉ *142 Wooster St., between Prince and W. Houston Sts., SoHo* 🖀 *212/475–0001* Ⓜ *Subway: F, V to Broadway–Lafayette* ✉ *27 E. 62nd St., between Park and Lexington*

Aves., Upper East Side ☎ *212/888–4539* Ⓜ *Subway: N, R, W, 4, 5, 6 to 59th St./Lexington Ave.* ✉ *341 Columbus Ave., at W. 76th St., Upper West Side* ☎ *212/799–5900* Ⓜ *Subway: 1, 2, 3, 9 to 72nd St.*

★ **De Vera.** The objets d'art and jewelry here all seem to have stories behind them. Many are antique and hint of colonial travels: Indian carvings, Japanese lacquer boxes, 19th-century British garnet earrings. Others exemplify modern forms of traditional workmanship, such as the Murano glass vases or incredibly lifelike glass insects. ✉ *1 Crosby St., at Howard St., SoHo* ☎ *212/625–0838* Ⓜ *Subway: N, R, Q, W, 6 to Canal St.*

Fishs Eddy. The dishes, china, and glassware for resale here come from all walks of crockery life—corporate dining rooms, failed restaurants, etc. New wares often look retro, such as a service with a ticker-tape border, and there are lots of oddball pieces such as finger bowls. ✉ *2176 Broadway, at W. 77th St., Upper West Side* ☎ *212/873–8819* Ⓜ *Subway: 1, 9 to 79th St.* ✉ *889 Broadway, at E. 19th St., Flatiron District* ☎ *212/420–9020* Ⓜ *Subway: L, N, Q, R, W, 4, 5, 6 to 14th St./Union Sq.* ✉ *1388 3rd Ave., near E. 79th St., Upper East Side* ☎ *212/737–2844* Ⓜ *Subway: 6 to 77th St.*

Hable Construction. Vivid colors, graphic shapes (stripes, dots, leaves), and a soft nap give these wool felt and cotton-linen pillows all-around warmth. Cotton canvas hats and beach totes come out in spring; appliqued felt stockings are hung up for the holidays. ✉ *230 Elizabeth St., between Prince and E. Houston Sts., NoLita* ☎ *212/343–8555* Ⓜ *Subway: R, W to Prince St.*

Jonathan Adler. Adler gets mid-20th-century modern and Scandinavian styles to lighten up with his striped, striated, or curvy handmade pottery (ranging from a $30 vase to a chunky $400 lamp) as well as the hand-loomed wool pillow covers, rugs, and throws with blunt graphics (stripes, crosses, circles). ✉ *47 Greene St., between Broome and Grand Sts., SoHo* ☎ *212/941–8950* Ⓜ *Subway: N, R, Q, W, 6 to Canal St.*

Maurice Villency. The company may be venerable, but the furniture is strictly modern. The lines cut sharp corners for a boxy sofa and curve for a chaise or ottoman, but they're always uncluttered. This flagship introduces home accessories, too, including kimonos and vases. ✉ *929 3rd Ave., at E. 57th St., Midtown East* ☎ *212/725–4840* Ⓜ *Subway: N, R, W, 4, 5, 6 to 59th St./Lexington Ave.*

Mood Indigo. For a retro rush, this shop lets you drift through Stork Club paraphernalia, Bakelite bangles, novelty salt-and-pepper sets, cobalt-glass martini shakers, and seemingly endless rows of Fiestaware. ✉ *181 Prince St., between Sullivan and Thompson Sts., SoHo* ☎ *212/254–1176* Ⓜ *Subway: R, W to Prince St.*

★ **Moss.** International designers, many of them Italian or Scandinavian, put a fantastic spin on even the most utilitarian objects, which are carefully brought together by Murray Moss at his store–cum–design museum. The latest innovations from Jasper Morrison, Ted Muehling, and Philippe Starck are interspersed with vintage Baccarat crystal and classic chair designs from Frank Gehry. A recent expansion (the new Moss Gallery is next to the original space) has allowed the collection to grow even more. ✉ *146–152 Greene St., between W. Houston and Prince Sts., SoHo* ☎ *212/204–7100* Ⓜ *Subway: R, W to Prince St.*

Mxyplyzyk. Hard to pronounce (*mixy plit sick*) and hard to resist, this is a trove of impulse buys—creative riffs on household standbys such as dishes (here, covered in psychedelic patterns or made from old vinyl LPs), handbags (made to look like boccie balls), and toothbrush holders (shaped like giant teeth). ⊠ *125 Greenwich Ave., at W. 13th St., Greenwich Village* ☎ *212/989–4300* Ⓜ *Subway: A, C, E, L to 14th St./8th Ave.*

Nina Griscom. Another socialite has joined the commercial fray, allowing those of us without a bold-face name to sample the rarified style. The objets d'art, furniture, and jewelry here have an exotic–organic appeal, with natural materials like ivory, sandalwood, and coral turning up as candlesticks, decorative boxes, and chunky cuff bracelets. ⊠ *958 Lexington Ave., at E. 70th St., Upper East Side* ☎ *212/717–7373* Ⓜ *Subway: 6 to E. 68th St.*

★ **Olatz.** The wife and muse of painter Julian, Olatz Schnabel modeled her linen shop on a historic Havana pharmacy after the couple visited Cuba. The black-and white checkerboard floors and mint-green walls breathe a sort of lazy, faded elegance, a spot-on backdrop to her collection of luxurious sheets, blankets, and pajama sets, all of which have sky-high thread counts and are bordered with bold stripes or intricate damask embroidery. ⊠ *43 Clarkson St., between Hudson and Greenwich Sts., Greenwich Village* ☎ *212/255–8627* Ⓜ *Subway: 1, 9 to Houston St.*

Pylones. Even the most utilitarian items get a goofy, colorful makeover from this French company. Toasters and thermoses are coated in stripes or flowers, hairbrushes have pictures of frogs or ladybugs on their backs, and whisks are reimagined as squid. There are plenty of fun gifts for less than $20, such as old-fashioned robot toys and candy-colored boxes. ⊠ *69 Spring St., between Crosby and Lafayette Sts., SoHo* ☎ *212/431–3244* Ⓜ *Subway: 6 to Spring St.*

Restoration Hardware. There's a touch of retro goodness in the wares here, such as bathroom and cabinet fixtures, tools, a smattering of furniture and lamps, and cleaning supplies, plus little buy-mes like bar towels and bookends. ⊠ *935 Broadway, at E. 22nd St., Flatiron District* ☎ *212/260–9479* Ⓜ *Subway: R, W to 23rd St.*

Scully & Scully. Leather footstools in animal shapes and small pieces of reproduction antique furniture exemplify this store's high-WASP style. ⊠ *504 Park Ave., between E. 59th and E. 60th Sts., Upper East Side* ☎ *212/755–2590* Ⓜ *Subway: N, R, W, 4, 5, 6 to 59th St./Lexington Ave.*

Shabby Chic. The linens and upholstered furnishings here all look invitingly soft and faded, like what you'd find in grandmother's beach cottage. Pastel toiles and rose-pattern fabrics also adorn lampshades, nightgowns, and pajamas. ⊠ *83 Wooster St., between Spring and Broome Sts., SoHo* ☎ *212/274–9842* Ⓜ *Subway: 6 to Spring St.*

Steuben. The bowls and vases make for knockout table centerpieces, but if all this shopping gives you sweaty palms, wrap your fingers around a miniature sculpted-animal hand cooler, then head downstairs to view one of the rotating glass exhibitions. ⊠ *667 Madison Ave., between E. 60th and E. 61st Sts., Upper East Side* ☎ *212/752–1441* Ⓜ *Subway: N, R, W to 5th Ave./59th St.*

Terence Conran Shop. The small glass pavilion beneath the 59th Street Bridge caps this British-style monger's vast underground showroom of kitchen and garden implements, fabrics, furniture, and glassware. Even the shower curtains are cool here. ✉ *407 E. 59th St., at 1st Ave., Midtown East* ☎ *212/755–9079* Ⓜ *Subway: N, R, W to 59th St./Lexington Ave.*

Troy. In this spare space, the clean lines of Lucite, leather, cedar, and resin furniture and home accessories may well wreak havoc with your credit card. In addition to the seriously sleek furnishings, you can also find slightly less-imposing items like stone-shape lamps in Murano glass, teakwood serving trays, and creative ceramic tableware. ✉ *138 Greene St., between Prince and W. Houston Sts., SoHo* ☎ *212/941–4777* Ⓜ *Subway: R, W to Prince St.*

Vitra. A newcomer to the retail market but a seasoned vet in the realm of furniture design, Vitra is the source of many of mid-20th-century modernism's most iconic pieces. The S-curved molded plastic Panton chairs, George Nelson's wall clocks and "marshmallow" sofa, the Eames chairs—they're all here. If you can't swing for the real thing, check out the miniature replicas. ✉ *29 9th Ave., at W. 13th St., Meatpacking District* ☎ *212/929–3626* Ⓜ *Subway: A, C, E to 14th St.*

Waterworks. While bathroom fittings may not be on the top of your shopping list, Waterworks is more than a faucet shop. European toiletries, brushed-steel tissue holders and soap dishes, and comb-and-brush sets in wood, resin, and pewter are all here to tempt you. Best of all are the super-plush towels, which can be customized with your choice of embroidery, piping, and monogram. ✉ *225 E. 57th St., between 2nd and 3rd Aves., Midtown East* ☎ *212/371–9266* Ⓜ *Subway: N, R, W, 4, 5, 6 to 59th St./Lexington Ave.* ✉ *469 Broome St., at Greene St., SoHo* ☎ *212/966–0605* Ⓜ *Subway: 6 to Spring St.; J, M, N, Q, R, W, Z, 6 to Canal St.*

William-Wayne & Co. Silver julep cups, Viennese playing cards, butler's trays, candelabras made from coral, and other whimsical decorative items all vie for your attention at this shop. ✉ *40 University Pl., at E. 9th St., Greenwich Village* ☎ *212/533–4711* Ⓜ *Subway: 6 to Astor Pl.* ✉ *846 Lexington Ave., at E. 64th St., Upper East Side* ☎ *212/737–8934* Ⓜ *Subway: 6 to 68th St./Hunter College* ✉ *850 Lexington Ave., at E. 64th St., Upper East Side* ☎ *212/288–9243* Ⓜ *Subway: 6 to 68th St./Hunter College.*

Jewelry, Watches & Silver

Most of the world's premier jewelers have retail outlets in New York, and the nation's wholesale diamond center is on West 47th Street between 5th and 6th avenues.

A La Vieille Russie. Stop here to behold bibelots by Fabergé and others, enameled or encrusted with jewels. ✉ *781 5th Ave., at E. 59th St., Midtown East* ☎ *212/752–1727* Ⓜ *Subway: N, R, W to 5th Ave./59th St.*

Asprey. Having split from Garrard, Asprey has spread its net to cater to all kinds of luxury tastes, from leather goods and rare books to polo equipment and cashmere sweaters. Its claim to fame, though, is jewelry; its own eponymous diamond cut has A-shaped facets. ✉ *725 5th Ave., at E. 56th St., Midtown East* ☎ *212/688–1811* Ⓜ *Subway: F to 5th Ave.*

Beads of Paradise. Enjoy a rich selection of African trade-bead necklaces, earrings, and rare artifacts. You can also create your own designs. ⊠ *16 E. 17th St., between 5th Ave. and Broadway, Flatiron District* ☎ *212/ 620–0642* Ⓜ *Subway: 4, 5, 6, N, R, Q, W to 14th St./Union Sq.*

Bulgari. This Italian company is certainly not shy about its name, which encircles gems, watch faces, even lighters. There are beautiful, weighty rings, pieces mixing gold with stainless steel or porcelain, and the latest Astrale line, which incorporates delicate motifs, like concentric circles of small diamonds, into drop earrings and necklaces. ⊠ *730 5th Ave., at W. 57th St., Midtown West* ☎ *212/315–9000* Ⓜ *Subway: N, R, W to 5th Ave.* ⊠ *783 Madison Ave., between E. 66th and E. 67th Sts., Upper East Side* ☎ *212/717–2300* Ⓜ *Subway: 6 to 68th St./Hunter College.*

Cartier. Pierre Cartier allegedly won the 5th Avenue mansion location by trading two strands of perfectly matched natural pearls with Mrs. Morton Plant. The jewelry is still incredibly persuasive, from such established favorites as the interlocking rings to the more recent additions such as the handcufflike Menotte bracelets. ⊠ *653 5th Ave., at E. 52nd St., Midtown East* ☎ *212/753–0111* Ⓜ *Subway: E, V to 5th Ave./53rd St.* ⊠ *828 Madison Ave., at E. 69th St., Upper East Side* ☎ *212/472– 6400* Ⓜ *Subway: 6 to 68th St./Hunter College.*

Chanel Fine Jewelry. Besides the showstopper pieces based on Chanel's own jewels, there are stars and comets sparkling with diamonds and gold worked into a quilted design. ⊠ *733 Madison Ave., at E. 64th St., Upper East Side* ☎ *212/535–5828* Ⓜ *Subway: 6 to 68th St./Hunter College.*

David Yurman. The signature motifs here—cables, quatrefoil shapes— add up to a classic, go-anywhere look, while the use of semiprecious stones keeps prices within reason. ⊠ *729 Madison Ave., at E. 64th St., Upper East Side* ☎ *212/752–4255* Ⓜ *Subway: 6 to 68th St./Hunter Collge.*

Dinosaur Designs. Translucent and colorful, this antipodean work uses an untraditional medium: resin. Some look like semiprecious stone, such as onyx or jade; the rest delve into stronger colors like aqua or crimson. Cruise the stacks of chunky bangles and cuffs or rows of rings; prices start under $50. There's some striking tableware, too. ⊠ *250 Mott St., between Prince and E. Houston Sts., NoLita* ☎ *212/680–3523* Ⓜ *Subway: R, W to Prince St.*

Femmegems. Finicky tastes can be as choosy as they like here. On one side dangle necklaces and bracelets designed by the staff, on the other hang strands of stones ready for customization. Pick out the beads you like (mostly semiprecious such as topaz, carnelian, and aquamarine), fish out a porcelain or carved-stone pendant, and have a unique bauble assembled in short order. ⊠ *280 Mulberry St., between Prince and E. Houston Sts., NoLita* ☎ *212/625–1611* Ⓜ *Subway: R, W to Prince St.*

Fragments. This spot glitters with pieces by nimble new jewelry designers, many of them local. Most use semiprecious stones—you could try on turquoise-bead shoulder-duster earrings, an oversize opal ring, or a tourmaline pendant—but a few bust out the sapphires and rubies. ⊠ *116 Prince St., between Greene and Wooster Sts., SoHo* ☎ *212/334–9588* Ⓜ *Subway: R, W to Prince St.* ⊠ *997 Madison Ave., between E. 77th and 78th Sts., Upper East Side* ☎ *212/537–5000* Ⓜ *Subway: 6 to E. 77th St.*

Fred Leighton. If you're in the market for vintage diamonds, this is the place, whether your taste is for tiaras, art deco settings, or sparklers once worn by a Vanderbilt. ⊠ *773 Madison Ave., at E. 66th St., Upper East Side* ☎ *212/288–1872* Ⓜ *Subway: 6 to 68th St./Hunter College.*

H. Stern. Sleek designs pose in an equally modern 5th Avenue setting; smooth cabochon-cut stones, most from South America, glow in pale wooden display cases. The designers make notable use of semiprecious stones such as citrine, tourmaline, and topaz. ⊠ *645 5th Ave., between E. 51st and E. 52nd Sts., Midtown East* ☎ *212/688–0300* Ⓜ *Subway: E, V to 5th Ave./53rd St.* ⊠ *301 Park Ave., between E. 49th and E. 50th Sts., in Waldorf-Astoria, Midtown East* ☎ *212/753–5595* Ⓜ *Subway: 6 to 51st St.*

Harry Winston. Ice-clear diamonds of impeccable quality sparkle in Harry Winston's inner sanctum. They're set in everything from emerald-cut solitaire rings to wreath necklaces resembling strings of flowers. No wonder the jeweler was immortalized in the song "Diamonds Are a Girl's Best Friend." ⊠ *718 5th Ave., at W. 56th St., Midtown West* ☎ *212/245–2000* Ⓜ *Subway: F to 57th St.*

Jacob & Co. The designs at the new home of Diamond District legend "Jacob the Jeweler" are anything but subtle; in Jacob's parlance, bigger is better. Diamond-encrusted watches (favored by such celebs as Paris Hilton, P. Diddy, and Busta Rhymes) are nearly saucer-size, and carats for rings go up into the double-digits. If you're not blinded by the glare, head to the back of the shop for a giggle at some of the novelty items: giant pendants shaped like guitars, dice, and Jesus. ⊠ *48 E. 57th St., between 5th and Madison Aves., Midtown West* ☎ *212/719–5887* Ⓜ *Subway: N, R, W, 4, 5, 6 to 59th St./Lexington Ave.*

James Robinson. This family-owned business sells handmade flatware, antique silver, fine estate jewelry, and 18th- and 19th-century china (mostly in sets, rather than individual pieces). ⊠ *480 Park Ave., at E. 58th St., Midtown East* ☎ *212/752–6166* Ⓜ *Subway: N, R, W, 4, 5, 6 to 59th St./Lexington Ave.*

Jean's Silversmiths. Where to find a replacement for the butter knife that's missing from your great-aunt's set? Try this dusty, crowded shop. ⊠ *16 W. 45th St., between 5th and 6th Aves., Midtown West* ☎ *212/575–0723* Ⓜ *Subway: B, D, F, V to 42nd St.*

Me + Ro. Eastern styling has gained these designers a cult following. The Indian-inspired, hand-finished gold bangles and earrings covered with tiny dangling rubies or sapphires may look bohemian, but the prices target the trust-fund set. ⊠ *241 Elizabeth St., between Prince and E. Houston Sts., NoLita* ☎ *917/237–9215* Ⓜ *Subway: R, W to Prince St.*

Mikimoto. The Japanese originator of the cultured pearl, Mikimoto presents a glowing display of high-luster pearls. Besides the creamy strands from their own pearl farms, check out the dazzlingly colored South Sea pearls, dramatic black-lip and silver-lip varieties, and rare conch pearls. ⊠*730 5th Ave., between W. 56th and W. 57th Sts., Midtown West* ☎*212/457–4600* Ⓜ *Subway: F to 57th St.*

Objets du Désir. The wall-hung cases juxtapose terrifically different jewelry styles; one might display dainty clusters of pearls and filigree, while its neighbor could glower with punky stud bracelets and silver skull rings. One great recent find: a cuff etched with a free-form street map of Manhattan. ✉ *241 Mulberry St., between Prince and Spring Sts., No-Lita* ☎ *212/334–9727* Ⓜ *Subway: 6 to Spring St.*

Robert Lee Morris. Gold and silver take on bold, sculptural shapes here; cuff bracelets are chunky but fluidly curved, and necklaces and earrings have dangling hammered disks for a "wind chime" effect. Some pieces incorporate diamonds; others have semiprecious stones like turquoise or citrine. ✉ *400 West Broadway, between Broome and Spring Sts., SoHo* ☎ *212/431–9405* Ⓜ *Subway: C, E to Spring St.*

Stuart Moore. Many of the Teutonic designs are minimalist, almost in-dustrial-seeming: diamonds are set in brushed platinum, and some rings and cufflinks have a geometric, architectural aesthetic. Pieces here tend to be modest in scale. ✉ *128 Prince St., at Wooster St., SoHo* ☎ *212/941–1023* Ⓜ *Subway: R, W to Prince St.*

Ten Thousand Things. Exquisitely delicate, the designs at this boutique in-corporate tiny beads of Peruvian opal, chrysophase, ruby, sapphire, and red coral. ✉ *423 W. 14th St., Meatpacking District* ☎ *212/352–1333* Ⓜ *Subway: A, C, E to 14th St.*

Fodor'sChoice ★ **Tiffany & Co.** The display windows can be soigné, funny, or just plain breathtaking. Alongside the $80,000 platinum-and-diamond bracelets, a lot here is affordable on a whim—and everything comes wrapped in that unmistakable Tiffany blue. ✉ *727 5th Ave., at E. 57th St., Mid-town East* ☎ *212/755–8000* Ⓜ *Subway: N, R, W to 5th Ave./59th St.*

Tourneau. Each of these stores stocks a wide range of watches, but the three-level 57th Street TimeMachine, a high-tech merchandising ex-travaganza, steals the scene. A museum downstairs has timepiece ex-hibits, both temporary and permanent. The shops carry more than 70 brands, from status symbols such as Patek Philippe, Cartier, and Rolex, to more casual styles by Swatch, Seiko, and Swiss Army. ✉ *500 Madi-son Ave., between E. 52nd and E. 53rd Sts., Midtown East* ☎ *212/758–6098* Ⓜ *Subway: 6 to 51st St./Lexington Ave.; E, V to Lexington–3rd Aves./53rd St.* ✉ *12 E. 57th St., between 5th and Madison Aves., Mid-town East* ☎ *212/758–7300* ✉ *200 W. 34th St., at 7th Ave., Midtown West* ☎ *212/563–6880* Ⓜ *Subway: A, C, E, 1, 2, 3 to 34th St./Penn Station* ✉ *10 Columbus Circle, at W. 59th St., Midtown West* ☎ *212/823–9425* Ⓜ *Subway: 1, 9, A, C, B, D to Columbus Circle.*

Van Cleef & Arpels. The jewelry here (lots of classically set diamonds and floral motifs) is sheer perfection. ✉ *744 5th Ave., at W. 57th St., Mid-town West* ☎ *212/644–9500* Ⓜ *Subway: E, F, N, R to 5th Ave.*

Versani. Silver teams up with all kinds of materials here: leather, denim, and snakeskin as well as semiprecious stones. There's a good selection of silver rings and pendants under $40. ✉ *152 Mercer St., between Prince and W. Houston Sts., SoHo* ☎ *212/941–9919* Ⓜ *Subway: R, W to Prince St.* ✉ *227 Mulberry St., between Prince and Spring Sts., NoLita* ☎ *212/431–4944* Ⓜ *Subway: 6 to Spring St.*

Lingerie

Agent Provocateur. The bustiest mannequins in Manhattan vamp in the front window of this British underpinnings phenom. Showpieces include boned corsets, lace sets with contrast-color trim, bottoms tied with satin ribbons, and a few fetish-type leather ensembles. A great selection of stockings is complemented by the garter belts to secure them. ⊠ *133 Mercer St., between Prince and Spring Sts., SoHo* ☎ *212/965–0229* Ⓜ *Subway: R, W to Prince St.*

Eres. These sheer mesh and lace underthings prove that simple can be sexy. There's also a line of beautifully cut swimsuits that are all the rage on the French Riviera. ⊠ *621 Madison Ave., between E. 58th and E. 59th Sts., Midtown East* ☎ *212/223–3550* Ⓜ *Subway: N, R, W to 5th Ave.* ⊠ *98 Wooster St., between Prince and Spring Sts., SoHo* ☎ *212/ 431–7300* Ⓜ *Subway: R, W to Prince St.*

La Perla. From the Leavers lace, soutache, and embroidery to unadorned tulle, these underthings are so perfect they've inspired a trilogy of books. Look for the sets of sheer underwear embroidered with the days of the week in Italian—a grown-up alternative to Bloomie's classic bloomers. ⊠ *803 Madison Ave., between E. 67th and E. 68th Sts., Upper East Side* ☎ *212/459–2775* Ⓜ *Subway: 6 to 68th St./Hunter College* ⊠ *93 Greene St., between Prince and Spring Sts., SoHo* ☎ *212/219–0999* Ⓜ *Subway: R, W to Prince St.*

La Petite Coquette. Among the signed photos on the walls is one of ulti-mate authority—from Frederique, longtime Victoria's Secret model. The store's own line of silk slips, camisoles, and other underpinnings comes in a range of colors, and as befits the name, they have special pe-tite cuts. ⊠ *51 University Pl., between E. 9th and E. 10th Sts., Green-wich Village* ☎ *212/473–2478* Ⓜ *Subway: R, W to 8th St.*

Le Corset. This lovely boutique naturally stocks its namesake, plus lacy underwear and negligees from such designers as Chloe and Collette Din-nigan, and even powder-pink vintage slips and girdles. ⊠ *80 Thomp-son St., between Spring and Broome Sts., SoHo* ☎ *212/334–4936* Ⓜ *Subway: C, E to Spring St.*

Mixona. The minx-at-heart will have a field day among the lace-encrusted Aubade and the gauzy bras of Passion Bait. Some lines trace back to such major design houses as Blumarine and D & G. There are usually good finds on the sales racks in back. ⊠ *262 Mott St., between Prince and E. Houston Sts., NoLita* ☎ *646/613–0100* Ⓜ *Subway: R, W to Prince St.*

3 7 = 1 Atelier. The ethereal silk chiffon pieces here bring delicacy to a new level. Many are made to match various skin tones, and the use of ribbon and fine seams, rather than elastics, mean that you might forget you're wearing anything at all. ⊠ *37 Crosby St., between Broome and Grand Sts., NoLita* ☎ *212/226–0067* Ⓜ *Subway: 4, 5, 6 to Canal St.*

Luggage, Leather Goods & Handbags

Altman Luggage. Great bargains (a Samsonite Pullman for a little more than $100) are the thing at this discount store, which also stocks tough Timberland and Jansport backpacks. ⊠ *135 Orchard St., between De-lancey and Rivington Sts., Lower East Side* ☎ *212/254–7275* Ⓜ *Sub-way: F, J, M, Z to Delancey St./Essex St.*

Anya Hindmarch. While some of these divine British handbags in calf, satin, or velvet are ready for a very proper occasion, others cut loose with funny silk-screened photos or sequinned designs of candy or painkillers. ⊠ *29 E. 60th St., between Madison and Park Aves., Upper East Side* ☎ *212/750–3974* Ⓜ *Subway: N, R, W to 5th Ave./59th St.* ⊠ *115 Greene St., between Prince and Spring Sts., SoHo* ☎ *212/343–8147* Ⓜ *Subway: R, W to Prince St.*

Bottega Veneta. The signature crosshatch weave graces leather handbags, slouchy satchels, and shoes; the especially satisfying brown shades extend from fawn to deep chocolate. ⊠ *699 5th Ave., between E. 54th and E. 55th Sts., Midtown East* ☎ *212/371–5511* Ⓜ *Subway: N, R, W, 4, 5, 6 to 59th St./Lexington Ave.*

Crouch & Fitzgerald. Since 1839 this store has offered an unimpeachable selection of hard- and soft-sided luggage, as well as a huge number of attaché cases. ⊠ *400 Madison Ave., at E. 48th St., Midtown East* ☎ *212/755–5888* Ⓜ *Subway: B, D, F, V to 47th–50th St./Rockefeller Center.*

Fendi. Once known for its furs, Fendi is now synonymous with decadent handbags. The purses are beaded, embroidered, and fantastically embellished within an inch of their lives, resulting in prices that skyrocket over $1,000. Fancy leathers, furs, and other accessories are available, too. ⊠ *755 Madison Ave., between E. 65th and E. 66th Sts., Upper East Side* ☎ *212/734–8910* Ⓜ *Subway: 6 to 68th St.*

Fine & Klein. Among the Orchard Street veterans, this is a reliable stop for handbags. Some purses bear a marked resemblance to those of well-known designers. ⊠ *119 Orchard St., between Rivington and Delancey Sts., Lower East Side* ☎ *212/674–6720* Ⓜ *Subway: F, J, M, Z to Delancey St./Essex St.*

Flight 001. Frequent flyers can one-stop-shop at this travel-theme store. Carry-on bags, passport holders, and personal-size down pillows share shelves with mini-alarm clocks, satin sleep masks, and mellow music CDs for soothing frazzled nerves. ⊠ *96 Greenwich Ave., between W. 12th and Jane Sts., Greenwich Village* ☎ *212/691–1001* Ⓜ *Subway: 1, 9 to Christopher St./Sheridan Sq.*

Furla. Shoulder bags, oblong clutches, and roomy totes can be quite proper or attention-getting, from a cocoa-brown, croc-embossed zipper-top to a patent leather, cherry red purse. ⊠ *598 Madison Ave., at E. 57th St., Midtown East* ☎ *212/980–3208* Ⓜ *Subway: N, R, 4, 5, 6 to 59th St.* ⊠ *727 Madison Ave., between E. 63rd and E. 64th Sts., Upper East Side* ☎ *212/755–8986* Ⓜ *Subway: N, R, W, 4, 5, 6 to 59th St./Lexington Ave.*

Henry Beguelin. The aroma of leather pervades this boutique on the ground floor of the Hotel Gansevoort, and it's no wonder: everything here, even the floor, is made from it. Many of the pieces have an ethnic-bohemian look, with fringe and beading on jackets and swingy skirts. ⊠ *18 9th Ave., at W. 13th St., Meatpacking District* ☎ *212/647–8415* Ⓜ *Subway: A, C, E to 14th St.*

Hiponica. Some of these breezy, colorful handbags come trimmed with grosgrain ribbon or with a coin-purse-like snapping closure. Others open like mini garment bags to disclose a wealth of inner pockets. ⊠ *238 Mott St., between Prince and Spring Sts., NoLita* ☎ *212/966–4388* Ⓜ *Subway: 6 to Bleecker St.*

Jamin Puech. Many of these bags have a sense of wanderlust; the colors, embroideries, fringes, and fabrics may suggest Morocco or Polynesia, and they can cost as much as an off-season plane ticket to the Continent. ⊠ *247 Elizabeth St., between E. Houston and Prince Sts., No-Lita* ☎ *212/431–5200* Ⓜ *Subway: R, W to Prince St.*

Judith Leiber. A door handle twinkling with Swarowski crystals signals the entrance to the Kingdom of Sparkle. Instantly recognizable handbags are completely frosted in crystals, from simple, colorful rectangles to minaudières shaped like animals or flowers. Crystals also spangle the heels of satin pumps and the bows of oversized (to cut the glare?) sunglasses. ⊠ *680 Madison Ave., at E. 61st St., Upper East Side* ☎ *212/223–2999* Ⓜ *Subway: 4, 5, 6 to E. 59th St.*

Kate Spade. These eminently desirable (and oft-copied) handbags in lush-color leather, tweed, and canvas have a classic but kicky retro style. Totes and shoulder bags are lined in fun fabrics; wicker baskets for summer are jazzed with bright leather accents, or shaped like birdhouses. The expanded Broome Street shop also carries shoes, hats and scarves, linens, and sunglasses. Around the corner at **Jack Spade** (⊠ 56 Greene St., between Broome and Spring Sts., SoHo ☎ 212/625–1820 Ⓜ Subway: C, E to Prince St.), Kate's husband peddles his own line of bags, dopp kits, and other men's accessories in a nostalgic setting. The original storefront on Thompson Street now carries travel accessories. ⊠ *454 Broome St., between Mercer and Greene Sts., SoHo* ☎ *212/274–1991* Ⓜ *Subway: C, E to Spring St.* ⊠ *59 Thompson St., between Spring and Broome Sts., SoHo* ☎ *212/965–8654.*

Longchamp. Its nylon bags have become an Upper East Side staple and can be spotted everywhere in the Hamptons. The store carries the entire line of luggage, wallets, and totes in a rainbow of colors. ⊠ *713 Madison Ave., between E. 63rd and E. 64th Sts., Upper East Side* ☎ *212/223–1500* Ⓜ *Subway: N, R, W, 4, 5, 6 to 59th St./Lexington Ave.*

★ **Louis Vuitton.** In the mammoth new 57th Street store, vintage examples of Vuitton's famous monogrammed trunks float above the fray on the ground floor, where shoppers angle for the latest accessories. Joining the initials are the Damier check pattern and colorful striated leathers, not to mention devastatingly chic clothes and shoes designed by Marc Jacobs. ⊠ *1 E. 57th St., at 5th Ave., Midtown East* ☎ *212/758–8877* Ⓜ *Subway: E, V to 5th Ave./53rd St.* ⊠ *116 Greene St., between Prince and Spring Sts., SoHo* ☎ *212/274–9090* Ⓜ *Subway: R, W to Prince St.*

Lulu Guinness. Hit this lavender-upholster salon for such whimsically retro accessories as handbags adorned with appliqué, beads, and bows, polka-dot scarves and cosmetic cases, or umbrellas patterned with poodles. ⊠ *394 Bleecker St., between W. 11th and Perry Sts., Greenwich Village* ☎ *212/367–2120* Ⓜ *Subway: 1, 9 to Christopher St.*

Manhattan Portage. You know you want one, so visit the source of the messenger-bag fad. Although they're a-dime-a-dozen around these parts, these sturdy nylon and canvas numbers cost real money—$20–$100—and will impress the folks back home. ⊠ *333 E. 9th St., between 1st and 2nd Aves., East Village* ☎ *212/995–5490* Ⓜ *Subway: 6 to Astor Pl.*

Sigerson Morrison. Ready to seduce your shoulder as well as your feet, Sigerson Morrison devises bags in calfskin, pigskin, suede, and the occasional fabric, often equipped with zippered exterior pockets for cell phones and other things you need close at hand. ✉ *242 Mott St., between Prince and E. Houston Sts., NoLita* ☎ *212/941–5404* Ⓜ *Subway: R, W to Prince St.*

T. Anthony. The trademark coated-canvas luggage with leather trim can be classic (black or beige) or eye-catching (red or purply blue). Those who like to carry it all with them can outfit themselves with hatboxes and shirt cases, plus totes, trunks, and hard- and soft-sided suitcases. ✉ *445 Park Ave., at E. 56th St., Midtown East* ☎ *212/750–9797* Ⓜ *Subway: E, V to 5th Ave./53rd St.*

Museum Stores

Metropolitan Museum of Art Shop. Of the three locations, the store in the museum has a phenomenal book selection, as well as posters, art videos, and computer programs. Reproductions of jewelry, statuettes, and other *objets* fill the gleaming cases in every branch. ✉ *5th Ave., at E. 82nd St., Upper East Side* ☎ *212/879–5500* Ⓜ *Subway: 4, 5, 6 to 86th St.* ✉ *113 Prince St., between Greene and Wooster Sts., SoHo* ☎ *212/614–3000* Ⓜ *Subway: R, W to Prince St.* ✉ *15 W. 49th St., between 5th and 6th Aves., Rockefeller Center, Midtown West* ☎ *212/332–1360* Ⓜ *Subway: B, D, F, V to 47th–50th Sts./Rockefeller Center.*

Museum of Arts and Design. The tie-ins to ongoing exhibits can yield beautiful handmade glassware, unusual jewelry, or enticing textiles. ✉ *40 W. 53rd St., between 5th and 6th Aves., Midtown West* ☎ *212/956–3535* Ⓜ *Subway: E, V to 5th Ave./53rd St.*

Museum of Modern Art Design and Book Store. The redesigned MoMA expanded its in-house shop with a huge selection of art posters and more than 2,000 titles on painting, sculpture, film, and photography. Across the street is the **MoMA Design Store** (✉ *44 W. 53rd St., between 5th and 6th Aves., Midtown West* ☎ *212/767–1050* Ⓜ *Subway: E, V to 5th Ave./53rd St.*), where you can find Frank Lloyd Wright furniture reproductions, vases designed by Alvar Aalto, and lots of clever trinkets. The SoHo branch combines most of the virtues of the first two, although its book selection is smaller. It also has the city's only cache of Muji, a line of addictively inexpensive and minimalist daily necessities like notebooks and aluminum card carriers. ✉ *11 W. 53rd Sts., between 5th and 6th Aves., Midtown West* ☎ *212/708–9700* Ⓜ *Subway: E, V to 5th Ave./53rd St.* ✉ *81 Spring St., between Broadway and Crosby St., SoHo* ☎ *646/613–1367* Ⓜ *Subway: 6 to Spring St.*

Museum of the City of New York. Satisfy your curiosity about NYC's past, present, or future with this terrific selection of books, cards, toys, and photography posters. If you've something classic in mind, look for the Tin Pan Alley tunes and stickball sets. ✉ *1220 5th Ave., at E. 103rd St., Upper East Side* ☎ *212/534–1672* Ⓜ *Subway: 6 to 103rd St.*

Paper, Greeting Cards & Stationery

Industries Stationery. The datebooks, calendars, and paper goods here are all clean-lined and bold. Journals might have wooden or bright yellow leather covers, and notecards are patterned in Marimekko-ish designs. ✉ *91 Crosby St., between Prince and Spring Sts., SoHo* ☎ *212/334–4447* Ⓜ *Subway: N, R to Prince St.*

Fodor'sChoice **Kate's Paperie.** Heaven for avid correspondents and gift-givers, Kate's
★ rustles with fabulous wrapping papers, ribbons, blank books, writing
implements of all kinds, and more. ⊠ *561 Broadway, between Prince
and Spring Sts., SoHo* ☎ *212/941–9816* Ⓜ *Subway: R, W to Prince St.*
⊠ *8 W. 13th St., between 5th and 6th Aves., Greenwich Village* ☎ *212/
633–0570* Ⓜ *Subway: F, V to 14th St.* ⊠ *1282 3rd Ave., between E.
73rd and E. 74th Sts., Upper East Side* ☎ *212/396–3670* Ⓜ *Subway:
6 to 77th St.* ⊠ *140 W. 57th St., between 6th and 7th Ave., Midtown
West* ☎ *212/459–0700* Ⓜ *Subway: F to 57th St.*

Smythson of Bond Street. Keep notes on your purchases, deepest thoughts,
or conquests in softbound leather diaries with appropriate gilded titles
such as "Passions & Pleasures" or "Juicy Gossip." They also carry blue
blood–worthy array of stationery, address books, and buttery leather
travel accessories. ⊠ *4 W. 57th St., between 5th and 6th Aves., Midtown West* ☎ *212/265–4573* Ⓜ *Subway: F to 57th St.*

Untitled. One wall groans with art books, the other flutters with all kinds
of greeting cards. There's also a long row of motley postcards alpha-
betized by topic, such as Degas pastels and fruit-crate labels. ⊠ *159 Prince
St., between Thompson St. and West Broadway, SoHo* ☎ *212/982–2088*
Ⓜ *Subway: C, E to Spring St.*

Performing Arts Memorabilia

Drama Book Shop. The comprehensive stock here includes scripts, scores,
and librettos. ⊠ *250 W. 40th St., between 7th and 8th Aves., Midtown
West* ☎ *212/944–0595* Ⓜ *Subway: A, C, E to 42nd St./Port Authority.*

Motion Picture Arts Gallery. Vintage posters enchant collectors here: the
selections range from such classics as *Citizen Kane* and *His Girl Friday*
to more recent blockbusters. The shop is closed weekends and Monday. ⊠ *133 E. 58th St., between Park and Lexington Aves., 10th fl.,
Upper East Side* ☎ *212/223–1009* Ⓜ *Subway: N, R, W, 4, 5, 6 to 59th
St./Lexington Ave.*

Movie Star News. It's hard to doubt their claim that they have the world's
largest variety of movie photos and posters as you flip through images
from blockbusters, cult faves, and memorable bombs. A poster of a New
York film such as *Manhattan, The Royal Tenenbaums,* or *Taxi Driver*
makes for a good souvenir for under $20. Behind the counter are signed
photos of many of the stars seen on the posters. ⊠ *134 W. 18th St., between 6th and 7th Aves., Chelsea* ☎ *212/620–8160* Ⓜ *Subway: 1, 2,
3, 9 to 14th St.*

One Shubert Alley. Souvenir posters, tees, and other knickknacks memo-
rializing past and present Broadway hits reign at this theater district shop.
⊠ *1 Shubert Alley, between W. 44th and W. 45th Sts., Midtown West* ☎ *212/
944–4133* Ⓜ *Subway: N, R, Q, S, W, 1, 2, 3 to 42nd St./Times Sq.*

Triton Gallery. Theatrical posters large and small can be found here, and
the selection is democratic, with everything from Marlene Deitrich's *Blue
Angel* to Ralph Macchio film flops are represented. ⊠ *323 W. 45th St.,
between 8th and 9th Aves., Midtown West* ☎ *212/765–2472* Ⓜ *Subway: A, E to 42nd St./Port Authority.*

Shoes

For dressy, expensive footwear, Madison Avenue is always a good bet, but West 8th Street between 5th and 6th avenues is what most New Yorkers mean when they refer to Shoe Street; it's crammed with small shoe-storefronts that hawk funky styles, from steel-toe boots to outrageous platforms.

Men's & Women's Shoes

Bally. A few curveballs, like olive green or slate blue wing tips, liven up the mostly conservative selection. Carry-ons and clothing, such as deer-skin or lamb jackets, join the shoe leather. ⊠ *628 Madison Ave., at E. 59th St., Midtown East* ☎ *212/751–9082* Ⓜ *Subway: N, R, W, 4, 5, 6 to 59th St./Lexington Ave.*

Camper. These Euro-fave walking shoes, with their sturdy leather uppers and nubby rubber soles, have also proved popular on the cobble-stone streets of SoHo. Comfort is a priority; all the slip-ons and lace-ups here have generously rounded toes and a springy feel. ⊠ *125 Prince St., at Wooster St., SoHo* ☎ *212/358–1841* Ⓜ *Subway: R, W to Prince St.*

Cole-Haan. No longer wedded to staid moccasin styles, Cole-Haan has of late broken into stylish territory. Shoes for both sexes now come in exotic skins like python and crocodile; for warm weather, check out the orange suede thongs for men and metallic stiletto sandals for women. The handbag line is much more playful, too. ⊠ *620 5th Ave., at Rockefeller Center, Midtown West* ☎ *212/765–9747* Ⓜ *Subway: E, V to 5th Ave./53rd St.* ⊠ *667 Madison Ave., at E. 61st St., Upper East Side* ☎ *212/421–8440* Ⓜ *Subway: N, R, W, 4, 5, 6 to 59th St./Lexington Ave.* ⊠ *10 Columbus Circle, at W. 59th St., Midtown West* ☎ *212/823–9420* Ⓜ *Subway: 1, 9, A, C, B, D to Columbus Circle.*

J. M. Weston. Specially treated calfskin for the soles and handcrafted construction have made these a French favorite; they could also double the price of your outfit. High heels, a more recent addition to the selection, started gradually with stacked-heel pumps. ⊠ *812 Madison Ave., at E. 68th St., Upper East Side* ☎ *212/535–2100* Ⓜ *Subway: 6 to 68th St./Hunter College.*

John Fluevog Shoes. The inventor of the Angelic sole (protects against water, acid . . . "and Satan"), Fluevog designs chunky, funky shoes and boots. ⊠ *250 Mulberry St., at Prince St., NoLita* ☎ *212/431–4484* Ⓜ *Subway: R, W to Prince St.*

Otto Tootsi Plohound. Downtown New Yorkers swear by this large selection of supercool shoes. Many, including the store's own line, are Italian-made. Styles range from Tyrolean fur boots to vampy Dries Van Noten pumps to Paul Smith rain booties with swirly-print soles. ⊠ *413 West Broadway, between Prince and Spring Sts., SoHo* ☎ *212/925–8931* Ⓜ *Subway: C, E to Spring St.* ⊠ *273 Lafayette St., between Prince and E. Houston Sts., East Village* ☎ *212/431–7299* Ⓜ *Subway: R, W to Prince St.* ⊠ *137 5th Ave., between E. 20th and 21st Sts., Flatiron District* ☎ *212/460–8650* Ⓜ *Subway: F, V to 23rd St.* ⊠ *38 E. 57th St., between Park and Madison Aves., Midtown East* ☎ *212/231–3199* Ⓜ *Subway: N, R, W, 4, 5, 6 to 59th St./Lexington Ave.*

Salvatore Ferragamo. Elegance typifies these designs, from black-tie patent to weekender ankle boots. The company reworks some of their women's styles from previous decades, like the girlish Audrey (as in Hepburn) flat, available in the original black or seasonal takes like bone or leopard. The larger of the two stores is the flagship on 5th Avenue. ⊠ *655 5th Ave., at E. 52nd St.* ☎ *212/759–3822* Ⓜ *Subway: E, V to 53rd St.* ⊠ *124 Spring St., at Greene St., SoHo* ☎ *212/226–4330* Ⓜ *Subway: C, E to Spring St.*

Sigerson Morrison. The details—just-right T-straps, small buckles, interesting two-tones—make the women's shoes irresistible. Prices rise above $300, so the sales are big events. ⊠ *28 Prince St., between Mott and Elizabeth Sts., NoLita* ☎ *212/219–3893* Ⓜ *Subway: F, V to Broadway–Lafayette St.*

Stuart Weitzman. The broad range of styles, from wing tips to strappy sandals, is enhanced by an even wider range of sizes and widths. ⊠ *625 Madison Ave., between E. 58th and E. 59th Sts., Midtown East* ☎ *212/ 750–2555* Ⓜ *Subway: N, R, W, 4, 5, 6 to 59th St./Lexington Ave.* ⊠ *10 Columbus Circle, at W. 59th St., Midtown West* ☎ *212/823–9560* Ⓜ *Subway: 1, 9, A, C, B, D to Columbus Circle.*

Men's Shoes

Billy Martin's. Quality hand-tooled and custom-made boots for the Urban Cowboy are carried here. To complete the look, you can also find everything from suede shirts to turquoise-and-silver belts. ⊠ *220 E. 60th St., between 2nd and 3rd Aves., Upper East Side* ☎ *212/861–3100* Ⓜ *Subway: N, R, 4, 5, 6 to 59th St.*

Church's English Shoes. The high quality of these shoes is indisputable; you could choose something highly polished for an embassy dinner, a loafer or a crepe-sole suede ankle boot for a weekend, or even a black-and-white spectator style worthy of Fred Astaire. ⊠ *689 Madison Ave., at E. 62nd St., Upper East Side* ☎ *212/758–5200* Ⓜ *Subway: N, R, 4, 5, 6 to 59th St.*

John Lobb. These British shoes often use waxed leather, the better to contend with London levels of damp. Ankle boots with padded collars or zips join the traditional oxfords and derbys; some shoes have elegantly tapered toes. ⊠ *680 Madison Ave., between E. 62nd and E. 61st Sts., Upper East Side* ☎ *212/888–9797* Ⓜ *Subway: N, R, 4, 5, 6 to 59th St.*

Santoni. Those who equate Italian with slightly flashy haven't seen these discreet, meticulously finished, handmade shoes. ⊠ *864 Madison Ave., between E. 70th and E. 71st Sts., Upper East Side* ☎ *212/794–3820* Ⓜ *Subway: 6 to 68th St./Hunter College.*

Women's Shoes

Christian Louboutin. Bright-red soles are the signature of Louboutin's delicately sexy couture slippers and stilettos, and his latest, larger downtown store has carpeting to match. The pointy-toe creations come trimmed with brocade, tassels, buttons, or satin ribbons. ⊠ *941 Madison Ave., between E. 74th and E. 75th Sts., Upper East Side* ☎ *212/ 396–1884* Ⓜ *Subway: 6 to 77th St.* ⊠ *59 Horatio St., between Hudson and Greenwich Sts., Meatpacking District* ☎ *212/255–1910* Ⓜ *Subway: A, C, E to 14th St.*

Hollywould. Colorful ballet flats with long grosgrain ties close ranks along the floorboards, and cinematic high heels patrol the shelves above. Padded soles make even the most soaring pumps surprisingly wearable. ⊠ *198 Elizabeth St., between Prince and Spring Sts., NoLita* ☎ *212/ 343–8344* Ⓜ *Subway: 6 to Spring St.*

Jimmy Choo. Pointy toes, low vamps, narrow heels, ankle-wrapping straps—these British-made shoes are undeniably hot to trot, and sometimes more comfortable than they look. ⊠ *716 Madison Ave., between E. 63rd and E. 64th Sts., Upper East Side* ☎ *212/759–7078* Ⓜ *Subway: 6 to 68th St./Hunter College* ⊠ *645 5th Ave., at E. 51st St., Midtown East* ☎ *212/593–0800* Ⓜ *Subway: B, D, F, V to 47th–50th Sts./Rockefeller Center.*

★ **Lace.** Perch on a princessy chair to try on hard-to-find European styles, perhaps some glam scrunchy boots by Gaspard Yurkievich, chunky-heel Vivienne Westwoods, or poised Martine Sitbon pumps. ⊠ *223 Mott St., between Prince and Spring Sts., NoLita* ☎ *212/941–0528* Ⓜ *Subway: 6 to Spring St.*

Manolo Blahnik. These are, notoriously, some of the most expensive shoes money can buy. They're also devastatingly sexy, with pointed toes, low-cut vamps, and spindly heels. Mercifully, the summer stock includes flat (but still exquisite) sandals; look for gladiator styles with ankle laces, or thongs embellished with sparkly beads. Pray for a sale. ⊠ *31 W. 54th St., between 5th and 6th Aves., Midtown West* ☎ *212/582–3007* Ⓜ *Subway: E, V to 5th Ave./53rd St.*

Robert Clergerie. Not without its sense of fun, this place is often best in summer, when the sandal selection includes curvaceous soles and beaded starfish shapes. ⊠ *681 Madison Ave., between E. 61st and E. 62nd Sts., Upper East Side* ☎ *212/207–8600* Ⓜ *Subway: N, R, W, 4, 5, 6 to 59th St./Lexington Ave.*

Tod's. Diego Della Valle's coveted driving moccasins, casual loafers, and boots in colorful leather, suede, and ponyskin are right at home on Madison Avenue. An increasing selection of high heels is bent on driving sales, rather than cars. ⊠ *650 Madison Ave., near E. 60th St., Upper East Side* ☎ *212/644–5945* Ⓜ *Subway: N, R, W to 5th Ave./59th St.*

Unisa. Try on a gentle riff on a current trend, from bow-top slides to driving mocs; most pairs are under $150, sometimes well under. ⊠ *701 Madison Ave., between E. 62nd and E. 63rd Sts., Upper East Side* ☎ *212/753–7474* Ⓜ *Subway: N, R, W to 5th Ave./59th St.*

Souvenirs of New York City

Major tourist attractions keep their gift shops well stocked, and dozens of souvenir shops dot the Times Square area. If you're looking for grungier souvenirs of downtown (T-shirts with salty messages, tattoos), troll St. Marks Place between 2nd and 3rd avenues in the East Village.

City Store. Discover all kinds of books and pamphlets that explain New York City's government from pocket maps, NYPD T-shirts, and cocktail napkins printed with subway routes to manhole-cover coasters and a New York City scented candle (don't worry, it smells like apple pie, not exhaust). It's closed weekends. ⊠ *1 Centre St., at Chambers St., Lower Manhattan* ☎ *212/669–8246* Ⓜ *Subway: 4, 5, 6 to City Hall/Brooklyn Bridge.*

New York City Transit Museum Gift Shop. In the symbolic heart of NYC's transit system, all the store's merchandise is somehow linked to the MTA, from "straphanger" ties to skateboards decorated with subway-line logos. ⊠ *Grand Central Terminal, at Vanderbilt Pl. and E. 42nd St., Midtown East* ☎ *212/878–0106* Ⓜ *Subway: 4, 5, 6, 7 to 42nd St./Grand Central Terminal.*

New York Firefighter's Friend. NYFD logo tees join firefighter-theme toys and books, plus a few vintage items. The shop, though not officially affiliated with the fire department, donates a portion of its proceeds to widows' and children's funds for firefighters lost in the World Trade Center attacks. A similar shop carrying New York Police Department merchandise is next door. ⊠ *263 Lafayette St., between Prince and Spring Sts., SoHo* ☎ *212/226–3142* Ⓜ *Subway: R, W to Prince St.; 6 to Spring St.*

The Pop Shop. Images from the late Keith Haring's unmistakable pop art cover a wealth of paraphernalia, from backpacks and umbrellas to key chains. ⊠ *292 Lafayette St., between Houston and Prince Sts., SoHo* ☎ *212/219–2784* Ⓜ *Subway: R, W to Prince St.*

Sporting Goods

The NBA Store. Push through the bronze-armed door and you'll find yourself in a basketball temple. Every imaginable item having to do with pro b-ball is here, from jerseys, hats, and bags emblazoned with team logos to balls signed by Yao Ming and Larry Bird. Players grin in the digital-photo station, but they also make live appearances on the store's half-court. ⊠ *666 5th Ave., at W. 52nd St., Midtown West* ☎ *212/515–6221* Ⓜ *Subway: E, V to 5th Ave./53rd St.*

NikeTown. A fusion of fashion and sports arena, Nike's "motivational retail environment" is its largest sports-gear emporium. Inspirational quotes in the floor, computer-driven foot sizers, and a heart-pumping movie shown on an enormous screen in the entry atrium make it hard to leave without something in the latest wick-away fabric or footwear design. ⊠ *6 E. 57th St., between 5th and Madison Aves., Midtown East* ☎ *212/891–6453* Ⓜ *Subway: E, V to 5th Ave./53rd St.*

Paragon Sporting Goods. Tennis rackets, snowshoes, kayaks, swim goggles, scuba gear, croquet mallets: Paragon stocks virtually everything any athlete needs, no matter what the sport. It keeps up with the trends (heart-rate monitors) and doesn't neglect the old-fashioned (Woolrich shirts). ⊠ *867 Broadway, at E. 18th St., Flatiron District* ☎ *212/255–8036* Ⓜ *Subway: L, N, Q, R, W, 4, 5, 6 to 14th St./Union Sq.*

Toys & Games

Most of these stores are geared to children, but a few shops that cater to grown-up toy-lovers are mixed in. During February's Toy Week, when out-of-town buyers come to place orders for the next Christmas season, the windows of the Toy Center at 23rd Street and 5th Avenue display the latest thing. In addition to the stores listed below, *see* Pylones *in* Home Decor.

American Girl Place. No toy pink convertibles here; instead, the namesake dolls are historically themed, from "Felicity" of colonial Virginia to "Kit" of Depression-era Cincinnati. Each character has her own affiliated books, furniture, clothes, and accessories. There's a doll hairdressing station, a café, and even a theater showing a musical based on the dolls' stories. ⊠ *609 5th Ave., at E. 49th St., Midtown East* ☎ *212/371–2220* Ⓜ *Subway: B, D, F, V to 47th–50th Sts./Rockefeller Center.*

Classic Toys. Collectors and children scrutinize the rows of miniature soldiers, toy cars, and other figures. It's a prime source for toy soldiers from Britain's Ltd., the United Kingdom's top manufacturer. ⊠ *218 Sullivan St., between Bleecker and W. 3rd Sts., Greenwich Village* ☎ *212/674–4434* Ⓜ *Subway: A, C, E, F, V to W. 4th St./Washington Sq.*

Compleat Strategist. This store puts on a great spread—from board games and classic soldier sets to fantasy games. ⊠ *11 E. 33rd St., between 5th and Madison Aves., Murray Hill* ☎ *212/685–3880* Ⓜ *Subway: 6 to 33rd St.*

Dinosaur Hill. These toys leave the run-of-the-mill far behind, with mini bongo drums, craft kits, jack-in-the-boxes, and a throng of marionettes and hand puppets, from mermaids to farmers to demons. ⊠ *306 E. 9th St., between 2nd and 1st Aves., East Village* ☎ *212/473–5850* Ⓜ *Subway: R, W to 8th St.; 6 to Astor Pl.*

Fodor'sChoice **F.A.O. Schwarz.** Back in business and better than ever, this children's par-
★ adise more than lives up to the hype. The ground floor is a zoo of extraordinary stuffed animals, from cuddly $20 teddies to towering, life-size elephants and giraffes (with larger-than-life prices to match). F.A.O. Schweets stocks M&Ms in every color of the rainbow; upstairs, you can dance on the giant musical floor keyboard, browse through Barbies wearing Armani and Juicy Couture, and design your own customized Hot Wheels car. ⊠ *767 5th Ave., at E. 58th St., Midtown East* ☎ *212/644–9400* Ⓜ *Subway: 4, 5, 6 to E. 59th St.*

Geppetto's Toy Box. Many toys here are handmade, from extravagantly costumed dolls and furry animal hand puppets to lots of tried-and-true favorites such as Lego, building blocks, and rubber duckies. ⊠ *10 Christopher St., at Greenwich Ave., Greenwich Village* ☎ *212/620–7511* Ⓜ *Subway: 1, 9 to Christopher St./Sheridan Sq.*

Kidding Around. This unpretentious shop is piled high with old-fashioned wooden toys, Playmobil and Brio sets, and a fun selection of hand puppets. The costume racks are rich with dress-up potential. ⊠ *60 W. 15th St., between 5th and 6th Aves., Flatiron District* ☎ *212/645–6337* Ⓜ *Subway: L, N, Q, R, W, 4, 5, 6 to 14th St./Union Sq.*

Kid Robot. Even if you've never heard of Urban Vinyl Toys which, in quainter times, were simply referred to as "action figures," you can get a kick out of this shop, where adult and kid collectors flock to stock up on the latest toys from Asian designers. ⊠ *126 Prince St., between Greene and Wooster Sts., SoHo* ☎ *212/966–6688* Ⓜ *Subway: N, R to Prince St.*

Toys "R" Us. The Times Square branch of this megastore is so big that a three-story Ferris wheel revolves inside. With all the movie tie-in merchandise, video games, old favorites like pogo sticks, stuffed animals, and what seems to be the entire Mattel oeuvre, these stores have a lock on sheer volume. ⊠ *1514 Broadway, at W. 44th St., Midtown West* ☎ *800/869–7787* Ⓜ *Subway: 1, 9, N, R, Q, W to 42nd St./Times Sq.*

World of Disney New York. You'll be flooded with merchandise relating to Disney films and characters—pajamas, toys, figurines, you name it. There's also the largest collection of Disney animation art in the country. ⊠ *711 5th Ave., between E. 55th and E. 56th Sts., Midtown East* ☎ *212/702–0702* Ⓜ *Subway: F to 57th St.*

Wine

Acker Merrall & Condit. Known for its selection of red burgundies, this store has knowledgeable, helpful personnel. ⊠ *160 W. 72nd St., between Amsterdam and Columbus Aves., Upper West Side* ☎ *212/787–1700* Ⓜ *Subway: 1, 2, 3, 9 to 72nd St.*

Astor Wines & Spirits. Plain and fluorescent-lighted it may be, but this is a key spot for everything from well-priced champagne to Poire William to Riesling. ⊠ *12 Astor Pl., at Lafayette St., East Village* ☎ *212/674–7500* Ⓜ *Subway: 6 to Astor Pl.*

Best Cellars. In a novel move, the stock here is organized by the wine's characteristics (sweet, fruity) rather than region—and not only that, the prices are amazingly low, running between $10 and $14 a bottle. ⊠ *1291 Lexington Ave., between E. 86th and E. 87th Sts., Upper East Side* ☎ *212/426–4200* Ⓜ *Subway: 4, 5, 6 to 86th St.*

Garnet Wines & Liquors. Its fine selection includes champagne at prices that one wine writer called "almost charitable." ⊠ *929 Lexington Ave., between E. 68th and E. 69th Sts., Upper East Side* ☎ *212/772–3211* Ⓜ *Subway: 6 to 68th St./Hunter College.*

Morrell & Company. Peter Morrell is a well-regarded and very colorful figure in the wine business; his store reflects his expertise. Free wine tastings are held several times a month (for serious oenophiles, ask about the rare vintage auctions). Next door is his café, where dozens of fine wines are available by the glass. ⊠ *1 Rockefeller Plaza, at W. 49th St., Midtown West* ☎ *212/688–9370* Ⓜ *Subway: B, D, F, V to 47–50 Sts./Rockefeller Center.*

Sherry-Lehmann. This New York institution is an excellent place to go for good advice and to browse through sales on intriguing vintages. ⊠ *679 Madison Ave., between E. 61st and E. 62nd Sts., Upper East Side* ☎ *212/838–7500* Ⓜ *Subway: N, R, W, 4, 5, 6 to 59th St./Lexington Ave.*

Union Square Wine & Spirits. The store stocks a great selection and has a regular schedule of wine seminars and special tasting events. ⊠ *33 Union Sq. W, at W. 16th St, Flatiron District* ☎ *212/675–8100* Ⓜ *Subway: L, N, Q, R, W, 4, 5, 6 to 14th St./Union Sq.*

Vintage New York. The vintages here, from cabernet sauvignon all the way to gewürztraminer, hail exclusively from New York State. Try your top choices at the tasting bar in the back; every wine sold is available by the glass. The business is open seven days a week. ⊠ *482 Broome St., at Wooster St., SoHo* ☎ *212/226–9463* Ⓜ *Subway: J, M, N, Q, R, W, Z, 6 to Canal St.* ⊠ *2492 Broadway, between W. 92nd and W. 93rd Sts., Upper West Side* ☎ *212/721–9999* Ⓜ *Subway: 6 to 96th St.*

WORD OF MOUTH

"[Four Seasons] is the best of the best. Rooms are huge and many offer outstanding views of the New York skyline as well as furnished balconies. All have walk-in closets and gigantic bathrooms."

—jfd

"The [Inn on 23rd] was the perfect base for it all. We stayed in the Cabin Room, spacious, spotless, I want that couch! The neighborhood and the location are perfect."

—Nancy

"[Le Parker Meridien has a] great hall, marble, and very high ceilings. Great park views available. Above all, the swimming pool . . . pure delight, you're swimming on top of the world, and you can sunbathe on the rooftop."

—Sophie

Updated by
Melissa
Klurman

NEW YORK LIFE WEAVES IN AND OUT OF THE CITY'S HOTELS. Whether a New Yorker is invited to a wedding, a premiere, or dinner, there's a fair chance it will take place in one of Manhattan's luxurious old stand-bys or in one of the latest chic newcomers. When epicures gather for gastronomic adventure, odds are it will be in a hot spot such as Matsuri in the Maritime Hotel. For world-class cuisine and power dining, the elite gather at such upscale boîtes as Alain Ducasse in the Essex House, Town in Chambers, and Jean-Georges at Trump International Hotel and Towers. And when a TV reporter wants to interview a celebrity, an intimate suite at the Lowell is often the spot of choice. New York hotels grant a loftier standard of service and glamour to locals and visitors alike.

It's always amusing to observe upscale New York hotel trends, which filter down not only to second-tier hostelries, but also to residences far and wide. One ubiquitous visual element is the bed crowned with an oversize, high-style headboard that manages to condense a hotel's style into a few square feet of metaphor. Did we mention sensual textures and fabrics such as mohair, Tibetan wool, and Ultrasuede? Or innovative use of lighting technology and color? With the city at the center of the art world, it's no wonder that at several newer hotels, every room and hallway is an informal gallery, from the Gansevoort's display of local artists to the vintage cityscape photos at the Park South Hotel. Increasingly, you can find such high-tech accessories as plasma TVs, portable phones, and wireless Internet service. At almost all the top and middle-ranking hotels you can be pampered with 300-plus thread count sheets and goose-down duvets and you can often have plush robes, terry-cloth slippers, and designer toiletries.

Many visitors to New York cram themselves into hotels in the hectic Midtown area, but it's worth noting that Manhattan is so small and dense that other neighborhoods are often just as convenient for travelers. Several less-touristed areas, such as Gramercy, Murray Hill, and the Upper East Side, offer a far more accurate sense of the pace and feel of New York life. For those who seek the most exciting lodging experience, nearly every upscale New York hotel has an extravagant penthouse or specialty suite. Even if you're accustomed to staying in a standard room at a luxury hotel, for a similar price you might consider staying in one of these spectacular spaces at a less credentialed hotel. The Alchemist Suite in the Dylan is a Gothic wonder with soaring ceilings, while the penthouse duplex at the Mansfield is slightly down at the heel, but grand.

Lower Manhattan

★ $$$–$$$$ 🏨 **Ritz-Carlton New York, Battery Park.** Sweeping views over the Statue of Liberty, Ellis Island, and lower Manhattan set the scene for this elegant tower on the tip of Manhattan. The hotel is an oasis of fine living; the luxurious, large rooms and suites with plush fabrics and furnishings seem more like expensive living rooms than hotel rooms. The superlative staff includes a bath butler who can fill your deep soaking tub with anything from rose petals to rubber duckies. Take advantage of the quiet weekends to sample the Kobe beef at 2 West restaurant or imbibe at the View bar with its spectacular sightlines of lady liberty. ✉ 2

West St., at Battery Pl., Battery Park 10004 ☎ *212/344–0800 or 800/ 241–3333* 🖷 *212/344–3801* ⊕ *www.ritzcarlton.com* 📼 *254 rooms, 44 suites* ⚴ *Restaurant, minibars, cable TV with video games, in-room DVD, in-room data ports, 2 bars, piano, laundry service, concierge, Internet, meeting rooms, parking (fee), no-smoking rooms* ▭ *AE, D, DC, MC, V* Ⓜ *Subway: 1, 9, N, R, W to Rector St.*

$$$ 🔲 **Millennium Hilton.** This sleek black tower directly across the street from the World Trade Center site was badly damaged by the disaster but was renovated and reopened in less than two years. The business-class modern, beige-and-wood rooms have a streamlined look, with contoured built-in desks and night tables as well as enormous plasma TVs; almost all have expansive views reaching to both the Hudson and the East rivers. The health club has an Olympic-size pool with windows that look out on St. Paul's Church. ⊠ *55 Church St., between Dey and Fulton Sts., Lower Manhattan 10007* ☎ *212/693–2001 or 800/445–8667* 🖷 *212/ 571–2317* ⊕ *www.hilton.com* 📼 *463 rooms, 102 suites* ⚴ *2 restaurants, room service, in-room safes, minibars, cable TV, in-room data ports, indoor pool, gym, health club, massage, 3 bars, piano, babysitting, dry cleaning, laundry service, concierge, business services, meeting rooms, parking (fee)* ▭ *AE, D, DC, MC, V* Ⓜ *Subway: R, W to Cortlandt St.*

$$ 🔲 **Embassy Suites Hotel New York.** Directly across from the World Trade Center site is Manhattan's first Embassy Suites Hotel. As the name suggests, every one of the modern rooms here is at least a one-bedroom suite, with a living area that includes a pull-out sofa, dining table, microwave oven, and refrigerator. Not only is this hotel practical and reasonably priced, but it's also unusually attractive with original contemporary artwork in the atrium and lobby. Take advantage of the complimentary evening cocktail reception and breakfast bonanza. ⊠ *102 North End Ave., at Murray St., Lower Manhattan 10281* ☎ *212/945–0100 or 800/362–2779* 🖷 *212/945–3012* ⊕ *www.embassynewyork.com* 📼 *463 suites* ⚴ *Restaurant, room service, in-room fax, in-room safes, refrigerators, in-room data ports, bar, concierge, business services, meeting rooms, parking (fee)* ▭ *AE, D, DC, MC, V* ⏍◎▯ *BP* Ⓜ *Subway: N, R, W to Cortlandt St.*

★ **$–$$** 🔲 **Holiday Inn Wall Street.** You know the future has arrived when a Holiday Inn provides T-1 Internet access in every room, express check-in lobby computers that dispense key cards, and both Web TV and Nintendo on 27-inch televisions. Half the rooms have desktop PCs, and on the "smart floor" wireless laptops and printers are at the ready. The comfortable rooms are surprisingly spacious—many have 14-foot ceilings. Thoughtful touches include ergonomically designed workspaces, full-length mirrors that open to reveal ironing boards, and oversize showerheads that simulate falling rain. ⊠ *15 Gold St., at Platt St., Lower Manhattan 10038* ☎ *212/232–7700 or 800/465–4329* 🖷 *212/425– 0330* ⊕ *www.holidayinnwsd.com* 📼 *136 rooms, 1 suite* ⚴ *Restaurant, room service, in-room safes, minibars, cable TV with movies and video games, in-room data ports, gym, bar, dry cleaning, laundry service, Internet, business services, meeting rooms, parking (fee), some pets allowed (fee), no-smoking floors* ▭ *AE, D, DC, MC, V* Ⓜ *Subway: A, E, J, M, 2, 3, 4, 5 to Fulton St./Broadway Nassau.*

Whatever your preference, your hotel will have a significant impact on the quality of your stay in New York. Choose carefully. Some are visual dreamscapes, others offer the kind of service that is effective without being overly attentive, but many are simply adequate places to sleep. The lodgings we list are the cream of the crop in each price category. Properties are assigned price categories based on the range from their least expensive standard double room at high season (excluding holidays) to the most expensive. We always list the facilities that are available—but we don't specify whether they cost extra: when pricing accommodations, always ask what's included and what costs extra.

11

Services Unless otherwise noted in the individual descriptions, all the hotels listed have private baths, central heating, air-conditioning, and private phones. Almost all hotels have data ports and phones with voice mail, as well as valet service. Most large hotels have video or high-speed checkout capability, and many can arrange babysitting.

Pools are a rarity, but most properties have gyms or health clubs, and sometimes full-scale spas; hotels without facilities usually have arrangements for guests at nearby gyms, sometimes for a fee. Among those hotels with pools (all listed in this chapter) are Hotel Gansevoort, Le Parker Meridien, the Mandarin Oriental, the Peninsula, the Millennium Hilton, the Millennium Hotel New York UN Plaza, Trump International Hotel and Towers, and the New York Marriott Brooklyn; on the other end of the price spectrum is the Vanderbilt YMCA.

Bringing a car to Manhattan can be the source of any number of headaches and can significantly add to your lodging expenses. Many properties in all price ranges do have parking facilities, but they are often at independent garages that charge as much as $20 or more per day, and valet parking can cost up to $60 a day. The city's exorbitant 18¾% parking tax makes leaving your lemon out of the Big Apple a smart idea.

New York has gone to great lengths to attract family vacationers, and hotels have followed the family-friendly trend. One result is that properties that once drew mostly business travelers are finding themselves suddenly full of families—and are scrambling to add child-friendly amenities. Some properties provide such diversions as Web TV and in-room video games; others have suites with kitchenettes and fold-out sofa beds. Most full-service Manhattan hotels provide roll-away beds, babysitting, and stroller rental, but be sure to make arrangements when booking the room, not when you arrive. Ask the reservations agent specific questions, since the list of services and amenities is constantly expanding.

Reservations Hotel reservations are an absolute necessity when planning your trip to New York—hotels fill up quickly, so book your room as far in advance as possible. Fierce competition means properties undergo frequent improvements, especially during July and August, so when booking inquire about any ongoing renovations lest you get a room within earshot of noisy construction. In this ever-changing city, travelers can find themselves temporarily, and most inconveniently, without commonplace amenities such as room service or spa access if their hotel is upgrading.

Once you decide on a hotel, use a major credit card to guarantee the reservation—another essential in a market where "lost" reservations are not unheard of. When signing in, take a pleasant but firm attitude; if there's a mix-up, chances are the outcome will be an upgrade or a free night.

What It Costs
With square footage coming at a hefty premium in this town, some accommodations provide more space for more money, while others can only entreat you with more amenities. The style-conscious set seduced by Ian Schrager's Paramount and Hudson hotels or at Midtown's Dream Hotel pay for cell-size rooms in exchange for the exciting public spaces, while spacious rooms at hotels like the Inn at Irving Place and the Kitano attract those who hanker for privacy. It's up to you to choose your priority: do you yearn for Bulgari toiletries, a restaurant in the building, spectacular views, or room to maneuver? If it's a bargain you long for, that's one amenity few New York hotels provide. But don't be put off by printed rates—the priciest hotels often have deals that cut room rates nearly in half. Be sure to ask about promotional rates and to check the hotel's Web site, and Web sites Fodors.com, Travelscape.com, Hoteldiscounts.com, and Hotres.com, as well as Expedia.com and Orbitz.com.

WHAT IT COSTS In New York City				
	$$$$	$$$	$$	$	¢
FOR 2 PEOPLE	over $475	$350–$475	$225–$350	$110–$225	under $110

Prices are for a standard double room, excluding 13.625% city and state taxes.

$ **Best Western Seaport Inn.** This thoroughly pleasant, restored 19th-century building is one block from the waterfront, close to South Street Seaport. Its cozy, librarylike lobby has the feel of a Colonial sea captain's house, though the reasonably priced rooms are clearly those of a chain hotel. For around $25–$35 extra, you can have a room with a whirlpool tub and/or an outdoor terrace with a view of the Brooklyn Bridge. ⊠ 33 Peck Slip, between Front and Water Sts., Lower Manhattan 10038 ☎ 212/766-6600 or 800/468-3569 ☐ 212/766-6615 ⊕ www.bestwestern.com ➪ 72 rooms ⚄ In-room safes, refrigerators, cable TV with video games, in-room VCRs, in-room data ports, gym, dry cleaning, laundry service, parking (fee), no-smoking floors ☐ AE, D, DC, MC, V ⓜ Subway: A, E, 2, 3, 4, 5 to Fulton St./Broadway Nassau.

Chinatown, SoHo & TriBeCa

$$$ **Mercer Hotel.** Owner Andre Balazs, known for his Château Marmont Fodor'sChoice in Hollywood, has a knack for channeling a neighborhood sensibility. ★ Here, it's SoHo loft all the way. In the hushed lobby, the reception desk

is unmarked. Guest rooms are generously sized with long entryways, high ceilings, and walk-in closets. Dark African woods and custom-designed furniture upholstered in muted solids lend serenity. The bathrooms steal the show with their decadent two-person marble tubs—some surrounded by mirrors—but beware: not all rooms come with a tub. Downstairs is the happening Mercer Kitchen, where the cool still congregate. ⊠ *147 Mercer St., at Prince St., SoHo 10012* ☎ *212/966–6060 or 888/918–6060* 🖷 *212/965–3838* ⊕ *www.mercerhotel.com* 🛏 *67 rooms, 8 suites* ⟁ *Restaurant, room service, in-room safes, minibars, cable TV with movies and video games, in-room VCRs, 2 bars, concierge, In-room Internet, business services, some pets allowed, no-smoking rooms* ▤ *AE, D, DC, MC, V* Ⓜ *Subway: N, R, W to Prince St.*

★ **$$$** 🏨 **60 Thompson.** A superb and original design by Thomas O'Brien, along with a popular lounge and restaurant, instantly anchored this stunning hotel into the downtown scene. The generous use of dark woods and full-wall leather headboards gives the retro-classic rooms a welcoming warmth; a decadent touch are the FatWitch brownies at turn-down. Marble-swathed bathrooms have oversize showers, mosaic tile floors, and Philosophy bath products. Chic Thai restaurant Kittichai on the ground floor has patio dining and a gold-suffused bar; rooftop lounge A60 is a warm-weather haven for hipsters. ⊠ *60 Thompson St., between Broome and Spring Sts., SoHo 10012* ☎ *212/431–0400* 🖷 *212/431–0200* ⊕ *www.60thompson.com* 🛏 *90 rooms, 11 suites* ⟁ *Restaurant, room service, in-room fax, in-room safes, minibars, cable TV with movies, in-room DVDs, in-room VCRs, in-room data ports, 2 bars, concierge, Internet, meeting rooms, parking (fee); no-smoking rooms* ▤ *AE, D, DC, MC, V* Ⓜ *Subway: C, E to Spring St.*

$$ 🏨 **SoHo Grand.** This hardy pioneer of SoHo's hotel boom still holds its own against newer arrivals. Public spaces as well as guest rooms use an industrial chic design to mimic the original architecture of the neighborhood. Comfortable contemporary rooms are mainly focused on the view out the 8-foot windows; bathrooms are stark but have deep soaking tubs. The high-ceiling lounge is outfitted in pony and mohair, but better yet is the large outdoor yard area where you can have a drink or meal and then spread out on the grassy lawn—the only one of its kind at a city hotel. ⊠ *310 West Broadway, at Grand St., SoHo 10013* ☎ *212/965–3000 or 800/965–3000* 🖷 *212/965–3244* ⊕ *www.sohogrand.com* 🛏 *365 rooms, 2 suites* ⟁ *Restaurant, room service, in-room safes, minibars, cable TV with movies, in-room VCRs, in-room data ports, exercise equipment, gym, hair salon, massage, 2 bars, babysitting, dry cleaning, laundry service, concierge, Internet, business services, meeting rooms, parking (fee), some pets allowed, no-smoking rooms, no-smoking floor* ▤ *AE, D, DC, MC, V* Ⓜ *Subway: 6, J, M, N, Q, R, W to Canal St.*

$$ 🏨 **Tribeca Grand.** Enter this industrial-looking giant via a curving, 30-foot cleft-stone ramp and you can find yourself looking up into an eight-story atrium onto which all rooms open. Movie- and music-industry types hang out at the Church Lounge—a bar, café, and dining room—well into the night, sometimes to the dismay of quiet-minded guests. Twin glass elevators housed in a steel cage whisk you to hallways overlooking the atrium. Modern-design rooms have low platform beds, large workspaces,

Best Western Seaport Inn ...**30**

Carlton Arms ...**7**

Chelsea Inn ...**11**

Chelsea Savoy Hotel **13**

Cosmopolitan ..**25**

Embassy Suites **26**

The Gershwin ...**4**

Holiday Inn Downtown **23**

Holiday Inn Wall Street **29**

Hotel Gansevoort ...**15**

Hotel Giraffe ...**6**

Hotel on Rivington **18**

Howard Johnson's Express Inn ...**19**

The Inn at Irving Place ...**8**

Inn on 23rd ...**12**

Larchmont Hotel **17**

Maritime **14**

Mercer Hotel ..**20**

Millennium Hilton **27**

New York Marriott Brooklyn **31**

Park South Hotel **5**

Ritz-Carlton New York Battery Park **28**

Roger Williams Hotel **1**

Second Home on Second Avenue **10**

60 Thompson ...**21**

SoHo Grand ...**22**

Thirty Thirty Hotel **3**

Tribeca Grand **24**

W New York Union Square ...**9**

Washington Square Hotel ..**16**

Wolcott Hotel ...**2**

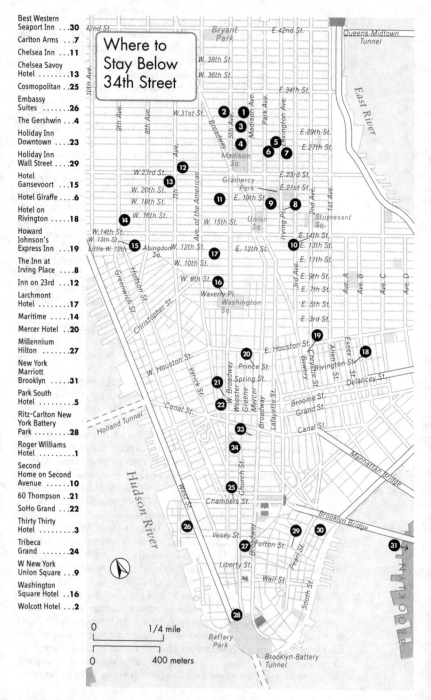

and podlike bathrooms with aluminum consoles reminiscent of airplanes. Like its sister, the SoHo Grand, the Tribeca Grand welcomes pets. ⊠ *2 Ave. of the Americas, between Walker and White Sts., TriBeCa 10013* ☎ *212/519–6600 or 800/965–3000* ☐ *212/519–6700* ⊕ *www.tribecagrand.com* ↪ *203 rooms, 6 suites* ♿ *Restaurant, café, room service, in-room fax, in-room safes, minibars, cable TV with movies and video games, in-room VCRs, in-room data ports, gym, bar, dry cleaning, laundry service, concierge, Internet, business services, meeting rooms, parking (fee), some pets allowed, no-smoking rooms, no-smoking floors* ▤ *AE, D, DC, MC, V* Ⓜ *Subway: A, C, E to Canal St.*

$ 🏨 **Cosmopolitan.** For those on a budget, this spot is one of the better buys, especially if you want a room with a private bath. The decor is modern and clean, and the location is ideal for exploring Chinatown, Little Italy, Wall Street, SoHo, and the South Street Seaport. The building dates to 1850, and amazingly Abraham Lincoln slept here. A repeat clientele comes for the "miniloft" rooms. ⊠ *95 West Broadway, at Chambers St., TriBeCa 10007* ☎ *212/566–1900 or 888/895–9400* ☐ *212/566–6909* ⊕ *www.cosmohotel.com* ↪ *105 rooms* ♿ *In-room data ports, gym, babysitting, dry cleaning, laundry service, concierge, parking (fee)* ▤ *AE, DC, MC, V* Ⓜ *Subway: 1, 2, 3, 9, A, C to Chambers St.*

$ 🏨 **Holiday Inn Downtown.** Historical features such as oversize arched windows, high ceilings, and a classic exterior remain in this former factory building, but the lobby is a cross-cultural affair mixing marble and Asian accents. Excellent dim sum at Pacifica Restaurant attracts plenty of Asian business travelers. Many Europeans and young budget travelers are also drawn by the reasonable rates and proximity to Little Italy, TriBeCa, and SoHo. The rooms are standard issue, but clean and well maintained, and they do have nice touches such as in-room coffeemakers and CD players. The staff is well trained and works hard to please. Nearby is bustling Canal Street. ⊠ *138 Lafayette St., near Canal St., Chinatown 10013* ☎ *212/966–8898 or 800/465–4329* ☐ *212/966–3933* ⊕ *www.holidayinn-nyc.com* ↪ *215 rooms, 12 suites* ♿ *Restaurant, room service, refrigerators, cable TV with movies, in-room data ports, bar, dry cleaning, laundry service, concierge, parking (fee), no-smoking floors* ▤ *AE, D, DC, MC, V* Ⓜ *Subway: 6, M, N, Q, R, W to Canal St.*

Greenwich Village

$$$ 🏨 **Hotel Gansevoort.** Modern and hip, the hotel is a shining beacon in the trendy Meatpacking District. Most notable is the extensive rooftop deck comprising a heated 45-foot pool, myriad terraces, a restaurant where complimentary breakfast is served, and happening bar–lounge that fills with late-night scene-seekers. Sleek, sexy rooms have sweeping views of the city or the Hudson River; slate-and-marble bathrooms have unique showers that double as steam rooms. Original NYC-centric artwork, including Warhols and local gallery pieces, hangs in rooms and hallways. Downstairs, Japanese restaurant Ono has a vibrant Asian interior and an extensive outdoor bar and lounge space. ⊠ *18 9th Ave., at 13th St., Greenwich Village 10014* ☎ *212/206–6700 or 877/426–7386* ☐ *212/255–5858* ⊕ *www.hotelgansevoort.com* ↪ *166 rooms, 21 suites* ♿ *2*

CloseUp

KIDS IN TOW

MANY NEW YORK HOTELS *go out of their way to accommodate families with special amenities and family-size rooms.* However, just because a hotel says they're child-friendly doesn't always translate to true kid-welcoming style. Ask questions such as if cribs come with linens, whether there are high chairs and children's menus in the dining room, and if there's in-house babysitters. Here are some of the top picks for traveling with kids.

SUITE LIFE Space is at a premium in New York hotels, and if you have more than two people in a standard room, you'll really start to feel the squeeze. The answer? A suite, where you can spread out in style. The **Embassy Suites Hotel New York** (⇨ Lower Manhattan), a tried-and-true option of any family, is even more kid friendly in NYC since it's in the same building as a multiplex movie theater and several reasonably priced dining options. A great uptown choice is **The Milburn Hotel** (⇨ Upper West Side), where for less than $200 you'll score a one-bedroom suite with kitchen facilities. The hotel also has a library with children's books and family movies to watch on your in-room VCR, all gratis. With newly renovated, super-spacious suites, **Affinia Fifty** (⇨ Midtown East) is the family hotel of choice on the residential East Side.

LUXE LIFE Just because you have children in tow doesn't mean your dream of a pampering vacation needs to go down the drain. Several top New York hotels go out of their way to accommodate families. The **Ritz-Carlton**'s two hotels (⇨ Lower Manhattan & Midtown West) offer special healthy children's menus, rubber-duck filled baths, and toy menus from FAO Schwartz. The Battery Park location even has children's etiquette classes the first Saturday of the month. At **The Pierre** (⇨ Upper East Side), your little one can

luxuriate in a children's bathrobe while perusing the menu of children's favorites that includes everything from Fruit Loops to Kraft Macaroni and Cheese not to mention the complimentary cookies and milk served in bed. The hotel can also find a babysitter with as little as five hours notice.

NEW YORK SPECIAL Hotel QT (⇨ Midtown West) might make the perfect respite with teens in tow. There's a funky lobby pool; a lobby kiosk that stocks sweets with which to fill the in-room refrigerators; and rooms have ingenious bunk beds that levitate out of the walls and have their own plasma TVs—all in the heart of Times Square. At the hipster **Hotel on Rivington** (⇨ East Village & the Lower East Side), a special family suite has two full bedrooms, one with two sets of bunk beds and a big bin of toys, two full baths, and a Japanese tub that could easily fit four preschoolers. Bonus points: the hotel is across from Economy Candy.

Family friendly **Le Parker Meridien** (⇨ Midtown West) has a large pool, a restaurant that serves decadent breakfast foods such as chocolate French toast until 3 PM, and another dining spot that serves nothing but burgers and shakes. Kid heaven. Upon check-in at the **Omni Berkshire Place** (⇨ Midtown East), kids get a goodie bag and a backpack loaner. Both contain toys galore from cards and puzzles to coloring books and bedtime reading. On the room's Web TV, kids can log on to ⊕ www.omnikidsrule.com to participate in polls and contests.

restaurants, room service, in-room safes, cable TV with movies, in-room data ports, Wi-Fi, pool, gym, spa, bar, dry cleaning, laundry service, concierge, business services, meeting rooms, parking (fee), some pets allowed ⊟ *AE, MC, V* ⊚*l CP* Ⓜ *Subway: A, C, E, L to 14th St.*

$ Ⓗ **Washington Square Hotel.** This low-key hotel with a distinguished history and a Continental feel is catercorner to Washington Square Park's magnificent arch. Most striking is the intimate bar, entered through an ornate wrought iron and gleaming brass gate brought over from Paris, and decorated with mosaic floors and elegant mirrors. Request one of the lovely, crimson-fuschia colored renovated rooms. Its proximity to New York University, however, keeps it busy with visiting parents. ⊠ *103 Waverly Pl., at MacDougal St., Greenwich Village 10011* ☎ *212/777–9515 or 800/222–0418* 🖷 *212/979–8373* ⊕ *www.washingtonsquarehotel. com* ↩ *160 rooms* ⌂ *Restaurant, in-room safes, cable TV, in-room data ports, Wi-Fi, gym, massage, bar, meeting rooms* ⊟ *AE, MC, V* ⊚*l CP* Ⓜ *Subway: A, B, C, D, E, F, V to W. 4th St./Washington Sq.*

¢–$ Ⓗ **Larchmont Hotel.** You might miss the entrance to this beaux-arts town
Fodor'sChoice   house, whose geranium boxes and lanterns blend right in with the old
★   New York feel of West 11th Street. If you don't mind shared bathrooms and no room service, the residential-style accommodations are all anyone could ask for, for the price. The small rooms have a tasteful safari theme; your own private sink and stocked bookshelf will make you feel right at home. Guests have use of a communal kitchen and a Continental breakfast is included. ⊠ *27 W. 11th St., between 5th and 6th Aves., Greenwich Village 10011* ☎ *212/989–9333* 🖷 *212/989–9496* ⊕ *www. larchmonthotel.com* ↩ *60 rooms, none with bath* ⌂ *Café, fans, business services, no-smoking rooms* ⊟ *AE, D, DC, MC, V* ⊚*l CP* Ⓜ *Subway: A, B, C, D, E, F, V to W. 4th St./Washington Sq.*

The East Village & the Lower East Side

★ $$–$$$ Ⓗ **Hotel on Rivington.** The hip Lower East Side finally gets a hotel cool enough to call its own. What's pleasantly surprising here, considering its off-the-beaten-path location, is just how refined, comfortable, and cutting-edge the rooms are. If you like baths, request a room with a super-deep, two-person Japanese soaking tub. Steam showers have glass walls that look onto the street ("privacy" curtains are available on request) and bathrooms have heated floors. High-tech wake up calls remotely open the blinds on the floor-to-ceiling windows. Most rooms have balconies. The public areas have an Alice-through-the-looking-glass feeling, with amorphous entryways and velvet settees. ⊠ *107 Rivington St., between Ludlow and Essex Sts., Lower East Side 10002* ☎ *212/475–2600 or 800/915–1537* 🖷 *212/ 475–5959* ⊕ *www.hotelonrivington.com* ↩ *110 rooms* ⌂ *Restaurant, room service, in-room safes, minibars, in-room data ports, cable TV with movies, Wi-Fi, Japanese baths, bar, lounge, dry cleaning, laundry service, concierge, meeting rooms, parking (fee), some pets allowed* ⊟ *AE, D, DC, MC, V* Ⓜ *Subway: F, J, M, Z to Delancey/Essex Sts.*

$ Ⓗ **Howard Johnson's Express Inn.** This hotel at the nexus of East Village
Fodor'sChoice   and Lower East Side nightlife is perfect if you want to check out the down-
★   town scene. A corner location increases your chances of having a view

ROMANTIC RETREATS

EVEN IF YOU LIVE IN NEW YORK, *treat yourself to a stay in one of these romantic hotels where you can order everything from breakfast in bed to a rose-petal filled bath.*

*At the **Ritz-Carlton New York, Battery Park** (⇨ Lower Manhattan), your wish is their command. Take advantage of lower-than-normal weekend rates to book a Liberty Suite, with sweeping views of the Statue of Liberty. A quick call to the concierge before you arrive can take care of everything from having champagne and strawberries waiting on your arrival to a silver-framed picture of your sweetie by the bedside. A bath butler can then fill your marble tub with a potion of bath oils and flower petals. If you're here in February, don't miss a trip to the penthouse Chocolate Bar with its aphrodisiacal chocolate and champagne buffet.*

***The Inn at Irving Place** (⇨ Flatiron District & Gramercy) does romance the old-*

fashioned way, with four-poster beds, fireplaces, fur throws, and lots of privacy in an elegant 1800s brownstone. The complimentary breakfast is served on fine bone china either in the cozy sitting room or in bed.

*All of the rooms at the **Library Hotel** (⇨ Midtown East) have a certain inviting charm that makes them a good choice for a romantic weekend away, but if your looking for a little mood reading, ask for the Erotic Literature room or the Love room, curated by Dr. Ruth.*

---

when you eventually rise to meet the day, and next door is a century-old knish bakery. The tastefully done rooms each have enough space for a desk; a few have hot tubs or microwaves and mini-refrigerators. With amenities such as in-room hair dryers, irons, coffeemakers, and voice mail, plus free local calls, you're getting more than your money's worth in New York's hotel market. ⊠ *135 E. Houston St., at Forsyth St., Lower East Side 10002* ☏ *212/358–8844 or 800/446–4656* 🖷 *212/ 473–3500* ⊕ *www.hojo.com* 🛏 *46 rooms* ⚶ *Some microwaves, cable TV, in-room data ports, laundry service, no-smoking floors* ▤ *AE, D, DC, MC, V* ❙❭❙ *CP* Ⓜ *Subway: F, V to 2nd Ave.*

¢–$ 🏨 **Second Home on Second Avenue.** The rooms at this budget hotel are themed: modern, Caribbean, Peruvian, skylight, and tribal. Local calls are free; a skylight illuminates common areas; and the staff is friendly. Not all rooms, however, have private baths. This is a popular place, so book well in advance. ⊠ *221 2nd Ave., between 13 and 14th Sts., East Village 10002* ☏ *212/677–3161* ⊕ *secondhome.citysearch.com* 🛏 *7 rooms, 2 with bath* ⚶ *Cable TV* ▤ *AE, D, DC, MC, V* Ⓜ *Subway: 4, 5, 6, L, N, Q, R, W to 14th St./Union Sq.; L to 3rd Ave.*

Flatiron District & Gramercy

$$–$$$$ **The Inn at Irving Place.** The city's most romantic small inn occupies two
Fodor's Choice grand 1830s town houses just steps from Gramercy Park. Its cozy tea
★ salon (complete with a working fireplace), antiques-filled living room,
and original curving banister evoke a more genteel era. Rooms have or-
namental fireplaces, four-poster beds with embroidered linens, wood shut-
ters, and glossy cherrywood floors. The room named after Madame
Olenska (the lovelorn Edith Wharton character) has a bay window with
sitting nook. In the morning, steaming pots of tea and coffee are served
in the tea salon, along with a free Continental breakfast including home-
made pastries and breads. ⌧ *56 Irving Pl., between E. 17th and E. 18th
Sts., Gramercy 10003* ☎ *212/533–4600 or 800/685–1447* 🖷 *212/533–
4611* ⊕ *www.innatirving.com* ⇆ *5 rooms, 6 suites* ♺ *Restaurant, room
service, minibars, refrigerators, cable TV with movies, in-room VCRs,
in-room data ports, massage, bar, dry cleaning, laundry service, business
services, parking (fee); no kids under 8* ▤ *AE, D, DC, MC, V* ❙⃝❙ *CP*
Ⓜ *Subway: 4, 5, 6, L, N, Q, R, W to 14th St./Union Sq.*

$$$ **W New York Union Square.** Starwood's W Hotel brand has owned Union
Square since it bought the landmark Guardian Life building at the
park's northeast corner. Both the interior and exterior of the 1911
beaux arts–style building retain many original granite and limestone details. Modernism permeates each room, from shiny sharkskin bed coverings to overstuffed velvet armchairs. Generally, the service staff look
as though they just stepped out of a photo shoot, and at times it feels
like that's where they'd rather be. Celebrity chef Todd English's first New
York restaurant, Olives, and the comfortable lobby bar draw huge
crowds. ⌧ *201 Park Ave. S, at E. 17th St., Flatiron District 10003* ☎ *212/
253–9119 or 877/946–8357* 🖷 *212/779–0148* ⊕ *www.whotels.com*
⇆ *270 rooms, 16 suites* ♺ *Restaurant, café, room service, in-room fax,
in-room safes, minibars, cable TV with movies, in-room DVDs, in-room
VCRs, in-room data ports, Web TV, gym, health club, massage, spa, 2
bars, babysitting, dry cleaning, laundry service, concierge, Internet,
business services, meeting rooms, parking (fee), some pets allowed; no-
smoking rooms, no-smoking floors* ▤ *AE, D, DC, MC, V* Ⓜ *Subway:
4, 5, 6, L, N, Q, R, W to 14th St./Union Sq.*

Murray Hill

$$$–$$$$ **The Kitano.** A large Botero bronze of a stylized dog presides over the
Asian-inspired airy marble lobby of this luxe hotel with an austere
grandeur. Handsome cherry and mahogany furnishings, Japanese tea mak-
ers, and watercolor still lifes impart an air of serenity to the rooms; sound-
proof windows make them among Manhattan's quietest. The Nadaman
restaurant is known for high-price but authentic Japanese cuisine; the
second-floor lounge hosts a jazz band on Friday nights. For business meet-
ings, two of the top-floor banquet rooms have floor-to-ceiling glass
doors leading to expansive balconies with dazzling city views. ⌧ *66 Park
Ave., at E. 38th St., Murray Hill 10016* ☎ *212/885–7000 or 800/548–
2666* 🖷 *212/885–7100* ⊕ *www.kitano.com* ⇆ *131 rooms, 18 suites* ♺ *2*

restaurants, room service, in-room fax, in-room safes, in-room hot tubs, minibars, cable TV with movies, in-room data ports, Web TV, bar, babysitting, dry cleaning, laundry facilities, laundry service, concierge, business services, meeting rooms, parking (fee), no-smoking floors ▭ AE, D, DC, MC, V Ⓜ *Subway: 6 to 33rd St.*

$–$$$$ 🏨 **W New York–The Court and W New York–The Tuscany.** Big black "W"s transform guest-room headboards into billboards at these self-consciously stylish sister properties. The design-for-design's-sake lobbies might strike some as cold, but an exceedingly attentive staff goes a long way toward warming things up. Spacious rooms have vaguely Oriental black-and-blond wood furnishings and ottomans with chenille throws (which can be purchased through the in-room W catalog). Both uphold the W chain's hip nightlife standards with Tuscany's Cherry, a rock-and-roll vision in red; the Court's popular Wet Bar; and the starkly elegant, steamship-deco Icon restaurant. *Court* ✉ *130 E. 39th St., between Lexington and Park Aves., Murray Hill 10016* ☎ *212/685–1100 or 877/946–8357* 🖷 *212/ 889–0287* ⊕ *www.whotels.com* 🛏 *Court: 150 rooms, 48 suites; Tuscany: 110 rooms, 12 suites* ⚐ *Restaurant, café, room service, in-room safes, minibars, cable TV with movies, in-room VCRs, in-room data ports, exercise equipment, gym, massage, spa, 2 bars, babysitting, dry cleaning, laundry service, concierge, business services, meeting rooms, parking (fee), no-smoking rooms, no-smoking floors ▭ AE, D, DC, MC, V* ✉ *Tuscany* ✉ *120 E. 39th St., near Lexington Ave., Murray Hill 10016* ☎ *212/779–7822, 800/223–6725 for reservations* 🖷 *212/696–2095* Ⓜ *Subway: 4, 5, 6, 7, S to 42nd St./Grand Central.*

$$$ 🏨 **70 Park Avenue.** Kimpton hotels have something of a cult following with design enthusiasts, and whether you're one of the devout or not, you should be pleased with New York's first offering from this contemporary hotel group. The lobby with its limestone fireplace and thick-pillowed couches replicates a well-appointed living room, and is the location for complimentary evening cocktails. The rest of the hotel channels a prosperous Park Avenue abode; neutral-palette rooms have ultrasuede chairs and couches, plasma TVs, and woven silk blankets. Silverleaf Tavern serves a modern-American menu, and the bar is comfortable even if you're alone. ✉ *70 Park Ave., at 38th St., Murray Hill 10016* ☎ *212/973–2400 or 800/ 707–2752* 🖷 *212/973–2401* ⊕ *www.70parkavenuehotel.com* 🛏 *201 rooms, 4 suites* ⚐ *Restaurant, room service, in-room safes, in-room data ports, in-room DVD/CD, Wi-Fi, bar, laundry service, concierge, meeting rooms, some pets allowed; no-smoking rooms ▭ AE, D, DC, MC, V* Ⓜ *Subway: 6 to 33rd St.*

$$–$$$ 🏨 **Hotel Giraffe.** Inspired by the colors and sleek lines of European Moderne, this retro-glam property aspires to the sophisticated style of the 1920s and 1930s. Guest rooms with 10-foot ceilings are adorned with antique-rose velveteen armchairs, sorbet-hue sheer curtains, and pearlized platinum wall covers. Deluxe rooms have French doors opening onto private balconies from which you can survey Park Avenue. For the ultimate in entertaining (or an exorbitant romantic getaway), reserve the spectacular penthouse suite with baby grand piano and rooftop garden. The civilized service here includes complimentary breakfast, coffee beverages, and weekday evening champagne reception. ✉ *365 Park Ave. S, at E.*

26th St., Murray Hill 10016 ☎ *212/685–7700 or 877/296–0009* 🖷 *212/685–7771* ⊕ *www.hotelgiraffe.com* ⟳ *52 rooms, 21 suites* ⚹ *Restaurant, room service, in-room safes, minibars, cable TV, in-room VCRs, in-room data ports, Wi-FI, 2 bars, piano, dry cleaning, laundry service, concierge, business services, parking (fee), no-smoking rooms, no-smoking floors* ▤ *AE, DC, MC, V* ⎮◎⎮ *CP* Ⓜ *Subway: 6 to 28th St.*

$$ 🏨 **Jolly Hotel Madison Towers.** The Italian Jolly Hotels chain brings a European air to this friendly hotel on a residential Murray Hill corner, combining an Italian aesthetic with an art deco design. The tasteful, traditional rooms have elegant cherry furniture and travertine marble bathrooms. Deluxe rooms on the top floors have a sleek, contemporary design, grand bathrooms with separate soaking tubs, and views of the Empire State Building. Cinque Terre serves Northern Italian cuisine, and the cozy Whaler Bar has a fireplace and a wood-beam ceiling. A separate concession on the premises offers shiatsu massage and a Japanese sauna. Note that the name appears as "Madison Towers" on the flags marking the entrance. ✉ *22 E. 38th St., between Madison and Park Aves., Murray Hill 10016* ☎ *212/802–0600 or 800/225–4340* 🖷 *212/447–0747* ⊕ *www.jollymadison.com* ⟳ *238 rooms, 6 suites* ⚹ *Restaurant, in-room safes, minibars, cable TV with movies and video games, in-room data ports, Wi-Fi, massage, sauna, steam room, bar, dry cleaning, laundry service, concierge, Internet, business services, meeting rooms, parking (fee), some pets allowed, no-smoking floors* ▤ *AE, DC, MC, V* Ⓜ *Subway: 6 to 33rd St.*

★ **$$** 🏨 **Morgans.** Überhotelier Ian Schrager launched New York's boutique hotel craze way back in 1984 when he opened this hipster, but Morgans is still up-to-the-minute. Comfortable rooms have a minimalist, high-tech look, with low-lying, futonlike beds, long window seats, and original Mapplethorpe photographs; the tiny but functional bathrooms have steel surgical sinks and poured-granite floors. An incredibly friendly and hospitable staff is one of the reasons that the hotel is filled with return guests. The chic Asia de Cuba created the Latin-fusion craze and is still standing-room only. The cavelike, candlelight Morgans Bar downstairs also lives up to all its hype. ✉ *237 Madison Ave., between E. 37th and E. 38th Sts., Murray Hill 10016* ☎ *212/686–0300 or 800/334–3408* 🖷 *212/779–8352* ⊕ *www.ianschragerhotels.com* ⟳ *87 rooms, 26 suites* ⚹ *Restaurant, room service, in-room safes, minibars, refrigerators, cable TV with movies, in-room VCRs, in-room data ports, 2 bars, babysitting, dry cleaning, laundry service, concierge, Internet, business services, meeting rooms, parking (fee), some pets allowed, no-smoking rooms, no-smoking floors* ▤ *AE, D, DC, MC, V* Ⓜ *Subway: 4, 5, 6, 7, S to 42nd St./Grand Central.*

$$ 🏨 **Roger Williams Hotel.** A masterpiece of industrial chic, the cavernous
Fodor's Choice Rafael Viñoly–designed lobby—clad with sleek maple walls accented with
★ fluted zinc pillars—was dubbed "a shrine to modernism" by *New York* magazine. Rooms have a clean California beach feel—the parent hotel is in Santa Monica—with blond-birch furnishings, chartreuse enamel bathroom accents, and brightly colored quilts and pillows. A small splurge will buy you an upgrade to a room with a full-size terrace; you'll make up the fee with the bargain $12, NYC-specialty-filled, buffet breakfast. ✉ *131 Madison Ave., at E. 31st St., Murray Hill 10016*

☏ *212/448–7000 or 877/847–4444* 🖷 *212/448–7007* ⊕ *www. rogerwilliamshotel.com* 🛏 *185 rooms, 2 suites* ♿ *Restaurant, room service, cable TV, in-room VCRs, in-room data ports, exercise equipment, gym, bar, piano, concierge, Internet, business services, parking (fee), no-smoking rooms, no-smoking floors* ▭ *AE, D, MC, V* †⦿† *CP* Ⓜ *Subway: 6 to 33rd St.*

$–$$ 🏨 **Park South Hotel.** In this beautifully transformed 1906 office building, restful rooms are smartly contemporary although they've retained some period detailing. Beware rooms with half-size closets and those that overlook noisy 27th street; try instead for views of the Chrysler Building. The New York flavor permeates from a mezzanine library focusing on local history to the ubiquitous black-and-white photos of city scenes from the 1880s through 1950s. The Black Duck bar and restaurant warms patrons with its wood-burning fireplace. Unlike some boutique hotels where locals have made the lounges their watering holes, you won't have to contend with crowds here. ✉ *122 E. 28th St., between Lexington and Park Aves., Murray Hill 10016* ☏ *212/448–0888 or 800/315–4642* 🖷 *212/448–0811* ⊕ *www.parksouthhotel.com* 🛏 *141 rooms* ♿ *Restaurant, in-room fax, cable TV, in-room DVDs, in-room data ports, gym, bar, dry cleaning, laundry service, concierge, business services* ▭ *AE, D, DC, MC, V* †⦿† *CP* Ⓜ *Subway: 6 to 28th St.*

¢–$$ 🏨 **The Gershwin Hotel.** Young, foreign travelers flock to this budget
Fodor'sChoice hotel–cum–hostel, housed in a converted 13-story Greek Revival build-
★ ing adjacent to the Museum of Sex. A giant Plexiglas and metal sculpture of glowing pods by Stefan Lindfors creeps down the facade and winds its way into the lobby. With Andy Warhol as muse, there's pop art on every floor. Rooms are painted in bright colors. Dormitories have 2 to 10 beds and a remarkable $33 to $53 rate. On any given night there's something going on—film series, stand-up comedy, performance art— at this slightly cheesy center for avant-garde activities. ✉ *7 E. 27th St., between 5th and Madison Aves., Murray Hill 10016* ☏ *212/545–8000* 🖷 *212/684–5546* ⊕ *www.gershwinhotel.com* 🛏 *120 rooms, 64 beds in dorm rooms, 12 suites* ♿ *Restaurant, café, cable TV, bar, Internet, no-smoking floors; no TV in some rooms* ▭ *AE, MC, V* Ⓜ *Subway: 6, R, W to 28th St.*

$ 🏨 **Thirty Thirty Hotel.** The former Martha Washington women's residence is still haunted by many of its female senior-citizen tenants, who remain in the building despite the fact that a busy hotel has been built around them. This is an efficient and pleasant place, with a friendly staff. The rooms are clean, modern, simple, and sparsely decorated in dusty shades of beige, purple, and green. For a few dollars more you can upgrade to a room with a kitchenette. ✉ *30 E. 30th St., between Park Ave. S and Madison, Murray Hill 10016* ☏ *212/689–1900 or 800/497–6028* ⊕ *www. thirtythirty-nyc.com* 🛏 *243 rooms* ♿ *Room service, some kitchenettes, cable TV with movies, in-room data ports, dry cleaning, laundry service, Internet* ▭ *AE, D, DC, MC, V* Ⓜ *Subway: 6, R, W to 28th St.*

$ 🏨 **Wolcott Hotel.** Edith Wharton stayed at this unassuming hotel back when it was a beaux-arts glamour palace. Now students, international travelers, and conventioneers grab the unimpressive rooms' impressively low rates. Tilt your head back when you enter the lobby and the chandeliers, marble columns, and ornate moldings will give you an idea of the grandeur that was once here. Now, however, rooms are tiny and the furnishings old, and the elevator is old and slow. The location, however, is still one of the best in New York. ✉ *3 W. 31st St., between 5th Ave. and Broadway, Murray Hill 10001* ☎ *212/268–2900 or 212/563–0096* ⊕ *www.wolcott.com* ↪ *180 rooms* ⚹ *In-room safes, cable TV with movies and video games, gym, laundry facilities, laundry service, concierge, business services* ▭ *AE, MC, V* Ⓜ *Subway: B, D, F, N, Q, R, V, W to 34th St./Herald Sq.*

¢ 🏨**Carlton Arms.** So creepy, it's cool—every wall and ceiling in this bohemian dive is covered with a mural. Each room has a theme, such as the Versailles Room with its outré symphony of trompe l'oeil trellises and classical urns and the "child's dream" room with its puzzle-covered floor and a bed the shape of a car with monsters underneath. But these are tame compared to the room devoted to sadomasochism. Children are allowed, but you may consider leaving them with relatives. All rooms have double-glaze windows; many are almost free of furniture, and some of baths, and none have TVs or phones. ✉ *160 E. 25th St., at 3rd Ave., Murray Hill 10010* ☎ *212/684–8337, 212/679–0680 for reservations* ⊕ *www.carltonarms.com* ↪ *54 rooms, 20 with bath* ⚹ *Some pets allowed; no room phones, no room TVs* ▭ *MC, V* Ⓜ *Subway: R, W to 28th St.*

Chelsea

$$ 🏨 **Maritime Hotel.** The soaring white-ceramic tower that is the Maritime earns the title of the first luxury hotel in the heart of the Chelsea gallery scene. And with the Meatpacking District two blocks away, you are near the some of the city's chicest boutiques and hippest nightclubs. Rooms here resemble modern ship's cabins, with burnished teak paneling, sea-blue drapes and bed accents, and large porthole windows that face the Hudson River skyline. Matsuri, the cavernous Japanese restaurant below the hotel, is an experience in itself. ✉ *363 W. 16th St., at 9th Ave., Chelsea 10011* ☎ *212/242–4300* 🖷 *212/242–1188* ⊕ *www.themaritimehotel. com* ↪ *120 rooms, 4 suites* ⚹ *2 restaurants, room service, in-room safes, minibars, cable TV, in-room DVDs, in-room data ports, bar, dry cleaning, concierge, Internet, business services, no-smoking rooms* ▭ *AE, MC, V* Ⓜ *Subway: A, C, E to 14th St.*

$ 🏨 **Chelsea Savoy Hotel.** Affordable rates and a friendly though often harried young staff make this a sensible choice. Jade-green carpets, butterscotch wood furniture, and perhaps a framed van Gogh print enliven the small, basic rooms. The Bull Run Grill is next to the bland lobby. ✉ *204 W. 23rd St., at 7th Ave., Chelsea 10011* ☎ *212/929–9353 or 866/929–9353* 🖷 *212/741–6309* ⊕ *www.chelseasavoynyc.com* ↪ *90 rooms* ⚹ *Restaurant, café, room service, in-room safes, refrigerators, cable TV, in-room data ports, bar, no-smoking rooms* ▭ *AE, MC, V* Ⓜ *Subway: F, V to 23rd St.*

$ 🏨 **Inn on 23rd.** Innkeepers Annette and Barry Fisherman were inspired to restore this 19th-century commercial building in the heart of Chelsea, making each of the guest rooms spacious and unique. One exotic and elegant room is outfitted in bamboo, another in the art moderne style

LODGING ALTERNATIVES

Apartment Rentals

If you want a home base that's roomy enough for a family and comes with cooking facilities, consider a furnished rental. These can save you money, especially if you're traveling with a group. Home-exchange directories sometimes list rentals as well as exchanges.

International agents include: **Hideaways International** (⌧ 767 Islington St., Portsmouth, NH 03801 ☎ 603/430–4433 or 800/843–4433 🖷 603/430–4444 ⊕ www.hideaways.com), annual membership $185. **Hometours International** (⌧ 1108 Scottie La., Knoxville, TN 37919 ☎ 865/690–8484 or 866/367–4668 ⊕ thor.he. net/~hometour/).

Local agents include: **Abode Limited** (⌀ Box 20022, New York, NY 10028 ☎ 800/835–8880 or 212/472–2000 ⊕ www.abodenyc.com) arranges rentals of furnished apartments. **A Hospitality Company** (⌧ 515 Madison Ave., 25th fl., New York, NY 10001 ☎ 800/987–1235 or 212/813–2244 🖷 212/813–9001 ⊕ www.hospitalitycompany.com). **Manhattan Getaways** (⌀ Box 1994, New York, NY 10022 ☎ 212/956–2010 ⊕ www.manhattangetaways.com).

Bed-and-Breakfasts

Most bed-and-breakfasts in New York City are residential apartments. B&Bs booked through a service may be either hosted (you're the guest in someone's quarters) or unhosted (you have full use of someone's vacated apartment, including kitchen privileges). Reservation services include: **All Around the Town** (⌧ 270 Lafayette St., Suite 804, New York, NY 10012 ☎ 212/334–2655 or 800/443–3800 🖷 212/675–6366 ⊕ www.newyorkcitybestbb. com). **Bed-and-Breakfast (and Books)** (⌧ 35 W. 92nd St., Apt. 2C, between Central Park W and Columbus Ave., Upper West Side, New York, NY 10025

🖷🖷 212/865–8740 please call only weekdays 10 AM–5 PM). **Bed-and-Breakfast in Manhattan** (⌀ Box 533, New York, NY 10150 ☎ 212/472–2528 🖷 212/988–9818). **Bed-and-Breakfast Network of New York** (⌧ 134 W. 32nd St., Suite 602, between 6th and 7th Aves., Midtown West, New York, NY 10001 ☎ 212/645–8134 or 800/900–8134 ⊕ www. bedandbreakfastnetny.com). **City Lights Bed-and-Breakfast** (⌀ Box 20355, Cherokee Station, New York, NY 10021 ☎ 212/737–7049 🖷 212/535–2755 ⊕ www.citylightsbedandbreakfast.com). **Manhattan Getaways** (⌀ Box 1994, New York, NY 10101 ☎ 212/956–2010 ⊕ www.manhattangetaways.com). **Manhattan Home Stays** (⌀ Box 20684, Cherokee Station, New York, NY 10021 ☎ 212/249–6255 🖷 212/265–3561 ⊕ www.manhattanstays.com). **New World Bed and Breakfast** (⌧ 150 5th Ave., Suite 711, between 19th and 20th Sts., Gramercy, New York, NY 10011 ☎ 212/675–5600, 800/443–3800 in U.S. 🖷 212/675–6366). **New York Habitat** (⌧ 307 7th Ave., Suite 306, between 27th and 28th Sts., Chelsea, New York, NY 10001 ☎ 212/647–9365 🖷 212/627–1416 ⊕ www.nyhabitat.com). **West Village Reservations** (⌀ Village Station, Box 347, New York, NY 10014-0347 ☎ 212/614–3034 🖷 425/920–2384).

Home Exchanges

If you would like to exchange your home for someone else's, join a home-exchange organization, which will send you its updated listings of available exchanges for a year and will include your own listing in at least one of them. It's up to you to make specific arrangements. Exchange clubs include: **HomeLink International** (⌀ Box 47747, Tampa, FL 33647 ☎ 813/975–9825 or 800/638–3841 🖷 813/910–8144 ⊕ www.homelink.org); $110 yearly for a listing, online access, and catalog; $70 without catalog. **Intervac U.S** (⌧ 30

Corte San Fernando, Tiburon, CA 94920 ☎ 800/756–4663 ≞ 415/435–7440 ⊕ www.intervacus.com); $125 yearly for a listing, online access, and a catalog; $65 without catalog.

Hostels

No matter what your age, you can save on lodging costs by staying at hostels. In some 4,500 locations in more than 70 countries around the world, Hostelling International (HI), the umbrella group for a number of national youth-hostel associations, offers single-sex, dorm-style beds and, at many hostels, rooms for couples and family accommodations. Membership in any HI national hostel association, open to travelers of all ages, allows you to stay in HI-affiliated hostels at member rates; one-year membership is about $28 for adults (C$35 for a two-year minimum membership in Canada, £14 in the U.K., A$52 in Australia, and NZ$40 in New Zealand); hostels charge about $10–$30 per night. Members have priority if the hostel is full; they're also eligible for discounts around the world, even on rail and bus travel in some countries.

In New York, hostels are often full of international travelers.

To contact the organizations: **Hostelling International—USA** (⊠ 8401 Colesville Rd., Suite 600, Silver Spring, MD 20910 ☎ 301/495–1240 ≞ 301/495–6697 ⊕ www.hiusa.org). **Hostelling International—Canada** (⊠ 205 Catherine St., Suite 400, Ottawa, Ontario K2P 1C3 ☎ 613/237–7884 or 800/663–5777 ≞ 613/237–7868 ⊕ www.hihostels.ca). **YHA England and Wales** (⊠ Trevelyan House, Dimple Rd., Matlock, Derbyshire DE4 3YH, U.K. ☎ 0870/870–8808, 0870/770–8868, or 0162/959–2600 ≞ 0870/770–6127 ⊕ www.yha.org.uk). **YHA Australia** (⊠ 422 Kent St., Sydney, NSW 2001 ☎ 02/9261–1111 ≞ 02/9261–1969 ⊕ www.yha.com.au). **YHA**

New Zealand (⊠ Level 1, Moorhouse City, 166 Moorhouse Ave., Box 436, Christchurch ☎ 03/379–9970 or 0800/278–299 ≞ 03/365–4476 ⊕ www.yha.org.nz).

Hotels

All hotels listed have private bath unless otherwise noted.

Toll-Free Numbers Best Western ☎ 800/528–1234 ⊕ www.bestwestern.com. **Choice** ☎ 800/424–6423 ⊕ www.choicehotels.com. **Clarion** ☎ 800/424–6423 ⊕ www.choicehotels.com. **Days Inn** ☎ 800/325–2525 ⊕ www.daysinn.com. **Embassy Suites** ☎ 800/362–2779 ⊕ www.embassysuites.com. **Fairfield Inn** ☎ 800/228–2800 ⊕ www.marriott.com. **Four Seasons** ☎ 800/332–3442 ⊕ www.fourseasons.com. **Hilton** ☎ 800/445–8667 ⊕ www.hilton.com. **Holiday Inn** ☎ 800/465–4329 ⊕ www.ichotelsgroup.com. **Howard Johnson** ☎ 800/446–4656 ⊕ www.hojo.com. **Hyatt Hotels & Resorts** ☎ 800/233–1234 ⊕ www.hyatt.com. **Inter-Continental** ☎ 800/327–0200 ⊕ www.ichotelsgroup.com. **La Quinta** ☎ 800/531–5900 ⊕ www.lq.com. **Marriott** ☎ 800/228–9290 ⊕ www.marriott.com. **Le Meridien** ☎ 800/543–4300 ⊕ www.lemeridien.com. **Omni** ☎ 800/843–6664 ⊕ www.omnihotels.com. **Quality Inn** ☎ 800/424–6423 ⊕ www.choicehotels.com. **Radisson** ☎ 800/333–3333 ⊕ www.radisson.com. **Ramada** ☎ 800/228–2828, 800/854–7854 international reservations ⊕ www.ramada.com. **Renaissance Hotels & Resorts** ☎ 800/468–3571 ⊕ www.renaissancehotels.com/. **Ritz-Carlton** ☎ 800/241–3333 ⊕ www.ritzcarlton.com. **Sheraton** ☎ 800/325–3535 ⊕ www.starwood.com/sheraton. **Sleep Inn** ☎ 800/424–6423 ⊕ www.choicehotels.com. **Westin Hotels & Resorts** ☎ 800/228–3000 ⊕ www.starwood.com/westin.

of the 1940s. Although it's small and homey, the inn provides private baths and satellite TV in all rooms, an elevator, and, of course, breakfast. ⊠ *131 W. 23rd St., between 6th and 7th Aves., Chelsea 10011* ☎*212/ 463–0330* 🖷 *212/463–0302* ⊕ *www.innon23rd.com* ➫ *13 rooms, 1 suite* ᗉ *In-room data ports, Wi-Fi, Internet; no smoking* ⊟ *AE, MC, V* ⏐◎⏐ *CP* Ⓜ *Subway: F, V to 23rd St.*

¢–$ 🏨 **Chelsea Inn.** The eclectic, country ambience here is a refreshing change from the characterless hotels that dominate this price category. Housed in an old brownstone, it's a favorite of young budget travelers, who don't mind not having an elevator and appreciate the funky style and in-room cooking facilities. (Most rooms have kitchenettes; others have a refrigerator and sink.) Rooms, with shared or private bath, are a hodgepodge of country quilts and thrift-shop antiques. A few in back overlook a little courtyard with an ivy-draped fence, and quiet prevails even though next door sits one of the largest gay bars in town. ⊠ *46 W. 17th St., between 5th and 6th Aves., Chelsea 10011* ☎ *212/645–8989 or 800/ 640–6469* 🖷 *212/645–1903* ⊕ *www.chelseainn.com* ➫ *26 rooms, 4 with bath* ᗉ *In-room safes, some kitchenettes, some microwaves, refrigerators, cable TV* ⊟ *AE, D, MC, V* ⏐◎⏐ *CP* Ⓜ *Subway: 4, 5, 6, L, N, Q, R, W to 14th St./Union Sq.; F, V to 14th St.*

Midtown West

★ $$$$ 🏨 **Mandarin Oriental.** No standard hotel rooms in Manhattan are larger or luxer than those at the Mandarin. Black-enamel furniture is embellished with Asian-inspired silver draw pulls; silk-encased throw pillows nearly cover the plush beds; marble-ensconced bathrooms are larger than some New York apartments. Since the hotel begins on the 35th floor, views of the city, especially Central Park, are paramount; even the swimming pool has floor-to-ceiling windows and park vistas. Contemporary art, notably two glass sculptures by Dale Chihuly, graces the cavernous public spaces; the hotel also contains an elaborate spa, glass-enclosed lounge, and high-end Asiate restaurant. You will pay for all this pleasure—rates start at $650 per night. ⊠ *80 Columbus Circle, at 60th St., Midtown West 10019* ☎ *212/805–8800* 🖷 *212/805–8888* ⊕ *www.mandarinoriental.com* ➫ *203 rooms, 48 suites* ᗉ *Restaurant, room service, minibars, cable TV, in-room DVDs, in-room data ports, pool, gym, spa, bar, dry cleaning, laundry service, concierge, business services* ⊟ *AE, D, DC, MC, V* Ⓜ *Subway: A, B, C, D, 1, 9 to 59th St./Columbus Circle.*

$$$$ 🏨 **Ritz-Carlton New York, Central Park South.** A luxurious retreat with stellar views of Central Park, the former St. Moritz hotel is easily one of the top properties in the city. No request is too difficult for the superlative Ritz staff, one reason the hotel's a favorite of celebrities and royalty. Quietly elegant rooms and suites are sumptuous without feeling stiff or stuffy, with high thread-count sheets and rich plush fabrics throughout. Exceptional French cuisine is served at jewel-box Atelier restaurant and the La Prairie salon is a pampering treat. ⊠ *50 Central Park S, at 6th Ave., Midtown West 10019* ☎ *212/308–9100 or 800/241–3333* 🖷 *212/ 207–8831* ⊕ *www.ritzcarlton.com* ➫ *237 rooms, 40 suites* ᗉ *Restaurant, room service, minibars, in-room safes, cable TV with movies, in-*

FodorsChoice ★

room DVDs, in-room data ports, gym, spa, massage, bar, lobby lounge, babysitting, Internet, dry cleaning, laundry service, concierge, meeting rooms, some pets allowed, no-smoking floors ▭ *AE, D, DC, MC, V* Ⓜ *Subway: F, V to 57th St.*

$$$–$$$$ 🏨 **Essex House, a Westin Hotel.** The lobby of this stately Central Park South property is an art deco masterpiece, with inlaid marble floors and bas-relief elevator doors. Reproductions of Chippendale or Louis XV antiques decorate guest rooms, all of which have marble bathrooms and luxuriously comfortable beds. The top 20 floors of the hotel, called the St. Regis Club, provides even more lavish rooms, all with park views, as well as butler service. For all-out decadence, book a table at Michelin-starred chef Alain Ducasse's restaurant, where caviar and truffles are de rigueur and prix fixe dinners starting at $150 buy you your table for the entire evening. ✉ *160 Central Park S, between 6th and 7th Aves., Midtown West 10019* ☎ *212/247–0300 or 800/937–8461* 📠 *212/315–1839* ⊕ *www.westin.com/essexhouse* 🛏 *526 rooms, 79 suites* ♿ *2 restaurants, room service, in-room fax, in-room safes, minibars, cable TV, in-room VCRs, in-room data ports, exercise equipment, gym, health club, spa, bar, babysitting, dry cleaning, laundry service, concierge, Internet, business services, meeting rooms, parking (fee), no-smoking rooms* ▭ *AE, D, DC, MC, V* Ⓜ *Subway: F, N, R, Q, W to 57th St.*

$$$–$$$$ 🏨 **Le Parker Meridien.** This chic midtown hotel provides two things that don't always come together in New York: sleek styling and top-of-the-line service. The lobby's striking atrium combines cherry paneling, hand-painted columns, and contemporary art. Crisp, modern rooms include low platform beds, rotating ceiling-to-floor entertainment units, Aeron chairs, CD players, and Central Park or skyline views. A 15,000-square-foot health club has a glass-enclosed rooftop pool and spa services. Norma's serves the morning meal from 6:30 AM to 3 PM; the discreetly hidden Burger Joint is a neighborhood favorite. ✉ *118 W. 57th St., between 6th and 7th Aves., Midtown West 10019* ☎ *212/245–5000 or 800/543–4300* 📠 *212/307–1776* ⊕ *www.parkermeridien.com* 🛏 *701 rooms, 249 suites* ♿ *2 restaurants, room service, in-room safes, minibars, microwaves, cable TV, in-room DVD/VCRs, in-room data ports, indoor pool, health club, hot tub, massage, sauna, spa, basketball, racquetball, bar, babysitting, dry cleaning, laundry service, concierge, Internet, business services, meeting rooms, parking (fee), some pets allowed, no-smoking rooms, no-smoking floors* ▭ *AE, D, DC, MC, V* Ⓜ *Subway: B, D, E, N, Q, R, W to 57th St.*

$$$–$$$$ 🏨 **Rihga Royal.** This discreet establishment—the only luxury all-suites hotel in Manhattan—has a loyal following among celebrities and business travelers. Each of its contemporary-style suites—many of them quite spacious—has a living room, bedroom, and large marble bath with glass-enclosed shower and separate tub. Some suites have French doors and bay windows, and the pricier Pinnacle Suites include personalized business cards, cellular phones, printer-copiers, and even complimentary town-car service from and to airports. The hotel's spectacular Sunday brunch has become a local favorite. ✉ *151 W. 54th St., between 6th and 7th Aves., Midtown West 10019* ☎ *212/307–5000 or 800/937–*

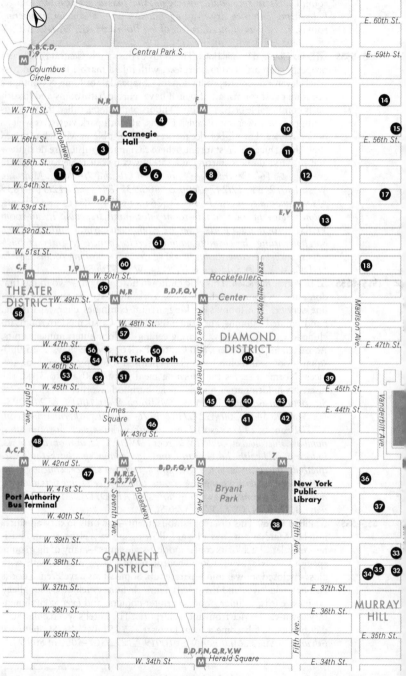

E. 60th St.

E. 59th St.

**A,B,C,D,
1,9**

Columbus
Circle

Central Park S.

N,R

F

W. 57th St.

Broadway

Carnegie
Hall

④

⑭

⑮

E. 56th St.

W. 56th St.

⑩

W. 55th St.

③

⑨

⑪

W. 54th St.

①

②

⑤ ⑥

⑧

⑫

⑰

⑦

W. 53rd St.

B,D,E

E,V

W. 52nd St.

⑬

⑥①

W. 51st St.

⑥⓪

C,E

1,9

⑱

W. 50th St.

Rockefeller Plaza

⑤⑨

THEATER
DISTRICT

W. 49th St.

Rockefeller

N,R

B,D,F,Q,V

Center

⑤⑧

W. 48th St.

⑤⑦

DIAMOND
DISTRICT

W. 47th St.

⑤⑥

⑤⓪

E. 47th St.

⑤⑤ ⑤④

TKTS Ticket Booth

⑤⑨

Eighth Ave.

W. 46th St.

⑤③

⑤②

⑤①

Avenue of the Americas

W. 45th St.

⑤⑨

E. 45th St.

Vanderbilt Ave.

Times
Square

⑤⑤ ⑤④ ⑤⓪

⑤③

W. 44th St.

⑤①

⑤②

E. 44th St.

Madison Ave.

⑥⑥

W. 43rd St.

A,C,E

⑥⑧

7

W. 42nd St.

B,D,F,Q,V

⑥⑦

**N,R,S
1,2,3,7,9**

Bryant
Park

New York
Public
Library

⑥⑥

Port Authority
Bus Terminal

W. 41st St.

Seventh Ave.

Broadway

(Sixth Ave.)

⑥⑦

W. 40th St.

⑥⑧

GARMENT
DISTRICT

W. 39th St.

⑥⑥

W. 38th St.

⑥④ ⑥⑤ ⑥②

W. 37th St.

E. 37th St.

MURRAY
HILL

W. 36th St.

E. 36th St.

Fifth Ave.

W. 35th St.

E. 35th St.

Fifth Ave.

B,D,F,N,Q,R,V,W

W. 34th St.

Herald Square

E. 34th St.

5454 🖨 212/765–6530 ⊕ *www.rihgaroyalny.com* 🛏 *500 suites*
⟡ *Restaurant, room service, in-room fax, in-room safes, in-room hot*
tubs, kitchenettes, minibars, refrigerators, cable TV with movies and video
games, in-room VCRs, in-room data ports, gym, health club, massage,
bar, babysitting, dry cleaning, laundry service, concierge, Internet, busi-
ness services, meeting rooms, parking (fee), no-smoking floors ▤ *AE,*
D, DC, MC, V Ⓜ *Subway: B, D, E to 7th Ave.; N, Q, R, W to 57th St.*

$$–$$$$ 🏨 **The Bryant Park.** Carved out of the bones of the former American Ra-
diator Building that towers over the New York Public Library and Bryant
Park, this brilliant blend of '20s Gothic Revival exterior and sleekly
modern rooms delivers the pizzazz worthy of the city's moniker, Gotham.
Rooms are furnished at the apex of minimalist chic with sumptuous traver-
tine bathrooms, hardwood floors with Tibetan rugs, and killer views. Since
it's at the apex of Fashion Week activities, expect a designer-filled crowd
and a runway-feel in the stark red lobby. Both the restaurant and bars
here are popular with the after-work crowd. ✉ *40 W. 40th St., between*
5th and 6th Aves., Midtown West 10018 ☎ *212/869–0100 or 877/640–*
9300 🖨 *212/869–4446* ⊕ *www.bryantparkhotel.com* 🛏 *107 rooms, 22*
suites ⟡ *Restaurant, room service, in-room safes, minibars, cable TV with*
movies, in-room data ports, Web TV, gym, health club, massage, spa,
steam room, 2 bars, dry cleaning, laundry service, concierge, Internet,
business services, meeting rooms, parking (fee), some pets allowed (fee),
no-smoking floors ▤ *AE, DC, MC, V* Ⓜ *Subway: B, D, F, V to 42nd*
St.; 7 to 5th Ave.

$$–$$$$ 🏨 **City Club Hotel.** Like Cary Grant's ocean-liner suites, City Club rooms
are brisk, bright, and masculine, with Jonathan Adler ceramics, base-
ball photos from the '50s, Hermes bathroom products, and "City Club"
banner wool blankets. The bathroom marble is chocolate color, and the
wallpaper flecked with mica. Privacy, not publicity, is the emphasis at
this luxe property owned by young man-about-town Jeff Klein and designed by celebrity decorator Jeffrey Bilhuber. The lobby is tiny, and guests
who wish to drink are sent across the street to the Royalton. Top chef
Daniel Boulud opened his db Bistro Moderne downstairs. ✉ *55 W. 44th*
St., between 5th and 6th Aves., Midtown West 10036 ☎ *212/921–*
5500 🖨 *212/944–5544* ⊕ *www.cityclubhotel.com* 🛏 *62 rooms, 3*
suites ⟡ *Restaurant, minibars, cable TV with movies, in-room DVDs,*
in-room data ports, parking (fee), no-smoking rooms ▤ *AE, D, DC,*
MC, V Ⓜ *Subway: B, D, F, V to 42nd St.; 7 to 5th Ave.*

$$–$$$$ 🏨 **The Muse.** In the heart of the theater district, the Muse has a display of
artwork that includes photos of such "muses" as Katharine Hepburn and
Nureyev. Fans of the hotel rave about the oversize rooms and bathrooms,
super-comfortable beds, and thoughtful touches such as luxe bathroom
goodies and complimentary business cards. Note that although the prime
Theater District location may be a draw for some, the noise that may ac-
company it is also part of the atmosphere. The hotel's stagelike restau-
rant, District, serves globally influenced American cuisine. ✉ *130 W.*
46th St., between 6th and 7th Aves., Midtown West 10036 ☎ *212/485–*
2400 or 877/692–6873 🖨 *212/485–2900* ⊕ *www.themusehotel.com*
🛏 *200 rooms, 19 suites* ⟡ *Restaurant, room service, in-room safes,*
minibars, cable TV with movies, in-room data ports, gym, massage, bar,

dry cleaning, laundry service, concierge, business services, meeting rooms, parking (fee), some pets allowed, no-smoking floors ▤ *AE, D, DC, MC, V* Ⓜ *Subway: B, D, F, V to 47–50 Sts./Rockefeller Center.*

$$$ ⌸ **Chambers.** Midtown is the new downtown in David Rockwell's gorgeous showcase, where more than 500 works of art hang and each guest-room floor has a mural installation. Loftlike rooms with hand-troweled cement walls are decorated warmly, and the bathroom floors of poured concrete shimmer with glass mosaic tiles. After entering through the magnificent carved teak doors and passing through the intimate yet grand lobby with soaring ceilings, double-sided fireplace, and Hugo Boss–uniformed staff, head downstairs to the restaurant Town, which also provides room service, for one of the most sublime culinary experiences around. ⊠ *15 W. 56th St., off 5th Ave., Midtown West 10019* ☎ *212/974–5656 or 866/ 204–5656* 🖶 *212/974–5657* ⊕ *www.chambershotel.com* 🔊 *72 rooms, 5 suites* ⌂ *Restaurant, in-room safes, minibars, cable TV with movies, in-room DVDs, in-room data ports, massage, bar, lounge, babysitting, dry cleaning, laundry service, concierge, parking (fee), some pets allowed, no-smoking floors* ▤ *AE, D, DC, MC, V* Ⓜ *Subway: F, V to 57th St.*

★ $$$ ⌸ **The Iroquois.** Built during the Depression, this once prosaic hotel is now among the city's better boutique properties, and significantly more modern than its traditional exterior. Service is smiling and top-notch, and rooms are a quiet retreat from the frenetic neighborhood. Children can enjoy in-room Nintendo systems and pint-size Frette bathrobes. The large, restful cream-and-white standard rooms have ultracomfortable beds, and the marble-and-brass bathrooms contain phones and pedestal sinks. Off the tiny lobby are a homey reading area with a laptop, a bar, and the intimate and refined Triomphe restaurant. ⊠ *49 W. 44th St., between 5th and 6th Aves., Midtown West 10036* ☎ *212/840–3080 or 800/332–7220* 🖶 *212/398–1754* ⊕ *www.iroquoisny.com* 🔊 *105 rooms, 9 suites* ⌂ *Restaurant, room service, in-room safes, minibars, cable TV with movies and video games, in-room data ports, gym, health club, massage, sauna, bar, dry cleaning, laundry service, concierge, Internet, business services, meeting rooms, parking (fee), no-smoking floors* ▤ *AE, D, DC, MC, V* Ⓜ *Subway: B, D, F, V to 42nd St.; 7 to 5th Ave.*

$$$ ⌸ **The Mansfield.** Built in 1901 as lodging for distinguished bachelors, this small, clubby hotel has an Edwardian sensibility from the working fireplace in the lounge to the lobby's coffered ceiling and marble and cast-iron staircase. Rooms, with their black-marble bathrooms, dark-wood venetian blinds, and sleigh beds, never disappoint. And suites are especially grand. A machine dispenses complimentary 24-hour coffee and tea, and the hotel's swank M Bar serves cocktails, caviar, and desserts until midnight. For a romantic, if refined, getaway, ensconce yourself in the duplex penthouse suite. ⊠ *12 W. 44th St., between 5th and 6th Aves., Midtown West 10036* ☎ *212/944–6050 or 800/255–5167* 🖶 *212/764–4477* ⊕ *www.mansfieldhotel.com* 🔊 *124 rooms, 25 suites* ⌂ *Room service, in-room safes, some microwaves, refrigerators, cable TV, in-room VCRs, bar, cinema, concert hall, library, dry cleaning, laundry service, concierge, Internet, business services, meeting rooms, parking (fee), some pets allowed, no-smoking rooms, no-smoking floors* ▤ *AE, D, DC, MC, V* Ⓜ *Subway B, D, F, V to 42nd St.*

$$$ 🏨 **The Royalton.** During the '90s, the lobby restaurant "44" started the craze of local A-listers meeting and greeting in hotel boîtes. Although many of the movers and shakers have moved on, the minimalist Philippe Starck space with its sumptuous sofas and secluded Vodka Bar still gives off a cool vibe. Before you can get to your room, you'll have to transverse this hipster lounge, and then feel your way down the dimly lit hallways. Guest rooms have low-lying, custom-made beds, tasteful lighting, and fresh flowers. Some of the rooms have working fireplaces, and all have CD players. Slate bathrooms with stainless-steel and glass fixtures may also include round, two-person tubs. ⊠ *44 W. 44th St., between 5th and 6th Aves., Midtown West 10036* 🕿 *212/869–4400 or 800/635–9013* 🖷 *212/575–0012* ⊕ *www.ianschragerhotels.com* 📮 *141 rooms, 27 suites* ♨ *Restaurant, room service, in-room safes, minibars, refrigerators, cable TV, in-room VCRs, in-room data ports, exercise equipment, gym, massage, bar, babysitting, dry cleaning, laundry service, concierge, business services, meeting rooms, parking (fee), some pets allowed, no-smoking rooms* ▤ *AE, DC, MC, V* Ⓜ *Subway: B, D, F, V to 42nd St.*

$$$ 🏨 **Sofitel New York.** The European hotel group's property is a dramatic, contemporary 30-story curved tower overlooking 5th Avenue. The place feels professional, with a spacious, quiet lobby, an elegant French brasserie (Gaby, named for a Parisian model who made a name for herself in the Big Apple in the 1920s), and courteous staff who are always on hand. Upstairs, the rooms are what you expect to find in a big corporate hotel—lots of earth tones and mahogany—but what they lack in aesthetics they more than make up for in simple comforts; the best rooms have balconies and views of the Chrysler Building. ⊠ *45 W. 44th St., between 5th and 6th Aves., Midtown West 10036* 🕿 *212/354–8844* 🖷 *212/782–3002* ⊕ *www.sofitel.com* 📮 *398 rooms, 52 suites* ♨ *Restaurant, room service, minibars, cable TV with movies, in-room data ports, gym, massage, bar, dry cleaning, laundry service, concierge, Internet, business services, meeting rooms, parking (fee), no-smoking floors* ▤ *AE, D, DC, MC, V* Ⓜ *Subway: B, D, F, V to 42nd St.*

$$$ 🏨 **The Time Hotel.** This spot half a block from the din of Times Square tempers trendiness with a touch of humor. A ridiculously futuristic glass elevator—eggshells line the bottom of the shaft—transports guests to the second-floor lobby. In the adjoining bar, nature videos lighten up the low-flung, serious gray-scale furnishings. The smallish guest rooms, each themed on one of the primary colors—red, yellow, or blue—have mood lighting and even specific "color" aromas that create a unique, if contrived, hotel experience. ⊠ *224 W. 49th St., between Broadway and 8th Ave., Midtown West 10019* 🕿 *212/320–2900 or 877/846–3692* 🖷 *212/245–2305* ⊕ *www.thetimeny.com* 📮 *164 rooms, 29 suites* ♨ *Restaurant, room service, in-room fax, in-room safes, minibars, refrigerators, cable TV with movies, in-room VCRs, gym, bar, dry cleaning, laundry service, concierge, business services, parking (fee), no-smoking floors* ▤ *AE, D, DC, MC, V* Ⓜ *Subway: 1, 9, C, E to 50th St.; R, W to 49th St.*

★ **$$$**   🏨 **Warwick.** Astonishingly, this palatial hotel was built by William Randolph Hearst in 1927 as a private hotel for his friends and family. The midtown favorite is well placed for the Theater District. The marble-floor lobby buzzes with activity; the Randolph restaurant is on one side and

Murals on 54, a Continental restaurant, is on the other. Handsome, Regency-style rooms have soft pastel color schemes, mahogany armoires, and marble bathrooms, and some have fax machines. The Cary Grant suite was the actor's New York residence for 12 years, and encapsulates a more refined moment in New York glamour. ⊠ 65 W. 54th St., at 6th Ave., Midtown West 10019 ☎ 212/247–2700 or 800/223–4099 ☎ 212/713–1751 ⊕ www.warwickhotels.com ↘ 359 rooms, 67 suites ⌂ 2 restaurants, room service, in-room safes, minibars, cable TV with movies and video games, in-room data ports, Wi-Fi, exercise equipment, gym, bar, babysitting, dry cleaning, laundry service, concierge, Internet, business services, meeting rooms, parking (fee), no-smoking rooms ⊟ AE, DC, MC, V Ⓜ Subway: E, V to 5th Ave.; N, Q, R, W to 57th St.

$$–$$$ ▦ **The Algonquin.** Even Matilda the resident cat, who holds court in the parlorlike lobby, seems to know that the draw here is the ghost of its literary past. Hordes of literary enthusiasts fill the lobby; signed works of former Round Table raconteurs can be checked out of the library, and their witticisms grace guest room doors. New Yorker cartoon strewn wallpaper covers hallways. Small and boxy, the rooms, though spotless, have a less than cheerful feel, but the hotel has been upgraded to meet a higher technological standard. The renowned Oak Room is one of the city's premier cabaret performance venues, and the publike Blue Bar makes visitors from around the world feel at home. ⊠ 59 W. 44th St., between 5th and 6th Aves., Midtown West 10036 ☎ 212/840–6800 or 800/555–8000 ☎ 212/944–1419 ⊕ www.algonquinhotel.com ↘ 150 rooms, 24 suites ⌂ 2 restaurants, room service, in-room safes, cable TV with movies, in-room data ports, gym, bar, cabaret, library, dry cleaning, laundry service, concierge, Internet, business services, meeting rooms, parking (fee), no-smoking floors ⊟ AE, D, DC, MC, V Ⓜ Subway: B, D, F, V to 42nd St.

$$–$$$ ▦ **Hilton New York.** New York City's largest hotel and the epicenter of the city's hotel-based conventions, the Hilton has a Vegas-size range of business facilities, eating establishments, and shops, all designed for convenience. Considering the size of this property, guest rooms are well maintained, and all have coffeemakers, hair dryers, and ironing boards. A variety of local ethnic cuisines is available at the New York Marketplace, a mall-style food court in the hotel lobby. ⊠ 1335 6th Ave., between W. 53rd and W. 54th Sts., Midtown West 10019 ☎ 212/586–7000 or 800/445–8667 ☎ 212/315–1374 ⊕ www.newyorktowers.hilton.com ↘ 2,079 rooms, 2 penthouses, 5 suites ⌂ 2 restaurants, café, room service, in-room safes, minibars, cable TV, in-room data ports, gym, health club, hair salon, hot tub, massage, sauna, 2 bars, sports bar, shops, babysitting, dry cleaning, laundry service, concierge, concierge floors, business services, parking (fee) ⊟ AE, D, DC, MC, V Ⓜ Subway: B, D, F, V to 47th–50th Sts./Rockefeller Center.

$$–$$$ ▦ **Marriott Marquis.** This brash behemoth in the heart of the Theater District is a place New Yorkers love to hate. With its own little city of restaurants, a sushi bar, shops, meeting rooms, and ballrooms—there's even a Broadway theater—it virtually defines "over-the-top." As at other Marriotts, all of the nearly 2,000 rooms here look alike and are pleasant and functional. Some have more dramatic urban views than others. The

View, the revolving restaurant and bar on the 49th floor, provides one of the most spectacular panoramas in New York, but it's only open in the evening. Make a reservation to get in. ✉ *1535 Broadway, at W. 45th St., Midtown West 10036* ☎ *212/398–1900 or 800/843–4898* 🖶 *212/704–8930 or 212/704–8931* ⊕ *www.marriott.com* ⤢ *1,889 rooms, 58 suites* ☖ *3 restaurants, café, coffee shop, room service, in-room safes, minibars, cable TV, in-room data ports, exercise equipment, health club, hair salon, hot tub, massage, 3 bars, theater, babysitting, dry cleaning, laundry service, concierge, Internet, business services, meeting rooms, parking (fee), some pets allowed, no-smoking rooms* 🚭 *AE, D, DC, MC, V* Ⓜ *Subway: 1, 2, 3, 7, 9, S, N, Q, R, W to 42nd St./Times Sq.*

★ **$$–$$$** 🏨 **The Michelangelo.** Italophiles will feel that they've been transported to the good life in the boot at this deluxe hotel, whose long, wide lobby lounge is clad with multihue marble and Veronese-style oil paintings. Upstairs, the decor of the relatively spacious rooms (averaging 475 square feet) varies. You can choose contemporary, neoclassic, art deco, or French country—all have marble foyers and marble bathrooms equipped with bidets and oversize 55-gallon tubs. The larger rooms have sitting areas and king beds. Complimentary cappuccino, pastries, and other Italian treats are served each morning in the baroque lobby lounge. ✉ *152 W. 51st St., at 7th Ave., Midtown West 10019* ☎ *212/765–1900 or 800/237–0990* 🖶 *212/581–7618* ⊕ *www.michelangelohotel.com* ⤢ *123 rooms, 55 suites* ☖ *Restaurant, room service, in-room fax, in-room safes, minibars, cable TV with movies, in-room DVDs, in-room data ports, exercise equipment, gym, bar, babysitting, dry cleaning, laundry service, concierge, business services, meeting rooms, parking (fee), no-smoking floors* 🚭 *AE, D, DC, MC, V* ⦿ *CP* Ⓜ *Subway: B, D, E to 7th Ave.; 1, 9 to 50th St.; B, D, F, V to 47th–50th Sts./Rockefeller Center.*

$$–$$$ 🏨 **The Paramount.** The Paramount caters to a somewhat bohemian, fashionable, yet cost-conscious clientele. The tiny rooms—many guests remark on how they can touch both walls while sitting on the bed—have white furnishings and walls, gilt-framed headboards, and conical steel bathroom sinks. In the lobby, a sheer platinum wall and a glamorous sweep of staircase lead to the Mezzanine Restaurant, where you can enjoy cocktails or dinner while gazing down on the action below. The bar, once fiercely trendy, draws a somewhat diluted crowd now that other Whiskey Bars have opened in many of the W Hotels around town. Hotel drawbacks include limited room amenities and a sometimes harried staff. The hotel has been sold to the Hard Rock Hotel group and may close for a period during what's being billed as a multi-million dollar refurbishment. ✉ *235 W. 46th St., between Broadway and 8th Aves., Midtown West 10036* ☎ *212/764–5500 or 800/225–7474* 🖶 *212/354–5237* ⊕ *www.hardrock.com* ⤢ *590 rooms, 10 suites* ☖ *2 restaurants, café, room service, in-room safes, minibars, cable TV, in-room VCRs, in-room data ports, gym, 2 bars, dry cleaning, laundry service, concierge, Internet, business services, meeting rooms, no-smoking floors* 🚭 *AE, D, DC, MC, V* Ⓜ *Subway: 1, 2, 3, 7, 9, S, N, Q, R, W to 42nd St./Times Sq.*

$$–$$$ 🏨 **The Shoreham.** This is a miniature, low-attitude version of the ultra-cool Royalton—and it's comfortable to boot. Almost everything is metal or of metal color, from perforated steel headboards (lighted from behind) to steel sinks in the shiny, tiny bathrooms to the silver-gray carpets. Pleasant touches include CD players and cedar-lined closets. There's complimentary Continental breakfast as well as free cappuccino and other hot drinks in the lobby, and the Shoreham Restaurant & Bar serves an eclectic, light menu of sandwiches and salads. ⊠ *33 W. 55th St., between 5th and 6th Aves., Midtown West 10019* ☎ *212/247–6700 or 877/847–4444* 🖷 *212/765–9741* ⊕ *www.shorehamhotel.com* 🖅 *174 rooms, 37 suites* ⟁ *Restaurant, room service, in-room safes, cable TV, in-room VCRs, bar, babysitting, dry cleaning, laundry service, concierge, Internet, business services, parking (fee), some pets allowed, no-smoking floors* ⊟ *AE, D, DC, MC, V* ⓧ| *CP* Ⓜ *Subway: E, V to 5th Ave.*

$$–$$$
Fodor'sChoice
★

🖫 **W Times Square.** Times Square finally goes hip on a grand scale with the opening of this super-sleek 57-floor monolith, the flagship of the white-hot W line. After passing through an entrance of cascading, glass-enclosed water, you alight to the seventh-floor lobby where Kenneth Cole–clad "welcome ambassadors" await. The Jetsons experience continues in the space-age, white-on-white lobby and the futuristic rooms with their glowing resin boxes and multiple shades of gray. The bi-level Blue Fin restaurant with its sushi bar and floor-to-ceiling windows caps the architectural wonderment. ⊠ *1567 Broadway, at W. 47th St., Midtown West 10036* ☎ *212/930–7400 or 877/946–8357* 🖷 *212/930–7500* ⊕ *www. whotels.com* 🖅 *466 rooms, 43 suites* ⟁ *Restaurant, café, room service, in-room safes, minibars, cable TV with movies, in-room DVDs, in-room data ports, exercise equipment, gym, massage, 4 bars, shop, dry cleaning, laundry service, concierge, Internet, business services, parking (fee), some pets allowed (fee), no-smoking rooms, no-smoking floors* ⊟ *AE, D, DC, MC, V* Ⓜ *Subway: 1, 2, 3, 7, 9, S, N, Q, R, W to 42nd St./Times Sq.*

$–$$$
🖫 **The Hudson.** From the bower-draped lobby to the dark-wall rooms with their whiter-than-white furnishings, the Hudson is yet another extravaganza from the team of Ian Schrager and Philippe Starck. One thousand rooms are squeezed into 23 floors, some as small as 150 square feet, and service is at a minimum. Tight quarters are balanced by low (by Manhattan standards) rates, but if you're staying here, it's for the atmosphere, not the accommodations. Some bathrooms have see-through shower walls, and all have a supply of candles. Like a posh living room, the garden-lounge is one of the most coveted outdoor spaces in town. ⊠ *356 W. 58th St., between 8th and 9th Aves., Midtown West 10019* ☎ *212/554–6000* 🖷 *212/554–6001* ⊕ *www.hudsonhotel.com* 🖅 *1,000 rooms, 2 suites* ⟁ *Restaurant, room service, in-room safes, in-room data ports, health club, massage, bar, laundry service, concierge, business services, meeting rooms, parking (fee)* ⊟ *AE, D, DC, MC, V* Ⓜ *Subway: 1, 9, A, B, C, D to 59th St./Columbus Circle.*

$$
🖫 **The Blakely.** The cozy English clubhouse–like lobby sets the tone for this hotel, formerly the Gorham, with lots of maple and cherry paneling and wainscoting, large library chairs, and leather-bound books along the walls. Fully equipped kitchenettes and large work areas make the spacious rooms a bargain, and the dark woods and rich fabrics are stylish enough to make the hotel a favorite of Louis Vuitton employees. Abboccato, the well-reviewed Italian restaurant, provides room service. The location across from City Center is a boon to arts lovers. ⊠ *136 W. 55th St., be-*

tween 6th and 7th Aves., Midtown West 10019 ☎ *212/245–1800 or 800/735–0710* 🖷 *212/582–8332* ⊕ *www.blakelynewyork.com* 🛏 *57 rooms, 54 suites* ⚭ *Restaurant, room service, in-room safes, kitchenettes, microwaves, refrigerators, cable TV, in-room data ports, Wi-Fi, exercise equipment, gym, massage, dry cleaning, laundry service, concierge, Internet, business services, parking (fee), no-smoking rooms, no-smoking floors* ▤ *AE, DC, MC, V* Ⓜ *Subway: N, Q, R, W to 57th St.*

$$ 🏨 **Casablanca.** This Morocco comes by way of Disney: mosaic tiles, framed Berber scarves and rugs, and a mural of a North African city. Rattan furniture, ceiling fans, and Moroccan-style wood shutters dress up the smallish and mysteriously tatty rooms, which have elaborately tiled bathrooms. In the spacious lounge with a fireplace, a piano, a 41-inch movie screen, and bookshelves stocked with Bogart-abilia, join guests for the popular nightly wine-and-cheese fest and free Continental breakfast in the morning. ⊠ *147 W. 43rd St., between 6th Ave. and Broadway, Midtown West 10036* ☎ *212/869–1212 or 888/922–7225* 🖷 *212/391–7585* ⊕ *www.casablancahotel.com* 🛏 *48 rooms, 5 suites* ⚭ *Restaurant, room service, in-room safes, minibars, refrigerators, cable TV, in-room VCRs, in-room data ports, lounge, piano, babysitting, dry cleaning, laundry service, Internet, business services, meeting rooms, parking (fee), no-smoking floors* ▤ *AE, DC, MC, V* ❑ *CP* Ⓜ *Subway: 1, 2, 3, 7, 9, S, N, Q, R, W to 42nd St./Times Sq.*

$$ 🏨 **Dream Hotel.** A Kafkaesque dream by way of hotelier Vikram Chatwal, this midtown scenester focuses more on style than comfort. The lobby oddly combines an awesome two-story cylindrical neon-lighted aquarium, an unsettling two-story photograph of a tattooed woman, and a copper sculpture of Catherine the Great. Step off the elevator onto your floor and you'll be met with a jarring neon photograph; rooms are almost as disquieting—stark white walls, black furniture, and light box desks that glow from within. Stay here if you love things modern: plasma TVs, complimentary iPod use, a Deepak Chopra spa, and a velvet-rope rooftop bar scene. ⊠ *210 W. 55th St., at Broadway, Midtown West 10019* ☎ *212/247–2000 or 866/437–3266* 🖷 *212/974–0595* ⊕ *www.dreamny.com* 🛏 *208 rooms, 20 suites* ⚭ *Restaurant, room service, in-room safes, minibars, cable TV with movies, in-room data ports, exercise equipment, spa, massage, 3 bars, dry cleaning, laundry service, concierge, meeting rooms, some pets allowed (fee), parking (fee)* ▤ *AE, D, DC, MC, V* Ⓜ *Subway: N, Q, R, W to 57th St.*

$$ 🏨 **Flatotel.** Its name gives it away. This 46-story tower started life as British-built condominium apartments (flats), but has been transformed into a hotel full of spacious, minimalist rooms. At cocktail time, the contemporary leather-couch filled lobby lounge is a hub of genteel carousing; later, diners sup at the Milan-style Moda, which spills outside in good weather. The beds are custom-designed with attached night-lights and anchored at their feet by built-in drawers, and fitted with goose-down duvets and luxe linens. Bathrooms have oversize marble Jacuzzi tubs. ⊠ *135 W. 52nd St., between 6th and 7th Aves., Midtown West 10019* ☎ *212/887–9400 or 800/352–8683* 🖷 *212/887–9442 for reservations, 212/887–9795 for guests* ⊕ *www.flatotel.com* 🛏 *210 rooms, 70 suites* ⚭ *Restaurant, room service, in-room safes, kitchenettes, minibars, microwaves, re-*

frigerators, cable TV, in-room data ports, exercise equipment, gym, bar, concierge, Internet ⊟ *AE, DC, MC, V* Ⓜ *Subway: B, D, E to 7th Ave.; 1, 9 to 50th St.; B, D, F, V to 47th–50th Sts./Rockefeller Center.*

$$ Ⓣ **Hilton Times Square.** The Hilton Times Square sits atop a 335,000-square-foot retail and entertainment complex that includes a 25-theater movie megaplex and Madame Tussaud's Wax Museum. The building has a handsome Mondrian-inspired facade, but room decor is chain-hotel bland. Nonetheless, the rooms are comfortable and larger than at many chains, with amenities from in-room coffeemakers to CD players to bathrobes. The hotel is efficiently run and the staff is pleasant. Because all guest rooms are above the 21st floor, many afford excellent views of Times Square and midtown. Restaurant Above is off the "sky lobby" on the 21st floor. ⊠ *234 W. 42nd St., between 7th and 8th Aves., Midtown West 10036* ☎ *212/642–2500 or 800/445–8667* 🖷 *212/840–5516* ⊕ *www.hilton.com* ⇆ *444 rooms, 15 suites* ⚫ *Restaurant, room service, in-room safes, minibars, cable TV with movies, in-room data ports, gym, bar, babysitting, laundry service, concierge, business services, meeting rooms, some pets allowed, parking (fee); no-smoking rooms, no-smoking floors* ⊟ *AE, D, DC, MC, V* Ⓜ *Subway: 1, 2, 3, 7, 9, S, N, Q, R, W to 42nd St./Times Sq.*

$$ Ⓣ **Renaissance.** This link in the Marriott chain is a business hotel, but vacationers often take advantage of its low promotional rates and its location at the head of Times Square. For the businessperson, each spacious and plush room comes with a work desk, a duo of two-line speakerphones, call waiting, a fax, and a voice-mail system. For the diva, the marble bathrooms have deep soaking tubs and a princess phone. Elevators lead from street level to the third-floor art deco–style reception area. On the lobby floor are two bars and Foley's Restaurant & Bar, a restaurant with up-close views of Times Square. ⊠ *714 7th Ave., between W. 47th and W. 48th Sts., Midtown West 10036* ☎ *212/765–7676 or 800/628–5222* 🖷 *212/765–1962* ⊕ *www.renaissancehotels.com* ⇆ *300 rooms, 5 suites* ⚫ *Restaurant, room service, in-room safes, minibars, cable TV with movies, in-room data ports, exercise equipment, gym, massage, 2 bars, babysitting, dry cleaning, laundry service, concierge, Internet, business services, meeting rooms, parking (fee), some pets allowed (fee), no-smoking floors* ⊟ *AE, D, DC, MC, V* Ⓜ *Subway: R, W to 49th St.; 1, 9 to 50th St.*

$$ Ⓣ **The Westin New York at Times Square.** The Westin changed the skyline of midtown with this soaring skyscraper that subtly mimics the flow of the city—look for subway patterns in the carpets and the city reflected on the building's exterior. A thoughtful staff helps make the cavernous lobby and throngs of guests tolerable. Exceptionally large rooms are blissfully quiet and built to give you optimal views—especially the light-filled corner rooms. The much-noted Heavenly Bed and double shower heads are indeed praiseworthy, but for even more comfort, spa floor rooms come with massage chairs, aromatherapy candles, and other pampering pleasures. ⊠ *270 W. 43rd St., at 8th Ave., Midtown West 10036* ☎ *212/201 2700 or 866/837–4183* 🖷 *212/201–2701* ⊕ *www.westinny.com* ⇆ *737 rooms, 126 suites* ⚫ *Restaurant, café, room service, in-room fax, in-room safes, minibars, cable TV with movies, in-room data ports,*

Wi-Fi, gym, health club, massage, spa, 2 bars, babysitting, dry cleaning, laundry service, concierge, business services, meeting rooms, parking (fee), some pets allowed, no-smoking rooms, no-smoking floors ▭ *AE, D, DC, MC, V* Ⓜ *Subway: A, C, E to 42nd St./Times Sq.*

$–$$ 🏨 **Ameritania Hotel.** Guests at this busy crash pad just off Broadway are divided pretty evenly: half come for business, half for pleasure. Dimly lighted hallways create a feeling of perpetual nighttime—an impression that lingers in the bedrooms, where black-metal furniture dominates. Rates may drop by as much as $100 a night off-season, depending on occupancy. ✉ *230 W. 54th St., at Broadway, Midtown West 10019* ☎ *212/ 247–5000 or 888/664–6835* 🖷 *212/247–3316* ⊕ *www.nychotels.com/ ameritania.html* ⇄ *207 rooms, 12 suites* ♦ *Room service, some in-room safes, cable TV with movies, in-room data ports, bar, dry cleaning, laundry service, concierge, business services, parking (fee), no-smoking rooms* ▭ *AE, D, DC, MC, V* ⎪◎⎪ *CP* Ⓜ *Subway: B, D, E to 7th Ave.*

$–$$ 🏨 **Belvedere Hotel.** This affordable hotel has some fun with its art deco café and playful floor patterning, but the rooms are surprisingly conservative, with patterned bedspreads and curtains and traditional wooden headboards (an odd juxtaposition to the modern art prints on the walls). Still, the rooms are large enough for kitchenettes and have two full beds if you need them (you can also request a queen- or king-size bed). ✉ *319 W. 48th St., between 8th and 9th Aves., Midtown West 10036* ☎ *212/ 245–7000 or 888/468–3558* 🖷 *212/245–4455* ⊕ *www.newyorkhotel. com* ⇄ *398 rooms, 2 suites* ♦ *Restaurant, café, in-room safes, kitchenettes, microwaves, refrigerators, cable TV with video games, in-room data ports, shop, dry cleaning, laundry facilities, laundry service, concierge, Internet, business services, parking (fee)* ▭ *AE, D, DC, MC, V* Ⓜ *Subway: C, E to 50th St.*

★ **$–$$** 🏨 **Broadway Inn.** In the heart of the theater district, this Midwestern-friendly B&B welcomes with a charmingly comfy brick-walled reception room with hump-backed sofa, bentwood chairs, fresh flowers, and stocked book shelves that encourage lingering. Impeccably clean neo-deco–style rooms with black-lacquer beds are basic, but cheerful. An extra $70 or $80 gets you a suite with an additional fold-out sofa bed, and a kitchenette hidden by closet doors. ✉ *264 W. 46th St., between Broadway and 8th Ave., Midtown West 10036* ☎ *212/997–9200 or 800/826–6300* 🖷 *212/768– 2807* ⊕ *www.broadwayinn.com* ⇄ *28 rooms, 12 suites* ♦ *Some kitchenettes, some microwaves, refrigerators, cable TV, some in-room data ports, concierge, parking (fee), no-smoking rooms* ▭ *AE, D, DC, MC, V* Ⓜ *Subway: 1, 2, 3, 7, 9, N, Q, R, S, W to 42nd St./Times Sq.*

★ **$–$$** 🏨 **Hotel QT.** Giving budget a good name is this Times Square hotel by Andre Balazs, best known for the stylish Mercer Hotel. The unique lobby centers on a raised pool with peep-show-like windows that overlook the bar. Upstairs, rooms are modern, dorm-room in size, but have upscale hotel touches such as feather-pillow-topped mattresses, rainhead showers, and DVD players to accompany the flat-screen TVs. There's no work space, no bathtubs, and double rooms have bunk beds sprouting out of the wall; but you can't beat the price—rooms start at just $125, including Continental breakfast—and the location is as central as they come. ✉ *125 W. 45th St., between 5th and 6th Aves., Mid-*

town West 10036 ☎ *212/354–2323* 🖷 *212/302–8585* ⊕ *www.hotelqt. com* ⇆ *140 rooms* ⎴ *In-room data ports, in-room safes, refrigerators, cable TV with movies, in-room DVDs, Wi-Fi, indoor pool, gym, sauna, steam room, bar* ⊟ *AE, DC, MC, V* ⎟⍉⎟ *CP* Ⓜ *Subway: B, D, F, V to 42nd St.; 7 to 5th Ave.*

$–$$ 🖷 **Wellington Hotel.** This large, old-fashioned property's main advantages are reasonable prices and its proximity to Central Park and Carnegie Hall. The lobby has an aura of faded glamor, from the lighted-up red awning outside to the chandeliers and ornate artwork inside. The hotel appeals to families, groups, and those traveling on a budget. Rooms are small, baths are serviceable, and the staff is helpful. ✉ *871 7th Ave., at W. 55th St., Midtown West 10019* ☎ *212/247–3900 or 800/652–1212* 🖷 *212/ 581–1719* ⊕ *www.wellingtonhotel.com* ⇆ *500 rooms, 100 suites* ⎴ *Restaurant, coffee shop, microwaves, cable TV with movies, hair salon, bar, laundry facilities, laundry service, parking (fee), no-smoking floors* ⊟ *AE, D, DC, MC, V* Ⓜ *Subway: N, Q, R, W to 57th St.*

¢–$$ 🖷 **Quality Hotel and Suites.** This small prewar hotel shares its block with a plethora of Brazilian restaurants and is near many theaters and Rockefeller Center. The peculiar lobby has a narrow corridor that snakes off around a corner and is decorated with some rather handsome art deco Bakelite lamps. The rooms are very plain, but most are well maintained and clean. This block is one of midtown's most deserted at night, so travelers should be alert. ✉ *59 W. 46th St., between 5th and 6th Aves., Midtown West 10036* ☎ *212/790–2710 or 800/567–7720* 🖷 *212/290–2760* ⊕ *www.applecorehotels.com* ⇆ *209 rooms* ⎴ *Cafeteria, in-room safes, cable TV with movies and video games, in-room data ports, hair salon, bar, business services, meeting rooms, parking (fee), no-smoking rooms* ⊟ *AE, D, DC, MC, V* Ⓜ *Subway: B, D, F, V to 47th–50th Sts./Rockefeller Center.*

$ 🖷 **Hotel Edison.** This offbeat old hotel is a popular budget stop for tour groups from both the United States and abroad. The simple, serviceable guest rooms are clean and fresh, but the bathrooms tend to show their age. The loan-shark murder scene in *The Godfather* was shot in what is now Sofia's restaurant, and the pink-and-blue plaster Edison Café, known half jokingly as the Polish Tea Room, is a theater-crowd landmark consistently recognized as New York City's best coffee shop. ✉ *228 W. 47th St., between Broadway and 8th Ave., Midtown West 10036* ☎ *212/840–5000 or 800/637–7070* 🖷 *212/596–6850* ⊕ *www. edisonhotelnyc.com* ⇆ *770 rooms, 30 suites* ⎴ *Restaurant, coffee shop, cable TV, Wi-Fi, gym, hair salon, 2 bars, piano, dry cleaning, Internet, business services, meeting rooms, airport shuttle, parking (fee), no-smoking rooms* ⊟ *AE, D, DC, MC, V* Ⓜ *Subway: C, E to 50th St.*

¢–$ 🖷 **Portland Square Hotel.** You can't beat this theater district old-timer for value, given its clean, simple rooms that invite with flower-print bedspreads and curtains. James Cagney once lived in the building, and—as the story goes—a few of his Radio City Rockette acquaintances lived upstairs. *Life* magazine used to have its offices here, and the original detailing evokes old New York. There are no no-smoking rooms, but if you check into one with a smoky scent, they'll move you to another. Rooms on the east wing have oversize bathrooms. ✉ *132 W. 47th St.,*

CloseUp

HOTEL HIBERNATION

For some travelers, a hotel is an ends to a mean, a place to rest their head after the real business of the day—either corporate or sightseeing—is done. But for more and more people, the hotel is the destination—the reason they've come to the city in the first place. Whether it's a New Yorker with an airshaft view who wants a panorama of the Statue of Liberty; a couple who wants a break from braving the winter cold with a chance to order room service, eat a fine dinner without donning a coat, and then taking in some shopping all within an enclosed space; or a harried mom who wants to visit a spa and then return to her room still wearing her bathrobe and slippers—New York is the perfect place to do it.

Too cold to go outside? Check into one of the enormous rooms at **Mandarin Oriental** (⇨ Midtown West), stare out at the sweeping vistas of icy Central Park, and then wander down to Asiate for sumptuous French dishes with a Japanese accent. Across from the restaurant and slightly to the left is MOBar, where a saketini is the drink of choice. The next morning, use the secret passageway on the third floor to access the Time Warner Center. You can take a tour of CNN, stock-up on provisions at Whole Foods, buy a T-shirt at J Crew, and then stop by Jazz at Lincoln Center, which has performance space here, for tickets to a show. Still have some cash in your wallet? Book a table at Per Se, Masa, or Café Gray, all of which reap in accolades from foodies. Then you can walk a few hundred yards back to your room with nary a hair blown out of place.

A change from the ordinary that won't break the bank? Check out **The Gershwin Hotel** (⇨ Murray Hill). Even though rooms here aren't luxe, they'll let you try a bit of bohemia on for size. Taste some tapas at the restaurant and lounge, then take in a poetry slam, live music, and a young vibe at the performance space off the lobby.

A healthful retreat? The **W New York** (⇨ Midtown East), on Lexington Avenue, has one of the most deluxe spas in the city, Bliss49, where you can spend a full day being pampered and pedicured; then head down to the health-oriented restaurant Heartbeat, for a restorative treat.

Somewhere to enjoy the summer weather? Head straight to the **Hotel Gansevoort** (⇨ Greenwich Village). The entire roof here has been turned into an enchanted outdoor space with a full-size heated swimming pool illuminated with colored lights and livened up with an underwater stereo system. At night there's a happening bar scene up high; at street level, wander through the lobby into scene-stealing Ono. Not only is the Japanese sushi and robitaki excellent, but the outdoor space here looks like South Beach's Delano hotel, with a dining room hovering over a reflecting pool and private lounge rooms with plasma TVs and curtains to shut out the crowds. Of course, it's privacy you want, you could just hop the elevator back up to your room. How convenient!

between 6th and 7th Aves., Midtown West 10036 ☏ *212/382–0600 or 800/388–8988* 🖷 *212/382–0684* ⊕ *www.portlandsquarehotel.com* 🛏 *142 rooms, 112 with bath* ⚲ *In-room safes, cable TV, gym, laundry facilities, Internet, business services* ▭ *AE, MC, V* Ⓜ *Subway: R, W to 49th St.*

Midtown East

$$$$ 🏨 **The Drake.** Off Park Avenue in the center of corporate Manhattan, this Swissôtel property caters to business travelers with modern, comfortable rooms that are a cut above the average corporate variety. The deco-style accommodations are a welcome alternative to the traditional look of many hotels in this price category. The Q-56 restaurant is sleek and contemporary, and a branch of Fauchon—the first time this luxury food emporium ventured beyond Paris—has a shop and a lovely tearoom off the lobby. ✉ *440 Park Ave., at E. 56th St., Midtown East 10022* ☏ *212/421–0900 or 800/372–5369* 🖷 *212/371–4190* ⊕ *www.swissotel.com* 🛏 *387 rooms, 109 suites* ⚲ *Restaurant, tea shop, room service, in-room fax, in-room safes, minibars, some refrigerators, cable TV, in-room data ports, gym, health club, massage, sauna, spa, steam room, bar, babysitting, dry cleaning, laundry service, concierge, Internet, business services, meeting rooms, parking (fee), some pets allowed* ▭ *AE, D, DC, MC, V* Ⓜ *Subway: 4, 5, 6, N, Q, R, W to 59th St./Lexington Ave.*

$$$$ 🏨 **Four Seasons.** Architect I. M. Pei designed this limestone-clad stepped
Fodor'sChoice spire amid the prime shops of 57th Street. Everything here comes in epic
★ proportions—from the rooms averaging 600 square feet (and *starting* at $595) to the sky-high Grand Foyer, with French limestone pillars, marble, onyx, and acre upon acre of blond wood. The soundproof guest rooms have 10-foot-high ceilings, enormous English sycamore walk-in closets, and blond-marble bathrooms with tubs that fill in 60 seconds. If you really want epic, a night in the one-bedroom penthouse suite may run to $19,000. ✉ *57 E. 57th St., between Park and Madison Aves., Midtown East 10022* ☏ *212/758–5700 or 800/487–3769* 🖷 *212/758–5711* ⊕ *www.fourseasons.com* 🛏 *300 rooms, 68 suites* ⚲ *Restaurant, room service, in-room fax, in-room safes, minibars, some microwaves, cable TV, in-room DVDs, in-room data ports, gym, health club, massage, sauna, spa, steam room, bar, lobby lounge, piano, babysitting, dry cleaning, laundry service, concierge, business services, meeting rooms, car rental, parking (fee), some pets allowed, no-smoking floors* ▭ *AE, D, DC, MC, V* Ⓜ *Subway: 4, 5, 6, N, Q, R, W to 59th St./Lexington Ave.*

$$$$ 🏨 **New York Palace.** Connected mansions built in the 1880s by railroad baron Henry Villard create the base of this palatial hotel. The lobby, with its sweeping staircases, golden chandeliers, and arched colonnades fit for royalty, is host to New American restaurant Istana. Standard rooms in the main section of the hotel are traditional in style and quite large, but a bit worn around the edges. Better options are rooms in the tower that vary between modern or classic depending on the floor, have more luxe decor and bathrooms, separate check-in, and more attentive service. Many rooms, including the 7,000-square-foot health club, have terrific views of St. Patrick's Cathedral. ✉ *455 Madison Ave., at E. 50th St., Midtown East 10022* ☏ *212/888–7000 or 800/697–2522* 🖷 *212/*

303–6000 ⊕ www.newyorkpalace.com ➡ 809 rooms, 88 suites ⚙ Restaurant, room service, in-room fax, in-room safes, minibars, some refrigerators, cable TV with movies, in-room data ports, health club, massage, spa, 2 bars, babysitting, dry cleaning, laundry service, concierge, business services, meeting rooms, some pets allowed, no-smoking rooms, no-smoking floors ⊟ AE, D, DC, MC, V Ⓜ Subway: 6 to 51st St./Lexington Ave.; E, V to Lexington–3rd Aves./53rd St.

$$$$ 🏨 **The Peninsula.** Step past the beaux arts facade of this 1905 gem and into the luxurious lobby with original art nouveau accents. Guest rooms, many with sweeping views down 5th Avenue, have a modern sensibility. The high-tech amenities are excellent, from a bedside console that controls the lighting, sound, and thermostat for the room to a TV mounted over the tub for bath-time viewing (in all but standard rooms). Thoughtful service extends to the complimentary selection of bottled waters in each room to same-day laundry service. The rooftop health club, indoor pool, and seasonal open-air bar—which is something of a local hot spot—all have dazzling views of midtown. ✉ 700 5th Ave., at E. 55th St., Midtown East 10019 ☎ 212/247–2200 or 800/262–9467 🖶 212/903–3943 ⊕ www.peninsula.com ➡ 185 rooms, 54 suites ⚙ 2 restaurants, room service, in-room fax, in-room safes, minibars, cable TV with movies, in-room data ports, Wi-Fi, indoor pool, gym, health club, hair salon, hot tub, massage, sauna, spa, steam room, 2 bars, lobby lounge, lounge, babysitting, dry cleaning, laundry service, concierge, business services, meeting rooms, parking (fee), some pets allowed, no-smoking floors ⊟ AE, D, DC, MC, V Ⓜ Subway: E, V to 5th Ave.

★ $$$$ 🏨 **The St. Regis.** A one-of-a-kind New York classic, this 5th Avenue beaux arts landmark is a hive of activity in its unparalleled public spaces. The King Cole Bar is an institution in itself with its famous Maxfield Parrish mural. Guest rooms, all serviced by accommodating butlers, are straight out of the American Movie Channel, with high ceilings, crystal chandeliers, silk wall coverings, Louis XVI antiques, and world-class amenities such as Tiffany silver services. Marble bathrooms, with tubs, stall showers, and double sinks, are outstanding. ✉ 2 E. 55th St., at 5th Ave., Midtown East 10022 ☎ 212/753–4500 or 800/325–3589 🖶 212/787–3447 ⊕ www.stregis.com ➡ 222 rooms, 44 suites ⚙ Restaurant, room service, in-room fax, in-room safes, minibars, cable TV, in-room VCRs, in-room data ports, gym, health club, hair salon, massage, sauna, shops, babysitting, dry cleaning, laundry service, concierge, business services, meeting rooms, parking (fee), no-smoking rooms, no-smoking floors ⊟ AE, D, DC, MC, V Ⓜ Subway: 7 to 5th Ave.; B, D, F, V to 42nd St.

$$$–$$$$ 🏨 **Waldorf-Astoria.** The lobby of this landmark 1931 art deco masterpiece, full of murals, mosaics, and elaborate plaster ornamentation, features a grand piano once owned by Cole Porter and still played daily. Astoria-level rooms have the added advantages of great views, fax machines, and access to the Astoria lounge, where a lovely, free afternoon tea is served. The Bull and Bear Bar is a 1940s throwback complete with cigar smoke, miniature soda bottles, and no-nonsense barkeeps. Well known to U.S. presidents and other international luminaries, the ultra-exclusive Waldorf Towers (the 28th floor and above) has a separate entrance and management. ✉ 301 Park Ave., between E. 49th and E.

50th Sts., Midtown East 10022 ☎ *212/355–3000 or 800/925–3673*
🖷 *212/872-7272* ⊕ *www.waldorfastoria.com* ➷ *1,176 rooms, 276
suites* ⚭ *4 restaurants, room service, in-room fax, some in-room safes,
minibars, refrigerators, cable TV with movies, in-room data ports, gym,
health club, hair salon, massage, sauna, steam room, 3 bars, piano,
shops, babysitting, dry cleaning, laundry service, concierge, concierge floors,
business services, meeting rooms, parking (fee), some pets allowed, no-
smoking floors* ▤ *AE, D, DC, MC, V* Ⓜ *Subway: 6 to 51st St./Lexington
Ave.; E, V to Lexington–3rd Aves./53rd St.*

$$–$$$$ 🏨 **Sherry-Netherland.** The marble-lined lobby of this grande dame wows
with fine, hand-loomed carpets, crystal chandeliers, and wall friezes
from the Vanderbilt mansion. White-gloved attendants man the eleva-
tors. Many floors of the hotel are private residences and all hotel rooms
are privately owned and individually decorated but adhere to the rigid
standards of the hotel. The utterly luxurious suites have separate living
and dining areas, crystal chandeliers, and serving pantries, and many have
decorative fireplaces, antiques, and glorious marble baths. The cramped
and stupendously expensive Harry Cipriani's provides room service (a
liter of water costs about $20). Continental breakfast is complimentary
for guests, and at lunch it's the best people-watching in town. ⊠ *781
5th Ave., at E. 59th St., Midtown East 10022* ☎ *212/355–2800 or 800/
247-4377* 🖷 *212/319–4306* ⊕ *www.sherrynetherland.com* ➷ *30 rooms,
23 suites* ⚭ *Restaurant, room service, in-room fax, in-room safes, re-
frigerators, cable TV, in-room VCRs, gym, hair salon, massage, bar, dry
cleaning, laundry service, concierge, Internet, business services, meeting
rooms, parking (fee)* ▤ *AE, D, DC, MC, V* ⦿ *CP* Ⓜ *Subway: N, R,
Q, W to 5th Ave.*

$$–$$$$ 🏨 **W New York.** Window boxes filled with grass, bowls heaped with green
apples, flowing curtains, and vast floor-to-ceiling windows that pour sun-
light into the airy lobby all conjure up a calming outdoor vibe here. Quite
a trick considering a hopping bar and a sunken sitting area flanks the
reception area. Although tiny, rooms are rich in natural materials, and
soothe with elements such as feather beds and slate-floor baths instead
of the ubiquitous polished marble. Downstairs, Heartbeat Restaurant
serves heart-healthy foods; the attached Whiskey Blue draws a young,
hip, and moneyed crowd; and an uptown sibling of Bliss Spa draws le-
gions of beauty devotees. ⊠ *541 Lexington Ave., between E. 49th and
E. 50th Sts., Midtown East 10022* ☎ *212/755–1200 or 877/946–8357*
🖷 *212/319–8344* ⊕ *www.whotels.com* ➷ *652 rooms, 61 suites*
⚭ *Restaurant, snack bar, room service, in-room fax, in-room safes,
minibars, cable TV, in-room data ports, health club, massage, 2 spas,
steam room, bar, lobby lounge, dry cleaning, laundry facilities, laundry
service, concierge, business services, meeting rooms, no-smoking floors*
▤ *AE, D, DC, MC, V* Ⓜ *Subway: 6 to 51st St./Lexington Ave.; E, V
to Lexington–3rd Aves./53rd St.*

$$$ 🏨 **Affinia Fifty.** This hotel has a distinctly businesslike mood, but it's also
supremely comfortable for families or other leisure travelers. A top to
bottom renovation modernized the spacious rooms, called suites here,
all of which have a clean, modern design with oversize chairs and couches,
kitchen facilities, and plenty of space to stretch out. And for the busi-

ness travelers, the second floor club lounge is devoted to complimentary business services, including snacks and beverages. There's no restaurant in the hotel, but a restaurant next door provides room service. ⊠ 155 E. 50th St., at 3rd Ave., Midtown East 10022 ☎ 212/751–5710 or 800/637–8483 📠 212/753–1468 ⊕ www.affinia.com 🛏 56 rooms, 138 suites △ Room service, in-room safes, kitchens, kitchenettes, microwaves, refrigerators, cable TV, in-room data ports, exercise equipment, gym, health club, dry cleaning, laundry facilities, laundry service, concierge, Internet, parking (fee), no-smoking floors ▤ AE, D, DC, MC, V Ⓜ Subway: 6 to 51st St./Lexington Ave.; E, V to Lexington–3rd Aves./53rd St.

$$$ ▦ **The Alex.** The goal of the David Rockwell–designed Alex is to create a soothing environment for business travelers on long-term stays. Japanese-influenced rooms use unobtrusive sliding panels with nature prints to hide away the rooms' many gadgets. What remains is a clean, calm space where you can truly appreciate attentive details such as kitchenettes with Gaggenau rangetops and SubZero refrigerators; nightstands that turn into leather desktops; and flatscreen bathroom TVs that you can watch from the impressively deep bathtubs. James Beard Foundation winner Marcus Samuelsson runs Asian-influenced Riingo restaurant, which also provides room service. ⊠ 205 E. 45th St., between 2nd and 3rd Aves., Midtown East 10017 ☎ 212/867–5100 📠 212/867–7878 ⊕ www.thealexhotel.com 🛏 73 rooms, 130 suites △ Restaurant, room service, some kitchens, minibars, cable TV, in-room DVDs, in-room data ports, Wi-Fi, gym, spa, bar, concierge, business services ▤ AE, MC, V Ⓜ Subway: 4, 5, 6, 7, S to 42nd St./Grand Central.

$$$ ▦ **Omni Berkshire Place.** Omni Berkshire's East Coast flagship hotel brings sophistication to the Omni name. Old-World maps hang in the reception area, which leads to a dramatic, two-story atrium lounge with a fireplace, an elaborately stained dark-wood floor, and a piano. The earthtone spacious guest rooms have a contemporary simplicity as well as plush bedding, tasteful furnishings, spacious bathrooms, and Web TV. Kids receive their own welcome bag of treats. ⊠ 21 E. 52nd St., between 5th and Madison Aves., Midtown East 10022 ☎ 212/753–5800 or 800/843–6664 📠 212/754–5020 ⊕ www.omnihotels.com 🛏 352 rooms, 44 suites △ Restaurant, room service, in-room fax, in-room safes, minibars, cable TV with movies and video games, Wi-Fi, exercise equipment, health club, massage, bar, babysitting, dry cleaning, laundry facilities, laundry service, concierge, Internet, business services, meeting rooms, parking (fee), some pets allowed (fee), no-smoking floors ▤ AE, D, DC, MC, V Ⓜ Subway: E, V to 5th Ave.

$$$ ▦ **The Regency.** Rough-hewn travertine punctuated by Regency-style furnishings, potted palms, and burnished gold sconces lines an understated lobby—the better to cloak heads of state and other VIP guests in modesty. The modern guest rooms have taupe-color silk wallpaper, velvet throw pillows, and polished Honduran mahogany, but the smallish bathrooms with their marble countertops are unspectacular. Goose-down duvets and ergonomic leather desk chairs reinforce the pleasingly modern feel. Feinstein's at the Regency hosts some of the hottest (and priciest) cabaret acts in town, and 540 Park has become a destination in its own right among restaurant-savvy locals. ⊠ 540 Park Ave., at E. 61st St., Mid-

town East 10021 ☎ *212/759–4100 or 800/235–6397* 🖷 *212/826–5674* ⊕ *www.loewshotels.com* ⇙ *266 rooms, 86 suites* ⌕ *Restaurant, room service, in-room fax, in-room safes, some kitchenettes, minibars, refrigerators, cable TV, in-room VCRs, in-room data ports, gym, hair salon, massage, sauna, bar, lobby lounge, cabaret, babysitting, dry cleaning, laundry service, concierge, business services, meeting rooms, parking (fee), some pets allowed, no-smoking floors* ☰ *AE, D, DC, MC, V* Ⓜ *Subway: 4, 5, 6, N, Q, R, W to 59th St./Lexington Ave.*

$$–$$$ 🏨 **Beekman Tower.** Three blocks north of the United Nations, this jazzy 1928 hotel is an art deco architectural landmark. Its swanky Top of the Towers lounge, a rooftop bar with live piano, is a superb place to take in the view of the East River and beyond; downstairs, the Zephyr Grill looks out on 1st Avenue. Suites, which range from studios to one-bedrooms, are all very spacious, and all have kitchens. Rooms are attractively decorated with chintz and dark-wood furniture, and all have separate sitting areas. The one-bedroom suites have dining tables as well. ✉ *3 Mitchell Pl., at 1st Ave. and E. 49th St., Midtown East 10017* ☎ *212/ 320–8018 or 800/637–8483* 🖷 *212/465–3697* ⊕ *www.affinia.com* ⇙ *174 suites* ⌕ *2 restaurants, room service, in-room fax, in-room safes, kitchenettes, minibars, microwaves, cable TV, in-room data ports, Wi-Fi, exercise equipment, gym, 2 bars, lounge, piano bar, dry cleaning, laundry facilities, laundry service, concierge, Internet, business services, meeting rooms, parking (fee), no-smoking floors* ☰ *AE, D, DC, MC, V* Ⓜ *Subway: 6 to 51st St./Lexington Ave.; E, V to Lexington–3rd Aves./53rd St.*

$$–$$$ 🏨 **The Benjamin.** From the elegant marble-and-silver lobby with 30-foot ceilings and a sweeping staircase to the argon gas–filled windows that reduce street noises to near whispers, this place pleases in ways seen and unseen. Elegant rooms are done in warm beiges and golds, extensive in-room offices come with personalized business cards, and you can choose from more than a dozen pillow options for your plush bed. A small spa and clubby restaurant make it easy to relax here. Note that no rooms have two beds, so the clientele leans toward business travelers and couples. ✉ *125 E. 50th St., at Lexington Ave., Midtown East 10022* ☎ *212/715–2500 or 888/423–6526* 🖷 *212/715–2525* ⊕ *www. thebenjamin.com* ⇙ *109 rooms, 100 suites* ⌕ *Restaurant, room service, in-room safes, kitchenettes, minibars, cable TV, in-room data ports, gym, health club, massage, spa, bar, babysitting, dry cleaning, laundry service, concierge, concierge floors, business services, meeting rooms, parking (fee)* ☰ *AE, D, DC, MC, V* Ⓜ *Subway: 6 to 51st St./Lexington Ave.; E, V to Lexington–3rd Aves./53rd St.*

$$–$$$ 🏨 **Crowne Plaza at the United Nations.** This 20-story building built in 1931 is in historic Tudor City, a stone's throw from the United Nations and Grand Central Terminal. Interior spaces are classic and unassuming, with marble floors, handmade carpets, and hardwood reproduction furniture upholstered in brocades and velvets. The traditional, well-kept rooms all come with CD players, irons and ironing boards, and coffeemakers. ✉ *304 E. 42nd St., between 1st and 2nd Aves., Midtown East 10017* ☎ *212/986–8800 or 800/879–8836* 🖷 *212/297–3440* ⊕ *www. ichotelsgroup.com* ⇙ *300 rooms, 14 suites* ⌕ *Restaurant, room ser-*

*vice, in-room safes, minibars, cable TV, in-room data ports, exercise equip-
ment, gym, massage, sauna, spa, bar, lounge, babysitting, dry cleaning,
laundry service, concierge, Internet, business services, meeting rooms,
parking (fee), some pets allowed (fee), no-smoking rooms* ▭ *AE, D, DC,
MC, V* Ⓜ *Subway: 4, 5, 6, 7, S to 42nd St./Grand Central.*

$$–$$$ ▦ **The Dylan.** This 1903 beaux arts–style building with ornate plaster-
work on its facade and a stunning marble staircase spiraling up its three
floors once housed the Chemists Club. The 11-foot ceilings give the modern guest rooms a touch of grandeur, and the Carrara cut-marble bathrooms show the hotel's opulent intentions. Soaring columns and vaulted
ceilings make the splendid Alchemy Suite—built in the 1930s to repli-
cate a medieval laboratory—a Gothic confection. ⊠ *52 E. 41st St., between Park and Madison Aves., Midtown East 10017* ☎ *212/338–
0500* 🖷 *212/338–0569* ⊕ *www.dylanhotel.com* ↷ *107 rooms, 2 suites*
⟐ *Restaurant, in-room safes, minibars, in-room data ports, gym, health
club, bar, concierge, business services, meeting rooms* ▭ *AE, D, DC,
MC, V* Ⓜ *Subway: 4, 5, 6, 7, S to 42nd St./Grand Central.*

★ **$$–$$$** ▦ **Library Hotel.** Boutiquey and bookish, this handsome landmark brown-
stone (1900) gets its inspiration from the New York Public Library. Each
of its 10 floors is dedicated to one of the 10 categories of the Dewey Dec-
imal System; undersize modern rooms are stocked with art and books rel-
evant to a subtopic such as erotica, astronomy, or biography—let your
interests guide your room choice. The staff is incredibly hospitable and
the whole property is old-leather-armchair comfortable, whether you're
unwinding in front of the library fireplace, partaking of the complimentary wine and cheese or Continental breakfast, or relaxing in the roof garden. ⊠ *299 Madison Ave., at E. 41st St., Midtown East 10017* ☎ *212/
983–4500 or 877/793–7323* 🖷 *212/499–9099* ⊕ *www.libraryhotel.com*
↷ *60 rooms* ⟐ *Restaurant, room service, in-room safes, minibars, cable
TV with movies, in-room VCRs, in-room data ports, massage, bar, 3 lounges,
babysitting, dry cleaning, laundry service, concierge, Internet, business services, meeting rooms, parking (fee), no-smoking floors* ▭ *AE, DC, MC,
V* ⦿⊙ *CP* Ⓜ *Subway: 4, 5, 6, 7, S to 42nd St./Grand Central.*

$$–$$$ ▦ **Millennium Hotel New York UN Plaza.** A name change and major ren-
ovation have modernized this sky-high tower near the United Nations.
Rooms, which begin on the 28th floor, have breathtaking views, make
generous use of warm woods and neutral tones, and have an array of
up-to-the-minute telecommunications gadgets. The multilingual staff caters
to a discerning clientele that includes heads of state. The views also dazzle from the elegant 27th-floor pool and health club, and the rooftop
tennis court attracts name players. Service throughout the hotel is first-
rate, and the business center is open until 11 PM. ⊠ *1 United Nations
Plaza, at E. 44th St. and 1st Ave., Midtown East 10017* ☎ *212/758–
1234 or 866/866–8086* 🖷 *212/702–5051* ⊕ *www.millenniumhotels.com*
↷ *387 rooms, 40 suites* ⟐ *Restaurant, room service, in-room fax, in-
room safes, some kitchens, minibars, cable TV with movies, in-room
data ports, tennis court, indoor pool, health club, massage, sauna, bar,
shop, babysitting, dry cleaning, laundry service, concierge, business services, meeting rooms, parking (fee), no-smoking floors* ▭ *AE, D, DC,
MC, V* Ⓜ *Subway: 4, 5, 6, 7, S to 42nd St./Grand Central.*

$$ 🏨 **Hotel Elysée.** Best known as the site of the Monkey Bar, a legendary watering hole, this intimate, Euro-style hotel has relatively affordable rates, given its location. All guests have access to the comfortable Club Room, where complimentary coffee, tea, and snacks are available all day. You can grab a breakfast pastry there in the morning and free wine and hors d'oeuvres on weeknights—a blessing, since room service is limited and there are no minibars in the guest rooms. Many of the old-world guest rooms have terraces. ✉ *60 E. 54th St., between Madison and Park Aves., Midtown East 10022* ☎ *212/753–1066 or 800/535–9733* 🖷 *212/ 980–9278* ⊕ *www.elyseehotel.com* 🛏 *86 rooms, 15 suites* ♻ *Restaurant, room service, in-room safes, some kitchenettes, microwaves, refrigerators, cable TV, in-room VCRs, in-room data ports, massage, bar, piano, babysitting, dry cleaning, laundry service, concierge, Internet, business services, meeting rooms, parking (fee), no-smoking floors* 🖃 *AE, D, DC, MC, V* 🍽 *CP* Ⓜ *Subway: E, V to 5th Ave.*

★ **$$** 🏨 **Roger Smith.** The elusive Roger Smith (see if *you* can find out who he is) lends his name to this colorful boutique hotel and adjacent gallery. Riotous murals cover the walls in Lily's, the café. The art-filled rooms are homey and comfortable, and some have stocked bookshelves and fireplaces. An eclectic mix of room service is provided by five local restaurants. Guests have access to the nearby New York Sports Club ($10 fee). Rates can drop by as much as $75 per night in winter and summer, so ask when booking. A complimentary Continental breakfast is included. ✉ *501 Lexington Ave., between E. 47th and E. 48th Sts., Midtown East 10017* ☎ *212/755–1400 or 800/445–0277* 🖷 *212/758–4061* ⊕ *www. rogersmith.com* 🛏 *102 rooms, 28 suites* ♻ *Restaurant, room service, some kitchenettes, refrigerators, cable TV with movies and video games, in-room data ports, massage, bar, babysitting, dry cleaning, laundry service, Internet, meeting rooms, parking (fee), some pets allowed, no-smoking floors* 🖃 *AE, D, DC, MC, V* 🍽 *CP* Ⓜ *Subway: 6 to 51st St./Lexington Ave.; E, V to Lexington–3rd Aves./53rd St.*

$–$$ 🏨 **The Fitzpatrick Manhattan Hotel.** This cozy hotel south of Bloomingdale's brings Irish charm to the New York hotel scene, which might explain why Irish citizens ranging from Gregory Peck to the Chieftains have all been guests. More than half of the units are suites, and all have golden draperies and carpets and traditional dark-wood furniture. Guests have free access to the Excelsior Athletic Club next door. Fitzer's, the publike bar at the heart of the hotel, is as welcoming as any in Dublin. ✉ *687 Lexington Ave., at E. 57th St., Midtown East 10022* ☎ *212/355–0100 or 800/367–7701* 🖷 *212/355–1371* ⊕ *www.fitzpatrickhotels.com* 🛏 *40 rooms, 52 suites* ♻ *Restaurant, room service, some in-room safes, some kitchenettes, minibars, some refrigerators, cable TV with movies and video games, in-room data ports, health club, massage, bar, pub, babysitting, dry cleaning, laundry service, concierge, business services, meeting rooms, airport shuttle, parking (fee), no-smoking rooms* 🖃 *AE, D, DC, MC, V* Ⓜ *Subway: 4, 5, 6, N, Q, R, W to 59th St./Lexington Ave.*

$–$$ 🏨 **The Melrose Hotel New York.** A women's residence club from 1927 to 1981, the Melrose, formerly the Barbizon, was home at various times to Grace Kelly, Joan Crawford, and Liza Minelli. The lobby has a beautiful marble-and-limestone floor and gilt chairs with mohair upholstery.

Guest rooms, decorated in shades of shell-pink or celadon, are modest but pleasant. The on-site health club has a lap pool. Since most rooms are minuscule, ask for one of the few larger ones when booking; some tower suites have balconies and Jacuzzis. If you want space at any cost, ask for the penthouse suite, which has a lovely view of Central Park. ⊠ *140 E. 63rd St., at Lexington Ave., Midtown East 10021* ☎ *212/838–5700 or 800/635–7673* 🖷 *212/888–4271* ⊕ *www.melrosehotel.com* ⟲ *274 rooms, 32 suites* ⚷ *Café, room service, in-room safes, some in-room hot tubs, minibars, cable TV, some in-room VCRs, in-room data ports, indoor pool, health club, hair salon, massage, spa, bar, babysitting, dry cleaning, laundry service, concierge, business services, parking (fee), no-smoking rooms* ▭ *AE, D, DC, MC, V* Ⓜ *Subway: 4, 5, 6, F, N, R, W to 59th St./Lexington Ave.*

$ 🏨 **The Bentley.** A great budget-price hotel is certainly welcome in the often-pricey Bloomingdale's neighborhood. Although the lobby is minimal, the pocket-size library is inviting and has free cappuccino round-the-clock. Rooms are relatively large compared to other hotels in the same price category. Sheets are Belgian, toiletries are boutiquey—the whole place is reminiscent of a small European hotel. Noise can sometimes be a problem on the lowest floors, so request a high floor, preferably with a view of the East River. The 21st floor restaurant has wonderful river and city vistas. Rates can go as low as $100 here. ⊠ *500 E. 62nd St., at York Ave., Midtown East 10021* ☎ *212/644–6000 or 888/664–6835* 🖷 *212/207–4800* ⊕ *www.nychotels.com* ⟲ *200 rooms* ⚷ *Restaurant, room service, cable TV with movies, Wi-Fi, laundry service; no-smoking rooms* ▭ *AE, D, DC, MC, V* Ⓜ *Subway: 4, 5, 6, F, N, R, W to 59th St./Lexington Ave.*

¢–$ 🏨 **Pickwick Arms Hotel.** This no-frills but convenient East Side establishment is regularly booked solid by bargain hunters. Privations you endure to save a buck start and end with the lilliputian size of some rooms, all of which have cheap-looking furnishings; some doubles have bunkbeds. However, some rooms look over the Manhattan skyline, and all are renovated on a regular basis. There's also a rooftop garden. ⊠ *230 E. 51st St., between 2nd and 3rd Aves., Midtown East 10022* ☎ *212/355–0300 or 800/742–5945* 🖷 *212/755–5029* ⊕ *www.pickwickarms.com* ⟲ *360 rooms, 175 with bath* ⚷ *Café, some refrigerators, cable TV, in-room data ports, bar, airport shuttle, parking (fee)* ▭ *AE, DC, MC, V* Ⓜ *Subway: 6 to 51st St./Lexington Ave.; E, V to Lexington–3rd Aves./53rd St.*

¢–$ 🏨 **Vanderbilt YMCA.** Of the various Manhattan Ys that provide overnight accommodations, this one has the best facilities, including a full-scale fitness center and pools. Rooms are little more than dormitory-style cells, each with a bed (bunks in doubles), dresser, and TV; singles have desks. Only six rooms have phones and private baths (these cost extra), but communal showers and toilets are clean. The Turtle Bay neighborhood is safe and convenient; Grand Central Terminal and the United Nations are both a few blocks away. ⊠ *224 E. 47th St., between 2nd and 3rd Aves., Midtown East 10017* ☎ *212/756–9600* 🖷 *212/752–0210* ⊕ *www.ymcanyc.org* ⟲ *375 rooms, 6 with bath* ⚷ *Restaurant, refrigerators, 2 indoor pools, fitness classes, gym, health club, hot tub, massage, sauna, steam room, basketball, volleyball, laundry facilities, meeting* *rooms, airport shuttle; no phones in some rooms* ▭ *AE, MC, V* Ⓜ *Subway: 6 to 51st St.*

Upper East Side

★ **$$$$** 🏨 **The Carlyle.** European tradition and Manhattan swank come together at New York's most lovable grand hotel. Everything about this Madison Avenue landmark suggests refinement, from rooms decorated with fine antique furniture and artfully framed Audubons and botanicals, to the first-rate service. Cabaret luminaries Barbara Cook and Bobby Short take turns holding court at the clubby Café Carlyle, but the canny Peter Mintun steals the show at Bemelmans Bar. Discreet whispers of change, such as the impeccable Thierry Despont–designed suite atop the hotel and the elegant new "C" logos on certain elevator doors, enrich the hotel's ambience, which to some still feels a bit stuffy and old school. ✉ *35 E. 76th St., between Madison and Park Aves., Upper East Side 10021* 🖀 *212/744–1600* ⊕ *www.thecarlyle.com* 🛏 *145 rooms, 52 suites* ⚭ *Restaurant, café, room service, in-room fax, in-room safes, some in-room hot tubs, kitchenettes, minibars, microwaves, cable TV, in-room VCRs, in-room data ports, gym, health club, massage, spa, bar, dry cleaning, laundry service, concierge, business services, meeting room, parking (fee), some pets allowed, no-smoking floors* ▭ *AE, DC, MC, V* Ⓜ *Subway: 6 to 77th St.*

$$$$ 🏨 **Hotel Plaza Athénée.** At this elegant French property in a building of a certain age, no two rooms share the same floor plan and all have ample space. Even the most modest rooms have sitting areas with inviting sofas, and generous closet space. Handsomely furnished suites come with dining tables or dining rooms, and 12 suites have balconies. Rooms above the 12th floor have over-the-rooftops views. The Bar Seine is a romantic Moroccan fantasy, and the restaurant Arabelle serves world-class food. Ask about weekend packages, which can be much less expensive than the standard rates. ✉ *37 E. 64th St., at Madison Ave., Upper East Side 10021* 🖀 *212/734–9100 or 800/447–8800* 🖷 *212/772–0958* ⊕ *www.plaza-athenee.com* 🛏 *115 rooms, 35 suites* ⚭ *Restaurant, room service, some in-room faxes, in-room safes, some kitchenettes, minibars, refrigerators, cable TV, in-room data ports, exercise equipment, gym, health club, massage, bar, lounge, babysitting, dry cleaning, laundry service, concierge, Internet, business services, meeting rooms, parking (fee), some pets allowed, no-smoking floors* ▭ *AE, D, DC, MC, V* Ⓜ *Subway: 6 to 68th St./Hunter College.*

$$$–$$$$ 🏨 **The Pierre.** The Pierre remains a grand presence among the Four Seasons hotel group's properties, all of which are known for their exceptional service (the staff will scan an image for a business presentation or hand wash your delicates). As ornate as the Four Seasons hotel on 57th Street is minimalist, the Pierre's landmark building owes a lot to the Palace of Versailles, with chandeliers, murals depicting putti, and Corinthian columns in the Rotunda lounge. Chintz and dark wood adorn the grand and traditional guest rooms, whose gleaming black-and-white art deco bathrooms are spacious for New York. ✉ *2 E. 61st St., between 5th and Madison Aves., Upper East Side 10021* 🖀 *212/838–8000 or 800/332–3442* 🖷 *212/758–1615* ⊕ *www.fshr.com* 🛏 *149*

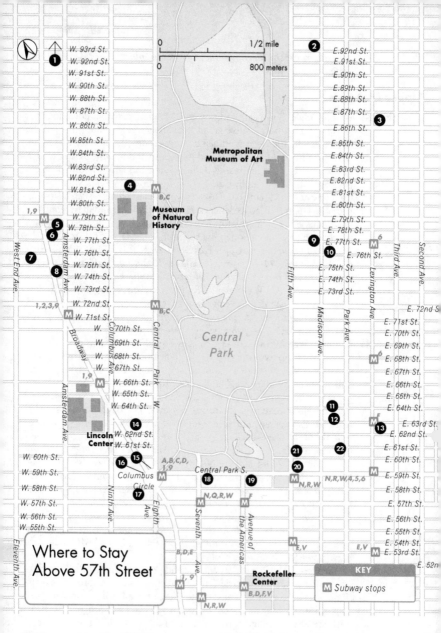

Where to Stay Above 57th Street

KEY

M Subway stops

rooms, 52 suites 🖒 2 restaurants, room service, in-room fax, in-room safes, minibars, cable TV, in-room data ports, exercise equipment, health club, hair salon, massage, bar, babysitting, dry cleaning, laundry service, concierge, Internet, business services, meeting rooms, travel services, parking (fee), some pets allowed, no-smoking floors ⊟ AE, D, DC, MC, V Ⓜ Subway: N, R, W to 5th Ave.

$$$
Fodor'sChoice
★
🖫 **The Lowell.** This old-money refuge was built as an upscale apartment hotel in the 1920s and still delivers genteel sophistication. Guest rooms have all the civilized comforts of home, including stocked bookshelves, luxe bathrooms, and even umbrellas. Thirty-three of the suites have working fireplaces, and 11 have private terraces, the better for spying on posh neighboring abodes. A gym suite has its own fitness center, and a garden suite has two beautifully planted terraces. Most of the rooms have been redecorated in a more modern, streamlined style with less chintz and no patterns. The Pembroke Room serves a fine afternoon tea, and the Post House serves some of the best steaks in town. ⊠ 28 E. 63rd St., between Madison and Park Aves., Upper East Side 10021 ☎ 212/838–1400 or 800/221–4444 🖷 212/319–4230 ⊕ www.lhw.com ⏎ 23 rooms, 47 suites 🖒 2 restaurants, room service, in-room fax, in-room safes, kitchenettes, minibars, refrigerators, cable TV, in-room VCRs, in-room data ports, exercise equipment, health club, massage, bar, babysitting, dry cleaning, laundry service, concierge, Internet, business services, parking (fee), some pets allowed ⊟ AE, D, DC, MC, V Ⓜ Subway: 4, 5, 6, N, R, W to 59th St./Lexington Ave.; F to 63rd St./Lexington Ave.

$$–$$$
🖫 **Hotel Wales.** Every effort has been made to retain the turn-of-the-20th-century mood of this 1901 Carnegie Hill landmark—from the cavernous lobby to the Pied Piper parlor, where vintage children's illustrations cover the walls. A complimentary European-style breakfast is served in the parlor, along with free coffee and cappuccino; on a nice day head up to the rooftop terrace with your treats. Guest rooms are small, but they do have fine oak woodwork, and all are equipped with CD players. Most of the suites face Madison Avenue; the lovely Sarabeth's Restaurant, a local favorite for brunch, is in the hotel. ⊠ 1295 Madison Ave., between E. 92nd and E. 93rd Sts., Upper East Side 10128 ☎ 212/876–6000 or 877/847–4444 🖷 212/860–7000 ⊕ www.waleshotel.com ⏎ 46 rooms, 41 suites 🖒 Restaurant, room service, in-room safes, some kitchenettes, minibars, cable TV with video games, in-room VCRs, gym, bar, babysitting, dry cleaning, laundry service, Internet, business services, parking (fee), some pets allowed, no-smoking floors ⊟ AE, D, DC, MC, V ⍑◎⍒ CP Ⓜ Subway: 6 to 96th St.

★ **$$–$$$**
🖫 **The Mark.** A member of the Mandarin Oriental hotel group, the Mark, whose motto is "No jacket, no tie, no attitude," is refreshingly unpretentious considering its luxurious atmosphere. A petite art deco marble lobby leads into a clubby bar where even lone women travelers feel comfortable, and to the Mark's restaurant, where afternoon tea is served. Elegant bedrooms have English and Italian furnishings and prints and deep soaking tubs in the sleek marble bathrooms. Special touches here include hidden pantries with small kitchenettes in many of the rooms, a free shuttle to Wall Street, and complimentary cell phones. ⊠25 E. 77th St., at Madison Ave., Upper East Side 10021 ☎212/

744–4300 or 800/843–6275 🖷212/472–5714 ⊕*www.mandarinoriental. com* ➾ *122 rooms, 54 suites* ⚘ *Restaurant, room service, in-room fax, in-room safes, some kitchenettes, minibars, cable TV, in-room VCRs, in-room data ports, exercise equipment, health club, massage, sauna, steam room, bar, babysitting, dry cleaning, laundry service, concierge, Internet, business services, meeting rooms, parking (fee), some pets allowed, no-smoking floors* ▤ *AE, D, DC, MC, V* Ⓜ *Subway: 6 to 77th St.*

$ 🏨 **The Franklin.** The Upper East Side's hippest, funkiest hotel has a pint-size lobby decorated with black granite, brushed steel, and cherrywood. Most rooms are also tiny (some measure 100 square feet), but what they lack in size they make up for in style: all have custom-built steel furniture, gauzy white canopies over the beds, cedar closets, and CD players. Added bonuses are the generous complimentary breakfast, fresh fruit in the evenings, and 24-hour cappuccino. ✉ *164 E. 87th St., between Lexington and 3rd Aves., Upper East Side 10128* ☎ *212/369–1000 or 877/847–4444* 🖷 *212/894–5220* ⊕ *www.franklinhotel.com* ➾ *50 rooms* ⚘ *In-room safes, cable TV, in-room VCRs, in-room data ports, Wi-Fi, lounge, library, dry cleaning, laundry service, no-smoking floors* ▤ *AE, DC, MC, V* ◯❙ *CP* Ⓜ *Subway: 4, 5, 6 to 86th St.*

Upper West Side

$$$$ 🏨 **Trump International Hotel and Towers.** Rooms and suites in this expensive, showy hotel resemble mini-apartments: all have fully equipped kitchens with black-granite countertops, entertainment centers with stereos and CD players, and mini-telescopes, which you can use to gaze through the floor-to-ceiling windows. Creamy-beige marble bathrooms are equipped with Jacuzzis and Frette bathrobes, and slippers hang in the closets. Complimentary cellular phones and personalized stationery and business cards are also provided. The restaurant, Jean-Georges, is one of the city's finest, and for a price a Jean-Georges's sous-chef will prepare a meal in your kitchenette. ✉ *1 Central Park W, between W. 59th and W. 60th Sts., Upper West Side 10023* ☎ *212/299–1000 or 888/448–7867* 🖷 *212/299–1023* ⊕ *www.trumpintl.com* ➾ *37 rooms, 130 suites* ⚘ *Restaurant, café, room service, in-room fax, in-room safes, in-room hot tubs, kitchenettes, minibars, microwaves, refrigerators, cable TV, in-room DVD/ VCR, in-room data ports, indoor pool, gym, health club, massage, sauna, spa, steam room, bar, babysitting, dry cleaning, laundry service, concierge, Internet, business services, meeting rooms, parking (fee), no-smoking rooms, no-smoking floors* ▤ *AE, D, DC, MC, V* Ⓜ *Subway: 1, 9, A, B, C, D to 59th St./Columbus Circle.*

$$ 🏨 **Excelsior.** Directly across the street from the American Museum of Natural History, this well-kept spot rubs shoulders with fine prewar doorman apartment buildings (make sure to spring for a room with museum views). Fine traditional rooms come with amenities such as Web TV, a pants press, and an iron and ironing board. The second-floor breakfast room serves a good, if slightly pricey for the neighborhood, breakfast. The library lounge, with leather sofas, a cozy fireplace, and tables with built-in game boards, is an unexpected plus. ✉ *45 W. 81st St., between*

Central Park W and Columbus Ave., Upper West Side 10024 ☎ *212/ 362–9200 or 800/368–4575* 🖷 *212/721–2994* ⊕ *www.excelsiorhotelny. com* ⤶ *118 rooms, 80 suites* ⚹ *Restaurant, coffee shop, in-room fax, in-room safes, in-room data ports, Wi-Fi, gym, library, dry cleaning, laundry service, concierge, meeting rooms, some pets allowed, no-smoking floors* ☰ *AE, D, DC, MC, V* Ⓜ *Subway: B to 81st St.*

$$ 🏨 **On the Ave.** A slice of sophistication and service on the Upper West Side, this reasonably priced boutique hotel appeals to those who will do anything to avoid midtown. There's no restaurant, but the amenities in the basic rooms, like hair dryers and terry robes, are more than adequate, and penthouse floors and the all-guest-access balcony terrace on the 16th floor afford views of Central Park and/or the Hudson River. On the Ave combines modern style—unlike most of the other moderately priced Upper West Side hotels—with comfort. It gives guests a little taste of what it's like to live in New York. ✉ *2178 Broadway, at W. 77th St., Upper West Side 10024* ☎ *212/362–1100 or 800/509–7598* 🖷 *212/787–9521* ⊕ *www.ontheave-nyc.com* ⤶ *230 rooms, 24 suites* ⚹ *Room service, in-room safes, in-room data ports, babysitting, dry cleaning, laundry service, concierge, Internet, business services, parking (fee), some pets allowed, no-smoking floors* ☰ *AE, D, DC, MC, V* Ⓜ *Subway: 1, 9 to 79th St.*

★ **$–$$** 🏨 **Hotel Beacon.** The Upper West Side's best buy for the price is three blocks from Central Park and Lincoln Center, and footsteps from Zabar's gourmet bazaar. All of the generously sized rooms and suites include marble bathrooms, kitchenettes with coffeemakers, pots and pans, stoves, and ironing facilities. Closets are huge, and some of the bathrooms have Hollywood dressing room–style mirrors. High floors have views of Central Park, the Hudson River, or the midtown skyline; the staff here is especially friendly and helpful. ✉ *2130 Broadway, at W. 75th St., Upper West Side 10023* ☎ *212/787–1100 or 800/572–4969* 🖷 *212/787–8119* ⊕ *www.beaconhotel.com* ⤶ *120 rooms, 110 suites* ⚹ *Café, in-room safes, kitchens, kitchenettes, microwaves, refrigerators, cable TV, babysitting, laundry facilities, business services, meeting rooms, parking (fee), no-smoking rooms* ☰ *AE, D, DC, MC, V* Ⓜ *Subway: 1, 2, 3, 9 to 72nd St.*

$ 🏨 **The Lucerne.** The landmarked facade of this exquisite building has more pizzazz than the predictable guest rooms, with their requisite darkwood reproduction furniture and chintz bedspreads. Health-conscious adults might like the gym on the top floor, with its city views, and children may be glued to the in-room Nintendo games. Service is the hotel's strong suit, and their popular restaurant Nice Matin is one of the better ones on the Upper West Side. The affluent residential neighborhood is filled with an impressive array of boutiques and gourmet food shops, and the American Museum of Natural History is a short walk away. ✉ *201 W. 79th St., at Amsterdam Ave., Upper West Side 10024* ☎ *212/ 875–1000 or 800/492–8122* 🖷 *212/721–1179* ⊕ *www.thelucernehotel. com* ⤶ *142 rooms, 42 suites* ⚹ *Restaurant, room service, some kitchenettes, some microwaves, some refrigerators, cable TV with movies and video games, in-room data ports, Web TV, gym, bar, lobby lounge, babysitting, dry cleaning, laundry service, concierge, Internet, business* *services, meeting rooms, parking (fee), no-smoking floors* ▤ *AE, D, DC, MC, V* Ⓜ *Subway: 1, 9 to 79th St.*

$ 🏨 **The Milburn Hotel.** In a converted prewar apartment building on a quiet, residential side street, this small bohemian hotel has a lobby that resembles a Bavarian castle, with a hanging tapestry, black-and-white marble floors, and abundant gilt. Spacious rooms are homey and a notch classier than your usual value-conscious hostelry; all have kitchenettes equipped with a microwave and coffeemaker (Zabar's is blocks away). Half the rooms here are one-bedroom suites, and the hotel is especially popular with families—there's even a children's book-filled library. The location is convenient to Lincoln Center, Central Park, and a host of shops and dining establishments, ✉ *242 W. 76th St., between Broadway and West End Ave., Upper West Side 10023* ☎ *212/362–1006 or 800/833–9622* 📠 *212/721–5476* ⊕ *www.milburnhotel.com* 🛏 *50 rooms, 50 suites* ⎐ *In-room safes, kitchenettes, microwaves, cable TV, in-room VCRs, Wi-Fi, laundry facilities* ▤ *AE, DC, MC, V* Ⓜ *Subway: 1, 9 to 79th St.*

¢–$ 🏨 **YMCA West Side.** Although the fitness center here is not quite as polished as the one at the Vanderbilt YMCA in Midtown East, you can't beat this Y for value, location, and atmosphere. Two blocks from Lincoln Center and a short jaunt from Central Park, it's housed in a building that looks like a Spanish cloister, with gargoyles adorning its arched neo-Byzantine entrance. Rooms are as tiny as jail cells, but red carpeting and spreads make them a little more cheerful. Those with private bath cost extra. ✉ *5 W. 63rd St., at Central Park W, Upper West Side 10023* ☎ *212/875–4100 or 800/348–9622* 📠 *212/875–1334* ⊕ *www.ymcanyc.org* 🛏 *500 rooms, 33 with bath* ⎐ *Cafeteria, cable TV, 2 indoor pools, health club, massage, sauna, steam room, paddle tennis, racquetball, squash, laundry facilities, Internet, meeting rooms, airport shuttle; no room phones, no smoking* ▤ *AE, MC, V* Ⓜ *Subway: 1, 9, A, B, C, D to 59th St./Columbus Circle.*

¢ 🏨 **Malibu Studios Hotel.** This youth-oriented budget crash pad could almost pass for a college dorm, especially given its proximity to Columbia University. Although it's farther north than you may care to venture, it's in a lively, safe neighborhood and the price is unheard-of for New York City. Double-occupancy rooms have private or shared baths; every room has a TV, CD player, and a desk with a writing lamp. ✉ *2688 Broadway, between W. 102nd and W. 103rd Sts., Upper West Side 10025* ☎ *212/222–2954 or 800/647–2227* 📠 *212/678–6842* ⊕ *www.malibuhotelnyc.com* 🛏 *150 rooms, 100 with bath* ⎐ *Restaurant, room service, some cable TV, in-room data ports, dry cleaning, laundry service, Internet, business services, no-smoking rooms* ▤ *MC, V* Ⓜ *Subway: 1 to 103rd St.*

Brooklyn

$$ 🏨 **New York Marriott Brooklyn.** Don't discount staying in Brooklyn. What Manhattan hotel has room for an Olympic-length lap pool, an 1,100-car garage, and even a dedicated Kosher kitchen? Large (if plain) guest rooms are enhanced by niceties such as 11-foot ceilings, massaging showerheads, and rolling desks. Beautiful trompe l'oeil ceilings transform the multilevel foyer into a virtual open-air atrium. Major subway lines only a block away make for a mere 10-minute commute into Manhattan. Five-minute walks bring you to the Brooklyn Bridge's pedestrian path and the charming neighborhood of Brooklyn Heights. Marriott is preparing to add more than 250 rooms to this popular property. ⊠ *333 Adams St., between Johnson and Willoughby Sts., Downtown Brooklyn 11201* ☎ *718/246–7000 or 800/843–4898* 🖷 *718/246–0563* ⊕ *www.marriott.com/nycbk* 🛏 *355 rooms, 21 suites* ⚊ *Restaurant, room service, in-room fax, in-room safes, minibars, cable TV, in-room data ports, indoor pool, health club, hot tub, massage, sauna, bar, babysitting, dry cleaning, laundry service, concierge, Internet, business services, meeting rooms, airport shuttle, parking (fee), no-smoking floors* ▭ *AE, D, DC, MC, V* Ⓜ *Subway: 2, 3, 4, 5 to Borough Hall.*

BOOKS & MOVIES

Books

Most New York bookstores have a section dedicated to generic and obscure titles on the city. Guides delve into specific neighborhoods and subcultures, and architecture and design books devote themselves to only one feature, be it cast-iron buildings, art deco details, or stone carvings. Photography books and historical accounts of any era or ethnic group abound. Many of the books listed here are penned by hard-nosed journalists who have written or edited for one of the city's daily newspapers for years.

ART & ARCHITECTURE. Nathan Silver's *Lost New York* documents historic buildings wiped out by development as well as the effect these places had on city dwellers. The visionary architect Rem Koolhaas's *Delirious New York: A Retroactive Manifesto for Manhattan* captures the city's spirit better than many literal histories. *Inside New York* has gorgeous photographs of hard-to-see New York interiors. Robert A. M. Stern has published a several-volume history of New York architecture for serious scholars. The 24-panel fold-out in Matteo Pericoli's *Manhattan Unfurled* reveals two 22-foot drawings of Manhattan's east and west side skylines; his *Manhattan Within* is similar, looking outward this time from Central Park.

Abstract expressionism and pop art came out of New York in the mid-20th century. Intellectual Serge Guilbart links art to general culture during the cold war era in *How New York Stole the Idea of Modern Art*. The classic *The New York School: A Cultural Reckoning* by Dore Ashton examines the artistic world between the 1930s and 1950s. For three decades Henry Geldzahler was a huge advocate of abstract art and served the movement well when curating American art at the Metropolitan Museum of Art. His writing on New York art, such as *Making It New*, is always a pleasure. *Making the Mummies Dance: Inside the Metropolitan Museum of Art*, by the institution's former director Thomas Hoving, illuminates the politics and triumphs of art-collecting. Tom Wolfe turns his satiric eye on art critics in *The Painted Word*.

BLACK, JEWISH & PUERTO RICAN NEW YORK. The black experience in New York City has been fictionalized in Ralph Ellison's *Invisible Man*, James Baldwin's *Go Tell It on the Mountain*, and Claude Brown's *Manchild in the Promised Land*. For a portrait of 1920s Harlem, try *When Harlem Was in Vogue*, by David Levering Lewis. For a look at the experience of black Caribbean women in Brooklyn, turn to Paule Marshall's fiction. Brilliant non-fiction includes Jervis Anderson's *This Was Harlem*, and Ralph Ellison's essay "Harlem is Nowhere" in *Shadow and Act*.

The history of New York's Jews can be traced in such books as *World of Our Fathers*, by Irving Howe; *Call It Sleep*, by Henry Roth; *New York Jew*, by Alfred Kazin; *The Promise* and *The Chosen*, by Chaim Potok; and *Our Crowd*, by Stephen Birmingham. A classic of New York Puerto Rican (aka "Nuyorican") fiction is Piri Thomas's *Down These Mean Streets*. Poet-playwright-actor of the Lower East Side, Miguel Piñero's first book of explosive poetry is *La Bodega: Sold Dreams*.

FICTION. *Wonderful Town* is a terrific collection of *New Yorker* stories set in New York, with selections from Lorrie Moore, Isaac Bashevis Singer, John Updike, and Jamaica Kincaid. *The Bonfire of the Vanities*, by Tom Wolfe, is a sprawling novel set in such divergent precincts as the opulent Upper East Side, the ghettoes of the Bronx, and the labyrinthine criminal justice system. Don DeLillo's *Underworld* is an epic that begins in Yankee Stadium, National Book Award winner *Charming Billy* by Alice McDermott portrays an Irish-American family in Bayside, Queens, and Jonathan Ames's hilarious and moving *The Extra Man* spans New York from the world of elegant Upper East Side ladies and their walkers to Times Square transsexual bars. The ill-used subject of *The Nanny Diaries*, by Emma McLaughlin and Nicola Kraus, spills the beans on what it can be like to work for a Park Avenue family as callous as it is wealthy.

In the lyrical *Shackling Water*, by Adam Mansbach, a 19-year-old saxophonist devoted to jazz struggles to stay the course between his Harlem boardinghouse and a downtown jazz club. *Bringing out the Dead* draws on author Joe Connelly's experience as a paramedic in New York. The young narrator in Jay McInerney's *Bright Lights, Big City* works at a *New Yorker*–like magazine by day and by night explores a tense nightlife built up around downtown clubs and restaurants. In *The Devil Wears Prada*, Lauren Weisberger's stand-in aspires to work at *The New Yorker*, but instead she's assistant to a woman bearing more than a passing resemblance to *Vogue*'s editor, Anna Wintour.

The SoHo art world and Manhattan real estate market set the scene for *The Third Eye*, an eerie confessional-style novel written by David Knowles. Other notable New York novels include *The Mambo Kings Play Songs of Love*, by Oscar Hijuelos; *The New York Trilogy*, by Paul Auster; and *People Like Us*, by Dominick Dunne.

Novels set in 19th-century New York include Henry James's moving *Washington Square*; Edith Wharton's *The House of Mirth* and *The Age of Innocence*; Stephen Crane's *Maggie, a Girl of the Streets*; Jack Finney's *Time and Again*; and *The Waterworks*, by E. L. Doctorow. The 20th century unfolds in F. Scott Fitzgerald's *The Beautiful and the Damned*, John Dos Passos's *Manhattan Transfer*, John O'Hara's *Butterfield 8*, Mary McCarthy's *The Group*, James Baldwin's *Another Country*, J. D. Salinger's *The Catcher in the Rye*, and Chang-rae Lee's *Native Speaker*. New York short stories come from O. Henry, Damon Runyon, John Cheever, Bernard Malamud, Grace Paley, and Isaac Bashevis Singer.

GUIDEBOOKS. *Up & Coming* by art dealer Michael Steinberg points out where to see the freshest faces in the art scene—both their galleries and favorite restaurants. *AIA Guide to New York City*, by Elliot Willensky and Norval White, is the definitive guide to the city's architecture. The *WPA Guide to New York City*, a 1939 product of the Federal Writers Project, includes prints, photos, a section on the 1939 World Fair, and a bibliography. *In Old New York*, written by journalist Thomas Janvier in 1894, tours New York's neighborhoods and has etchings and maps.

HISTORY & JOURNALISM General histories include a witty early account of New York, *Knickerbocker's History of New York*, by Washington Irving; the heavily illustrated *Columbia Historical Portrait of New York*, by John Kouwenhoven; and *The Historical Atlas of New York City*, by Eric Homberger. The Pulitzer Prize–winning *Gotham: A History of New York City to 1898* is by Edwin Burrows and Mike Wallace. Other solid histories are Brit expat Michael Pye's *Maximum City: The Biography of New York* (now out-of-print) and Oliver E. Allen's anecdotal volume *New York, New York*, with awe-inspiring accounts of the robber barons of the industrial revolution. Colson Whitehead's *The Colossus of New York* is a lyric group of essays covering the mundane annoyances of the city as well as its grandeur. *The Great Port* (out-of-print), Jan Morris details the origins of New York commerce, while in *Manhattan '45* she reconstructs New York as it greeted returning GIs in 1945.

The celebrated caricaturist Al Hirshfeld chronicled Broadway and other Gotham hotspots for over 75 years. His work can be found in such books as *Hirschfeld's New York*, with text by Clare Bell; *Hirschfeld's Harlem*; and *The Speakeasies of 1932*, written with Gordon Kahn.

Photographs and quotes from characters of the time enrich the historical survey *New York,* by Ric Burns and James Sanders, which follows the themes of the endless documentary Burns directed on the subject. The more than 4,000 entries in *Encyclopedia of New York,* edited by Kenneth T. Jackson, amount to an engrossing guide to every aspect of city life— politics, saloons, bagels, garbage collection, you name it.

Cultural Histories. *New York Intellect,* by Thomas Bender, is a fascinating history of the emergence of the city's philosophical circles, from the 19th-century founders of the Metropolitan Museum and the New York Public Library to the 20th-century editors of the *Partisan Review.* Christine Stansell's *American Moderns: Bohemian New York and the Creation of a New Century* is a smart, readable, and skeptical account of downtown freethinkers and free-lovers during the turn of the 20th century; Anne Douglas's *Terrible Honesty: Mongrel Manhattan in the 1920s* captures the personalities of the Roaring '20s, from Greenwich Village to Harlem. *You Must Remember This,* by Jeff Kisseloff, is an oral history of ordinary New Yorkers remembering life in their neighborhoods in the late 1880s through the mid-1940s. Joe DiMaggio, Frank Sinatra, and other New York characters are interviewed by Gay Talese in the out-of-print *Fame and Obscurity,* in which he also uncovers the regular folk who fill the city's odd and unusual occupations.

Tom Wolfe's *Radical Chic,* a classic snapshot of the late 1960s, when the Black Panthers dined at the Leonard Bernsteins, still retains its bite. *Positively 4th Street: The Lives and Times of Joan Baez, Bob Dylan, Mimi Baez Farina, and Richard Farina* by David Hajdu is a romp through Village coffeehouses with the musicians who brought folk music back to the masses. *Please Kill Me,* edited by Legs McNeil and Gillian McCain, is an eye-popping oral history of New York punk rockers, including the Ramones, Blondie, and the Velvet Un-

derground. Nothing brings back the fast-flying 1970s and '80s better than *The Andy Warhol Diaries*—except for Patrick McMullen's gigantic *so80s: A Photographic Diary of a Decade* and its casual snaps of nightclubbers of all persuasions. James St. James's *Party Monster: A Fabulous But True Tale of Murder in Clubland,* which takes as its subject the promoter and murderer Michael Alig, is an equally mordant look at the self-consciously decadent nightlife of the late '80s and early '90s.

New York's Politics. New York politics has always been colorful, maybe too colorful, and there are dozens of accounts to prove it. *Once Upon a Time in New York,* by author and critic Herbert Mitgang, narrates the Jazz Age rivalry between New York State governor Franklin Roosevelt and corrupt New York City mayor Jimmy Walker. Other political tales can be found in *The Great Mayor: Fiorello H. LaGuardia and the Making of the City of New York,* a biography of the Depression-era mayor by Alyn Brodsky, and Robert Caro's Pulitzer Prize–winning *The Power Broker,* 1,300-plus pages chronicling the career of the often despotic parks commissioner Robert Moses.

New York's Underbelly. In *Low Life,* Luc Sante writes about the cops, gangs, saloons, and politicians of 19th-century New York. *Weegee's World,* the catalog from an exhibition of the legendary photojournalist's work, is a visual equivalent to Sante's history. *The Gangs of New York,* the semi-factual book that inspired Martin Scorsese's movie of the same name, is an account of ethnic gangs in the late 1800s written by 1920s author Herbert Ashbury. Timothy J. Gilfoyle reveals how common prostitution was in 19th-century New York in *City of Eros.* With *Infamous Manhattan* by Andrew Roth in hand, you can walk your way to famous Gotham crime scenes. For a better understanding of what it was like to fight all that crime, look into *My Father's Gun: One Family, Three Badges, One Hundred Years in the*

NYPD, in which author Brian McDonald traces the lives of his grandfather, father, and brother—all policemen.

The Heart of the World, by Nik Cohn, is a vivid block-by-block account of shady but amusing characters living and working along Broadway. Booksellers, panhandlers, and street dwellers on a West Village corner spent years divulging their lives and outlook to sociologist Mitchell Duneier, who shares their experience in *Sidewalk.* At the other end of the economic spectrum is *Den of Thieves,* by former *Wall Street Journal* editor James B. Stewart. The dirt gets dished on greedy traders of the 1980s, detailing the deeds of Michael Milken and Ivan Boesky among others.

LITERARY ANTHOLOGIES & COLLECTIONS. To sample New York City essays from all the usual suspects—Walt Whitman, Herman Melville, E. B. White (his 1949 classic "Here is New York"), Henry James, Ralph Ellison, Langston Hughes, Elizabeth Bishop, Edna St. Vincent Millay, Jane Jacobs, and Dawn Powell—dip into Phillip Lopate's anthology *Writing New York.* Bill Harris and Mike Marquese edited the now out-of-print *New York: An Anthology,* which organizes writing from New Yorkers such as Theodore Dreiser and Kathy Acker around themes such as "mammon," "city of orgies," and "acts of creation." *Mirror for Gotham,* by Bayrd Still, collects the thoughts of visitors since New York was New Amsterdam. Shaun O'Connell's *Remarkable, Unspeakable New York* is a survey of New York as represented in fiction, drama, travel writing, and memoirs by writers such as Edith Wharton, James Baldwin, and Sylvia Plath.

Writers for *The New Yorker* magazine have preserved the texture of 20th-century New York life. *Back Where I Came From,* by A. J. Liebling describes neighborhood characters, as does Mark Singer's *Mr. Personality,* which chronicles lives of five brothers who are all building superintendents, as well as the activities of retired men who meet each day at a courthouse to follow criminal trials. Joseph Mitchell's *Up in the Old Hotel* is a collection of fiction and journalism that he wrote between the 1930s and the 1960s. These stories cover such topics as McSorley's, the bar that claims to be the oldest in New York; the self-styled King of the Gypsies; and life along the East River.

MEMOIRS. American writers and editors often move to New York because it's the center of the publishing industry. Many of these migrants write about the lives they find here, complementing the perspective of native-born authors. Federico Garcia Lorca's *Poet in New York,* written during a nine-month trip just after the Wall Street crash of 1929, records his response to the city's brutality, loneliness, and greed. A great memoir of New York bohemia is Samuel Delany's *The Motion of Light in Water.* Brendan Behan's *New York* describes the city's seedy sides, and Mary McCarthy's *Intellectual Memoirs* captures its left-wing circles. Dan Wakefield tells stories about meeting and drinking with such figures as Jack Kerouac and James Baldwin in *New York in the Fifties.* Anatole Broyard writes about that same era in *Kafka Was the Rage,* a description of his coming of age as a literary critic in Greenwich Village, and James McCourt's *Queer Street* is an attempt to reconstruct pre-Stonewall gay and lesbian life

In *New York Days* Willie Morris writes about arriving in town as a young journalist from Mississippi, then describes his stint as editor of *Harper's* magazine during its heyday as a venue for new journalism. Bronx native Jerome Charyn's *Metropolis* dives into the same period, with sharply different results. In works that blur memoir and fiction, Charyn tells the story of his 1940s Bronx childhood through *The Dark Lady from Belorusse: A Memoir,* and *The Black Swan: A Memoir.* Other good accounts are *Christopher Morley's New York,* a mid-1920s reminiscence; *Walker in the City,* by Alfred

Kazin; *Apple of My Eye,* a lighthearted memoir of writing a New York guidebook, by Helene Hanff; *Paul Auster's New York;* Eileen Myles's *Chelsea Girls;* and *Manhattan When I Was Young,* by Mary Cantwell.

MYSTERIES & NOIR. Mysteries set in New York City range from Dashiell Hammett's urbane 1933 novel *The Thin Man* to Rex Stout's series of Nero Wolfe mysteries. Jonathan Lethem's Tourettes-stricken detective in *Motherless Brooklyn* has to deal with both mobsters and religious cults. Caleb Carr's *The Alienist* and *Angel of Darkness* are thrillers set in 19th-century New York. In *Manhattan Nocturne,* Colin Harrison tells the story of a tabloid reporter who falls in love with a beautiful widow and investigates the murder of her filmmaker husband. *While My Pretty One Sleeps,* by Mary Higgins Clark, Kinky Friedman's *Greenwich Killing Time,* Heather Lewis's *The Second Suspect,* Mike Lupica's *Dead Air,* and *Unorthodox Practices,* by Marissa Piesman, are some other mysteries with a good sense of the place.

TALES FROM THE KITCHEN. *Kitchen Confidential,* by chef Anthony Bourdain, is a rip-roaring account of the rough-edged personalities that prepare some of New York's finest meals. At the opposite extreme is the military precision captured in *The Fourth Star,* by Leslie Brenner, which documents a single year at chef Daniel Boulud's esteemed restaurant, Daniel.

FOR THEATER LOVERS. A glamorous theater life is remembered in *Act One,* the timeless autobiography of playwright and director Moss Hart (1904–61). *The Season,* written by William Goldman in 1969, is an in-depth look at what makes Broadway successes and failures. *Rewrites* is Neil Simon's memoir. Brooks Atkinson's *Broadway* and the oral history *It Happened on Broadway* capture the glory days when the Great White Way debuted playwrights including Kaufman and Hart, Eugene O'Neill, Arthur Miller, Edward Albee, and Tennessee Williams, and musical the-

ater figures such as Rodgers and Hammerstein, David Merrick, Jerome Robbins, and Stephen Sondheim. Walter Kerr's criticism, such as *The Theater in Spite of Itself* and *The Decline of Pleasure,* is worth volumes of academic history. Frank Rich's *Hot Seat* chronicles the years from 1980 to 1993, which produced David Mamet and Sam Shepard.

Movies

Anyone who became enthralled with New York through the movies, or anyone interested in a good cinematic read should check out *Celluloid Skyline,* by James Sanders. Set-design illustrations, photos, and a 13-page filmography round out his exploration on how Hollywood added to the myths of New York.

Prepare to fall in love with the city via a vicarious tour with guide Timothy "Speed" Levitch, the loquacious subject of the documentary *The Cruise* (1998). His rapture with the city comes out in lavish, poetic, and hyper praise from his pulpit atop a double-decker Gray Line bus. Director Ric Burns has tackled the city's history in the 14-plus hour *New York: A Documentary Film* (1999). Perhaps the quintessential New York City movie is *Breakfast at Tiffany's* (1961), directed by Blake Edwards and based on Truman Capote's novella from 1958. Another classic, *On the Town,* (1949) stars Gene Kelly and Frank Sinatra as sailors on a 24-hour leave. You can get a sneak peak at Big Apple sights with *The Muppets Take Manhattan* (1984).

Filmmaker Woody Allen has filmed almost all his movies in Manhattan. (He says he likes to be able to go home and get a sweater.) *Annie Hall* (1977), *Manhattan* (1979), *Hannah and Her Sisters* (1987), *Crimes and Misdemeanors* (1989), *Alice* (1990), *Manhattan Murder Mystery* (1993), and *Everyone Says I Love You* (1996) are a few.

Director Martin Scorsese has made some of his best films in New York, including *Mean Streets* (1973), *Taxi Driver* (1976),

New York, New York (1977), *Raging Bull* (1980), *The King of Comedy* (1983), *Goodfellas* (1991), and *The Age of Innocence* (1993). *Gangs of New York* (2002) depicts the rivalries between the native-born and more recent immigrants in 1800s New York.

The late Bronx-born Alan J. Pakula used New York City masterfully in a number of his films. Jane Fonda took home an Oscar for her performance in *Klute* (1971), and Meryl Streep won for *Sophie's Choice* (1982). Other Pakula films featuring New York City are *Rollover* (1981), *Presumed Innocent* (1990), and his final film, *The Devil's Own* (1997). Sidney Lumet's films of misfits and police corruption include *Serpico* (1973) and *Dog Day Afternoon* (1975), both starring Al Pacino.

Some of director Paul Mazursky's most entertaining films have New York settings: *Next Stop, Greenwich Village* (1976), *An Unmarried Woman* (1978), and *Enemies, A Love Story* (1989), based on the novel by Isaac Bashevis Singer. Joan Micklin Silver portrays the Lower East Side in different eras in *Hester Street* (1975) and *Crossing Delancey* (1988).

Neil Simon films with city locations include *Barefoot in the Park* (1967), *The Odd Couple* (1968), *The Out-of-Towners* (1970; remade in 1999), *The Goodbye Girl* (1977), and *Brighton Beach Memoirs* (1986).

Spike Lee has perfected his very Brooklyn aesthetic with such films as *Do the Right Thing* (1990), *Crooklyn* (1994), and *Son of Sam* (1999). Jennie Livingston's documentary *Paris Is Burning* (1990) explores the fascinating gay black subculture of drag balls. *I Like It Like That* (1994), directed by Darnell Martin, deals with a feisty single mother in the Bronx. Lou Reed, Jim Jarmusch, and Madonna make appearances in the vignettes of *Blue in the Face* (1995) and Harvey Keitel and a host of high-calibre actors star in *Smoke* (1995), both set in Brooklyn and both collaborations of Wayne Wang and Paul Auster.

Downtown 81, filmed in 1981 but completed in 2001, employs the late painter Jean-Michael Basquiat in a semiautobiographical role amid the garbage- and graffiti strewn East Village and Lower East Side of the 1980s. Jeffrey Wright played the title role in *Basquiat* (1996), a version of the wunderkind artist's rise and fall as a darling of the 1980s art scene. Whit Stillman's nostalgic *Metropolitan* (1990) and *The Last Days of Disco* (1998) have some great scenes of New York interiors and WASP folkways. The HBO series *Sex and the City* was filmed on location, and for a time even jaded New Yorkers flocked to the same shops and bars that the four protagonists graced with their overpriced shoes. *Piñero* (2001), Benjamin Pratt portrays the late Latino poet-actor who grew up on the Lower East Side and went on to found the Nuyorican Poets Café. His spoken-word performances were precursors to hip-hop and rap.

Other New York City–set movies include *The Women* (1939), *The Naked City* (1945), *The Lost Weekend* (1948), *All About Eve* (1950), *Sweet Smell of Success* (1957), *Auntie Mame* (1959), *Love with the Proper Stranger* (1963), *Up the Down Staircase* (1967), *Wait Until Dark* (1967), *The Producers* (1967), *Rosemary's Baby* (1968), *Midnight Cowboy* (1969), *Diary of a Mad Housewife* (1970), *The Way We Were* (1973), *Network* (1976), *Saturday Night Fever* (1978), *Hair* (1979), *Kramer vs. Kramer* (1979), *Dressed to Kill* (1980), *Fame* (1980), *Ghostbusters* (1984), *Moonstruck* (1987), *New York Stories* (1989), *Sea of Love* (1989), *Night and the City* (1992), *A Bronx Tale* (1993), *Household Saints* (1993), *Little Odessa* (1994), *City Hall* (1996), *I Shot Andy Warhol* (1996), *Donnie Brasco* (1997), *A Perfect Murder* (1998), *Joe Gould's Secret* (1999), *The Royal Tenenbaums* (2001), *Chelsea Walls* (2001), *Changing Lanes* (2002), *Maid in Manhattan* (2002), and *Two Weeks Notice* (2002).

INDEX

NOTES

NOTES

NOTES

NOTES

FODOR'S KEY TO THE GUIDES

Caribbean

AMERICA'S **GUIDEBOOK LEADER** PUBLISHES GUIDES FOR **EVERY KIND OF TRAVELER**. CHECK OUT OUR MANY SERIES AND FIND YOUR **PERFECT MATCH**.

FODOR'S GOLD GUIDES
America's favorite travel-guide series offers the most detailed insider reviews of hotels, restaurants, and attractions in all price ranges, plus great background information, smart tips, and useful maps.

COMPASS AMERICAN GUIDES
Stunning guides from top local writers and photographers, with gorgeous photos, literary excerpts, and colorful anecdotes. A must-have for culture mavens, history buffs, and new residents.

FODOR'S 25 BEST / CITYPACKS
Concise city coverage in a guide plus a foldout map. The right choice for urban travelers who want everything under one cover.

FODOR'S AROUND THE CITY WITH KIDS
Up to 68 great ideas for family days, recommended by resident parents. Perfect for exploring in your own backyard or on the road.

SEE IT GUIDES
Illustrated guidebooks that include the practical information travelers need, in gorgeous full color. Perfect for travelers who want the best value packed in a fresh, easy-to-use, colorful layout.

FODOR'S FLASHMAPS
Every resident's map guide, with 60 easy-to-follow maps of public transit, parks, museums, zip codes, and more.

FODOR'S LANGUAGES FOR TRAVELERS
Practice the local language before you hit the road. Available in phrase books, cassette sets, and CD sets.

THE COLLECTED TRAVELER
These collections of the best published essays and articles on various European destinations will give you a feel for the culture, cuisine, and way of life.